Research in Psychology
Methods and Design

Sixth Edition

C. James Goodwin
Western Carolina University

WILEY

To Susan

VICE PRESIDENT & EXECUTIVE PUBLISHER   Jay O'Callaghan
EXECUTIVE EDITOR   Christopher T. Johnson
ASSISTANT EDITOR   Eileen McKeever
EXECUTIVE MARKETING MANAGER   Danielle Torio
SENIOR PRODUCTION EDITOR   Trish McFadden
COVER DESIGNER   Madelyn Lesure
PRODUCTION MANAGEMENT SERVICES   Laserwords Maine
MEDIA EDITOR   Bridget O'Lavin
PHOTO EDITOR   Hilary Newman
COVER PHOTO   ©Media Bakery

This book was set in Bembo by Laserwords and printed and bound by R.R. Donnelley & Sons, Inc. (Crawfordsville). The cover was printed by Phoenix Color.

This book is printed on acid-free paper. ∞

To order books or for customer service, please call 1-800-CALL WILEY (225–5945).

Library of Congress Cataloging-in-Publication Data

Goodwin, C. James.
  Research in psychology methods and design / C. James Goodwin.—6th ed.
    p. cm.
  Includes bibliographical references and index.
  ISBN 978-0-470-52278-3 (cloth)
  1. Psychology—Research—Textbooks. 2. Psychology—Research—Methodology—Textbooks.
3. Psychology, Experimental—Textbooks. I. Title.
  BF76.5.G64 2010
  150.72—dc22

                                                                        2009014320

Printed in the United States of America

10 9 8 7 6 5 4

Preface

The Philosophy of the Text

In the process of preparing six editions of this text, I have been guided by several strong beliefs. First, I would like students to develop a clear sense of how experimental psychologists think and how they do their work. Thus, the student using this book will encounter thorough discussions of the nature of psychological science and how it differs from pseudoscience, the logic of scientific thinking, and the manner in which experimental psychologists (a) develop ideas and hypotheses for research, (b) design their studies, (c) carry them out, (d) analyze them, and (e) draw reasoned conclusions from them. Second, I want students to understand that psychologists use a variety of methods in their attempts to understand psychological phenomena. Although the book's main focus is on the experimental method, there is thorough treatment of numerous other research strategies. Third, because I believe that researchers must always be aware of the ethical dimensions of their research, I have placed the ethics chapter early in the book (Chapter 2) and have included some additional discussion of ethics (Ethics Boxes) in *every* chapter in the book after Chapter 2. Fourth, because I have a love for psychology's history and believe that nobody can understand psychology's present without knowing something of its past, I have incorporated some of the history of experimental psychology into the text. Recognizing that my text is for a methods course and not for a history course, however, I have only included historical information that illuminates important methodological concepts. Fifth, and perhaps most important, although I believe that doing psychological science is a joyful activity, it has been my experience that some students enter the course with a sense of dread. They believe it will be boring, difficult, and not especially relevant for them. To counter this, I have taken pains to write a student-friendly book that is appealing (lots of interesting descriptions of real research), understandable (clear writing in an interactive, conversational style), and valuable (sharpening important critical thinking skills).

The Organization of the Text

The book includes twelve chapters, an epilogue, and several useful appendices. By thoroughly explaining the scientific way of thinking and contrasting it with nonscientific and pseudoscientific thinking, the opening chapter lays the groundwork for all that follows. Chapter 2 is devoted to research ethics and concerns how the American Psychological Association's most recent code of ethics is applied to research with both human participants and animal subjects. The problem of scientific fraud is also discussed. Chapter 3 examines the question of how ideas for research originate and explains the continually evolving relationship between theory and research. It also helps students learn to use psychology's most important electronic database (PsycINFO) and provides some tips about how to do a literature review. Issues related to measurement and data analysis are the focus of Chapter 4, which leads up to four consecutive chapters on the experimental method, psychology's most important method because of the kind of conclusion (causal) that can be drawn from it. There is a basic introduction to the experimental method (Chapter 5), a discussion of control problems in experimental research (Chapter 6), and two chapters devoted to experimental design (Chapter 7 on single-factor designs and Chapter 8 on factorial designs). Descriptions of other methodological strategies follow in subsequent chapters. These include correlational research (Chapter 9); quasi-experimental designs, applied research, and program evaluation (Chapter 10); research using "small *N*" designs (Chapter 11); and two varieties of descriptive research, observational research and surveys (Chapter 12). The appendices describe how to prepare the (in)famous APA-style research report, reprint the APA ethics codes for human research, and provide feedback for the some of the end-of-chapter applications exercises. Note the word "some." So that you as instructors can use some of these materials for homework assignments, I have given students feedback on approximately half of the exercises, in Appendix C. Answers to the remaining exercises can be found in the electronic Instructor's Resources (www.wiley.com/college/goodwin).

At various points in the text, there are boxed sections of three general types. *Origins* boxes supply interesting information about the historical roots of experimental psychology and show how various research concepts and methods (e.g., the questionnaire) were created and have evolved over the years. *Classic Studies* boxes describe well-known experiments (e.g., Bandura's Bobo studies) that illustrate particular research designs and/or methodological issues. Finally, the previously mentioned *Ethics* boxes reflect my belief that a consideration of research ethics should occur in more than just a single chapter. The ethics boxes consider such topics as informed consent, the operation of subject pools, and the proper use of surveys.

It is not uncommon for methods texts to begin with simple descriptive methods (observation, survey, etc.), move through correlational and quasi-experimental methods, and eventually reach the experimental method. There is certainly some logic to this organizational scheme, but it is not the scheme I have chosen to use. Rather, when teaching the course some years ago, I was always disturbed by how late in the semester students were encountering such things as factorial designs—who wants to be figuring out interactions while they are still digesting the Thanksgiving turkey? I wanted to get to experiments sooner in the semester because I wanted to be able to spend time on them if students ran into trouble. Also, because most of my labs used experimental designs, I wanted students to have some understanding of the studies they were running during the semester. So my chapter organization reflects the way I teach the course—I like to get to experiments as soon as possible. Reviewers of the text have been divided on the issue, with most liking the current organization, but some preferring to start with descriptive methods. I have been pleased to learn, however, that a number of reviewer/colleagues who like to begin the course with descriptive methods have been using my text anyway, and simply changing the chapter sequence to suit themselves. Thus, it is worth noting that the text is to some degree modular and can be taught using several different arrangements of chapters.

If Your Course Combines Research Methods and Statistics

In recent years, a number of psychology departments have taken their stand-alone statistics and methodology courses and combined them into two sequential courses that fully integrate statistics and methodology. The rationale for this is the unquestioned interdependence of the two. For instructors teaching in this way, the issue then becomes what to do for a text—statistics texts don't have enough methodology and methodology texts don't have enough statistics. One solution is to use a text specifically written for the integrated course. A few are beginning to appear on the market, but the choices are limited at this point. Another strategy is to adopt both a stat text and a methods text, telling students that they will be using both books both semesters, so the cost won't be any greater than taking a traditional statistics course followed by a methods course. The problem with this second strategy is that statistics texts and methodology texts often use inconsistent language and slightly different statistical symbol systems. Students can easily be confused about the *t* test for dependent groups in their methodology text and the *t* test for correlated samples in their statistics text, failing to realize that the two are identical. To solve this problem, I have coordinated the rewriting of this book with Robert and John Witte, who write a successful statistics text for Wiley (*Statistics*), now in its ninth edition. That is, I have changed some of my statistical language and symbols so that they match theirs exactly, and I have included occasional references to their fine book. Thus, if you are teaching a combined course and wish to use separate statistics and methods texts, adopting my book along with the Witte text will guarantee you consistency both in the language and the statistical symbols.

Pedagogical Features of the Text

For the student, this text has several features designed to facilitate learning. These include:

- At the start of each chapter, a brief preview of what is to be found in the chapter and a set of specific learning objectives for the chapter.
- Throughout each chapter, periodic Self Tests, set off in small boxes, enabling the student to test comprehension for a portion of a chapter just completed.
- At the end of each chapter, a comprehensive summary of important points, a set of Review Questions, a set of Applications Exercises, and answers to the

Self Tests. The review questions are short essay questions for discussion and reflection. These review questions are not just definitional; they ask students to apply some of the concepts learned in the chapter and to think critically about them. The applications exercises include thought questions and problems to solve that require using the concepts learned in the chapter. There is feedback to about half of these exercises in Appendix C. The online Instructor's Manual includes feedback for the remaining exercises, which enables instructors to assign some of the end-of-chapter exercise as graded homework.

• Key terms and concepts appear in **boldface** print throughout the book and they are collected in a Glossary at the end of the book. To make it easier to find where the descriptions of the Glossary terms are in the text, I have structured the Subject Index so that the text page where a glossary term is first defined is boldfaced.

• Throughout the text, there are numerous concrete examples of real research, used to illustrate various methodological points and to enhance critical thinking. These include *forty* detailed descriptions (called "Research Examples") and dozens of other, briefer descriptions.

Electronic Resources

There are several electronic resources available for students and instructors. They can be found here:

www.wiley.com/college/goodwin

Simply go to the site, find my textbook and click on Student or Instructor Resources. Students can get to the materials directly; instructors must register with Wiley because some of the materials (e.g., test bank) are password-protected. Here's what can be found.

For the Instructor:

• An Instructor's Manual, organized by chapter, which provides numerous ideas for in-class exercises, lecture elaborations, homework, and so on (many taken from psychology's best journal for teachers, *Teaching of Psychology*). It also includes the answers for those end-of-chapter Applications Exercises that students won't find in Appendix C.

• A Test Bank for each chapter that includes both objective (multiple choice and fill-in-the-blank) items and written questions (short essays and comprehensive, integrative essays).

• A set of PowerPoint slides to accompany the chapters.

• A Laboratory Manual—a set of materials and instructions that will enable you to collect data in 20 different experiments.

• Everything that is to be found in the Student materials.

For the Student:

- Accompanying this text and available from the Wiley website is an electronic Study Guide. The Study Guide includes concept questions for students to answer as they work their way through chapters, sample objective test items (fill-ins, matching, and multiple choice) with detailed feedback, and applications exercises similar to the ones found at the ends of chapters in the main text.

- The Study Guide also includes two important aids for statistical analysis:

  - Detailed descriptions about how to calculate various statistical analyses by hand (e.g., t tests, ANOVA); this has been coordinated carefully with the Witte's statistics text and replaces the Appendix C that appeared in earlier editions of this text.

  - Because many departments rely on SPSS for statistical analysis, I have included a detailed step-by-step SPSS Guide that my students have found useful over the years.

Acknowledgments

This project would not have been started, much less completed and evolved into a sixth edition, without the encouragement and support of many people, most notably my dear wife of forty-plus years (Susan, retired now, but a former corporate auditor good at keeping me on task, yet willing to let me sneak out for an occasional semi-guilt-free 18 holes of mountain golf) and my children (Kerri, a university professor and cognitive psychologist, and Charles, a full-time project geologist for an environmental consulting firm and part-time graduate student). The hundreds of students who have passed through my research methods course have been my principal source of inspiration in writing the book—during the years before I started writing the first edition, many of them told me to stop complaining about the textbook being used at the time and write my own. I would especially like to acknowledge Aimee Faso Wright, who was the leader of a group of students interested in cognitive mapping and was the senior author of the sample study on that topic in Appendix A. I'm delighted that she has earned a Ph.D. in pharmacology, and only mildly disappointed that experimental psychology lost her.

To Darryl Bruce, my dissertation director, I owe a great debt. He first showed me just how exciting research in psychology could be during my grad school days in Tallahassee. Today, he is happily retired in beautiful Nova Scotia, which gives Susan and me an excuse to visit a place with (relatively) cheap lobster. I would also like to thank two of my colleagues in the Society for the Teaching of Psychology (APA's Division 2), Wayne Weiten and Steve Davis. At the very beginning of the project, both were instrumental in convincing me that I actually could write a book, and both continue to provide support, encouragement, and friendship.

Thanks also go to the stalwart and thoughtful reviewers for the text. Sixth edition reviewers included:

Chad Galuska, College of Charleston

Michael Marcell, College of Charleston

Christine Selby, Husson College

Stephen D. O'Rourke, The College of New Rochelle

Finally, the editors, production team, and marketing staff at Wiley have continued to be first rate, making the entire process a breeze (or at least much less onerous than I had any reason to expect). I am especially grateful for the editorial support of Chris Johnson and Eileen McKeever, and for the skillful production work of Mark Sehestedt and his team at Laserwords Maine.

CONTENTS

CHAPTER 5

Introduction to Experimental Research   167

CHAPTER 6

Control Problems in Experimental Research   205

CHAPTER **12**

Observational and Survey Research Methods   451

APPENDIX B

The Ethics Code of the American Psychological Association 533

APPENDIX C

Answers to Selected End-of-Chapter Applications Exercises 539

Summary of
Research Examples

CHAPTER 1

Scientific Thinking in Psychology

Preview & Chapter Objectives

Welcome to what might be the most important course you will take as an undergraduate student of psychology. This opening chapter begins by trying to convince you that a methods course is essential to your education, whether or not you have a future as a research psychologist. The chapter then proceeds with an introduction to the ways in which we come to know things in our world. Some of our knowledge derives from our reliance on authority figures, other knowledge results from our use of logical reasoning, and we have often heard that experience is the best teacher. All these approaches to knowledge have merit, but each is also flawed. Research psychologists rely on scientific thinking as a way to truth, and this opening chapter carefully examines the general nature of science, describes the scientific way of thinking, and contrasts it with pseudoscientific thinking. Distinguishing science from pseudoscience is especially important for psychology, because some things that are promoted as ''psychological truth'' (e.g., the ability to measure and evaluate personality by examining someone's handwriting) are actually examples of pseudoscience rather than true science. The chapter closes with a discussion of the goals for a scientific psychology and brief introductions to the work of two of experimental psychology's shining stars, Eleanor Gibson and B. F. Skinner. They both illustrate the passion that research psychologists show for their work. When you finish this chapter, you should be able to:

- Defend the need for a research methods course in a psychology curriculum.
- Explain how the overall purpose of a methods course differs from other courses in the psychology curriculum.
- Identify and evaluate nonscientific ways of knowing about things in the world.
- Describe the nature of science as a way of knowing.
- Describe the attributes of science as a way of knowing, which assumes determinism and discoverability; makes systematic observations; produces public, data based, but tentative knowledge; asks answerable questions; and develops theories capable of disproof.
- Distinguish science from pseudoscience and recognize the attributes of pseudoscientific thinking.
- Describe the main goals of research in psychology and relate them to various research strategies to be encountered later in the book.

In the preface to his weighty two-volume *Principles of Physiological Psychology*, published in 1874, the German physiologist Wilhelm Wundt boldly and unambiguously declared that his text represented "an attempt to mark out a new domain of *science*" (Wundt, 1874/1904; italics added). Shortly after publishing the book, Wundt established his now famous psychology laboratory at Leipzig, Germany, attracting students from all over Europe as well as from the United States. American universities soon established their own laboratories, about twenty of them by 1892 (Sokal, 1992). In that same year the American Psychological Association (APA) was founded, and before long it ratified a constitution identifying its purpose as "the advancement of Psychology as a *science*. Those who are eligible for membership are engaged in this work" (Cattell, 1895, p. 150; italics added). Thus, for psychology's pioneers, both in Germany and in the United States, the "new psychology" was to be identified with laboratory science. It gradually forged an identity separate from the disciplines of physiology and philosophy to become the independent science it is today.

For the early psychologists, the new psychology was to be a science of mental life, the goal being to understand exactly how human consciousness was structured and/or how it enabled people to adapt to their environments. In order to study the mind scientifically, however, generally agreed-on methods had to be developed and taught. Hence, students of the new psychology found themselves in laboratories learning the basic procedures for studying mental processes. Indeed, one of psychology's most famous early texts was a two-volume (four if the instructor's manuals are included) laboratory manual published right after the turn of the twentieth century by Cornell's eminent experimental psychologist, E. B. Titchener. The manuals were in use in lab courses well into the 1930s and they were instrumental in training a generation of experimental psychologists (Tweney, 1987).

Although the particular methods have changed considerably over the years, today's psychology departments continue this long tradition of teaching the tools of the trade to psychology students. From the very beginning of psychology's history, teaching research methodology has been the heart and soul of the psychology curriculum. Of course, students understandably tend to be suspicious of the argument that they are required to take a research methods course because "we've always done it that way." There should be other reasons to justify taking the course. There are.

Why Take This Course?

The most obvious reason for taking a course in research methods is to begin the process of learning how to do research in psychology. My ideal scenario would be for you to become fascinated by research, decide that you would like to do some, get your feet wet as an undergraduate (e.g., collaborate with a professor and perhaps present your research at a research conference), go to graduate school and complete a doctorate in psychology, begin a career as a productive researcher, get lots of publications and win lots of grants, achieve tenure, and eventually be named recipient of the APA's annual award for "Distinguished Scientific Contributions"! Of course, I'm also a realist and know that most psychology majors have interests other than doing research, most do not go on to earn doctorates, most who earn doctorates do not become productive researchers, and very few productive scholars win prestigious APA awards. If you won't be a famous research psychologist some day, are there still reasons to take this course? Sure.

For one thing, a course in research methods provides a solid foundation for other psychology courses in more specific topic areas (social, cognitive, developmental, etc.). This is an important reason why your psychology department requires you to take a methodology course. The difference between the methods course and these other courses is essentially the difference between *process* and *content*. The methods course teaches a *process* of acquiring knowledge about psychological phenomena that is then applied to all the specific *content* areas represented by other courses in the psychology curriculum. A social psychology experiment in conformity might be worlds apart in subject matter from a cognitive psychology study on eyewitness memory, but their common thread is method—the way in which researchers gain their knowledge about these phenomena. Fully understanding textbook descriptions of research in psychology is much easier if you know something about the methods used to arrive at the conclusions.

To illustrate, take a minute and look at one of your other psychology textbooks. Chances are that virtually every paragraph makes some assertion about behavior that either includes a specific description of a research study or at least makes reference to one. On my shelf, for example, is a social psychology text by Myers (1990) that includes the following description of a study about the effects of violent pornography on male aggression (Donnerstein, 1980). Myers wrote that the experimenter "showed 120 . . . men either a neutral, an erotic, or an aggressive-erotic (rape) film. Then the men, supposedly as part of another experiment, 'taught' a male or female confederate some nonsense syllables by choosing how much shock to administer for incorrect answers. The men who had watched the rape film administered markedly stronger shocks—but only toward female victims'' (Myers, 1990, p. 393). While reading this description, someone unfamiliar with experimental design might get the general idea, but someone familiar with methodology would also be registering that the study was at the very least a 2 (sex of the confederate) × 3 (film condition) between-subjects factorial design resulting in a type of interaction effect that takes precedence over any main effects; that the two independent variables (film type, victim sex) were both manipulated variables, thereby strengthening the causal interpretation of the results; and that the ''victims'' were not really shocked but were clued in to the purposes of the study (i.e., they were confederates).[1] Also, the thoughts ''I wonder what would happen if there was more of a delay between viewing the film and the learning part of the study?'' or ''I wonder how female participants would react in a replication of the study?'' might also float through the mind of someone in tune with the kind of ''what do we do next?'' thinking that accompanies knowledge of research methodology.

A second reason for taking experimental psychology is that even if you never collect a single piece of data after completing this course, knowledge of research methods will make you a more informed and critical consumer of information. We are continually exposed to claims about behavior from sources ranging from the people around us who are amateur psychologists (i.e., everyone) to media accounts ranging from the sublime (an account in a reputable magazine about research on the relationship between TV watching and aggressiveness) to the ridiculous (the tabloid headlines you read while waiting in line to pay for groceries). While the latter can be dismissed without much difficulty (for most people), a professional writer unaware of the important distinction between experimental and correlational research might have penned the TV study. Consequently, the article might describe a correlational study hinting at cause and effect more than is justified, a mistake you'll have no difficulty recognizing once you have finished Chapter 9. Another example might be a claim that while under hypnosis, people can be transported back to the moment of their birth, thereby gaining some great insight into the origins of their problems. When you learn about ''parsimonious'' explanations in Chapter 3, you will be highly suspicious about such a claim and able to think of several alternative explanations for the reports given by patients about their alleged birth experiences. Similarly, you will learn to become skeptical about the claims made by those who believe the ''subliminal'' CD they just bought is the cause of the weight they just lost, or by those who believe that their child's IQ can be raised by listening to classical music (the so-called ''Mozart effect'').

Third, there is a very pragmatic reason for taking a methods course. Even if you have no desire to become a research psychologist, you might like to be a professional practitioner of psychology some day. Like researchers, practitioners must earn an advanced degree, preferably the doctorate. Even for future clinical psychologists, counselors, and school psychologists, graduate school almost certainly

---

[1] All the jargon in this sentence will be part of your everyday vocabulary by the time you finish this course.

means doing some research, so a course in methodology is an obvious first step to learning the necessary skills. Furthermore, your chances of getting into *any* type of graduate program in the first place are improved significantly if you (a) did well in undergraduate research methods and statistics courses and (b) were involved in doing some research as an undergraduate. A study by Norcross, Hanych, and Terranova (1996), which examined the undergraduate courses most likely to be required for admission to graduate school, found that the methods course was ranked second, just behind statistics, while specific content courses (e.g., developmental and abnormal psychology) were not required by very many programs.[2]

Once you become a professional psychologist, your research skills will be invaluable. Even if you aren't an active researcher, you will need to keep up with the latest research in your area of expertise and to be able to read research critically. Furthermore, good clinical work involves essentially the same kind of thinking that characterizes the laboratory scientist—hypotheses about a client's problems are created and tested by trying out various treatments, and the outcomes are systematically evaluated. Also, if you work for a social service agency, you may find yourself dealing with accreditation boards or funding sources and they will want to know if your psychological services are effective. As you will discover in Chapter 10, research evaluating program effectiveness touches the lives of most professional psychologists.

Only a minority of psychology majors becomes professional psychologists, of course, yet a research methods course can help develop the kinds of skills that employers look for in bachelor's level job applicants. By the time you have completed this course, for example, you should be better at critical and analytical thinking, precise writing, and logical argument. In addition, you will know how to analyze, summarize, and interpret empirical data, search for information in libraries and electronic databases, and present the results of your research in a clear and organized fashion. Your computer skills will also improve—you will either learn or increase your existing skill with some statistical software package (e.g., SPSS) and you might also become more familiar with presentation software (e.g., PowerPoint). To learn more about the kinds of skills you will begin to develop in the methods course, you might take a peak ahead to the Epilogue and the section called "what I learned in my research methods course."

Finally, a course in research methods introduces you to a particular type of thinking. As mentioned above, other psychology courses deal with specific content areas and concentrate on what is known about topic X. The methods course, however, focuses more on the process by which knowledge of X is acquired. That process is centered on scientific thinking, and it is deeply ingrained in all research psychologists. Before detailing the features of the scientific way of thinking, however, let me first describe some of the other ways in which we arrive at our knowledge of the world.

---

[2] In an analysis of 1554 graduate programs, it was found that 85.2% "required" or "preferred" statistics. The percentages were 66.0% for the research methods course, 35.9% for "childhood/developmental," and 32.5% for "abnormal/psychopathology."

✓ Self Test 1.1

1. How does a research methods course differ from a course in social psychology?
2. When graduate schools in psychology examine student transcripts, which courses are they most likely to want to see?
3. Even if you never get involved in research after taking the research methods course, why is taking a research methods course valuable?

Ways of Knowing

Take a moment and reflect on something that you believe to be true. The belief could be something as simple as the conviction that lobster should be eaten only in Maine, or it could be something as profound as the belief in a personal God. How do we arrive at such beliefs?

Authority

Whenever we accept the validity of information from a source that we judge to be expert or influential in some way, then we are relying on **authority** as a source of our knowledge. As children we are influenced by and believe what our parents tell us (at least for a while), as students we generally accept the authority of textbooks and professors, as patients we take the pills prescribed for us by doctors and believe they will have beneficial effects, and so on. Of course, relying on the authority of others to establish our beliefs overlooks the fact that authorities can be wrong. Some parents pass along harmful prejudices to their children, textbooks and professors are sometimes wrong or their knowledge is incomplete or biased, and doctors can miss a diagnosis or prescribe the wrong medicine.

On the other hand, we do learn important things from authority figures, especially those who are recognized as experts in particular fields. Thus, we read *Consumer Reports*, watch the Weather Channel, and (sometimes) pay attention when the medical community cautions us about our chronic lack of exercise and poor eating habits. Also, it doesn't stretch the concept of authority to consider the giants in the arts and literature as authority figures who can teach us much about ourselves and others. Who can read Shakespeare or Dickens or Austen without gaining valuable insights about human nature?

Use of Reason

We sometimes arrive at conclusions by using logic and reason. For example, given the statements (sometimes called premises):

Primates are capable of using language.

Bozo the chimp is a primate.

It is logical for us to conclude that Bozo the chimp has the ability to use language. I think you can see the problem here—the logic is flawless, but the conclusion depends on the truth of the first two statements. The second one might be OK and easy to verify, but the first one could be subject to considerable debate, depending, among other things, on how language is defined. Psycholinguists have been arguing about the issue for years. The key point is that the value of a logically drawn conclusion depends on the truth of the premises, and it takes more than logic to determine whether the premises have merit.

The American pragmatist philosopher Charles Peirce pointed out another difficulty with the use of reason and logic—it can be used to reach opposing conclusions, easily observed in political discussions. Peirce labeled the use of reason, and a developing consensus among those debating the merits of one belief over another, the **a priori method** for acquiring knowledge. Beliefs are deduced from statements about what is thought to be true according to the rules of logic. That is, a belief develops as the result of logical argument, before a person has direct experience with the phenomenon at hand (*a priori* translates from the Latin as "from what comes before"). With more than a hint of sarcasm, Peirce pointed out that the *a priori* method was favored by metaphysical philosophers, who could reason eloquently to reach some truth, only to be contradicted by other philosophers who reasoned just as eloquently to the opposite truth. On the question of whether the mind and the body are one or two different essences, for instance, a "dualist" might develop a sophisticated argument for the existence of two fundamentally different essences, the physical and the mental, while a "monist" might develop an equally compelling argument that mental phenomena can be reduced to physical phenomena (e.g., the mind *is* the brain). The outcome of the *a priori* approach, Peirce argued, is that philosophical beliefs go in and out of fashion, with no real "progress" toward truth.

Experience

Another important way of coming to know things is through our experiences in the world. This is **empiricism**—the process of learning things through direct observation or experience, and reflection on those experiences. You will see shortly that asking "empirical questions" is an important component of scientific thinking, and there is certainly some truth in the old saying that "experience is the best teacher." Yet it can be dangerous to rely solely on one's experiences when trying to determine the truth of some matter. The difficulty is that our experiences are necessarily limited and our interpretations of our experiences can be influenced by a number of what social psychologists refer to as "social cognition biases." For example, one of these biases is called **belief perseverance** (Lepper, Ross, & Lau, 1986). Motivated by a desire to be certain about one's knowledge, it is a tendency to hold on doggedly to a belief, even in the face of evidence that would convince most people that the belief is false. It is likely that these beliefs form when the individual hears some "truth" being continuously repeated, in the absence of contrary information. Thus, many college students in the 1960s strongly believed in the idea of a generation gap and accepted as gospel the saying "Don't trust anyone over the age of 30." (Of course, these same people are now 70 or older and some of them are deeply suspicious of anyone younger than 30.)

Belief perseverance often combines with another preconception called a **confirmation bias**, a tendency to search out and pay special attention to information that supports one's beliefs, while ignoring information that contradicts a belief (Wason & Johnson-Laird, 1972). For instance, persons believing in extrasensory perception (ESP) will keep close track of instances when they were "thinking about Mom, and then the phone rang and it was her!" Yet they ignore the far more numerous times when (a) they were thinking about Mom and she didn't call and (b) they weren't thinking about Mom and she did call. They also fail to recognize that if they talk to Mom about every two weeks, their frequency of "thinking about Mom" will increase near the end of the two-week interval, thereby increasing the chances of a "hit." Strongly held prejudices include both belief perseverance and confirmation bias. Racists, for example, refuse to consider evidence disconfirming the prejudice and pay attention to and seek out information consistent with the prejudice. They will argue that experience is indeed the best teacher and that their experience has taught them about the superiority of their own group and the inferiority of members of group X.

Another social cognition bias is called the **availability heuristic**, and it occurs when we experience unusual or very memorable events and then overestimate how often such events typically occur (Tversky & Kahneman, 1973). Thus, people who watch a lot of crime shows on TV misjudge their chances of being crime victims, and because spectacular plane crashes are given more attention in the media than car accidents, some people cannot believe the fact that air travel is considerably safer than travel by automobile. An example of an availability heuristic of relevance to students is what happens when students change their answers on multiple-choice tests. Many students believe that the most frequent outcome of answer changing is that an initially correct answer will be changed to a wrong one. Students tend to hold that belief because when such an event does occur, it is painful and hence memorable (i.e., available to memory), perhaps making the difference between an A and a B on a test. Also, once the belief starts to develop, it is strengthened whenever the same kind of outcome does occur (confirmation bias), and it doesn't take too many instances before a strong belief about answer changing develops (i.e., belief perseverance begins). It is not uncommon to hear students tell others not to change answers but to "go with your initial gut feeling." The problem is that students usually overlook cases when they change from one wrong multiple-choice alternate to another wrong one, or when they change from a wrong alternative to the correct one. It is only the memorable situation, changing from right to wrong answer, that damages their score ("I had it right! And I changed it!"). That such a belief in the effects of answer changing is erroneous can be concluded from studies showing that, in fact, the most likely outcome (about 58% of the time) is that a changed answer will go from wrong to correct. On the other hand, changing from the correct answer to a wrong one happens only about 20% of the time and the remaining 22% of outcomes are those in which the change is from one wrong answer to another (Benjamin, Cavell, & Shallenberger, 1984). If you are saying to yourself there is no way this can be true, and I suspect you might indeed be saying that to yourself, then you have some idea of the strength of belief perseverance, confirmation bias, and the availability heuristic.

Our experiences can be an indispensable and important guide to life's difficulties, but we also need to be aware of their limits. Social cognition biases such as the ones described here (not to mention several others—check out any social psychology textbook) can work together to distort the beliefs we develop from our experiences in the world.

The Ways of Knowing and Science

The most reliable way to develop a belief, according to Charles Peirce, is through the method of science. Its procedures allow us to know "real things, whose characters are entirely independent of our opinions about them" (Tomas, 1957, p. 25). Thus, Peirce believed that the chief advantage of science lies in its objectivity, which he considered to be the opposite of subjectivity. That is, for Peirce, to be objective is to avoid completely any human bias or preconception. Before discussing the nature of science and scientific thinking in detail, however, it is important to point out that scientists are just as human as everyone else. They rely on authority, they often argue with each other in an *a priori* fashion, and they are prone to social cognition biases in the process of learning from their experiences.

Concerning bias, scientists sometimes hold on to a pet theory or a favored methodology long after others have abandoned it, and they occasionally seem to be less than willing to entertain new ideas. Charles Darwin once wrote half seriously that it might be a good idea for scientists to die by age 60, because after that age, they "would be sure to oppose all new doctrines" (cited in Boorstin, 1985, p. 468). On the other hand, the historian of science Thomas Kuhn (1970) argued that refusing to give up on a theory, in the face of a few experiments questioning that theory's validity, can have the beneficial effect of ensuring that the theory receives a thorough evaluation. Thus, being a vigorous advocate for a theory can ensure that it will be pushed to its limits before being abandoned by the scientific community. The process by which theories are evaluated, evolve, and sometimes die will be elaborated in Chapter 3.

Research psychologists can also be influenced by authority. The "authorities" are usually other scientists, and experts are certainly more likely to be reliable sources than not. Nonetheless, researchers should know better than to assume automatically that something is true simply because a reputable scientist said it was true. Rather, scientists are normally guided by the motto engraved on the entrance to the headquarters of the British Royal Society—"Nullius in Verba"—which encourages them to "take nobody's word for it; see for yourself" (cited in Boorstin, 1985, p. 394). Of course, "seeing for yourself" also opens up the dangers of uncritically relying on experience.

Peirce's *a priori* method (the use of reason) is frequently found in science to the extent that scientists argue with each other, trying to reach a rational consensus on some issue, but often failing to do so (e.g., whether to use the computer as a useful metaphor for the brain). As you will see in Chapter 3, they also rely on the rules of logic and inductive/deductive reasoning to develop ideas for research and to evaluate research outcomes. But while scientific thinking includes elements of the nonscientific ways of knowing described thus far, it has a number of distinct attributes. It is to the nature of science that we now turn.

✓ Self Test 1.2

1. If you fail to question anything in this textbook, you will be relying too heavily on ____ as a way of knowing.
2. Some students think they should never change answers on multiple-choice tests. What does this have to do with the availability heuristic?

Science as a Way of Knowing

The way of knowing that constitutes science in general and psychological science in particular involves a number of interrelated assumptions and characteristics. First, researchers assume **determinism** and **discoverability**. Determinism simply means that events, including psychological ones, have causes, and discoverability means that by using agreed-upon scientific methods, these causes can be discovered, with some degree of confidence. Even with the best of methods, research psychologists do not expect to predict psychological phenomena with 100% certainty, but they have faith that psychological phenomena occur with some regularity and that the regularities can be investigated successfully. Let us examine the determinism assumption in more detail. This will be followed by a discussion of the other attributes of science as a way of knowing.

Science Assumes Determinism

Students are often confused after reading that psychologists regard human behavior as "determined." They sometimes assume this means "predestined" or "predetermined." It doesn't. A believer in absolute predestination thinks that every event is determined ahead of time, perhaps by God, and develops a fatalistic conviction that one can do little but accept life as it presents itself. However, the traditional concept of determinism, as used in science, contends simply that all events have causes. Some philosophers argue for a strict determinism, which holds that the causal structure of the universe enables the prediction of all events with 100% certainty, at least in principle. Most, however, influenced by twentieth-century developments in physics and the philosophy of science, take a more moderate view that could be called probabilistic or **statistical determinism**. This approach argues that events can be predicted, but only with a probability greater than chance. Research psychologists take this position.

Yet the concept of determinism, even the "less than 100%" variety, is troubling because it seems to require that we abandon our belief in free will. If every event has a cause, so the argument goes, then how can one course of action be freely chosen over another? The psychologist would reply that if determinism is not true at least to some degree, then how can we ever know anything about behavior? Imagine for a moment what it would be like if human behavior was completely unpredictable. How could you decide whether to marry Ed or Ted? How could you decide whether or not to take a course from Professor Jones?

Of course, there are multiple factors influencing behavior, and it is difficult to know for sure what someone will do at any one moment. Nonetheless, behavior follows certain patterns and is clearly predictable. For example, because we know that children will often do things that work effectively for them, it is not hard to predict a tantrum in the toy department of a crowded store if that behavior has yielded toys for a child in that store in the past. And because behavior learned in one setting tends to "generalize" to similar environments, it isn't hard to predict a tantrum in Wal-Mart for the child whose tantrums have worked effectively in Kmart.

Concerning the matter of free choice, the positivist philosopher of science Rudolph Carnap argued that free choice is actually meaningless unless determinism is true, because choices should be made on some reasonable basis and there can be no such basis for a choice unless the world is lawful. According to Carnap, without "causal regularity, . . . it is not possible to make a free choice at all. A choice involves a deliberate preference for one course of action over another. How could a choice possibly be made if the consequences of alternative courses of action could not be foreseen?" (1966, p. 220). In short, Carnap argued that the idea of free choice has no meaning unless determinism is in fact true! Thus, deciding between Ed and Ted as a marriage partner makes sense only if you know certain things that are predictable about them (e.g., Ed is more reliable). Deciding whether to take Professor Jones's course might hinge on her reputation for being predictably fair in treating students.

It is clear to researchers that in order for choice to have any meaning for humans, events in the world must be somewhat predictable. Thus, when the psychologist investigates behavior and discovers regularities, this does not eliminate or even limit human freedom. Indeed, if Carnap is correct, such research may actually enhance our ability to choose by increasing our knowledge of the alternatives.

Most research psychologists believe that the issue about the existence of free will cannot be settled one way or the other by science. Rather, whether the choices we make in life are freely made or not is a philosophical matter, and our personal belief about free will must be an individual decision, arrived at through the use of reason (perhaps supplemented with reflection on our experiences and/or the ideas of authority figures). The best that psychologists can do is to examine scientifically such topics as (a) the extent to which behavior is influenced by a strong belief in free will, (b) the degree to which some behaviors are more "free" than others (i.e., require more conscious decision making), and (c) what the limits might be on our "free choices" (Baumeister, 2008).

Science Makes Systematic Observations

A major attribute of science as a way of knowing is the manner in which science goes about the business of searching for regularities in nature. All of us do a lot of observing in our daily lives, and we draw conclusions about things based on those observations. But we also know, from the earlier discussion of experience as a way of knowing, that experience is susceptible to such biases as belief perseverance, confirmation bias, and the availability heuristic. Science also bases its findings on observations, but they are made much more systematically than our everyday observations. The scientist's systematic observations include using (a) precise definitions of the phenomena being measured, (b) reliable and valid measuring tools that yield useful and interpretable data, (c) generally accepted research methodologies, and (d) a system of logic for drawing conclusions and fitting those conclusions into general theories. In a sense, the rest of this book is an elaboration of the sentence you just read.

Science Produces Public Knowledge

Another important characteristic of science as a way of knowing is that its procedures result in knowledge that can be publicly verified. This was the attribute that Peirce found most appealing about science—its **objectivity**. For Peirce, being objective meant eliminating such human factors as expectation and bias. The objective scientist was believed to be almost machine-like in the search for truth. Today, however, nobody believes that scientists can separate themselves from their already-existing attitudes, and to be objective does not mean to be devoid of such normal human traits. Rather, an objective observation, as the term is used in science, is simply one that can be verified by more than one observer. In science this usually takes the form of defining the terms and research procedures precisely enough so that any other person can systematically repeat the study, presumably achieving the same observable outcome. That is, science produces knowledge that is public knowledge. This process of repeating a study to determine if its results occur reliably is called "replication" and you will learn more about it in Chapter 3. In general, as results are replicated, public confidence in the reality of some psychological phenomenon is increased. On the other hand, questions are raised when results cannot be replicated. As you will learn in the next chapter, a failure to replicate is also how scientific fraud is sometimes suspected and then uncovered.

Of course, in order to repeat a study, one must know precisely what was done in the original one. This is accomplished by means of a prescribed set of rules for describing research projects. These rules are presented in great detail in the *Publication Manual of the American Psychological Association* (American Psychological Association, 2001), a useful resource for anyone reporting research results or writing any other type of psychology paper. Appendix A, a guide to writing a lab report in APA format, is based on the manual and provides a good introduction to writing the report.

Objectivity in psychological science has been a problem historically. When psychology first emerged as a new science, it defined itself as the "science of mental life" and one of its early methods was called **introspection**. This procedure varied considerably from one laboratory to another, but it was basically a form of precise self-report. Participants in an experiment would perform some task and then provide a detailed description of their conscious experience of the task. To give you some sense of what introspection was actually like, read Box 1.1 before going any further. It shows you an example of a verbatim introspective description in an experiment on attention, and it shows how introspective thinking was a part of the everyday cognition of early psychologists (and the final quote in the Box shows how some researchers can get a little carried away in their enthusiasm for science).

Box 1.1

ORIGINS—A Taste of Introspection

The following introspective account is from a 1913 study by Karl Dallenbach dealing with the phenomenon of attention. Introspectors were instructed to listen to two metronomes set at different speeds and to count the number of beats between coincident beats (i.e., both metronomes hitting at the same instant). While counting, they were also asked to perform some other task, such as continuously adding numbers out loud. Needless to say, these tasks severely tested the limits of attention. After finishing a session, one introspector reported:

> The sounds of the metronomes, as a series of discontinuous clicks, were clear in consciousness only four or five times during the experiment, and they were especially bothersome at first. They were accompanied by strain sensations and unpleasantness. The rest of the experiment my attention was on the adding, which was composed of auditory images of the numbers, visual images of the numbers, sometimes on a dark gray scale which was directly ahead and about three feet in front of me. . . . When these processes were clear in consciousness, the sounds of the metronomes were very vague or obscure. (Dallenbach, 1913, p. 467)

Notice that the introspector attempted to describe everything that happened in consciousness while performing the task, including sensory events ("strain"), emotion ("unpleasant"), and imagery, both auditory and visual. Also, the difficulty in keeping multiple tasks equally "clear in consciousness" led Dallenbach to conclude that attention was severely limited, a finding later rediscovered by more modern research on "selective" attention (e.g., Broadbent, 1958).

Scientific thinking does not disappear when the scientist leaves the lab. Instead, thinking scientifically becomes the core of the scientist's everyday thinking. Thus, psychologists during the heyday of introspection often thought in introspectionist terms, even when they were far from the lab. In their letters to each other, for example, they would often reflect on some recent event by describing their conscious experience of it. The following example shows how some researchers can get a bit carried away. The excerpt is from an 1893 letter from Lightner Witmer, director of the laboratory at the University of Pennsylvania, to Hugo Münsterberg, director of the laboratory at Harvard University. It was a "what I did on my summer vacation" type of letter. After describing the joys of dissecting a human skull to map out the musculature related to emotional expressions, Witmer chronicled an unusual firsthand experiment on pain:

> I let a horse throw me from his back, allowing me to drop on my shoulder and head. I showed a beautiful case of loss of consciousness before the act.... I not only do not remember mounting and the horse running, but I forgot almost everything that happened.... [F]rom the time I got up in the morning till I regained complete consciousness ... I can form no continuous series of events. My head was bad for a while but is all right now, but my arm has served the purpose of quite a number of experiments as it still continues quite painful at times.... The psychological side of my afflictions will form the basis of at least three lectures next fall. (Witmer, 1893)

Witmer apparently recovered, and went on to have a distinguished career, which included the creation of psychology's first clinic near the end of the nineteenth century. He also coined the term "clinical psychologist."

The problem with introspection was that although introspectors underwent rigorous training that attempted to eliminate the potential for bias in their self-observations, the method was fundamentally subjective—I cannot verify your introspections and you cannot verify mine. The problem motivated psychologists like John B. Watson to argue that if psychology was to be truly "scientific," it needed to measure something that was directly observable and could be verified objectively (i.e., by two or more observers). Behavior fit the bill for Watson, and his vigorous arguments that the basic data of psychology ought to be observable and measurable actions earned him the title of "founder of behaviorism" as a school of thought. Today, the term "behavior" is part of psychology's definition in every introductory textbook of psychology.

With behavior as the data to be measured, the modern researcher investigating attention would not ask for detailed introspective accounts, as Dallenbach did in Box 1.1, but would design an experiment in which conclusions about attention could be drawn from some easily observed behavior in the Dallenbach task, such as the number of addition errors made while the participant was trying to keep track of the metronome activity. Presumably, two independent observers could agree on the number of errors that occurred in the task, making the experiment open to public verification.

Science Produces Data-Based Conclusions

Another attribute of science as a way of knowing is that researchers are **data-driven**. That is, like the character in the middle at the bar in Figure 1.1, who is undoubtedly a scientist of some kind, research psychologists expect conclusions about behavior to be supported by the evidence of objective information gathered through some systematic procedure. For instance, a claim made by a college admissions director

"Are you just pissing and moaning, or can you verify what you're saying with data?"

FIGURE 1.1 On the importance of data-based conclusions. (© The New Yorker Collection 1999 Edward Koren from cartoonbank.com. All Rights Reserved).

that "this year's incoming class is better prepared than any in recent memory" (an annual claim at some schools) would compel the scientific thinker to respond, "Let's see the data for this year and the past few years," and "What do you mean by better prepared?" Furthermore, researchers try to judge whether the data given to support some claim are adequate for the claim to be made. Hence, if someone asserts that talking on a cell phone adversely affects driving, the scientist immediately begins to wonder about the type and amount of data collected, how the terms were defined in the study (e.g., driving performance), the exact procedures used to collect the data, the type of statistical analysis that was done, and so on.

This attitude can be detected easily in research psychologists. They even find themselves thinking about how data might bear on the problems they encounter in daily living. Even a neighbor's offhand observation about the tomato crop being better this year might generate in the researcher's mind a host of data-related questions to test the claim (How exactly did you count the tomatoes during the past two years? Did you measure the number picked per day or the number that ripened per day? How did you define "ripe"? What do you mean by "better"?). Of course, there are certain hazards resulting from this kind of thinking, including a tendency for the neighbor to begin avoiding you. Sometimes the "driven" (as in compelled) part of the term "data-driven" seems to be the operative term!

A personification of the data-driven attitude taken to extremes can be found in the life of Sir Francis Galton, a nineteenth-century British jack-of-all-sciences, whose interests ranged from geography to meteorology to psychology. His importance for correlational research will be examined in Chapter 9. Galton was obsessed with the idea of collecting data and making data-based conclusions. Thus, he once measured interest in various theater productions by counting the number of yawns that he could detect during performances; he studied association by counting the number of related ideas occurring to him on his morning walks; and he collected data on species differences and age-related hearing loss by inventing a device, called the "Galton whistle," that produced sounds of various pitches (Galton, 1883/1948). Concerning hearing loss, the fun that Galton had in collecting the data is clear from this quote:

> On testing different persons I found there was a remarkable falling off in the power of hearing high notes as age advanced.... It is an only too amusing experience to test a party of persons of various ages, including some rather elderly and self-satisfied personages. They are indignant at being thought deficient in the power of hearing, yet the experiment quickly shows that they are absolutely deaf to shrill [i.e., high pitch] tones which the younger persons hear acutely, and they commonly betray much dislike to the discovery. (Galton, 1883/1948, p. 277)

Galton's most unusual attempt to draw a data-based conclusion was his controversial study on the "efficacy of prayer" (Galton, 1872). Like his cousin, Charles Darwin, Galton was skeptical about religion and decided to test empirically the notion that prayers "worked." If prayers were effective, he reasoned, then sick people who pray for a return to health should recover sooner than those who do not. Similarly, people who do a lot of praying for a living (i.e., the clergy) or who are the object of a great deal of prayer (i.e., the king and queen of England) should live longer than the general population. None of these predictions proved to be true, however. For instance, by digging through biographical dictionaries, Galton found that eminent members of the clergy lived for an average of 66.42 years and members of the royal family lasted 64.04 years; lawyers, on the other hand (presumably less likely to be the object of prayer), made it to a virtually identical average of 66.51 years (data from Forrest, 1974, p. 112). Galton was understandably criticized for his rather simplistic idea of the purpose of prayer, and his article on prayer was initially rejected (three times) as being "too terribly conclusive and offensive not to raise a hornet's nest" (cited in Forrest, 1974, p. 111), but the study certainly illustrates a conviction for drawing conclusions based on data.

Science Produces Tentative Conclusions

Related to the data-driven attitude that characterizes researchers is the recognition that conclusions drawn from data are always tentative, subject to future revision based on new research. That is, science is a self-correcting enterprise, its conclusions never absolute, yet there is confidence that research will eventually get one ever closer to the truth. The attitude was nicely described by Damasio (1994), in the context of research on the brain.

I have a difficult time seeing scientific results, especially in neurobiology, as anything but provisional approximations, to be enjoyed for a while and discarded as soon as better accounts become available. But skepticism about the current reach of science, especially as it concerns the mind, does not imply diminished enthusiasm for the attempt to improve provisional explanations. (p. xviii)

The tentative nature of scientific research is a feature of scientific thinking that is often difficult for the general public to understand, because people seem to believe that the outcome of well-executed scientific research will be the authoritative and the final answer to some question. This belief is the basis for the frustration often felt when some new finding reported in the news seems to contradict what was reported just a few years before. You can probably think of many examples that have been in the news in recent years. For example, current thinking about hormone replacement therapy (HRT) for menopausal women is that it might cause more problems (e.g., increased risk of breast cancer, blood clots, and stroke) than it solves, yet early research enthusiastically supported HRT because of its benefits in reducing the uncomfortable symptoms of menopause (e.g., hot flashes) and strengthening bone tissue, thereby fighting osteoporosis. It is easy to see how a woman undergoing HRT for several years, based on the old recommendation, would be upset to learn about new findings. She would be likely to say, as you have undoubtedly heard someone say under similar circumstances, "Why can't they (scientists) make up their minds?" The frustration is reasonable, but it is based on a fundamental misunderstanding of science. It is true that some findings have a greater degree of certainty than others, because they are based on a larger body of consistent evidence, but all findings are subject to rethinking, based on new research. Especially in the early decades of research on some phenomenon, it is likely that divergent findings will occur. Compared to most people, scientists have a relatively high tolerance for ambiguity and a willingness to be patient with the progress of science. In the long run, they have faith that the proficient use of science will lead to increasing confidence about the truth of some phenomenon (refer back to the Damasio quote again).

This attribute of science, its tentative nature, makes a large contrast with the nonscientific thinking described in the previous section of this chapter. Beliefs not based in science, because they bring social cognition biases into play, tend to be resistant to change. Beliefs based on scientific methodology, however, are always subject to change based on new data. Individual scientists might be reluctant to give up on their own data easily, but science as a whole proceeds because new information, if based on good science and replicated, eventually cannot be ignored. And there is an important lesson here for everyday critical thinking—we should always be open to new data and new ideas, willing to change our minds in the face of good evidence.

Science Asks Answerable Questions

As mentioned earlier, empiricism is a term that refers to the process of learning things through direct observation or experience. **Empirical questions** are those that can be answered through the systematic observations and techniques that characterize scientific methodology. They are questions that are precise enough to allow specific predictions to be made. As you will learn in Chapter 3, asking questions is the first step of any research project. How to develop a good empirical question and convert it into a testable hypothesis will be one theme of that chapter.

We can begin to get an idea about what constitutes empirical questions, however, by contrasting them with questions that cannot be answered empirically. For example, recall that Peirce used the mind-body question to illustrate the *a priori* method (use of reason). Philosophers argued both sides of the question for many years (they're still at it!), and Peirce wasn't optimistic about the issue ever being resolved. Whether the mind and the body are two separate essences or one is simply not an empirical question. However, there are a number of empirical questions that *can* be asked that are related to this issue. For instance, it is possible to ask about the influence of mental activity (mind) on physical health (body) by asking the empirical question "What are the effects of psychological stress on the immune system?" Also, it is possible to look at the body's influence on mental states by asking how physical fatigue affects problem-solving ability in some task.

Although research psychologists believe that the scientific approach is the ideal way to answer questions, it is worth pointing out that there are many questions in our lives that science *cannot* answer adequately. These questions include such things as whether a deity exists or whether people are fundamentally good or evil. These are certainly important questions, but they cannot be answered scientifically.[3] Of course, it is possible to investigate empirically such things as the specific factors that lead people to believe in a deity or that lead them to do good or bad things. Thus, potential empirical questions might include these:

> ✓ Does a belief in God increase with age (i.e., proximity to death)?
> ✓ Does helping behavior decline if the cost of helping outweighs the benefit?

Science Develops Theories That Can Be Disproven

When developing research studies, an early step in the process is to take the empirical question and develop it into a **hypothesis**, which is a prediction about the study's outcome. That is, prior to having empirical data, the hypothesis is your best guess about the answer to your empirical question. For the two empirical questions just asked, for instance, we might develop these hypotheses:

> ✓ With increasing age, especially after age 40, the strength of an average person's belief in God will increase systematically.

---

[3]I have often had discussions with a very good friend of mine, a philosophy professor, about our two disciplines and the kinds of questions we examine. The conversations, in a nutshell, went like this:

Him: Unlike psychologists, philosophers ask important questions.

Me: Unlike philosophers, psychologists ask answerable questions.

We were both right, of course.

✓ In a helping behavior situation, as the physical costs associated with helping increase, the probability of helping behavior occurring decreases.

As you will learn in the Chapter 3 discussion of theory, hypotheses often develop as logical deductions from a **theory**, which is a set of statements that summarize what is known about some phenomena and propose working explanations for those phenomena. A critically important attribute of a good theory is that it must be precise enough so that it can be disproven, at least in principle. This concept is often referred to as **falsification** (elaborated in Chapter 3—you could take a look ahead to Box 3.3 for a great historical example of falsification). That is, theories must generate hypotheses producing research results that could come out as the hypothesis predicts (i.e., support the hypothesis and increase confidence in the theory) or could come out in the opposite direction (i.e., fail to support the hypothesis and raise questions about the theory). Research that consistently fails to support hypotheses derived from a theory eventually calls a theory into question and can lead to its abandonment.

The requirement that theories be open to falsification might seem obvious, but there have been instances in psychology's history when theories, even popular ones, have been strongly criticized for not being precise enough to meet the criterion of potential disproof. Freud's famous theory is the one most often used to illustrate the point. Many elements of Freud's theories were vaguely defined, at least initially, making it difficult to put the theories to a strong test. As you are about to learn, one of the hallmarks of pseudoscientific theories is that they actively avoid this criterion of disproof.

To sum up this section on science as a way of knowing, I would describe research psychologists as "skeptical optimists." They are open to new ideas and optimistic about using scientific methods to test these ideas, but at the same time they are tough-minded—they won't accept claims without good evidence. Also, researchers are constantly thinking of ways to test ideas scientifically, they are confident that truth will emerge by asking and answering empirical questions, and they are willing (sometimes grudgingly) to alter their beliefs if the answers to their empirical questions are not what they expected.

One final point. Although I have been describing the attitudes and behaviors of psychological scientists, it is important to realize that virtually all of the points made in this section of the chapter are relevant to you as a developing critical thinker. To reiterate a point made earlier, it is not essential for you to become a researcher for the lessons of this book to have value for you. All of us could benefit from using the attributes of scientific thinking to be more critical and analytical about the information we are exposed to every day.

✓ Self Test 1.3

1. Textbook definitions of psychology always include the term "behavior." What does this have to do with the concept of objectivity?
2. What is an empirical question? Give an example.
3. What is the difference between a theory and a hypothesis?

Psychological Science and Pseudoscience

Because everyone is interested in human behavior, it is not surprising that many claims are made about its causes and inner workings. Many of those claims are based on legitimate scientific inquiry, of course, following the rules of the game that you will learn about in this text and carried out by the skeptical optimists I just described. That is, we know much about behavior as a result of relying on the kinds of thinking and the specific methods that characterize legitimate science. However, many claims are made in the name of psychological science using methods and ways of thinking that are not truly scientific but merely pseudoscientific ("pseudo-" is from the Greek word for "false"). In general, the term **pseudoscience** is applied to any field of inquiry that appears to use scientific methods and tries hard to give that impression, but is actually based on inadequate, unscientific methods and makes claims that are generally false. The Sidney Harris cartoon in Figure 1.2 portrays an unfortunate truth about pseudoscience—its popular appeal. What differentiates true science from pseudoscience is an important thing to know.

FIGURE 1.2   The unfortunate popularity of pseudoscience (© 1998 by Sidney Harris).

Recognizing Pseudoscience

Those living in the late nineteenth century could send away to the New York firm of Fowler and Wells for a "Symbolic Head and Phrenological Map" for 10 cents. For another $1.25, the head and map would be accompanied by a copy of *How to Read Character: A New Illustrated Handbook of Phrenology and Physiognomy* (Anonymous Advertisement, 1881). Thus equipped, people would then be in a position to measure character "scientifically" through an analysis of the shape of their skull.

Those of us living in the early twenty-first century can visit any one of dozens of websites and, for about $30, order "subliminal" CDs promising to improve our lives. Several sites will even let us download subliminal messages that will flash on our computers while we work. By merely listening to these CDs (or working on the computer), without any additional effort, we supposedly can improve memory, lose weight, stop smoking, improve self-esteem, increase our work productivity, and even become smarter students. Thus equipped, we are then able to solve life's problems with minimal effort ("just relax, turn on the CD, and your subconscious will do all the work for you").

As these two examples suggest, people are willing to pay for self-knowledge or self-improvement, especially if the methods appear to be scientific and take little effort to implement and understand. Both nineteenth-century phrenology and the twentieth-first century subliminal self-help industry are pseudoscientific, and both illustrate the main features of the pseudosciences—they try hard to associate with true science, they rely primarily on anecdotal and testimonial evidence, they sidestep the falsification criterion, and they reduce complex phenomena to overly simplistic concepts.

Associates with True Science

Pseudosciences do everything they can to give the appearance of being scientific. In some cases, the origins of a pseudoscience can be found in true science; in other instances, the pseudoscience confuses its concepts with genuine scientific ones. Phrenology illustrates the former, subliminals the latter.

Phrenology originated in legitimate attempts to demonstrate that different parts of the brain had identifiably different functions, and it can be considered one of the first systematic theories about the localization of brain function (Bakan, 1966). Phrenologists believed that (a) different personality and intellectual attributes ("faculties") were associated with different parts of the brain (see Figure 1.3), (b) particularly strong faculties resulted in larger brain areas, and (c) skull measurements yielded estimates of the relative strengths of faculties. By measuring skulls, therefore, one could measure personality.

Phrenology remained popular into the early years of the twentieth century, even though it had been discredited in a brilliant series of studies by the French physiologist Pierre Flourens by the mid-1800s (see Box 1.2). By the second half of the nineteenth century, despite being abandoned by scientists, phrenology as big business flourished: Phrenological societies were formed, popular journals were established, and phrenological analysis was used for everything from choosing a career to hiring an honest servant. Even if a theory is discredited within the scientific community, then, it can still find favor with the public. This creates

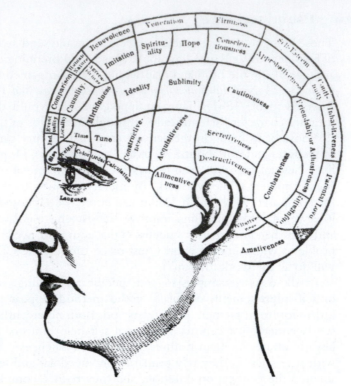

FIGURE 1.3   A skull showing the locations of the various
faculties proposed by phrenologists (Granger Collection).

special problems for psychology as a science because it isn't difficult for virtually any
type of theory about human behavior to have some popular appeal. The subliminal
self-help business is a good recent example.

Subliminal messages and their supposed influence on human behavior first
achieved widespread notoriety in the 1950s when James Vicary, a marketing
researcher, claimed that sales of popcorn and soda increased dramatically when
subliminal messages to "eat popcorn" and "drink Coca-Cola" were embedded in
a film being shown at a theater in New Jersey. Presumably, while filmgoers were
watching the movie, their minds were being manipulated without their knowledge
by the messages that were said to be below the threshold of conscious awareness, but
accessible to the unconscious mind. Despite the lack of any independent verification
of the increase in sales and the fact that Vicary later retracted his claim (Pratkanis,
Eskenazi, & Greenwald, 1994), this episode continues to be reported by devotees
as the "classic" example of the power of subliminal messages.

How are subliminal self-help CDs said to work? When playing one, the
listener typically hears soothing music or nature sounds (e.g., ocean waves and
the occasional seagull). Supposedly, subliminal messages such as "you can lose all
the weight you'd like" are played at a volume too faint to be heard consciously,
but detected nonetheless by the unconscious mind. The unconscious then is said

Box 1.2

CLASSIC STUDIES — Disproving Phrenology

In 1846, a brief volume (144 pages) with the title *Phrenology Examined* appeared. Its author was Pierre Flourens (1794–1867), a distinguished French physiologist and surgeon known for demonstrating the role of the ear's semicircular canals in balance, for locating the respiratory center in the medulla oblongata, and for discovering the anesthetic properties of chloroform (Kruta, 1972). He was also phrenology's worst enemy. He certainly did not mince words, declaring:

> The entire doctrine of [phrenology] is contained in two fundamental propositions, of which the first is, that understanding resides exclusively in the brain, and the second, that each particular faculty of the understanding is provided in the brain with an organ proper to itself.
>
> Now, of these two propositions, there is certainly nothing new in the first one, and perhaps nothing true in the second one. (Flourens, 1846/1978, p. 18)

To disprove the phrenologists' claims, Flourens took an experimental approach to the problem of localization, using the method of *ablation*. Rather than wait for natural experiments to occur in the form of accidental brain damage, Flourens removed specific sections of the brain and observed the effects. If the result of an ablation is an inability to see, then presumably the area of the removed portion has something to do with vision.

Flourens's attack on phrenology consisted of showing that specific areas of the brain that were alleged by phrenologists to serve function X in fact served function Y, and that the cerebral cortex operated as an integrated whole rather than as a large collection of individual faculties located in specific places. One focus of his research was the cerebellum. To the phrenologists, this portion of the brain controlled sexual behavior and was the center of the faculty of "amativeness." In his celebrated *Outlines of Phrenology*, for instance, Johann G. Spurzheim (1832/1978) argued that sexuality "appears with the development of this part, and is in relation to its size" (p. 28). Apparently thinking of some anecdotal data, Spurzheim pointed out that sometimes the cerebellum "is of great magnitude in children, and then its special function, the propensity we treat of, appears in early life" (p. 28).

Flourens would have none of it. First, he ridiculed the circular logic of assigning "faculties" to a certain behavior and then explaining that same behavior by pointing to the faculties:

> [W]hat sort of philosophy is that, that thinks to explain a fact by a word? You observe . . . a penchant in an animal . . . a taste or talent in a man; *presto*, a particular faculty is produced for each one of the peculiarities, and you suppose the whole matter to be settled. You deceive yourself; your *faculty* is only a

word,—it is the name of a fact,—and all the difficulty [of explanation] remains where it was before. (Flourens, 1846/1978, p. 39; italics in the original)

Flourens had little trouble ruling out (falsifying) the idea that the cerebellum had anything to do with sexual motivation. By carefully removing portions of the cerebellum, he showed that it was the center of motor coordination. Thus, pigeons deprived of the organ were unable to coordinate wing movements in order to fly, and dogs were unable to walk properly and were observed staggering, falling down, and bumping into objects they could normally avoid. Sexual motivation was unaffected. With other animals, Flourens removed varying amounts of the cerebral cortex and found a general relationship between the amount destroyed and the seriousness of the ensuing problem. He could find no indication of distinct functions ("faculties") residing in specific areas of the cortex.

Flourens effectively destroyed phrenology, but the issue of localization of function did not by any means disappear, and other physiologists soon demonstrated that the cortex had a greater degree of localization than Flourens was willing to grant. Paul Broca, for example, demonstrated that a relatively small area of the left frontal lobe of the cortex, later named for him, seemed to control the production of speech. For more on this issue of localization, take your department's courses in history and systems of psychology and biological psychology.

to influence the person's behavior in some unspecified fashion. Part of the CD's appeal is that the buyer is led to believe that dramatic self-improvement can be made with minimal effort—once the message is firmly in the unconscious, the individual will be driven by some powerful internal force and won't have to expend any serious effort on the conscious level.

Part of the marketing strategy is to convince potential buyers that the technology has a strong basis in established science. Indeed, there is a great deal of legitimate research on sensory thresholds, some of it showing that certain behaviors can be influenced by stimuli that are below the normal threshold of conscious reporting. In studies of semantic priming, for example, participants are first shown a screen that might contain a word (e.g., "infant"). The word is flashed very rapidly and followed by a "masking" stimulus, which has the effect of making it virtually impossible for participants to verbally report the word just presented. That is, the word has been shown subliminally, below the threshold for conscious recognition. Participants next see a sequence of letters presented rapidly. Some form words, others don't, and the task is to respond as quickly as possible when a true word has been recognized. Researchers (e.g., Marcel, 1983) have consistently found that words (e.g., "child") that are semantically related to the subliminal word ("infant") are recognized more quickly than unrelated words (e.g., "chair"). "Child" will not be recognized more quickly than "chair" unless "infant" has been presented subliminally first. In short, the process of word recognition has been "primed" by the initial subliminal stimulus.

Any connection between this research on priming and the effects of subliminal CDs on behavior, however, is purely coincidental. It is a long way from having a small effect on word recognition to having a persuasive effect on the complex behaviors involved with such tasks as trying to lose weight. And as you might have guessed, research that directly evaluates the effects of subliminal CDs on behavior regularly show that the CDs by themselves have *no effect at all*. Instead, any changes that occur are the result of other factors, such as the person's expectations about what should happen (e.g., Greenwald, Spangenberg, Pratkanis, & Eskenazi, 1991). You will read about one of these studies in Chapter 7 when you learn about different kinds of control groups. Just as Flourens's research derailed phrenology, modern researchers have shown that subliminal self-help CDs are equally pseudoscientific and a waste of your money.

Relies on Anecdotal Evidence

A second feature of pseudoscience, and one that helps explain its popularity, is the reliance on and uncritical acceptance of **anecdotal evidence**, specific instances that seem to provide evidence for some phenomenon. Thus, phrenology data consisted mostly of a catalogue of examples: a thief with a large area of "acquisitiveness," a priest with an overdeveloped bump for "reverence," a prostitute with excessive "amativeness." Subliminal advocates use the same approach. Their websites are filled with testimonials from people who have (apparently) improved their lives after using the CDs. In the area of weight loss, for example, where there is a long history of searching for a quick fix, reading about someone losing 20 pounds merely by lounging in the recliner and listening to seagulls can be irresistible. Anecdotal evidence has immediate appeal to the uncritical reader.

There is nothing wrong with accumulating evidence to support a theory; even anecdotal examples like the ones mentioned are not automatically disqualified. The problem occurs when one relies exclusively on anecdotes or makes more of them than is warranted. The difficulty is that anecdotal evidence is selective; examples that don't fit are ignored (you might recognize this as another example of a confirmation bias). Hence, there may be some thieves with a particular skull shape, but in order to evaluate a specific relationship between skull configuration X and thievery, one must know (a) how many people who are thieves do not have configuration X and (b) how many people who have configuration X aren't thieves. Without having these two pieces of information, there is no way to determine if there is anything unusual about a particular thief or two with skull shape X. The identical problem occurs with subliminals—the websites never report stories about people buying CDs and then failing to lose weight.

One other reason to distrust a glowing testimonial is that it often results from a phenomenon familiar to social psychologists—**effort justification** (Aronson & Mills, 1959). Following from Leon Festinger's theory of cognitive dissonance (elaborated in the Chapter 3 discussion about theory), the idea is that after people expend significant effort, they feel compelled to convince themselves that the effort was worthwhile. After spending $30 on a subliminal CD and a few dozen hours listening to it, we don't like to think that we've thrown away hard-earned money and wasted valuable time. To reduce the discomfort associated with the possibility that we've been had, we convince ourselves that the investment of time and money was a good one, and we may develop some extra motivation to change our behavior, at least in the short term.

Sidesteps Disproof

As you learned earlier in this chapter, one of the hallmarks of a good scientific theory is that it is stated precisely enough to be put to the stern test of disproof (falsification). In pseudoscience this does not occur, even though on the surface it would seem that both phrenology and the effects of subliminals would be easy to disprove. Indeed, as far as the scientific community is concerned, disproof has occurred for both.

Advocates of pseudosciences such as phrenology and subliminals have had to confront claims of disproof and the accompanying skepticism of legitimate scientists. Not all thieves have bumps in just the right places and not everyone listens to a CD and loses weight. Apologists respond to these threats rather creatively. Instead of allowing an apparent contradiction to hurt the theory, they sidestep the problem by rearranging the theory a bit or by adding some elements to accommodate the anomaly. Consequently, the apparent disproof winds up being touted as further evidence in support of the theory! For example, if a known pacifist nonetheless had a large area of destructiveness, a clever phrenologist would find even larger areas of cautiousness, benevolence, and reverence, and these would be said to offset or suppress the violent tendencies. Likewise, when responding to a study showing that subliminals have no measurable effects, defenders of subliminals might argue that that CDs work through unconscious processes that are beyond the reach of conventional scientific methodology. That is, subliminals clearly work (after all, look at all our testimonials), and if science fails to find evidence to support the effects, there must be something wrong with the science. Furthermore, if someone fails to benefit, they must be experiencing some kind of unconscious motivational block (i.e., it's your fault, not the subliminal message). Thus, for pseudoscience, any negative outcome can be explained or, more accurately, explained away. Yet a theory that explains all possible outcomes fails as a theory because it can never make specific predictions. If a pacifist can have either a large or a small area of destructiveness, how can we use skull shape to predict whether someone will be a pacifist? If subliminals may or may not produce weight loss, depending on whether the mysterious unconscious accepts or blocks the messages, how can its effects be reliably predicted? In general, if a theory is said to be, by definition, beyond the reach of scientific disproof, on what rational basis can its effects be shown to be valid?

Another way that disproof is sidestepped by pseudoscience is that research reports in pseudoscientific areas are notoriously vague and they are never submitted to reputable journals with peer review systems in place. As you recall, one of science's important features is that research produces public results, reported in books and journals that are available to anyone. More important, scientists describe their research with enough precision that others can replicate the experiment if they wish.

This does not happen with pseudoscience, where the research reports are usually vague or incomplete and, as seen earlier, heavily dependent on anecdotal support.

Reduces Complex Phenomena to Overly Simplistic Concepts

A final characteristic of pseudoscience worth noting is that these doctrines take what are actually very complicated phenomena (the causes of behavior and personality; the factors that bring about the kinds of life changes that would produce permanent weight loss) and reduce them to overly simplistic concepts. This, of course, has great consumer appeal, especially in psychology. Trying to figure out and improve behavior is a universal human activity, and if the process can be simplified, either by measuring someone's head, listening to a CD, determining someone's astrological sign, or interpreting one's handwriting, then many people will be taken in by the apparent ease of the explanations. Please note that the actual simplicity of the explanatory concepts is often masked by an apparent complexity of the measuring devices used in many of the pseudosciences. Thus, the phrenologists went through an elaborate set of skull measurements to measure faculties. Similarly, graphologists, alleged to be able to tell you all you need to know about yourself by analyzing your handwriting, often measure dozens of features of handwriting (e.g., slant angles). And those advocating for the effects of subliminal messages cloak their explanations in complicated descriptions of unconscious processes and brain activities.

In sum, pseudoscience is characterized by (a) a false association with true science, (b) a misuse of the rules of evidence by relying excessively on anecdotal data, (c) a lack of specificity that avoids a true test of the theory, and (d) an oversimplification of complex processes. Perhaps because of our enormous interest in behavior, pseudoscientific approaches to psychology are not hard to find in any historical era, and many people seem to have difficulty seeing the inherent weaknesses in pseudoscientific doctrines. As you develop your skills as a critical thinker by taking this research methods course, however, you should be able to distinguish valid psychological science from that which merely pretends to be.

The Goals of Research in Psychology

Scientific research in psychology has four interrelated goals. Researchers hope to develop complete descriptions of behaviors, to be able to make predictions about future behavior, and to be able to provide reasonable explanations of behavior. Furthermore, they assume that the knowledge derived from their research will be applied so as to benefit people, either directly or eventually. Each of these goals will be elaborated in later chapters of the book.

Description

To provide a good **description** in psychology is to identify regularly occurring sequences of events, including both stimuli or environmental events and responses or behavioral events. For example, a description of aggressive behavior in some primate species might include a list of the situations in which fighting is most likely to occur (e.g., over food), the types of threat signals that might precede actual combat (e.g., baring teeth), and the form of the fight itself (e.g., attacks directed at nonvital areas like shoulders and haunches). Description also involves classification, as when someone attempts to classify various forms of aggressive behavior (e.g., fighting vs. predation). Providing a clear, accurate description is an obvious yet essential first step in any scientific endeavor; without it, predictions cannot be made and explanations are meaningless. Some research in psychology is primarily descriptive in nature. For example, most observational and survey/questionnaire research falls into this category. You will learn more about this research in Chapter 12.

Prediction

To say that behavior follows **laws** is to say that regular and predictable relationships exist between variables. The strength of these relationships allows **predictions** to be made with some degree of confidence. After describing numerous primate fights, for example, it might become clear that after two animals fight over food and one wins, the same two animals won't fight again. If they both spot a banana at the same time, the winner of the initial battle might display a threat gesture and the loser of that first fight will probably go away. If that series of events happened often enough, the researchers could make predictions about future encounters between these animals and, more generally, between animals who are winners and losers of fights. One of the primary strengths of correlational research, as you will learn in Chapter 9, is that it is useful for making predications. A correlation between SAT scores and college GPA enables admissions departments at colleges to use SAT scores to predict success in college (up to a point).

Explanation

The third goal of the experimenter is **explanation**. To explain some behavior is to know what caused it to happen. The concept of causality is immensely complex, and its nature has occupied philosophers for centuries. Experimental psychologists recognize the tentative nature of explanations for behavior, but they are generally willing to conclude that X is causing Y to occur if they conduct an experiment in which they systematically vary X, control all other factors that could affect the results, and observe that Y occurs with some probability greater than chance and that variations of Y can be predicted from the variations in X. That is, X and Y are said to "covary," or occur together, and because X occurs first, it is said to be the cause of Y. Furthermore, they will have confidence in the causal explanation to the extent that (a) the explanation makes sense with reference to some theory or some already existing sets of laws and (b) other possible explanations for Y occurring in the presence of X can be effectively ruled out. The process of theory building, and of how empirical research is derived from and affects the development of theory, will be elaborated in Chapter 3. For now, simply be aware that causality is a complicated process involving covariation, experimental control, a time sequence with cause preceding effect, a theoretical structure, and the ruling out of alternative explanations. As you will see, starting in Chapter 5, research psychologists believe that, within some limits, causal conclusions can be drawn from a type of research called experimental research.

Application

This final goal of psychological science, **application**, refers simply to the various ways of applying those principles of behavior learned through research. Psychologists assume that because of the knowledge derived from the research they do, it is possible for people's lives to change for the better. Hence, research on the factors influencing depression enables therapists to help people diagnosed with depression, research on aggression can help parents raise their children more effectively, and so on.

✓ Self Test 1.4

1. How did pseudoscientific phrenologists get around the problem of falsification (disproof)?
2. What is anecdotal evidence and why is it often useless as a way to support the truth of some claim?
3. In psychological science, what is a law, and with which goal is it associated?

A Passion for Research in Psychology (Part I)

This chapter began by listing several reasons why the research methods course is essential. Besides tradition and the obvious fact that the course is step 1 on the road to becoming a researcher in psychology, these reasons include helping you understand the content of other psychology courses better, making you a critical consumer of research information, improving your chances of getting into graduate school or getting a job, and giving you an appreciation for the nature of science as a way of knowing. All this is fine, but, in my opinion, the single most important reason to learn how to do research in psychology is that, simply put, doing research can be great fun. It is challenging, frustrating at times, and the long hours in the lab can be tedious, but few researchers would exchange their careers for another. What could be more satisfying than getting an idea about behavior, putting it to the test of a research study, and having the results come out just as predicted? Who could not be thrilled about making some new discovery about behavior that might improve people's lives?

The attitude of seeing a research career as an ideal life is apparent in the remarkable final paragraph of a chapter written by the behaviorist Edward Tolman for a book series about various theoretical approaches to psychology. After describing his famous theory of learning, Tolman concluded by saying, in part:

> The [theory] may well not stand up to any final canons of scientific procedure. But I do not much care. I have liked to think about psychology in ways that have proved congenial to me. Since all the sciences, and especially psychology, are still immersed in such tremendous realms of the uncertain and the unknown, the best that any individual scientist … can do [is] to follow his own gleam and his own bent, however inadequate they may be. In fact, I suppose that actually this is what we all do. *In the end, the only sure criterion is to have fun. And I have had fun.* (Tolman, 1959, p. 152; italics added)

Let me wrap up this opening chapter with brief examples of how two legendary experimental psychologists became almost obsessively devoted to their work and found great satisfaction in it.

Eleanor Gibson (1910–2002)

On June 23, 1992, Eleanor Gibson (Figure 1.4a) was awarded the National Medal of Science by President George H. W. Bush. It is the highest honor a president can confer on a scientist. Gibson, then 82, was honored for a lifetime of research in developmental psychology, studying topics ranging from how we learn to read to how depth perception develops. She was perhaps best known to undergraduates for her "visual cliff" studies (Figure 1.4b).

(a)   (b)

FIGURE 1.4   (a) Eleanor Gibson (Associated Press, Cornell University/© AP/Wide World Photos). (b) Early research with the visual cliff (Topham Picturepoint/The Image Works).

Gibson was the prototype of the devoted researcher who persevered even in the face of major obstacles. In her case the burden was sexism. This she discovered on arrival at Yale University in 1935, eager to work in the lab of Robert Yerkes, well known for his work both in comparative psychology and mental testing. She was astounded by her first interview with him. As she later recalled, "He stood up, walked to the door, held it open, and said, 'I have no women in my laboratory'" (Gibson, 1980, p. 246).

Undaunted, Gibson eventually convinced the great behaviorist Clark Hull that she could be a scientist and finished her doctorate with him. Then in the late 1940s, she went to Cornell University with her husband, James Gibson (another famous name, this time in perception research). Eleanor labored there as an unpaid research associate for sixteen years before being named professor.[4] It was during this period of uncertain status that she completed her work on perceptual development. Some sense of her excitement about this research is evident from her description of how the visual cliff experiments first came about.

Briefly, the project evolved out of some perceptual development research with rats that she was doing with a Cornell colleague, Richard Walk. They were both curious about depth perception. In the army, Walk had studied training programs for parachute jumpers, and at Cornell's "Behavior Farm," Gibson had observed newborn goats avoid falling from a raised platform. She also had a "long-standing aversion to cliffs, dating from a visit to the Grand Canyon" (Gibson, 1980, p. 258). With a lab assistant, Gibson

> hastily put together a contraption consisting of a sheet of glass held up by rods, with a piece of wallpaper under one side of it and nothing under the other side except the floor many feet below.
>
> A few rats left over from other experiments got the first try.... We put a board about three inches wide across the division between the surface with flooring and the unlined glass, and put the rats on the board. Would they descend randomly to either side?
>
> What ensued was better than we had dared expect. All the rats descended on the side with textured paper under the glass. We quickly inserted some paper under the other side and tried them again. This time they went either way. We built some proper apparatus after that, with carefully controlled lighting and so on.... *It worked beautifully.* (Gibson, 1980, p. 259; italics added)

Gibson and Walk (1960) went on to test numerous species, including, of course, humans. The visual cliff studies, showing the unwillingness of eight-month-olds to cross the "deep side," even with Mom on the other side, are now familiar to any student of introductory psychology.

---

[4]Cornell did not pay her a salary during this time, but she earned stipends via the many successful research grants that she wrote (e.g., from the Rockefeller Foundation, National Science Foundation, U.S. Office of Education).

B. F. Skinner (1904–1990)

If you ask students to name a famous psychologist other than Freud, many will say "B. F. Skinner" (Figure 1.5), who is modern psychology's most famous scientist. His work on operant conditioning created an entire subculture within experimental psychology called the "experimental analysis of behavior." Its philosophy and the methods associated with it will be explored in Chapter 11.

Skinner's (three-volume—he wasn't shy) autobiography provides a marvelous glimpse of his life and work, and the following quote illustrates his almost childlike fascination with making a new discovery. It is from a period when Skinner had just completed his doctorate at Harvard and was staying on there as a prestigious Research Fellow. In early 1932, he was studying a number of different conditioning phenomena, including extinction. In his words:

> My first extinction curve showed up by accident. A rat was pressing the lever in an experiment on satiation when the pellet dispenser jammed. I was not there at the time, and when I returned *I found a beautiful curve*. The rat had gone on pressing although no pellets were received. . . .
>
> The change was more orderly than the extinction of a salivary reflex in Pavlov's setting, and *I was terribly excited*. It was a Friday afternoon and there was no one in the laboratory who I could tell. All that weekend I crossed streets with particular care and avoided all unnecessary risks to protect my discovery from loss through my accidental death. (Skinner, 1979, p. 95; italics added)

Note the use of the word "beauty" in both the Gibson and the Skinner quotes. Gibson's visual cliff experiment "worked beautifully" and Skinner found a "beautiful curve." The language reflects the strong emotion that is often felt by research scientists completely immersed in their work.

FIGURE 1.5   B. F. Skinner as a young graduate student at Harvard, circa 1930 (UPI/Corbis-Bettmann).

B. F. Skinner also had a healthy skepticism toward those (including most writers of research methods texts) who describe the scientific method as a series of specific steps to be completed. In an article chronicling how he eventually produced the apparatus associated with his name, the Skinner box, he articulated a number of informal "rules" of scientific conduct (Skinner, 1956). One of them captures the passion and curiosity of the best scientific thinkers: "When you run into something fascinating, drop everything else and study it" (p. 223).

Throughout the remainder of this book, you will be learning the tools of the experimental psychology trade and will be reading about the work of other psychologists who are committed researchers in love with their work. My greatest hope is that by the time you have completed this book, you will be hooked on research and want to contribute to our growing collection of knowledge about what makes people behave the way they do. And while I don't want you to ignore your other studies, I do hope that you will find research in psychology so fascinating that you will be tempted to "drop everything else and study it."

Chapter Summary

Why Take This Course?

The research methods course is at the core of the psychology curriculum. It should be taken by all psychology majors because it provides the foundation for doing research in psychology, serves as a basis for understanding other content courses in psychology, makes one a more critical consumer of information about behavior, is essential for admission to graduate studies, and teaches scientific thinking.

Ways of Knowing

Our knowledge of the world around us often derives from our experiences and how we interpret them, our reliance on the authority of others, and our use of reason. These sources of knowledge can be quite valuable, but they can also lead to error. Our experiences can be subject to social cognition biases (e.g., belief perseverance, availability heuristic, confirmation bias), authorities can be wrong, and while reason and logic are essential for critical thinking, reasonable arguments in the absence of empirical evidence can be unproductive in the search for truth. Research psychologists rely heavily on scientific thinking as a way of knowing and understanding behavior.

Science as a Way of Knowing

Research psychologists assume that human behavior is lawful and predictable and that using scientific methods can lead to the discovery of regularities in behavior. Science relies on observations that are more systematic than those made in everyday life, and produces knowledge that is open to public verification (i.e., it is said to be objective—verifiable by more than a single observer); historically, the emphasis on objectivity led to a shift from using introspection as a method to using methods that measured specific behaviors. Science also requires conclusions about the causes of behavior to be data-based, but scientists recognize that their data-based conclusions are tentative and could change, depending on the outcomes of future studies. The questions asked by scientific researchers are referred to as empirical questions—they are answerable through the use of recognized scientific methods. Scientists also develop theories that are precise enough to meet the test of disproof. Research psychologists are skeptical optimists—optimistic about discovering important things about behavior, but skeptical about claims made without solid empirical support.

Psychological Science and Pseudoscience

It is important to distinguish legitimate scientific inquiry from pseudoscience. The latter is characterized by a deliberate attempt to associate itself with true science, by relying on anecdotal evidence (e.g., glowing testimonials), by developing theories that are too vague to be adequately tested with scientific methods and fail the test of disproof, and by a tendency to explain complicated phenomena with overly simplistic concepts.

The Goals of Scientific Psychology

Research in psychology aims to provide clear and detailed descriptions of behavioral phenomena, to develop laws that enable scientists to predict behavior with some probability greater than chance, and to provide adequate explanations of the causes of behavior. The results of psychological research can also be applied to change behavior directly.

A Passion for Research in Psychology (Part I)

Psychological scientists tend to be intensely curious about behavior and passionate about their work. As a relatively young discipline, psychology has more questions than answers, so doing research in psychology can be enormously rewarding. The joy of doing research can be seen in the lives and work of famous psychologists such as Eleanor Gibson (the visual cliff studies) and B. F. Skinner (the discovery and promotion of operant conditioning).

Chapter Review Questions

At the end of each chapter you will find a set of short essay questions for review. You should study the chapter thoroughly before attempting to answer them. You might consider working through them with a lab partner or with a study group. There are additional review questions, along with detailed feedback, at the online Study Guide, which you can access by going to www.wiley.com/college/goodwin. The review material includes multiple choice, fill in the blank, and matching items.

1. Explain why it would be a good idea to take a research methods course prior to taking courses in such areas as social, abnormal, and cognitive psychology.

2. As ways of knowing, what are the shortcomings of authority and what Peirce called the *a priori* method?

3. Explain how various social cognition biases should make us cautious about the old saying that "experience is the best teacher."

4. According to Carnap, determinism must exist in order for free choice to have meaning. Explain the logic of his argument.

5. Using the historical example of introspection to illustrate, explain how research psychologists use the term objectivity.

6. What is an empirical question? Give an example of an empirical question that would be of interest to someone studying the relationship between religion and health.

7. Describe the essential attributes of science as a way of knowing.

8. Research psychologists are said to be "skeptical optimists." What does this mean?

9. Pseudosciences are criticized for relying on anecdotal evidence. What kind of evidence is this and why is it a problem?

10. Pseudosciences do what they can to appear scientific. How do those trying to sell you a subliminal self-help CD accomplish this?

11. Research in psychology is said to have four related goals. Describe them.

12. In order for research psychologists to feel confident that they have found a "cause" for some phenomenon, what conditions have to be met?

Applications Exercises

In addition to review questions, the end of each chapter will include "applications" exercises. These will be problems and questions that encourage you to think like a research psychologist and to apply what you have learned in a particular chapter. For each chapter, in order to give you some feedback, I will provide you with answers to some of the items (about half) in Appendix C. Your instructor will have a complete set of answers to all the exercises.

Exercise 1.1   Asking Empirical Questions

For each of the following nonempirical questions, think of an empirical question that would be related to the issue raised and lead to a potentially interesting scientific study.

1. Is God dead?
2. What is truth?
3. Are humans naturally good?

4. Are women morally superior to men?
5. What is beauty?
6. What is the meaning of life?

Exercise 1.2   Thinking Critically About an Old Saying

You have probably heard the old saying that "bad things come in threes." Use what you have learned about the various ways of knowing and about pseudoscientific thinking to explain how such a belief might be formed and why it is hard to convince a believer that there are problems with the saying. From what you have learned about scientific thinking, explain what needs to be made clearer in order to examine this "theory" more critically. That is, what needs to be precisely defined to determine if the saying is really true?

Exercise 1.3   Arriving at a Strong Belief

Consider people who have a strong belief in a personal God who, they believe, directs their daily lives. Using the various ways of knowing described in this chapter, explain how such a belief might form and be maintained.

Exercise 1.4   Graphology

The basic idea behind the pseudoscience of graphology is that the way you form your letters is a reflection of your personality. For example, a graphologist might report that you are shy or withdrawn if your writing is small and cramped. Do a simple Google search for "graphology." You will find hundreds of sites. Examine two sites very carefully—one promoting graphology and one that is a more skeptical analysis.

a. Consider each of the main aspects of pseudoscience. How might each apply in the case of graphology?

b. Even though we have not begun to discuss research design, you probably have some sense of what an experiment is like. Design a basic study that might be a good test of graphology's claim.

Exercise 1.5   Social Cognition and the Psychic Hotline

There are a surprising number of otherwise normal people who regularly consult psychics for advice about how to live their lives. Explain how believing in psychic ability might result from or be strengthened by:

a. belief perseverance

b. confirmation bias

c. availability heuristic

Answers to Self Tests:

✓ **1.1.**

1. A methods course teaches a process (of doing research) that applies to other content courses (e.g., social psychology).
2. Statistics (Research Methods is a close second).
3. Improves your ability to be a critical consumer of information.

✓ **1.2.**

1. Authority.
2. When students change answers and happen to get the item wrong (statistically less likely than changing an answer and getting it right), the outcome sticks out in their memory because it is painful (loss of points).

✓ **1.3.**

1. Behaviors can be measured and agreement among observers can occur.
2. An empirical question is one that can be answered with data collected from a study using scientific procedures. An example: What percentage of students reading this book take the self tests?
3. A theory summarizes what is known about some phenomenon and provides a tentative explanation; a hypothesis is a research prediction that can be deduced from a theory.

✓ **1.4.**

1. Phrenologists sidestepped disproof about one faculty by using other faculties to explain the apparent anomaly.
2. Anecdotal evidence involves using specific examples to support a general claim (they are also known as testimonials); they are problematic because those using such evidence fail to report instances that do not support the claim.
3. A law is a regularly occurring relationship. It applies to the goal of prediction.

CHAPTER 2

Ethics in Psychological Research

Preview & Chapter Objectives

This second chapter will introduce you to the most recent version (2002), of the ethics code formulated by the American Psychological Association (APA); it directs psychological scientists in the planning, execution, and reporting of their research. The code includes guidelines for psychological research that uses both human participants and animals.[1] The topic is presented early in the text because of its importance—ethical issues must be addressed at all stages of the research process. When you finish this chapter, you should be able to:

- Describe the origins of the APA ethics code.

- Articulate the code's five general principles, especially as they apply to research in psychology, and distinguish between the code's general principles and its specific standards.

---

[1] Humans are animals, too, of course. When I use the term "animal research," I am referring to research with nonhuman animals.

- Describe the role of the Institutional Review Board (IRB) in the research process and what needs to be done by the researcher to achieve IRB approval of research.
- Explain when research proposals are exempt from IRB review, eligible for expedited review, or in need of a full formal review.
- Explain why the decision-making processes of IRBs have occasionally been controversial.
- Identify the essential features of a researcher's ethical responsibility when completing psychological research using adult human participants.
- Describe historical examples of research, both in medical and psychological research, that raised serious ethical questions.
- Identify the ethical principles involved when completing research using children and those from special populations (e.g., prisoners, nursing home residents).
- Describe how the ethics code applies to research that involves the Internet.
- Describe the arguments for and against the use of animals in psychological research.
- Identify the essential features of a researcher's ethical responsibility when completing psychological research using animal subjects.
- Identify the varieties of scientific dishonesty, how it can be detected, and understand some of the reasons why misconduct sometimes occurs in science.

A system of **ethics** is a set of "standards governing the conduct of a person or the members of a profession" (*American Heritage Dictionary*, 1992, p. 630). As members of the profession of psychology, researchers are obligated to follow the code of ethics established by the APA. When conducting research in psychology, our ethical obligations encompass several areas. Research psychologists must (a) treat human research participants with respect and in a way that maintains their rights and dignity, (b) care for the welfare of animals when they are the subjects of research, and (c) be scrupulously honest in the treatment of data. This chapter will examine each of these broad topics.

Before beginning to study the APA code of ethics, you should read Box 2.1, which describes one of psychology's best-known studies and two other lesser-known experiments. The Little Albert experiment is often depicted as a pioneering investigation of how children develop fears, but it also serves well as a lesson in dubious ethical practice. Also, in the name of psychological science, other infants have been subjected to repeated pinpricks in a study on adaptation to pain and have spent up to 14 months in relative isolation.

Developing the APA Code of Ethics

Psychologists in the United States published their first code of ethics in 1953 (APA, 1953). This 171-page document was the outcome of about 15 years of discussion within the APA, which had created a temporary committee on Scientific

Box 2.1

CLASSIC STUDIES—Infants at Risk

In this chapter you will be learning about an ethics code that is quite elaborate and finely tuned. In fact, you might start to think that the code is unnecessarily complex and that the good judgment of psychological researchers would surely prevent research participants from coming to serious harm. After reading about the following three studies, however, it should be clear why the creation of an ethics code was needed.

One of psychology's most frequently cited studies (Watson & Rayner, 1920) has come to be known as the "Little Albert" study. The authors were the famous behaviorist John B. Watson and Rosalie Rayner, a graduate student who eventually became Watson's second wife. The study used just one child, an 11-month-old boy given the pseudonym of Albert B. The purpose of the study was to see if Albert could be conditioned to be afraid. Although it included serious methodological weaknesses and some replication attempts failed (Harris, 1979), it has become a "classic" study in psychology's history, routinely appearing in general psychology textbooks.

Watson and Rayner (1920) first determined that Albert had no natural fear of a white rat, but would react with a strong fear response if a steel bar was struck with a hammer just behind his head (Figure 2.1). The procedure was to pair the loud noise with the rat. When Albert would reach out to touch the rat, "the bar was struck immediately behind his head" (p. 4). His response? "The infant jumped violently and fell forward, burying his face in the mattress" (p. 4). After several trials, the loud noise was no longer needed—Albert developed a powerful association and was terrified of the rat. Because of generalization to similar stimuli, he was also afraid of a rabbit, a fur coat, and cotton wool (it is also clear from the film that Watson made that the unfortunate Albert was also quite afraid of Watson). Watson and Rayner made no attempt to remove the fear, even though they had access to the infant for a full month after the conditioning (instead, they used the month to see if the fear would persist—and it did).

It is difficult to hold Watson and Rayner responsible for ethical guidelines that were published 33 years after they conducted the Little Albert study. Historical events need to be evaluated in the context of their own times. It is clear, however, that the researchers were aware that some persons might object to the study, that "a certain responsibility attaches to such a procedure" (Watson & Rayner, 1920, p. 3). They decided to proceed because Albert seemed to be a strong, healthy child. Watson also justified the study by arguing that because Albert would learn such fears in real life *anyway*, he might as well learn them in a way that would advance science.

Watson and Rayner haven't been the only psychologists who used questionable judgment while studying infants. Two other examples are studies by Myrtle McGraw and by Wayne Dennis, both published in 1941. McGraw (1941) was interested in the maturation of the nervous system in the first few years of life, a legitimate topic

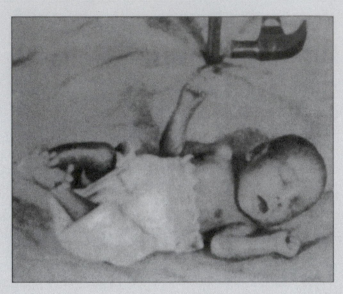

FIGURE 2.1 Loud noise producing fear in a child, from a film made by Watson of his infant research (including the Little Albert study); this still photo was taken from the film and reprinted by Watson in his *Psychological Care of Infant and Child* (1928). The photo shows what happens when "[a] steel bar is struck with a hammer near [the infant's] head" (p. 26). (From PSYCHOLOGICAL CARE OF INFANT AND CHILD by John B. Watson. Copyright 1928 by W. W. Norton & Company. Used by permission of W. W. Norton & Company, Inc.).

of study. Her method, however, was to apply repeated "pin pricks" to the cheeks, abdomens, arms, and legs of 75 different infants "at repeated intervals from birth to four years" (p. 31). The pin pricks evidently did not penetrate the skin, being delivered by a "blunt sterile safety pin" (p. 31), but they certainly caused some distress, as is clear from McGraw's descriptions of the reactions to the stimulus. For example, she wrote that the "most characteristic response consists of diffuse bodily movements accompanied by crying, and possibly a local reflex withdrawal of the stimulated member" (p. 32). Eventually, it appears that just the mere sight of McGraw heading their way with pin in hand was enough to stress the children—"With advancing development it will be observed that perception of the pin or of the approaching arm of the adult provokes fussing, crying, or withdrawal reactions on the part of this child" (p. 33).

Dennis (1941) was interested in studying how a child's development in the first year would be affected by reducing environmental and social stimulation. From the University of Virginia Hospital, Dennis and his wife were able to "obtain" a pair of female twins "because the mother was unable to provide for them" (p. 149). The Dennises offered the impoverished mother "temporary care of the twins in return for the privilege of studying them" (p. 149). The twins spent *14* months in the Dennis household, kept most of the time in a nursery room that afforded minimal views of the outside (sky and the top of a tree) and contained limited furniture and no toys. Dennis and his wife only interacted with them during feeding, bathing, and diaper changing, and "carefully refrained from rewarding or punishing the subjects for any action" (p. 150). Dennis reported delays in motor development, but claimed no serious adverse effect. He concluded that during the first year, social interactions and environmental stimulation had minimal adverse effect on children. He made little of the fact that the twins also were behind in language development, an outcome that wouldn't surprise modern developmental psychologists. Later in the chapter, you will learn that research psychologists sometimes use animals in procedures that would not be considered appropriate for humans, and raising them in isolation is an example. In 1941, however, Dennis apparently had no misgivings about subjecting infants to an impoverished environment.

The Watson, McGraw, and Dennis studies were not completed by callous and unconcerned researchers, but by people who believed they were advancing science, but they were operating in the absence of a code of ethical conduct that might have given them pause. The studies, which cause us to cringe today, make the need for an ethics code clear.

and Professional Ethics in the late 1930s. The committee soon became a standing committee to investigate complaints of unethical behavior (usually concerned with the professional practice of psychology) that occasionally were brought to its attention. In 1948, this group recommended the creation of a formal code of ethics. Under the leadership of Nicholas Hobbs, a new committee on Ethical Standards for Psychology was formed and began what became a 5-year project (Hobbs, 1948).

We have seen in Chapter 1 that psychologists are trained to think scientifically. What is noteworthy about the Hobbs committee is that, in keeping with psychology's penchant for relying on data before drawing conclusions, it opted for an empirical approach to forming the code. Using a procedure called the **critical incidents** technique, the committee surveyed the entire membership of the APA (there were about 7,500 members then), asking them to provide examples of "incidents" of unethical conduct that they knew about firsthand and "to indicate what [they] perceived as being the ethical issue involved" (APA, 1953, p. vi). The request yielded over 1,000 replies. Although most of the replies concerned the practice of psychology (e.g., psychotherapy), some of the reported incidents involved the conduct of research (e.g., research participants being harmed unnecessarily). The committee organized the replies into a series of several drafts that were published in *American Psychologist*, the association's primary journal. The APA's Council of Directors accepted the final version in 1952 and published it the next year. Although it was concerned mainly with professional practice, one of its sections was called "Ethical Standards in Research."

Over the years the code has been revised several times, most recently in 2002. It currently includes a set of five general principles, which are excerpted in Table 2.1,

TABLE **2.1**   *General Principles of the APA Code of Ethics*

Principle A: Beneficence and Non-Malfeasance

Psychologists strive to benefit those with whom they work and take care to do no harm. In their professional actions, psychologists seek to safeguard the welfare and rights of those with whom they interact professionally and other affected persons, and the welfare of animal subjects of research. . . . Because psychologists' scientific and professional judgments and actions may affect the lives of others, they are alert to and guard against . . . factors that might lead to misuse of their influence. . . .

Principle B: Fidelity and Responsibility

Psychologists establish relationships of trust with those with whom they work. They are aware of their professional and scientific responsibilities. . . . Psychologists uphold professional standards of conduct, clarify their professional roles and obligations, accept appropriate responsibility for their behavior, and seek to manage conflicts of interest that could lead to exploitation or harm. . . .

Principle C: Integrity

Psychologists seek to promote accuracy, honesty, and truthfulness in the science, teaching, and practice of psychology. . . . In situations in which deception may be ethically justifiable to maximize benefits and minimize harm, psychologists have a serious obligation to consider . . . their responsibility to correct any resulting mistrust or other harmful effects that arise from the use of such techniques.

Principle D: Justice

Psychologists recognize that fairness and justice entitle all persons access to and benefit from the contributions of psychology. . . . Psychologists exercise reasonable judgment and take precautions to insure that their potential biases, the boundaries of their competence, and the limitations of their expertise do not lead to or condone unjust practices.

Principle E. Respect for Peoples' Rights and Dignity

Psychologists respect the dignity and worth of all people, and the rights of individuals to privacy, confidentiality, and self-determination. Psychologists are aware that special safeguards may be necessary to protect the rights and welfare of persons or communities whose vulnerabilities impair autonomous decision-making. Psychologists are aware of and respect cultural, individual, and role differences. . . . Psychologists try to eliminate the effect on their work of biases . . . , and they do not knowingly participate in or condone activities of others based upon such prejudices.

and 89 standards, clustered into the 10 general categories listed in Table 2.2. The general principles are "aspirational" in their intent, designed to "guide and inspire psychologists toward the very highest ideals of the profession" (APA, 2002, p. 1062), while the standards establish specific rules of conduct and provide the basis for any charges of unethical conduct.[2]

---

[2]The APA has established procedures for evaluating claims of ethical misconduct and for punishing those found guilty of misconduct. There is even a link allowing psychologists to report "critical incidents." For more information, visit www.apa.org/ethics.

TABLE 2.2   *The Ten Categories of Ethical Standards in the 2002 Code*

Category		Examples of Standards
1. Resolving Ethical Issues	1.01	Misuse of psychologists' work
[8]	1.05	Reporting ethical violations
2. Competence	2.01	Boundaries of competence
[6]	2.04	Bases for scientific and professional judgments
3. Human Relations	3.01	Unfair discrimination
[12]	3.06	Conflict of interest
4. Privacy and Confidentiality	4.01	Maintaining confidentiality
[7]	4.04	Minimizing intrusions on privacy
5. Advertising/Public Statements	5.01	Avoidance of false or deceptive statements
[6]		
	5.04	Media presentations
6. Record Keeping and Fees	6.01	Documentation of professional and scientific work and maintenance of records
[7]		
	6.07	Referrals and fees
7. Education and Training	7.01	Design of education and training programs
[7]		
	7.03	Accuracy in teaching
8. Research and Publication	8.02	Informed consent to research
[15]	8.12	Publication credit
9. Assessment	9.02	Use of assessments
[11]	9.05	Test construction
10. Therapy	10.02	Therapy involving couples or families
[10]	10.10	Terminating therapy

The five general principles reflect the philosophical basis for the code as a whole. You should read the fuller descriptions in Table 2.1, but as they apply to research, they involve the following:

- *Beneficence and Non-Malfeasance* establishes the principle that psychologists must constantly weigh the benefits and the costs of the research they conduct and seek to achieve the greatest good in their research.
- *Fidelity and Responsibility* obligates researchers to be constantly aware of their responsibility to society and reminds them always to exemplify the highest standards of professional behavior in their role as researchers.
- *Integrity* compels researchers to be scrupulously honest in all aspects of the research enterprise.
- *Justice* obligates researchers to treat everyone involved in the research enterprise with fairness and to maintain a level of expertise that reduces the chances of their work showing any form of bias.

- *Respect for People's Rights and Dignity* translates into a special need for research psychologists to be vigorous in their efforts to safeguard the welfare and protect the rights of those volunteering as research participants.

✓ Self Test 2.1

1. What was the critical incidents technique?
2. The first general principle of the APA ethics code is "beneficence and non-malfeasance." What does this mean for the researcher?

Ethical Guidelines for Research with Humans

In the 1960s, a portion of the original ethics code was elaborated into a separate code of ethics for research with human participants. An APA committee modeled on the Hobbs committee and headed by a former member of it, Stuart Cook, used the same critical incidents procedure and published an ethics code specifically for researchers in 1973 (APA, 1973); it was revised in 1982 (APA, 1982), and again as part of the general revisions of 1992 and 2002. The specific APA Standards regarding research are found in category 8 of the code (Table 2.2 has samples of standards in all 10 categories) and the research standards are reprinted in full in Appendix B. For the rest of the chapter, whenever I make reference to a specific standard, I will refer to the identifying number, so you will be able to find the precise wording in the Appendix. The standards for research with human participants include making a judgment that the benefits of the research outweigh the costs, gaining the informed consent of those participating in the study, and treating the research volunteers well during the course of the study and after it has been completed.[3]

Judging Benefits and Costs: The IRB

All research on human behavior imposes some burden on those participating in the study. At a minimum, people are asked to spend time in an experiment when they could be doing something else. At the other extreme, they are sometimes placed in potentially harmful situations. In the name of psychological science, human **research participants** (or **subjects**)[4] have received electrical shocks, have been told that they failed some apparently easy test, and have been embarrassed in any number of ways. That such experiences can be distressing is clearly illustrated by

---

[3]Another useful source of information about the ethical treatment of human research participants is the Office for Human Research Protections in the Department of Health and Human Services. Its website is www.hhs.gov/ohrp/.
[4]Until recently, research psychologists routinely used the term *subject* to refer to any research participant, human or animal, whose behavior was being measured in a study. Starting with the fourth edition of its publication manual, in 1994, however, the APA recommended a change in this usage. At least with regard to most humans

one of social psychology's most famous series of studies, the obedience research of Stanley Milgram (1963, 1974).

In the guise of a study on the effects of physical punishment on learning, Milgram induced volunteers to obey commands from an authority figure, the experimenter (a part of the research team and a high school biology teacher in real life). Playing the role of teachers, participants were told to deliver what they thought were high-voltage shocks (no shocks were actually given) to another apparent volunteer (also a member of the research team and a railroad payroll auditor in real life) who was trying, without much success, to accomplish a memory task. A surprisingly high percentage of subjects complied with the "orders" to deliver shock, and, in doing so, most became quite distressed. In his original study, Milgram (1963) reported that he had

> observed a mature and initially poised businessman enter the laboratory smiling and confident. Within 20 minutes he was reduced to a twitching, stuttering wreck, and was rapidly approaching a point of nervous collapse. (p. 377)

As you might guess, Milgram's research has been controversial. He was sharply criticized for exposing his volunteers to extreme levels of stress, for producing what could be long-term adverse effects on their self-esteem and dignity, and, because of the degree of deception involved, for destroying their trust in psychologists (Baumrind, 1964).

The basic dilemma faced by Milgram and every other researcher is to weigh the scientific value of the study being planned (a benefit) against the degree of intrusion on those contributing data to the study (a cost). On one hand, experimental psychologists believe strongly in the need to conduct psychological research on a wide range of topics. Indeed, they believe that failing to investigate some topic abdicates one's responsibility as a scientist. If the ultimate goal is to improve the human condition (the "beneficence" principle), and if knowledge about behavior is essential for this to occur, then clearly it is essential to learn as much as possible. On the other hand, as we have just seen, research can create discomfort for those participating in it, although very few studies come anywhere near the Milgram experiments in terms of the level of stress experienced by subjects. When planning a research study, the experimenter always faces the conflicting requirements of (a) producing meaningful research results that could ultimately increase our knowledge of behavior and add to the general good, and (b) respecting the rights and welfare of the study's participants and causing them no harm. Clearly, Milgram

---

(nonhuman animals and preverbal infants were still to be referred to as "subjects"), APA recommended that writers use "research participant" or "participant" instead of "subject," apparently on the grounds that the latter term is somehow biased and dehumanizing. Furthermore, even though the change was only described as a recommendation, it has taken on the rule of law as the years have gone by—just try publishing anything in an APA journal with the term "subject" in it. Some prominent researchers (Roediger, 2004) have challenged this switch in terminology, though, arguing that the term "subject" does not demean anyone, that the term is more efficient linguistically (two as opposed to four syllables), and that it reflects historical continuity. I agree with Roediger, and because this is not an APA publication, I am under no obligation to bow to their dictates. But it is also true that whichever term is used, it is certain to be used a lot in a methods text. So for the sake of avoiding a monotonous repetition of the same term, I will compromise and use both terms interchangeably throughout the text.

reached the conclusion that the potential value of his research outweighed the potential dangers of his procedures. He was motivated by questions about the Nazi Holocaust (Milgram was Jewish) and deeply concerned about the problem of obedience to authority. Did the Holocaust reflect some basic flaw in the German psyche? Or is the tendency to obey authority to be found in all of us, produced when the circumstances are right? (The latter, Milgram eventually concluded—situations can be powerful.)

An integral part of the process of planning a study involves consulting with others. Informally, this can mean asking colleagues to examine a research plan for compliance with ethical guidelines. A formal process also exists, however, and it concerns a group called the **Institutional Review Board** or **IRB**. This group consists of at least five people, usually faculty members from several departments and including at least one member of the outside community and a minimum of one nonscientist (Department of Health and Human Services, 1983). In 1974, as part of the National Research Act, the federal government mandated that IRBs be in place for any college or university receiving federal funds for research. Today they are found in virtually all colleges and universities, whether or not federal funding is involved. Researchers seeking IRB approval typically submit to the board a rationale for the study and a description of research procedures, a statement about potential risks to participants, how these risks will be alleviated and why they can be justified, a copy of the study's "informed consent" form, and any copies of materials to be used in the experiment. IRBs distinguish between proposals that are *exempt* from full review, those eligible for *expedited review*, and those requiring a full *formal review*. For research in psychology, proposals that are exempt from full review include studies conducted in an educational setting for training purposes (e.g., asking students like you to test each other on reaction time in the lab as part of a course requirement), purely naturalistic observation studies of public behavior, survey research that does not assess sensitive topics, and archival research. Proposals receiving expedited reviews include many of the typical psychology laboratory experiments in basic processes such as memory, attention, or perception, in which participants will not experience uncomfortable levels of stress or have their behavior manipulated in any significant fashion. All other research requires a formal review by the full IRB. As you might guess, there are gray areas concerning decisions about exempt, expedited, and full review. Hence, it is common practice for universities to ask that *all* research be given some degree of examination by the IRB. Sometimes, different members of an IRB might be designated as "first step" decision makers—identifying those proposals that are exempt, granting approval (on behalf of the full board) for expedited proposals, and sending on to the full board only those proposals in need of consideration by the entire group. At medium and large universities, where the number of proposals might overwhelm a single committee, departmental IRBs are sometimes created to handle the expedited reviews (Murphy, 1999).

IRBs provide an effective safeguard for participants, researchers, and universities, but they have been controversial for four reasons. One issue has been the extent to which IRBs should be judging the details of research procedures and designs (Kimmel, 2007). Researchers legitimately object to nonspecialists (e.g., philosophy professors) passing judgment on procedures they may not understand or research traditions they fail to appreciate (e.g., staging "accidents" in research on helping behavior). On the other hand, there are ethical implications of a poorly designed study. If it is seriously flawed methodologically, its results will be worthless, its subjects could be harmed needlessly, and, at the very least, the time of the subjects will be wasted. At least one prominent researcher has suggested that IRBs should include methodology experts (Rosenthal, 1994). A second issue concerns the perception among some researchers that it is very difficult to win IRB approval of "basic" research (i.e., investigating fundamental psychological processes, such as perception—see Chapter 3 for a full discussion of basic versus applied research). IRB members unfamiliar with some specific research area might fail to see the relevance of a proposed study in basic science, for instance, yet might easily be able to comprehend an applied research study. For instance, it could be difficult for an IRB member to see the justification for a laboratory experiment in which subjects see meaningless shapes that vary according to some specific dimensions, and then try to pick them out later in a recognition test. On the other hand, a study examining the ability to recognize people filmed on bank video cameras might appear to be more important and could gain IRB approval more easily. Third, some researchers complain that IRBs can be overzealous in their concern about risk, weighing it more heavily than warranted, relative to the scientific value of a study. For instance, a researcher described by Kimmel (2007) was unable to obtain IRB approval for a study in which people were asked to detect tones of varying loudness. Despite the fact that no tone was louder than conversational speech, the IRB insisted that listening to the tones "entailed a slight risk to [subjects'] welfare" (p. 283). The researcher refused to concede the point, argued with the IRB for three years, had no recourse for appeal, and eventually switched to animal research, stating that "the composition of animal welfare committees [was] a bit more reasonable" (p. 283). Obviously, not all IRBs are this arbitrary and inflexible, but the lack of an appeal process beyond the IRB is a serious problem. Some research has suggested that researchers, if they believe they have been treated unfairly by an IRB, might go as far as to omit from their IRB proposals some aspects of their procedure that IRBs could find objectionable. For example, Keith-Spiegel and Koocher (2005) reported one incident in which a researcher "writes, in elaborate detail, content he knows will likely bore readers ... , while omitting or distorting elements of his projects that he believes might cause his IRB to balk. He has used this technique for his last seven proposals, and every one gained approval without question" (p. 340). A fourth issue that concerns psychologists is that IRBs sometimes overemphasize a biomedical research model to evaluate proposals. As a result, they sometimes ask researchers to respond to requests that are not relevant for most psychological research. For example, they might ask that the consent form include information about procedures or alternative courses of treatment available to those who choose not to participate in the study (Azar, 2002). This makes sense for research evaluating the effectiveness of some medical treatment, but makes no sense in most psychological research, where the alternative to participating is simply not to participate. One unfortunate consequence of these four issues is a lack of consistency among different IRBs. You might not be surprised to learn that the exact same IRB proposal can be approved by one IRB and rejected by another (Ceci & Bruck, 2009).

An important component of the IRB decision about a proposal involves determining the degree of **risk** to be encountered by participants. Sometimes there is no risk at all, as when experimenters observe public behavior and do not intervene in any way. At other times, subjects in a study may be "at risk" or "at minimal risk." The distinction is not razor sharp but is based on the degree to which the people being studied find themselves in situations similar to "those ordinarily encountered in daily life or during the performance of routine physical or psychological examinations or tests" (Department of Health and Human Services, 1983, p. 297). Hence, subjects facing situations like those encountered in daily living that might involve some stress, but not a substantial amount, are considered to be "at minimal risk." If the risks, physical or mental, are greater than that, participants are said to be "at risk." For instance, people would be at minimal risk in a sports psychology study investigating whether training in visual imagery techniques leads to better athletic performance than the absence of such training. However, if that same study investigated whether the improvement due to training in imagery could be reduced by having participants ingest low or moderate doses of some drug, the degree of risk to participants would obviously be higher and require more careful scrutiny by an IRB.

When there is minimal or no risk, IRB approval is usually routinely granted through an expedited review, or the proposal will be judged to be exempt from review. However, when participants are "at risk," a full IRB review will occur, and experimenters must convince the committee that the value of the study outweighs the risk and that the study could not be completed in any other fashion, and they must scrupulously follow the remaining ethical guidelines to ensure that those contributing data are informed and well treated.

One final point about IRB approval is that when conducting research outside of the university environment, a researcher might have to satisfy more than a single review board. A health psychologist, for instance, might be using a local wellness center as a location for studying adherence to an exercise program. In addition to gaining university IRB approval, the researcher might have to get the OK from the center's research committee before proceeding with the study.

Informed Consent and Deception in Research

Consider the following scenario. You decide to sign up for a psychology experiment. The "sign-up room" has a table with several folders on it, each giving a brief description of a study and providing sign-up information. A study on "problem solving" looks interesting, so you sign up. You show up at the appropriate time and place and, after being given some initial instructions by an experimenter, you and another participant are left alone and given some anagrams to solve (anagrams are sets of letters that have to be unscrambled to make a word). After five minutes or so, the other person seems to be getting upset about the difficulty of the task and then storms out of the room. The experimenter returns, asks you a series of identifying questions about the other person who just left (e.g., "Could you describe what she was wearing?"), and then asks you to identify this person from a set of photos. The experimenter then informs you that the real purpose of the study was eyewitness identification accuracy, not anagram problem solving. How would you react to this?

A central feature of the APA code is the concept of **informed consent** (Standard 8.02), the notion that in deciding whether to participate in psychological research, human participants should be given enough information about the study's purpose and procedures to decide if they wish to volunteer. For example, the use of painful procedures in a study (e.g., electric shock, regardless of how mild it is) must be disclosed. On the other hand, Standard 8.07 indicates that subjects might experience **deception** in a study if it is determined by the researcher, and agreed to by the IRB, that the study could not be done in any other fashion. That is, participants might not be told the complete details of a study at its outset or they might be misled about some of the procedures or about the study's purpose, as in the eyewitness memory example you just read. Researchers argue that in the absence of deception in certain studies, participants would not act naturally. If you knew you were in a study on eyewitness identification and that the anagrams didn't matter, so the argument goes, you wouldn't bother much with the anagrams. Instead, you'd be trying to memorize the features of the other person in the room, a behavior that would not occur under normal circumstances. How can these apparently contradictory concepts of consent and deception be reconciled?

One could argue that truly informed consent should never result in people being deceived about the purposes of the study. Some (e.g., Baumrind, 1985) have recommended eliminating deception in all psychology experiments, on the grounds that people in positions of trust (i.e., experimenters) should not be lying to others (i.e., participants). The outcome of deceptive research, she believes, is that participants could become mistrustful of experts and perhaps even cynical about the legitimacy of psychology as a science. Others (e.g., Geller, 1982) have argued that the need for "truth in advertising" could be met by forewarning those thinking about participating in a deception. They could be given a general rationale for deception during the consent procedure, told that some form of deception would probably occur in the study, and assured that all would be revealed at the end. Forewarning has been criticized, however, on the grounds that subjects would spend more time trying to figure out the true purpose of the study than they would behaving naturally, and that many would refuse to participate, thereby reducing the generality of the results of the study (Resnick & Schwartz, 1973).

Several alternatives to deception have been suggested, including naturalistic observation and qualitative interview procedures. Greenberg (1967), for example, suggested using a simulation procedure in which people are told the complete purpose of a study ahead of time and are then asked to role-play someone who did not know the purpose ahead of time. Studies (e.g., Miller, 1972) evaluating this idea have not been very supportive, however. There is a difference between behaving naturally and acting the way you think you are supposed to act; consequently, it's not surprising that role-playing subjects and naive subjects behave differently. Furthermore, there is evidence that participants who are fully informed ahead of time about the purpose of an experiment behave differently from those who aren't informed. For instance, a study by Gardner (1978) looked at the effects of noise as a stressor for some who were fully informed about the noise and others who weren't. The usual finding is that noise disrupts concentration and reduces performance on a variety of tasks, especially if the noise is unpredictable. Gardner, however, found that noise failed to have adverse effects on those who were first given complete information about the study, including the explicit direction that they could leave the study at any time. Apparently, the information about being able to leave increased the participants' *feeling of control* over the situation, and even the unpredictable noise didn't bother them. Other research (e.g., Sherrod, Hage, Halpern, & Moore, 1977) has shown consistently that an increased perception of control over one's fate generally acts to reduce stress. Thus, fully informing participants in a study on the effects of unpredictable noise might produce an outcome that fails to discover the bad effects of such noise. In order to examine thoroughly the variables influencing the relationship between unpredictable noise as a stressor and performance on some tasks, it seems that some degree of deception is needed.

Milgram's obedience studies provide a further illustration of why psychologists sometimes withhold information about the true purpose of the study at the beginning of the experiment. We've seen that Milgram told his subjects he was investigating the effects of punishment on learning. Teachers (the real subjects) tried to teach a list of word pairs to the learner, believing they were shocking him for errors (see Figure 2.2). Milgram was not really interested in learning, of course. Rather, he wanted to know whether his volunteers would (a) continue to administer apparent shocks of increasing voltage to a learner who was in discomfort and not learning much or (b) disobey the experimenter and stop the experiment. The outcome: Few people disobeyed. In the original study, 26 out of 40 continued shocking the learner even when the voltage level seemed to reach 450 and *nobody* disobeyed until the level reached 300 volts (Milgram, 1963)! If Milgram had informed his "teachers" that he was interested in seeing whether they would obey unreasonable commands, would the same results have occurred? Certainly not. Blind obedience to authority is not something that people value highly, so subjects told ahead of time they are in a study of obedience would surely be less compliant than they otherwise might be. The key point is that researchers want their participants to take the task seriously, to be thoroughly involved in the study, and to behave as naturally as possible. For that to happen, deception is sometimes necessary. Please keep in mind, however, that the Milgram study is an extreme example of deception. Although deception studies with elaborate "cover stories" are more likely to be found in social psychology than in other research areas (Korn, 1997), the level of deception is minor in most research. Typically, it involves the withholding of some information about the study rather than an elaborate story that creates the impression that the study concerns topic A when it really involves topic B. That is, most deception research involves omitting some information in the consent process, rather than actively misleading participants about what they are to encounter (Fischman, 2000). For instance, participants in a memory study might be given a series of five word lists to study and recall, one at a time. At the end of the session, although not initially informed of it, they might be asked to recall as many words as they could from all five lists. Information about that final recall would be omitted from the consent procedure to get a better measure of the memory for all of the lists, uncontaminated by extra rehearsal.

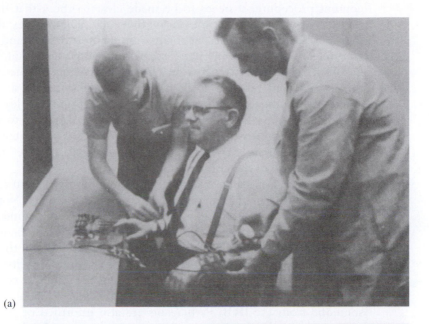

(a)

(b)

FIGURE 2.2   (a) The "learner" in Stanley Milgram's experiment being prepared for an experimental session; (b) the apparatus used by the "teacher" to (apparently) deliver shocks to the learner. From Milgram (1974) (© 1965 by Stanley Milgram. From the film "Obedience" distributed by the New York University Film Library).

Although subjects might not be told everything about the study during the consent procedure, it needs to be made clear to them that they can discontinue their participation at any time during the study. That is, they should be aware that they can leave the experiment at any time without penalty and with no pressure to continue. This "quit at any time" stipulation would have sunk Milgram's proposal, had IRBs been in existence when he completed his obedience research. During the sequence of learning trials, if the teacher-participant showed any hesitation about continuing to administer shocks to the bumbling learner (and almost all participants did), the experimenter was trained by Milgram to say things like "The experiment requires that you continue" or "it is absolutely essential that you continue" (Milgram, 1963, p. 374). This clearly violates the "feel free to leave any time" provision of the consent standard.[5]

Figure 2.3 displays an example of a simple consent form for adult participants that I have used in an experiment on cognitive mapping. Note that it has several features. Potential volunteers agree to participate after learning the general purpose of the study (but not the specific hypotheses), the basic procedure, and the amount of time for the session. In addition, participants understand that they can leave the session at any time without penalty, that strict confidentiality will be upheld, and that if there are any lingering questions about the study or complaints to be made about their treatment as participants, there are specific people to contact, including someone from the IRB. Participants are also informed of any risk that might be encountered in the study (virtually none, in this case). Lastly, participants are given the opportunity to receive a summary of the final results of the study, once it has been completed.

A feature that is new to the 2002 revision of the ethics code is a more detailed set of provisions for research that is designed to test the effectiveness of some treatment program that could provide benefits, but could also be ineffective and perhaps even harmful (Smith, 2003), a program to alleviate panic attacks, for instance. It is found in Standard 8.02b, which tells researchers to be sure to inform participants that the treatment is experimental (i.e., not shown to be effective yet), that some specific services will be available to the control group at the end of the study, and that services will be available to participants who exercise their right to withdraw from the study or who choose not to participate after reading the consent form. Participants must also be informed of the method by which people have been assigned to the experimental and the control group(s).

Although informed consent is essential in most research in psychology, it is important to note that consent is not required for research that is exempt from full review. As Standard 8.05 indicates, consent is not needed in studies using anonymous questionnaires, for data that have already been collected for

---

[5]For years the Milgram study has been considered the "experiment that could never be replicated," because of the ethical issues involved. Recently, however, such a replication did occur at Santa Clara University (Burger, 2009), although substantial modifications were made to Milgram's original procedure (e.g., not insisting that subjects continue, stopping the experiment earlier than Milgram did, screening subjects carefully). Despite the methodological changes designed to placate his university IRB, Burger found levels of obedience similar to those found by Milgram.

Procedure

- Experimenter welcomes the participant, describes the general nature of the study, and asks the individual to consent to participate.

- Individual reads over the form, asks questions perhaps, then signs or does not sign two copies of the consent form.

- The participant is given one of the copies of the form.

An Experiment on Cognitive Mapping

The purpose of this research is to determine how accurately people can point to geographic locations. If you choose to participate, you will first complete a pointing-to-target task, in which you will try to estimate the geographical direction of four different targets on or near campus, while also indicating how confident you are about the accuracy of your pointing. You will then be asked to fill out four brief surveys, all having to do with your thoughts and attitudes about your cognitive mapping experience and spatial skill. The experiment will take about 20 minutes and, at its conclusion, the purposes of the study will be explained to you in greater detail and we will answer any questions you might have. Except for some minor uncertainty or frustration about not being able to locate geographical targets accurately, there is no risk to you in the study. The study has been approved by the university's Institutional Review Board (IRB). If you have any questions or concerns about your participation in the study or about the study in general, you may contact me directly (Jim Mapman, at ___), the project director, Dr. Smith (___), or the Chair of the IRB, Dr. Jones (___).

Consent

I, _____, state that I am over 18 years of age and that I agree to participate in a research study being conducted by _____ of the Psychology Department. I have been informed that my participation in this study is voluntary, that I may withdraw my participation at any time without penalty, and that all data that I contribute will remain confidential. I understand that I will be making judgments about the geographical locations of objects and that I will receive a complete explanation at the end of my participation. I understand that the study involves no serious risk.

_____   _____
Signature of Participant   Date

_____   _____
Signature of Researcher   Date

If you would like to receive a summary of the results at the conclusion of the study, please write your e-mail address here: _____

FIGURE 2.3 A version of a consent form for research with human participants.

another purpose (archival data), for classroom projects in which data collection is for demonstration purposes, and for certain employment-related data collection exercises. Also, consent is not needed for observational studies that occur in certain locations. The key is whether the setting is a public one—if the study occurs in a place where anyone could be observed by anyone else, then consent is not needed (Koocher & Keith-Spiegel, 1998).

Consent procedures evolved from the aftermath of historical abuses, most notably the medical research that occurred in Germany during World War II, using concentration camp inmates as human guinea pigs. In the name of medical science, Nazi doctors and scientists such as Josef Mengele completed horrific studies. To measure human endurance and capacity for survival, for instance, inmates were immersed in ice water, injected with gasoline, or deliberately exposed to infectious and deadly diseases, among other things. At their Nuremberg trials in the late 1940s, the doctors defended their actions by arguing that voluntary consent didn't really exist in any medical research of the time and that the long-term importance of their research outweighed any adverse consequences to a few participants. Their argument failed, they were convicted, and the presiding tribunal wrote what was called the Nuremberg Code. It became the basis for all subsequent codes of medical research ethics as well as the consent portion of the APA ethics code, establishing the principle that consent must be informed, competent, and voluntary, and that the person giving it must be able to comprehend the situation involved (Faden & Beauchamp, 1986).

Although the experiments performed on concentration camp victims are the most dramatic and appalling examples of consent violations, problems have occurred in the United States as well. See Box 2.2 for brief descriptions of cases in which (a) severely retarded children were infected with hepatitis in order to study the development of the illness, (b) poor southern black men with syphilis were left untreated for years and misinformed about their health, also for the purpose of learning more about the time course of the disease, and (c) Americans, usually soldiers, were given large doses of LSD without their knowledge.

Box 2.2

ETHICS—Historical Problems with Informed Consent

The research activities of doctors in the Third Reich are unprecedented in their callousness and cruelty. Nonetheless, there are cases in the United States of research projects that have provoked intensely critical reactions and have invited comparisons, albeit remote, to the Nazi doctors. Three famous examples are the Willowbrook hepatitis study, the Tuskegee syphilis study, and project MK-ULTRA.

At Willowbrook, an institution housing children with varying degrees of mental retardation, an experiment began in 1956 and continued into the 1970s in which approximately one in ten new admissions was purposely infected with hepatitis. The parents were told of the procedure and agreed to it, but it was later shown that they might have felt pressured into giving consent. Also, the study violated the principle that research using the mentally disabled as participants should not be done unless it "relates immediately to the etiology, pathogenesis, prevention, diagnosis, or treatment of mental disability itself" (Beauchamp & Childress, 1979, p. 182). The Willowbrook study was investigating hepatitis, not mental disability.

The study was initiated because hepatitis was rampant at the institution, partly due to a high proportion of severely retarded children who could not be toilet trained. At one point in the 1950s, there were 5,200 residents; of those, 3,800 had IQs lower than 20 and more than 3,000 were not toilet trained (Beauchamp & Childress, 1979). Even with the staff's best efforts, conditions were generally unsanitary and led to the spread of the disease. By deliberately infecting new admissions and placing them in a separate ward but not treating them, the researchers hoped to study the development of the disease under controlled conditions. Those in charge of the project defended it on the grounds that the children would almost certainly contract the disease anyway, so why not have them contract it in such a way that more could be learned about it? Indeed, while the study has been legitimately criticized on consent grounds, it did contribute to the understanding of hepatitis and improved treatment of the disease.

The Tuskegee study was designed to examine the physical deterioration of persons suffering from advanced syphilis (Jones, 1981). Beginning in the early 1930s, about 400 poor black men from the rural South were diagnosed with the disease and deliberately left untreated. They were never informed about the nature of the disease, nor were they told its name; doctors simply informed them that they had "bad blood." Also, local physicians agreed not to treat the men. Given the poverty of the participants, it was not difficult to induce (coerce?) them to visit the clinic periodically (free rides and a hot meal), where blood tests and other examinations were done. The project continued into the early 1970s, even though it was clear by the late 1940s that the subjects were dying at twice the rate of a control group and were developing significantly more medical complications (Faden & Beauchamp, 1986). Defenders of the study argued that, when it began in the 1930s, there was no effective treatment for the disease and little knowledge of it. Like Willowbrook, the Tuskegee study contributed to our understanding of a serious disease, but was overshadowed by the consent violations.

While the chief investigators in both the Willowbrook and Tuskegee studies were misguided in their abuse of informed consent, they had a sincere desire to learn as much as possible about two devastating diseases, hepatitis and syphilis. The third example of a consent violation, unfortunately, lacked even the justification of an eventual medical benefit. This was a project launched by the Central Intelligence Agency (CIA) to expose unknowing human participants to the drug LSD in order to gauge the drug's ability as a weapon. The project was created in the early 1950s, during the "cold war" between the United States and the Soviet Union. Prompted by an erroneous intelligence report that the Soviets were buying up the world's supply of LSD (Thomas, 1995), CIA leadership approved a program to determine if LSD could be used to cause mental confusion in an enemy or render captured spies defenseless. Over a period of about ten years, the CIA sponsored numerous studies on unwitting participants, often soldiers, but sometimes members of the general public. Soldiers signed consent forms, but the forms said nothing about the potential effects of the drug and were designed mostly to ensure that soldiers would not reveal their participation. That secrecy was important is clear from an internal CIA memo that read, in part,

> Precautions must be taken . . . to conceal these activities from the American public. . . . The knowledge that the Agency is engaging in unethical and illicit activities would have serious repercussions in political and diplomatic circles. (cited in Grose, 1994, p. 393)

What went on during MK–ULTRA? Projects included giving soldiers LSD and then putting them in isolation, giving them the drug and then performing a lie detection task, examining the effects of repeated doses (over 77 consecutive days in one case), and even surreptitiously giving the drug to men visiting prostitutes in a CIA-financed brothel, with agents observing behind two-way mirrors (Thomas, 1995). This latter study was code-named by a CIA humorist—it was called "Operation Midnight Climax."

At least two people died as part of MK–ULTRA and numerous others were adversely affected by it. Here is a typical case, as described in the 1994 Rockefeller Report, the results of a congressional investigation into 50 years of CIA-sponsored biological experimentation:

> In 1957, ___ volunteered for a special program to test new military protective clothing. He was offered various incentives to participate in the program, including a liberal leave policy. . . . During the 3 weeks of testing new clothing, he was given two or three water-size glasses of a liquid containing LSD to drink. Thereafter, Mr. ___ developed erratic behavior and even attempted suicide. He did not learn that he had received LSD . . . until 18 years later, as a result of congressional hearings in 1975. (Rockefeller Report, 1994)

The CIA did not bother to inform either Congress or the President about MK–ULTRA. The program ground to a halt in 1963, not because of any ethical misgivings on the part of the CIA, but primarily because the studies had not yielded useful military information. Congressional investigators discovered it in the mid-1970s and eventually issued a full report and a rebuke (Grose, 1994).

Informed Consent and Special Populations

Not all research subjects are capable of giving consent, due to such factors as age or disability, and some persons might experience undue coercion to volunteer for research (e.g., prisoners). In these circumstances, additional procedures apply. For example, the Society for Research in Child Development (SRCD) follows a set of guidelines that build on and amplify some of the provisions of the code for adults. Thus, because children might not be able to fully understand a consent form, their parents or legal guardians are the ones who give consent. Nonetheless, unless the participant is an infant or is otherwise not capable of skilled language use, researchers are obligated to inform the child about the study and to gain what is referred to as **assent**. That is, researchers give the child as much information as possible to gauge whether the child is willing to participate. According to the SRCD code, assent occurs when "the child shows some form of agreement to participate without necessarily comprehending the full significance of the research necessary to give informed consent" (Society for Research in Child Development, 1996, p. 337). Assent also means that the researcher has a responsibility to monitor experiments with children and to stop them if it appears that undue stress is being experienced. A parent may give informed consent for a study on the effects of TV violence on children's aggressive behavior, but the parent won't be in the room when the film is shown. It is up to the researcher to be sensitive enough to remove the child from the task at hand (and repair the damage) if the stress level is too high.

In addition to the assent provision, the SRCD code requires that additional consent be obtained from others who might be involved with the study in any way. For example, this would include teachers when a study includes their students. The code also cautions researchers about incentives that might be used in the study, either to induce a willingness to participate, or as rewards for the tasks completed in the study. The rewards "must not unduly exceed the range of incentives that the child normally receives" (p. 337). Also, researchers should not use the potential rewards as an inducement to gain the child's assent; indeed, rewards should not even be mentioned until after the parents have given full informed consent (Scott-Jones, 2000). Finally, the SRCD code mirrors the provisions of the code for adults, but warns researchers to be even more vigilant in certain areas. These include the decisions about balancing scientific gain against risk to participants, the level of deception that can be justified, and the reporting of the study's results.

Additional provisions for the protection of participants exist with other special populations. Thus, legal guardians must give truly informed consent for research with people who are confined to institutions (e.g., the Willowbrook case). Second, it is imperative to ensure that participants do not feel coerced into volunteering for a study. This is a problem very difficult to avoid in environments such as prisons, because even with the best intentions of researchers, prisoners might not believe that their failure to volunteer won't cost them at some time in the future and perhaps even affect their future parole status. In general, researchers tend to rely on simple material rewards (e.g., money) and make it clear to prisoners that their participation will not be noted in any way in their parole records (Diener & Crandall, 1978). As was the case for the SRCD code for research with children, the inducements to participate must be reasonable.

A study by Spelt in the late 1940s is an example of a historical case in which extra inducements probably exposed participants to some harm, and for which no consent was obtained. Spelt (1948) tried to classically condition fetuses during the final month of their mother's pregnancy. There was no consent ("Not that the Ss knew they were taking part in an experiment"—p. 339) and the women were induced to participate by being "guaranteed free care in the hospital's obstetrical ward when they came to term" (p. 339). Part of the experiment involved taking

X-rays of the women's abdomens, thereby exposing the fetuses to radiation. Although the dangers of radiation exposure were not fully known at the time, there was enough knowledge of potential risks that should have given the researchers some pause. And the procedure, pairing the conditioned stimulus of vibrating the abdomen's surface with unconditioned stimulus of a loud noise (shades of Watson and Rayner), in order to produce fetal kicking, evidently sent two women into premature labor!

Another issue with confined populations is confidentiality (Kimmel, 2007). While normal guidelines for disguising the identity of participants apply, researchers are legally obligated to break confidentiality under circumstances that involve a clear danger (e.g., a prisoner participant reveals that he is about to kill another prisoner). Finally, as illustrated in Box 2.3 in the Willowbrook case, research with confined populations should be designed for the expressed purpose of providing knowledge that will in some way benefit the members of that population.

Treating Participants Well

Several portions of the ethics code are designed to ensure that volunteers are treated fairly and with respect during their participation, that they receive complete information about the study at its conclusion, that any stress they encounter is relieved, and that their participation is kept in confidence. It is important to note that this responsibility extends to everyone involved in the running of the study, from the primary researcher to the graduate students or undergraduates who might actually run the experimental sessions.

We have already seen that the experimental psychologist must make an estimate of the amount of risk to participants, with greater amounts of risk creating a greater burden to justify the study. This problem of risk and potential harm is addressed in the standards relating to consent and deception and once more in Standard 8.08, which makes it clear that responsibility does not end with the conclusion of the experimental session. After the experiment is over, the researcher has an additional task. It is called **debriefing**, during which the experimenter answers questions the participants might have and fills them in about the purpose(s) of the study. It is not absolutely essential that participants be informed about *all* aspects of the study immediately after their participation. Standard 8.08(b)—"[I]f scientific or humane values justify delaying or withholding this information, psychologists take reasonable steps to reduce the harm"—makes it clear that, in some circumstances, the immediate debriefing can be incomplete. This situation occurs most frequently when there is some deception involved, college students are the population under study, and the experimenter is concerned about participants talking to other potential participants (classmates). The problem, sometimes referred to as **leakage**, can ruin a study. Even in a relatively minor deception, subjects who go into the experimental session knowing something that is unknown to naïve subjects will certainly be influenced by their knowledge. There is evidence that leakage occurs (e.g., Diener, Matthews, & Smith, 1972), especially in situations where participants can easily interact with each other (e.g., college students). One common solution is to provide information about the general nature of the research during debriefing, and then to provide full information of results to participants after the experiment has been completed. Recall that the last line of the sample consent form (Figure 2.3) provides an opportunity for subjects to receive a final summary of the study's results.

In general, debriefing can serve two related purposes, referred to by Holmes (1976a, 1976b) as "dehoaxing" and "desensitizing." **Dehoaxing** means revealing the purpose of the experiment to participants, and the hypotheses being tested, and **desensitizing** refers to the process of reducing any stress or other negative feelings that might have been experienced in the session. Subjects are also informed that, if they wish, they may have their data removed from the data set.

The amount of time spent in debriefing depends on the complexity of the study, the presence and degree of deception, and the level of potential distress. In a study involving deception, a debriefing session often begins by asking participants if they thought the study had a purpose other than the one initially described. This enables the experimenter to determine if the deception was effective; it also provides a lead-in, allowing the experimenter to reveal more about the study. It is at this time that the experimenter tries to justify the deception (e.g., emphasizing the importance of getting one's true reactions) and begins to alleviate any stress involved. Participants "taken in" by the experiment's cover story are told that their behavior reflects the effectiveness of the cover story, not any personal weakness on their part. That is, subjects in many types of studies can be assured that the situation they experienced had powerful effects on their behavior, that their reactions don't reflect any individual inadequacies, and that others reacted similarly (Holmes, 1976b). In most cases, dehoaxing amounts to explaining the importance of eliciting natural behaviors and discussing the nature of the research topic being studied.

A properly conducted debriefing sometimes lasts longer than the experimental session, and several studies have shown that participants who are thoroughly debriefed evaluate the research experience positively. One study even showed that, compared to nondeceived subjects, those in deception studies actually rated their experiences higher in both enjoyment and educational value, apparently because the debriefing was more extensive (Smith & Richardson, 1983). One result of an effective debriefing is that skilled experimenters can better understand their current study and improve future ones. Participants can be asked for their ideas about revising the procedure in order to learn more about the problem being studied. In many cases, their descriptions of what they were thinking about during the experiment can be of immense help in interpreting the data and planning the next study.

The importance of leaving people with a good feeling about their research participation cannot be overstated. Yet it can be a difficult business, especially when deception is involved. Consider the Milgram experiment again—what must that debriefing have been like? In fairness to Milgram, he was apparently sensitive to the emotional health of his subjects. After the study was completed, he sent them a questionnaire about their experience (84% said they were glad they had participated) and a five-page report describing the results and their significance. He also completed a one-year follow-up study in which a psychiatrist examined 40 former participants and found "no evidence...of any traumatic reactions" (Milgram, 1974, p. 197).

Studies surveying research volunteers have found that fears of excessive harm in psychological research might be exaggerated; participants seem to understand and accept the rationale for deception (Christensen, 1988). One survey even found that college students were considerably more lenient than professional psychologists in their judgments about the ethical appropriateness of four hypothetical studies involving such things as experimentally produced stress and alterations of self-esteem (Sullivan & Deiker, 1973). Other research shows that objections by subjects about participating in psychological research seem to center more on their concern about being bored than being harmed (Coulter, 1986). On the other hand, it has been argued that post-experiment surveys of participants are biased, especially if deception has been involved. Having been misled and perhaps embarrassed in the study, deceived participants might respond positively to surveys as part of the process of convincing themselves that the study was worth their time and effort (Baumrind, 1985)—another example of an *effort justification* (refer back to Chapter 1). A study by Fisher and Fyrberg (1994) avoided this post-deception survey problem by asking students who had not yet been participants in research to evaluate three published studies involving various forms of deception. They found that students believed participants would be embarrassed or made uncomfortable in the studies and that debriefing, while essential, would not completely alleviate the negative feelings. Yet, when asked to make an overall cost-benefit assessment of the three studies described, 90%, 73%, and 79% (depending on the described study) of the students judged the scientific merit of the research to be sufficient to justify the deceptions involved.

One last aspect of treating participants well concerns privacy and **confidentiality**. Research participants should be confident that their identities will not be known by anyone other than the experimenter and that only group or disguised data will be reported. The only exceptions to this occur in cases when researchers might be compelled by law to report certain things disclosed by participants (e.g., child abuse, clear intent to harm oneself or another). In research that could involve such disclosure, researchers should word the consent form to make it clear that confidentiality could be limited (Folkman, 2000). The basic right to privacy also applies to research outside of the laboratory that might affect people in daily living situations. We'll see in the next chapter, when laboratory and field research are compared, that concerns over invading the privacy of people going about their daily business keeps many researchers within the protected confines of the laboratory.

In summary, in research using human participants, our ethical obligations include:

- Developing a study in which the overall benefits outweigh the overall costs
- Not doing anything that would cause harm to participants
- Gaining the informed consent of participants (under most circumstances)
- Assuring volunteers that they can quit the study at any time, without penalty
- Providing some form of debriefing
- Assuring participant confidentiality and that they will remain anonymous

Research Ethics and the Internet

Because the Internet has altered life dramatically in the twenty-first century, you won't be surprised to learn that research in psychology has been affected by the electronic world. Electronic research ("e-research") of interest to psychologists falls into two broad categories (Anderson & Kanuka, 2003). First, some websites are designed to collect data from those signing into the sites. This happens most frequently in the form of online surveys and questionnaires, but can involve other forms of data collection as well. For example, at some sites, computer users can sign in as participants in a perception study and have their data added to a large database of participant data (e.g., http://psychexps.olemiss.edu). In other cases, subjects sign in to sites controlled by researchers on their own campus, and complete a study electronically (e.g., filling out a survey created on software such as *Survey Monkey*). Although there hasn't been a great deal of research on the issue, it appears that data collected electronically correspond reasonably well and yield the same results as data collected in a more traditional fashion (McGraw, Tew, & Williams, 2000). The second form of e-research involves a researcher studying the behavior of Internet users. This research ranges from examining the frequency of usage of selected websites to analyses of the content of web-based interactions (e.g., monitoring the activity of a chat room). For both types of e-research, the basic principles of the ethics code continue to apply, but research involving the Internet introduces some unique ethical problems for the researcher. The problems have even resulted in the development of a code of ethics for Internet-based research, created by an organization called the Association of Internet Research. The code can be found at www.aoir.org/reports/ethics.pdf. The American Association for the Advancement of Science has also prepared guidelines for IRBs that have to decide whether to approve e-research. See www.aaas.org/spp/sfrl/projects/intres/report.pdf.

For e-research in which computer users contribute data, problems relating to informed consent and debriefing exist. During a normal informed consent procedure, the experimenter can quickly clear up any confusion or misunderstanding on the part of participants, and can be reasonably sure that participants have read the consent form before signing. Consent forms can be used easily enough in e-research, but there is no opportunity for researchers to answer questions and no way to know if the consent form has been read. Another consent problem concerns age—researchers can post warnings that participants need parental consent if they are under age 18, but it is impossible to monitor compliance. Debriefing is also problematic. A good debriefing session is interactive, with questions asked and answered, but with e-research, there is no guarantee that participants will even be there to read the debriefing information. One click and the participant is gone without being debriefed. Furthermore, if deception is involved, while the dehoaxing part of debriefing can be managed by presenting clear information, the desensitizing part will be difficult if not impossible to accomplish.

E-research involving the collection of information from computer users involves an additional set of problems. Issues of consent and debriefing continue, but a major issue concerns privacy and confidentiality (Kraut, Olson, Banaji, Bruckman, Cohen, & Couper, 2004). As you recall from the general discussion of informed consent earlier in this chapter, consent is not required for studies that are purely observational and individual behavior is observed in public places. With e-research, the interesting and as yet unresolved question is whether such activities as chat rooms, discussion boards, and listservs are public forums or private discussions. For the researcher, the best general guideline is be faithful to the general principles of the code (Table 2.1) and to consult frequently with colleagues and the local IRB during the planning stages of e-research. For the user of chat rooms, discussion boards, and listservs, it is important to be aware that, in the absence of sophisticated encryption software, messages posted are "out there," available to anyone with an Internet connection. The best advice is to think of the messages you post as having about the same level of privacy as postcards.

Concerning confidentiality, researchers using Internet surveys, responded to by those using their own personal computer, need to take steps to ensure that the user's identity remains protected. This can mean taking steps to ensure that "cookies" (a tool that can be used to track information about a user) are not left on the user's computer as a result of taking the survey; also, users need to be assured that if their computer's identity (e.g., an IP address) is returned with the survey, that the researcher will discard the information (Pollick, 2007).

✓ **Self Test 2.2**

1. You wish to do a study comparing two different memory improvement techniques. Which category of the IRB approval process will apply in this case?
2. How does the APA define informed consent?
3. Milgram's procedure probably would not have gained IRB approval. What was the most obvious problem?
4. At the end of an experimental session, what is the experimenter obligated to do and what are the two parts to this obligation?

Ethical Guidelines for Research with Animals

As you recall from your course in general psychology, psychologists occasionally use animals as research subjects. Although some people have the impression that psychologists seem to study rats more than people, the truth is that animal research involves a relatively small proportion of the total research done in psychology—about 7–9% (Gallup & Suarez, 1985a), and the vast majority of studies use rats, mice, and birds as subjects. Nonetheless, many of psychology's important contributions to human welfare are based on a foundation of research with animals (Domjan & Purdy, 1995).

Animals are used in psychological research for several reasons. Methodologically, their environmental, genetic, and developmental histories can be easily controlled;

ethically, most experimental psychologists take the position that, with certain safeguards in place, animals can be subjected to procedures that could not be used with humans. Consider Eleanor Gibson's visual cliff research again (Gibson & Walk, 1960; refer back to Chapter 1). Thirty-six 6- to 14-month-old infants were placed in the middle of the apparatus, and although they were quite willing to crawl around on the "shallow" side, they hesitated to crawl onto the glass surface over the "deep" side. This shows that they were able to perceive depth and apparently were aware of some of its consequences. Does this mean that depth perception is innate? No, because these infants had 6 to 14 months of learning experience with distance perception. To control for this experience, it would have been necessary to raise infants in complete visual isolation, a procedure that was obviously out of the question (although as you recall from Box 2.1, Dennis (1941) felt no qualms about subjecting infants to an impoverished environment). Such an isolation procedure *is* feasible with animals, however, in part because the isolation does not have to be long—animals develop the ability to move through their environments very quickly, sometimes in a matter of minutes. So Gibson and Walk tested a variety of species from rats to kittens to lambs, isolating them from birth (i.e., no specific visual experiences) until they could move around competently and then testing them on the visual cliff. They discovered that depth perception, at least as measured in the cliff apparatus, is built into the visual system, at least for those species that rely heavily on vision.

The Issue of Animal Rights

The use of animals in research is an emotional and controversial issue (not a new one, though—see Box 2.3). Animal rights activists have denounced the use of animals in studies ranging from medical research to cosmetics testing. The majority of animal activists confine their activities to sincere argument and nonviolent protest, and work hard to live a life that is consistent with their moral stance (Herzog, 1993). In some cases, however, activism has led to animal laboratories being vandalized and animals released from labs. During the 1980s, for example, animal rights extremists vandalized approximately 100 research facilities housing animals (Adler, 1992). The problem was severe enough to produce federal legislation, the Animal Enterprise Protection Act of 1992, specifically outlawing such vandalism and setting stiff penalties, and the Animal Enterprise Terrorism Act of 2006, which took an even harder line. In recent years, an alarming trend has been for some groups to target researchers directly, not just their labs. In the fall of 2008, for instance, two researchers at the University of California at Vera Cruz were the targets of firebombs (the car of one, the home of another).

What is the case against the use of animals as research subjects? Some argue that humans have no right to consider themselves superior to any other sentient species, that is, any species capable of experiencing pain (Singer, 1975). Sentient animals are said to have the same basic rights to privacy, autonomy, and freedom from harm as humans and therefore cannot be subjugated by humans in any way, including participation in any form of research. Others skeptical of animal research take a position grounded in Judeo-Christian theology, arguing that humans have

Box 2.3

ORIGINS—*Antivivisection and the APA*

Considering the high visibility of the animal research controversy, you might think it is a fairly recent development. Not so. Actually, it has a long history, as documented nicely by the comparative psychologist and historian Donald Dewsbury (1990).

The term "vivisection" derives from the Latin *vivus*, or "alive," and refers to surgical procedures on live animals, historically done for scientific purposes. The antivivisection movement developed in nineteenth-century England, where activists' efforts contributed to the passage of England's Cruelty to Animals Act in 1876, a code similar in spirit to modern APA guidelines for animals. The antivivisection movement quickly spread to the United States; the American Antivivisection Society was founded in 1883 in Philadelphia. Antivivisectionists and animal researchers (including physiologists and early experimental psychologists) engaged in the same arguments that are heard today, with claims of unspeakable torture on the one side and justifications on scientific grounds on the other.

DREAM OF THE MEDICAL VIVISECTIONIST CRANK WHO WANTONLY AND CRUELLY OPERATED ON RATS, TO SEE THE EFFECT, FROM A "SCIENTIFIC" VIEW-POINT, OF THE LOSS OF THE DIFFERENT SENSES.

FIGURE 2.4 Antivivisectionist cartoon of Watson on the operating table. From Dewsbury (1990). (From *Journal of Zoophily*, 1907.)

One especially controversial series of studies concerned John B. Watson (again). In order to determine which senses were critical for maze learning, Watson did a series of studies in which he surgically eliminated senses one at a time to examine the effects on rats in mazes (Watson, 1907). The study caused an outcry when it was reported in the *New York Times* on December 30, 1906, and Watson was satirized in the cartoon in Figure 2.4 (from Dewsbury, 1990).

The APA established its first code for regulating animal research in the 1920s, well before creating the code for research with humans. A committee chaired by Robert Yerkes was formed in 1924, and the following year the APA adopted its recommendations. The committee proposed that laboratories create an open door policy in which "any accredited member . . . of a humane society [could] be permitted to visit a laboratory to observe the care of animals and methods of experimentation" (Anderson, 1926, p. 125), that journals require authors to be clear about the use of humane procedures in their research, that psychologists defend the need for animal research, both in the classroom and publicly, and that the APA maintain a standing committee on "precautions in animal experimentation" (Anderson, 1926, p. 125).

dominion over animals, but also a responsibility to protect them. This latter group recognizes the value of some research using animals, especially medical research, but rejects other types of experimentation on the grounds that researchers have inflicted needless pain and suffering when alternative approaches to the research would yield essentially the same conclusions. This argument has been quite salutary in reducing unnecessary research on animals by the cosmetics industry, for instance, but it has been applied to research in psychology as well. Psychological research with animals has been described as needlessly repetitive and concerned with trivial problems that have no practical human benefit. Critics have suggested that instead of using animals in the laboratory, researchers could discover all they need to know about animal behavior by observing animals in their natural habitats, by substituting nonsentient for sentient animals, or by using computer simulations. How do research psychologists respond?

Using Animals in Psychological Research

Most psychologists simply do not agree that sentient animals have rights equal to those of humans. While granting that humans have a strong obligation to respect and protect nonhuman species, the Judeo-Christian position, psychologists believe that humans can be distinguished from nonhumans because of our degree of awareness, our ability to develop culture and understand history, and especially our ability to make moral judgments. Although animals are remarkable creatures capable of complex cognition, they are "incapable of being moral subjects, of acting rightly or wrongly in the moral sense, of having, discharging, or breaching duties and obligations" (Feinberg, 1974, p. 46). Of course, differentiating between human and nonhuman species does not by itself allow the use of the latter by the former. Some psychologists (e.g., Ulrich, 1991) caution that there have been instances in which animals have not been treated well by research psychologists and that some research has been needlessly repetitive. Most psychologists argue, however, that the use of animals in research does not constitute exploitation and that the net effect of such research is beneficial rather than costly, for both humans *and* animals.

The most visible defender of animal research in psychology has been Neal Miller (1909–2002), a noted experimental psychologist. His research, on topics ranging from basic processes in conditioning and motivation to the principles underlying biofeedback, earned him the APA's Distinguished Scientific Contributions Award in 1959 and its Distinguished Professional Contributions Award in 1983. In "The Value of Behavioral Research on Animals" (1985), Miller argued that (a) animal activists sometimes overstate the harm done to animals in psychological research, (b) animal research provides clear benefits for the well-being of humans, and (c) animal research benefits animals as well. Concerning harm, Miller cited a study by Coile and Miller (1984) that examined five years' worth of published research in APA journals, a total of 608 studies, and found *no* instances of the forms of abuse claimed by activists. Also, examining the abuse claims shows that at least some of the alleged "abuse" may not be that at all, but merely seemed to be because of the inflammatory language used. For instance, Coile and Miller cited several misleading statements from activist literature including: "[The animals] are deprived of food and water to suffer and die slowly from hunger and thirst" (Coile & Miller, 1984, p. 700). This evidently refers to the common laboratory practice in conditioning experiments of depriving animals of food or water for 24 hours. Animals then placed in a conditioning procedure are motivated to work for the food or the water (e.g., solve a maze). Is this abuse? Perhaps not, considering that veterinarians recommend that most pets be fed just once a day (Gallup & Suarez, 1985b). On the other hand, some researchers argue that six hours without food is sufficient to create an adequate level of hunger for research purposes.

Miller argued that situations involving harm to animals during the research procedures are rare, used only when less painful alternatives cannot be used, and can be justified by the ultimate good that derives from the studies. This good applies to both humans and animals, and the bulk of his 1985 article was an attempt to document the kinds of good that derive from animal studies. First, he argued that while the long history of animal conditioning research has taught us much about general principles of learning, it also has had direct application to human problems. An early example of this was a device developed and tested by Mowrer and Mowrer (1938) for treating enuresis (excessive and uncontrolled bedwetting) that was based explicitly on the classical conditioning work involving Pavlov's dogs. Teaching machines and several forms of behavior therapy are likewise grounded in conditioning principles. More recently, animal research has directly influenced the development of behavioral medicine—the application of behavioral principles to traditional medical practice. Disorders ranging from headaches to hypertension to the disabilities following strokes can be treated with behavioral procedures such as biofeedback, and the essential principles of biofeedback were determined using animals as subjects.

Finally, Miller argued that animal research provides direct benefits to animals themselves. Medical research with animals has improved veterinary care dramatically, but behavioral research has also improved the welfare of various species. The study of animal behavior by research psychologists has led to the improvement of zoo environments, aided in nonchemical pest control, and discouraged coyote attacks on sheep by using taste avoidance conditioning as a substitute for lethal control. Behavioral research can even help preserve endangered species. Miller used the example of imprinting, the tendency for young ducklings and other species to follow the first stimulus that moves (usually the mother). Research on imprinting led to the procedure of exposing newly hatched condors to a puppet resembling an adult condor rather than to a normal human caretaker, thereby facilitating the bonding process for the incubator-raised bird and ultimately enhancing the survival of this threatened species.

One last point about using animals in psychological research is that most people seem to think that animal research has value. Surveys of psychologists (Plous, 1996a) and psychology majors (Plous, 1996b), for instance, indicate that although there is ambivalence about research in which animals experience pain and/or have to be put to death at the conclusion of the study, most psychologists and students of psychology believe that animal research in psychology is both justified and necessary. These views appear to be shared by students in general (Fulero & Kirkland, 1992; Gallup & Beckstead, 1988). Furthermore, the use of animals by research psychologists has not changed substantially in recent years as a consequence of pressure from animal rights groups. Although Gallup and Eddy (1990) reported that 14.7% of graduate programs that formerly had animal labs no longer have them, the decline was attributed more to changing research interests and cost rather than to pressure from animal rights protesters. Benedict and Stoloff (1991) found similar results among elite undergraduate colleges. More recently, in a survey of 110 undergraduate department chairpersons, Hull (1996) found virtually no change in their use of animal labs over a 5-year period; 47% reported using animals at the time of the survey, while 50% had used animals 5 years earlier. Hull's survey also revealed that departments using animals did not find APA and National Institutes of Health (NIH) guidelines difficult to follow and that the student response to the presence of an animal lab was mostly favorable. On the other hand, Plous (1996a) reported that strong support for animal research was higher among older than among younger psychologists, suggesting that animal research among psychologists, as well as animal labs for undergraduate psychology majors, may decline in the future.[6]

The APA Code for Animal Research

Standard 8.09 of the 2002 APA ethics code sketches the ethical guidelines for animal care and use; the details of the code are elaborated on the APA website (www.apa.org/science/anguide.html). Analogous to the IRB for human research,

---

[6] For more on this survey, refer to Chapter 12, where it is featured as a good example of survey research.

there should be an "Institutional Animal Care and Use Committee" (IACUC). Like an IRB, the animal use committee is composed of professors from several disciplines in addition to science, and includes someone from outside the university.[7] The guidelines for using animals deal with (a) the need to justify the study when the potential for harm to the animals exists, (b) the proper acquisition and care of animals, both during and after the study, and (c) the use of animals for educational rather than research purposes. The main theme of the code is the issue of balancing the scientific justification for a particular project with the potential for harm to the animals. Here are the highlights.

Justifying the Study

Just as the researcher studying humans must weigh the scientific value of the research against the degree of risk to the participants, the animal researcher must make the case that the "scientific purpose of the research [is] of sufficient potential significance as to outweigh any harm or distress to the animals used" (APA, 1985, p. 5). The "scientific purpose" of the study should fall within one of four categories. The research should "(a) increase knowledge of the processes underlying the evolution, development, maintenance, alteration, control, or biological significance of behavior, (b) determine the replicability and generality of prior research, (c) increase understanding of the species under study, or (d) provide results that benefit the health or welfare of humans or other animals" (www.apa.org/science/anguide.html).

The longest section of the guidelines identifies the range of procedures that can be used. In general, researchers are told that their requirement for a strong justification increases with the degree of discomfort to be experienced by the animals. In addition, they are told that appetitive procedures (i.e., use of positive reinforcement) should be substituted for aversive procedures as much as possible, that less stressful procedures should be preferred to more stressful ones, and that surgical procedures require special care and expertise. Researchers are also encouraged to try out painful procedures on themselves first, whenever feasible. Field research procedures should disturb the animals living in their natural habitat as little as possible.

Caring for the Animals

The research supervisor must be an expert in the care of the species of animals to be used, must carefully train all those who will be in contact with the animals, and must be fully aware of federal regulations about animal care. To further ensure proper care, a veterinarian must check the facilities twice annually and should be on call as a general consultant. The animals should be acquired from legitimate suppliers or bred in the laboratory. If wild animals are being studied, they must be trapped humanely.

Once an experiment has been completed, alternatives to destroying the animals should be considered. However, euthanasia is sometimes necessary, "either as a

---

[7]As with IRBs, animal use committees have been controversial. One study found, for instance, that the same proposals given to different IACUCs yielded highly inconsistent levels of approval (Plous & Herzog, 2001).

requirement of the research, or because it constitutes the most humane form of disposition of an animal at the conclusion of the research" (APA, 1985, p. 8). In such cases, the process must be "accomplished in a humane manner, appropriate for the species, under anesthesia, or in such a way as to ensure immediate death, and in accordance with procedures approved by the institutional animal care and use committee" (p. 8).

Using Animals for Educational Purposes

The guidelines are designed primarily to aid researchers who use animals, but animals are often used educationally to demonstrate specific behaviors, train students in animal research procedures, and give students firsthand experience in studying such well-known phenomena as classical and operant conditioning. Unlike the research situation, however, the educational use of animals does not result directly in new knowledge. Consequently, the educator is urged to use fewer rather than more animals to accomplish a given purpose and to consider a variety of alternative procedures. For example, instead of demonstrating the same principle (e.g., shaping) to an introductory psychology class with a new rat each semester, the instructor might do it once and make a video of the procedure for future classes.

Sometimes computer simulations of various phenomena can be substituted for live procedures; several reasonably accurate simulations of both classical and operant conditioning procedures exist. These simulations can be effective (and necessary in smaller schools that cannot keep up with federal regulations for the proper care of animals), but shaping a schematized rat to bar press is not quite the same as shaping a real rat. Students often experience a deep insight into the power of reinforcement contingencies when they witness them firsthand. Direct experiences with animals in undergraduate learning laboratories have motivated more than one student to become a research psychologist (Moses, 1991).

In summary, most psychologists defend the use of animals in behavioral research while recognizing the need to scrutinize closely the rationale for every animal study. Animal research has contributed greatly to our understanding of behavior and promises to help in the future search for solutions to AIDS, Alzheimer's disease, mental illness, and countless other human problems.

Scientific Fraud

There has been much discussion in recent years about fraud in science, with specific cases sparking debate about whether they represent just the occasional "bad apple" or, more ominously, the "tip of the iceberg." Obviously, scientists in general and research psychologists in particular are expected to be scrupulously honest in all of their scientific activities. Principle C (Integrity) of the 2002 code unambiguously states that psychologists "seek to promote accuracy, honesty, and truthfulness in the science, teaching, and practice of psychology" (APA, 2002, p. 1062). Furthermore, several of the specific standards of the code directly concern fraudulent research practices. This last section of the chapter addresses the following questions: What is scientific fraud? How prevalent is it, and how can it be detected? Why does it happen?

The *American Heritage Dictionary* (1992) defines fraud as "a deception deliberately practiced in order to secure unfair or unlawful gain" (p. 722). The two major types of fraud in science are (1) **plagiarism**, deliberately taking the ideas of someone else and claiming them as one's own, and (2) **falsifying data**. In the 2002 code, plagiarism is specifically condemned in Standard 8.11, and data falsification receives similar treatment in Standard 8.10. Plagiarism is a problem that can occur in all disciplines, and you will find further discussion of it in Appendix A, which concerns writing lab reports. Falsifying data, on the other hand, is a problem that happens only in science; it will be the major focus here.

Data Falsification

If there is a mortal sin in science, it is the failure to be scrupulously honest in managing the data, the foundation stones on which the entire enterprise is built. Thus, the integrity of data is an issue of pivotal importance. This type of fraud can take several forms. First and most extreme, a scientist fails to collect any data at all and simply manufactures it. Second, some of the collected data are altered or omitted to make the overall results look better. Third, some data are collected, but "missing" data are guessed at and created in a way that produces a data set congenial to the researcher's expectations. Fourth, an entire study is suppressed because its results fail to come out as expected. In each of these cases, the deception is deliberate and the scientist presumably "secures an unfair or unlawful gain" (e.g., publication, tenure).

The traditional view is that fraud is rare and easily detected because faked results won't be replicated (Hilgartner, 1990). That is, if a scientist produces a result with fraudulent data, the results won't represent some empirical truth. Other scientists, intrigued or surprised by this new finding, will try to reproduce it in their own labs and will fail to do so; the fraudulent findings will then be uncovered and eventually discarded. One hint of this kind of problem occurs if a researcher attempting to replicate a study, suspecting that something is odd about the original study, asks to see the raw data collected in the study in question. Scientists in psychology and other disciplines have a long history of being willing to share data and a refusal to do so would create suspicion about the "new" finding. Standard 8.14 of the code makes it clear that data sharing is expected from researchers. This situation, a failure to replicate, combined with an unwillingness to share data with colleagues, were the factors leading to the discovery of data falsification by a prominent Harvard social psychologist, Karen Ruggiero, in 2001. After the discovery, she was forced to print public retractions of the findings that she had published on the basis of the fabricated data (Murray, 2002).

In addition to failures to replicate findings, fraud may be detected (or at least suspected) during the normal peer review process. Whenever a research article is submitted for journal publication or a grant is submitted to an agency, it is reviewed by several experts, whose recommendations help determine whether the article will be published or the grant funded. Anything that seems odd probably will be detected by at least one of the reviewers. A third way of detecting fraud is when a researcher's collaborators suspect a problem. This happened in the 1980s in a series of studies that apparently made a breakthrough in the treatment of hyperactivity in retarded children. Stephen Breuning, while working at the University of Pittsburgh, produced data showing that stimulant drugs could be more effective than antipsychotic drugs for treating the problem (Holden, 1987). However, a colleague suspected that the data were faked, a charge that was upheld after a three-year investigation by the National Institute of Mental Health (NIMH), which had funded some of Breuning's research. In a plea bargain, Breuning pled guilty to two counts of submitting false data to NIMH; in exchange, NIMH dropped the charge that Breuning committed perjury during the investigation (Byrne, 1988).

One of the great strengths of science is the self-correction resulting from the replication process, peer reviews, and the honesty of colleagues. Indeed, this system has detected fraud numerous times, as in the Ruggiero and Breuning cases. But what if peers fail to notice something awry or if some fraudulent result is consistent with other, nonfraudulent findings (i.e., it replicates)? If the bogus results fit with other legitimate research outcomes, there is little reason to question them and the fraud may go undetected for years. Something like this might have occurred in one of psychology's best-known cases of apparent fraud ("apparent" because the case is still being debated).

The case involved one of Great Britain's most famous psychologists, Cyril Burt (1883–1971), a major player in the debate over the nature of intelligence. His twin studies are often cited as evidence for the idea that intelligence is mostly inherited from one's parents. His most important (and controversial) result was that identical twins had virtually the same IQ scores even if they were given up for adoption at birth and raised in different environments. His data went unchallenged for years and became assimilated into the literature on the heritability of intelligence. However, careful readers eventually noticed that in different publications describing the results with different numbers of twins, Burt kept reporting *exactly* the same statistical results (identical correlation coefficients). Such an outcome is highly unlikely mathematically. Furthermore, in most studies of separated identical twins, researchers try to exclude twin pairs who have been raised in similar environments. Hence, they are able to use only a percentage of the total number of twins available (less than half typically). Burt included all the twins in his study that he claimed to have at his disposal, arguing that in none of the cases were the twins placed into similar environments. This outcome is also virtually impossible, compared to other studies (Tucker, 1997).

Detractors have accused Burt of manufacturing the results to support his strong hereditarian and elitist beliefs, while defenders argued that he collected the data but became a forgetful and careless reporter with increasing age. It was also said in his defense that if he were intent on fraud, he surely would have done a better job of disguising it (e.g., not stating that he was able to use all of his twins). There is no question that something is wrong with Burt's data, and even his defenders concede that much of the data have little or no scientific value.

Analyzing the Burt affair has become a cottage industry (Green, 1992; Joynson, 1989; Samelson, 1992; Tucker, 1997), but for our purposes the point is that bad data, whether they result from error, oversight, or deliberate distortion, may fail to be noticed if they fit with other findings (i.e., if they are replicated elsewhere). This was the case with Burt; his data were quite similar to the findings from other, subsequent twin studies that were done properly (e.g., Bouchard & McGue, 1981).

It is worth mentioning that some commentators (e.g., Hilgartner, 1990) believe that while falsified data may go undetected because they replicate "good" data, they may not be detected for two other reasons as well. First, the sheer number of studies being published these days makes it easier for a bad study to slip through the cracks, especially if it isn't reporting some notable discovery that attracts widespread attention. Second, the reward system in science is structured so that new discoveries pay off, but scientists who spend their time "merely" replicating other work aren't seen as very creative. Consequently, the academic rewards elude them, and some questionable studies might escape the replication process.

The reward system is also believed to be part of the reason why fraud occurs in the first place. This brings us to the final question about fraud—why does it occur? Explanations range from individual (character weakness) to societal (a reflection of general moral decay in modern society), with reasons relating to the academic reward system somewhere in the middle. Scientists who publish are promoted, tenured, win grants, and influence people. Sometimes the attendant "publish or perish" pressures overwhelm the individual and lead the researcher (or the researcher's assistants) to cut some corners. It might begin on a small scale—adding, subtracting, or altering a few pieces of data to achieve the desired outcome—but expand over time.

What does this mean for you as a student researcher? At the very least, it means that you need to be compulsive about data. Follow procedures scrupulously and *never* succumb to the temptation to manufacture even a single piece of data. Likewise, never discard data from a participant unless there are clear procedures for doing so and these procedures are specified before the experiment begins (e.g., the participant doesn't follow instructions, the experimenter doesn't administer the procedure correctly). Finally, keep the raw data or, at the very least, the data summary sheets. Your best protection against a charge that your results seem unusual is your ability to produce the data on request. For more on research fraud and how it can be prevented, visit the site for the Office of Research Integrity at the U.S. Department of Health and Human Services (http://ori.dhhs.gov).

✓ Self Test 2.3

1. Miller argued that animal rights activists exaggerate when making claims about animal research. What were his other two arguments for the value of doing animal research in psychology?
2. What does the APA recommend about the use of animals for educational purposes?
3. Which facts first alerted researchers to the possibility of fraud in Ruggiero's research?

The importance of being aware of the ethical implications of the research you're doing cannot be overstated. It is the reason for placing this chapter early in the text, and it won't be the last you'll hear of the topic. If you glance back at the Table of Contents, for instance, you will notice that each of the remaining chapters includes an "Ethics Box" that examines such topics as privacy in field research, recruiting participants, using surveys responsibly, and being an ethically competent experimenter. On the immediate horizon, however, is a chapter that considers the problem of how to begin developing ideas for research projects.

Chapter Summary

Developing the APA Code of Ethics

In keeping with psychology's habit of relying on data-based principles, the APA developed its initial ethics code empirically, using a critical incidents procedure. The code for research using human participants was first published in 1953 and has been revised periodically since then, most recently in 2002. It consists of general principles guiding the behavior of psychologists (e.g., concern for others' welfare) and specific standards of behavior (e.g., maintaining the confidentiality of research participants), the violation of which can lead to censure.

Ethical Guidelines for Research with Humans

The APA code for research with humans provides guidance for the researcher in planning and carrying out the study. Planning includes doing a cost-benefit analysis that weighs the degree of risk imposed on participants against the scientific value of the research. The code also requires that subjects be given sufficient information to decide whether to participate (i.e., informed consent). Special care needs to be taken with children and with those who might feel coerced into participation (e.g., prisoners). Participants must be told that they are free to withdraw from the study without penalty and they must be assured of confidentiality. At the conclusion of their participation, they must receive a full debriefing. Institutional Review Boards (IRBs) have the responsibility for ensuring that research studies with human subjects are conducted according to the ethics code and federal law. Certain forms of deception are acceptable in psychological research, but the researcher must convince an IRB that the legitimate goals of the study can be met only through deception.

Ethical Guidelines for Research with Animals

APA guidelines for research with animal subjects concern the care and humane treatment of animals used for psychological research, provide guidance in deciding about appropriate experimental procedures, and cover the use of animals both for research and for educational purposes. Although animal rights proponents have argued that animal research in psychology is inappropriate, most research psychologists argue that such research can benefit both humans and animals.

Scientific Fraud

Plagiarism, presenting the ideas of another as one's own, and data falsification, the manufacturing or altering of data, are the most serious forms of scientific fraud. Although data falsification is often discovered because of repeated failures to replicate unreliable findings, it may remain undetected because (a) the fraudulent findings are consistent with legitimate outcomes or (b) the sheer mass of published work precludes much replication. The academic reward system sometimes creates pressures that lead to scientific fraud.

Chapter Review Questions

1. Distinguish between the "general principles" of the APA ethics code and the "standards" of the code. Describe any three of the general principles.

2. Describe the role of the IRB and the reasons why research psychologists have criticized IRBs.

3. What factors determine whether research proposals are exempt from IRB review, receive expedited review, or are subject to full review?

4. Distinguish between "consent" and "assent" and explain how both concepts are accomplished in research with children.

5. Describe the essential ingredients of an informed consent form to be used in research with adult research participants.

6. Why is deception sometimes used in psychological research? How can the use of deception be reconciled with the concept of informed consent?

7. Describe the two main purposes of a debriefing session.

8. Which ethical principles were violated in (a) the Willowbrook study, (b) the Tuskegee study, and (c) MK-ULTRA?

9. Use the Gibson visual cliff study to illustrate why psychologists sometimes use nonhuman species as research subjects.

10. Describe the arguments for and against the use of nonhuman species in psychological research.

11. What are the essential features of the APA code for animal research?

12. Describe the ways in which data falsification is usually discovered. Why does this type of fraud occur?

Applications Exercises

Exercise 2.1   Thinking Scientifically About the Ethics Code

From the standpoint of a research psychologist who is thinking scientifically, how would you design a study to evaluate the following claims that are sometimes made about the use of deception in research? That is, what kinds of empirical data would you like to have in order to judge the truth of the claims?

1. Deception should never be used in psychological research because once people have been deceived in a study, they will no longer trust any psychologist.

2. Researchers could avoid deception by instructing subjects to "imagine" that they are in a deception study; they are then asked to behave as they think a typical person would behave.

3. Psychologists are just fooling themselves; most participants see right through their deceptions and quickly understand the true purpose of a study.

4. Deception seldom works in research with university students, because they talk to each other about the studies in which they have participated and tell each other the "true" purpose of the studies.

Exercise 2.2   Recognizing Ethical Problems

Consider each of the following brief descriptions of actual research in social psychology. From the standpoint of the APA's code of ethics, which components could cause problems with an IRB? Explain how you might defend each study to an IRB.

1. The effect of crowding on stress was investigated in a public men's room. A member of the research team followed a subject into the bathroom and occupied either the urinal directly adjacent to the subject's or the next one down the line. Subjects were unaware that they were participating in a study. On the assumption that increased stress would affect urination, the amount of time it took for the subject to begin to urinate and the total time spent urinating were recorded by another researcher hidden in one of the stalls. As predicted, subjects' urination was more disrupted when the immediately adjacent urinal was occupied (Middlemist, Knowles, & Matter, 1976).

2. In a field experiment, a woman (who was actually part of the experiment) stood by her car on the side of a road. The car had a flat tire. To determine if modeling would affect the helping behavior of passing motorists, on some trials another woman with a flat tire was helped by a stopped motorist (all part of the staged event) about a quarter of a mile before the place where the woman waited for help. As expected, motorists were more likely to stop and help if they had just witnessed another person helping (Bryan & Test, 1967).

3. In the wake of the Watergate scandal, researchers wished to determine if average people could be induced to commit a crime, especially if they thought an arm of government would give them immunity from prosecution. Subjects

were recruited by the experimenter, posing as a private investigator, and asked to be part of a break-in at a local advertising agency that was said to be involved in tax fraud. Some subjects were told the IRS was organizing the break-in and promised immunity from prosecution; others weren't promised immunity. A third group was told that a competing advertising agency was leading the break-in, and a fourth group was not told who was behind the crime. The prediction that people would be most willing to participate for a government agency that promised immunity was confirmed; the experiment ended when participants either agreed or disagreed—no break-in actually occurred (West, Gunn, & Chernicky, 1975).

Exercise 2.3   Replicating Milgram

Describe what changes you think could be made to Milgram's basic obedience study in order to get it approved by an IRB today. Then track down Burger's description of his replication (Burger, 2009) and describe exactly what he did. On the basis of his study, do you think it is safe to conclude that Milgram's studies have been replicated and that people are just as obedient today as they were in the 1960s?

Exercise 2.4   Decisions about Animal Research

The following exercise is based on a study by Galvin and Herzog (1992) and is used with the permission of Hal Herzog. The idea is for you to play the role of a member of an IACUC (Institutional Animal Care and Use Committee) and make decisions about whether the following studies ought to gain approval from an IACUC (quoting from Galvin & Herzog, p. 265):

1. *Mice.* A neurobiologist proposes to amputate the forelimbs of newborn mice to study the relative influence of heredity and environment on the development of motor patterns (grooming).

2. *Rats.* A psychologist seeks permission to conduct a classroom learning demonstration. Rats are to be deprived of food for 23 hours and taught to press a lever for food reinforcements.

3. *Monkeys.* Tissue from monkey fetuses will be implanted into the brains of adult rhesus monkeys to explore the feasibility of neural transplantation as a treatment for Alzheimer's disease.

4. *Dogs.* Stray dogs awaiting euthanasia in an animal shelter are to be used to teach surgical techniques to veterinary students.

5. *Bears.* Wild grizzly bears will be anesthetized. Collars containing radio telemetry devices will be attached to their necks for a study of their social and territorial behavior patterns.

For each of these studies, do a cost-benefit analysis, indicate whether you would approve the study, and explain the reasons why or why not. In terms of the ethics code, indicate whether some changes in procedure might switch your decision from "reject" to "approve."

Answers to Self Tests:

✓ **2.1.**
1. The Hobbs committee used the procedure to collect examples of perceived ethical violations among psychologists.
2. It means researchers must always weigh the benefits of their research against the potential costs, in order to achieve the greatest good.

✓ **2.2.**
1. Expedited review.
2. The potential subject is given enough information about the study to make a reasoned decision about whether to participate.
3. His procedure violated the "quit any time" proviso.
4. Debriefing, with its two components, dehoaxing and desensitizing.

✓ **2.3.**
1. It benefits the well being of humans; it also benefits animals (e.g., zoos).
2. Use live animals as sparingly as possible.
3. A failure by others to replicate her research and her unwillingness to produce her raw data.

CHAPTER 3

Developing Ideas for Research in Psychology

Preview & Chapter Objectives

All research begins with a good question and this chapter is designed to help you develop such questions. The chapter begins by distinguishing among various forms of research methodology and elaborates on a concept introduced in Chapter 1—the empirical question. You will then learn how research can develop from everyday observations of behavior, from theory, and from questions left unanswered by research just completed. The chapter concludes with a brief description of PsycINFO, psychology's premier information database, and some advice about how to prepare a literature review. When you finish this chapter, you should be able to:

- Distinguish between and identify the value of (a) basic and applied research, (b) laboratory and field research, and (c) qualitative and quantitative research.

- Understand how a good empirical question requires the use of operational definitions.
- Describe research examples that develop from everyday observations and from serendipitous events.
- Describe the defining features of a theory in psychology and show how theories (a) lead to empirical research, (b) are influenced by the outcomes of research, and (c) need to be productive, parsimonious, and testable (i.e., capable of falsification).
- Understand the importance of the "What's next?" question and the value of research that simultaneously replicates and extends prior research.
- Show how creative thinking occurs in science.
- Use PsycINFO to search for information about research in psychology.
- Write a review of the literature on some research topic in psychology.

As one of the requirements for this course, or perhaps as an independent project, you may be asked to develop an idea for a research project, learn about other research that has been completed on the topic, and perhaps even carry out the study. You might react to this assignment with a feeling that the screen has gone blank, accompanied by a mounting sense of panic. Take heart—this chapter has come along just in time. When you finish it, you may not find ideas for research projects flowing freely into your mind, but you should at least have some good ideas about where to start and how to proceed. Before looking at the sources of ideas for research, however, let us categorize the varieties of psychological research.

Varieties of Psychological Research

Research in psychology can be classified along several dimensions. One relates to the Chapter 1 description of research goals and distinguishes among studies designed primary to describe, predict, or explain. Research can also be classified as (a) basic or applied research, (b) laboratory or field research, and (c) quantitative or qualitative research.

Basic versus Applied Research

Some research in psychology concerns describing, predicting, and explaining the fundamental principles of behavior and mental processes; this activity is referred to as **basic research**. Traditionally, those involved in basic research in psychology have studied such topics as sensation and perception, learning, memory and cognition, and basic neurological and physiological processes as they relate to psychological phenomena. On the other hand, **applied research** is so named because it has direct and immediate relevance to the solution of real-world problems. To illustrate the distinction, consider some research in the area of attention capacity (a topic with a long history—recall the Dallenbach (1913) study in Box 1.1). A *basic* research study might investigate the ability of people to simultaneously carry out two different information-processing tasks in a laboratory. The researcher might examine the effects of the similarity of the tasks, their difficulty, and so on. One well-established method involves "shadowing" in a "dichotic listening" task, a technique pioneered by Cherry (1953) and Broadbent (1958) in England. A research participant in this type of experiment wears a set of earphones, with two messages coming in simultaneously, one to each ear. The task is to focus attention on one message and shadow it—that is, while the message in one ear (the "attended" ear) is being heard, the subject tries to repeat the message verbatim, as it is being heard. Of interest is what happens to the message coming into the other (i.e., the "nonattended") ear. In general, researchers find that when people are asked about information in the nonattended ear, they have a very difficult time recalling any of it, unless it is especially meaningful to them (e.g., their name). The shadowing research has led to the development of several theories of attention, which you can learn about when you take a cognitive psychology course. For our purposes, it is a good example of basic research—research designed to discover basic properties of the cognitive process of attention.

An *applied* study on attention capacity might examine the limits of attention for a real-world task with important practical implications—using a cell phone while driving a car, for example. This activity is clearly a problem, with some surveys showing that at least 85% of drivers report using their phone while driving (Hunt & Ellis, 2004) and other studies showing that a substantial number of people are on their phones when they have accidents (Redelmeier & Tibshirani, 1997). An interesting series of studies by Strayer and Johnston (2001) is a good illustration of an applied research project; it examined how carrying on a cell phone conversation could affect simulated driving performance. In one of their studies, college-aged participants performed a computer-tracking task involving skills analogous to those involved in driving. They either performed this task by itself ("single-task mode") or performed it while doing a second task ("dual-task mode"). One of the second tasks was "a *shadowing* task in which the participants performed the simulated-driving task while they repeated words that the experimenter read to them over a handheld cell phone" (p. 464, italics added). The other dual task created even more of a cognitive burden—after hearing each word, instead of repeating it back, participants had to generate a new word starting with the final letter of the word said to them. See the connection with basic research? Knowing the attention literature like the backs of their hands, Strayer and Johnston immediately thought of adapting a basic research methodology, shadowing, to an applied research study.

You might not be too surprised about the results of this study. Although "driving" performance was not affected too much by the shadowing task, it deteriorated sharply when subjects did the word generation task—focusing attention on the word generation interfered with driving. You might be more surprised about the results of a second study reported by Strayer and Johnston in the same 2001 article. They compared driving simulation performance when subjects were talking on cell phones that were either hands-free or handheld. Although those folks trying to sell hands-free phones base their marketing on the idea that their product is safer than a handheld phone, the study showed that both forms of cell phone use produced poor performance and the two forms of cell phoning did *not* differ from each other. They also found that while cell phone talking adversely affected driving, listening to books on tape or just listening to the radio did not affect the driving performance. They concluded that the problem with cell phones was not the distraction caused by holding a phone with one hand and driving with the other, or the act of listening to verbal material, but by the attentional demands of the conversation reducing the capacity for the driving task. Neat study.

It is sometimes believed that applied research is more valuable than basic research because an applied study seems to concern more relevant problems and to tackle them directly. It could be argued, however, that a major advantage of basic research is that the principles and procedures (e.g., shadowing) can potentially be used in a variety of applied situations, even though these uses aren't considered when the basic research is being done. Nonetheless, basic research is a frequent target of politicians (and some IRBs, as you recall from the last chapter), who bluster about the misuse of tax dollars to fund research that doesn't seem very "useful." The charges are easy to make and tend to resonate with voters; after all, a major component of the American national character is the high value we place on the practical and the useful. Even those committed to a program of basic research recognize that grant funds are easier to obtain when the research appears to be useful. In an interview after being elected president of the Association for Psychological Science (APS), for instance, the noted experimental psychologist Richard F. Thompson acknowledged that "[m]any of us who have been basic scientists have come to feel that to justify our existence we, too, have really got to try to develop applications to the problems of society" (Kent, 1994, p. 10).

One final point about the basic/applied distinction is that, in some cases, what is learned from basic research can be useful in an applied project that is from a completely different topic area. For instance, the serial position effect, the tendency to recall information from the beginning and end of a list better than information from the middle, is a well-known finding from basic research on memory. One might not immediately think that serial position would be especially relevant for applied research on how people navigate through the environment without getting lost, yet that is exactly what happened in a study by Cornell, Heth, Kneubuhler, and Sehgal (1996). Eight- and twelve-year-olds were led on a complicated route in a campus setting and then asked to retrace their route. A serial position effect similar to the one found in basic memory research occurred—both age groups did rather well at the beginning and end of the route, and they made most of their errors in the middle of the route. Cornell et al. even converted the serial position data into probability estimates of where the children were most likely to become lost. They concluded that such information could aid police searches for missing children.

If it is true that basic research often leads to applications, it is also the case that applied research outcomes frequently have relevance for basic research, providing evidence that either supports or refutes theories. Supporting a capacity theory of attention was not Strayer and Johnston's (2001) goal, but the study did just that. Similarly, the research on navigating through the environment is applied research, but its findings also increased the generality of the serial position phenomenon.

The Setting: Laboratory versus Field Research

Another way of classifying studies is by location. As is evident from the above labels, the distinction hinges on whether the study occurs inside or outside the controlled environment of a laboratory. **Laboratory research** allows the researcher greater control: Conditions of the study can be specified more precisely, and participants can be selected and placed in the different conditions of the study more systematically. On the other hand, in **field research**, the environment more closely matches the situations we encounter in daily living. Although field research is often applied research and laboratory research is often basic research, you should know that some basic research takes place in the field and some applied research takes place in the laboratory.

Laboratory research is sometimes criticized for being ''artificial'' and far removed from the situations encountered in everyday life. It is clear, however, that laboratory research has yielded important knowledge about behavior and a case can be made that there are more important considerations when judging the quality of research than mere correspondence to daily living. Social psychologist Elliot Aronson (2007), for example, made a distinction between mundane and experimental realism. **Mundane realism** refers to how closely a study mirrors real-life experiences. **Experimental realism** concerns the extent to which a research study, which can occur either in the laboratory or in the field, ''has an impact on the subjects, forces them to take the matter seriously, and involves them in the procedures'' (p. 411). It is the experimental realism of the study that counts, according to Aronson. If participants are involved in the study and taking it seriously, then the researcher can draw valid conclusions about behavior. The Milgram experiments on obedience, discussed in Chapter 2, don't have much mundane realism—we are unlikely to find ourselves zapping someone who fails to learn a word list for us. Milgram's volunteers were clearly involved in the experiment, however, and his studies have strong experimental realism. Milgram's research was controversial, but it shed important light on the factors influencing the phenomenon of obedience to authority.

Proximity to everyday life is the strength of field research, but there are other reasons for conducting research away from the lab. On the basis of their studies of cognitive functioning of children from India infected with intestinal parasites, for instance, Sternberg and Grigorenko (1999) argued that research in the field has several strengths. First, conditions in the field often cannot be duplicated in a laboratory. Sternberg and Grigorenko studied children living in cramped quarters in 113° heat, with the smell of excrement from open sewers almost overwhelming. Such conditions can hardly be created in a laboratory, if for no other reason than an IRB probably would not allow it. A second reason to do field research is to confirm the findings of laboratory studies and perhaps to correct misconceptions or oversimplifications that might derive from the safe confines of a laboratory. A third reason is to make discoveries that could result in an immediate difference in the lives of the people being studied. Fourth, although field research is ordinarily associated with applied research, it is also a good setting in which to do basic research. Sternberg and his colleagues have studied the effects of parasitic infections in numerous locations around the globe, and one focus of their work is to test hypotheses derived from Sternberg's theories about the basic nature of intelligence.

Some researchers combine both laboratory and field research within a single series of studies; a classic example is a project by Dutton and Aron (1974). They were interested in testing a hypothesis from a two-factor theory of romantic love: People experiencing strong physical arousal may sometimes misinterpret that arousal as love (the two factors in the theory are physiological arousal and a cognitive interpretation of the arousal). In their field study they created a situation in which males experienced different degrees of anxiety while encountering an attractive female. Dutton and Aron wanted to see if part of the arousal connected with anxiety would be misinterpreted as physical attraction for the female. They used two locations over a river in a national park in British Columbia, Canada. One was a swaying 5-foot-wide, 450-foot-long suspension bridge featuring a 230-foot drop to the river (Figure 3.1). The other was a solid wooden bridge just 10 feet over the river. In both locations, attractive female confederates approached males and asked them for help with a psychology project on how scenic attractions could influence creativity. Agreeable participants were asked some routine questions (e.g., had they visited the park before) and then given a supposed test for creativity—shown an ambiguous drawing of a woman (from a test called the Thematic Apperception Test, or TAT), they were asked to create a story about her. The men also were given the female experimenter's phone number in case they had further questions about the project. Compared to males encountered on the "safe" bridge, which presumably aroused little anxiety, males on the suspension bridge had more sexual imagery in their written TAT stories and they were more likely to call the female confederate (50 percent of the males on the swaying bridge called, while only 12.5 percent from the solid bridge called). As a further indication that it was the attractive female that produced these effects, Dutton and Aron repeated the study with *male*

FIGURE 3.1 The suspension bridge used in Dutton and Aron's (1974) study of romance in high places (John de Visser/Masterfile).

experimenters approaching male subjects on both bridges. No effects occurred (i.e., same outcome on both the high and low bridge).

These suspension bridge results came out as predicted, but Dutton and Aron (1974) were rightly concerned that the results could have other interpretations, a problem not uncommon in field research. Perhaps the males who took the suspension bridge were just more adventurous than the other males who crossed on the safer bridge. To account for this possibility, Dutton and Aron recruited subjects for a *laboratory* experiment with the same essential design. Male participants were told the study concerned the effects of electrical shock on learning. Also in the lab was an attractive female who appeared to be another participant but was actually an **experimental confederate** (i.e., working for the experimenter and part of the experimental procedure). Half of the participants were led to believe that they would be experiencing a strong ("quite painful") shock; the remaining subjects were told the shock was a "mere tingle" (p. 515). Hence, the first group was expected to experience greater anxiety than the second (just as the high bridge creates more anxiety than the low one). The results? As in the field study, males experiencing more anxiety showed more sexual imagery in their TAT stories; and on an attractiveness measure, they were more physically attracted to the female than those experiencing less anxiety. Thus, the lab study reinforced the findings of the field study that males could misinterpret anxiety as physical attraction. Together, the studies supported the two-factor theory of love.

The Dutton and Aron study shows that field research and laboratory research can converge on the same conclusion. To the extent that such an outcome occurs, it strengthens the argument that both types of research are important and necessary. But is the Dutton and Aron outcome an isolated event? Can it be said in general that the results of laboratory research mirror the results of field research? Apparently so, at least in some areas. Anderson, Lindsay, and Bushman (1999) examined several topics within social psychology and found a large collection (288 studies in all) of laboratory and field studies that investigated the same topics. For example, in the area of aggression, they matched up lab and field studies investigating the effects of anonymity on aggressive behavior. What they discovered was a high degree of correspondence between the results found in and outside the lab. Such an outcome provides aid and comfort to laboratory researchers who tire of hearing about the "artificiality" of their studies, and to field researchers who tire of hearing about how their studies lack the controls that enable firm conclusions to be drawn.

One last point about the decision on where to locate a study concerns ethics. Besides providing increased control, researchers often prefer the laboratory to the field because of problems with informed consent and privacy. In laboratory research, it is relatively easy to stick closely to the ethics code. In the field, however, it is difficult, and sometimes impossible, to provide informed consent and debriefing; in fact, in some situations, the research procedures might be considered an invasion of privacy. Consequently, field studies can face a greater challenge from an IRB, and field researchers must show that the importance of their study justifies some of the risks involved. On the other hand, as seen in the Sternberg and Grigorenko (1999) example, IRBs might not allow the conditions of some field settings to be simulated in a laboratory. Before leaving this topic, please read Box 3.1, which considers privacy invasion in field research from a legal angle.

Box 3.1

ETHICS—*A Matter of Privacy*

Unlike laboratory research, field research sometimes causes problems with informed consent, freedom to leave the study, debriefing, and invasion of privacy. An interesting study by Silverman (1975) illustrates why researchers are sometimes hesitant about doing field studies. He gave descriptions of ten published field studies to two lawyers and asked them to judge whether the procedures might violate any laws or if there seemed to be any invasion of privacy. The procedures, based on actual studies in social psychology, included having a confederate fall down in a subway car to see if anyone would help, leaving cars in different places to see if they would be vandalized, going to shoe stores and trying on many pairs of shoes, and asking for small amounts of money from passersby.

The two lawyers gave almost the *opposite* responses. Lawyer 1 believed that intent and a concern for the greater good were the key factors. The studies were designed for the ultimate good of increasing our knowledge of human behavior and not for the personal gain of the scientist. He believed that if charges were brought against the psychologist, the judge would "seek a balance between degree of annoyance and degree of legitimate purpose" (Silverman, 1975, p. 766). Lawyer 2, however, felt that in several of the studies there would be grounds not just for a civil suit on the part of individuals not wanting to be subjects of research (i.e., invasion of privacy), but for criminal action on the grounds of harassment, fraud, criminal trespass, and even disorderly conduct! Note that even with psychologist-friendly lawyer 1, the researcher could still wind up in court.

Silverman was disconcerted enough by the responses to bring the description of the subway helping behavior study to a judge for his considered opinion about whether civil or criminal charges could be brought. In general, the judge sided with lawyer 1, at least on the issue of criminal charges, but also pointed out that experiments in the field might have unforeseen consequences that could result in a negligence suit. In short, for the psychologist considering doing research in the field, there are some serious risks that do not occur in the laboratory.

By the way, you might be interested to know that lawyer 1, who didn't think the researcher would be in great jeopardy, was a successful criminal defense lawyer accustomed to seeing his clients charged but then acquitted. Lawyer 2's specialty was in medical law; he usually "defended the legal rights of patients and subjects in medical practice and research" (Silverman, 1975, p. 767). In his mind, "research psychologists invading privacy" fell into the same category as "doctors harming patients."

Quantitative versus Qualitative Research

Most research in psychology is quantitative in nature. That is, with **quantitative research**, the data are collected and presented in the form of numbers—average scores for different groups on some task, percentages of people who do one thing or another, graphs and tables of data, and so on. In recent years, however, a number of research psychologists have begun doing what is known as **qualitative research**, sometimes borrowing techniques from sociologists and anthropologists. Qualitative research is not easily classified, but it often includes studies that collect interview information, either from individuals or groups; it sometimes involves detailed case studies; or it sometimes involves carefully designed observational studies. What these various forms of qualitative research have in common is that results are presented not as statistical summaries, but as analytical narratives that summarize the project's main outcomes. A good illustration of a qualitative study is some research by Walker (1996), who wondered if sex differences in the control of a TV remote would affect relationships among couples. Her primary method was to conduct semistructured interviews with 36 couples that were either married or cohabiting and had been together for at least a year. First, as is common in qualitative research, a portion of the questions resulted in responses that could be quantified—for instance, in response to a question about control over the remote when both partners were watching TV, Walker determined that women had control 20% of the time, men 80% of the time. Most of the description, however, was a qualitative analysis, a narrative based on several open-ended questions in the interview, along with quotes from the interview to illustrate conclusions. Among other things, subjects were asked (they were interviewed individually) how they decided on programs to watch together, what their frustrations might be during this process, and what they would like to change about the process. Unlike descriptions of results in quantitative studies, which focus on the numerical data and the statistical analysis of it, results in qualitative studies often take longer to describe and include quotes that are said to represent typical responses. For example, in the Walker study, a common theme was that men seemed to take it for granted that they would control the remote. As one man reported, "I should probably let her 'drive' sometimes, but [it] would bug me too much not to be able to do it" (p. 819). Another, attempting without too much success to sound fair-minded, said "I just say I want to watch something, and if she wants to watch something really bad, I will let her watch what she wants to watch" (p. 819). Walker concluded that when both partners were watching TV, men usually had control over what was being watched, and that, in general, what should be a leisure activity could be a source of stress and misunderstanding instead.

Research that is partly or wholly qualitative in nature will be described in Chapter 10's discussion of program evaluation, Chapter 11's discussion on case studies, and in Chapter 12 in the context of observational research and interviews.

Asking Empirical Questions

Whether a research project (a) concerns basic or applied research, (b) occurs in the lab or the field, or (c) is primarily quantitative or qualitative in nature, it always begins with a question. As you recall from Chapter 1, I referred to these as **empirical questions**. They have two important features: They must be answerable with data, qualitative and/or quantitative, and their terms must be precisely defined.

We saw in Chapter 1 that questions like "Are people good or evil?" and "Is there a personal God?" are interesting and important, and individuals can reach their own conclusions about them. However, the questions are not answerable with the evidence of empirical data. Of course, there are some questions related to good, evil, and religion that *are* empirical questions. These include:

✓ What is the relationship between belief in God and fear of death?
✓ Does belief in God influence the pain threshold of terminally ill patients?
✓ What is the effect of having an altruistic sibling on one's tendency to donate blood?

Notice that each of these questions allows data to be collected in some form. Before such data can be collected, however, these questions must be refined even further. This task can be referred to as "operationalizing" the terms in the question. The process of defining terms precisely is the second feature of an empirical question.

Operational Definitions

The term **operationism** originated in the 1920s in physics, with the publication of *The Logic of Modern Physics* (1927) by the Harvard physicist Percy Bridgman. Bridgman argued that the terminology of science must be totally objective and precise, and that all concepts should be defined in terms of a set of operations to be performed. These types of definitions came to be called **operational definitions**. The length of some object, for instance, could be defined operationally by a series of agreed-on procedures. In Bridgman's words, the "concept of length is therefore fixed when the operations by which length is measured are fixed; that is, the concept of length involves as much as and nothing more than a set of operations" (Bridgman, 1927, p. 5).

Given the tendency of experimental psychologists to emulate the older sciences, especially physics, it is not surprising that the psychological community embraced operationism when it first appeared. A strict operationism did not last very long in psychology, however, in part because equating a concept with a set of operations creates an arbitrary limitation on the concept. For psychologists the problem with operationism boiled down to how to accomplish it in practice when dealing with such complex psychological phenomena as aggression, creativity, depression, and so on. Among physicists it might not be difficult to agree on a set of operations for measuring the length of a line, but how does one operationalize a concept like "aggression"? Even if psychologists could agree that the term refers to a behavior that reflects some intent to harm (Aronson, 2007), exactly what behaviors are to be measured? In the aggression literature over the years, the term has been operationalized as behaviors ranging from the delivery of electrical shocks to horn honking by car drivers to pressing a button that makes it hard for someone else to complete a task. Are these behaviors measuring the same phenomenon?

Despite this problem with the *strict* use of operational definitions, the concept has been of value to psychology by forcing researchers to define clearly the terms of their studies (Hilgard, 1987). This is especially important when you consider that most research in psychology concerns concepts that are open to numerous definitions. For instance, suppose a researcher is interested in the effects of hunger on maze learning. "Hunger" is a term that can mean several things and is not easily determined in a rat. How can you tell if a rat is hungry? The solution is to operationalize the term. You could define it operationally in terms of a procedure (e.g., not feeding the rat for 12 hours—it's reasonable to assume that the operation would produce hunger) or in terms of a behavior (creating a situation in which the rat has to work hard to earn food—it's reasonable to assume that a nonhungry rat wouldn't perform the task).

One important result of the precision resulting from operational definitions is that it allows experiments to be repeated. *Replication*, an important feature of any science, was mentioned briefly in Chapters 1 and 2, and will be elaborated later in the chapter. Research psychologists are not greatly troubled by the limitations imposed by having to define terms of their studies operationally because, in the long run, the requirement for precision increases confidence in the veracity of theories about behavior. Psychologists use the concept of **converging operations**, which refers to the idea that our understanding of some behavioral phenomenon is increased when a series of investigations, all using slightly different operational definitions and experimental procedures, nonetheless converge on a common conclusion. Thus, if the results of several studies on the effects of hunger on maze learning reached the same conclusion, even though each used different operational definitions for hunger and for learning, then confidence would be high that a lawful relationship between hunger and maze learning had been established.

Developing fruitful empirical questions in psychology is a skill that takes some practice and involves a gradual narrowing from a broad topic to a specific question. These questions can have several different origins, as I will describe in the following sections. Empirical questions may evolve out of (a) everyday observations of behavior, (b) the need to solve a practical problem, (c) attempts to support or refute a theory, or (d) unanswered questions from a study just completed. Furthermore, researchers with some creative thinking skills are especially good at developing ideas for research.

✓ Self Test 3.1

1. Consider the psychological phenomenon of attention. Give an example of basic research on attention and applied research on attention.
2. Milgram's obedience study was low on mundane reality but high on experimental reality. Explain.
3. The study on male vs. female control of the TV remote illustrated how two types of research can be combined in the same study. Which two types?

Developing Research from Observations
of Behavior and Serendipity

All of us have had the experience of observing behavior and wondering what caused it. Why does Norma get so angry when she misses a short putt, while Jeff, who misses just as many, shrugs it off and comments on how fortunate he is to be avoiding work? Why is Aunt Ethel able to recall vivid details of World War II, yet unable to remember what she did yesterday? Why do some students eagerly volunteer to give blood, while others would not consider it? Why do some young children seem to be very outgoing, while others, perhaps in the same family, seem to be painfully shy? And on and on.

These same questions occur to experimental psychologists, and are often the starting point for developing empirical questions. For Robert Sternberg, noted for his research on varieties of intelligence and the nature of human love, simple observations of daily life are his principle source of inspiration:

> All of my ideas (almost) come from watching people—myself, students I work with, my kids, my relationships with people, other people's relationships, and so on....The point is that in psychology, there is no better data source than the people around you. I've never found books or lectures or labs as good as real experience for getting ideas. (R. J. Sternberg, personal communication, May 18, 1993)

One of psychology's classic studies originated this way. The Russian psychologist Bluma Zeigarnik, a student of the famous German psychologist Kurt Lewin, gave 164 participants a series of simple tasks, each requiring a few minutes to finish. They included such things as constructing a cardboard box, making a clay figure, completing puzzles, and performing arithmetic and other mental tasks. Each person was allowed to complete half of the tasks, but was interrupted and not allowed to finish the other half. To ensure that the interruption was clearly felt to be a disruption, Zeigarnik "always chose a time when the subject was most engrossed in his work" (1927/1967, p. 303). What she found was that the interrupted tasks were about twice as likely to be recalled as the uninterrupted ones. This phenomenon—memory is better for incomplete rather than completed tasks—is today called the "Zeigarnik effect."

The idea for the study came from an activity well known to graduate students —sitting in a coffee shop talking about research. Lewin and his students often met informally for hours at a time at a cafe across the street from their laboratory in Berlin. The group couldn't help noticing that one of the waiters could remember what each student had ordered without writing it down. Soon after the bill was paid, however, the waiter had no memory of the orders. Could it be that before the bill was settled, the situation was "incomplete" and the waiter needed to keep the information in mind? Zeigarnik was intrigued, the study was designed, and the rest, as they say, is history.

A more modern example of observations leading to research comes from the social psychological research on helping behavior, which developed out of several well-publicized cases of failure to help. Most notable among them was the Kitty Genovese case in 1964, in which a woman was attacked several times and eventually murdered in New York City, in full view of a number of witnesses, none of whom even made an anonymous phone call to police. As John Darley, one of the leading researchers in the area of altruism and helping behavior, recalled later:

> Certainly the precipitating event for us all was the murder of a young lady in New York, the now famous Kitty Genovese case the *New York Times* picked up. A young lady was murdered, but sadly that's a rather typical incident. What was atypical was that thirty-eight people in her apartment building watched out their windows while this happened, and none of them did much in the way of helping. Bibb [Latané, Darley's co-worker] and I were having dinner together one night shortly thereafter. Everybody was talking about it and so were we....We probably sketched out the experiments on a tablecloth that day. (Krupat, 1975, p. 257)

The Kitty Genovese case led Darley and Latané to conduct a series of experiments showing that unresponsive bystanders aren't simply uncaring; they often assume that someone else will help if there are other people around (Darley & Latané, 1968). The study of helping behavior is now well established, as you can tell by looking at any modern social psychology text, which invariably includes an entire chapter on the topic of helping.

Serendipitous observations can also lead to research. **Serendipity**, the act of discovering something while looking for something else entirely, has been a source of numerous important events in the history of science. It can happen when a scientist is wrestling with a difficult research problem and some chance event accidentally provides the key, or it might occur when something goes wrong in an experiment, such as an apparatus failure. Skinner's experience with extinction curves following an apparatus breakdown, described in Chapter 1, is a good example of a serendipitous finding. Another involves the accidental discovery of feature detectors in the brain. To examine the origins of some research that led eventually to a Nobel Prize for David Hubel and Torsten Wiesel, read Box 3.2.

Besides resulting from observations about everyday behavior, research can also derive from specific everyday problems that are in need of solution. This is especially true of applied research, the focus of Chapter 10. For now, an example will illustrate the point. To improve the ability of its students to survive their opening semester, a college might create a special seminar for freshman students. Empirically thinking administrators might establish an applied research project that compares a group of first-year students in an experimental seminar with a comparable group of other first-year students receiving the more typical freshman orientation. The research outcome would then influence decisions about the future of the program.

Box 3.2

ORIGINS—Serendipity and Edge Detectors

Some of the most important research in the second half of the twentieth century on the physiology of the visual system was triggered by a serendipitous finding in the Harvard laboratory of David Hubel and Torsten Wiesel (Hubel & Wiesel, 1959). They were investigating the behavior of single neurons at various points in the visual pathway to see if the neurons could be made to fire in response to certain stimuli. Their experimental setup consisted of a screen on which various stimuli could be projected and seen by a cat with its head held stationary and an electrode implanted within a single cell of its visual system. (Even in the 1950s, procedures were precise enough to isolate the activity of single neurons.)

Hubel and Wiesel were hoping the neuron would fire in response to black or white dots projected onto the cat's retina. Their first efforts were frustrating:

> The position of the microelectrode tip, relative to the cortex, was unusually stable, so much so that we were able to listen in on one cell for a period of about nine hours. We tried everything short of standing on our heads to get it to fire. (Hubel, 1988, p. 69)

Nothing happened. Yet Hubel and Wiesel persevered, eventually concentrating on one area of the retina. Oddly, passing the dot over that area sometimes produced neuron firing, but not reliably. As they described it:

> After about five hours of struggle, we suddenly had the impression that the glass [slide] with the dot was occasionally producing a response, but the response seemed to have little to do with the dot. *Eventually we caught on: it was the sharp but faint shadow cast by the edge of the glass as we slid it into the slot that was doing the trick.* We soon convinced ourselves that the edge worked only when its shadow was swept across one small part of the retina and that the sweeping had to be done with the edge in one particular orientation. Most amazing was the contrast between the machine-gun discharge when the orientation of the stimulus was just right and the utter lack of a response if we changed the orientation or simply shined a bright flashlight into the cat's eyes. (Hubel, 1988, pp. 69–70; italics added)

The unexpected discovery that cells ("edge detectors") in the visual system were specialized to respond to edges and contours set at specific orientations was just the beginning. Hubel and Wiesel went on to develop an extensive research program identifying the types of stimuli that would trigger cells at all levels of the visual system; it won them the Nobel Prize in 1981. Their work also reflects the passion for doing research that was illustrated in Chapter 1 with the work of Gibson and Skinner. In

> discussing the years spent studying receptive fields for vision, roughly from 1950 to 1980, Hubel wrote:
>
> > I count myself lucky to have been around in that era, a time of excitement and fun. Some of the experiments have been arduous, or so it has often seemed at 4:00 A.M., especially when everything has gone wrong. But 98 percent of the time the work is exhilarating. There is a special immediacy to neurophysiological experiments; we can see and hear a cell respond to the stimuli we use and often realize, right at the time, what the responses imply for brain function. (Hubel, 1988, p. vii)

Developing Research from Theory

Chapter 1 included a brief discussion of theory, making the point that science as a way of knowing includes the creation of theories that have testable hypotheses. The chapter also described explanation as an important goal for research psychology. The process of developing these explanations is, in essence, the process of theory building and theory testing. In this section we'll take a more detailed look at what a theory is, the reciprocal relationship between theory construction and data collection, the logical processes involved, and the criteria for determining whether theories have value.

The Nature of Theory

A **theory** in psychology is a set of logically consistent statements about some phenomenon that (a) best summarizes existing empirical knowledge of the phenomenon, (b) organizes this knowledge in the form of precise statements of relationships among variables (i.e., laws), (c) provides a tentative explanation for the phenomenon, and (d) serves as the basis for making predictions about behavior. These predictions are then tested with research. A theory is considered to be a working truth, always subject to revision pending the outcome of empirical studies (remember from the Chapter 1 description of scientific thinking that "science produces tentative conclusions").

Theories differ in terms of their scope. Some aim to cover broad expanses of behavior and are general theories—Erik Erikson's famous theory of how our personality is developed and operates throughout the life span is an example. More frequently, however, a theory is more focused on some specific aspect of behavior. In social psychology, for instance, cognitive dissonance theory concerns decision making and how people resolve inconsistencies; in abnormal psychology, learned helplessness theory attempts to account for psychological depression. Theories also differ in terms of their level of precision, with some being stated in strict mathematical terms and others described more simply as a set of logically connected statements.

As an example of how theories originate and evolve, and to illustrate several important features of theories, let's consider the theory of cognitive dissonance in more detail. First proposed in 1957 by the renowned social psychologist Leon Festinger, this theory was remarkably simple in conception, yet widely applicable to all sorts of phenomena. It helps explain why and how people rationalize the decisions they make, how attitudes and behaviors relate, and how people justify the contradictions of their lives. The theory was especially prominent in the 1960s and 1970s, but it also remains an important force even today, as evidenced by a recent book (dedicated to the memory of Festinger, who died in 1989) describing current developments in the theory (Harmon-Jones & Mills, 1999). The essence of the theory is the proposal that whenever people hold two opposing cognitions at the same time, a state of discomfort, called "cognitive dissonance," is created. Cognitive dissonance is an example of what psychologists refer to as a **construct**. A construct is a hypothetical factor that is not observed directly; its existence is inferred from certain behaviors and assumed to follow from certain circumstances. Hence, cognitive dissonance is assumed to exist following circumstances of cognitive inconsistency and presumably leads to certain predictable behaviors.

The person experiencing dissonance is motivated to reduce the discomfort and bring the cognitions back into harmony and consistency, according to Festinger (1957). Dissonance reduction can come about by several means—one or both of the cognitions could be altered, behavior could be changed, or additional cognitions could be added to bring the two dissonant cognitions into consonance. Consider smoking, for example. This is a common activity, carried on by people who frequently hear or read about the dangers of smoking. The cognitions "I am smoking" and "Smoking can kill me" do not fit together very well. They create dissonance. One way to reduce the dissonance is to change the first cognition and stop smoking, and many people do, but nicotine is an addictive drug and quitting is easier said than done.[1] A second alternative is to alter the second cognition, perhaps by questioning the conclusiveness of the evidence for the ill effects of smoking (an option much harder to sustain today than it was when Festinger proposed the theory in 1957). A third option is to add cognitions that bridge the two original ones. For instance, the person might say, "OK, this smoking might be bad for me in one sense, but it helps me keep my weight down and all my friends smoke, so it helps me socially, and some really cool people in movies smoke, so it can't be all that bad." The process of reducing dissonance, then, can alter behavior (smoking stops) or shape beliefs and attitudes (smoking has some benefits that offset the risks).

An important feature of any theory is its continual evolution in light of new data. No theory is ever complete and, as you will learn shortly, Festinger's was no exception. Its development beyond the initial formulation nicely illustrates the reciprocal relationship between theory and data and demonstrates an important attribute of a good theory—its ability to make predictions that lead to new research. This requires some elaboration.

---

[1]The smoking example was the first one used by Festinger in his book, ironic because Festinger was a heavy smoker. Just before his death from liver cancer, he announced, reducing dissonance right to the very end, "Make sure everyone knows that it wasn't lung cancer!" (Zajonc, 1990, p. 662).

The Relationship Between Theory and Data

The move from theory to data involves the logical process of **deduction**, reasoning from a set of general statements toward the prediction of some specific event. With regard to theory, deduction takes the form of the scientist reasoning that if the theory is correct, then research outcome X can be predicted and should occur with some probability greater than chance. The prediction about specific outcomes that is derived this way from a theory is called a **hypothesis**, which in general can be considered a reasoned prediction about some empirical result that should occur under certain circumstances. These hypotheses lead to the design of a study, which produces results as predicted or fails to produce them. In the former case the theory is supported, and in the latter it is not. If the theory is supported by a large body of research, confidence is high that the theory is good; to put it another way, we could say that *inductive* support for the theory increases when individual experiments keep producing the results as predicted. **Induction** is the logical process of reasoning from specific events (the results of many experiments) to the general (the theory).

Of course, experiments don't always come out as expected. The experiment might not be a good test of the hypothesis (e.g., bad choice of operational definitions for the variables being studied in an experiment), it might have some methodological flaws, or it might just be the odd experiment that just didn't work. Also, measurements of psychological phenomena are imperfect, so a failed experiment could be the result of some form of "measurement error" (more on this concept in the next chapter). Consequently, one unexpected result seldom calls a theory into question. If results repeatedly fail to support the theory, however, especially if they occur in different laboratories, confidence in the theory begins to wane and it may be discarded or, more likely, altered.

Note that in the above two paragraphs I have avoided saying things like "a successful outcome 'proves' a theory to be true" and "a bad result 'disproves' a theory." This is because scientists hesitate to use the words "prove" and "disprove" when discussing theories and data, both on logical *and* on practical grounds.

On *strictly logical* grounds, it is impossible to prove a theory to be true, while it is possible to disprove a theory. To understand why requires a brief side trip to the rules of conditional ("if ... then") logic. Assume for the moment that all known crows are black. This statement can take the conditional form "If the bird is a crow, then it is certain that it will be black." Now suppose you see a bird that happens to be black. Can it be concluded that "therefore it must be a crow"? No, because other birds besides crows could be black. To conclude that this observed black bird must be a crow is to commit the logical fallacy known as "affirming the consequent." The situation can be summarized as follows:

> **Logical fallacy of affirming the consequent:**
> If the bird is a crow, then it will be black.
> Here's a black bird.
> Therefore, it must be a crow.

On the other hand, suppose you observe a yellow bird. Can you conclude that "therefore, it cannot be a crow"? Yes, because it has been asserted that all known crows are black. In conditional logic this conclusion is known as a "modus tollens." Thus:

Logically correct modus tollens:

If the bird is a crow, then it will be black.

Here's a yellow bird.

Therefore, it cannot be a crow.

This distinction between affirming the consequent and a modus tollens can be applied directly to theory testing. The "if . . . then" statement takes this form: "If theory X is true, then result Y can be expected to occur." Consider dissonance theory again. Festinger used the theory to make predications about what happens after people make difficult decisions. What makes some decisions hard is the fact that both alternatives have positive and negative attributes to them. Deciding which house to buy would be a snap if everything about house A was good and everything about house B was bad. But, in reality, both A and B have good and bad things about them. However the decision is actually made, Festinger predicted that dissonance would occur immediately after the final choice, because the person would have chosen something that had some negative attributes and rejected something with some positive attributes. The cognition "I am a good decision maker," is dissonant with the cognition "I've just chosen something with negative features and rejected something with positive features." To reduce dissonance, Festinger proposed that the person would make cognitive changes that would accentuate the positive features of the chosen alternative and the negative features of the rejected alternative ("Because my new house is so close to the highway, I can get to work really fast; that other house was so far up the mountain that it would have added 15 minutes to the commute, not to mention wear and tear on the brakes"); at the same time, the homebuyer would be expected to downplay the negative features of what was chosen and the positive features of what was not chosen ("The highway noise at my new house is easy to get used to; I suppose the other house had a nice view, but it would have been hidden by fog half the time").

In terms of a conditional statement, Festinger's prediction might have gone like this: "If dissonance theory is correct, then, after a difficult decision, the values placed on the attributes of the selected and rejected alternatives will alter in a specific way that will reduce dissonance." This could lead to a study in which individuals would choose between two attractive items, then, at some later time, evaluate both the chosen and nonchosen item in some fashion. Several studies like this were completed in the early years of dissonance theory, and the outcomes supported dissonance theory. For example, Brehm (1956) asked women to rate appliances; then, as a reward for participating in the study, he let them pick an appliance from two that had been rated similarly. Some time later, when asked to rate all of the appliances again, the ratings shifted—of the two appliances, the chosen one increased its rating, while the rating for the rejected appliance actually went down.

Now, as interesting as this supporting evidence might be, it cannot prove dissonance theory to be true, because of the problem of affirming the consequent:

If dissonance theory is true, then the appliance ratings will change as predicted.

The ratings did indeed change.

Therefore, dissonance theory is proven true.

You can see that the conclusion about the theory being true (i.e., proven) cannot be made because the ratings might have changed for some *other* reason having nothing to do with dissonance theory (just like other birds besides crows can be black). What can be said—and the careful scientist will never say more than this—is that the experiment "supports" or "is consistent with" the theory.

What if the appliance ratings didn't change or perhaps changed in the opposite direction? On logical grounds, this would be a modus tollens and the theory could be considered not true (i.e., disproven):

If dissonance theory is true, then the appliance ratings will change as predicted.

The ratings did not change.

Therefore, dissonance theory is not true.

Please note, however, my earlier comment that when discussing research results, scientists don't usually say things like "prove" and "disprove" on both logical and *practical* grounds. We've seen that to conclude that dissonance theory is proven because the ratings changed is to commit the fallacy of affirming the consequent. To conclude that the theory is disproven because the ratings failed to change might be technically correct (i.e., a modus tollens) but would be a most imprudent decision to make. As mentioned earlier, single experiments can fail to come out as predicted for any number of reasons, and to abandon a theory after just one problematic study is an outcome that simply never happens in science. Even strong disconfirming evidence, while it could have the effect of identifying some of the limits of some theory, probably won't destroy the theory. Theories are indeed discarded, but only when scientists lose confidence in them, and this takes a while, occurring only after predictions have been repeatedly disconfirmed in a number of laboratories and some competing theory arrives and begins to look more attractive.

Theories may be supported and theories may be discarded, but what happens most frequently is that they evolve as research accumulates and as challenges to the theory appear. Festinger, reflecting on dissonance theory thirty years after its birth, had this to say about the fate of theories: "One doesn't ask about theories, can I show that they are wrong or can I show that they are right, but rather one asks, how much of the empirical realm can it handle and how must it be modified and changed as it matures" (Festinger, 1999, p. 383). Evolution is exactly what happened in the case of cognitive dissonance. For example, one of Festinger's students, Elliot Aronson (who distinguished between mundane and experimental realism earlier in this chapter, and who is featured in this book's Epilogue), proposed that dissonance and the subsequent motivation to reduce it would be most potent when one of the cognitions related to an important aspect of the self-concept and threatened the self.

For example, Aronson would argue that the dissonance involved in smoking results from an inconsistency between what the person is doing (smoking) and a part of the self-concept that says "I am smart when it comes to my health." Aronson and his students completed a number of studies supporting the importance of the self-concept in dissonance situations (e.g., Aronson & Mettee, 1968).

Attributes of Good Theories

Some theories are judged by history to be more effective than others, and those judged to be good are characterized by several features. The most obvious one is **productivity**—good theories advance knowledge by generating a great deal of research, a trait that clearly can be applied to dissonance theory. Hundreds of studies have been done over the years. Two other attributes of good theories, falsification and parsimony, require some elaboration.

Falsification

A popular misconception about theories in psychology is that the ultimate goal is to produce one that will be so good that it will explain every possible outcome. In fact, however, a theory that appears to explain everything is seriously flawed. To understand why, we need to look at an approach to testing theories first advocated by the philosopher of science Karl Popper (1959), clearly implied in what you just read about proving and disproving theories, and mentioned briefly in the Chapter 1 discussion of scientific thinking ("science develops theories that can be disproven").

According to Popper, science proceeds by setting up theories and then attempting to disprove or falsify them. Theories that are continually resistant to **falsification** are accepted as possibly true (with the emphasis on "possibly"). Recall my earlier comment that confidence in a theory increases as inductive support accumulates. This confidence never becomes absolute, however, because of the limits of induction. For example, one hundred specific examples of birds could be found that would inductively support the conclusion "All birds can fly," yet it takes just a single nonflying bird (e.g., a kiwi) to destroy the general conclusion. Similarly, one hundred predictions derived from a theory could support a theory, but one disconfirmation could disprove it via modus tollens reasoning. Of course, we've already seen that on practical grounds, one disconfirmation will *never* lead to a wholesale abandonment of a theory. Nonetheless, Popper's argument suggests that disconfirmation carries greater weight than confirmation. At the very least, it requires that disconfirmations be investigated thoroughly.

As you recall from Chapter 1, one of the attributes of pseudoscience is its tendency to "sidestep disproof." This is just another way of saying the pseudoscientific theories fail the test of falsification. Phrenology illustrates the point. As you recall, by arranging the theory so that it could explain (more accurately, explain away) all possible anomalies, phrenologists managed to create the appearance of an infallible theory. In fact, by explaining everything, it failed to predict anything. Would a large area of "acquisitiveness" mean that a person would be a thief? According to phrenology, it might, but if the acquisitiveness faculty was offset by a large area of "modesty," it might not. So a large acquisitiveness area may or may not produce a thief. This failure to predict isn't good enough.

A common criticism of Popper's falsification approach is that it fails to take into account the everyday psychology of doing research, in the sense that most researchers in the midst of their programs of research, like the phrenologists, develop a sense of ownership and tend to get more excited about supportive evidence than outcomes that question their theories. There is some truth to this, but, unlike phrenologists and other pseudoscientists, however, real scientists clearly recognize the importance of falsification thinking. Even though researchers might hope to find support for their own theories, they are always trying to design experiments that can rule out one explanation or another. For example, think back to the applied research study on the effects of cell phone use on driving (Strayer & Johnston, 2001), described earlier in this chapter. As you recall, one of their comparisons was between subjects using a hands-free device and others using a handheld phone. The purpose of the handheld versus hands-free comparison was to test the theory that the problem with cell phone use in a car has to do with the ability to use both hands while driving, not with the attention demands. But because performance was poor in *both* groups, Strayer and Johnston were able to rule out (falsify) the idea that a hands-free cell phone solves the problem of using cell phones in cars. One of psychology's most famous examples of a "rule it out" approach involves the investigation of a famous horse with alleged mathematical and reading abilities. Take a moment and read Box 3.3, which chronicles the case of Clever Hans, a horse with intellectual skills more apparent than real.

Box 3.3

CLASSIC STUDIES—Falsification and Der Kluge Hans

In Berlin at the turn of the twentieth century, the best show in town, except perhaps for the just-opened subway, could be found in the courtyard adjacent to a stable on Griebenow Street. There the spectator would encounter a horse (Figure 3.2) that appeared to have remarkable intellectual powers. When asked to multiply four by four, the horse would tap his front hoof 16 times and stop. Adding, subtracting, multiplying, and dividing didn't challenge the remarkable animal, known to the German public as Clever (*Kluge* in German) Hans. Even fractions and decimals were no problem. When asked to add 2/5 and 1/2, the horse would tap out 9 for the numerator and 10 for the denominator (Sanford, 1914). The horse (apparently) could also read and spell, using a system of tapping that translated letters into numbers (as you might guess, Hans was not a speed reader).

If you've been developing your scientific thinking skills, I imagine you're a bit skeptical about this horse that read and did math better than some of your friends. Skeptics existed then too and one of them, Oskar Pfungst, provides us with a wonderful example of falsification thinking. Pfungst set out to see if he could rule out

FIGURE 3.2   Clever Hans at work (Mary Evans Picture Library/The Image Works).

intelligence as an explanation for the behavior of the horse, while at the same time trying to find a more reasonable explanation for what the horse was actually doing.

A special commission including scientists and animal trainers concluded that the horse's trainer, Wilhelm von Osten, was not a fraud, but Pfungst suspected that the owner might be giving the animal subtle cues about how to respond. He reasoned that if this were the case, then the horse would be correct only if the questioner knew the answer.

Testing the hypothesis that the horse would not know the answer unless the questioner did was easy. Pfungst simply set up several tests in which the questioner knew the correct answer sometimes but not at other times. For example, Pfungst had questioners hold up a card with a number on it. When the questioner was allowed to see the number before holding it up, the horse tapped out the number correctly 98% of the time. However, if the questioner was not allowed to look at the card before the horse did, Hans was correct only 8% of the time (Fernald, 1984). So much for mathematical ability. In a series of similar tests, Pfungst was able to rule out (falsify) the idea that Hans could also use language.

Thus, Hans was clearly getting information about the correct answer from the person asking the question. How this occurred was still a puzzle that Pfungst eventually solved. To make a long story short, he was able to determine that the horse was responding to slight visual cues from the questioner. Whenever someone asked a question, that person would bend forward very slightly or move his or her eyes down without being aware of it (in effect, glancing down at the horse's hoof to see if it would start tapping). Hans learned that the movement was a signal to begin responding. When Hans reached the correct answer, the person would straighten up or glance up, again just slightly and without awareness, but enough to signal Hans that it was time to stop.

The Clever Hans case illustrates two other points besides the falsification strategy of Pfungst. By showing that the horse's abilities were not due to a high level of intelligence but could be explained adequately in terms of the simpler process of learning to respond to two sets of visual cues (when to start and when to stop), Pfungst provided a more *parsimonious* explanation of the horse's behavior. Second, if von Osten was giving subtle cues that influenced behavior, then perhaps experimenters in general might subtly influence the behavior of participants when the experimenter knows what the outcome will be. We'll return to this point in Chapter 6—it is an example of what is called *experimenter bias*.

Parsimony

Besides being stated precisely enough to be falsified, good theories are also **parsimonious**. This means, ideally, that they include the minimum number of constructs and assumptions that are necessary to explain the phenomenon adequately and predict future research outcomes. If two theories are equal in every way except that one is more parsimonious, then the simpler one is generally preferred.

In psychology, the idea is normally attributed to the late-nineteenth-century British comparative psychologist Conwy Lloyd Morgan. He lived at a time when the theory of evolution was prompting naturalists to look for evidence of mental processes in animals (such as intelligence in horses like Clever Hans), hence supporting the Darwinian notion of continuity among species. This search produced a number of excessive claims, including the notion that moths approach candles because they are curious, that beavers show foresight and planning in their dam-building activities, that scorpions can experience depression and commit suicide, and that ants are in the "habit of keeping domestic pets" (Romanes, 1886, p. 83). While not ruling out the idea of consciousness in animals, Morgan argued that behavior should be explained in the simplest terms possible, yet still be sufficient to explain the behavior. His famous statement, which has come to be known as "Lloyd Morgan's Canon," was that "[i]n no case may we interpret an action as the outcome of the exercise of a higher psychical faculty, if it can be interpreted as the outcome of the exercise of one which stands lower in the psychological scale" (Morgan, 1903, p. 53). Instead of attributing logical reasoning to the dog that lifts a latch to get out of the yard, for example, Morgan would explain the behavior more simply (i.e., more parsimoniously) as an example of trial and error learning. The dog tries many behaviors to get out of the yard, and eventually hits on one that works. That behavior gradually becomes strengthened with repeated success, and the animal has learned to escape. No logical thinking needed in this case.

In psychology a good illustration of parsimony is a comparison of Freudian and behaviorist theories about why five-year-old boys imitate their fathers. The Freudian explanation requires acceptance of a large number of assumptions and constructs, including ideas about the unconscious control of behavior, infantile sexuality, Oedipal feelings, castration anxiety, repression, and identification with the aggressor. Briefly, the young boy is said to desire his mother sexually, but to fear being harmed by his father if the desire is discovered. Consequently, he represses the desire into the unconscious and identifies with the aggressive father, reasoning (unconsciously) "if I act exactly like Dad, maybe Mom will love me like she loves him." Learning theory simply assumes that (a) behaviors that are reinforced will tend to occur again in similar situations in the future and (b) parents are likely to notice and reinforce imitative behaviors. Learning theory is clearly more parsimonious than its Freudian counterpart in this instance, while still providing an adequate explanation for the imitation behavior and a basis for predicting future behavior.

Misunderstandings about Theories

One final point here is that theories are often misunderstood. For example, here are several statements that I know you have heard before, each showing a failure to understand the true nature of theory:

- "It's not a fact; it's only a theory."
- "It's just a theory; there's no proof."
- "Here's my theory about that."

From what you now know, you should be able to see the problems with these statements. The first two are variations on the same theme and are often encountered in discussions about Darwin's theory of evolution. Both reflect a serious misunderstanding of the relationship between theory and data. You now know that theories represent "working truths" about some phenomenon, *always* subject to revision based on new data, but reflecting the most reasonable current understanding of the phenomenon. "Facts" are the results of research outcomes that add inductive support for theories or fail to support theories. As you know from the discussion of the fallacy of affirming the consequent, theories can never be absolutely "proven" to be true. They can only be accepted with varying degrees of confidence, depending on the strength of the empirical support (and Darwin's theory is perhaps the most strongly supported theory in the history of science). Think of it this way—theories never become facts; rather, they serve to explain facts. The third statement above could reflect a reasonably accurate understanding of theory, but normally the person saying it means "hypothesis," not "theory."

Developing Research from Other Research

To a large extent, this section on developing ideas for research is an extension of what was just described about the reciprocal relationship between theory and data, but research deriving from other research occurs even when theory development is not the prime focus. Sometimes researchers simply want to investigate some phenomenon to discover regular, predictable relationships between variables (i.e., to discover laws of behavior) and are not very concerned about theory building. Skinner's operant conditioning research (Chapter 11) falls into this category.

I believe the most common sources of ideas for research in psychology are unanswered questions from studies just completed. Psychologists seldom conduct individual experiments that are separate from each other; instead, they build **programs of research**, a series of interrelated studies. You won't often find someone doing a study on helping behavior and then switching to do a study on aggression. Rather, researchers become involved in a specific area of investigation and conduct a series of investigations in that area that may last for years and may extend to many other researchers with an interest in the topic. The conclusion of one project invariably leads to another because while experiments answer some empirical questions, they also typically raise new ones. The research of Festinger and his colleagues and students on cognitive dissonance is a good example of a research program lasting decades.

One unmistakable indication of how research leads to other research can be seen by scanning any issue of a typical psychology journal. Look at the authors of a specific publication; then look to see if those same names appear in the reference sections of the publication as authors of similar studies. As an illustration, in the first two issues of the journal *Psychological Science* (perhaps psychology's best research journal) for 2008, there are 32 different research articles. The authors of the articles reference other work by themselves in 25 of the 32 articles. Although some of this may be a normal human tendency to cite one's own work, for the most part it reflects the fact that researchers simply don't do single experiments—they establish systematic programs of interconnected experiments. Experiments lead to more experiments.

Research Teams and the "What's Next?" Question

If you asked research psychologists to describe their day-to-day existence, you would get a wide variety of answers, but one general principle would emerge: Few researchers work by themselves. Rather, they assemble **research teams** within their laboratories that operate under what has been called an "apprenticeship" model (Taylor, Garner, & Hunt, 1959). Typically, the team will include a senior researcher, Dr. X, several graduate students who are working for Dr. X, and perhaps two or three highly motivated undergraduates who have convinced Dr. X of their interest and willingness to work odd hours and perhaps clean animal cages. The undergraduates normally work under the direction of the graduate students, who, in turn, are the apprentices of the professor. This hierarchical team will have several experiments going on at once, and team members will spend long hours in the lab collecting data and analyzing them. Also, they will often find themselves sitting around a table in the coffee house across the street, not unlike Lewin and his students, discussing research projects in various stages of completion while consuming large amounts of caffeine. When discussing completed projects, team members will use what could be called "what's next?" thinking—given the outcome of this study, what should we do next? At some point in the conversation, someone will get an idea and ask the single most frequently heard question in conversations among research psychologists: "What do you think would happen if we did X?" The "X" refers to a rough idea for a study, and "what do you think would happen?" is a request for predictions about the outcome. The question will lead to a lively discussion in which the group will refine the idea or perhaps decide it is unworkable and think about the next "what's next?" question that comes up. If the idea is pursued, some procedure will be created, tried in the next few days in trial runs that are sometimes called **pilot studies**, revised or refined further (additional coffee involved here), and eventually shaped into a tightly designed study that is then completed.

The pilot study is an invaluable way to determine such things as the clarity of your instructions to subjects, the difficulty of the task you might have created, the believability of a cover story (if your study involves deception), the duration of the experiment, and the adequacy of the materials you have created. For example, a study by Schlagman, Schulz, and Kvavilashvili (2006) examined the so-called "positivity" effect in autobiographical memory—a tendency for us to be more likely to recall positive experiences as we grow older. The plan was to give young and old subjects a notebook in which to record specific types of memories that occurred to them spontaneously during the course of a week. Each page of the notebook included a number of questions for subjects to answer about their memories (e.g., the mood they were in when the memory came to them). The researchers had no idea how many pages to include in the notebook, eventually settling on twenty after doing a pilot study.

[P]articipants were provided with a diary in the form of a notebook, which contained 20 questionnaires, one to be completed for each involuntary memory experienced. This number of questionnaires was provided because, in an earlier pilot study, none of the participants who were supplied with 50 questionnaires recorded more than 20 memories in a 1-week period. (p. 164)

Once completed, a research study seldom stands by itself. Instead, its outcome almost always leads to another study, often designed to clarify some unanswered question of the first study or extend the findings in new directions. To illustrate, consider these two studies on face recognition by Burton, Wilson, Cowan, and Bruce (1999). In their initial study they wondered about our ability to recognize people shown in typical surveillance videos, where the visual quality is often poor. They compared participants who already knew the people on a video with others unfamiliar with the people being filmed. A third group consisted of police officers in training (presumably learning to be good at recognizing crooks on surveillance tapes of bank robberies). They found that subjects relatively familiar with the people on the tape performed rather well on a recognition task, while those in the other two groups fared poorly. Given this outcome, and thinking along "what's next?" lines, Burton and his research team wondered about the basis for the accurate recognition when participants knew the people on the tapes. Was it the faces, the overall body shapes, or perhaps the way the people on the tapes walked? This question led to the obvious next study, in which tapes were edited to obscure faces, bodies, or the gaits of the people on the video. They discovered that recognition performance was still quite good with body and gait obscured, but when viewers could not see the faces of those on the surveillance tape, accuracy disappeared. In short, the second study followed nicely from the first, and answered a question raised by the first study.

Thus, research in psychology (a) usually involves a continuous series of interrelated studies, each following logically from the prior one; (b) is often a communal effort, combining the efforts of several people who are immersed in the same narrowly specialized research area; and (c) is very unstructured in its early, creative stages. This lack of structure was noted some time ago by a panel of distinguished experimental psychologists brought together in 1958 by the Education and Training Board of the APA and charged with making recommendations about graduate training in experimental psychology. They described "the process of doing research—that is, of creating and building a science of psychology—[as] a rather informal, often illogical and sometimes messy-looking affair. It includes a great deal of floundering around in the empirical world, sometimes dignified by names like 'pilot studies' and 'exploratory research'" (Taylor, Garner, & Hunt, 1959, p. 169).

One fairly recent development in "what's next?" question asking is the extension of the concept of a research team far beyond the confines of a single laboratory. In the electronic age, it is quite common for researchers on different campuses to interact electronically. These digital conversations often include descriptions of a proposed method preceded by the famous question, "What do you think would happen if we did this?" Thus, while being separated by thousands of miles, researchers can nonetheless carry on the kind of informal discussion that leads to creative research. They can even drink coffee while communicating electronically, assuming they keep the liquid far enough away from the keyboard.

For you as a student, then, one fruitful strategy for getting ideas for research is to begin reading some published research. As you begin to read journal articles about research studies, be thinking in "what's next?" terms. Here are some specific tips:

✓ Could the next study test a suggestion made in the Discussion section of the article you read?

✓ The authors of the study you just read will offer some kind of explanation for their results. Could the next study test this explanation by setting up a study that compares it to some other explanation?

✓ The study you just read might draw a general conclusion about some phenomenon, but you might think the conclusion would be more likely to apply to one type of person rather than to another. Your next study could see if the conclusions of the study just read apply to certain types of persons (e.g., introverts but not extroverts).

✓ Could the next study extend the findings to another age group or socioeconomic group?

✓ Could the next study extend the findings to a different culture?

✓ Could the procedures used in the study you just read be adapted for other kinds of research problems?

Replication and Extension

Many studies that follow on the heels of completed studies will be similar enough to be considered replications but different enough so that they are not exact duplicates of prior research. In other words, they include both replication and extension. As research psychologists normally use the term, **replication** refers to a study that duplicates some or all of the procedures of some prior study. **Extension**, on the other hand, resembles a prior study and usually replicates part of it, but goes further and adds at least one new feature. Furthermore, in studies that are extensions, the term **partial replication** is often used to refer to that part of the study that replicates some portion of the earlier work. Sometimes the term "exact replication" or "direct replication" is used to describe a point-for-point duplication of some other study.

Exact replication was a procedure used for training purposes in Pavlov's famous laboratory in Russia. Whenever new workers came into the lab, their first experiment would be to replicate some previous study (Babkin, 1949). Thus, Pavlov had a continuous system of checking on results while new researchers developed the skills to eventually carry on extensions of earlier findings. In general, however, exact replications seldom occur for the simple reason that researchers don't get promoted and tenured if all they do is repeat what someone else has done. Normally, exact replications occur only when serious questions are raised about some finding. For instance, if several researchers are trying to extend some finding and their studies include a partial replication that fails to come out as expected, it may be necessary to go back to the original study and do an exact replication to determine if the finding really was reliable. And, as you recall from Chapter 2, failures to replicate sometimes lead to the discovery of scientific fraud.

A good example of a case where questions were raised about a finding, which in turn led to an exact replication, is a study by Steele, Bass, and Crook (1999) with the title "The Mystery of the Mozart Effect: Failure to Replicate." The researchers were reacting to an earlier study by Rauscher, Shaw, and Ky (1993) that seemed to show a short-term improvement in spatial skill following brief exposure to Mozart's music. The possibility that listening to the music could increase ability was dubbed the Mozart effect. There had been several (failed) attempts at replication, but the studies had not been exact replications. Steele et al., however, duplicated the Rauscher et al. study in all its essential aspects, and failed to find any evidence whatsoever for the effect. Consequently, few psychologists believe such an effect really exists. As you might guess, however, given the Chapter 1 discussion of pseudoscience, the Mozart effect lives on among the gullible, despite the absence of any convincing evidence. There is even a website where you can purchase various Mozart CDs designed to make your child smarter. Caveat emptor.

A study by Marean, Werner, and Kuhl (1992) is a good example of how research can replicate and extend at the same time. These researchers were interested in whether infants as young as two months old could categorize different vowel sounds. The study was an extension of earlier work showing that six-month-olds had this categorizing ability. Marean et al. wondered if the ability developed even earlier than age six months. Their study tested two- and three-month-old children, and as a partial replication of the earlier study, included six-month-olds as well. Basically, the study showed that as early as two months, children showed different reactions to two different vowels spoken by the same person but did not react differently to two different persons speaking the same vowel. That is, they were discriminating by the general category of a vowel sound, not by the individual acoustic features of two different voices.

Creative Thinking in Science

One element of the research-generating process that has been implied several times in this chapter, but not dealt with directly, is scientific creativity. It is one thing to say that research can be generated from simple observations, from theory, or from the outcomes of other studies, but the jump from these sources of research ideas to the actual research study does not occur automatically. At some point, the experiment must be *created*. Sometimes the study follows logically from what preceded it and may be minimally creative, but at other times, a creative leap occurs.

Creative thinking in research design involves a process of recognizing meaningful connections between apparently unrelated ideas and seeing those connections as the key to developing the study. Such thinking does not occur in a vacuum, however, but rather in the context of some problem to be solved by a scientist with considerable knowledge of the problem at hand. As the famous biologist Louis Pasteur put it, "chance favors the prepared mind" (cited in Myers, 1992, p. 335). Thus, serendipity does not by itself produce an idea for a research study; the serendipitous event must be seen by the scientist immersed in a topic as the missing piece that solves the problem at hand. This is one reason why researchers work in teams—the presence of several minds increases the chances that someone will have an idea that someone else on the team will see as the missing piece to the puzzle.

To examine a specific example of scientific creativity, consider maze learning. Ask a psychologist to name famous pieces of research equipment, and mazes will be at or near the top of the list. Although the maze reached its peak of popularity in the period 1920–1940, it is still an important tool used to study such things as learning, spatial behavior, and drug effects. Credit for the first maze learning study with rats belongs to Willard Small of Clark University, who completed his studies near the end of the nineteenth century (Small, 1900).

How did Small get the idea of putting rats in mazes? Along with his laboratory colleague, Linus Kline, he was interested in rat behavior, in particular the rat's "home-finding tendencies." In a discussion with Edmund Sanford, director of Clark's lab, Kline described some tunnels he had observed "made by large feral rats to their nests under the porch of an old cabin. . . . These runways were from three to six inches below the surface of the ground and when exposed during excavation presented a veritable maze" (Miles, 1930, p. 331). The term "maze" apparently made a connection for Sanford, and he suggested that Kline build a maze himself. In particular, Sanford proposed using as a model the well-known Hampton Court maze, England's popular people-size labyrinth.

With other projects under way, Kline passed along the idea to Small, who built a 6 × 8-foot wire mesh maze, changing the Hampton Court maze's trapezoidal shape (Figure 3.3a) to rectangular (Figure 3.3b), but keeping the design the same. Small ran several studies examining how rats learned the maze; the Hampton design became common in the early decades of the twentieth century, and thus began a rats-in-mazes tradition that continues to the present day.[2]

The story is a good illustration of scientific creativity. Scientists (Kline and Small) knowledgeable in some research area (animal behavior) were wrestling with a difficult problem (how to study home finding in the rat). An offhand comment (Kline's recollections of rats tunneling under a porch) combined with Sanford's familiarity with the Hampton Court maze produced a link between seemingly unrelated events, and the problem was solved—the way to study a rat's home-finding tendencies was to create an apparatus modeled on a famous maze in England.

It is worth noting that while a thorough knowledge of one's field may be a prerequisite to creative thinking in science, the blade is double-edged; this knowledge can sometimes create rigid patterns of thinking that inhibit creativity. Scientists occasionally become so accustomed to a particular method or so comfortable with a particular theory that they fail to consider alternatives, thereby reducing the chances of making new discoveries. Consider maze learning again.

The maze has contributed a great deal to our understanding of basic learning processes, and its invention illustrates scientific creativity at its best. However, the apparatus has also led to many dead ends, so to speak. Once established as a standard apparatus, the maze occasionally hindered creativity, leading researchers to narrow the focus of their work to situations that were relevant to mazes but to little else.

---

[2]Incidentally, although critics sometimes refer to the maze as an example of the "artificiality" of laboratory research in psychology (i.e., no mundane reality for the rat), it is worth noting that Small's original intent in using the maze was not to create a sterile environment but one close to the rat's world, or, as Small (1900) put it, to create "as little difference as possible between the conditions of experiment and of ordinary experience" (p. 209).

(a)

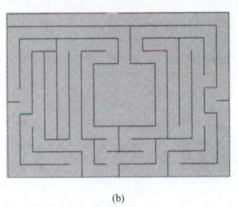

(b)

FIGURE 3.3 (a) The Hampton Court maze on a busy day (Georg Gerster/Photo Researchers). (b) Small's adaptation of the Hampton Court maze design for his pioneering study of maze learning in rats.

The phenomenon of "centrifugal swing" is an example. Investigated heavily in the 1920s and 1930s, it was said to be a tendency for an animal to emerge from one turn in a maze (presumably at high speed) and swing by centrifugal force to the far wall. This would then influence the direction of its next turn. This swing was contrasted with a "forward-moving tendency." Dozens of studies attempted to tease out the factors that would produce either a swing or a forward move (e.g., Schneirla, 1929). The studies were elegantly designed and they no doubt helped develop the research skills of a number of experimental psychologists, but the research had no importance beyond the maze apparatus itself and shed no light on fundamental learning processes.

Perhaps the famous behaviorist E. C. Tolman was only half serious when he closed his 1937 APA presidential address by professing that "everything important in psychology ... can be investigated in essence through the ... analysis of the determiners of rat behavior at a choice-point in a maze" (cited in Hilgard, 1978, p. 364). His comment, however, shows that the focus on an existing apparatus can narrow scientific thinking. The origins of scientific equipment such as mazes may reveal creative thinking at its best (e.g., Sanford's idea to use the Hampton Court maze), but innovation can be dampened once an apparatus or a research procedure becomes established.

✓ Self Test 3.3

1. What is the goal of a "what's next?" question?
2. What is a study like if it "replicates" and "extends" some research finding?
3. What is the point of Pasteur's comment that "chance favors the prepared mind"?

Reviewing the Literature

Research projects do not develop in a vacuum. The psychologists involved in a program of research are thoroughly familiar, not just with the work of their own lab, but also with the work done in other labs conducting similar research. Those researchers deriving experiments from theory are likewise familiar with the research concerning the theory in question. Even the experimenter who gets an idea for a study after making a casual observation often makes that observation within the context of some related knowledge or some problem at hand. How is one's knowledge of the literature acquired?

Computerized Database Searches

Chances are that you have already used an electronic database to search for information. Some common ones are JSTOR, Science Direct, and Academic Search Premier. And you have undoubtedly started many of your searches by simply relying on Google (what you might not know is that you can search for scientific literature on a subset of Google called Google Scholar). In psychology, the APA's PsycINFO Services provides a variety of electronic search tools. The primary database, from which all of the others are derived, is called PsycINFO. It includes references to journal articles, doctoral dissertations, technical reports, books, and book chapters. It includes journal articles dating back to 1887, the year when American psychology's first successful journal, the *American Journal of Psychology*, was founded. It includes more than 2.5 million abstracts, covers literature published in more than 2,400 journals, and is updated weekly. The features of PsycINFO are constantly being improved, so for the most up-to-date information, you should check out PsycINFO's website at www.apa.org/psycinfo.

As a student, you will be most likely to find PsycINFO among the list of electronic databases on your library's website. It can appear in several different-looking formats, depending on how your library subscribes. Regardless of which service is used, however, the basic features of PsycINFO are the same. The best way to learn the mechanics of using PsycINFO is to sit at your computer and experiment, perhaps starting by working your way through the "help" screens. The APA also publishes various guides (e.g., there is one that can be downloaded from www.apa.org/databases/training/searchguides.html), and reference librarians are always happy to assist you as well.

Once your search has produced specific research articles, you can ask PsycINFO to show you the "records" for them. These can then be printed or downloaded to your computer. Figure 3.4 shows you what a typical PsycINFO record for a journal article looks like (you should recognize the article as one featured earlier in

Title:	Driven to distraction: Dual-task studies of simulated driving and conversing on a cellular telephone.
Pub. Yr.:	2001
Author(s):	Strayer, David L.; Johnston, William A.
Affiliation:	U Utah, Department of Psychology
Source:	Psychological Science. Vol. 12(6), Nov. 2001, 462–466.
Abstract:	Dual-task studies assessed the effects of cellular-phone conversations on performance of 48 Ss (aged 18–30 yr) on a simulated driving task. Performance was not disrupted by listening to radio broadcasts or listening to a book on tape. Nor was it disturbed by a continuous shadowing task using a handheld phone, ruling out, in this case, dual- task interpretations associated with holding the phone, listening, or speaking. However, significant interference was observed in a word-generation variant of the shadowing task, and this deficit increased with the difficulty of driving. Moreover, unconstrained conversations using either a handheld or a hands-free phone resulted in a twofold increase in the failure to detect simulated traffic signals and slower reactions to those signals that were detected. The authors suggest that cellular phone use disrupts performance by diverting attention to cognitive context other than the one immediately associated with driving.
Key Phrase:	Dual task studies; cellular phone usage; driving task; radio listening; shadowing task; slower reaction times; diverting attention
Descriptors:	Attention, distractibility, driving behavior, reaction time, telephone systems
Population:	Human; male; female
Age Group:	Adulthood (18 yrs and older)
References:	21 (this is usually followed by a list of the references in the article)

FIGURE 3.4 A portion of the PsycINFO record for the study by Strayer and Johnston (2001) on the effects of cell phone use on driving.

this chapter concerning cell phones). As you can see, each record includes several important categories of information. These categories are called "fields," and they include, among other things, the article's title and its author(s), all of the needed reference information (journal, volume, page numbers), an abstract of the article, and descriptors (terms that can be used to search further). Reading the abstracts will tell you whether the article is especially relevant for you. If so, depending on your library's subscription to the database, you can probably download and print a .pdf copy of the article itself.

Search Tips

Experience is the best teacher of PsycINFO, but there are some guidelines that can help you become a proficient user. First, when PsychINFO first appears on your screen, it will be in a basic search mode. You should immediately find the "advanced search" button and click on it. This will enable you to search more precisely. For example, you can then search by such fields as author, article title, and/or year of publication. You can also choose various search "limiters." Thus, you could choose a "publication type" search, a neat device for focusing on specific types of articles. One of my interests is the history of psychology, for example, and I can search specifically for "obituaries." Other publication types that can be chosen include "longitudinal studies," "experimental replications," "literature review," and "meta analysis." These last two types of search can be especially useful because they will find articles that summarize the results of many other articles. The reference sections of these literature reviews and meta analyses alone will have great value in your research. Be especially primed to notice articles in the journal *Psychological Bulletin* and chapters in the book series *Annual Review of Psychology*. Both publish long literature reviews that are potential gold mines because they also contain extensive reference lists. Once you begin finding good articles on your topic of choice, you can use the reference sections of the actual articles as a means of further search. From these references you might pick up some new search terms, and you can identify names of researchers who seem to publish a lot on the topic.

Another search tip is to use the "and" function to narrow the search, and the truncation function to avoid narrowing it too much. For example, suppose you are taking social psychology and looking for articles on altruism, our tendency to help others in need. Furthermore, suppose you want to examine altruism from the standpoint of evolutionary psychology. If you ask PsycINFO to just find records with the word "altruism" in them, you will retrieve too many records. The search I just completed to illustrate this point yielded 3,378 records (by the time you read this, the number will be much higher). When I asked PsycINFO to search for "altruism AND evolutionary psychology," however, there were many fewer records—81. That is a much more manageable number, of course, but it might occur to you that there must be more than 81 articles dealing with this topic. There are. By asking for "evolutionary psychology," I eliminated records that included just the terms "evolution" or "evolutionary." To solve the problem, the evolutionary psychology term could be "truncated" (i.e., shortened). This is done by using only the first few key letters and adding an asterisk. For example, using "evol★" will retrieve all of the terms that begin with those four letters, including evolutionary, evolution, evolved, and evolving. When I asked for "altruism and evol★," 530 records appeared. This is better than 81, but way too many to look at them all. Fortunately, however, when it lists the results of a search, PsycINFO lists the items by date, with the most recent ones appearing first. It is always a good idea to look at the most recent articles first (their Reference sections will tell you the most important earlier articles), so even with 530 records available, searching the most recent ones will give you a good start. Of the 530 records I found today, the first 14 were published in 2008.

As you become proficient in using PsycINFO, you will begin to identify useful information about your topic of interest. As you begin to read some of this information, and perhaps talk it over with other students or professors, you will start to know the literature. (You should carefully examine Table 3.1 for some tips on how to read a psychology research article effectively). This knowledge, in turn, will put you in a better position to develop ideas for research, formulate them

TABLE 3.1   *Getting the Most Out of Reading Journal Articles*

At some point in your research methods course, perhaps as part of an assignment to complete a literature review, you will find yourself reading research articles that have been published in one of the psychology journals. It is important to keep in mind that journal articles were not written for an undergraduate audience; rather, they are aimed at other professional researchers. Hence, they can be hard to read. Here are some tips to make the task easier:

- Get as much as you can out of the Abstract. This is an overall summary of the research and probably the easiest section of the paper to read and understand—read it several times.

- In the opening paragraph or two of the Introduction, look for a general statement of the problem being studied. By the way, this part of the paper will not have a label called "Introduction," but it will include everything between the Abstract and the section labeled "Method."

- Near the end of the Introduction, probably in the final paragraph, look for statements of the hypothesis or hypotheses being tested in the study. These hypotheses will emerge out of the problem statement and the research questions raised by the studies that will have been described in the middle part of the introduction (the literature review portion of the Introduction). Write down the hypotheses and keep them in mind as you continue reading. Don't be concerned if the word "hypothesis" does not appear. Instead, you might see words like "prediction" and "expect."

- In the Method section, pay careful attention to the description of the procedure and experimental design. Try to place yourself in the role of a participant in the study and develop a clear idea of what the participants had to do in the study. If it's an experimental study, identify and write down the independent and dependent variables (you've encountered these terms in your general psychology course and you'll learn much more about them in Chapter 5).

(continued)

TABLE 3.1 *(continued)*

- The Results section might be especially difficult, because it will include some statistical information and symbols that will seem bizarre. A good Results section will have a clear verbal description of what the results were, however, and the graphs and tables should be helpful. In a well-written Results section, you should be able to understand the gist of what happened in the study without looking at a single number.

- The last main part of the article is the Discussion section. It often begins with a paragraph that summarizes the main results, so if the Results section is Greek to you, there's still hope. The main purpose of the Discussion section is to explain the results with reference to the original hypotheses, so the writer will be making connections back to the Introduction. The researcher will also address weaknesses that might have existed in the study, or alternative explanations for the results. A final thing to look for in the Discussion is a description of what research should be done next (the "What's Next?" question). This part of the Discussion section, which points toward future research, is a great source of ideas for research. If your assignment involves doing a literature search and then developing a research proposal, this "future directions" portion of the Discussion is where you'll get some excellent ideas.

as empirical questions, and develop them into testable hypotheses. With a good research hypothesis in hand, you are ready to begin designing a study that will provide some answers to your empirical question. The problem of design will be dealt with shortly. First, however, it is necessary to introduce you to some of the basics about the data that you will be collecting.

Chapter Summary

Varieties of Psychological Research

Basic research in psychology aims to discover fundamental principles of behavior, while applied research is undertaken with specific practical problems in mind. Both basic and applied research can take place either in the laboratory or in a field setting. Laboratory research allows greater control, but field research more closely approximates real-life situations. Research that involves participants in the procedures (i.e., has experimental reality), even if it places people in situations far removed from everyday living, can yield important information about behavior. Most research in psychology is quantitative in nature, involving numerical data subjected to statistical analysis, but recent years have seen an increase in what is called qualitative research (e.g., content analysis of structured interviews).

Asking Empirical Questions

The initial step in any research project is to formulate an empirical question—one that can be answered with the evidence of objective data. Empirical questions include terms that are defined precisely enough (i.e., operationally) to allow replication to occur. Several studies on the same topic might use different operational definitions of terms, yet might converge ("converging operations") on the same general conclusion about behavior (e.g., frustration leads to aggression).

Developing Research from Observations and Serendipity

Some research ideas derive from reflection on everyday observations, especially of events that are unusual enough to attract one's attention. Specific problems to be solved also lead to research; much of the applied research in general and program evaluation research in particular develops this way. Sometimes we observe events that occur unexpectedly or accidentally. Serendipity is the act of discovering something by accident; serendipitous events often yield ideas for further research. The discovery of edge detectors in vision is an example.

Developing Research from Theory

Theories summarize and organize existing knowledge, provide a basis for making predictions, and provide a working explanation about some phenomenon. There is a reciprocal relationship between theory building and research. Empirical questions can be deduced from theory; these questions lead to specific hypotheses and then to the design of experiments. The conclusions of the completed experiments then either support or fail to support the theory. Theories cannot be proven to be true, although they can be disproven, at least in principle. Actually, however, a theory is discarded only after a consensus develops that it is consistently failing to make good predictions. In most cases, theories evolve to take into account the accumulating knowledge about some phenomenon. Theories in psychology are useful to the extent that they generate research that increases our understanding of behavior. Also, good theories are parsimonious and stated precisely enough to be falsified by well-designed research.

Developing Research from Other Research

Researchers in psychology seldom think in terms of isolated experiments. Instead, they produce programs of research, series of interrelated experiments within a specific area. They continually use the results of experiments as starting points for the next experiment. Research programs often include studies that involve replications or partial replications of existing findings, along with extensions into new areas.

Creative Thinking in Science

Scientific creativity occurs when researchers make connections among ideas or events that other people perceive to be unrelated. The creative scientist must be knowledgeable in a particular research area and is prepared to notice the relevance of events apparently unrelated to the problem at hand.

Reviewing the Literature

Empirical questions occur more frequently to the investigator who knows the research literature in a particular area. Most searching is done electronically using such tools as PsycINFO.

Chapter Review Questions

1. What is the essential difference between basic and applied research? Use the basic "shadowing" and applied cell phone studies to illustrate.
2. What are the comparative advantages and disadvantages of research completed in and out of the laboratory?
3. In the Dutton and Aron study of romance in "high places," why did the researchers believe it was necessary to complete the laboratory study, given the results of their field study?
4. Give three different operational definitions of hunger and explain why research using all three could result in what is called converging operations.
5. What is a theory in psychology, and what are the attributes of good theories?
6. Use cognitive dissonance theory to illustrate the reciprocal relationship between theory and data. Be sure to work the terms deduction, induction, and hypothesis into your answer.
7. Explain why you are unlikely to hear scientists say that a theory has been *proven* to be true. Be sure to work the logical fallacy of affirming the consequent into your answer.
8. Theories can be "disproven" on the basis of a research outcome, but that never actually happens in science. Explain.
9. Explain how the Clever Hans study illustrates the importance of (a) a falsification strategy, and (b) the use of parsimonious explanations.
10. What are pilot studies, and what purpose do they serve?
11. Use the origins of maze learning to illustrate the process of creative thinking in science.
12. Describe any three tips that will facilitate searches in PsycINFO.

Applications Exercises

Exercise 3.1   What's Next?

Consider each of the following research outcomes. If you were a part of the research team, (a) what might you suggest as the next study to do, and (b) what do you predict would happen (i.e., what would the hypothesis be)?

1. College students are shown a video of a male college-age student driving an expensive car while talking on a cell phone. Asked to give their impressions of the driver, the students rate him high on the following attributes: egotistical, extroverted, and unconcerned for others.

2. In a study of aggression, some preschool boys see cartoons with violent themes, while other boys see interesting but nonviolent cartoons. Later, given a chance to be aggressive, children in the first group hit a punching bag more frequently and with greater force than children in the second group.

3. In a direction-finding study that takes place at a central point on campus, college students are asked to point as accurately as they can in the direction of four major cities, two of them more than 200 miles from campus, and two less than 20 miles from campus. The students are more accurate for the closer cities.

4. In a memory experiment in which a list of 30 words is to be memorized, college students recall more words if they study while listening to a violin concerto than when they listen to bluegrass.

Exercise 3.2   Replicating and Extending Milgram's Obedience Research

Consider Milgram's obedience study, highlighted in Chapter 2 in the context of ethics. As you recall, subjects playing the role of "teachers" thought they were in a study of the effect of punishment on learning. A "learner," who was in on the deception and in the adjacent room, pretended to make numerous errors and the teacher's job was to shock the learner for each error and increase the voltage by 15 volts for each successive error. Milgram was interested in discovering the point, from 15 to 450 volts, at which the teacher/subject would stop the experiment, thereby showing disobedience. Describe how you might vary the procedure in subsequent studies to test these hypotheses:

1. Because of their greater compassion, women teachers would be more likely to disobey the male experimenter, especially if the learner was also a woman.

2. The more the experimenter is perceived as a genuine and legitimate authority, the greater the level of obedience.

3. Subjects delivered lots of shocks because they simply enjoyed doing it—after all, everyone is a bit sadistic.

4. There will be more disobedience if the learner clearly has a health problem (e.g., cardiac symptoms).

Exercise 3.3   Creating Operational Definitions

Create two different operational definitions for each of the following psychological constructs.

1. frustration

2. cognitive dissonance

3. anxiety

4. sense of direction

Exercise 3.4   Confirmation Bias

We have seen in this chapter that one strategy used by scientists is to arrive at some empirical conclusion by ruling out or *falsifying* alternative explanations. But this strategy is difficult to develop, as the following exercise from Wason and Johnson-Laird (1972, pp. 172–173) shows. Try it.

Imagine that you are holding four cards and each has a letter printed on one side and a number printed on the other. As you look at the front side of the cards, this is what you see:

E   K   4   7

Your task is to decide which cards have to be turned over in order to determine whether the following rule is true or not:

If a card has a vowel on the front side, then it has an even number on the back side.

Which cards would you turn over? (*Hint*: Think in falsification terms—which cards, if turned over, would falsify or disprove the statement?)

Exercise 3.5   Searching PsycINFO

Using PsycINFO, find records for any five of the articles referenced in this chapter. For each of the five articles, (a) find another article by the same author, and (b) find another article on the same topic that was published within the last three years.

Answers to Self Tests:

✓ **3.1.**

1. Basic → a dichotic listening experiment that varied the message in the nonattended ear.

   Applied → an experiment on how cell phone use while driving affects driving.

2. The experimental setting would not be encountered in real life (mundane reality), but subjects were deeply involved in the procedure and took it very seriously (experimental reality).

3. Qualitative and quantitative.

✓ **3.2.**

1. Everyday observations of behavior.

2. The research comes out as hypothesized, and the researcher concludes that the theory has therefore been proven true.

3. Trial and error learning is a simpler explanation, while still being adequate as an explanation.

✓ **3.3.**

1. It gets researchers thinking about the next logical experiment, following upon a study that has just been completed.

2. This means some research outcome has been repeated, and the study also includes some additional findings that go beyond the original research outcome.

3. Serendipity by itself won't produce scientific creativity; the scientist also must have a certain degree of knowledge about the phenomenon in question.

CHAPTER 4

Measurement and Data Analysis

Preview & Chapter Objectives

In this chapter we begin taking a close look at the data produced by research in psychology. Specifically, we will examine the range of behaviors measured in psychological research, the factors determining whether these measures are of any value, and a system for classifying what are called scales of measurement. The chapter also introduces (and, for most of you, I hope, reviews) the important distinction between descriptive and inferential statistics, and introduces the process of hypothesis testing. When you finish this chapter, you should be able to:

- Recognize the variety of behavioral measures used when conducting research in psychology.
- Understand what psychologists mean by a construct (e.g., visual imagery) and how measurable behaviors (e.g., reaction time) are developed and used to study constructs.

- Know what it means to say that a behavioral measure is reliable and relatively free from measurement error.
- Know what it means to say that a behavioral measure is valid, and distinguish several forms of validity (content validity, criterion validity, construct validity).
- Identify the defining features of nominal, ordinal, interval, and ratio scales of measurement, and know when each should be used.
- Summarize data effectively using measures of central tendency (e.g., mean), measures of variability (e.g., standard deviation), and visual displays (e.g., stem and leaf displays).
- Understand the logic of hypothesis testing and what is involved in making an inferential analysis of data.
- Describe the criticisms that have been made of hypothesis testing and alternatives that have been suggested (e.g., confidence intervals).
- Understand what is meant by (a) effect size and (b) the power of a statistical test, and know the factors that enhance power.

You know from Chapter 1 that research psychologists are "data-driven," insisting that conclusions about behavior be based on data collected via scientific methods. Deciding precisely which behaviors to measure, how to take the measurements, and how to make sense of the resulting collection of numbers is no simple task. This chapter begins the discussion of the relationship between data and psychological knowledge.

What to Measure—Varieties of Behavior

The variety of behaviors measured by experimental psychologists is virtually unlimited. What gets measured ranges from overt behavior (e.g., rats running through a maze) to self-report (e.g., college students filling out an attitude survey) to recordings of physiological activity (e.g., blood pressure readings from senior citizens). To illustrate the rich variety of behaviors measured in psychological research, consider just a few examples from the literature:

1. A study on "span of apprehension in schizophrenic patients as a function of distractor masking and laterality" (Elkins, Cromwell, & Asarnow, 1992) investigated attention-span limitations in patients diagnosed with schizophrenia. The behavior measured was whether or not the participants could accurately name the target letters in different circumstances. Compared with nonschizophrenic controls, the schizophrenic patients did poorly when asked to identify target letters appearing in an array of distracting letters.

2. A study on the "effects of respite from work on burnout: vacation relief and fade-out" (Westman & Eden, 1997) looked at the effects of a vacation on perceived stress and degree of burnout for clerical workers in an electronics firm. On three different occasions, before, during, and after a vacation, researchers measured (a) perceptions of job stress with eight items from a

survey instrument called the "Job Characteristics Questionnaire," and (b) job burnout with a twenty-one-item "Burnout Index." Participants also filled out a "Vacation Satisfaction Scale." Initially, high stress and burnout scores dropped precipitously during the vacation, but the effect was very short-lived. By three weeks after the vacation, stress and burnout levels were back at the pre-vacation level.

3. A study on the "effects of deindividuation on stealing among Halloween trick-or-treaters" (Diener, Fraser, Beaman, & Kelem, 1976) observed the candy- and money-taking behavior of children in a field study during Halloween night. The behavior observed (from behind a screen by an experimenter) was whether children took extra amounts of candy, and/or took money that was in a nearby bowl, when the woman answering the door briefly left the room. When given an opportunity to steal, the children were most likely to succumb to temptation when (a) they were in groups rather than alone, and (b) anonymous (i.e., not asked their name) rather than known.

4. A study of "task-related arousal of Type A and Type B persons" (Holmes, McGilley, & Houston, 1984) compared two types of subjects (A and B) on a digit span task (listen to a list of numbers, then repeat them back accurately) that varied in difficulty. While performing the task, several physiological measures of arousal were taken, including systolic and diastolic blood pressure. Compared with more laid-back Type B subjects, hard-driving type A subjects showed elevated blood pressure, especially when the task increased in difficulty.

Developing Measures from Constructs

From these examples you can see that researchers measure behavior in many ways. But how do they decide what to measure? Where do they get the idea to measure attention by seeing which letters can be selected accurately from an array, job burnout by giving a specific survey, moral behavior by observing candy taking, or arousal by measuring blood pressure?

In part, they know what to measure because they know the literature in their area of expertise, and so they know what measures are used by other investigators. They also develop ideas for new measures by modifying commonly used measures, or perhaps by creatively seeing a new use for an old measure. Finally, they develop measures out of the process of refining the constructs of interest in the study. Let me elaborate.

When a researcher is planning a study, one of the first decisions is to define the constructs to be used in the project as precisely as possible. Sound familiar? It should, because we are talking about *operational definitions* again. Part of the design for any study involves taking the constructs of interest, which by definition are not directly observable, and deciding which behaviors will adequately reflect those constructs. In the previous examples, each researcher was faced with the task of taking some phenomenon and turning it into a manageable experiment by carefully defining the constructs in terms of measurable behaviors. Table 4.1 summarizes those four examples in terms of the constructs studied and how they were operationalized into specific behaviors.

TABLE 4.1 *Sample Constructs and How They Are Measured*

Construct	Behavior to Measure the Construct
Attention span	Letter identification accuracy
Burnout	Score on self-reported Burnout Index
Honesty	Amount of candy or money taken
Arousal	Systolic and diastolic blood pressure

One thing you may notice is that none of these constructs (attention, burnout, honesty, arousal) is directly observable—each must be inferred from the measures used to investigate it. This process is repeated over and over in psychology and allows the research psychologist to ask some empirical questions that might seem impossible to answer at first glance. Let's consider in greater detail two specific examples of procedures frequently used to investigate questions that, at first glance, might seem difficult, if not impossible, to answer empirically:

✓ Do preverbal infants understand the concept of gravity?
✓ Can you demonstrate that people use visual images?

The measures used to study these seemingly nonempirical questions are as simple as recording (a) how long an infant looks at something and (b) how long it takes people to make decisions.

Research Example 1—Habituation

Do infants have a concept of gravity? How could you ever find out? You cannot ask them directly, of course, but the question can be asked indirectly via a technique in which the amount of time a baby spends looking at different stimuli is measured. This "habituation" procedure involves showing an infant the same stimulus repeatedly and then changing to a new stimulus. From other research on "preferential looking," it is known that infants prefer to look at events that are new to them (Spelke, 1985), so if the same stimulus is presented repeatedly, they lose interest (i.e., they stop looking). The term habituation is defined as a gradual decrease in responding to repeated stimuli. If a new stimulus is presented *and* it is recognized as something new or unusual, the infant will increase the time spent looking at it. So if looking time in response to stimuli decreases and then suddenly increases, you can infer that the infant has noticed something new.

With this in mind, consider a delightful study by Kim and Spelke (1992). They compared 5- and 7-month-olds and concluded that some type of basic understanding of gravity develops during that two-month period of infancy. To produce habituation, infants were first shown repeated film clips of balls speeding up while rolling down inclined planes, as depicted in the first frame of Figure 4.1.[1] This event reflects the natural effect of gravity on a ball rolling down a hill. After habituation occurred (i.e., looking time decreased after repeated trials), the infants

---

[1] For control purposes, Kim and Spelke (1992) also included a second set of trials, starting with the habituation event of a ball slowing down while going up the incline.

| Habituation event (downward acceleration) | Natural test event (slowing down) | Unnatural test event (speeding up) |

FIGURE 4.1   Stimulus items from Kim and Spelke's (1992) habituation study.

encountered either a "natural test event" (middle frame), a ball slowing down while going up a hill, or an "unnatural test event" (third frame), a ball speeding up while going up the hill. Notice that the natural test event differs from the habituation event in two ways, direction and speed, while the unnatural event differs only in one way, direction. Simply in terms of how much one of the test events differed from the habituation event, it seems reasonable to expect the infants to perceive the natural event as novel (two factors changed) and to look longer at it than at the unnatural one (one factor changed). Indeed, the 5-month-old infants did just that. The 7-month-olds, however, looked at the *unnatural* event more, presumably because it violated what gravity dictates, whereas the natural event continued to be consistent with the law of gravity displayed in the habituation events. Hence, the younger infants noticed changes in the total number of stimulus dimensions, while the older ones noticed changes violating the law of gravity. From the measures of preferential looking, then, Kim and Spelke concluded that the infants, at least the 7-month-olds, possessed some form of understanding of the concept of gravity.

Research Example 2—Reaction Time

Do we use visual images as part of our cognitive processing? How could you find out? Of course, you could ask, but if someone says, "Yes, I'm using images," how could you be sure about what the person was doing? That is, you would be confronting the same problem that brought about the demise of introspection as a method—its lack of objectivity. You could, however, ask people to perform some task that would produce one type of behavior if images were being used and a different type of behavior if images weren't being used. That was the strategy behind a well-known series of studies by Shepard and his colleagues of what is termed "mental rotation."

Look at the two pairs of geometric objects in Figure 4.2. Could each right-hand object of each pair be the same as the left-hand object, but merely rotated to a different position? Or is it a different object altogether? How did you decide? Shepard and Metzler (1971) asked participants to make these decisions but went one step further and recorded *how long it took* for them to decide. Their rationale was that if participants solve these problems by taking the left-hand object and turning it mentally (i.e., using a visual image) until it overlaps the right-hand object, then the rotation process will take a certain amount of time. Furthermore, the greater the degree of mental rotation that is required to reach the overlap point, the more

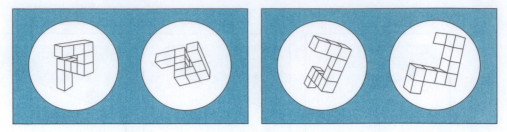

FIGURE 4.2　Stimulus items from Shepard and Metzler's (1971) mental rotation studies.

time the process should take. I think you can see where this is going. Shepard and Metzler systematically varied the degree of rotation and found that as the angle increased, so did the amount of time needed to make the decision—in fact, the graph of the results showed almost a perfect linear relationship between the angle of rotation in the drawings and the amount of time needed for a decision. From these measures of reaction time, then, they inferred that mental imagery was occurring.

Reaction time is one of psychology's oldest and most enduring methods, but the rationale for its use has changed over the years. For more on its origins and evolution as a tried-and-true method in experimental psychology, see Box 4.1.

Box 4.1

ORIGINS—*Reaction Time: From Mental Chronometry to Mental Rotation*

The use of reaction time in psychology can be traced to the work of F. C. Donders (1818–1889), a Dutch physiologist, who argued that times for mental events could be determined by calculating the differences between the reaction times for different kinds of tasks (Boring, 1950). His idea ushered in a flood of research on what became known as "mental chronometry" or the "complication experiment." Researchers would measure the time for a simple reaction (SRT): A single response made as quickly as possible after perceiving a single stimulus, a red light, for instance. The task could then be "complicated" by displaying one of two stimuli and telling the person to respond to only one of them. This could be called discrimination reaction time (DRT) because the person first had to discriminate between the two stimuli, such as a red and a green light, and then respond. DRT includes SRT plus the mental event of "discrimination," so subtracting SRT from DRT yields the time taken for the mental event of discrimination:

$$DRT = SRT + \text{discrimination}$$
$$\therefore \text{discrimination} = DRT - SRT$$

The procedure could be elaborated even more, with additional mental events subtracted out, and these studies generated a great deal of excitement at the end of the nineteenth century because psychology was trying to establish itself as a science, and what could be more scientific than to have mental events measured to the fraction of a second? The procedure was especially popular in Wundt's laboratory at Leipzig and was quickly imported to the United States, as you can see from Figure 4.3, which shows a reaction time experiment in progress at Clark University in 1892.

Unfortunately, it soon became apparent that problems existed with the procedure. In particular, some reaction times were faster than predicted from the complication logic, others slower. Oswald Külpe, one of Wundt's students, pointed out the fatal flaw—mental events don't combine in a simple additive fashion to form more complicated events. Rather, a complex mental event has a quality all its own that is more than the sum of simpler events.

Although Külpe's arguments effectively ended mental chronometry, and reaction time as a method declined in use during the heyday of behaviorism (roughly 1930–1950), it has subsequently enjoyed a resurgence in several areas of cognitive psychology. The idea is no longer to measure the precise times of mental events but to test predictions from cognitive theories. The mental rotation studies are a good example. Shepard predicted that if mental rotation occurs in the minds of participants, then this mental activity should take a certain amount of time (Shepard & Metzler, 1971). Larger degrees of rotation should take greater amounts of time and, as you have seen, this indeed occurred.

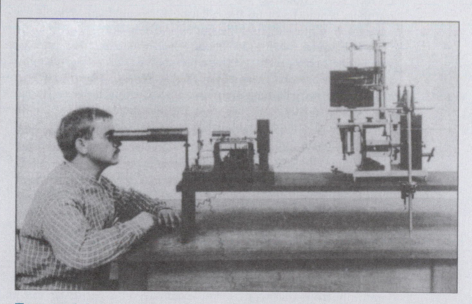

FIGURE 4.3 Reaction time study in progress at Clark University, circa 1892. The response will be made by releasing a telegraph key with the right hand as quickly as possible when the stimulus is seen through the tube.

Evaluating Measures

How can you tell if some measure of behavior is any good? What accounts for the confidence with which psychologists use such things as preferential looking, reaction time, IQ tests, surveys of burnout, blood pressure, and so on? To answer the question requires a discussion of two key factors: reliability and validity.

Reliability

In general, a measure of behavior is said to be **reliable** if its results are repeatable when the behaviors are remeasured. Reaction time is a good example; its high reliability is one reason for its popularity over the years. Someone responding to a red light in .18 second on one trial will almost certainly respond with just about the same speed on other trials, and practically all of the trials will be in the general vicinity of .18 second. Similarly, scores on the Graduate Record Exam (GRE) are reasonably reliable. Someone with a combined score of 950 on the GRE general test would probably score close to that a second time and would be very unlikely to reach a score like 1450.

From these two examples, you can see why reliability is essential in any measure. Without it, there is no way of determining what a score on a particular measure *means*. Presumably, in reaction time you're trying to determine how fast someone is. If the reaction times vary wildly, there is no way to answer the question. Likewise, if GRE scores bounced 400 or 500 points from one testing session to another, the numbers would be of no use whatsoever to graduate schools because they would have no way of estimating the student's true score.

A behavioral measure's reliability is a direct function of the amount of **measurement error** present. If there is a great deal of error, reliability is low, and vice versa. No behavioral measure is perfectly reliable, so some degree of measurement error occurs with all measurement. That is, every measure is some combination of a hypothetical true score plus some measurement error. Ideally, measurement error is low enough so that the observed score is close to the true score.

The reaction time procedure provides a good illustration of how measurement error works and how it affects reliability. As in the earlier example, suppose a person takes .18 second on a reaction time trial. Is this the *true* measure of speed? Probably not, a conclusion easily reached when you notice that for the following five trials this same person's reaction times are:

.16 sec   .17 sec   .19 sec   .17 sec   .19 sec

These scores vary (slightly) because some degree of measurement error contributes to each trial. This error is caused by several possible factors, some of which operate randomly from trial to trial. For example, on a particular trial the person might respond faster than the true score by guessing that the stimulus was about to be presented or slower because of a momentary lapse of attention. Also, some systematic amount of error could occur if, for example, the experimenter signaled the participants to get ready just before turning on the stimulus, and the amount of time between the ready signal and the stimulus was constant from trial to trial. Then the participants could learn to anticipate the stimulus and produce reaction times that would be systematically faster than true ones.

Despite the presence of a small degree of measurement error, the above scores do cluster together pretty well, and the reaction times certainly would be judged more reliable than if the scores following the .18 second one were these:

.11 sec   .21 sec   .19 sec   .08 sec   .33 sec

With scores ranging from less than a tenth of a second to a third of a second, it is difficult to say what the person's real speed is.

When scores are reliable, therefore, the researcher can assign some meaning to their magnitude. Reliability also allows the researcher to make more meaningful comparisons with other sets of scores. For example, comparing the first set of scores above (.16, .17, etc.) with the ones below reveals a clear difference in basic speed of response:

.23 sec   .25 sec   .21 sec   .22 sec   .24 sec

It is probably fair to say that the true reaction time of this second person is slower than the person described earlier (.16, .17, etc.).

There are ways of calculating reliability, but this is seldom done in experimental research. Rather, confidence in the reliability of a measure develops over time, a benefit of the replication process. For example, the habituation and reaction time procedures have been used often enough and yielded consistent enough results for researchers to be highly confident about their reliability.

Reliability *is* assessed more formally in research that evaluates the adequacy of any type of psychological test. These are instruments designed to measure such constructs as personality factors (e.g., extroversion), abilities (e.g., IQ), and attitudes (e.g., political beliefs). They are usually paper-and-pencil tests in which a person responds to questions or statements of some kind. In the study mentioned earlier on burnout and vacations, participants filled out several self-report measures, including one called the BI, or Burnout Index. Analyses designed to establish the reliability of this kind of test require the use of correlational statistical procedures. For example, the test could be given on two occasions and the similarity of the two sets of results could be determined. Unless dramatic changes are taking place in the participant's life, the scores on two measurements with the BI should be similar. The degree of similarity is expressed in terms of a correlation (high similarity = strong correlation). The specifics of this kind of statistical analysis, especially as it relates to the whole area of psychological testing, will be explained more fully in Chapter 9.

Validity

A behavioral measure is said to be **valid** if it measures what it has been designed to measure. A measure of burnout should truly measure the phenomenon of burnout and should not measure some different construct. A test of intelligence should measure intelligence and not something else.

Conceptually, the simplest level of validity is called **content validity.** This type of validity concerns whether or not the actual content of the items on a test "makes sense" in terms of the construct being measured. It comes into play right at the start of the process of creating a test, because it concerns the precise wording of the test items. A measure of burnout, for example, would be more likely to measure such things as perceived job stress than it would be to measure vocabulary, and the opposite would be true about a measure of intelligence. Furthermore, with a complex construct that might have many attributes, such as intelligence, content validity also concerns whether the measure includes items that assess each of the attributes. Content validity is sometimes confused with **face validity,** which is not actually a "valid" form of validity at all (Anastasi & Urbina, 1997). Face validity concerns whether the measure seems to be valid to those who are taking it, and it is important only in the sense that we want those taking our tests and filling out our surveys to take the task seriously. Of course, a test can seem to make sense to those taking it and still not be a valid test. Most of the surveys found in popular magazines ("What's Your Sex Appeal Index?") fit into this category.

A more critical test of validity is called **criterion validity,** which concerns whether the measure (a) can accurately forecast some future behavior or (b) is meaningfully related to some other measure of behavior. For a test to be useful as an IQ test, for example, it should (a) do a reasonably good job of predicting how well a child will do in school and (b) produce results similar to those produced by other known measures of intelligent behavior. It is called "criterion" validity because the measure in question is related to some outcome or criterion. In the examples just used, the criterion variables would be (a) future grades in school and (b) scores on an already established test for intelligence. As with reliability estimates, criterion validity research is correlational in nature and occurs primarily in research on psychological testing. You'll see criterion validity again in Chapter 9.

A third form of validity, **construct validity,** concerns whether a test adequately measures some construct, and it connects directly with what is now a familiar concept to you—the operational definition. As you recall from Chapter 3, a construct is some hypothetical factor that has been developed as part of a theory to help explain some phenomenon (e.g., cognitive dissonance) or created as a shorthand term for a cluster of related behaviors (e.g., self-esteem). Constructs are never observed directly, so we develop operational definitions for them, as a way of investigating them empirically, and then develop measures for them. For example, "aggression" is a construct that in a particular study might be operationally defined as the number of shocks that subjects believe they are delivering to another subject. Another example: "Emotional intelligence" is a construct operationally defined as a score on a paper-and-pencil test with items designed to identify those skilled at reading the emotions of others. Construct validity relates to whether a particular measurement truly measures the construct; it is similar to theory in the sense that it is never established or destroyed with a single study and is never proven for the same reason that theories are never proven. Rather, confidence in construct validity accumulates gradually and inductively as research produces supportive results.

Research establishing criterion validity also helps to establish construct validity, but construct validity research also includes other procedures said to establish what are known as convergent and discriminant validity. Scores on a test measuring some construct should be related to scores on other tests that are theoretically related to the construct (**convergent validity**), but not related to scores on other tests that are theoretically unrelated to the construct (**discriminant validity**). Consider, for example, the construct of *self-efficacy*. This is a construct first developed by Bandura (1986) and it refers to "judgments of [our] capabilities to organize and execute courses of action required to attain designated types of performances" (p. 391). Students with a high degree of self-efficacy about their schoolwork, for instance, believe that they have good academic skills, know what to do to get good grades, and tend to get good grades. To increase confidence in the construct validity of a test designed to measure self-efficacy, for example, one might compare self-efficacy scores with those on already-established tests of locus of control and self-confidence. Locus of control (LOC) concerns our personal beliefs about the causes of what happens to us. Those with an internal LOC believe that they control what happens to them (by working hard, for instance), while those with an external LOC believe that outside forces (luck, for instance) determine what happens to them. I think you can see that someone with a high level of self-efficacy should probably also be someone with an internal LOC. Thus, research showing a strong relationship between the two would strengthen the construct validity of the self-efficacy measure because convergent validity would have been demonstrated. On the other hand, self-confidence is not necessarily related to self-efficacy. Someone with high self-efficacy might indeed be self-confident, but lots of people with high self-confidence might be confident for the wrong reasons and not be high in self-efficacy. You have probably met some people who put on a display of self-confidence, but don't have much substance to back it up. So research showing that measures of self-efficacy and self-confidence are not related or only weakly related would establish discriminant validity for the measure of self-efficacy.

Research Example 3 — Construct Validity

As a concrete example of construct validity research, consider this study by Mayer & Frantz (2004). They developed a test called the Connectedness to Nature Scale (CNS), which was designed to measure individual differences in "levels of feeling emotionally connected with the natural world" (p. 503). They hoped the scale would be useful in predicting environmentally friendly behavior (e.g., recycling, not littering). Here are a few of the items from the scale:

- ✓ I think of the natural world as a community to which I belong.
- ✓ I have a deep understanding of how my actions affect the natural world.
- ✓ Like a tree can be part of a forest, I feel embedded within the broader natural world.
- ✓ My personal welfare is independent of the welfare of the natural world.

Those scoring high and therefore having a large amount of the construct "connectedness to nature" would agree with the first three statements and disagree with the fourth one.

Mayer and Frantz (2004) completed a series of studies on their new scale, examining both reliability and validity. To evaluate the construct validity of the CNS, they gave the test to a wide range of adults (i.e., not just college students), along with another test called the NEP ("New Ecological Paradigm") scale, a survey about "their lifestyle patterns and time spent outdoors" (p. 505). The NEP scale (Dunlap, Van Liere, Mertig, & Jones, 2000) measures cognitive beliefs about ecological issues (sample item—"We are approaching the limit of the number of people the earth can support."). Mayer and Frantz also gathered data on participants' ecological behaviors (e.g., how often they turned off the lights in vacant rooms), scholastic aptitude (this part of the research used college students and collected SAT data), and a measure of social desirability (scoring high on this test means wanting to make oneself look good). They expected the CNS and NEP to be related and they were—people scoring high on one were likely to score high on the other. This outcome supported convergent validity, as did the finding that high CNS scores predicted ecological behavior and outdoor lifestyle patterns. They also expected that CNS scores would *not* be related to SAT scores or to the measure of social desirability and this also happened (discriminant validity).

This brief description only scratches the surface of Mayer and Frantz's (2004) article, which included five different experiments, but it should give you a sense of what is involved in trying to establish the construct validity of a new measuring tool, in this case the Connectedness to Nature Scale.

Reliability and Validity

For a measure to be of any value in psychological research, it must be sufficiently reliable and valid. Reliability is important because it enables one to have some confidence that the measure taken is close to the true measure. Validity is important because it tells you if the measure actually measures what it is supposed to measure, and not something else. Note that validity assumes reliability, but the converse is not true. Measures can be reliable but not valid; valid measures must be reliable, however.

A simple example illustrates this. In Chapter 1 you learned something about nineteenth-century phrenology, a popular theory claiming that you could measure a person's "faculties" by examining skull contour. From the discussion of reliability, you should recognize that phrenological measures of the skull were highly reliable—the distance between a point 2 inches above your left ear and 2 inches above your right ear will not change very much if measured on two separate occasions. However, to say that the measure is an indication of the faculty of "destructiveness" is quite another matter. We know that skull contour measurement is not a valid measure of destructiveness because it doesn't make much sense to us today (content validity), fails to predict aggressive behavior (criterion validity), and does not fit well with other research on constructs relating to destructiveness, such as impulsiveness, or with research on brain function (construct validity).

The issues of reliability and validity have ethical implications, especially when measures are used to make decisions affecting people's lives. Students are accepted or not accepted into college or graduate school, job applicants are hired or not hired, and people are given a psychiatric diagnosis and treatment, all on the basis of measurements of ability or behavior. If those measures fail the tests of reliability and validity, then the decisions will not be made in a fair and just fashion. If you were applying for a job and your score on some test was to be the determining factor, you would be justifiably upset to learn that the test was neither very reliable nor valid.

One final point. The concept of validity has been discussed here in the context of measurement. As you will see in the next chapter, however, measures of psychological constructs are not the only things judged to be valid or not. Validity also extends more broadly to the entire research project being undertaken. Strictly in the context of measurement, validity concerns whether the tool being used measures what it is supposed to measure. In the broader realm of the entire research project, validity concerns whether the experiment has been properly conducted and whether the hypothesis in question has been properly tested. This point will be elaborated in Chapter 5.

Scales of Measurement

Whenever a behavior is measured, numbers are assigned to it in some fashion. We say that someone responded in 3.5 seconds, scored 120 on an IQ test, or finished third best in a crossword puzzle test. We also talk of placing individuals into categories as a consequence of what they do or some characteristic they possess. These examples illustrate four different ways of assigning numbers to events, that is, four different **measurement scales.** A clear understanding of these scales is an important prelude to a discussion of statistics (this chapter's next main topic), because the type of measurement scale being used helps determine the appropriate statistical analysis to be completed. Confusion over measurement scales is behind the problem experienced by Dilbert in Figure 4.4.

Nominal Scales

Sometimes the number we assign to events serves only to classify them into one group or another. When this happens, we are using what is called a **nominal scale** of measurement. Studies using these scales typically assign people to categories

DILBERT reprinted by permission of United Feature Syndicate, Inc.

FIGURE 4.4 Problems with scales of measurement.

(e.g., male, female) and count the number of people falling into each category. We use nominal scales when we ask empirical questions like these:

✓ Comparing male and female joggers, who is more likely to run during the morning and who is more likely to run in the evening?

✓ If you divide people with mental illness into those who are shy and those who are outgoing, will introverts be more likely to be suffering from anxiety disorders than extroverts?

✓ When you change answers on a multiple-choice test, are you more likely to improve your score or hurt it?

This last example was an empirical question that has been asked in a number of studies, including a recent one by Kruger, Wirtz, and Miller (2005). In addition to illustrating the use of a nominal scale, the study is also a good example of why research often beats popular opinion—I suspect the results will surprise you. The researchers examined answer changing by students on a multiple-choice midterm general psychology exam. They simply counted the number of answer changes by looking for and counting erasure marks on the answer sheets. For the 1,561 students in the study, they counted a total of 3,291 changes. The categories they used were:

1. changing an answer from the right alternative to a wrong alternative (right → wrong)

2. changing an answer from a wrong alternative to the right alternative (wrong → right)

3. changing an answer from one wrong alternative to another wrong alternative (wrong → wrong)

What Kruger and his colleagues discovered was that the most frequent outcome was category 2—from wrong to right. This happened 1,690 times, 51% of the total number of changes recorded. Changing from right to wrong happened 838 times (25%), and changing from one wrong answer to another wrong one occurred 763 times (23%). Notice that I converted the frequency counts into percentages. This makes the results easier to understand and is common practice with nominal scale data.

So do you believe the results? Probably not—the idea that changing answers is likely to hurt you is a powerful myth among college students. The reason relates back to the social cognition biases you learned about in Chapter 1, the availability heuristic and the confirmation bias. Answer changing that lowers a score (i.e., right → wrong) certainly happens, and when it does, it sticks out as a painful memory (lowered my score!); if it happens again, it confirms the bias. On the other hand, answer changing that isn't painful (i.e., wrong → right) doesn't stick out in memory; it is just part of the larger category of "stuff I knew and got right." Trust me, though, the idea that you shouldn't change answers because it will lower your score, along with the complementary myth, "go with your first hunch and never look back," are simply not supported by research. And it is not just this one study—Kruger, Wirtz, and Miller (2005) simply replicated a result that has been consistently found in at least thirty-three other studies (Kersting, 2005).

Ordinal Scales

Ordinal scales of measurement are basically sets of rankings, showing the relative standing of objects or individuals. College transcripts, for example, often list a student's general class rank: 1st, 2nd, 3rd, 50th, and so on. From these rankings you can infer that one student had higher grades than another. Relative standing is the *only* thing you know, however. Dan, Fran, and Jan would be ranked 1, 2, and 3 in each of the following cases, even though Dan is clearly superior to Fran and Jan as a student only in the second case:

Case 1		Case 2	
Dan's GPA	4.0	Dan's GPA	4.0
Fran's GPA	3.9	Fran's GPA	3.2
Jan's GPA	3.8	Jan's GPA	3.0

Studies using ordinal scales ask empirical questions like these:

✓ If a child ranks five toys and is given the one ranked third, will the ranking for that toy go up or down after the child has played with it for a week?

✓ Do students rank textbook authors in the sciences and in the humanities differently when they are told the sex of the writers?

✓ How do young versus old people rank ten movies that vary in the levels of the amount of sex and aggression found in them?

A good example of the use of an ordinal scale is a study by Korn, Davis, and Davis (1991). Historians of psychology and department chairpersons were asked to list, in rank order from 1 to 10, the psychologists they considered to have made the most important contributions to the field. Two sets of rankings were solicited: one for the top 10 of "all time" and the second for a "contemporary" top 10. The returns were then summarized to yield a picture of eminence in psychology. Who topped the chart? B. F. Skinner was considered the most eminent contemporary psychologist by both historians and chairpersons. Department chairs also ranked Skinner first for all time; historians, who tended to select psychologists from earlier periods for their all-time list, dropped Skinner to eighth place and put Wundt on top.

Interval Scales

Most research in psychology uses interval or ratio scales of measurement. **Interval scales** extend the idea of rank order to include the concept of equal intervals between the events that are ordered. Research using psychological tests of personality, attitude, and ability are the most common examples of studies typically considered to involve interval scales. Scores on intelligence tests, for example, are usually assumed to be arranged this way. Someone with an IQ of 120 is believed to be more intelligent (granting, for the sake of illustration, that IQ measures intelligence) than someone else with an IQ of 110. Furthermore—and this is the defining feature of an interval scale—the difference in intelligence between people with IQs of 120 and 110 is assumed to be the same quantity as the difference between people with IQs of 110 and 100. In other words, each single point of increase in an IQ score is believed to represent the same amount of increase in intelligence—the intervals are equal. Note the word "assumed," however; some psychologists consider IQ (and scores on most personality tests as well) to be an example of an ordinal scale, arguing that it is difficult, if not impossible, to be sure about the equal-interval assumption in this case. Most accept the inclusion of IQ as an example of an interval scale, though, partly for a practical reason: Psychologists prefer to use interval and ratio scales generally because data on those scales allow more sophisticated statistical analyses and a wider range of them.

The brief description earlier of the study of burnout used several measures (e.g., Vacation Satisfaction Scale) that illustrate interval scales. Also, take a look at Box 4.2, which describes a classic set of studies in which interval scales were used in an attempt to show that our body type influences the kind of person we are.

Box 4.2

CLASSIC STUDIES—Measuring Somatotypes on an Interval Scale: Hoping for 4–4–4

You have already learned that phrenologists speculated about the relationship between some physical characteristic (skull contour) and what a person was like. Phrenology seems almost quaint to us today, but the idea of a relationship between physical characteristics and personality has endured. A twentieth century attempt to explore the connection was made by William Sheldon (1940, 1942).

Sheldon tried to define human physique in terms of a scale of measurement that went beyond some prior attempts that produced a set of discrete "body types." After examining about 4,000 photos of naked college men, he developed a system of classifying physiques in terms of three 7-point interval scales. Each scale reflected the degree to which the men displayed three ideal body types: endomorphy (fat), mesomorphy (muscular), and ectomorphy (thin). Everyone was assumed to have some degree of each of the physiques, with one of them usually predominant. Thus, an extremely round person might be labeled a 7–1–1, while a very thin person would be a 1–1–7, and Arnold Schwarzenegger (when he was in shape) would be a 1–7–1. A 4–4–4 would be a perfectly balanced person (Sheldon assessed himself as a 3.5–3.5–5). The set of numbers applied to a particular man was called his "somatotype."

After measuring somatotypes, Sheldon set out to measure personality types. These, he believed, also fell into three categories that could be measured on 7-point interval scales that would summarize the results of several personality tests. He labeled the categories "viscerotonia," "somatotonia," and "cerebrotonia." Generally, viscerotonics were sociable, fun-loving, slow-moving, even-tempered, and very interested in food. Somatotonics were aggressive, self-centered, and risk-taking, and cerebrotonics were shy and secretive, preferred to be alone, and tended to pursue intellectual tasks.

Sheldon's final step was to see if somatotypes related to personality types. You will not be surprised to learn that these pairs occurred together most often:

> endomorph—viscerotonia
>
> mesomorph—somatotonia
>
> ectomorph—cerebrotonics

Sheldon believed that body type led the individual to develop a certain personality, but critics pointed out that the relationships were not that strong and could be accounted for in different ways. Being an endomorph could cause someone to like food, but couldn't a strong liking for food create an endomorph?

The issues surrounding Sheldon's work were complex, and his theory has been discredited for a number of reasons. For example, stereotypical biases influenced the measurements, all of which were made by Sheldon (i.e., both the somatotype and the temperament measurements). For our purposes, Sheldon's research is a classic example of trying to quantify human personality and relate it to a person's physical attributes on some measurable scale of physique, in this case an interval scale of measurement.

It is important to note that with interval scales, a score of zero is simply another point on the scale—it does not mean a complete absence of the quantity being measured. The standard example is temperature. Zero degrees Celsius or Fahrenheit does not mean an absence of heat; it is simply a point on the scale that means, "put your sweater on." Likewise, if a test of anxiety has scores ranging from 0 to 20, a score of 0 is simply the lowest point on the scale and does not mean the complete absence of anxiety, just a very low score (actually, on tests like this, the lowest total score is more likely to be a "1" or greater, not "0").

Ratio Scales

On a **ratio scale,** the concepts of order and equal interval are carried over from ordinal and interval scales, but, in addition, the ratio scale has a true zero point. That is, for ratio scores, a score of zero means the complete absence of the attribute being measured. For instance, an error score of zero, attained by a rat running a maze, means the absence of any wrong turns. Ratio scales are typically found in studies using physical measures such as height, weight, and time. The case studies earlier in this chapter on habituation and reaction time both illustrate the use of a ratio scale.

✓ Self Test 4.1

1. Suppose the average discrimination reaction time is .28 sec. If the average simple reaction time is .19 sec, then how long would the mental event of "discrimination" take, according to Donders' method?
2. Suppose I claim that head size is a good measure of IQ and my measure is head circumference. Is the measure reliable? Valid? Explain.
3. In the Dilbert cartoon, which measurement scale was Dilbert using? What about Liz?

Statistical Analysis

The first sentence in a self-help book called *The Road Less Traveled* (Peck, 1978) is "Life is difficult" (p. 15). This is a belief that seems to be shared by many students taking a course in statistics, who readily identify with the confused character in Figure 4.5. I won't try to convince you that doing statistics compares with lying on a Florida beach in February, but I hope you'll come to see that part of the excitement of doing research in psychology is completing an analysis of the data you've painstakingly collected and finding out whether or not something *actually* happened in the study. I've seen mature, responsible adults holding their breath

FIGURE 4.5 A common perception of statistics.

while waiting for the results of a statistical analysis to appear on the screen, then reduced to anguish or raised to ecstasy moments after looking at the magic numbers in front of them. So, if you develop a passion for doing research in psychology, much of your emotion will be invested in dealing with the subtleties of statistical analysis.

My goal here is to introduce you to statistical thinking and the kinds of statistical analysis that you'll encounter when doing research in psychology. Ideally, you have already taken a course in statistics. If not, you should take one as soon as possible, especially if you have any desire to go to graduate school in psychology. Believe it or not, when graduate schools list the courses that they especially look for in applicants to their programs, the statistics course is number 1, just ahead of research methods (refer back to the 1996 survey by Norcross, Hanych, & Terranova, described in Chapter 1). I'll cover some of the essentials of statistical analysis, but there is no substitute for a complete course (or two).

You will find information about statistics popping up throughout the rest of the book, for the simple reason that designing research in psychology cannot be separated from the statistical analysis of that research. In this chapter, you will learn about (a) the difference between descriptive and inferential statistics, (b) the logic of hypothesis testing, and (c) some recent recommendations about statistical analysis.

Descriptive and Inferential Statistics

The most fundamental distinction between types of statistics is between those called "descriptive" and those referred to as "inferential." The difference parallels the distinction between samples and populations. You will learn more about sampling in Chapter 12; for now, just be aware that a **population** consists of all members of some defined group, while a **sample** is some subset of that group. Simply put, **descriptive statistics** summarize the data collected from the sample of participants in your study, and **inferential statistics** allow you to draw conclusions about your data that can be applied to the wider population.

Descriptive Statistics

In essence, descriptive statistical procedures enable you to turn a large pile of numbers that cannot be comprehended at a glance into a very small set of numbers that can be more easily understood. Descriptive statistics include measures of central tendency, variability, and association, presented both numerically and visually (e.g., in graphs). In this chapter, we'll consider the more common procedures for measuring central tendency and variability. Measures of association (coefficients of correlation) will be covered in Chapter 9.

To illustrate measures of central tendency and variability, consider some sample data from a hypothetical memory study in which 20 people study and then try to recall a list of 25 words. Each number in the data set below represents the number of words recalled by one of the 20 participants.

16	18	19	19
18	19	15	21
14	16	15	17
17	20	17	15
18	17	18	18

You can easily see that communicating the results of this study requires something more than just showing someone this pile of 20 numbers. Instead, you could try to identify a *typical* score or what is called a "measure of central tendency." The most common measure of central tendency used by research psychologists is the **mean,** or arithmetic average, which is found simply by adding the scores together and dividing by the total number of scores. Thus:

$$\overline{X} = \frac{\Sigma X}{N}$$

where

$\overline{X}$ = the mean (pronounced "ex-bar")
ΣX = the sum of the individual scores
N = the total number of scores in the sample

For the memory data:

$$\overline{X} = \frac{\Sigma X}{N} = (16 + 18 + 14 + \ldots 18)/20 = 347/20 = 17.35$$

Two other measures of central tendency are the median and the mode. The **median** is the score in the exact middle of a set of scores. Half of the scores will be higher and half will be lower than the median. To determine the median by hand, the first step is to arrange the scores in sequence, from the lowest to the highest score. For the memory data, this produces:

14 15 15 15 16 16 17 17 17 17   18 18 18 18 18 19 19 19 20 21

⇑

The next step is to determine the **median location,** the place in the sequence of scores where the median will lie (Witte & Witte, 2007). It is determined by the formula:

$$\text{Median location} = \frac{N + 1}{2}$$

For the memory data, the median location is $(20 + 1)/2 = 10.5$, which means that it falls midway between the 10th and the 11th numbers in the sequence. Counting from left to right, you can see that the 10th number is a 17 and the 11th number is an 18 (I've marked this point in the sequence above with an arrow). The median is an average of the two numbers immediately adjacent to the median location (17 and 18), 17.5 in this case. It is the exact middle of the set of scores—there are 10 scores on either side of this median.

The median is sometimes used when a set of scores includes one or two that are very different from the rest; when this outcome occurs, the mean gives a distorted view of the typical score. Scores that are far removed from other scores in a data set are known as **outliers.** For instance, suppose the IQ scores of the five teachers in your psychology department were 93, 81, 81, 95, and 200 (the outlier is probably the IQ of the person teaching the research methods course). The mean IQ score, which happens to be 110 (you should check this), gives a false impression that the psychology faculty as a whole is above average (average IQ is 100). The median gives a better estimate of a typical IQ in this case. Thus, the median location is equal to $(5+1)/2 = 3$, and with the scores lined up in sequence, the third number is 93:

$$81 \quad 81 \quad \mathbf{93} \quad 95 \quad 200$$
$$\Uparrow$$

Clearly, the median IQ of 93 is a much better indication of the typical intellectual capacity to be found in this hypothetical psychology department. In general, the presence of outliers makes median a better choice than mean when describing central tendency.

The **mode** is the score occurring most frequently in a set of scores. It is 81 in the psychology department IQ example. The mode for the hypothetical memory scores is one more than the median—a score of 18 occurs five times, more often than any other score. Because there are no unusually high or low scores in the memory data set, the mean (17.35), median (17.5), and mode (18) are quite close to each other, and each is a good measure of central tendency.

Measures of central tendency are obviously needed to summarize data. Less obvious but equally important, the amount of variability in any set of scores needs to be described. Suppose you are the pro at a local country club, ready to begin giving lessons to one group of five golfers at 8:00 and another group at 9:00. You measure their ability by determining their normal score (i.e., number of strokes) for nine holes. Here are the data:

8:00 group:	50	52	58	46	54
9:00 group:	36	62	50	72	40

Notice that the mean is the same for both sets of golfers: $260/5 = 52$ strokes. The pro will have plenty to say to both groups. The second group, however, creates much more of a problem. The scores there go from 36 (quite good) to 72 (ouch!). In the 8:00 group, however, the scores are generally close to each other—all five are at about the same ability level. Clearly, before starting the lessons, the pro would like to know more than the mean score for the group.

The simplest and crudest measure of variability is the **range**—the difference between the high and low scores of a group. For memory data presented earlier, the range is 7 (21 − 14). For the golf lesson example, the 8:00 group has a range of 12 (58 − 46), whereas the range for the 9:00 class is a whopping 36 (72 − 36). The range provides a rough estimate of variability, but it doesn't tell you any more than the difference between the most extreme scores. A more comprehensive measure of variability, the one used most often when reporting summary data, is the standard deviation.

The **standard deviation** for a set of sample scores is an estimate of the average amount by which the scores in the sample distribution deviate from the mean score. Table 4.2 shows you how to calculate one, using what is called the definition formula. For the scores in the hypothetical memory study, one standard deviation is equal to 1.81 words. For the golf lesson example, the standard deviation for the 8:00 class is 4.47 strokes, whereas the one for the 9:00 group is 15.03 strokes.

A third measure of variability is the **variance,** which is the number produced during the standard deviation calculation just prior to taking the square root (3.29 for the memory scores—see Table 4.2). So variance is standard deviation squared. Variance is seldom reported when listing descriptive statistics because it represents the units of measurement squared (e.g., ''words recalled squared''). It is, however, the central feature of perhaps the most common inferential procedure found in psychology—the ''analysis of variance,'' described in more detail in Chapters 7 and 8.

Finally, under some circumstances, researchers will calculate an **interquartile range.** It is useful for exactly the same reason that a median is sometimes useful—when there are outliers. The interquartile range is the range of scores between the bottom 25% of scores (25th percentile) and the top 25% of scores (75th percentile). The procedure is simple. First, divide the data set in two at the median. Then find the midpoint for the data below the median (call it Q1—it's the 25th percentile) and the midpoint for the data above the median (Q3, or the 75th percentile). The interquartile range (IQR) is equal to Q3 - Q1. Consider the memory data again:

14 15 15 15 16   16 17 17 17 17   18 18 18 18 18   19 19 19 20 21

⇑   ⇑   ⇑

Q1   median   Q3

Q1 = 16   Q3 = 18.5   IQR = Q3 − Q1 = 18.5 − 16 = 2.5

Notice that the IQR would not change if outliers were present. For example, if the first two memory scores were 3 and 4 instead of 14 and 15, the IQR would still be 2.5 (and the median would still be 17.5).

Measures of central tendency and variability are universal features of any description of data, but researchers also like to examine the entire set of scores at one time. Just looking at the data set doesn't help, but there are other ways to organize the scores so that they present a visual image that is meaningful. One way to accomplish this is by creating what is called a **histogram.** This is a graph that shows the number of times each score occurs or, if there is a large number of scores, how often scores within a defined range occur. The first step is to create a **frequency distribution,**

TABLE 4.2   *Calculating Standard Deviations*

If you are using a statistical package (e.g., SPSS), standard deviations will be printed out as part of the analysis anytime you ask for descriptive statistics. Likewise, most calculators include some basic statistical functions, including standard deviations, which can be calculated automatically for you. However, there is value in understanding what a standard deviation truly reveals, and that comes only from calculating one or two by hand, using what is called the "definition" formula (so called because the essence of the definition of the standard deviation concept becomes apparent during the calculations). This will give you the best insight into the nature of a standard deviation, which is a measure of the amount that each score deviates from the mean. Here's how it works for the memory scores:

Step 1. Calculate the mean score:
$$\overline{X} = \Sigma X/N = 347/20 = \mathbf{17.35}$$

Step 2. Calculate deviation scores (small x) by subtracting the mean from each individual score (big X). Notice that if you add up all of the deviation scores, they sum to zero (which makes a good check on your accuracy of calculating the deviation scores). Next, square each deviation score. This eliminates minus numbers and ensures some positive number when these numbers are added up to produce a sum of X-squares $\rightarrow \Sigma x^2$.

X	$\overline{X}$	x	x^2
16	17.35	−1.35	1.8225
18	17.35	.65	.4225
14	17.35	−3.35	11.2225
. . .	. . .	. . .	. . .
18	17.35	.65	.4225

$$\Sigma x^2 = 62.55 = SS$$

This Σx^2 is the sum of squared deviations, or sometimes just called the "sum of squares" and abbreviated SS.

Step 3. Calculate the standard deviation (SD) by dividing the sum of squared deviations (Σx^2 or SS) by sample size (minus 1), and then taking the square root (to reverse the effects of squaring the deviation scores):
$$SD = \sqrt{\Sigma x^2/(N-1)}$$
$$= \sqrt{62.55/19}$$
$$= \sqrt{3.29}$$
$$= \mathbf{1.81}$$

One final note: If a standard deviation indicates an "average" amount of variability, you might wonder why the Σx^2 is divided by $N-1$ and not just by N. It has to do with the fact that we are dealing with a sample here and not the population. When you have all of the population data, the denominator in an SD calculation is in indeed N. But with sample data, when we are trying to estimate what is going on in the population, it is possible to be a little off in that estimation, because the sample might just include some odd data, and statistical calculations like to take the conservative route. So it is conservative to slightly overestimate the standard deviation, and dividing by $N-1$ does just that, producing a slightly higher number ($SD = 1.81$) than dividing by N (which produces an SD of 1.77—you should check this).

a table that records the number of times that each score occurs. The frequency distribution of scores for the memory study looks like this:

Score	Frequency	Frequency as Asterisks
14	1	★
15	3	★★★
16	2	★★
17	4	★★★★
18	5	★★★★★
19	3	★★★
20	1	★
21	1	★

Plotting the histogram is easy once this table of frequencies has been created. Simply place the actual score values on the *X*-axis of a graph and the frequency of occurrence on the *Y*-axis; then draw the bars appropriately. The result should look like Figure 4.6. Notice that taking the pattern of asterisks from the frequency distribution and rotating it 90° results in the equivalent of Figure 4.6.

Another thing to note about the histogram is that it bulges somewhat near the middle and is relatively flat at each end. This is a distribution of scores that roughly approximates what would happen if you created a histogram for the entire population, not just for the twenty people in the sample described here. Such

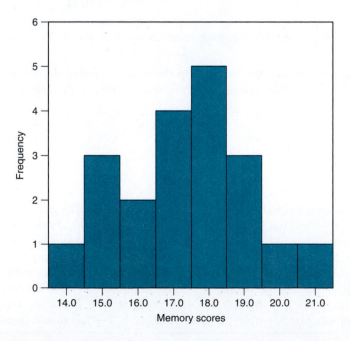

FIGURE 4.6 A histogram of scores on a memory test.

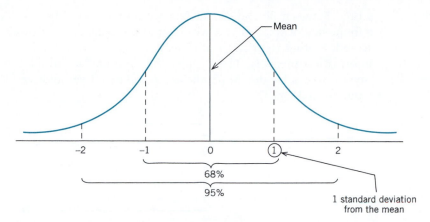

FIGURE 4.7 The normal curve.

a population distribution is the familiar bell-shaped curve known as the **normal curve** or normal distribution—see Figure 4.7.

The normal curve is a frequency distribution just like one for the memory scores, except that instead of being an *actual* (or "empirical") distribution of sample scores, it is a *hypothetical* (or "theoretical") distribution of what all the scores in the population would be like if everyone was tested. The mean score, as well as the median and the mode, are all in the exact middle of a normal distribution. A key point in statistical analysis is that if empirical distributions of scores resemble the normal distribution, then the mathematical properties of the normal distribution can be used to draw conclusions about the empirical distribution.

In the normal curve in Figure 4.7, notice that I have marked two standard deviations on either side of the mean. From the mathematical properties of the curve, it is possible to know that about two-thirds or 68% of all the scores in a population of scores fall within a single standard deviation on either side of the mean. Furthermore, about 95% of all scores fall within two standard deviations on either side of the mean. Obviously, scores that fall beyond two standard deviations are rare; they occur only 5% of the time. You might even describe such events as significant, as in "statistically significant." Keep this concept in mind; we'll return to it shortly.

In addition to frequency distributions and histograms, another common approach to displaying a data set meaningfully is to construct what is called a **stem and leaf display** (Tukey, 1977). Such displays are often used when there is such a wide range of scores that a simple frequency distribution and histogram would be cumbersome. For example, if you gave 20 persons a test for shyness and the scores ranged from 10 to 70, a simple frequency distribution like the one for the memory data would be huge and the histogram would have an *X*-axis a mile long. The problem can be solved by grouping the data into intervals (10–19, 20–29, 30–39, etc.). Each bar on a histogram would reflect the number of scores within that interval. Note, however, that grouping the data in this manner results in the loss of some information. If there were six people in the shyness example who scored between 30 and 39, all you would see would be the one bar representing a frequency of six, and you wouldn't know what each of those six people actually scored. With a stem and leaf display, however, you would be able to know this information precisely. Here's how the stem and leaf display works. Suppose the shyness scores for the 20 people are as follows (I've boldfaced the 6 people in the range from 31 to 39):

49	22	**33**	46
36	64	**39**	41
41	57	43	59
36	47	**32**	57
43	67	**37**	43

In the stem and leaf display with two-digit numbers, the "stem" will be the left-hand digit and the "leaf" will be the right-hand digit. Thus, for the first number, 49, the stem is 4 and the leaf is 9. For a 36, the stem is 3 and the leaf is 6. To organize the stems and leafs into a display, the first step is to arrange the numbers in ascending order, as you would when looking for the median (scores of 30–39 are again boldfaced). Hence:

22 **32 33 36 36 37 39** 41 41 43 43 43 46 47 49 57 57 59 64 67

Then list the stems in a left-hand column and the leaves corresponding to each stem in a right-hand column, like this:

Stems	Leaves
2	2
3	**236679**
4	11333679
5	779
6	47

If you rotate the stem and leaf display 90° and imagine covering over the leaf numbers to create solid bars, you would have the equivalent of a histogram for grouped data. Notice the advantage of a stem and leaf display over a normal histogram, though. For example, in the range 30–39, the histogram would show a single bar that reached to the level of six on the Y-axis. On the stem and leaf display, however, you not only see the "height" of the scores in the range, you can also determine each of the actual scores.

    There are variations on the basic stem and leaf display. Displays for data with a relatively narrow range can be constructed with two stems for each digit in the tens column. The first stem is paired with the numbers 0–4 in the ones digit, while the second stem is paired with the numbers 5–9. Two sets of data can also be placed on a single, side-by-side stem and leaf display. The following stem and leaf display illustrates both variations on the basic display. See if you can make sense of it.

210	**4**	3
9887655	**4**	588
2221100	**5**	001
8665	**5**	67777899
10	**6**	0011223344
6	**6**	77899

What I hope you see is that the scores for the right-hand set are higher overall (relatively more in the 60s) than the scores for the left-hand set (relatively more in the 40s). If you count them up, you will also notice that there are more total scores in the right-hand set (30) than in the left-hand set (24).

In articles describing research outcomes, descriptive statistics are reported three ways. First, if there are just a few numbers to report (e.g., means and standard deviations for the two groups in an experiment), they are sometimes worked into the narrative description of the results. Second, the means and standard deviations might be presented in a table; third, they might be reported in the visual form of a graph. Descriptions of how to construct tables and graphs that conform to the guidelines of the APA can be found in the sample research report in Appendix A, and Chapters 7 and 8 include some information on graph making. Also, take a look at Box 4.3, which makes it clear that statistical analysis and graph making have an ethical dimension.

Box 4.3

ETHICS—Lying with Statistics

We've all been exposed to the deceptive use of statistical information. Although politicians might be the worst offenders, with writers of commercial ads perhaps a close second, statistics are abused frequently enough that many people tend to be skeptical about them, and you often hear people say things like "Statistics don't really tell you anything useful—you can make them do anything you'd like." Is this really true?

Certainly there are decisions to be made about how to present data and what conclusions to draw from them. You can be reasonably confident that articles published in reputable journals, having gone through a tough peer review process, are reporting statistical analyses that lead to defensible conclusions. What you need to be careful about are the uses of statistics in the broader public arena or by people determined to convince you that they know the truth or to get you to buy something.

Being informed about the proper use of statistics will enable you to identify these questionable statistical practices. Some things to be careful about were first described some time ago in Darrell Huff's famous *How to Lie with Statistics* (1954). The book begins with a well-known quote attributed to the British politician Benjamin Disraeli that sums up a common perception of statistics: "There are lies, damned lies, and statistics" (p. 2).

Here's an example of how to lie with statistics that relates specifically to the visual portrayal of data—graphs. Figure 4.8 is a graph that appeared briefly on the CNN website, reporting the results of a poll in 2005. At issue was a heart-breaking case in which a young Florida woman (Terry Schiavo) had fallen in a persistent vegetative state and was essentially brain dead. A battle was being fought between her husband, who wished to remove her feeding tube, and her parents, who believed she could recover. National politicians with axes to grind even became involved, never a good sign. The dispute eventually reached the Supreme Court, and it was decided that the feeding tube could be removed (she died shortly thereafter). The subsequent CNN poll about the case included this question: "Based on what you have heard or read about the case, do you agree with the court's decision to have the feeding tube removed?" Figure 4.8 was used to compare the results for Democrat, Republican, and Independent voters who responded. As you can see, a quick look makes it appear that Democrats were much more likely to agree with the Court's decision than Republicans or Independents. In fact the differences among them were quite small (8 percentage points) and happened to be within the margin of error for the survey.

This is a type of graph that Huff called a "Gee Whiz" graph, for obvious reasons: when you first look at it, you find yourself saying, "Gee whiz, what an huge

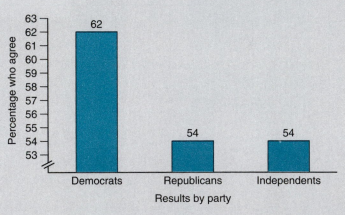

FIGURE 4.8 Graph as it appeared in the original reporting of the CNN/USA/Gallup poll.

difference!'' Democrats reading the graph might be inclined to think they are more reasonable than the other groups, while the other groups might think that Democrats value life less than they do. The problem, however, is that the percentages had been grossly exaggerated by using just a small range of numbers on the vertical or *Y*-axis, and by not starting the *Y*-axis at a percentage of zero. This strategy exaggerates small differences. A more reasonable labeling of the *Y*-axis yields the graph in Figure 4.9, which gives you a more truthful picture of the outcome—that no substantial differences among the groups occurred and that for all three groups, the majority agreed with the Court's decision. (*Note*: To their credit, CNN quickly recognized the problem and replaced the graph in Figure 4.8 with the more accurate one in 4.9).

The moral here is obvious: Beware the *Y*-axis. Be especially skeptical about graphs that seem to show large differences on a *Y*-axis that is not labeled, labeled ambiguously, labeled in very tiny gradations from top to bottom, and/or does not start at zero.

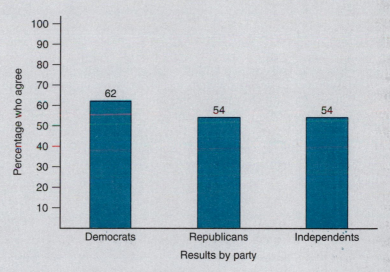

FIGURE 4.9 CNN'S corrected graph that more accurately reflects the data.

Inferential Statistics

Like most people, researchers need to believe their work is important. One way to accomplish this goal is to produce interesting research outcomes, results that apply beyond just the data collected in one study. That is, although a study looks at merely a small *sample* (a subset of the members of some defined group—50 college students, for instance) of all the data that could be collected, the researcher's hope is to arrive at a conclusion that will apply to the wider *population* (all the members of a defined group—all college students, for instance). After all, the idea of the whole research enterprise is to arrive at general laws of behavior.

To illustrate what an inferential analysis tries to accomplish, let's consider a hypothetical maze-learning study comparing rats fed immediately after reaching the end of a complicated maze with rats fed 10 seconds after reaching the end of the maze. Thus, the empirical question is whether immediate reinforcement results in faster maze learning than delayed reinforcement. Suppose the following results occurred for five rats in each group. Each score is the total number of trials the rat takes to learn the maze; learning is operationally defined as two consecutive errorless runs through the maze.

Rat #	Immediate Food	Rat #	Delayed Food
1	12	6	19
2	13	7	20
3	16	8	16
4	11	9	18
5	14	10	15

Notice that the scores within each column are not all the same, a result of slight differences between the five rats in each group and perhaps some other random factors. Despite the lack of absolute uniformity, however, it appears that the rats given immediate reinforcement learned the maze faster (i.e., require fewer trials).

Of course, we need more than a general impression resulting from a quick glance at the numbers. The first step is to calculate some descriptive statistics, such as the mean and standard deviation. They are:

	Immediate	Delayed
Mean	13.2	17.6
Standard deviation	1.9	2.1

On the average, at least for this sample, maze learning required more trials when the food reward was delayed. Also, the variability of the scores within each set, as reflected in the standard deviations, is fairly low and about the same for both groups. Can we conclude *in general* (i.e., with reference to the population of all rats) that immediate reinforcement speeds up maze learning? Not yet. What is needed is an inferential analysis of the data, which in this case involves hypothesis testing.[2]

---

[2]A second category of inferential analysis is called "estimation"; it involves estimating population values from individual sample scores.

✓ **Self Test 4.2**

1. If there are significant outliers, what is the best measure of (a) central tendency and (b) variability?
2. Consider the following numbers: 44, 30, 21, 35, 34, 41, 22, 45, 35, 48, 21, 30, 28, 37. Assuming an interval of 10, what will the "leaves" be for the "stem" of 3?
3. When reporting a mean, why is it also important to report a standard deviation?
4. Why is it difficult to interpret a graph if the *Y*-axis is not labeled?

Hypothesis Testing

The first step in testing hypotheses is to make the assumption that there is no difference in performance between the different conditions that you are studying, in this case between immediate and delayed rewards. This assumption is called the **null hypothesis** (null = nothing), symbolized H_0 and pronounced "h sub oh." The research hypothesis, the outcome you are *hoping* to find (fewer learning trials for rats receiving immediate reward), is called the **alternative hypothesis** or H_1. Thus, in your study, you hope to be able to disprove or reject H_0, thereby supporting (but not proving) H_1, the hypothesis close to your heart.

If this language sounds odd to you, think of it as analogous to what happens in a court of law. There, the accused person initially is presumed innocent. That is, the assumption is that the defendant has done nothing (null-thing) wrong. The job of the prosecution is to convince the jury of its alternative hypothesis, namely, that the defendant committed the crime. Like the prosecutor, the researcher must show that something indeed happened, namely, that the reinforcement delay influenced learning in our maze-learning example.

There can be only two outcomes to an inferential analysis. The differences you find between the two groups of rats could be due to some genuine, real, honest-to-goodness effect (e.g., reinforcement delay) or they could be due to chance. So the sample differences might mirror a true difference or they might not. Hence, an inferential statistical analysis yields only two results — you can either reject H_0 or fail to reject it. Failing to reject H_0 means you believe that any differences in the means (and studies almost always find some differences between groups) were most likely chance differences — you have failed to find a genuine effect that can be generalized beyond your sample. Rejecting H_0 means that you believe that an effect truly happened in your study and that the results can be generalized. In the maze example, rejecting H_0, that is, finding a statistically significant difference, means that it really does seem to be the case that immediate reinforcement aids maze learning.

The researcher's hypothesis (H_1) is never proven to be true in an absolute sense, just as defendants are never *absolutely* proven guilty: Guilt is said to be proven only beyond a reasonable doubt. Thus, H_0 can only be rejected (and at the same time

H_1 supported) with some degree of confidence, which is set by what is called the **alpha (α) level.** Technically, alpha refers to the probability of obtaining your particular results if H_0 (no true difference) is really true. By convention, alpha is set at .05 ($\alpha = .05$), but it can be set at other, more stringent, levels as well (e.g., $\alpha = .01$). If H_0 is rejected when alpha equals .05, it means that you believe the probability is very low (5 out of 100) that your research outcome is the result of chance factors. If it is not due to chance, then it must be due to something else, namely (you hope), the phenomenon you are studying, immediacy of reinforcement in this case.

The choice of .05 as the alpha level relates to the earlier discussion of the characteristics of the normal curve. Remember that for a normal distribution of scores, the probability that a given score will be more than two standard deviations from the mean is low, 5% or less. Such an event is rare. Similarly, when comparing two sets of scores, as in the maze study, one asks about the probability of the obtained difference between the means occurring if the truth was that no real difference existed (i.e., if H_0 is true). If that probability is low enough, we reject H_0 and decide that some real difference must be occurring. The "low enough" is the probability of 5%, or .05. Another way to put it is to say that the obtained difference between the sample means would be so unexpected (i.e., rare) if H_0 were true that we just cannot believe that H_0 is really true. We believe that something else happened (i.e., reinforcement delay really does slow down learning), so we reject H_0 and conclude that a "statistically significant" difference exists between the groups.

Type I and Type II Errors

Clear from the previous discussion is the fact that when you decide whether or not to reject H_0, you could be wrong. Actually, there are two kinds of errors you could make. First, you might reject H_0 and support H_1, get all excited about making some new breakthrough discovery, but be wrong. Rejecting H_0 when it is in fact true is called a **Type I error.** The chance of this happening is equal to the value of alpha, normally .05. That is, setting alpha at .05 and rejecting H_0 means that there is a 5% chance of making a Type I error—a 5% chance of thinking you have a real effect but being wrong. Type I errors are sometimes suspected when a research outcome fails several attempts at replication.

The other kind of mistake you could make is called a **Type II error.** This happens when you fail to reject H_0 but you are wrong. That is, you don't find a significant effect in your study, naturally feel depressed about it, but are in fact in error. There really is a true effect in the population; you just haven't found it in the sample you studied. Type II errors sometimes occur when the measurements used aren't very reliable or aren't sensitive enough to detect true differences between groups. As you will see in Chapter 10, this sometimes happens in program evaluation research. A program might indeed have a significant but small effect on those in it, but the measures used are too weak to pick up this subtle effect.

Table 4.3 summarizes the four possible outcomes of an inferential statistical analysis comparing two conditions of an experiment. As you can see, correct decisions result from rejecting H_0 when it is false and not rejecting H_0 when it is true. Erroneously rejecting H_0 produces a Type I error; a failure to reject H_0 when

TABLE **4.3** *Statistical Decision Making: Four Possible Outcomes of a Study Comparing Two Conditions, X and Y*

		The True State of Affairs	
		H_0 **is true:** There is no difference between X and Y	H_0 **is false:** There really is a difference between X and Y
Your Statistical Decision	**Fail to reject H_0:** In my study, I found no significant difference between X and Y, so I cannot reject H_0	**Correct decision**	**Type II error**
	Reject H_0: In my study, I found a significant difference between X and Y, so I reject H_0	**Type I error**	**Correct decision** (experimenter heaven)

H_0 is false is a Type II error. If it makes it easier to understand the terminology, you can make the following substitutions in Table 4.3:

For "Fail to Reject H_0," substitute:
—"You did the study, you went through all of the proper analyses, and what you came up with was zilch, nothing, zippo, no significant differences, and yes, you have good reason to be distraught, especially if this is your senior thesis project!"

For "Reject H_0," substitute:
—"You did the study, you went through all of the proper analyses, and the difference came out significant at the .05 level, and yes, your life now has meaning and you'll be able to impress your friends and especially your thesis director because you went through all of this work and you *actually found something!*"

For "H_0 is true," substitute:
—"Regardless of what might have occurred in your study, no true difference exists."

For "H_0 is false," substitute:
—"Regardless of what might have occurred in your study, a true difference does exist."

With the substitutions in mind, correct decisions mean either that (a) no real difference exists, which is OK because you didn't find one anyway, or (b) a real difference exists and you found it (experimenter heaven). A Type I error means there's no real difference, but you think there is because of the results of your particular study. A Type II error means there really is a difference, but you failed to find it in your study.

Inferential Analysis

An inferential statistical decision to reject or not reject the null hypothesis in a study like the maze-learning study depends on analyzing two general types of variability in the data. The first refers to the differences in the "number of trials to reach criterion" scores for the two groups of rats. These differences are caused by some combination of (a) systematic variance and (b) error variance. **Systematic variance** is the result of some identifiable factor, either the variable of interest (reinforcement delay) or some factor that you've failed to control adequately.[3] **Error variance** is nonsystematic variability due to individual differences between the rats in the two groups and any number of random, unpredictable effects that might have occurred during the study. Error variance also occurs within each group, also as a result of individual differences and other random effects, and accounts for the differences found there. Mathematically, many inferential analyses will calculate some form of ratio that takes this form:

$$\text{Inferential statistic} = \frac{\text{Variability between conditions (systematic + error)}}{\text{Variability within each condition (error)}}$$

The ideal outcome is to find that variability between conditions is huge and variability within each condition is relatively small.

As you can see, this outcome seems to occur for our hypothetical maze data. The differences between the two conditions are substantial—rats with immediate reinforcement learn the maze in fewer trials (13.2 < 17.6), whereas the scores within each condition cluster fairly close together, as reflected in the small standard deviations for each (1.9 and 2.1). The particular inferential test you would use in this case is called a "*t* test for independent samples," a procedure familiar to you if you have taken a basic course in statistics.

Interpreting Failures to Reject H$_0$

For academic researchers, the road to tenure and promotion passes through what I have called "experimenter heaven" (rejecting null hypotheses when there is indeed a true effect) but, of course, there are many times when the result of a study is a failure to reject H$_0$ (no significant differences occur). The typical reaction of a researcher to this second type of outcome result is unprintable in this family-oriented research methods text, but in fact, there might be circumstances when a failure to reject H$_0$ is not such a bad outcome. In general, it is important to note that interpreting failures to reject H$_0$ must be done with great caution. There might indeed be no difference to be found, or it could be that there is one, but you have failed to find it in your study (a Type II error). So if you are comparing, say, those who get a drug and those who don't, hoping to find that the drug improves memory, but you fail to find a significant difference between

---

[3]These uncontrolled factors, called "confounds," will be examined in depth in the next chapter.

the two groups, you're not allowed to say, "OK that settles it—there's no effect of this drug." On the other hand, and this is where replication once again comes into play, consistent failures to find differences can indeed be important outcomes in some circumstances. For example, as you will learn in the Chapter 7 discussion of yoked control groups, those who develop a new therapy (to cure extreme anxiety in this case) are obligated to provide evidence of its effectiveness. Several findings of no difference between the new therapy and a control group given no therapy would raise questions about the usefulness of the new approach.

For an example relevant to your life as students, consider a study by Vandehey, Marsh, and Diekhoff (2005). They examined the question of whether instructors should provide a full set of their lecture notes (typically on an instructor website) to students. Some argue that if students already have all of the notes, they don't have to worry about writing furiously in class, thereby missing some important points perhaps. But others have argued that if students have all of the notes, they won't come to class (why bother if the notes are posted online?). Over the course of a semester, Vandehey and his colleagues compared classes that provided full instructor notes, partial notes, or no notes. They found *no* significant differences in class attendance among any of the groups (no differences in course grades either). If this result holds up on replication (and some other studies have found slightly different results), it means that instructors providing all of their notes don't need to worry about teaching to empty classrooms.

Another implication of the failure to reject issue is that it is often (but not always) the case that nonsignificant findings do not get published. Yet, it could be that important research outcomes aren't becoming known. In research on sex differences, for example, research is more likely to be published if differences between males and females occur. Studies finding no differences were less likely to be published, and wind up being stored away in one's files—a phenomenon that has been called the **file drawer effect** (Rosenthal, 1979). A big problem occurs, however, if there are 10 published studies showing "males outperform females on X," no published studies showing the opposite or no differences, but 90 studies languishing in file drawers because no differences were found and the studies couldn't get published. Someone looking at "the literature" (i.e., the published research) would think that a genuine sex difference has been found, when, in fact, the evidence might be quite weak.

Going Beyond Hypothesis Testing

Although hypothesis testing and inferential analyses have a long history and have been the backbone of statistical decision making among psychologists, they have also been a focus of strong criticism. A major point of contention has been the all-or-none character of null hypothesis decision making, with the alpha level of .05 taking on seemingly magical properties (Cohen, 1994). Why, it is sometimes asked, is a difference between two means "significant" at the .05 level and another difference between another pair of means not significant at the .06 level? Studies producing these two outcomes are essentially identical in terms of the result, but one meets the magical .05 cutoff (and gets published), while the other one falls short (and gets stuffed into the file draw labeled "nonsignificant results"). Defenders of null hypothesis significance testing argue that providing a strong test before drawing a conclusion is not necessarily a bad thing; they also ask, if not .05 as a cutoff, then what should it be? .10? .15?

A beneficial effect of the argument has been an elaboration of the kinds of statistical analyses being done by research psychologists today. Based on recommendations from a special task force created by the APA (Wilkinson et al., 1999), researchers are starting to include several new features in their descriptions of statistical analyses. These include calculations of effect sizes, confidence intervals, and estimates of power. In addition, researchers are beginning to realize that even beyond statistical analysis, confidence in the validity of research outcomes requires a greater value being placed on the replication process. Kline (2004), for example, argued that it

> would make a very strong statement if journals and granting agencies required replication. This would increase the demands on the researcher and result in fewer published studies. The quality of what would be published might improve, however. A requirement for replication would also filter out some of the fad social science research topics that bloom for a short time but then quickly disappear. (p. 89)

Effect Size

The result of a null hypothesis significance test could be that a statistically significant difference between two groups or among multiple groups exists. But this outcome does not inform the researcher about the *size* of the difference(s). An effect size index is designed to do just that. **Effect size** provides an estimate of the magnitude of the difference among sets of scores, while at the same time taking into account the amount of variability in the scores. There are different types of effect size calculations for different kinds of research designs. All yield a statistic that enables the researcher to decide if the study produced a small, medium-sized, or large effect.[4]

One major advantage of calculating effect sizes is that it enables researchers to arrive at a common metric for evaluating diverse experiments. That is, if you examine 20 different studies designed to test the frustration–aggression hypothesis, each using different operational definitions of terms, different procedures, and different types of participants, an effect size can be calculated for each study and these effect sizes can be combined to yield an overall statistical conclusion about the generality of the relationship between frustration and aggression, across all the studies. This is precisely what is done in a type of study called a **meta-analysis.** Thus, a meta-analysis uses effect size analyses to combine the results from several (often, many) experiments that use the same variables, even though these variables are likely to have different operational definitions. For example, Anderson and Bushman (2001) combined the effect sizes from 35 different studies using more than 4,000 total participants to argue that playing violent video games increases

---

[4]One common measure of effect size is Cohen's *d* and a Google search for it will yield several sites that will automatically calculate effect size if you just plug in the means and standard deviations for two groups.

levels of aggressiveness in children and young adults. The outcome of a meta-analysis relates to the concept of converging operations, introduced in Chapter 3. In general, confidence in the generality of some conclusion increases when similar results occur, even though a variety of different methods and definitions of terms have been used.

Confidence Intervals

Calculating confidence intervals for specific means adds to the quality of the information provided in a description of results. In particular, a confidence interval is an inferential statistic, enabling the researcher to draw a conclusion about the population as a whole, based on the sample data. As you recall from my opening remarks about inferential statistics, drawing general conclusions is the name of the game for an inferential analysis. Using the hypothetical maze data again, the means and standard deviations can be supplemented with confidence intervals as follows:

	Immediate	Delayed
Mean	13.2	17.6
Standard deviation	1.9	2.1
Confidence Interval (95%)	10.8–15.6	15.0–20.2

A **confidence interval** is a range of values that is expected to include a population value with a certain degree of confidence. What a confidence interval tells us is that, based on the data for a sample, we can be 95% confident that the calculated interval captures the population mean.[5] Hence, there is a very good chance (95 out of 100) that the population mean for the immediately reinforced group is somewhere between 10.8 trials and 15.6 trials and that the population mean for the delayed group falls somewhere between 15.0 trials and 20.2 trials. Table 4.4 shows you how the first of these two intervals was calculated. As for the use of confidence intervals in drawing conclusions about an experiment, note that there is virtually no overlap in the intervals for the two groups in the maze study. The upper limit of the immediate group overlaps the lower limit for the delayed group, but just slightly. In general, nonoverlapping confidence intervals indicate a substantial difference between the two different conditions of the study—in our hypothetical study, delaying reinforcement seems to have a clear effect in slowing down learning (i.e., increasing the number of trials it takes to learn the maze).[6]

---

[5]Although the term "confidence interval" is seldom used when reporting the results of polls, it is in fact the key statistic yielding what is called the "margin of error," as in "The president currently has a 56% approval rating, with a margin of error of ± 4%."

[6]A second type of confidence interval also can be calculated, one that produces a range of mean differences for a study that compares two means. For more details on how to calculate and interpret a confidence interval around a mean difference, consult a statistics textbook (e.g., Witte & Witte, 2007).

TABLE 4.4 *Calculating a Confidence Interval*

Any time we calculate a sample mean, it is an estimate of the mean of the entire population, but only an estimate. A confidence interval around a sample mean is easy to calculate and the outcome is a range of scores. With some confidence (e.g., 95%), we can say that the population mean falls within that range. Here's how to calculate the 95% confidence interval (from 10.8 trials to 15.6 trials) for the immediately reinforced group in the hypothetical maze study. The formula for a confidence interval:

$$\text{Lower Limit} = LL = \overline{X} - t(s_{\overline{x}}) \quad \text{Upper Limit} = UL = \overline{X} = t(s_{\overline{x}})$$

$\overline{X}$ = the sample mean

t = a value from a table of critical values for the t distribution (your instructor will show you one); in this case, $N = 5$, so $df = 4$, and the tabled value is 2.78.

$s_{\overline{x}}$ = is called the standard error of the mean; if you took a large number of samples from a population and calculated means for each sample, the standard error is an estimate of how much these sample means would deviate from the population mean; the standard error of the mean is equal to the sample standard deviation divided by the square root of N; in this case it is equal to:

$$\frac{1.9}{\sqrt{5}} = .85$$

Calculate the Interval:

$$LL = \overline{X} - t(s_{\overline{x}}) = 13.2 - (2.78)(.85) = 13.2 - 2.36 = 10.84 = 10.8$$
$$UL = \overline{X} + t(s_{\overline{x}}) = 13.2 + (2.78)(.85) = 13.2 + 2.36 = 15.56 = 15.6$$

Hence, we can be 95% confident that the population mean (the true mean) is somewhere between 10.8 and 15.6 trials.

Power

When completing a null hypothesis significance test, one hopes to be able to reject H_0 when it is, in fact, false (the "experimenter heaven" cell of Table 4.3). The chance of this happening is referred to as the **power** of the statistical test. That is, a test is said to have high power if it results in a high probability that a difference that exists in reality will be found in a particular study. Note that there is an inverse relationship between power and a Type II error. This type of error, you will recall, occurs when a true effect exists, but the experiment fails to find a "significant difference." As power increases, the chances of a Type II error decrease, and vice versa. The probability of a Type II error occurring is sometimes referred to as β ("beta"). Power, then, is $1 - \beta$.

Power is affected by the alpha level (e.g., $\alpha = .05$), by the size of the treatment effect (effect size), and, especially, by the size of the sample used in the experiment. This latter attribute is directly under the experimenter's control, and researchers sometimes perform a "power analysis" at the outset of a study to help them make decisions about the best sample size for their study (consult a statistics text for more details on completing a power analysis).

Students are often frustrated when their study "doesn't come out" (i.e., no significant differences occur), an outcome that often results from a small sample size. That is, power was low and the chances of a Type II error are high—some effect might indeed have occurred in their study, but they failed to detect it. Increasing sample size, in a study that is well designed, is usually the best way to increase power. However, the other side of the power coin is that a huge sample size might produce a result that is statistically significant, but meaningless. That is, a tiny but statistically significant difference between groups might have little practical importance in a study with huge numbers of participants. For instance, suppose that, in a study evaluating the effects of orange juice on IQ, you include 5,000 people in each of two groups (orange juice vs. no orange juice), find a 2-point improvement in average IQ for the orange juice group and no change for the other group, and determine that the difference is significant at the .05 level. This is a test with very high power. Such a difference, however, would be of no real value. Two IQ points? Who cares? Part of the skill of becoming an accomplished researcher involves balancing considerations of power, effect size, significance level, and sample size.

✓ Self Test 4.3

1. A researcher believes that wild rats will learn to escape from a puzzle box more quickly than tame rats. What is H_0 in this study?
2. In the same study with rats, what kind of result would be considered a Type I error? Type II?
3. What is a meta-analysis and how does it relate to effect size?

Armed with some of the basic tools psychologists use to think about data, you are now ready to tackle the first of three chapters dealing with the experimental method, psychology's most powerful tool for trying to understand the intricacies of behavior and mental processes. We'll begin with a general introduction to the experimental method and then consider some control problems that occur with such research; third, we'll examine the features of the most common types of experimental designs.

Chapter Summary

What to Measure—Varieties of Behavior

The behaviors measured in psychological research range from overt actions to self-reports to physiological recordings; the measures chosen for a particular study will depend on the manner in which the study's constructs are operationally defined.

In many areas of psychological research, standard measures have developed over the years (e.g., preferential looking, reaction time).

Evaluating Measures

High-quality measures of behavior are both reliable and valid. To be reliable is to be repeatable and low in measurement error. Measures are valid if they actually measure what they are supposed to measure. Confidence in validity increases if a measure makes sense (content validity) and predicts future outcomes well (criterion validity). Construct validity means that the measurement being used is a good measure of the construct being studied (e.g., "connectedness to nature") and that the construct itself is useful for understanding some behavior. Valid constructs also show convergent and discriminant validity. Construct validity develops over time, when a research program investigating relationships between the construct being measured and related phenomena results in consistent, predictable outcomes.

Scales of Measurement

Data for psychological research can be classified into four different scales of measurement: nominal, ordinal, interval, and ratio. In a nominal scale, categories (e.g., male, female) are identified and the frequency of occurrences per category is the main research interest. Ordinal scales occur when events are placed in rank order. Interval and ratio scales both assume equal intervals between quantitatively increasing scores; only ratio scales have a true zero point, however. Traditionally, psychologists have preferred to rely on interval and ratio scales because of the wider range of statistical analyses available when these scales are used.

Statistical Analysis

Statistical analysis in psychology is an essential tool for understanding the meaning of research outcomes. Descriptive statistics are calculated for the sample of participants in a particular study. They provide a summary of results and include measures of central tendency (e.g., mean, median, mode) and variability (range, standard deviation, variance, interquartile range). For data with outliers, medians and interquartile ranges substitute for means and standard deviations. Data can be presented visually via graphical representation (e.g., histogram, stem and leaf display). Inferential statistics allow decisions about whether the results of a study are due to chance factors or appear to reflect some genuine relationship that can be applied to the larger population. The goal of null hypothesis significance testing is to reject the hypothesis of no difference (i.e., the null hypothesis) when a true difference indeed occurs. A Type I error happens when the null hypothesis is rejected but should not have been, and a Type II occurs when a true effect exists, but no statistically significant difference is found in the study. Another form of inferential analysis involves calculating confidence intervals. Information about the magnitude of some research outcome comes from determining effect size. A statistical test has high power if the chances are high that it will detect a true effect.

Chapter Review Questions

1. Describe the logic behind Donders' "mental chronometry" research. What was the basic flaw?

2. Define reliability and explain why phrenological measurements would have been highly reliable.

3. Define validity and explain why phrenological measurements would have failed a validity test.

4. Use the Connectedness to Nature Scale as an example to show how construct validity can be determined. Be sure to work convergent and discriminant validity into your answer.

5. Describe the essential difference between descriptive and inferential statistics.

6. Distinguish between means, median, and modes, and explain when a median is a better descriptor of central tendency than a mean.

7. When describing variability, what is an interquartile range and when is it most likely to be used?

8. Describe the purpose of a stem and leaf display and why it can be better than a histogram for displaying a set of scores.

9. Describe the basic logic of hypothesis testing and distinguish between Type I and Type II errors.

10. What are confidence intervals and how are they interpreted?

11. What is effect size and how does its calculation complement hypothesis testing?

12. What is meant by the power of a statistical test and how might power be enhanced?

Applications Exercises

Exercise 4.1   Scales of Measurement

For each of the following studies, indicate which scale of measurement (nominal, ordinal, interval, ratio) is being used for the behavior being measured.

1. Sally wishes to discover whether the children of Republicans and Democrats are more likely to major in the sciences, humanities, or business.

2. Fred decides to investigate whether rats that have learned one maze will learn a second one more quickly (i.e., show fewer errors) than naive rats.

3. Jim hypothesizes that children will rank different TV movies higher if they are in color but that adults' rankings won't be affected by color.

4. Nancy believes that somatotype changes with age, so she proposes to use Sheldon's scale to measure somatotypes for a group of people on their 10th, 15th, and 20th birthdays.

5. Susan is interested in the phenomenon of helping behavior and believes that whether or not someone helps will be influenced by weather—the chances of someone helping will be greater on sunny than on cloudy days.

6. John wishes to determine which of five new varieties of beer will be liked best (i.e., recognized as number 1) by the patrons of his bar.

7. Ellen is interested in how students perceive the safety of various campus buildings. She asks a sample of students to arrange a deck of cards in a pile, each containing the name of a campus building, with the safest building on top and the least safe building on the bottom.

8. Pat believes that those with an obsessive-compulsive disorder will make fewer formatting errors on APA-style lab reports than those without the disorder.

9. Jesse is interested in sex differences in shyness and gives a 15-item shyness test to groups of men and women. Each item has a statement (e.g., I have difficulty talking to strangers) that asks responders to rate on a scale from 1 (strongly disagree) through 5 (strongly agree).

10. Francis wishes to know whether age differences (comparing those in their 20s with those in their 50s) exist for those people who consider themselves either morning people (best able to perform cognitive tasks then) or evening people.

Exercise 4.2 H_0, H_1, Type I errors, and Type II errors

For each of the following studies, (a) identify the null hypothesis, (b) make your best guess about the alternative hypothesis—that is, what you would expect to happen in this study, (c) describe a research outcome that would be a Type I error, and (d) describe an outcome that would be a Type II error.

1. In a study of how well people can detect lying, male and female participants will try to detect deception in films of women lying in some parts of the film and telling the truth in other parts.

2. In a perception study, infants will be habituated to slides of normal faces and then shown faces with slight irregularities to see if they can detect the differences.

3. Patients with and without a diagnosis of depression will be asked to predict how they will do in negotiating a human maze.

4. Some athletes will be given training in a new imaging procedure that they are to use just prior to shooting foul shots; they will be compared with other athletes not given any special training.

Exercise 4.3   Practicing Statistical Analysis

Suppose you did a study comparing the critical thinking skills of psychology majors and philosophy majors. You collect the data found in the following table. Each number is a score on a test of critical and logical thinking. Scores can range from a low of 5 to a high of 80. Calculate a complete set of descriptive statistics, side-by-side stem and leaf displays, 95% confidence intervals, a *t* test, and an effect size index. On the basis of what you have calculated, what would you conclude from the study?

Psychology Majors	Philosophy Majors
67	58
53	62
74	44
60	51
49	51
55	47
65	43
72	55
60	61
63	67

Answers to Self Tests:

✓ **4.1.**
1. .09 sec (.28— .19 = .09).
2. The measure would be reliable—same circumference tomorrow as today; it would not be valid—for example, head size would not predict GPA (students with larger heads would probably not have larger GPAs).
3. Dilbert is using an interval scale, probably ranging from 1–10; Liz is using a ratio scale (time).

✓ **4.2.**
1. (a) median; (b) interquartile range.
2. 004557
3. Two sets of scores can have the same mean but different amounts of variability.
4. Small and meaningless differences in the data can be grossly exaggerated, resulting in a misleading interpretation of the data.

✓ **4.3.**
1. Wild and tame rats will be equal in their ability to escape.
2. Type I → wild rats are found to escape significantly faster than tame rats, but, in reality, the two types of rats are equal in their ability to escape.
    Type II → no significant difference in ability to escape is found in the study, but, in reality, wild rats are superior to tame rats.
3. Meta-analysis is a statistical tool for combining the results of multiple studies: What are taken from the various studies are the effects sizes, which are combined.

CHAPTER 5

Introduction to Experimental Research

Preview & Chapter Objectives

The middle four chapters of this text, Chapters 5 through 8, concern the design of experiments. The first half of Chapter 5 outlines the essential features of an experiment—varying factors of interest (the independent variables), controlling all other factors (extraneous variables), and measuring the outcome (dependent variables). In the second part of this chapter, you will learn how the validity of a study can be affected by how well it is designed. When you finish this chapter, you should be able to:

- Define a manipulated independent variable and identify examples that are situational, task, and instructional variables.

- Distinguish between experimental and control groups.

- Describe John Stuart Mill's rules of inductive logic and apply them to the concepts of experimental and control groups.

- Recognize the presence of confounding variables in an experiment and understand why confounding creates serious problems for interpreting the results of an experiment.
- Identify independent and dependent variables, given a brief description of any experiment.
- Distinguish between independent variables that are manipulated variables and those that are subject variables, and understand the interpretation problems that accompany the use of subject variables.
- Recognize the factors that can reduce the statistical conclusion validity of an experiment.
- Describe how construct validity applies to the design of an experiment.
- Distinguish between the internal and external validity of a study.
- Describe the various ways in which an experiment's external validity can be reduced.
- Describe and be able to recognize the various threats to an experiment's internal validity.
- Recognize that external validity might not be important for all research but that internal validity is essential.
- Understand the ethical guidelines for running a "subject pool."

When Robert Sessions Woodworth finally published his *Experimental Psychology* in 1938, the book's contents were already well known among psychologists. As early as 1909, Woodworth was giving his Columbia University students copies of a mimeographed handout called "Problems and Methods in Psychology," and a companion handout called "Laboratory Manual: Experiments in Memory, etc." appeared in 1912. By 1920, the manuscript filled 285 pages and was called "A Textbook of Experimental Psychology." After a 1932 revision, still in mimeograph form, the book finally was published in 1938. By then Woodworth's students were using it to teach their own students, and it was so widely known that the publisher's announcement of its publication said simply, "The Bible Is Out" (Winston, 1990).

The so-called Columbia bible was encyclopedic, with more than 823 pages of text and another 36 pages of references. After an introductory chapter, it was organized into 29 different research topics such as "memory," "maze learning," "reaction time," "association," "hearing," "the perception of color," and "thinking." Students wading through the text would learn about the methods used in each content area, and they would also learn virtually everything there was to know in 1938 about each topic.

The impact of the Columbia bible on the teaching of experimental psychology has been incalculable. Indeed, the teaching of experimental psychology today, and to some degree the structure of the book you're now reading, are largely cast in the mold set by Woodworth. In particular, he took the term "experiment," until then loosely defined as virtually any type of empirical research, and gave it the definition it has today. In particular, he contrasted experimental with correlational research, a distinction now taken for granted.

The defining feature of the experimental method was the manipulation of what Woodworth called an "independent variable," which would affect what he called the "dependent variable." In his words, the experimenter "holds all the conditions constant except for one factor which is his 'experimental factor' or his 'independent variable.' The observed effect is the 'dependent variable' which in a psychological experiment is some characteristic of behavior or reported experience" (Woodworth, 1938, p. 2). Although Woodworth did not invent the terms, he was the first to use them as they are used routinely today.

While the experimental method manipulates independent variables, the correlational method, according to Woodworth, "[m]easures two or more characteristics of the same individuals [and] computes the correlation of these characteristics. This method... has no 'independent variable' but treats all the measured variables alike" (Woodworth, 1938, p. 3). You will learn more about correlational research in Chapter 9. In this and the next three chapters, however, the focus will be on the experimental method, the researcher's most powerful tool for identifying cause-and-effect relationships.

Essential Features of Experimental Research

Since Woodworth's time, psychologists have thought of an **experiment** as a systematic research study in which the investigator directly varies some factor (or factors), holds all other factors constant, and observes the results of the variation. The factors under the control of the experimenter are called independent variables, the factors being held constant are referred to as extraneous variables, and the behaviors measured are called dependent variables. Before we examine these concepts more closely, however, you should read Box 5.1, which describes the logical foundations of the experimental method in a set of rules proposed by the British philosopher John Stuart Mill in 1843.

Box 5.1

ORIGINS—John Stuart Mill and the Rules of Inductive Logic

John Stuart Mill (1805–1873) was England's preeminent nineteenth-century philosopher. Although he was known primarily as a political philosopher, much of his work has direct relevance for psychology. For example, his book on *The Subjection of Women* (1869) argued forcefully and well ahead of its time that women had abilities equal to those of men and ought to be treated equally with men. Of importance for our focus on methodology, in 1843 he published *A System of Logic, Ratiocinative and Inductive, Being a Connected View of the Principles of Evidence, and the Methods of Scientific Investigation* (in those days, they liked to pack all they could into a title!). In his *Logic*, Mill argued for the creation of a science of psychology (he called it "ethology") on the grounds that, while it might not reach the level of precision of physics, it could do just as well as other disciplines that were considered scientific at the time (meteorology was the example he used). He also laid out a set of methods that form the logical basis for what you will learn in this chapter and in the chapter on correlation. The methods were those of "Agreement" and "Difference" (relevant for this chapter), and of "Concomitant Variation" (relevant for correlation, covered in Chapter 9).

Taken together, the methods of Agreement and Difference enable us to conclude, with a high degree of confidence, that some outcome, Y, was caused by some factor, X. The Method of Agreement states that if X is regularly followed by Y, then X is *sufficient* for Y to occur, and could be a cause of Y. That is, "if X, then Y." The Method of Difference states that if Y does not occur when X does not occur, then X is *necessary* for Y to occur—"if not X, then not Y." Taken together (what Mill called the "Joint Method"), the methods of Agreement and Difference provide the necessary and sufficient conditions (i.e., the immediate cause) for the production of Y.

To make this more concrete, suppose we are trying to determine if watching violent TV causes a child to be aggressive. "Watching violent TV" is X, and "aggression" is Y. If we can determine that every time a child watches violent TV (X), the result is some act of aggression (Y), then we have satisfied the Method of Agreement, and we can say that watching violent TV is enough (sufficient) to produce aggression. If the child watches violent TV (X), then aggression (Y) occurs ("If X, then Y"). If we can also show that whenever violent TV is not watched (not X), the child is not aggressive (not Y), then we can say that watching violent TV is necessary in order for aggression to occur. This satisfies the Method of Difference. If the child does not watch violent TV, aggression does not occur ("If not X, then not Y"). This combined outcome (Joint Method) would establish that watching TV causes aggression in children.

It is important to note that in the real world of research, the conditions described in these methods are never fully met. That is, it will be impossible to identify and measure the outcome of every instance of every child watching TV. Rather, the best one can do is to observe systematically as many instances as possible, under controlled conditions, and then draw conclusions with a certain amount of confidence. That is precisely what research psychologists do and, as you recall from the Chapter 1 discussion of scientific thinking, the reason why researchers regard all knowledge based on science to be tentative, pending additional research. As findings are replicated, confidence in them increases.

As you work through this chapter, especially at the point where you learn about studies with experimental and control groups, you will see that an experimental group (e.g., some children shown violent TV shows) accomplishes Mill's Method

> of Agreement, while a control group (e.g., other children not shown violent films) accomplishes the Method of Difference. Studies with both experimental and control groups meet the conditions of Mill's Joint Method.

Establishing Independent Variables

Any experiment can be described as a study investigating the effect of X on Y. The "X" is Woodworth's **independent variable**: it is the factor of interest to the experimenter, the one that is being studied to see if it will influence behavior (the "watching violent TV" in the John Stuart Mill example). It is sometimes called a "manipulated" factor or variable because the experimenter has complete control over it and is creating the situations that research participants will encounter in the study. As you will see, the concept of an independent variable can also be stretched to cover what are called nonmanipulated or subject variables, but, for now, let us consider only those independent variables that are under the experimenter's total control.

Independent variables must have a minimum of two *levels*. That is, at the very least, an experiment involves a comparison between two situations (or *conditions*). For example, suppose a researcher is interested in the effects of marijuana dosage on reaction time. In such a study, there have to be at least two different dosage levels in order to make a comparison. This study would be described as an experiment with "amount of marijuana" as the independent variable and "dosage 1" and "dosage 2" as the two levels of the independent variable. You could also say that the study has two conditions in it—the two dosage levels. Of course, independent variables can have more than two levels. In fact, there are distinct advantages to adding levels beyond the minimum of two, as you will see in Chapter 7 on experimental design.

Experimental research can be either basic or applied in its goals, and it can be conducted either in the laboratory or in the field (refer back to Chapter 3 to review these distinctions). Experiments that take place in the field are sometimes called **field experiments**. The term **field research** is a broader term for any empirical research outside of the laboratory, including both experimental studies and studies using nonexperimental methods.

Varieties of Independent Variables

The range of factors that can be used as independent variables is limited only by the creative thinking of the researcher. However, independent variables that are manipulated in a study tend to fall into three somewhat overlapping categories: situational, task, and instructional variables.

Situational variables refer to different features in the environment that participants might encounter. For example, in a helping behavior study, the researcher interested in studying the effect of the number of bystanders on the chances of help being offered might create a situation in which participants encounter a person in need of help. Sometimes the participant is alone with the person needing aid; at other times the participant and the victim are accompanied by a group of either three or six bystanders. In this case, the situational independent variable would be the number of potential helpers on the scene besides the participant, and the levels would be zero, three, and six bystanders.

Sometimes experimenters vary the type of task performed by subjects. One way to manipulate **task variables** is to give groups of participants different kinds of problems to solve. For instance, research on the psychology of reasoning often involves giving people different kinds of logical problems to determine the kinds of errors people tend to make. Similarly, mazes can differ in the degree of complexity, different types of illusions could be presented in a perception study, and so on.

Instructional variables are manipulated by asking different groups to perform a particular task in different ways. For example, children in a memory task who are all shown the same list of words might be given different instructions about how to memorize the list. Some might be told to form visual images of the words, others might be told to form associations between adjacent pairs of words, and still others might be told simply to repeat each word three times as it is presented.

Of course, it is possible to combine several types of independent variables in a single study. A study of the effects of crowding, task difficulty, and motivation on problem-solving ability could have participants placed in either a large or a small room, thereby manipulating crowding through the situational variable of room size. Some participants in each type of room could be given difficult crossword puzzles to solve and others less difficult ones—a task variable. Finally, an instructional variable could manipulate motivation by telling participants that they will earn either $1 or $5 for completing the puzzles.

Control Groups

In some experiments, the independent variable is whether or not some experimental condition occurs. The levels of the independent variable in this case are essentially 1 and 0; some get the treatment condition and others don't. In a study of the effects of TV violence on children's aggressive behavior, for instance, some children might be shown a violent TV program, while others don't get to see it, or see a nonviolent TV show. The term **experimental group** is used as a label for the first situation, in which the treatment is present. Those in the second type of condition, in which treatment is withheld, are said to be in the **control group**. Ideally, the participants in a control group are identical to those in the experimental group in all ways except that the control group participants do not get the experimental treatment. As you recall from Box 5.1, the conditions of the experimental group satisfy Mill's Method of Agreement (if violent TV, then aggression) and the control group can satisfy the Method of Difference (if no violent TV, then no aggression). Thus, a simple experiment with an experimental and a control group is an example of what Mill called the "Joint Method." In essence, the control group provides a baseline measure against which the experimental group's behavior can be compared. Think of it this way: control group = comparison group.

Please don't think that control groups are necessary in all research, however. It is indeed important to *control* extraneous variables, as you are about to learn, but control *groups* occur only in research when it is important to have a comparison with some baseline level of performance. For example, suppose you were interested in the construct "sense of direction," and wanted to know whether a specific training program would help people avoid getting lost in new environments. In that study, a reasonable comparison would be between a training group and a control group that did not get any training. On the other hand, if your empirical question concerns sex differences in sense of direction, the comparison will be between a group of males and a group of females—neither would be considered a control group. You will learn about several specialized types of control groups in Chapter 7, the first of two chapters dealing with experimental design.

Research Example 4—Experimental and Control Groups

A good example of a study with a simple comparison between an experimental and a control group is an experiment completed in The Netherlands by Geraerts, Bernstein, Merckelbach, Linders, Raymaekers, and Loftus (2008). Using a method developed by Elizabeth Loftus (featured in this book's Epilogue), researchers created a false memory in students (or not, in the control group) and then examined the effects of this false memory on their subsequent eating behavior. Students at Maastricht University were randomly placed into either an experimental or a control group. All the students went through a sequence of three sessions. In session one, everyone completed the same food history inventory, which included the statement "got sick after eating egg salad" (p. 750). Session two was held a week later, and subjects received feedback about the inventory they had completed, supposedly from a sophisticated computer program that compiled a "profile of their early childhood experiences with certain foods" (p. 750). At this point the independent variable was manipulated—in the midst of a detailed description of their supposed childhood experiences with food, some participants were told that as children they had a bad experience with egg salad and had been sickened by it. Those in the control group were *not* told this. All participants then filled out a second inventory (in part to see if those in the experimental group had been influenced by the false feedback). After this, they were thanked for their participation, given a misleading debriefing, and then told that as a reward for their service, they could stay for some food and drink. There were several choices of drinks, and five different types of sandwiches, including egg salad—so what they chose to eat was the dependent variable. Subjects in the experimental group were less likely to choose the egg salad than those in the control group.

To see if the manipulation had any lasting effects, all the participants were contacted again four months later and asked to participate in another study. They were led to believe that this study was not connected in any way with the first one (but it was). Specifically, they were told the new experiment involved a taste test and an assessment of food preferences. Among the items they were asked to evaluate were five types of sandwiches, including, you guessed it, egg salad. Subjects who had been in the experimental group, especially those showing (in a separate measure) that they believed they had been made sick by egg salad in their childhood, avoided the egg salad sandwiches; those in the control group did not.

Controlling Extraneous Variables

The second feature of the experimental method is that the researcher tries to control what are called **extraneous variables.** These are any variables that are not of interest to the researcher but which might influence the behavior being studied if they are not controlled properly. As long as these are held constant, they present no danger to the study. In the opening session of the Geraerts et al. (2008) egg salad study, for instance, every participant filled out exactly the same food history inventory; when given choices among sandwiches, they were always shown the same five types of sandwich. If a researcher fails to control extraneous variables, they can influence the behavior being measured in some systematic way. The result is called confounding. A **confound** is any uncontrolled extraneous variable that "covaries" with the independent variable and could provide an alternative explanation of the results. That is, a confounding variable changes at the same time that an independent variable changes (i.e., they "covary") and, consequently, its effect cannot be separated from the effect of the independent variable. Hence, when a study has a confound, the results could be due to the effects of *either* the confounding variable or the independent variable, or some combination of the two, and there is no way to decide among these alternatives. Confounded studies are uninterpretable.

To illustrate some obvious confounding, consider a verbal learning experiment in which a researcher wants to show that students who try to learn a large amount of material all at once don't do as well as those who spread their learning over several sessions. That is, massed practice (e.g., cramming the night before an exam) is predicted to be inferior to distributed practice. Three groups of students are selected, and each group is given the same chapter in a general psychology text to learn. Participants in the first group are given three hours on Monday to study the material. Participants in the second group are given three hours on Monday and three hours on Tuesday, and those in the final group get three hours each on Monday, Tuesday, and Wednesday. On Friday, all the groups are tested on the material (see Table 5.1 for the design). The results show that Group 3 scores the highest, followed by Group 2. Group 1 does not do well at all, and the researcher concludes that distributed practice is superior to massed practice. Do you agree with this conclusion?

TABLE 5.1   *Confounding in a Hypothetical Distribution of Practice Experiment*

	Monday	Tuesday	Wednesday	Thursday	Friday
Group 1	3	—	—	—	Exam
Group 2	3	3	—	—	Exam
Group 3	3	3	3	—	Exam

Note: The 3s in each column equal the number of hours spent studying five chapters of a general psychology text.

You probably don't (I hope), because there are two serious confounds in this study, both easy to spot. The participants certainly differ in how their practice is distributed (1, 2, or 3 days), but they *also* differ in how much total practice they get during the week (3, 6, or 9 hours). This is a perfect example of a confound—it is impossible to tell if the results are due to one factor (distribution of practice) or the other (total practice hours); the two factors covary perfectly. The way to describe this situation is to say "distribution of practice is confounded with total study hours." The second confound is perhaps less obvious but is equally problematic. It concerns the retention interval. The test is on Friday for everyone, but different amounts of time have elapsed between study and test for each group. Perhaps Group 3 did the best because they studied the material most recently and forgot the least amount. In this experiment, distribution of practice is confounded both with total study hours and with retention interval. Each confound by itself could account for the results, and the factors may also have interacted with each other in some way to provide yet another interpretation.

Look at Table 5.2, which gives you a convenient way to identify confounds. In the first column are the levels of the independent variable and in the final column are the results. The middle columns are extraneous variables that should be held constant through the use of appropriate controls. If they are not kept constant, then confounding exists. As you can see for the distributed practice example, the results could be explained by the variation in any of the first three columns, either individually or in some combination. To correct the confound problem in this case, you need to ensure that the middle two columns are constant instead of variable.

A problem that students sometimes have with understanding confounds is that they tend to use the term whenever they spot something in a study that might not be quite right. For example, suppose the distribution of practice study included the statement that only females were used in the study. Some students reading the description might think there's a confound here—sex. What they really mean is they believe both males and females ought to be in the study and that might indeed be the case, but sex is *not* a confound in this example. Sex would be a confound only if males were used just in one condition and females were used in one other condition. Then any group differences in the results could be due to the independent variable or to sex.

TABLE 5.2   *Identifying Confounds*

Levels of IV Distribution of Practice	EV 1 Study Hours	EV 2 Retention Interval	DV Retention Test Performance
1 day	3 hours	3 days	Lousy
2 days	6 hours	2 days	Average
3 days	9 hours	1 day	Great

IV = independent variable.
EV = extraneous variable.
DV = dependent variable.

In the Applications exercises at the end of the chapter you will be identifying confounds. You might find the task easier if you fit the problems into the Table 5.2 format. Take a minute and redesign the distributed practice study. How would you eliminate the confounding from these extraneous variables?

Learning to be aware of potential confounding factors and building appropriate ways to control for them is one of the scientific thinking skills that is most difficult to develop. Not all confounds are as obvious as the massed/distributed practice example. We'll encounter the problem occasionally in the remaining chapters and address it again shortly in the context of a discussion of what is called the internal validity of a study.

Measuring Dependent Variables

The third part of any experiment is measuring some behavior that is presumably being influenced by the independent variable. The term **dependent variable** is used to describe those behaviors that are the measured outcomes of experiments. If, as mentioned earlier, an experiment can be described as the effect of X on Y and ''X'' is the independent variable, then ''Y'' is the dependent variable. In a study of the effects of TV violence on children's aggressiveness (the example from Box 5.1 on Mill's rules), the dependent variable would be some measure of aggressiveness. In the distribution of practice study, it would be a measure of exam performance.

The credibility of any experiment and its chances of discovering anything of value depend partly on the decisions made about what behaviors to measure as dependent variables. We've already seen that empirical questions cannot be answered unless the terms are defined with some precision. You might take a minute and review the section on operational definitions in Chapter 3. When an experiment is designed, one key component concerns the operational definitions for the behaviors to be measured as dependent variables. Unless the behaviors are defined precisely, replication is impossible.

Deciding on dependent variables can be tricky. A useful guide is to know the prior research and use already-established dependent measures, those that have been shown to be reliable and valid. Sometimes you have to develop a new measure, however, and when you do, a brief pilot study might help you avoid two major problems that can occur with poorly chosen dependent variables—ceiling and floor effects. A **ceiling effect** occurs when the average scores for the different groups in the study are so high that no difference can be determined. This happens when your dependent measure is so easy that everyone gets a high score. Conversely, a **floor effect** happens when all the scores are extremely low because the task is too difficult for everyone, once again producing a failure to find any differences between groups.

One final point about variables. It is important to realize that a particular construct could be an independent, an extraneous, *or* a dependent variable, depending on the research problem at hand. An experiment might manipulate a particular construct as an independent variable, try to control it as an extraneous factor, or measure it as a dependent variable. Consider the construct of anxiety, for instance. It could be a manipulated independent variable by telling participants (instructional independent variable) that they will be experiencing shocks that will be either moderate or painful when they make errors on a simulated driving task. Anxiety could also be a factor that needs to be held constant in some experiments. For instance, if you wanted to evaluate the effects of a public speaking workshop on the ability of students to deliver a brief speech, you wouldn't want to videotape the students in one group without taping those in the other group as well. If everyone is taped, then the level of anxiety created by that factor (taping) is held constant for everyone. Finally, anxiety could be a dependent variable in a study of the effects of different types of exams (e.g., multiple choice vs. essay) on the perceived test anxiety of students during final exam week. Some physiological measures of anxiety might be used in this case.

Anxiety could also be considered a personality characteristic, with some people having more of it than others. This last possibility leads to the next topic.

✓ Self Test 5.1

1. In a study of the effects of problem difficulty (easy or hard) and reward size ($1 or $5 for each solution) on an anagram problem-solving task, what are the independent and dependent variables?
2. What are extraneous variables and what happens if they are not controlled properly?
3. Explain how frustration could be an independent, extraneous, or dependent variable, depending on the study.

Manipulated versus Subject Variables

Up to this point, the term independent variable has meant some factor directly manipulated by the researcher. An experiment compares one condition created by and under the control of the experimenter with another. However, in many studies, comparisons are also made between groups of people who differ from each other in ways other than those designed by the researcher. These comparisons are made between factors that are referred to variously as ex post facto variables, natural group variables, nonmanipulated variables, participant variables, or **subject variables,** which is the term I will use. They refer to already existing characteristics of the individuals participating in the study, such as sex, age, socioeconomic class, cultural group, intelligence, physical or psychiatric disorder, and any personality attribute you can name. When using subject variables in a study, the researcher cannot manipulate them directly but must *select* people for the different conditions of the experiment by virtue of the characteristics they already have.

To illustrate the differences between manipulated and subject variables, consider a hypothetical study of the effects of anxiety on maze learning in humans. You could *manipulate* anxiety directly by creating a situation in which one group is made anxious (told they'll be performing in front of a large audience perhaps), while a second group is not (no audience). In that study, any person who volunteers could potentially wind up in one group or the other. To do the study using a *subject* variable, on the other hand, you would select two groups differing in their characteristic levels of anxiety and ask each to try the maze. The first group would be those who were people who tended to be anxious all the time (as determined ahead of time, perhaps, by a personality test for anxiety proneness). The second group would include more relaxed types of people. Notice the major difference between this situation and one involving a manipulated variable. With anxiety as a subject variable, volunteers coming into the study cannot be placed into either of the conditions (anxious-all-the-time-Fred cannot be put into the low-anxiety group), but must be in one group or the other, depending on attributes they *already possess* prior to entering the study.

Some researchers, true to Woodworth's original use of the term, prefer to reserve the term independent variable for those variables directly manipulated by the experimenter. Others are willing to include subject variables as examples of a particular type of independent variable on the grounds that the experimenter has some degree of control over them by virtue of the decisions involved in selecting them in the first place and that the statistical analyses will be the same in both cases. I take this latter position and will use the term independent variable in the broader sense. However, whether this term is used broadly (manipulated + subject) or narrowly (manipulated only) is not important, providing you understand the difference between a manipulated variable and a nonmanipulated or subject variable, both in terms of how the groups are formed in the study, and the kinds of conclusions that can be drawn from each type of study.

Research Example 5 — Using Subject Variables

One common type of research using subject variables examines differences from one culture to another. Ji, Peng, and Nisbett (2000) provide a nice example. In a series of studies involving various cognitive tasks, they looked at the implications of the differences between those raised in Asian cultures and those raised in Western cultures. In general, they pointed out that Asian Americans, especially those with families from China, Korea, and Japan, have a "relatively holistic orientation, emphasizing relationships and connectedness" (p. 943) among objects, rather than on the individual properties of the objects themselves. Those from Western cultures, especially those deriving from the Greek "analytic" tradition, are "prone to focus more exclusively on the object, searching for those attributes of the object that would help explain and control its behavior" (p. 943).

This cultural difference led Ji et al. (2000) to make several predictions, including one that produced a study with two separate subject variables—culture and sex. They chose a cognitive task that has a long history, the rod and frame test (RFT). While sitting in a darkened room, participants in an RFT study see an illuminated square frame projected on a screen in front of them, along with a separate illuminated straight line (rod) inside the frame. The frame can be oriented to various angles by the experimenter and the participant's task is to move a device that changes the orientation of the rod. The goal is to make the rod perfectly vertical, regardless of the frame's orientation. The classic finding (Witkin & Goodenough, 1977) is that some people (field independent) are quite able to bring the rod into a true vertical position, disregarding the distraction of the frame, while others (field dependent) adjust the rod with reference to the frame and not with reference to true vertical. Can you guess the hypothesis? The researchers predicted that those from Asian cultures would be more likely to be field dependent than those from Western cultures. They also hypothesized greater field dependence for females, a prediction based on a typical finding in RFT studies. So, in replication terms (refer back to Chapter 3), part of this study (sex) involved replication and part (culture) involved extension.

Because the undergraduate population of the University of Michigan (where the study was conducted) included a large number of people originally from East Asia, Ji et al. (2000) were able to complete their study using students enrolled in general psychology classes there (in a few pages you'll be learning about "subject pools"). They compared 56 European Americans with 42 East Asian Americans (most from China, Korea, and Japan) who had been living in the United States for an average of about 2.5 years. Students in the two cultural groups were matched in terms of SAT math scores, and there were about an equal number of males and females in each group.

As you can see from Figure 5.1, the results supported both hypotheses (greater error on the Y-axis indicated a greater degree of field dependence). The finding about females being more field dependent than males was replicated, and that difference occurred in both cultures. In addition, the main finding was the consistent difference between the cultures—those from East Asian cultures were more field dependent than the European Americans. As Ji et al. (2000) described the outcome, the relative field independence of the Americans reflected their tendency to be "more attentive to the object and its relation to the self than to the field" (p. 951), while the field dependent Asians tended to be "more attentive to the field and to the relationship between the object and the field" (p. 952). One statistical point worth noting relates to the concept of an *outlier*, introduced in Chapter 4. Each subject did the RFT task 16 times and, on average, 1.2 of the scores was omitted from the analysis because they were significantly beyond the normal range of scores. Their operational definition of outlier was somewhat technical, but related to the distance from the interquartile range, another concept you recall from Chapter 4.

Only a study using *manipulated* independent variables can be called an experiment in the strictest sense of the term; it is sometimes called a "true" experiment (which sounds a bit pretentious and carries the unfortunate implication that other studies are "false"). Studies using independent variables that are *subject* variables are occasionally called ex post facto studies, natural groups studies, or quasi experiments ("quasi" meaning "to some degree" here).[1] Sometimes (often, actually) studies will include both manipulated and subject independent variables, as you will learn in Chapter 8. Being aware of the presence of subject variables is important because they affect the kinds of conclusions that can be drawn from the study's results.

---

[1] The term quasi-experimental design is actually a broader designation referring to any type of design in which participants cannot be randomly assigned to the groups being studied (Cook & Campbell, 1979). These designs are often found in applied research and will be elaborated in Chapter 10.

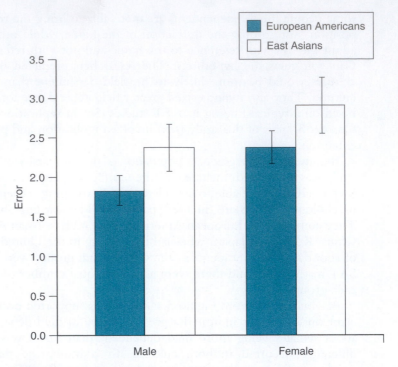

FIGURE 5.1   Sex and cultural differences in the rod and frame test,
from Ji, Peng, and Nisbett's (2000) cross-cultural study. Note the
vertical lines at the top of each bar; these are called "error bars,"
and they reflect the amount of variability around the mean.

Drawing Conclusions When Using Subject Variables

Put a little asterisk next to this section—it is extremely important. Recall from Chapter 1 that one of the goals of research in psychology is to discover explanations for behavior. That is, we wish to know what caused some behavior to occur. Simply put, with manipulated variables, conclusions about the causes of behavior can be made with some degree of confidence; with subject variables, causal conclusions cannot be drawn. The reason has to do with the amount of control held by the experimenter in each case.

With manipulated variables, the experiment can meet the criteria listed in Chapter 1 for demonstrating causality. The independent variable precedes the dependent variable, covaries with it, and, assuming that no confounds are present, can be considered the most reasonable explanation for the results. In other words, if you vary some factor and successfully hold all else constant, the results can be attributed *only* to the factor varied. In a confound-free experimental study with two groups, these groups will be essentially equal to each other (i.e., any differences will be random ones) in all ways except for the manipulated factor.

When using subject variables, however, the experimenter can also vary some factor (i.e., select participants having certain characteristics) but cannot hold all else constant. Selecting participants who are high or low on anxiety proneness does not guarantee that the two groups will be equivalent in other ways. In fact, they might be different from each other in several ways (in self-confidence, perhaps) that could influence the outcome of the study. When a difference between the groups occurs in this type of study, we cannot say that the differences were *caused* by the subject variable. In terms of the conditions for causality, although we can say that the independent variable precedes the dependent variable and covaries with it, we cannot eliminate alternative explanations for the relationship because certain extraneous factors cannot be controlled. When subject variables are present, all we can say is that the groups performed differently on the dependent measure.

An example from social psychology might help to clarify the distinction. Suppose you were interested in altruistic behavior and wanted to see how it was affected by the construct of "self-esteem." The study could be done in two ways. First, you could manipulate self-esteem directly by first giving participants a personality test. By providing different kinds of false feedback about the results of the test, both positive and negative, self-esteem could be raised or lowered temporarily. The participants could then be asked to do some volunteer work to see if those feeling good about themselves would be more likely to help.[2] A second way to do this study is to give participants a reliable and valid personality test for level of self-esteem and select those who score in the upper 25% and lower 25% on the measure as the participants for the two groups. Self-esteem in this case is a subject variable—half of the participants will be low self-esteem types, while the other half will be high self-esteem types. As in the first study, these two groups of people could be asked about volunteering.

In the first study, differences in volunteering can be traced *directly* to the self-esteem manipulation. If all other factors are properly controlled, the temporary feeling of increased or decreased self-esteem is the *only* thing that could have produced the differences in helping. In the second study, however, you cannot say that high self-esteem is the direct cause of the helping behavior; all you can say is that people with high self-esteem are more likely to help than those with low self-esteem. Your conclusion would then be limited to making educated guesses about the reasons why this might be true, because these participants may differ from each other in other ways unknown to you. For instance, high self-esteem types of people might have had prior experience in volunteering, and this experience might have had the joint effect of raising or strengthening their characteristic self-esteem and increasing the chances that they would volunteer in the future. Or they might

---

[2]Manipulating self-esteem raises ethical questions that were considered in a study described in Chapter 2 by Sullivan and Deiker (1973).

have greater expertise in the specific volunteering tasks (e.g., public speaking skills). As you will see in Chapter 9, this difficulty in interpreting research with subject variables is exactly the same problem encountered when trying to draw conclusions from correlational research.

Returning for a moment to the Ji, Peng, and Nibett (2000) study, which featured the subject variables of culture and gender, the authors were careful to avoid drawing conclusions about causality. The word "cause" never appears in their article, and the descriptions of results are always in the form "this group scored higher than this other group." In their words, "European Americans made fewer mistakes on the RFT than East Asians, . . . [and] men made fewer mistakes than women" (p. 950).

Before moving on to the discussion of the validity of experimental research, read Box 5.2. It identifies the variables in a classic study that you probably recall from your general psychology course—one of the so-called Bobo experiments that first investigated imitative aggression. Working through the example will help you apply your knowledge of independent, extraneous, and dependent variables, and will allow you to see how manipulated and subject variables are often encountered in the same study.

Box 5.2

CLASSIC STUDIES—Bobo Dolls and Aggression

Ask any student who has just completed a course in child, social, or personality psychology (perhaps even general psychology) to tell you about the Bobo doll studies. The response will be immediate recognition and a brief description along the lines of "Oh, yes, the studies showing that children will punch out an inflated doll if they see an adult doing it." A description of one of these studies is a good way to clarify further the differences between independent, extraneous, and dependent variables. The study was published by Albert Bandura and his colleagues in 1963 and is entitled "Imitation of Film-Mediated Aggressive Models" (Bandura, Ross, & Ross, 1963).

Establishing independent variables

The study included both manipulated and subject variables. The major manipulated variable was the type of experience that preceded the opportunity for aggression. There were four levels, including three experimental groups and a control group.

Experimental group 1: real-life aggression (children directly observed an adult model aggressing against the Bobo doll)

Experimental group 2: human-film aggression (children observed a film of an adult model aggressing against Bobo)

Experimental group 3: cartoon-film aggression (children observed a cartoon of "Herman the Cat" aggressing against a cartoon Bobo)

Control group: no exposure to aggressive models

The nonmanipulated independent variable (subject variable) was sex. Male and female children from the Stanford University Nursery School (mean age = 52 months) were the participants in the study. (Actually, there was also another manipulated variable; participants in groups 1 and 2 were exposed to either a same-sex or opposite-sex model.) The basic procedure of the experiment was to expose the children to some type of aggressive model (or not, for the control group), and then put them into a room full of toys (including Bobo), thereby giving them the opportunity to be aggressive themselves.

Controlling extraneous variables

Several possible confounds were avoided. First, in groups 1 and 2, the adults aggressed against a *5-foot* Bobo doll. When given a chance to pummel Bobo themselves, the children were put into a room with a *3-foot* Bobo doll. This kept the size relationship between person and doll approximately constant. Second, participants in all four groups were mildly frustrated before being given a chance to aggress. They were allowed to play for a few minutes with some very attractive toys and then were told by the experimenter that the toys were special and were being reserved for some other children. Thus, for *all* of the children, there was an approximately equivalent increase in their degree of emotional arousal just prior to the time when they were given the opportunity to be aggressive. Any differences in aggressiveness could be attributed to the imitative effects and not to any emotional differences between the groups.

Measuring dependent variables

Several different measures of aggression were used in this study. Aggressive responses were categorized as imitative, partially imitative, or nonimitative, depending on how closely they matched the model's behavior. For example, the operational definition of imitative aggressive behaviors included striking the doll with a wooden mallet, punching it in the nose, and kicking it. Partially imitative behaviors included hitting something else with the mallet and sitting on the doll but not hitting it. Nonimitative aggression included shooting darts from an available dart gun at targets other than Bobo and acting aggressively toward other objects in the room.

Briefly, the results of the study were that children in groups 1, 2, and 3 showed significantly more aggression than those in the control group, but the same amount of overall aggression occurred regardless of the type of modeling. Also, boys were more aggressive than girls in all conditions; some gender differences also occurred in the form of the aggression: girls "were more inclined than boys to sit on the Bobo

doll but [unlike the boys] refrained from punching it" (Bandura et al., 1963, p. 9).
Figure 5.2 summarizes the results.

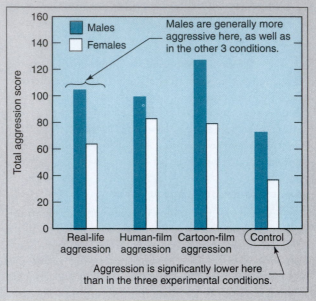

FIGURE 5.2   Data from Bandura, Ross, and Ross's Bobo study (1963) of the effects of imitation on aggression.

The Validity of Experimental Research

Chapter 4 introduced the concept of validity in the context of measurement. The term also applies to experiments as a whole. Just as a measure is valid if it measures what it is supposed to measure, psychological research is said to be valid if it provides the understanding about behavior that it is supposed to provide. This section of the chapter introduces four different types of validity, following the scheme first outlined by Cook and Campbell (1979) for research in field settings but applicable to any research in psychology. The four types of validity are statistical conclusion validity, construct validity (again), external validity, and internal validity.

Statistical Conclusion Validity

The previous chapter introduced you to the use of statistics in psychology. In particular, you learned about measurement scales, the distinction between descriptive and inferential statistics, and the basics of hypothesis testing. **Statistical**

conclusion validity concerns the extent to which the researcher uses statistics properly and draws the appropriate conclusions from the statistical analysis.

The statistical conclusion validity of a study can be reduced in several ways. First, researchers might do the wrong analysis or violate some of the assumptions required for performing a particular analysis. For instance, the data for a study might be measured using an ordinal scale, thereby requiring the use of a particular type of statistical procedure. The researcher, however, mistakenly uses an analysis that is appropriate only for interval or ratio data. Second, the researcher might selectively report some analyses that came out as predicted but might not report others (guess which ones?), a practice that most would consider fraudulent (see Chapter 2). The third example of a factor that reduces the statistical validity of a study concerns the reliability of the measures used. If the dependent measures are not reliable, there will be a great deal of error variability, which reduces the chances of finding a significant effect. If a true effect exits (i.e., H_0 should be rejected), but low reliability results in a failure to find that effect, the outcome would be a Type II error, thereby reducing the statistical conclusion validity.

The careful researcher decides on the statistical analysis at the same time that the experimental design is being planned. In fact, no experiment should ever be designed without giving thought to how the data will be analyzed.

Construct Validity

The previous chapter described construct validity in the context of measuring psychological constructs: It refers to whether a test truly measures some construct (e.g., self-efficacy, connectedness to nature). In experimental research, **construct validity** has a related meaning, referring to the adequacy of the operational definitions for *both* the independent and the dependent variables used in the study. In a study of the effects of TV violence on children's aggression, questions about construct validity could be (a) whether the programs chosen by the experimenter are the best choices to contrast violent with nonviolent television programming, and (b) whether the operational definitions and measures of aggression used are the best ones that could be chosen. If the study used violent cartoon characters (e.g., Elmer Fudd shooting at Bugs Bunny) compared to nonviolent characters (e.g., Winnie the Pooh), someone might argue that children's aggressive behavior is unaffected by fantasy; hence, a more *valid* manipulation of the independent variable, called "level of filmed violence," would involve showing children realistic films of people that varied in the amount of violence portrayed.

Similarly, someone might criticize the appropriateness of a measure of aggression used in a particular study. This, in fact, has been a problem in research on aggression. For rather obvious ethical reasons, you cannot design a study that results in subjects pounding each other into submission. Instead, aggression has been defined operationally in a variety of ways, some of which might seem to you to be more valid (e.g., angered participants led to believe they are delivering electric shocks to another person) than others (e.g., horn honking by frustrated drivers). As was true for the discussion of construct validity in the previous chapter when the emphasis was on measurement, the validity of the choices about exactly how to define independent and dependent variables develops over time as accumulated research fits into a coherent pattern.

External Validity

Experimental psychologists have been occasionally criticized for knowing a great deal about college sophomores and white rats and very little about anything else. This is, in essence, a criticism of **external validity,** the degree to which research findings generalize beyond the specific context of the experiment being conducted. For research to achieve the highest degree of external validity, it is argued, its results should generalize in three ways—to other populations, to other environments, and to other times.

Other Populations

The comment about rats and sophomores fits here. As we have seen in Chapter 2, part of the debate over the appropriateness of animal research has to do with how well this research provides explanations that are relevant for human behavior. Concerning sophomores, recall that Milgram deliberately avoided using college students, selecting adults from the general population as subjects for his obedience studies. The same cannot be said of most social psychologists, however. A survey by Sears (1986) of research in social psychology found that 75% of the research published in 1980 used undergraduates as participants. When Sears repeated the survey for research published in 1985, the number was 74%. And it is not just social psychologists whose studies feature a high percentage of college students—since it began publication in 1992, 86% of the empirical articles in the *Journal of Consumer Psychology* have used college student samples (Jaffe, 2005). Sears argued that the characteristics of college students as a population could very well bias the general conclusions about social phenomena. Compared to the general population, for instance, college students are more able cognitively, more self-centered, more susceptible to social influence, and more likely to change their attitudes on issues (Sears, 1986). To the extent that research investigates issues related to those features, results from students might not generalize to other groups, according to Sears. He suggested that researchers expand their databases and replicate important findings on a variety of populations. However, he also pointed out that many research areas (e.g., perception, cognition) produce outcomes relatively unaffected by the special characteristics of college students, and there is no question that students exist in large numbers and are readily available. One prominent memory researcher (Roediger, 2004) went as far as to argue that college students were the *ideal* subjects for his research—"[m]illions of years of evolution have designed a creature that is a learning and memorizing marvel. Students in my experiments have also been carefully selected through 12 or more years of education before they get to my lab. The world could not have arranged a more ideal subject" (p. 46). Some special ethical considerations apply when using college students, especially when recruiting them from introductory psychology courses. Box 5.3 outlines some guidelines for using a "subject pool" ethically.

Box 5.3

ETHICS—Recruiting Participants: Everyone's in the Pool

Most research psychologists are employed by colleges and universities and consequently find themselves surrounded by an available supply of participants for their research. Because students may not readily volunteer to participate in research, most university psychology departments establish what is called a **subject pool** or participant pool. The term refers to a group of students, typically those enrolled in introductory psychology classes, who are asked to participate in research as part of a course requirement. If you are a student at a large university, you have probably had this experience when you took introductory psychology. At a large university, if 800 students take general psychology each semester and each student signs up for three studies, that makes 2,400 participants available to researchers.

Subject pools are convenient for researchers, and they are defended on the grounds that research participation is part of the educational process (Kimmel, 2007). Ideally, students can acquire some insight into the research process by being in the middle of experiments and learning something about the psychological phenomena being investigated. To maintain the ''voluntary'' nature, students are given the opportunity to complete the requirement with alternatives other than direct research participation. Problems exist, however. A study by Sieber and Saks (1989), for example, found evidence that 89% of 366 departments surveyed had pools that failed to meet at least one of the APA's recommendations (below). Critics sometimes argue that the pools are not really voluntary, that alternative activities (e.g., writing papers) are often so onerous and time-consuming that students are effectively compelled to sign up for the research. On the other hand, a study by Trafimow, Madson, and Gwizdowski (2006) found that, when given a choice between research participation and a brief paper that was described as requiring exactly the same amount of effort as participation, most students opted for participation, and a substantial number (43.5% of those surveyed) indicated that participation in research while in general psychology had increased their interest in psychology.

Although there is potential for abuse, many psychology departments try to make the research experience educational for students. For example, during debriefing for a memory experiment, the participant/student could be told how the study relates to the information in the memory chapter of the text being used in the introductory course. Many departments also include creative alternative activities. These include having nonparticipating students (a) observe ongoing studies and record their observations, (b) participate in some community volunteer work, or (c) attend a research presentation by a visiting scholar and write a brief summary of it (Kimmel, 2007; McCord, 1991). Some studies have shown that students generally find research participation valuable, especially if researchers make an explicit attempt to tie the participation to the education occurring in the general psychology course (e.g., Landrum & Chastain, 1999; Leak, 1981).

The APA (1982, pp. 47–48) has provided some explicit guidelines about recruiting students as research participants, the main points being these:

- Students should be aware of the requirement before signing up for the course.
- Students should get a thorough description of the requirement on the first day of class, including a clear description of alternative activities if they opt not to serve as research subjects.
- Alternative activities must equal research participation in time and effort and, like participation, must have some educational value.
- All proposals for research using subject pools must have prior IRB approval.
- Special effort must be made to treat students courteously.
- There must be a clear and simple procedure for students to complain about mistreatment without their course grade being affected.
- All other aspects of the APA ethics code must be rigorously followed.
- The psychology department must have a mechanism in place to provide periodic review of pool policies.

The "college sophomore problem" is only one example of a concern over generalizing to other groups. Another has to do with gender. Some of psychology's most famous research has been limited by using only males (or, less frequently, only females), but drawing conclusions as if they apply to everyone. Perhaps the best-known example is Lawrence Kohlberg's research on children's moral development. Kohlberg (1964) asked adolescent boys (aged 10–16) to read and respond to brief accounts of various moral dilemmas. On the basis of the boys' responses, Kohlberg developed a six-stage theory of moral development that became a fixture in developmental psychology texts for years. At the most advanced stage, the person acts according to a set of universal principles based on preserving justice and individual rights.

Kohlberg's theory has been criticized on external validity grounds. For example, Gilligan (1982) argued that Kohlberg's model overlooked important gender differences in thinking patterns and in how moral decisions are made. Males may come to place the highest value on individual rights, but females tend to value the preservation of individual relationships. Hence, females responding to some of Kohlberg's moral dilemmas might not seem to be as morally "advanced" as males, but this is due to a biasing of the entire model because Kohlberg sampled only males, according to Gilligan.

Research psychologists also are careful about generalizing results from one culture to another. For example, "individualist" cultures are said to emphasize the unique person over the group, and personal responsibility and initiative are valued. On the other hand, the group is more important than the individual in "collectivist" cultures (Triandis, 1995). Hence, research conclusions based on just one culture might not be universally applicable. For example, Research Example 5 (above) found a cultural difference in field dependence. As another example, most children in the United States are taught to place great value on personal achievement. In Japan, on the other hand, children learn that if they stand out from the crowd, they might diminish the value of others in the group; individual achievement is not as valuable. One study found that personal achievement was associated with positive emotions for American students, but with *negative* emotions for Japanese students (Kitayama, Markus, Matsumoto, & Norasakkunkit, 1997). To conclude that feeling good about individual achievement is a universal human trait would be a mistake. Does this mean that all research in psychology should make cross-cultural comparisons? No. It just means that conclusions sometimes need to be drawn cautiously, and only with reference to the group studied in the research project.

Other Environments

Besides generalizing to other types of individuals, externally valid results are applicable to other stimulus settings. This problem is the basis for the occasional criticism of laboratory research mentioned in Chapter 3—it is sometimes said to be artificial and too far removed from real life. Recall from the discussion of basic and applied research (Chapter 3) that the laboratory researcher's response to criticisms about artificiality is to use Aronson's concept of experimental reality. The important thing is that people are involved in the study; mundane reality is secondary. In addition, laboratory researchers argue that some research is designed purely for theory testing and, as such, whether the results apply to real-life settings is less relevant than whether the results provide a good test of the theory (Mook, 1983).

Nonetheless, important developments in many areas of psychology have resulted from attempts to study psychological phenomena in real-life settings. A good example concerns the history of research on human memory. For much of the twentieth century, memory research occurred largely in the laboratory, where countless college sophomores memorized seemingly endless lists of words, nonsense syllables, strings of digits, and so on. The research created a comprehensive body of knowledge about basic memory processes that has value for the development of theories about memory and cognition, but whether principles discovered in the lab generalized to real-life memory situations was not clear. Change occurred in the 1970s, led by Cornell's Ulric Neisser. In *Cognition and Reality* (1976), he argued that the laboratory tradition in cognitive psychology, while producing important results, nonetheless had failed to yield enough useful information about information processing in real-world contexts. He called for more research concerning what he referred to as **ecological validity**—research with relevance for the everyday cognitive activities of people trying to adapt to their environment. Experimental psychologists, Neisser urged, "must make a greater effort to understand cognition as it occurs in the ordinary environment and in the context of natural purposeful activity. This would not mean an end to laboratory experiments, but a commitment to the study of variables that are ecologically important rather than those that are easily manageable" (p. 7).

Neisser's call to arms was embraced by many (but not all, of course) cognitive researchers, and the 1980s and 1990s saw increased study of such topics as eyewitness memory (e.g., Loftus, 1979) and the long-term recall of subjects learned in school, such as Spanish (e.g., Bahrick, 1984). Neisser himself completed an interesting analysis of the memory of John Dean (Neisser, 1981), the White House chief counsel who blew the whistle on President Richard Nixon's attempted cover-up of illegal activities in the Watergate scandal of the early 1970s. Dean's testimony before Congress precipitated the scandal and led to Nixon's resignation. Dean's 245-page account was so detailed that some reporters referred to him as a human tape recorder. As you might know, it was later revealed that the somewhat paranoid White House also tape-recorded the Oval Office meetings described by Dean. Comparing the tapes with Dean's testimony gave Neisser a perfect opportunity to evaluate Dean's supposedly photographic memory, which turned out to be not so photographic after all—he recalled the general topics of the meetings reasonably well but missed a lot of the details and was often confused about sequences of events. The important point for external validity is that Neisser's study is a good illustration of how our knowledge of memory can be enriched by studying phenomena outside of the normal laboratory environment.

Other Times

The third way in which external validity is sometimes questioned has to do with the longevity of results or the historical era during which a particular experiment was completed. A recent example is the study used to illustrate an ordinal scale in Chapter 4. Korn, Davis, and Davis (1991) found that department chairpersons ranked B. F. Skinner first on a list of top ten contemporary psychologists. But Skinner had died just the year before and his lifetime achievements were highly visible at the time. Replicating that study twenty years later might very well produce a different outcome. As an older example, some of the most famous experiments in the history of psychology are the conformity studies done by Solomon Asch in the 1950s (e.g., Asch, 1956). These experiments were completed during a historical period when conservative values were dominant in the United States, the "red menace" of the Soviet Union was a force to be concerned about, and conformity and obedience to authority were valued in American society. In that context, Asch found that college students were remarkably susceptible to conformity pressures. Would the same be true today? Would the factors that Asch found to influence conformity (e.g., group consensus) operate in the same way now? In general, research concerned with more fundamental processes (e.g., cognition) stands the test of time better than research involving social factors that may be embedded in some historical context.

A Note of Caution

Although external validity has value under many circumstances, it is important to point out that it is not often a major concern of a specific research project. Some (e.g., Mook, 1983) have even criticized the use of the term, because it carries the implication that research low in external "validity" is therefore "invalid." Yet there are many examples of research, completed in the laboratory under so-called artificial conditions, that have great value for the understanding of human behavior. Consider research on "false memory," for example (Roediger & McDermott, 1995). The typical laboratory strategy is to give people a list of words to memorize, including a number of words from the same category—"sleep," for instance. The list might include the words dream, bed, pillow, nap, and so on, but not the broader term sleep. When recalling the list, many people recall the word sleep and they are often confident that the word was on the list when they are given a recognition test. That is, a laboratory paradigm exists demonstrating that people can sometimes remember something with confidence that they did not experience. The phenomenon has relevance for eyewitness memory (jurors pay more attention to confident eyewitnesses, even if they are wrong), but the procedure is far removed from an eyewitness context. It might be judged by some to be low in external validity. Yet there is important research going on that explores the theoretical basis for false memory, determining, for instance, the limits of the phenomenon and exactly how it occurs (e.g., Goodwin, Meissner, & Ericsson, 2001). That research will eventually produce a body of knowledge that comprehensively explains the false memory phenomenon.

In summary, the external validity of some research finding increases as it applies to other people, places, and times. But must researchers design a study that includes many different groups of people, takes place in several settings, including "realistic" ones, and gets repeated every decade? Of course not. External validity is not determined by an individual research project—it develops over time as research is replicated in various contexts—and, as we have just seen, it is not always a relevant concern for research that is theory-based. Indeed, for the researcher designing a study, considerations of external validity pale compared to the importance of our next topic.

Internal Validity

The final type of experimental validity described by Cook and Campbell (1979) is called **internal validity**—the degree to which an experiment is methodologically sound and confound-free. In an internally valid study, the researcher feels confident that the results, as measured by the dependent variable, are directly associated with the independent variable and are not the result of some other, uncontrolled factor. In a study with confounding factors, as we've already seen in the massed/distributed practice example, the results will be uninterpretable. The outcome could be the result of the independent variable, the confounding variable(s), or some combination of both, and there is no clear way to decide between the different interpretations. Such a study would be quite low in internal validity.

✓ Self Test 5.2

1. Explain how "anxiety" could be both a manipulated variable and a subject variable.
2. In the famous "Bobo doll" study, what were the manipulated and the subject variables?
3. What is the basic difference between internal and external validity?
4. The study on the memory of John Dean was used to illustrate which form of validity?

Threats to Internal Validity

Any uncontrolled extraneous factor (i.e., the confounds you learned about earlier in the chapter) can reduce a study's internal validity, but there are a number of problems that require special notice (Cook & Campbell, 1979). These "threats" to internal validity are especially dangerous when control groups are absent, a problem that sometimes occurs in program evaluation research (Chapter 10). Many of these threats occur in studies that extend over a period of time during which several measures are taken. For example, participants might receive a pretest, an experimental treatment of some kind, and then a posttest, and maybe even a follow-up test. Ideally, the treatment should produce some positive effect that can be assessed by observing changes from the pretest to the posttest, changes that are maintained in the follow-up. A second general type of threat occurs when comparisons are made between groups that are said to be "nonequivalent." These so-called subject selection problems can interact with the other threats.

Studies Extending over a Period of Time

Do students learn general psychology better if the course is self-paced and computerized? If a college institutes a program to reduce test anxiety, can it be shown that it works? If you train people in various mnemonic strategies, will it improve their memories? These are all empirical questions that ask whether people will change over time as the result of some experience (a course, a program, memory training). To judge whether change occurred, one procedure is to evaluate people prior to the experience with what is known as a **pretest.** Then, after the experience, some **posttest** measure is taken. Please note that although I will be using pretests and posttests to illustrate several threats to internal validity, these threats can occur in any study extending over a period of time, whether or not pretests are used.

The ideal outcome for the examples I've just described is that, at the end of the time period for the study, people (a) know general psychology better than they did at the outset, (b) are less anxious in test taking than they were before, or

(c) show improvement in their memory. A typical research design includes pretests and posttesting, and compares experimental and control groups, with the latter not experiencing the treatment condition:

$$\text{Experimental:} \quad \text{pretest} \rightarrow \quad \textit{treatment} \rightarrow \quad \text{posttest}$$
$$\text{Control:} \quad \text{pretest} \quad\quad\quad \rightarrow \quad\quad \text{posttest}$$

If this type of procedure is run without a control group, there are several threats to internal validity. For example, suppose we are trying to evaluate the effectiveness of a college's program to help incoming students who suffer from test anxiety. That is, they have decent study skills and seem to know the material, but they are so anxious during exams that they don't perform well on them. During freshman orientation, first-year students fill out several questionnaires, including one that serves as a pretest for test anxiety. Let's assume that the scores can range from 20 to 100, with higher scores indicating greater anxiety. Some incoming students who score very high are asked to participate in the college's test anxiety program, which includes relaxation training, study skills training, and other techniques. Three months later these students are assessed again for test anxiety, and the results look like this:

pretest	**treatment**	**posttest**
90		70

Thus, the average pretest score of those selected for the program is 90, and the average posttest score is 70. Assuming that the difference is statistically significant, what would you conclude? Did the treatment program work? Was the change due to the treatment, or could other factors have been involved? I hope you can see that there are several ways of interpreting this outcome.

History and Maturation

Sometimes an event occurs between pre- and posttesting that produces large changes unrelated to the treatment program itself; when this happens, the study is confounded by the threat of **history.** For example, suppose the college in the above example decided that grades are counterproductive to learning and that all courses would henceforth be graded on a pass/fail basis. Furthermore, suppose this decision came after the pretest for test anxiety and in the middle of the treatment program for reducing anxiety. The posttest might show a huge drop in anxiety, but this result could very likely be due to the historical event of the college's change in grading policy rather than to the program. Wouldn't you be a little more relaxed about this research methods course if grades weren't an issue?

In a similar fashion, the program for test anxiety involves first-year students at the very start of their college careers, so pre–post changes could also be the result of a general **maturation** of these students as they become accustomed to college life. As you probably recall, the first semester of college was a time of real change in your life. Maturation, developmental changes that occur with the passage of time, is always a concern whenever a study extends over time.

Notice that if a control group is used, the experimenter can account for the effects of both history and maturation. These potential threats could be ruled out and the test anxiety program deemed effective if these results occurred:

Experimental:	**pretest**	*treatment*	**posttest**
	90		70
Control:	**pretest**		**posttest**
	90		90

On the other hand, either history or maturation or both would have to be considered as explanations for the changes in the experimental group if the control group scores also dropped to 70 on the posttest.

Regression

To regress is to go back, in this case in the direction of a mean score. Hence, the phenomenon I'm about to describe is sometimes called **regression to the mean.** In essence it refers to the fact that if score #1 is an extreme score, then score #2 will be closer to whatever the mean for the larger set of scores is. This is because, for a large set of scores, most will cluster around the mean and only a few will be far removed from the mean (i.e., extreme scores). Imagine you are selecting some score randomly from the normal distribution in Figure 5.3. Most of the scores center on the mean, so, if you make a random selection, you'll most likely choose a score near the mean (X on the left-hand graph of Figure 5.3). However, suppose you just happen to select one that is far removed from the mean (i.e., an extreme score—Y). If you then choose again, are you most likely to pick

a. the exact same extreme score again?

b. a score even more extreme than the first one?

c. a score less extreme (i.e., closer to the mean) than the first one?

My guess is that you've chosen alternative "c," which means that you understand the basic concept of regression to the mean. To take a more concrete example (refer to the right-hand graph of Figure 5.3), suppose you know that on the average (based on several hundred throws), Ted can throw a baseball 300 feet. Then he

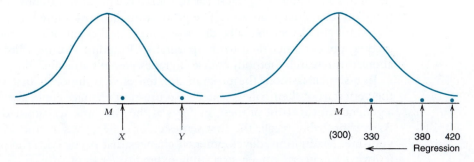

FIGURE 5.3   Regression to the mean.

throws one 380 feet. If you were betting on his *next* throw, where would you put your money?

a.   380 feet

b.   420 feet

c.   330 feet

Again, I imagine you've chosen "c," further convincing yourself that you get the idea of the regression phenomenon. But what does this have to do with our study about test anxiety?

In a number of pre-post studies, people are selected for some treatment because they've made an *extreme* score on the pretest. Thus, in the test anxiety study, participants were picked because on the pretest they scored very high for anxiety. On the posttest, their anxiety scores might improve (i.e., they will be lower than on the pretest), but the improvement could be a regression effect, at least in part, rather than the result of the memory improvement program. Once again, a control group of equivalent high-anxiety participants would enable the researcher to spot a possible regression effect. For instance, the following outcome would suggest that some regression might be involved,[3] but the program nonetheless had an effect over and above regression. Can you see why this is so?

Experimental:	**pretest**	*treatment*	**posttest**
	90		70
Control:	**pretest**		**posttest**
	90		80

Regression effects can cause a number of problems, and were probably the culprit in some early studies that erroneously questioned the effectiveness of the well-known Head Start program. That particular example will be taken up in Chapter 10 as an example of some of the problems involved in assessing large-scale, federally supported programs.

Testing and Instrumentation

Testing is considered to be a threat to internal validity when the mere fact of taking a pretest has an effect on posttest scores. There could be a practice effect of repeated testing, or some aspects of the pretest could sensitize participants to something about the program. For example, if the treatment program is a self-paced, computerized general psychology course, the pretest would be some test of knowledge. Participants might be sensitized by the pretest to topics about which they seem to know nothing; they could then pay more attention to those topics during the course and do better on the posttest as a result.

---

[3]Notice that the sentence reads, "might be involved," not "must be involved." This is because it is also possible that the control group's change from 90 to 80 could be due to one of the other threats. Regression would be suspected if these other threats could be ruled out.

Instrumentation is a problem when there are changes in the measurement instrument from pretest to posttest. In the self-paced general psychology course mentioned earlier, the pretest and posttest wouldn't be the same but would presumably be equivalent in level of difficulty. However, if the posttest happened to be easier, it would produce improvement that was more apparent than real. Instrumentation is sometimes a problem when the measurement tool involves observations. Those doing the observing might get better at it with practice, making the posttest instrument essentially different (more accurate in this case) from the pretest instrument.

Like the problems of history, maturation, and regression, the possible confounds of testing and instrumentation can be accounted for by including a control group. The only exception is that in the case of pretest sensitization, the experimental group might have a slight advantage over the control group on the posttest because the knowledge gained from the pretest might enable the experimental participants to focus on specific weaknesses during the treatment phase, whereas the control participants would be less likely to have that opportunity.

Participant Problems

Threats to internal validity can also arise from concerns over the individuals participating in the study. In particular, Cook and Campbell (1979) identified two problems.

Subject Selection Effects

One of the defining features of an experimental study with a manipulated independent variable is that participants in the different conditions are equivalent to each other in all ways except for the independent variable. In the next chapter you will learn how these equivalent groups are formed through random assignment or matching. If the groups are not equivalent, then **subject selection effects** might occur. For example, suppose two sections of a general psychology course are being offered and a researcher wants to compare a traditional lecture course with the one combining lecture and discussion groups. School policy (a) prevents the researcher from randomly assigning students to the two courses, and (b) requires full disclosure of the nature of the courses. Thus, students can sign up for either section. You can see the difficulty here. If students in the lecture plus discussion course outperform students in the straight lecture course, what caused the difference? Was it the nature of the course (the discussion element) or was it something about the students who *chose* that course? Maybe they were more articulate (hence, interested in discussion, and perhaps better students) than those in the straight lecture course. In short, there is a confound due to the selection of subjects for the two groups being compared.

Selection effects can also interact with other threats to internal validity. For example, in a study with two groups, some historical event might affect one group but not the other. This would be referred to as a history x selection confound (read as "history by selection"). Similarly, two groups might mature at different rates, respond to testing at different rates, be influenced by instrumentation in different ways, or show different degrees of regression.

One of psychology's most famous studies is (unfortunately) a good example of a subject selection effect. Known as the "ulcers in executive monkeys" study, it was a pioneering investigation by Joseph Brady in the area of health psychology. Brady investigated the relationship between stress and its physical consequences by placing pairs of rhesus monkeys in adjoining restraint chairs. One monkey, the "executive" (note the allusion to the stereotype of the hard-driving, stressed-out, responsible-for-everything business executive), could avoid mild shocks to its feet that were programmed to occur every twenty seconds by pressing a lever at any time during the interval. For the control monkey (stereotype of the worker with no control over anything), the lever didn't work and it was shocked every time the executive monkey let the twenty seconds go by and was shocked. Thus, both monkeys were shocked equally often, but only one monkey had the ability to control the shocks. The outcome was a stomach ulcer for the executive monkey, but none for the control monkey. Brady then replicated the experiment with a second pair of monkeys and found the same result. He eventually reported data on four pairs of animals (Brady, Porter, Conrad, & Mason, 1958), concluding that the psychological stress of being in command, not just of one's own fate but also of that of a subordinate, could lead to health problems (ulcers in this case).

The Brady study was widely reported in introductory psychology texts, and its publication in *Scientific American* (Brady, 1958) gave it an even broader audience. However, a close examination of Brady's procedure showed that a subject selection confound occurred. Specifically, Brady did not place the monkeys randomly in the two groups. Rather, all eight of them started out as executives in the sense that they were pretested on how quickly they would learn the avoidance conditioning procedure. Those learning most quickly were placed in the executive condition for the experiment proper. Although Brady didn't know it at the time, animals differ in their characteristic levels of emotionality and the more emotional ones respond most quickly to shock. Thus, he unwittingly placed highly emotional (and therefore ulcer-prone) animals in the executive condition and more laid-back animals in the control condition.

The first to point out the selection confound was Weiss (1968), whose better-controlled studies with rats produced results the *opposite* of Brady's. Weiss found that those with control over the shock, in fact, developed *fewer* ulcers than those with no control over the shocks.

Attrition

Participants do not always complete the experiment they begin. Some studies may last for a relatively long period of time, and people move away, lose interest, and even die. In some studies, participants may become uncomfortable and exercise their right to be released from further testing. Hence, for any number of reasons, there may be 100 participants at the start of the study and only 60 at the end. This problem sometimes is called subject mortality, or **attrition.** Attrition is a problem because, if particular types of people are more likely to drop out than others, then the group finishing the study is on average made up of different types of people than is the group that started the study. In essence, this produces a form of the subject selection problem because, in the final analysis, the group beginning the study is not equivalent to the group completing the study. Note that one way to test for differences between those continuing a study and those leaving it is to look at the pretest scores or other attributes at the outset of the study for both groups. If "attriters" and "continuers" are indistinguishable at the start of the study, then overall conclusions at the end of the study are strengthened, even with the loss through attrition.

✓ Self Test 5.3

1. Determined to get into graduate school, Jan takes the GRE nine times. In her first seven attempts, she always scored between 1050 and 1100, averaging 1075. On her eighth try, she gets a 1250. What do you expect her score to be like on her ninth try? Why?
2. How can attrition produce an effect that is similar to a subject selection effect?

This concludes our introduction to the experimental method. The next three chapters will elaborate—Chapter 6 begins by distinguishing between-subjects designs from within-subjects (or repeated measures) designs and describes a number of control problems in experimental research. In particular, it looks at the problems of creating equivalent groups in between-subjects designs, controlling for sequence effects in within-subjects designs, and the biasing effects that result from the fact that both experimenters and participants are humans. Chapters 7 and 8 look at a variety of research designs, ranging from those with a single independent variable (Chapter 7) to those with multiple independent variables, which are known as factorial designs (Chapter 8).

Chapter Summary

Essential Features of Experimental Research

An experiment in psychology involves establishing independent variables, controlling extraneous variables, and measuring dependent variables. Independent variables refer to the creation of experimental conditions or comparisons that are under the direct control of the researcher. Manipulated independent variables can involve placing participants in different situations, assigning them different tasks, or giving them different instructions. Extraneous variables are factors that are not of interest to the researcher, and failure to control them leads to a problem called confounding. When a confound exists, the results could be due to the independent variable or they could be due to the confounding variable. Dependent variables are the behaviors that are measured in the study; they must be defined precisely (operationally).

Manipulated versus Subject Variables

Some research in psychology compares groups of participants who differ from each other in some way before the experiment begins (e.g., gender, age, introversion). When this occurs, the independent variable of interest in the study is said to be selected by the experimenter rather than manipulated directly, and it is called a subject variable. Research in psychology frequently includes both manipulated and subject variables (e.g., Bandura's Bobo doll study). In a well-controlled study, conclusions about cause and effect can be drawn when manipulated variables are used but not when subject variables are used.

The Validity of Experimental Research

There are four ways in which psychological research can be considered valid. Valid research uses statistical analysis properly (statistical conclusion validity), defines independent and dependent variables meaningfully and precisely (construct validity), and is free of confounding variables (internal validity). External validity refers to whether the study's results generalize beyond the particular experiment just completed.

Threats to Internal Validity

The internal validity of an experiment can be threatened by a number of factors. History, maturation, regression, testing, and instrumentation are confounding factors especially likely to occur in poorly controlled studies that include comparisons between pretests and posttests. Selection problems can occur when comparisons are made between groups of individuals that are nonequivalent before the study begins (e.g., Brady's ulcers in executive monkeys study). Selection problems also can interact with the other threats to internal validity. In experiments extending over time, attrition can result in a type of selection problem—the small group remaining at the conclusion of the study could be systematically different from the larger group that started the study.

Chapter Review Questions

1. With anxiety as an example, illustrate the difference between independent variables that are (a) manipulated variables and (b) subject variables.

2. Distinguish between Mill's methods of Agreement and Difference, and apply them to a study with an experimental and a control group.

3. Use examples to show the differences between situational, task, and instructional independent variables.

4. What is a confound and why does the presence of one make it impossible to interpret the results of a study?

5. When a study uses subject variables, it is said that causal conclusions cannot be drawn. Why?

6. Describe the circumstances that could reduce the statistical conclusion validity of an experiment.

7. Describe the three types of circumstances in which external validity can be reduced.

8. Explain how the presence of a control group can help reduce the various threats to internal validity. Use history, maturation, or regression as specific examples.

9. Use the Brady study of "ulcers in executive monkeys" to illustrate selection effects.

10. What is attrition and why can it produce interpretation problems similar to subject selection problems?

Applications Exercises

Exercise 5.1   Identifying Variables

For each of the following, identify the independent variable(s), the levels of the independent variable(s), and the dependent variable(s). For independent variables, identify whether they are manipulated variables or nonmanipulated subject variables. For dependent variables, indicate the scale of measurement being used.

1. In a cognitive mapping study, first-year students are compared with seniors in their ability to point accurately to campus buildings. Some of the buildings are in the center of the campus along well-traveled routes; other buildings are on the periphery of the campus. Participants are asked to indicate (on a scale of 1 to 10) how confident they are about their pointing accuracy; the amount of error (in degrees) in their pointing is also recorded.

2. In a study of the effectiveness of a new drug in treating depression, some patients receive the drug while others only think they are receiving it. A third group is not treated at all. After the program is completed, participants complete the Beck Depression Inventory and are rated on depression (10-point scale) by trained observers.

3. In a Pavlovian conditioning study, hungry dogs (i.e., 12 hours without food) and not-so-hungry dogs (i.e., 6 hours without food) are conditioned to salivate to the sound of a tone by pairing the tone with food. For some animals, the tone is turned on and then off before the food is presented. For others, the tone remains on until the food is presented. For still others, the food precedes the tone. Experimenters record when salivation first begins and how much saliva accumulates for a fixed time interval.

4. In a study of developmental psycholinguistics, 2-, 3-, and 4-year-old children are shown dolls and asked to act out several scenes to determine if they can use certain grammatical rules. Sometimes each child is asked to act out a scene in

the active voice (Ernie hit Bert); at other times, each child acts out a scene in the passive voice (Ernie was hit by Bert). Children are judged by whether or not they act out the scene accurately (two possible scores) and by how quickly they begin acting out the scene.

5. In a study of maze learning, some rats are fed after reaching the end of the maze during the course of 30 trials; others aren't fed at all; still others are not fed for the first 15 trials but are fed for each of the 15 trials thereafter; a final group is fed for the first 15 trials and not fed for the last 15. The researcher makes note of any errors (wrong turns) made and how long it takes the animal to reach the goal.

6. In a helping behavior study, passersby in a mall are approached by a student who is either well dressed or shabbily dressed. The student asks for directions to either the public restroom or the Kmart. Nearby, an experimenter records whether or not people provide any help.

7. In a memory study, a researcher wishes to know how well people can recall the locations of items in an environment. Males and females are compared—each is shown a sheet of paper containing line drawings of 30 objects. They are then shown a second sheet in which some of the items have moved to a new location on the page and others have stayed in the same place. For half the subjects, the items on the sheet are stereotypically male-oriented (e.g., a football); the remaining subjects get stereotypically female-oriented items (e.g., a measuring cup).

8. In a study of cell phone use and driving, some participants try to perform as accurately as they can in a driving simulator (i.e., keep the car on a narrow road) while talking on a hand-held cell phone, others while talking on a hands-free phone, and yet others without talking on a phone at all. Half the subjects have two years of driving experience and the remaining subjects have four years of driving experience.

Exercise 5.2   Spot the Confound(s)

For each of the following, identify the independent and dependent variables, the levels of each independent variable, and find at least one extraneous variable that has not been adequately controlled (i.e., that is creating a confound). Use the format illustrated in Table 5.2.

1. A testing company is trying to determine if a new type of driver (club 1) will drive a golf ball greater distances than three competing brands (clubs 2–4). Twenty male golf pros are recruited. Each golfer hits 50 balls with club 1, then 50 more with 2, then 50 with 3, then 50 with 4. To add realism, the experiment takes place over the first four holes of an actual golf course—the first set of fifty balls is hit from the first tee, the second fifty from the second tee, and so on. The first four holes are all 380–400 yards in length, and each is a par 4 hole.

2. A researcher is interested in the ability of schizophrenic patients to judge different time durations. It is hypothesized that loud noise will adversely affect

their judgments. Participants are tested two ways. In the "quiet" condition, some participants are tested in a small soundproof room that is used for hearing tests. Those in the "noisy" condition are tested in a nurse's office where a stereo is playing music at a constant (and loud) volume. Because of scheduling problems, locked-ward (i.e., slightly more dangerous) patients are available for testing *only* on Monday and open-ward (i.e., slightly less dangerous) patients are available for testing *only* on Thursday. Furthermore, hearing tests are scheduled for Thursdays, so the soundproof room is available only on Monday.

3. An experimenter is interested in whether memory can be improved if people use visual imagery. Participants (all females) are placed in one of two groups—some are trained in imagery techniques, and others are trained to use rote repetition. The imagery group is given a list of twenty concrete nouns (for which it is easier to form images than abstract nouns) to study, and the other group is given twenty abstract words (ones that are especially easy to pronounce, so repetition will be easy), matched with the concrete words for frequency of general usage. To match the method of presentation with the method of study, participants in the imagery group are shown the words visually (on a computer screen). To control for any "compu-phobia," rote participants also sit at the computer terminal, but the computer is programmed to read the lists to them. After the word lists have been presented, participants have a minute to recall as many words as they can in any order that occurs to them.

4. A social psychologist is interested in helping behavior and happens to know two male graduate students who would be happy to assist. The first (Ned) is generally well dressed, but the second (Ted) doesn't care much about appearances. An experiment is designed in which passersby in a mall will be approached by a student who is either well-dressed Ned or shabbily-dressed Ted. All of the testing sessions occur between 8 and 9 o'clock in the evening, with Ned working on Monday and Ted working on Friday. The student will approach a shopper and ask for a quarter for a cup of coffee. Nearby, the experimenter will record whether or not people give money.

Exercise 5.3   Operational Definitions (Again)

In Chapter 3, you first learned about operational definitions and completed an exercise on the operational definitions of some familiar constructs used in psychological research. In this exercise, you are to play the role of an experimenter designing a study. For each of the four hypotheses:

a. identify the independent variable(s), decide how many levels of the independent variable(s) you would like to use, and identify the levels;

b. identify the dependent variable in each study (there will just be one dependent variable per item); and

b. create operational definitions for your independent and dependent variables.

1. People will be more likely to offer help to someone in need if the situation unambiguously calls for help.

2. Ability to concentrate on a task deteriorates when people feel crowded.

3. Good bowlers improve their performance in the presence of an audience, whereas average bowlers do worse when an audience is watching.

4. Animals learn a difficult maze best when they are moderately aroused. They do poorly in difficult mazes when their arousal is high or low. When the maze is easy, performance improves steadily from low to moderate to high arousal.

5. Caffeine improves memory, but only for older people.

6. In a bratwurst eating contest, those scoring high on a "sensation-seeking" scale will consume more, and this is especially true for fans of the Pittsburgh Steelers, compared with Baltimore Ravens fans.

Answers to Self Tests:

✓ **5.1.**

1. IVs = problem difficulty and reward size
    DV = number of anagrams solved

2. Extraneous variables are all of the factors that need to be controlled or kept constant from one group to another in an experiment; failure to control these variables results in a confound.

3. Frustration could be manipulated as an IV by having two groups, one allowed to complete a maze, and the other prevented from doing so. It could also be an extraneous variable being controlled in a study in which frustration was avoided completely. It could also be what is measured in a study that looked to see if self-reported frustration levels differed for those given impossible problems to solve, whereas others are given solvable problems.

✓ **5.2.**

1. As a manipulated variable, some people in a study could be made anxious ("you will be shocked if you make errors"), and others not; as a subject variable, people who are generally anxious would be in one group, and low anxious people would be in a second group.

2. Manipulated → the viewing experience shown to children.
    Subject → sex.

3. Internal → the study is free from methodological flaws, especially confounds.
    External → results generally beyond the confines of the study.

4. Ecological.

✓ **5.3.**

1. Somewhere around 1075 to 1100; regression to the mean.

2. If those who drop out are systematically different from those who stay, then the group of subjects who started the study will be quite different from those who finished.

CHAPTER 6

Control Problems in Experimental Research

Preview & Chapter Objectives

In Chapter 5 you learned the essentials of the experimental method—manipulating an independent variable, controlling everything else, and measuring the dependent variable. In this chapter we will begin by examining two general types of experimental design, one in which different groups of participants contribute data for different levels of the independent variable (between-subjects design) and one in which the same participants contribute data to all the levels of the independent variable (within-subjects design). As you are about to learn, there are special advantages associated with each approach, but there are also problems that have to be carefully controlled—the problem of equivalent groups for between-subjects designs, and problems of sequence for within-subjects designs. The last third of the chapter addresses the issue of bias and the ways of controlling it. When you finish this chapter, you should be able to:

- Discriminate between-subjects designs from within-subjects designs.
- Understand how random assignment can solve the equivalent groups problem in between-subjects designs.
- Understand when matching should be used instead of random assignment when attempting to create equivalent groups.
- Distinguish between progressive and carryover effects in within-subjects designs, and understand why counterbalancing normally works better with the former than with the latter.
- Describe the various forms of counterbalancing for situations in which participants are tested once per condition and more than once per condition.
- Describe the specific types of between- and within-subjects designs that occur in research in developmental psychology, and understand the problems associated with each.
- Describe how experimenter bias can occur and how it can be controlled.
- Describe how participant bias can occur and how it can be controlled.

In his landmark experimental psychology text, just after introducing his now famous distinction between independent and dependent variables, R. S. Woodworth emphasized the importance of *control* in experimental research. As Woodworth (1938) put it, "[w]hether one or more independent variables are used, it remains essential that all other conditions be constant. Otherwise you cannot connect the effect observed with any definite cause. The psychologist must expect to encounter difficulties in meeting this requirement." (p. 3). Some of these difficulties we have already seen. The general problem of confounding and the specific threats to internal validity, discussed in the previous chapter, are basically problems of controlling extraneous factors. In this chapter, we'll look at some other aspects of maintaining control: the problem of creating equivalent groups in experiments involving separate groups of subjects, the problem of sequence effects in experiments in which subjects are tested several times, and problems resulting from biases held by both experimenters and research participants.

Recall that any independent variable must have a minimum of two levels. At the very least, an experiment will compare condition A with condition B. Those who participate in the study might be placed in level A, level B, or both. If they receive either A *or* B but not both, the design is a **between-subjects design**, so named because the comparison of conditions A and B will be a contrast *between* two different groups of individuals. On the other hand, if each participant receives both levels A *and* B, you could say that both levels exist *within* each individual; hence, this design is called a **within-subjects design** (or, sometimes, a **repeated-measures design**). Let's examine each approach.

Between-Subjects Designs

Between-subjects designs are sometimes used because they must be used. If the independent variable is a subject variable, for instance, there is usually no choice. A study comparing introverts with extroverts requires two different groups of people, some shy, some outgoing. Unless the researcher could round up some multiple personalities, introverted in one personality and extroverted in another, there is no alternative but to compare two different groups. One of the few times a subject variable won't be a between-subject variable is when behaviors occurring at two different ages are being compared, and the same persons are studied at two different times in their lives (longitudinal design). Another possibility is when marital status is the subject variable, and the same people are studied before and after a marriage or a divorce. In the vast majority of cases, however, using a subject variable means that a between-subjects design will be used.

Using a between-subjects design is also unavoidable in some studies that use certain types of manipulated independent variables. That is, it is sometimes the case that when people participate in one level of an independent variable, the experience gained there will make it impossible for them to participate in other levels. This often happens in social psychological research and most research involving deception. Consider an experiment on the effects of the physical attractiveness of a defendant on recommended sentence length by Sigall and Ostrove (1975). They gave college students descriptions of a crime and asked them to recommend a jail sentence for the woman convicted of it. There were two separate between-subjects manipulated independent variables. One was the type of crime—either a burglary in which "Barbara Helm" broke into a neighbor's apartment and stole $2,200 (a fair amount of money in 1975), or a swindle in which Barbara "ingratiated herself to a middle-aged bachelor and induced him to invest $2,200 in a nonexistent corporation" (p. 412). The other manipulated variable was Barbara's attractiveness. Some participants saw a photo of her in which she was very attractive, others saw a photo of an unattractive Barbara (the same woman posed for both photos), and a control group did not see any photo. The interesting result was that when the crime was burglary, attractiveness paid. Attractive Barbara got a *lighter* sentence on average (2.8 years) than unattractive (5.2) or control (5.1) Barbara. However, the opposite happened when the crime was swindling. Apparently thinking that Barbara was using her good looks to commit the crime, participants gave attractive Barbara a harsher sentence (5.5 years) than they gave the unattractive (4.4) or control (4.4) Barbara.

You can see why it was necessary to run this study with between-subjects variables. For those participating in the Attractive-Barbara-Swindle condition, for example, the experience would certainly affect them and make it impossible for them to "start fresh" in, say, the Unattractive-Barbara-Burglary condition. In some studies, participating in one condition makes it impossible for the same person to be in a second condition. Sometimes, it is essential that each condition include uninformed participants.

While the advantage of a between-subjects design is that each subject enters the study fresh, and naive with respect to the procedures to be tested, the prime disadvantage is that large numbers of people may need to be recruited, tested, and debriefed during the course of the experiment. Hence, the researcher invests a great deal of energy in this type of design. For instance, my doctoral dissertation on memory involved five different experiments requiring between-subjects factors; more than 600 students trudged in and out of my lab before the project was finished!

Another disadvantage of between-subjects designs is that differences between the conditions could be due to the independent variables, but they might also be due to differences between the two groups. Perhaps the subjects in one group are smarter than those in the other group. To deal with this potential confound, deliberate steps must be taken to create what are called **equivalent groups**. These groups are equal to each other in every important way except for the levels of the independent variable. The number of equivalent groups in a between-subjects study corresponds exactly to the number of different conditions in the study, with one group of participants tested in each condition.

The Problem of Creating Equivalent Groups

There are two common techniques for creating equivalent groups in a between-subjects experiment. One approach is to use random assignment. A second strategy is to use matching, followed by random assignment.

Random Assignment

First, be sure you understand that random assignment and random selection are not the same. Random selection, to be described in Chapter 12, is a procedure for getting volunteers to come into your study. As you will learn, it is a process designed to produce a sample of individuals that reflects the broader population, and it is a common strategy in research using surveys. Random assignment, on the other hand, is a method for placing participants, once selected for a study, into the different groups. When **random assignment** is used, every person volunteering for the study has an equal chance of being placed in any of the groups being formed.

The goal of random assignment is to take individual difference factors that could influence the study and spread them evenly throughout the different groups. For instance, suppose you're comparing two presentation rates in a simple memory study. Further suppose that anxious participants don't do as well on your memory task as nonanxious participants, but you as the researcher are unaware of that fact. Some subjects are shown a word list at a rate of 2 seconds per word; others at 4 seconds per word. The prediction is that recall will be better for the 4-second group. Here are some hypothetical data that such a study might produce. Each number refers to the number of words recalled out of a list of 30. After each subject number, I've placed an "A" or an "R" in parentheses as a way of telling you which participants are anxious (A) and which are relaxed (R). Data for the anxious people are shaded.

Participant	2-Second Rate	Participant	4-Second Rate
S1(R)	16	S9 (R)	23
S2(R)	15	S10 (R)	19
S3(R)	16	S11 (R)	19
S4(R)	18	S12 (R)	20
S5(R)	20	S13 (R)	25
S6(A)	10	S14 (A)	16
S7(A)	12	S15 (A)	14
S8(A)	13	S16 (A)	16
M	15.00	M	19.00
SD	3.25	SD	3.70

If you look carefully at these data, you'll see that the three anxious participants in each group did worse than their five relaxed peers. Because there are an equal number of anxious participants in each group, however, the dampening effect of anxiety on recall is about the same for both groups. Thus, the main comparison of interest, the difference in presentation rates, is preserved—an average of 15 words for the 2-second group and 19 for the 4-second group.

Random assignment won't guarantee placing an equal number of anxious participants in each group, but in general the procedure has the effect of spreading potential confounds evenly among the different groups. This is especially true when large numbers of individuals are being assigned to each group. In fact, the greater the number of subjects involved, the greater the chance that random assignment will work to create equivalent groups of them. If groups are equivalent and if all else is adequately controlled, then you are in that enviable position of being able to say that your independent variable was responsible if you find differences between your groups.

You might think the actual process of random assignment would be fairly simple—just use a table of random numbers to assign each arriving participant to a group or, in the case of a two-group study, flip a coin. Unfortunately, however, the result of such a procedure is that your groups will almost certainly contain different numbers of people. In the worst-case scenario, imagine you are doing a study using 20 participants divided into two groups of 10. You decide to flip a coin as each volunteer arrives: heads, they're in group A; tails, group B. But what if the coin comes up heads all 20 times? Unlikely, but possible.

To complete a random assignment of participants to conditions in a way that guarantees an equal number of participants per group, a researcher can use **block randomization**, a procedure ensuring that each condition of the study has a participant randomly assigned to it before any condition is repeated a second time. Each "block" contains all of the conditions of the study in a randomized order. This can be done by hand, using a table of random numbers, but in actual practice researchers typically rely on a simple computer program to generate a sequence of conditions meeting the requirements of block randomization—you can find one at www.randomizer.org/.

One final point about random assignment is that the process is normally associated with laboratory research. In that environment, there is a high degree of control and it is not difficult to ensure that each person signing up for the study has an equal chance of being assigned to any of the conditions. Although it occurs less frequently, random assignment is also possible in some forms of field research as well. For example, some universities use a random assignment procedure to assign roommates, thereby providing an opportunity to examine systematically a number of factors affecting college students. For example, a study by Shook and Fazio (2008) examined the so-called "contact hypothesis," the idea that racial prejudice can be reduced when members of different races are in frequent contact with each other (and other factors, such as equal status, are in play). They found a university where roommates were randomly assigned to each other and designed an experiment to compare two groups of white first-year students—those randomly assigned to another white student and those randomly assigned to an African-American student. Over the course of a fall quarter, the researchers examined whether the close proximity of having an other-race roommate would affect prejudice in a positive way. In line with the contact hypothesis, it did.

Matching

When only a small number of subjects are available for your experiment, random assignment can sometimes fail to create equivalent groups. The following example shows you how this might happen. Let's take the same study of the effect of presentation rate on memory, used earlier, and assume that the data you just examined reflect an outcome in which random assignment happened to work. That is, there was an exact balance of five relaxed and three anxious people in each group. However, it is *possible* that random assignment could place all six of the anxious participants in *one* of the groups. This is unlikely, but it could occur (just as it's remotely possible for a perfectly fair coin to come up heads 10 times in a row). If it did, this might happen:

Participant	2–Second Rate	Participant	4–Second Rate
S1(R)	15	S9 (R)	23
S2(R)	17	S10 (R)	20
S3(R)	16	S11 (A)	16
S4(R)	18	S12 (A)	14
S5(R)	20	S13 (A)	16
S6(R)	17	S14 (A)	16
S7(R)	18	S15 (A)	14
S8(R)	15	S16 (A)	17
M	**17.00**	**M**	**17.00**
SD	**1.69**	**SD**	**3.07**

This outcome, of course, is totally different from the first example. Instead of concluding that recall was better for a slower presentation rate (as in the earlier example), the researcher in this case could not reject the null hypothesis ($17 = 17$) and would wonder what happened. After all, participants were randomly assigned, and the researcher's prediction about better recall for a slower presentation rate certainly makes sense. So what went wrong?

What happened was that random assignment in this case inadvertently created two decidedly nonequivalent groups—one made up entirely of relaxed people and one mostly including anxious folks. A 4-second rate probably does produce better recall, but the true difference was wiped out in this study because the mean for the 2-second group was inflated by the relatively high scores of the relaxed participants and the 4-second group's mean was suppressed because of the anxiety effect. Another way of saying this is that the failure of random assignment to create equivalent groups probably led to a Type II error (presentation rate really does affect recall; this study just failed to find the effect). To repeat what was mentioned earlier, the chance of random assignment working to create equivalent groups increases as sample size increases.

Note that the exact same outcome just described could also occur if you failed to make any effort to create equivalent groups. For example, suppose you just tested people as they signed up for your study, starting with the 2-second/item condition and then finishing with the 4-second/item condition. If you did that, it is conceivable that anxious subjects would be slower to sign up than relaxed subjects, resulting in the second group being composed mostly of anxious subjects.

A second general strategy for deliberately trying to create equivalent groups is to use what is called a matching procedure. In **matching**, participants are grouped together on some trait such as anxiety level, and then distributed randomly to the different groups in the experiment. In the memory study, "anxiety level" would be called a **matching variable**. Individuals in the memory experiment would be given some reliable and valid measure of anxiety, those with similar scores would be paired together, and one person in each pair would be randomly placed in the group getting the 2-second rate and the other would be put into the group with the 4-second rate. As an illustration of exactly how to accomplish matching in our hypothetical two-group experiment on memory, with anxiety as a matching variable, you should work through the example in Table 6.1.

Matching sometimes is used when the number of participants is small, and random assignment is therefore risky and might not yield equivalent groups. In order to undertake matching, however, two important conditions must be met. First, you must have good reason to believe that the matching variable will have a predictable effect on the outcome of the study. That is, you must be confident that the matching variable is correlated with the dependent variable. This was the case in our hypothetical memory study—anxiety clearly reduced recall and was therefore correlated with recall. When there is a high correlation between the matching variable and the dependent variable, the statistical techniques for evaluating matched-groups designs are sensitive to differences between the groups. On the other hand, if matching is done when there is a low correlation between the matching variable and the dependent variable, the chances of finding a true difference between the groups decline. So it is important to be careful when picking matching variables.

TABLE 6.1   *How to Use a Matching Procedure*

In our hypothetical study on the effect of presentation rate on memory, suppose that the researcher believes that matching is needed. That is, the researcher thinks that anxiety might correlate with memory performance. While screening subjects for the experiment, then, the researcher gives potential subjects a reliable and valid test designed to measure someone's characteristic levels of anxiety. For the sake of illustration, assume that scores on this test range from 10 to 50, with higher scores indicating greater levels of typical anxiety felt by people. Thus, a matching procedure is chosen, in order to ensure that the two groups of subjects in the memory experiment are equivalent to each other in terms of typical anxiety levels.

Step 1. Get a score for each person on the matching variable. This will be their score on the anxiety test (ranging from 10 to 50). Suppose there will be ten subjects ("Ss") in the study, five per group. Here are their anxiety scores:

S1: 32   S6: 45
S2: 18   S7: 26
S3: 43   S8: 29
S4: 39   S9: 31
S5: 19   S10: 41

Step 2. Arrange the anxiety scores in ascending order:

S2: 18   S1: 32
S5: 19   S4: 39
S7: 26   S10: 41
S8: 29   S3: 43
S9: 31   S6: 45

Step 3. Create five pairs of scores, with each pair consisting of quantitatively adjacent anxiety scores.
Pair 1: 18 and 19
Pair 2: 26 and 29
Pair 3: 31 and 32
Pair 4: 39 and 41
Pair 5: 43 and 45

Step 4. For each pair, randomly assign one subject to group 1 (2 sec/item) and one to group 2 (4 sec/item). Here's one possible outcome

	2 Sec/item Group	4 Sec/item Group
	18	19
	29	26
	31	32
	39	41
	45	43
Mean anxiety	**32.4**	**32.2**

Now the study can proceed with some assurance that the two groups are equivalent (32.4 is virtually the same as 32.2) in terms of anxiety.

Note: If more than two groups are being tested in the experiment, the matching procedure is the same up to and including step 2. In step 3, instead of creating pairs of scores, the researcher creates clusters equal to the number of groups needed. Then in step 4, the subjects in each cluster are randomly assigned to the multiple groups.

A second important condition for matching is that there must be some reasonable way of measuring or identifying participants on the matching variable. In some studies, participants must be tested on the matching variable first, then assigned to groups, and then put through the experimental procedure. Depending on the circumstances, this might require bringing participants into the lab on two separate occasions, which can create logistical problems. Also, the initial testing on the matching variable might give participants an indication of the study's purpose, thereby introducing bias into the study. The simplest matching situations occur when the matching variables are constructs that can be determined without directly testing the participants (e.g., Grade Point Average scores or IQ from school records), or by matching on the dependent variable itself. That is, in a memory study, participants could be given an initial memory test, then matched on their performance, and then assigned to 2-second and 4-second groups. Their preexisting memory ability would thereby be under control and the differences in performance could be attributed to the presentation rate.

One practical difficulty with matching concerns the number of matching variables to use. In a memory study, should I match the groups for anxiety level? What about intelligence level? What about education level? You can see that some judgment is required here, for matching is difficult to accomplish with more than one matching variable, and often results in having to eliminate participants because close matches sometimes cannot be made. The problem of deciding on and measuring matching variables is one reason why research psychologists generally prefer to make the effort to recruit enough volunteers to use random assignment, even when they might suspect that some extraneous variable correlates with the dependent variable. In memory research, for instance, researchers are seldom concerned about anxiety levels, intelligence, or education level. They simply make the groups large enough and assume that random assignment will distribute these potentially confounding factors evenly throughout the conditions of the study.

✓ Self Test 6.1

1. What is the defining feature of a between-subjects design? What is the main control problem that must be solved with this type of design?
2. Sal wishes to see if the type of font used when printing a document will influence comprehension of the material in the document. He thinks about matching on "verbal fluency." What two conditions must be in effect before this matching can occur?

Within-Subjects Designs

As mentioned at the start of this chapter, each participant is exposed to each level of the independent variable in a within-subjects design. Because everyone in this type of study is measured several times, you will sometimes see this procedure described as a repeated-measures design. One practical advantage of this design should be

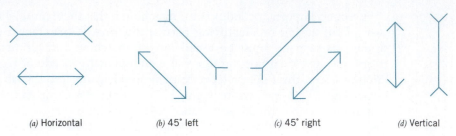

(a) Horizontal   *(b)* 45° left   *(c)* 45° right   *(d)* Vertical

FIGURE 6.1   Set of four Müller-Lyer illusions: horizontal, 45° left, 45° right, vertical.

obvious—fewer people need to be recruited. If you have a study comparing two conditions and you want to test 20 people in condition 1, you'll need to recruit 40 people for a between-subjects study, but only 20 for a within-subjects study.

Within-subjects designs are sometimes the only reasonable choice. In experiments in such areas as physiological psychology and sensation and perception, comparisons often are made between conditions that require just a brief amount of time to test but might demand extensive preparation. For example, a perceptual study using the Müller-Lyer illusion might vary the orientations of the lines to see if the illusion is especially strong when presented vertically (see Figure 6.1). The task might involve showing the illusion on a computer screen and asking the participant to tap a key that gradually changes the length of one of the lines. Participants are told to adjust the line until both lines are perceived to be the same length. Any one trial might take no more than five seconds, so it would be absurd to make the "illusion orientation" variable a between-subjects factor and use someone for a fraction of a minute. Instead, it makes more sense to make the orientation variable a within-subjects factor and give each participant a sequence of trials to cover all levels of the variable (and probably duplicate each level several times). And unlike the attractive/unattractive Barbara Helm study, serving in one condition would not make it impossible to serve in another.

One of psychology's oldest areas of research is in **psychophysics**, the study of sensory thresholds (e.g., a modern application is a hearing test). In a typical psychophysics study, subjects are asked to judge whether or not they can detect some stimulus or whether two stimuli are equal or different. Each situation requires a large number of trials and comparisons to be made within the same individual. Hence, psychophysics studies typically use just a few participants and measure them repeatedly. Research Example 6, which you will soon encounter, uses this strategy.

A within-subjects design might also be necessary when volunteers are scarce because the entire population of interest is small. Studying astronauts or people with special expertise (e.g., world-class chess players, to use an example you will see shortly) are just two examples. Of course, there are times when, even with a limited population, the design may require a between-subjects manipulation. Evaluating the effects of a new form of therapy for those suffering from a rare form of psychopathology requires comparing those in therapy with others in a control group not being treated.

Besides convenience, another advantage of within-subjects designs is that they eliminate the equivalent groups problem that occurs with between-subjects designs. Recall from Chapter 4 that an inferential statistical analysis comparing two groups examines the variability between experimental conditions with the variability within each condition. Variability between conditions could be due to (a) the independent variable, (b) other systematic variance resulting from confounding, and/or (c) nonsystematic error variance. Even with random assignment, a substantial portion of the error variance in a between-subjects design can result from individual differences between subjects in the different groups. But in a within-subjects design, any between-condition individual difference variance disappears. Let's look at a concrete example.

Suppose you are comparing two golf balls for distance. You recruit 10 professional golfers and randomly assign them to two groups of 5. After loosening up, each golfer hits one ball or the other. Here are the results:

Pros in the First Group	Golf Ball 1	Pros in the Second Group	Golf Ball 2
Pro 1	255	Pro 6	269
Pro 2	261	Pro 7	266
Pro 3	248	Pro 8	260
Pro 4	256	Pro 9	273
Pro 5	245	Pro 10	257
M	253.00	M	265.00
SD	6.44	SD	6.52

There are several things to note here. First, there is some variability within each group, as reflected in the standard deviation for each group. This is error variance due to individual differences within each group and to other random factors. Second, there is apparently an overall difference between the groups. The pros in the second group hit their ball farther than the pros in the first group. Why? Three possibilities:

a. Chance; perhaps this is not a statistically significant difference, and even if it is, there's a 5% chance that it is a Type I error if the null hypothesis (i.e., no real difference) is actually true.

b. The golf ball; perhaps the brand of golf ball hit by the second group simply goes farther (this, of course, is the research hypothesis).

c. Individual differences; maybe the golfers in the second group are stronger or more skilled than those in the first group.

The chances that the third possibility is a major problem are reduced by the procedures for creating equivalent groups described earlier. Using random assignment or matching allows you to be reasonably sure that the second group of golfers is approximately equal to the first group in ability, strength, and so on. Despite that, however, it is still possible that *some* of the difference between these groups can be traced back to the individual differences between the two groups. This problem simply does not occur in a within-subjects design, however. Suppose you repeated the study but used just the first five golfers, and each pro hit ball 1, and then ball 2. Now the table looks like this:

Pros in the First Group	Golf Ball 1	Golf Ball 2
Pro 1	255	269
Pro 2	261	266
Pro 3	248	260
Pro 4	256	273
Pro 5	245	257
M	253.00	265.00
SD	6.44	6.52

Of the three possible explanations for the differences in the first set of data, when there were two groups, explanation c can be eliminated for the second set. In the first set, the difference in the first row between the 255 and the 269 could be due to chance, the difference between the balls, or individual differences between pros 1 and 6, 2 and 7, and so on. In the second set, there is no second group of golfers, so the third possibility is gone. Thus, in a within-subjects design, individual differences are eliminated from the estimate of the amount of variability between conditions. Statistically, this means that, in a within-subjects design, an inferential analysis will be more sensitive to small differences between means than will be the case for a between-subjects design.

But wait. Are you completely satisfied that in the second case, the differences between the first set of scores and the second set could be due *only* to (a) chance factors and/or (b) the superiority of the second ball? Are you thinking that perhaps pro 1 actually changed in some way between hitting ball 1 and hitting ball 2? Although it's unlikely that the golfer will add 10 pounds of muscle between swings, what if some kind of practice or warm-up effect was operating? Or perhaps the pro detected a slight malfunction in his swing at ball 1 and corrected it for ball 2. Or perhaps the wind changed. In short, with a within-subjects design, a major problem is that once a participant has completed the first part of a study, the experience or altered circumstances could influence performance in later parts of the study. The problem is referred to as a **sequence** or **order effect**, and it can operate in several ways.

First, trial 1 might affect the participant in some way so that performance on trial 2 is steadily improved, as in the example of a practice effect. On the other hand, sometimes repeated trials produce gradual fatigue or boredom, and performance steadily declines from trial to trial. These two effects can both be referred to as **progressive effects** because it is assumed that performance changes steadily (progressively) from trial to trial. Also, some particular sequences might produce effects that are different from those of other sequences, what could be called a **carryover effect**. Thus, in a study with two basic conditions, experiencing the first condition before the second might affect the person much differently than experiencing the second before the first. For example, suppose you were studying the effects of noise on a problem-solving task using a within-subjects design. Let's say that participants will be trying to solve anagram problems (rearrange letters to form words) under some time pressure. In condition UPN (UnPredictable Noise), they have to solve the anagrams while distracting noises come from the next room, and these noises are presented randomly and therefore are unpredictable. In condition PN (Predictable Noise), the same total amount of noise occurs; however, it is not randomly presented but instead occurs in predictable patterns. If you put the people in condition UPN first (unpredictable noise), and then in PN (predictable noise), they will probably do poorly in UPN (most people do). This poor performance might discourage them and carry over to condition PN. They should do better in PN, but as soon as the noise begins, they might say to themselves, "Here we go again," and perhaps not try as hard. On the other hand, if you run condition PN first, the predictable noise, your subjects might do reasonably well (most people do), and some of the confidence might carry over to the second part of the study—UPN. ("Here comes the noise again, but I handled it before, I can handle it again.") When they encounter condition UPN in the second part of the study, they might do better than you would ordinarily expect. Thus, performance in condition UPN might be much worse in the sequence UPN–PN than in the sequence PN–UPN. Furthermore, a similar problem would occur for condition PN. In short, the sequence in which the conditions are presented, independently of practice or fatigue effects, might influence the study's outcome. In studies where carryover effects might be suspected, therefore, researchers often decide to use a between-subjects rather than a within-subjects design. Indeed, studies comparing predictable and unpredictable noise typically put people in two different groups.

The Problem of Controlling Sequence Effects

The typical way to control sequence effects in a within-subjects design is to use more than one sequence, a strategy known as **counterbalancing**. As is clear from the predictable versus unpredictable noise example, the procedure works better for progressive effects than for carryover effects. There are two general categories of counterbalancing, depending on whether participants are tested in each experimental condition just one time or are tested more than once per condition.

Testing Once Per Condition

In some experiments, participants will be tested in each of the conditions but tested only once per condition. Consider, for example, an interesting study by Reynolds (1992) on the ability of chess players to recognize the level of expertise in other chess players. He recruited 15 chess players with different degrees of expertise from various clubs in New York City and asked them to look at six different chess games that were said to be in progress (i.e., about 20 moves into the game). On each trial, the players examined the board of an in-progress game (they were told to assume that the pair of players of each game were of equal ability) and estimated the skill level of the players according to a standard rating system. The games were deliberately set up to reflect different levels of player expertise. Reynolds found that the more highly skilled of the 15 chess players made more accurate estimates of the ability reflected in the board setups they examined than did the less skilled players.

You'll recognize the design of the Reynolds study as including a within-subjects variable. Each of the 15 participants examined all six games. Also, you can see that it made sense for each game to be evaluated just one time by each player. Hence, Reynolds was faced with the question of how to control for any sequence effects that might be present. He certainly didn't want all 15 participants to see the six games in exactly the same order. How might he have proceeded?

Complete Counterbalancing

Whenever participants are tested once per condition in a within-subjects design, one solution to the sequence problem is to use **complete counterbalancing**. This means that every possible sequence will be used at least once. The total number of sequences needed can be determined by calculating $X!$, where X is the number of conditions, and "!" stands for the mathematical calculation of a "factorial." For example, if a study has three conditions, there are six possible sequences that can be used:

$$3! = 3 \times 2 \times 1 = 6$$

The six sequences in a study with conditions A, B, and C would be:

A B C	B A C
A C B	C A B
B C A	C B A

The problem with complete counterbalancing is that as the number of levels of the independent variable increases, the possible sequences that will be needed increase dramatically. There are six sequences needed for three conditions, but simply adding a fourth condition creates a need for 24 sequences ($4 \times 3 \times 2 \times 1$). As you can guess, complete counterbalancing was not possible in Reynolds' study unless he recruited many more than 15 chess players. In fact, with six different games (i.e., conditions), he would need to find 6! or 720 players to cover all of the possible sequences. Clearly, Reynolds used a different strategy.

Partial Counterbalancing

Whenever a subset of the total number of sequences is used, the result is called **partial counterbalancing** or, sometimes, "incomplete" counterbalancing This was Reynolds's solution; he simply took a random sample of the 720 possible sequences by ensuring that "the order of presentation [was] randomized for each subject" (Reynolds, 1992, p. 411). Sampling from the population of sequences is a common strategy whenever there are fewer participants available than possible sequences or when there is a fairly large number of conditions. Furthermore, modern computers make this a common strategy—it is easy to program a random sequence of conditions.

Reynolds sampled from the total number of sequences, but he could have chosen another approach that is used sometimes—the balanced **Latin square**. This device gets its name from an ancient Roman puzzle about arranging Latin letters in a matrix so that each letter appears only once in each row and each column (Kirk, 1968). The Latin square strategy is more sophisticated than simply choosing a random subset of the whole. With a perfectly balanced Latin square, you are assured that (a) every condition of the study occurs equally often in every sequential position, and (b) every condition precedes and follows every other condition exactly once. Work through Table 6.2 to see how to construct the following 6 × 6 Latin square. Think of each letter as one of the six games inspected by Reynolds's chess players.

A	B	F	C	E	D
B	C	**A**	D	F	E
C	D	B	E	**A**	F
D	E	C	F	B	**A**
E	F	D	**A**	C	B
F	**A**	E	B	D	C

I've boldfaced condition **A** (representing chess game setup #1) to show you how the square meets the two requirements listed in the preceding paragraph. First, condition A occurs in each of the six sequential positions (first in the first row, third in the second row, etc.). Second, A is followed by each of the other letters exactly one time. From the top to the bottom rows, (1) A is followed by B, D, F, nothing, C, and E, and (2) A is preceded by nothing, C, E, B, D, and F. The same is true for each of the other letters.

When using Latin squares, it is necessary for the number of participants to be equal to or be a multiple of the number of rows in the square. The fact that Reynolds had 15 participants in his study tells you that he didn't use a Latin square. If he had added three more chess players, giving him an N of 18, he could have randomly assigned three players to each of the six rows of the square ($3 \times 6 = 18$).

Testing More Than Once per Condition

In the Reynolds study, it made no sense to ask the chess players to look at any of the six games more than once. Similarly, if participants in a memory experiment are asked to study and recall four lists of words, with the order of the lists determined by a 4 × 4 Latin square, they will seldom be asked to study and recall any particular list a second time unless the researcher is specifically interested in the effects of repeated trials on memory. However, in many studies it is reasonable, even necessary, for participants to experience each condition more than one time. This often happens in research in sensation and perception, for instance. A look back at Figure 6.1 provides an example.

TABLE 6.2   *Building a Balanced 6 × 6 Latin Square*

In a balanced Latin square, every condition of the study occurs equally often in every sequential position, and every condition precedes and follows every other condition exactly once. Here's how to build a 6 × 6 square.

Step 1. Build the first row. It is fixed according to this general rule:

$$\text{A B "X" C "X} - 1\text{" D "X} - 2\text{" E "X} - 3\text{" F, etc.}$$

where A refers to the first condition of the study and "X" refers to the letter symbolizing the final condition of the experiment. To build the 6 × 6 square, this first row would substitute:

$$X = \text{the sixth letter of the alphabet} \rightarrow F$$
$$X - 1 = \text{the fifth letter} \rightarrow E$$

Therefore, the first row would be

$$\text{A B } \mathbf{F} \text{ (subbing for "X") C } \mathbf{E} \text{ (subbing for "X} - 1\text{") D}$$

Step 2. Build the second row. Directly below each letter of row 1, place in row 2 the letter that is next in the alphabet. The only exception is the F. Under that letter, return to the first of the six letters and place the letter A. Thus:

A B F C E D
B C A D F E

Step 3. Build the remaining four rows following the step 2 rule. Thus, the final 6 × 6 square is:

A B F C E D
B C A D F E
C D B E A F
D E C F B A
E F D A C B
F A E B D C

Step 4. Take the six conditions of the study and randomly assign them to the letters. A through F to determine the actual sequence of conditions for each row. Assign an equal number of participants to each row.

Note. This procedure works whenever there is an even number of conditions. If the number of conditions is odd, two squares will be needed—one created using the above procedure, and a second an exact reversal of the square created with the above procedure. For more details, see Winer, Brown, and Michaels (1994).

Suppose you were conducting a study in which you wanted to see if participants would be more affected by the illusion when it was presented vertically than when shown horizontally or at a 45° angle. Four conditions of the study are assigned to the letters A, B, C, and D:

A = horizontal

B = 45° to the left

C = 45° to the right

D = vertical

Participants in the study are shown the illusion on a computer screen and have to make adjustments to the lengths of the parallel lines until they perceive that the lines are equal. The four conditions could be presented multiple times to people according to one of two basic procedures.

Reverse Counterbalancing

When using **reverse counterbalancing**, the experimenter simply presents the conditions in one order, and then presents them again in the reverse order. In the illusion case, the order would be A–B–C–D, then D–C–B–A. If the researcher desires to have the participant perform the task more than twice per condition, and this is common in perception research, this sequence could be repeated as many times as necessary. Hence, if you wanted each participant to adjust each of the four illusions of Figure 6.1 six separate times, and you decided to use reverse counterbalancing, participants would see the illusions in this sequence:

A–B-C-D—D–C-B-A—A-B-C-D—D–C-B-A—A-B-C-D—D-C-B-A

Reverse counterbalancing was used in one of psychology's most famous studies, completed in the 1930s by J. Ridley Stroop. You've probably tried the Stroop task yourself—when shown color names printed in the wrong colors, you were asked to name the color rather than read the word. That is, when shown the word "RED" printed in blue ink, the correct response is "blue," not "red." Stroop's study is a classic example of a particular type of design described in the next chapter, so you will be learning more about his work when you encounter Box 7.1.[1]

Block Randomization

A second way to present a sequence of conditions when each condition is presented more than once is to use **block randomization**, the same procedure

---

[1] Although reverse counterbalancing normally occurs when participants are tested more than once per condition, the principle can also be applied in a within-subjects design in which participants see each condition only once. Thus, if a within-subjects study has six different conditions, each tested only once per person, half of the participants could get the sequence A–B-C-D-E-F, while the remaining participants experience the reverse order (F–E-D-C-B-A).

outlined earlier in the context of how to assign participants randomly to groups in a between-subjects experiment. Given the modern ease of having computers generate randomized sequences, this procedure is used more frequently than reverse counterbalancing. The basic rule of block randomization is that every condition occurs once before any condition is repeated a second time. Within each block, the order of conditions is randomized. This strategy eliminates the possibility that participants can predict what is coming next, a problem that can occur with reverse counterbalancing.

To use the illusions example again (Figure 6.1), participants would encounter all four conditions in a randomized order, then all four again but in a block with a new randomized order, and so on for as many blocks of four as needed. A reverse counterbalancing would look like this:

$$A–B–C–D—D–C–B–A$$

A block randomization procedure might produce either of these two sequences (among others):

$$B–C–D–A—C–A–D–B \quad or \quad C–A–B–D—A–B–D–C$$

To give you a sense of how block randomization works in an actual within-subjects experiment employing many trials, consider the following auditory perception study by Carello, Anderson, and Kunkler-Peck (1998).

Research Example 6—Counterbalancing with Block Randomization

Our ability to localize sound has been known for a long time—under normal circumstances, we are quite adept at identifying the location from which a sound originates. What interested Carello and her research team was whether people could identify something about the physical size of an object simply by hearing it drop on the floor. She devised the apparatus pictured in Figure 6.2 to examine the

FIGURE 6.2 The experimental setup for Carello, Anderson, & Kunkler-Peck (1998). After hearing a rod drop, participants adjusted the distance between the edge of their desk and the vertical surface facing them to match what they perceived to be the length of the rod.

question. Participants heard a wooden dowel hit the floor, and then tried to judge its length. They made their response by adjusting the distance between the edge of the desk they were sitting at and a movable vertical surface during a "trial," which was defined as having the same dowel dropped five times in a row from a given height. During the five drops, participants were encouraged to move the wall back and forth until they were comfortable with their decision about the dowel's size. In the first of two experiments, the within-subjects independent variable was the length of the dowel, and there were seven levels (30, 45, 60, 75, 90, 105, and 120 cm). Each participant judged dowel length three times for each dowel. The researchers counterbalanced the order of presenting the different dowel lengths, and the procedure they used was block randomization. That is, each of the seven lengths was tested in one random order, then in a second random order, then in a third. Note again an important feature of this block randomization procedure—each dowel length was tested once before being tested for a second time, and each was tested twice before being tested a third time.

Although you might think this length-judging task would be very difficult, the participants performed remarkably well. They did even better in a second experiment that replicated the first except that the seven dowel lengths were smaller (from 10 to 40 cm) than in experiment 1 (30 to 120 cm). Two other methodological features of these experiments are worth noting. First, they are a good example of the typical strategy in perception research—within-subjects designs requiring few participants and using many trials. A total of eight students participated in experiment 1 and six more performed in experiment 2, and each person performed the task 21 times. Second, recall the Chapter 3 discussion of pilot studies. Their purpose is to try out procedures and make slight adjustments if problems become apparent. Something similar happened in this research, although experiment 1 was not really a pilot study. One of the aspects of the experiment 1 procedure did lead to a change in experiment 2, however. In experiment 1, the dowels were dropped onto the floor. In experiment 2, they were dropped onto an elevated surface. Why? As Carello, Anderson, and Kunkler-Peck (1998) described it, the reason was a very practical one (and, reading between the lines, one for which the graduate students collecting the data were thankful). The change in procedure helped "to reduce the back and knee strain on the experimenter" (p. 212).

✓ **Self Test 6.2**

1. What is the defining feature of a within-subjects design? What is the main control problem that must be solved with this type of design?
2. If your IV has six levels, each tested just once per subject, why are you more likely to use partial counterbalancing instead of complete counterbalancing?
3. If participants are going to be tested more than one time for each level of the IV, what two forms of counterbalancing may be used?

Control Problems in Developmental Research

As you have learned, the researcher must weigh several factors when deciding whether to use a between-subjects design or a within-subjects design. There are some additional considerations for researchers in developmental psychology, where two specific varieties of these designs occur. These methods are known as cross-sectional and longitudinal designs.

You've seen these terms before if you have taken a course in developmental or child psychology. Research in these areas includes age as the prime independent variable—after all, the name of the game in developmental psychology is to discover how we change as we grow older. A **cross-sectional study** takes a between-subjects approach. A cross-sectional study comparing the language performance of 3-, 4-, and 5-year-old children would use three different groups of children. A **longitudinal study**, on the other hand, studies a single group over a period of time; it takes a within-subjects or repeated-measures approach. The same language study would measure language behavior in a group of 3-year-olds, and then study these same children when they turned 4 and 5.

The obvious advantage of the cross-sectional approach to the experiment on language is time; a study comparing 3-, 4-, and 5-year-olds might take a month to complete. If done as a longitudinal study, it would take at least two years. However, a potentially serious difficulty with some cross-sectional studies is a special form of the problem of nonequivalent groups and involves what are known as **cohort effects**. A cohort is a group of people born at about the same time. If you are studying three age groups, they differ not just simply in chronological age but also in terms of the environments in which they were raised. The problem is not especially noticeable when comparing 3-, 4-, and 5-year-olds, but what if you're interested in whether intelligence declines with age and decide to compare groups aged 40, 60, and 80? You might indeed find a decline with age, but does it mean that intelligence gradually decreases with age, or might the differences relate to the very different life histories of the three groups? For example, the 80-year-olds went to school during the Great Depression, the 60-year-olds were educated during the post–World War II boom, and the 40-year-olds were raised on TV. These factors could bias the results. Indeed, this outcome has occurred. Early research on the effects of age on IQ suggested that significant declines occurred, but these studies were cross-sectional (e.g., Miles, 1933). Subsequent longitudinal studies revealed a very different pattern (Schaie, 1988). For example, verbal abilities show minimal decline, especially if the person remains verbally active (moral: use it or lose it).

While cohort effects can plague cross-sectional studies, longitudinal studies also have problems, most notably with attrition (Chapter 5). If a large number of participants drop out of the study, the group completing it may be very different from the group starting it. Referring to the age and IQ example, if people stay healthy, they may remain more active intellectually than if they are sick all of the time. If they are chronically ill, they may die before a study is completed, leaving a group that may be generally more intelligent than the group starting the study. There are also potential ethical problems in longitudinal studies. As people develop and mature, they might change their attitudes about their willingness to participate. Most researchers doing longitudinal research recognize that informed consent is an ongoing process, not a one-time event. Ethically sensitive researchers will periodically renew the consent process in long-term studies, perhaps every few years (Fischman, 2000).

In trying to balance cohort and attrition problems, some researchers use a strategy that combines cross-sectional with longitudinal studies, a design referred to as a **cohort sequential design**. In such a study, a group of subjects will be selected and retested every few years, and then additional cohorts will be selected every few years and also retested over time. So different cohorts are continually being retested. To take a simple example, suppose you wished to examine the effects of aging on memory, comparing ages 55, 60, and 65. In the study's first year, you would recruit a group of 55-year-olds. Then every five years after that, you would recruit new groups of 55-year-olds, and retest those who had been recruited earlier. Schematically, the design for a study that began in the year 1960 and lasted for 30 years would look like this (the numbers in the matrix refer to the age of the subjects at any given testing point):

| | Year of the Study | | | | | | |
Cohort #	1960	1965	1970	1975	1980	1985	1990
1	55	60	65				
2		55	60	65			
3			55	60	65		
4				55	60	65	
5					55	60	65

So in 1960, you have a group of 55-year-olds that you test. Then in 1965, these same people (now 60 years old) would be retested, along with a new group of 55-year-olds. By year three (1970), you have cohorts for all three age groups. By 1990, combining the data in each of the diagonals would give you an overall comparison between those aged 55, 60, and 65. Comparing the data in the rows enables a comparison of overall differences between cohorts. In actual practice, these designs are more complicated, because researchers will typically start the first year of the study with a fuller range of ages. But the diagram gives you the basic idea. Perhaps the best-known example of this type of sequential design is a long series of studies by K. Warner Schaie (2005), known as the Seattle Longitudinal Study. It began in 1956, designed to examine age-related changes in various mental abilities. The initial cohort had 500 people in it, ranging in age from their early 20s to their late 60s (as of 2005, 38 of these subjects were still in the study, 49 years later!). The study has added a new cohort at 7-year intervals ever since 1956 and has recently reached the 50-year mark. In all, about 6,000 people have participated. In general, Schaie and his team have found that performance on mental ability tasks declines slightly with age, but with no serious losses before age 60, and the losses can be reduced by good physical health and lots of crossword puzzles. Concerning cohort effects, they have found that overall performance has been progressively better for those born more recently. Presumably, those born later in the twentieth century have had the advantages of better education, better nutrition, and so on.

The length of Schaie's Seattle project is impressive, but the world's record for perseverance in a repeated-measures study occurred in what is arguably the most famous longitudinal study of all time. Before continuing, read Box 6.1, which chronicles the epic tale of Lewis Terman's study of gifted children.

Box 6.1

CLASSIC STUDIES—The Record for Repeated Measures

In 1921, the psychologist Lewis Terman (1877–1956) began what became the longest-running repeated-measures design in the history of psychology. A precocious child himself, Terman developed an interest in studying gifted children. His doctoral dissertation, supervised by Edmund Sanford at Clark University in 1905, was his first serious investigation of giftedness; in it, he compared bright and dull local school children to see which tests might best distinguish between them (Minton, 1987). This early interest in giftedness and mental testing foreshadowed Terman's two main contributions to psychology. First, he took the intelligence test created by Alfred Binet of France and transformed it into the popular Stanford-Binet IQ test. Second, he began a longitudinal study of gifted children that continued long after he died.

Terman was motivated by the belief, shared by most mental testers of his day, that America should become a meritocracy. That is, he believed that positions of leadership should be held by those most *able* to lead. You can see how this belief led to his interests in IQ and giftedness. To bring about a meritocracy, there must be ways to recognize (i.e., measure) talent and nurture it.

Unlike his dissertation, which studied just 14 children, Terman's longitudinal study of gifted children was a mammoth undertaking. Through a variety of screening procedures, he recruited 1,470 children (824 boys and 646 girls). Most were in elementary school, but a group of 444 were in junior or senior high school (sample numbers from Minton, 1988). Their average IQ score was 150, which put the group roughly in the top 1% of the population. Each child was given an extensive battery of tests and questionnaires by the team of graduate students assembled by Terman. By the time the initial testing was complete, each child had a file of about 100 pages long (Minton, 1988)! The results of the first analysis of the group were published in more than 600 pages as the *Mental and Physical Traits of a Thousand Gifted Children* (Terman, 1925).

Terman intended to do just a brief follow-up study, but the project took on a life of its own. The sample was retested in the late 1920s (Burks, Jensen, & Terman, 1930), and additional follow-up studies during Terman's lifetime were published 25 (Terman & Oden, 1947) and 35 (Terman & Oden, 1959) years after the initial testing. Following Terman's death, the project was taken over by Robert Sears, a member of the gifted group and a well-known psychologist in his own right. In the foreword to the 35-year follow-up, Sears wrote: "On actuarial grounds, there is considerable likelihood that the last of Terman's Gifted Children will not have yielded his last report to the files before the year 2010!" (Terman & Oden, 1959, p. ix). Between 1960 and 1986, Sears produced five additional follow-up studies of the group, and he was working on a book-length study of the group as they aged when he died in 1989 (Cronbach, Hastorf, Hilgard, & Maccoby, 1990). The book was eventually published as *The Gifted Group in Later Maturity* (Holahan, Sears, & Cronbach, 1995).

There are three points worth making about this mega-longitudinal study. First, Terman's work shattered the stereotype of the gifted child as someone who was brilliant but socially retarded and prone to burnout early in life. Rather, the members of his group as a whole were both brilliant and well adjusted and they became successful as they matured. By the time they reached maturity, "the group had produced thousands of scientific papers, 60 nonfiction books, 33 novels, 375 short stories, 230 patents, and numerous radio and television shows, works of art, and musical compositions" (Hothersall, 1990, p. 353). Second, the data collected by Terman's team continues to be a source of rich archival information for modern researchers. For instance, studies have been published on the careers of the gifted females in Terman's group (Tomlinson-Keasy, 1990), and on the predictors of longevity in the group (Friedman, et al., 1995). Third, Terman's follow-up studies are incredible from the methodological standpoint of a longitudinal study's typical nemesis—*attrition*. The following figures (taken from Minton, 1988) are the percentage of living participants who participated in the first three follow-ups:

After 10 years: 92%

After 25 years: 98%

After 35 years: 93%

These are remarkably high numbers and reflect the intense loyalty that Terman and his group had for each other. Members of the group referred to themselves as "Termites," and some even wore termite jewelry (Hothersall, 1990). Terman corresponded with hundreds of his participants and genuinely cared for his special people. After all, the group represented the type of person Terman believed held the key to America's future.

Problems with Biasing

Because humans are always the experimenters and usually the participants in psychology research, there is the chance that the results of a study could be influenced by some human "bias," a preconceived expectation about what is to happen in an experiment. These biases take several forms but fall into two broad categories—those affecting experimenters and those affecting research participants. These two forms of bias often interact.

Experimenter Bias

As well as illustrating falsification and parsimony, the Clever Hans case (Box 3.3 in Chapter 3) is often used to show the effects of **experimenter bias** on the outcome of some study. Hans's trainer, knowing the outcome to the question "What is 3 times 3?," sent subtle head movement cues that were read by the apparently intelligent horse. Similarly, experimenters testing hypotheses sometimes may inadvertently do something that leads participants to behave in ways that confirm the hypothesis. Although the stereotype of the scientist is that of an objective, dispassionate, even mechanical person, the truth is that researchers can become rather emotionally involved in their research. It's not difficult to see how a desire to confirm some strongly held hypothesis might lead an unwary experimenter to behave (without awareness) in such a way as to influence the outcome of the study.

For one thing, biased experimenters might treat the research participants in the various conditions differently. Robert Rosenthal developed one procedure demonstrating this. Participants in one of his studies (e.g., Rosenthal & Fode, 1963a) were shown a set of photographs of faces and asked to make some judgment about the people pictured in them. For example, they might be asked to rate each photo on how successful the person seemed to be, with the interval scale ranging from −10 (total failure) to +10 (total success). All participants saw the same photos and made the same judgments. The independent variable was experimenter expectancy. Some experimenters were led to believe that most subjects would give people the benefit of the doubt and rate the pictures positively; other experimenters were told to expect negative ratings. Interestingly enough, the experimenter's expectancies typically produced effects on the subjects' rating behavior, even though the pictures were identical for both groups. How can this be?

According to Rosenthal (1966), experimenters can innocently communicate their expectancies in a number of subtle ways. For instance, on the person perception task, the experimenter holds up a picture while the participant rates it. If the experimenter is expecting a "+8" and the person says "−3," how might the experimenter act—with a slight frown perhaps? How might the participant read the frown? Might he or she try a "+7" on the next trial to see if this could elicit a smile or a nod from the experimenter? In general, could it be that experimenters in this situation, without even being aware of it, are subtly shaping the responses of their participants? Does this remind you of Clever Hans?

Rosenthal has even shown that experimenter expectancies can be communicated to subjects in animal research. For instance, rats learn mazes faster for experimenters who *think* their animals have been bred for maze-running ability than for those expecting their rats to be "maze-dull" (Rosenthal & Fode, 1963b). The rats, of course, are randomly assigned to the experimenters and are equal in ability. The key factor here seems to be that experimenters expecting their rats to be "maze-bright" treat them better; for example, they handle them more, a behavior known to affect learning.

It should be noted that some of the Rosenthal research has been criticized on statistical grounds and for interpreting the results as being due to expectancy when they may have been due to something else. For example, Barber (1976) raised questions about the statistical conclusion validity of some of Rosenthal's work. In at least one study, according to Barber, three of twenty experimenters reversed the expectancy results, getting data the opposite of the expectancies created for them. Rosenthal omitted these experimenters from the analysis and obtained a significant difference for the remaining seventeen experimenters. With all twenty experimenters included in the analysis, however, the difference disappeared. Barber also argued that, in the animal studies, some of the results occurred because experimenters simply fudged the data (e.g., misrecording maze errors). Another difficulty with the Rosenthal studies is that his procedures don't match what normally occurs in experiments; most experimenters test all of the participants in all conditions of the experiment, not just those participating in one of the conditions. Hence, Rosenthal's results might overestimate the amount of biasing that occurs.

Despite these reservations, the experimenter expectancy effect cannot be ignored; it has been replicated in a variety of situations and by many researchers other than Rosenthal and his colleagues (e.g., Word, Zanna, & Cooper, 1974). Furthermore, experimenters can be shown to influence the outcomes of studies in ways other than through their expectations. The behavior of participants can be affected by the experimenter's race and gender, as well as by demeanor, friendliness, and overall attitude (Adair, 1973). An example of the latter is a study by Fraysse and Desprels-Fraysse (1990), who found that preschoolers' performance on a cognitive classification task could be influenced by experimenter attitude. The children performed significantly better with "caring" than with "indifferent" experimenters.

Controlling for Experimenter Bias

It is probably impossible to eliminate experimenter effects completely. Experimenters cannot be turned into machines. However, one strategy to reduce bias is to mechanize procedures as much as possible. For instance, it's not hard to remove a frowning or smiling experimenter from the person perception task. With modern computer technology, participants can be shown photos on a screen and asked to make their responses with a key press while the experimenter is in a different room entirely.

Similarly, procedures for testing animals automatically have been available since the 1920s, even to the extent of eliminating human handling completely. E. C. Tolman didn't wait for computers to come along before inventing "a self-recording maze with an automatic delivery table" (Tolman, Tryon, & Jeffries, 1929). The "delivery table" was so called because it "automatically delivers each rat into the entrance of the maze and 'collects' him at the end without the mediation of the experimenter. Objectivity of scoring is insured by the use of a device which automatically records his path through the maze" (Tryon, 1929, p. 73). Today such automation is routine. Furthermore, computers make it easy to present instructions and stimuli to participants while also keeping track of data.

Experimenters can mechanize many procedures, to some degree at least, but the experimenter will be interacting with every participant nonetheless. Hence, it is important for experimenters to be given some training in how to be experimenters and for the experiments to have highly detailed descriptions of the sequence of steps that experimenters should follow in every research session. These descriptions are called research **protocols**.

Another strategy for controlling for experimenter bias is to use what is called a **double blind** procedure. This means simply that experimenters are kept in the dark (blind) about what to expect of participants in a particular testing session. As a result, neither the experimenters nor the participants know which condition is being tested—hence the designation "double." A double blind can be accomplished when the principal investigator sets up the experiment but a colleague (usually a graduate student) actually collects the data. Double blinds are not always possible, of course, as illustrated by the Dutton and Aron (1974) study you read about in Chapter 3. As you recall, female experimenters arranged to encounter men either on a suspension bridge swaying 230 feet over a river or on a solid bridge 10 feet over the same river. It would be a bit difficult to prevent those experimenters from knowing which condition of the study was being tested! On the other hand, many studies lend themselves to a procedure in which experimenters are blind to which condition is in effect. Research Example 7, which could increase the stock price of Starbucks, is a good example.

Research Example 7—Using a Double Blind

There is considerable evidence that as we age, we become less efficient cognitively in the afternoon. Also, older adults are more likely to describe themselves as "morning persons" (I am writing this on an early Saturday morning, so I think I'll get it right). Ryan, Hatfield, and Hofstetter (2002) wondered if the cognitive decline, as the day wears on, could be neutralized by America's favorite drug—caffeine. They recruited forty seniors, all 65 or older and self-described as (a) morning types and (b) moderate users of caffeine, and placed them in either a caffeine group or a decaf group (using Starbucks "house blends"). At each testing session, they drank a 12-ounce cup of coffee, either caffeinated or not; 30 minutes later, they were given a standardized memory test. The second independent variable was time of testing—either 8:00 A.M. or 4:00 P.M. Subjects were tested twice, once at each time (with a 5–11 day interval in between, making this a within-subjects factor).

The study was a double blind because the experimenters administering the memory tests did not know which participants had ingested caffeine, and the seniors did not know which type of coffee they were drinking. And to test for the adequacy of the control procedures, the researchers completed a clever "manipulation check" (you will learn more about this concept in a few paragraphs). At the end of the study, during debriefing, they asked the participants to guess whether they had been drinking the real stuff or the decaf. The accuracy of the seniors' responses was at chance level. In fact, most guessed incorrectly that they had been given regular coffee during one testing session and decaf at the other. All subjects ingested either caffeinated coffee or decaf at each session.

The researchers also did a nice job of incorporating some of the other control procedures you learned about in this chapter. For instance, the seniors were randomly assigned to the two different groups, and this random assignment seemed to produce the desired equivalent groups—the groups were indistinguishable in terms of age, education level, and average daily intake of caffeine. Also, counterbalancing was used to ensure that half of the seniors were tested first in the morning, then the afternoon, while the other half were tested in the sequence afternoon-morning.

The results? Time of day did not seem to affect a short-term memory task, but it had a significant effect on a more difficult longer-term task in which seniors learned some information, then had a 20-minute delay, then tried to recall the information, and then completed a recognition test for that same information. And caffeine prevented the decline for this more demanding task. On both the delayed recall and the delayed recognition tasks, seniors scored equally well in the morning sessions. In the afternoon sessions, however, those ingesting caffeine still did well, but the performance of those taking decaf declined. On the delayed recall task, for instance, here are the means (max score = 16). Also, remember from Chapter 4 that, when reporting descriptive statistics, it is important to report not just a measure of central tendency (mean), but also an indication of variability. So, in parentheses after each mean below, notice that I have included the standard deviations (*SD*).

$$\text{Morning with caffeine} \rightarrow \quad 11.8 \ (SD = 2.9)$$
$$\text{Morning with decaf} \rightarrow \quad 11.0 \ (SD = 2.7)$$
$$\text{Afternoon with caffeine} \rightarrow \quad 11.7 \ (SD = 2.8)$$
$$\text{Afternoon with decaf} \rightarrow \quad 8.9 \ (SD = 3.0)$$

So, if the word gets out about this study, the average age of Starbucks' clients might start to go up, starting around 3:00 in the afternoon. Of course, they will need to avoid the decaf.

Participant Bias

People participating in psychological research cannot be expected to respond like machines. They are humans who *know* they are in an experiment. Presumably they have been told about the general nature of the research during the informed consent process, but in deception studies they also know (or at least suspect) that they haven't been told everything. Furthermore, even if there is no deception in a study, participants may not believe it—after all, they are in a "psychology experiment," and aren't psychologists always trying to "psychoanalyze" people? In short, **participant bias** can occur in several ways, depending on what participants are expecting and what they believe their role should be in the study. When behavior is affected by the knowledge that one is in an experiment and is therefore important to the study's success, the phenomenon is sometimes called the **Hawthorne effect**, after a famous series of studies of worker productivity. To understand the origins of this term, you should read Box 6.2 before continuing. You may be surprised to learn that most historians believe the Hawthorne effect has been misnamed and that the data of the original study might have been distorted for political reasons.

Most research participants, in the spirit of trying to help the experimenter and contribute meaningful results, take on the role of the **good subject**, first described by Orne (1962). There are exceptions, of course, but, in general, participants tend to be very cooperative, to the point of persevering through repetitive and boring tasks, all in the name of psychological science. Furthermore, if participants can figure out the hypothesis, they may try to behave in such a way that confirms

Box 6.2

ORIGINS—*Productivity at Western Electric*

The research that led to naming the so-called Hawthorne effect took place at the Western Electric Plant in Hawthorne, Illinois, over a period of about 10 years, from 1924 to 1933. According to the traditional account, the purpose of the study was to investigate the factors influencing worker productivity. Numerous experiments were completed, but the most famous series became known as the Relay Assembly Test Room study.

In the Relay Assembly experiment, six female workers were selected from a larger group in the plant. Their job was to assemble relays for the phone company. Five workers did the actual assembly, and the sixth supplied them with parts. The assembly was a time-consuming, labor-intensive, repetitive job requiring the construction of some 35 parts per relay. Western Electric produced about seven million relays a year (Gillespie, 1988), so naturally they were interested in making workers as productive as possible.

The first series of relay studies extended from May 1927 through September 1928 (Gillespie, 1988). During that time, several workplace variables were studied (and confounded with each other, actually). At various times there were changes in the scheduling of rest periods, total hours of work, and bonuses paid for certain levels of production. The standard account has it that productivity for this small group quickly reached high levels and stayed there even when working conditions deteriorated. The example always mentioned concerned the infamous "12th test period" when workers were informed that the work week would increase from 42 to 48 hours per week, and that rest periods and free lunches would be discontinued. Virtually all textbooks describe the results somewhat like this:

> With few exceptions, no matter what changes were made—whether there were many or few rest periods, whether the workday was made longer or shorter, and so on—the women tended to produce more and more telephone relays. (Elmes, Kantowitz, & Roediger, 2006, p. 150)

Supposedly, the workers remained productive because they believed they were a special group and the focus of attention—they were part of an experiment. This is the origin of the concept called the *Hawthorne effect*, the tendency for performance to be affected because people know they are being studied in an experiment. The effect may be genuine, but whether it truly happened at Western Electric is uncertain.

A close look at what actually happened reveals some interesting alternative explanations. First, although accounts of the study typically emphasize how delighted the women were to be in this special testing room, the fact is that of the five original assemblers, two had to be removed from the room for insubordination and low output. One was said to have "gone Bolshevik" (Bramel & Friend, 1981).

(Remember, the Soviet Union was brand new in the 1920s, and the "red menace" was a threat to industrial America, resulting in things like a fear of labor unions.) Of the two replacements, one was especially talented and enthusiastic and quickly became the group leader. She apparently was selected because she "held the record as the fastest relay-assembler in the regular department" (Gillespie, 1988, p. 122). As you might suspect, her efforts contributed substantially to the high level of productivity.

A second problem with interpreting the relay data is a simple statistical problem. In the famous 12th period, productivity was recorded as output per week rather than output per hour, yet workers were putting in an extra six hours per week compared to the previous test period. If the more appropriate output per hour is used, productivity actually *declined* slightly (Bramel & Friend, 1981). Also, the women were apparently angry about the change, but afraid to complain lest they be removed from the test room, thereby losing bonus money. Lastly, it could have been that in some of the Hawthorne experiments, increased worker productivity could have been simply the result of feedback about performance, along with rewards for productivity (Parsons, 1974).

Historians argue that events must be understood within their entire political/economic/institutional context, and the Hawthorne studies are no exception. Painting a glossy picture of workers unaffected by specific working conditions and more concerned with being considered special ushered in the human relations movement in industry and led corporations to emphasize the humane management of employees in order to create one big happy family of labor and management. However, such a picture also helps to maintain power at the level of management and impede efforts at unionization, which some historians (e.g., Bramel & Friend, 1981) believe were the true motives behind the studies completed at Western Electric.

it. Orne used the term **demand characteristics** to refer to those aspects of the study that reveal the hypotheses being tested. If these features are too obvious to participants, they no longer act naturally and it becomes difficult to interpret the results. Did participants behave as they normally would or did they come to understand the hypothesis and behave so as to make it come true?

Orne demonstrated how demand characteristics can influence a study's outcome by recruiting students for a so-called sensory deprivation experiment (Orne & Scheibe, 1964). He assumed that subjects told that they were in such an experiment would expect the experience to be stressful and might respond accordingly. This indeed occurred. Participants who sat for four hours in a small but comfortable room showed signs of stress *only* if (a) they signed a form releasing the experimenter from any liability in case anything happened to them, and (b) the room included a "panic button" that could be pressed if they felt too stressed by the deprivation. Control participants were given no release form to sign, no panic button to press, and no expectation that their senses were being deprived. They did not react adversely.

The possibility that demand characteristics are operating has an impact on decisions about whether to opt for between- or within-subject designs. Participants serving in all of the conditions of a study have a greater opportunity to figure out the hypothesis(es). Hence, demand characteristics are potentially more troublesome in within-subject designs than in between-subjects designs. For both types of designs, demand characteristics are especially devastating if they affect some conditions but not others, thereby introducing a confound.

Besides being good subjects (i.e., trying to confirm the hypothesis), participants wish to be perceived as competent, creative, emotionally stable, and so on. The belief that they are being evaluated in the experiment produces what Rosenberg (1969) called **evaluation apprehension**. Participants want to be evaluated positively, so they may behave as they think the ideal person should behave. This concern over how one is going to look and the desire to help the experimenter often leads to the same behavior among participants, but sometimes the desire to create a favorable impression and the desire to be a good subject conflict. For example, in a helping behavior study, astute participants might guess that they are in the condition of the study designed to reduce the chances that help will be offered. On the other hand, altruism is a valued, even heroic, behavior. The pressure to be a good subject and support the hypothesis pulls the participant toward nonhelping, but evaluation apprehension makes the individual want to help. At least one study has suggested that when participants are faced with the option of confirming the hypothesis and being evaluated positively, the latter is the more powerful motivator (Rosnow, Goodstadt, Suls, & Gitter, 1973).

Controlling for Participant Bias

The primary strategy for controlling participant bias is to reduce demand characteristics to the minimum. One way of accomplishing this, of course, is through deception. As we've seen in Chapter 2, the primary purpose of deception is to induce participants to behave more naturally than they otherwise might. A second strategy, normally found in drug studies, is to use a placebo control group (elaborated in Chapter 7). This procedure allows for a comparison between those actually getting some treatment (e.g., a drug) and those who think they are getting the treatment but aren't. If the people in both groups behave identically, the effects can be attributed to participant expectations of the treatment's effects. You have probably already recognized that the caffeine study you just read about (Research Example 7) used this kind of logic.

A second way to check for the presence of demand characteristics is to do what is sometimes called a **manipulation check**. This can be accomplished during debriefing by asking participants in a deception study to indicate what they believe the true hypothesis to be (the "good subject" might feign ignorance, though). This was accomplished in Research Example 7 by asking participants to guess whether they had been given caffeine in their coffee or not. Manipulation checks can also be done during an experiment. Sometimes a random subset of participants in each condition will be stopped in the middle of a procedure and asked about the clarity of the instructions, what they think is going on, and so on. Manipulation checks are also used to see if some procedure is producing the effect it is supposed to produce. For example, if some procedure is supposed to make people feel anxious (e.g., telling participants to expect shock), a sample of participants might be stopped in the middle of the study and assessed for level of anxiety.

A final way of avoiding demand characteristics is to conduct field research. If participants are unaware that they are in a study, they are unlikely to spend any time thinking about research hypotheses and reacting to demand characteristics. Of course, field studies have problems of their own, as you recall from the discussion of informed consent in Chapter 2 and of privacy invasion in Chapter 3.

Although I stated earlier that most research participants play the role of "good subjects," this is not uniformly true, and some differences exist between those who truly volunteer and are interested in the experiment and those who are more reluctant and less interested. For instance, true volunteers tend to be slightly more intelligent and have a higher need for social approval (Adair, 1973). Differences between volunteers and nonvolunteers can be a problem when college students are asked to serve as participants as part of a course requirement; some students are more enthusiastic volunteers than others. Furthermore, a "semester effect" can operate. The true volunteers, those really interested in participating, sign up earlier in the semester than the reluctant volunteers. Therefore, if you ran a study with two groups, and Group 1 was tested in the first half of the semester and Group 2 in the second half, the differences found could be due to the independent variable, but they also could be due to differences between the true volunteers who sign up first and the reluctant volunteers who wait as long as they can. Can you think of a way to control for this problem? If the concept "block randomization" occurs to you, and you say to yourself "this will distribute the conditions of the study equally throughout the duration of the semester," then you've accomplished something in this chapter. Well done.

✓ Self Test 6.3

1. Unlike most longitudinal studies, Terman's study of gifted children did not experience which control problem?
2. Why does a double blind procedure control for experimenter bias?
3. How can a demand characteristic influence the outcome of a study?

To close out this chapter, read Box 6.3, which concerns the ethical obligations of those participating in psychological research. The list of responsibilities you'll find there is based on the assumption that research should be a collaborative effort between experimenters and participants. We've seen that experimenters must follow the APA ethics code. In Box 6.3 you'll learn that participants have some responsibilities too.

Box 6.3

ETHICS—Research Participants Have Responsibilities Too

The APA ethics code spells out the responsibilities that researchers have to those who participate in their experiments. Participants have a right to expect that the guidelines will be followed and, if not, there should be a clear process for registering complaints. But what about the subjects? What are their obligations?

An article by Jim Korn in the journal *Teaching of Psychology* (1988) outlines the basic rights that college students have when they participate in research, but it also lists the responsibilities of those who volunteer. They include

✓ Being responsible about scheduling by showing up for their appointments with researchers and arriving on time

✓ Being cooperative and acting professionally by giving their best and most honest effort

✓ Listening carefully to the experimenter during the informed consent and instructions phases and asking questions if they are not sure what to do

✓ Respecting any request by the researcher to avoid discussing the research with others until all the data have been collected

✓ Being active during the debriefing process by helping the researcher understand the phenomenon being studied

The assumption underlying this list is that research should be a collaborative effort between experimenters and participants. Korn's suggestion that participants take a more assertive role in making research more collaborative is a welcome one. This assertiveness, however, must be accompanied by enlightened experimenting that values and probes for the insights that participants have about what might be going on in a study. An experimenter who simply "runs a subject" and records the data is ignoring valuable information.

In the last two chapters, you have learned about the essential features of experimental research and some of the control problems that must be faced by those who wish to do research in psychology. We've now completed the necessary groundwork for introducing the various kinds of experimental designs used to test the effects of independent variables. So, let the designs begin!

Chapter Summary

Between-Subjects Designs

In between-subjects designs, individuals participate in just one of the experiment's conditions; hence, each condition in the study involves a different group of participants. Such a design is usually necessary when subject variables (e.g., gender) are being studied or when being in one condition of the experiment changes participants in ways that make it impossible for them to be in another condition. With between-subjects designs, the main difficulty is creating groups that are essentially equivalent to each other on all factors except for the independent variable.

The Problem of Creating Equivalent Groups

The preferred method of creating equivalent groups in between-subjects designs is random assignment. Random assignment has the effect of spreading unforeseen confounding factors evenly throughout the different groups, thereby eliminating their damaging influence. The chance of random assignment working effectively increases as the number of participants per group increases. If few participants are available, if some factor (e.g., intelligence) correlates highly with the dependent variable, and if that factor can be assessed without difficulty before the experiment begins, then equivalent groups can be formed by using a matching procedure.

Within-Subjects Designs

When each individual participates in all of the study's conditions, the study is using a within-subjects (or repeated-measures) design. For these designs, participating in one condition might affect how participants behave in other conditions. That is, sequence or order effects can occur, both of which can produce confounded results if not controlled. Sequence effects include progressive effects (they gradually accumulate, as in fatigue or boredom) and carryover effects (one sequence of conditions might produce effects different from another sequence). When substantial carryover effects are suspected, researchers usually switch to a between-subjects design.

The Problem of Controlling Sequence Effects

Sequence effects are controlled by various counterbalancing procedures, all of which ensure that the different conditions are tested in more than one sequence. When participants serve in each condition of the study just once, complete (all possible sequences used) or partial (a sample of different sequences or a Latin square) counterbalancing will be used. When participants serve in each condition more than once, reverse counterbalancing or block randomization can be used.

Control Problems in Developmental Research

In developmental psychology, the major independent variable is age, a subject variable. If age is studied between subjects, the design is referred to as a cross-sectional design. It has the advantage of efficiency, but cohort effects can occur, a special form of the problem of nonequivalent groups. If age is a within-subjects variable, the design is called a longitudinal design and attrition can be a problem. The two strategies can be combined in a cohort sequential design—selecting new cohorts every few years and testing each cohort longitudinally.

Problems with Biasing

The results of research in psychology can be biased by experimenter expectancy effects. These can lead the experimenter to treat participants in various conditions in different ways, making the results difficult to interpret. Such effects can be reduced by automating the procedures and/or using double blind control procedures. Participant bias also occurs. Participants might confirm the researcher's hypothesis if demand characteristics suggest to them the true purpose of a study or they might behave in unusual ways simply because they know they are in an experiment. Demand characteristics are usually controlled through varying degrees of deception; the extent of participant bias can be evaluated by using a manipulation check.

Chapter Review Questions

1. Under what circumstances would a between-subjects design be preferred over a within-subjects design?

2. Under what circumstances would a within-subjects design be preferred over a between-subjects design?

3. How does random selection differ from random assignment, and what is the purpose of the latter?

4. As a means of creating equivalent groups, when is matching most likely to be used?

5. Distinguish between progressive effects and carryover effects, and explain why counterbalancing might be more successful with the former than the latter.

6. In a taste test, Joan is asked to evaluate four dry white wines for taste: wines A, B, C, and D. In what sequence would they be tasted if (a) reverse counterbalancing or (b) block randomization were being used? How many sequences would be required if the researcher used complete counterbalancing?

7. What are the defining features of a Latin square and when is one likely to be used?

8. What specific control problems exist in developmental psychology with (a) cross-sectional studies and (b) longitudinal studies?

9. What is a cohort sequential design, and how does it improve on cross-sectional and longitudinal designs?

10. Describe an example of a study that illustrates experimenter bias. How might such bias be controlled?

11. What are demand characteristics and how might they be controlled?

12. What is a Hawthorne effect and what is the origin of the term?

Applications Exercises

Exercise 6.1   Between-Subject or Within-Subject?

Think of a study that might test each of the following hypotheses. For each, indicate whether you think the independent variable should be a between- or a within-subjects variable or whether either approach would be reasonable. Explain your decision in each case.

1. A neuroscientist hypothesizes that damage to the primary visual cortex is permanent in older animals.

2. A sensory psychologist predicts that it is easier to distinguish slightly different shades of gray under daylight than under fluorescent light.

3. A clinical psychologist thinks that phobias are best cured by repeatedly exposing the person to the feared object and not allowing the person to escape until the person realizes that the object really is harmless.

4. A developmental psychologist predicts cultural differences in moral development.

5. A social psychologist believes people will solve problems more creatively when in groups than when alone.

6. A cognitive psychologist hypothesizes that spaced practice of verbal information will lead to greater retention than massed practice.

7. A clinician hypothesizes that people with an obsessive–compulsive disorder will be easier to hypnotize than people with a phobic disorder.

8. An industrial psychologist predicts that worker productivity will increase if the company introduces flextime scheduling (i.e., work eight hours, but start and end at different times).

Exercise 6.2   Constructing a Balanced Latin Square

A memory researcher wishes to compare long-term memory for a series of word lists as a function of whether the person initially studies either four lists or eight lists. Help the investigator in the planning stages of this project by constructing the two needed Latin squares, a 4×4 and an 8×8, using the procedure outlined in Table 6.2.

Exercise 6.3   Random Assignment and Matching

A researcher investigates the effectiveness of an experimental weight-loss program. Sixteen volunteers will participate, half assigned to the experimental program and half placed in a control group. In a study such as this, it would be good if the average weights of the subjects in the two groups were approximately equal at the start of the experiment. Here are the weights, in pounds, for the 16 subjects before the study begins.

168	210	182	238	198	175	205	215
186	178	185	191	221	226	188	184

First, use a matching procedure as the method to form the two groups (experimental and control), and then calculate the average weight per group. Second, assign participants to the groups again, this time using random assignment (cut out 20 small pieces of paper, write one of the weights on each, then draw them out of a hat to form the two groups). Again, calculate the average weight per group after the random assignment has occurred. Compare your results to those of the rest of the class—are the average weights for the groups closer to each other with matching or with random assignment? In a situation such as this, what do you conclude about the relative merits of matching and random assignment?

Answers to Self Tests:

✓ **6.1.**
1. There is a minimum of two separate groups of subjects tested in the study, one group for each level of the IV; the problem of equivalent groups.
2. Sal must have a reason to expect verbal fluency to correlate with his dependent variable; he must also have a good way to measure verbal fluency.

✓ **6.2.**
1. Each subject participates in each level of the IV; sequence effects.
2. With six levels of the IV, complete counterbalancing requires a minimum of 720 subjects ($6 \times 5 \times 4 \times 3 \times 2 \times 1$), which could be impractical.
3. Reverse counterbalancing, or block randomization.

✓ **6.3.**
1. Attrition.
2. If the experimenter does not know which subjects are in each of the groups in the study, the experimenter cannot behave in a biased fashion.
3. If subjects know what is expected of them, they might be "good subjects" and not behave naturally.

CHAPTER 7

Experimental Design I: Single-Factor Designs

Preview & Chapter Objectives

Chapters 5 and 6 have set the stage for this and the following chapter. In Chapter 5, I introduced you to the experimental method; distinguished independent, extraneous, and dependent variables; considered the problem of confounding; and discussed several factors relating to the validity of psychology experiments. Chapter 6 compared between-subjects and within-subjects designs, described the basic techniques of control associated with each (e.g., random assignment, counterbalancing), and dealt with the problems of experimenter and subject bias in psychological research. With the stage now ready, this and the next chapter can be considered a playbill—a listing and description of the various designs that constitute experimental research in psychology. This chapter considers designs that feature single independent variables with two or more levels. Adding independent variables creates factorial designs, the main topic of Chapter 8. When you finish this chapter, you should be able to:

- Identify and understand the defining features of the four varieties of single-factor designs—independent groups, matched groups, nonequivalent groups, and repeated measures.

- Know when to use a *t* test for independent samples and when to use a *t* test for related samples, when doing an inferential analysis of a single-factor, two-level design.

- Explain the two different reasons for using more than two levels of an independent variable.

- Decide when to use a bar graph to present data and when to use a line graph.

- Understand why a 1-factor ANOVA, rather than multiple *t* tests, is the appropriate analysis when examining data from single-factor, multilevel studies.

- Construct an ANOVA source table for a 1-factor ANOVA for an independent groups design.

- Understand why post hoc statistical analyses typically accompany 1-factor ANOVAs for single-factor, multilevel studies.

- Understand the logic behind the use of three special types of control groups: placebo, waiting list, and yoked.

- Understand the ethical issues involved when using certain types of control groups.

In Chapter 3's discussion of scientific creativity, I used the origins of maze-learning research as an example. Willard Small's research, using a modified version of the Hampton Court maze, was just the first of a flood of studies on maze learning that appeared in the first two decades of the twentieth century. Most of the early research aimed to determine which of the rat's senses was critical to the learning process. You might recall from Box 2.3 of Chapter 2 that John Watson ran into trouble with "antivivisectionists" for doing a series of studies in which he surgically eliminated one sense after another and discovered that maze learning was not hampered even if rats were deprived of most of their senses. He concluded that rats rely on their muscle or kinesthetic sense to learn and recall the maze. In effect, the rat learns to take so many steps, and then turn right, and so on. To test his kinesthesis idea directly, he completed a simple yet elegant study with his University of Chicago colleague Harvey Carr. After one group of rats learned a complicated maze, Carr and Watson (1908) removed a middle section of the maze structure, thereby making certain portions of the maze shorter than before, while maintaining the same overall maze design. They predicted that rats trained on the longer maze might literally run into the walls when the maze was shortened. Sure enough, in a description of one of the rats, the researchers noted that it "ran into [the wall] with all her strength. Was badly staggered and did not recover normal conduct until she had gone [another] 9 feet" (p. 39). A second group of rats was trained on the shorter maze, and then tested on the longer one. These rats behaved similarly, often turning too soon and running into the sidewall of an alley, apparently expecting to find a turn there. Long after he left academia, John Watson remembered this study as one of his most important. Subsequent research on maze learning questioned the kinesthesis hypothesis, but the important point here is that good research does not require immensely complex research designs. In some cases, two groups will do just fine.

Single Factor—Two Levels

As you can see from the decision tree in Figure 7.1, there are four basic research designs involving one independent variable that has two levels, and they result from a series of decisions about the independent variable under investigation. First, the independent variable can be tested either between or within subjects. If it is tested between subjects, it could be either a manipulated or a subject variable. If the independent variable is manipulated, the design will be called either an **independent groups design**, if simple random assignment is used to create equivalent groups, or a **matched groups design**, if a matching procedure is used. As you recall from Chapter 6, decisions about whether to use random assignment or matching have to do with sample size and the need to be wary about extraneous variables that are highly correlated with the dependent variable. If a subject variable is being investigated, the groups are composed of different types of individuals

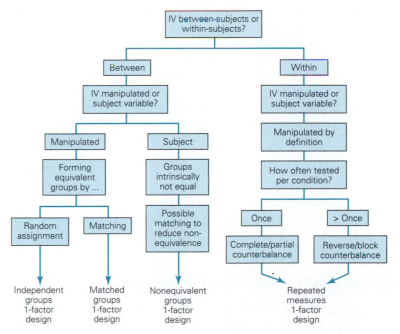

FIGURE 7.1 Decision tree—single-factor designs.

TABLE 7.1   *Attributes of Four Single-Factor Designs*

Types of Design	Minimum Levels of Independent Variable?	Independent Variable Between or Within?	Independent Variable Type?	Creating Equivalent Groups
Independent groups	2	between	manipulated	random assignment
Matched groups	2	between	manipulated	matching
Nonequivalent groups	2	between	subject	matching may reduce nonequivalence
Repeated measures	2	within	manipulated	n/a

(e.g., male/female, introverted/extroverted, liberal/conservative). This design is sometimes called an "ex post facto" design because the groups are formed "after the fact" of their already-existing subject characteristics; it has also been referred to as a "natural groups" design. I prefer the term **nonequivalent groups design**, because groups are made up of different kinds of individuals in this kind of design, and their differences make the groups by definition "nonequivalent." Researchers using these designs usually try to reduce the nonequivalence as much as possible by matching the groups on a variety of factors and controlling extraneous variables as much as they can. For instance, a nonequivalent groups study comparing males and females might select participants for each group that are about the same age and from the same socioeconomic class. Note that this kind of matching, in which subjects in one group are recruited so that they are comparable to those in the other group, is different from the kind of matching that occurs in the matched group design. In the latter, after matched pairs have been formed, they can be randomly assigned to the two groups (refer back to Table 6.1). In nonequivalent groups designs, random assignment is not possible—subjects are already in one group or another by virtue of being male or female, introverted or extroverted, and so on.

The fourth type of single-factor design is a **repeated-measures design**, used when the independent variable is tested within subjects. That is, each participant in the study experiences each level of the independent variable (i.e., is measured repeatedly). The major attributes of each of the four main types of designs are summarized in Table 7.1. Let's look at some specific examples.

Between-Subjects, Single-Factor Designs

Single-factor studies using only two levels are not as common as you might think. Most researchers prefer to use more complex designs, which often produce more elaborate and more intriguing outcomes. Also, few journal editors are impressed with single-factor, two-level designs. Nonetheless, there is a certain beauty in simplicity, and nothing could be simpler than a study comparing just two conditions. The following Research Examples illustrate three such experiments, one comparing independent groups, a second comparing matched groups, and a third comparing nonequivalent groups.

Research Example 8—Independent Groups

An example of an independent groups design using a single factor with two levels is a study by Kasser and Sheldon (2000), which looked at the relationship between insecurity and one's materialist leanings. Their idea for the study derived from the humanistic/existential tradition in psychology, which proposes that when people focus their lives on making lots of money and buying everything in sight, they do so out of a desire to overcome deep-rooted feelings of insecurity. Kasser and Sheldon decided to see if they could *create* a feeling of insecurity in research participants, and then determine if the insecurity influenced how they would respond to questions about financial and consumer issues. From some prior research, they knew that when people are reminded that their lives are finite (i.e., they will eventually and certainly die), the reminder creates feelings of anxiety and insecurity.

The defining feature of an independent groups design is random assignment of participants to groups, and that is exactly what happened in this study. Participants were assigned randomly to two groups. Those in the "mortality-salience" group were asked to write an essay on the "feelings and thoughts they had concerning their own death" (Kasser & Sheldon, 2000, p. 349). Those assigned to the second group wrote an essay on their "thoughts and feelings regarding listening to music" (p. 349). After writing the essays, participants completed a brief filler task and then were asked to think about their lives fifteen years into the future. The dependent variables in the study were the estimates they gave of their future income, the value of their future homes and possessions, how much they'd spend per year on travel, and so on. The prediction was that those participants thinking of their own future demise (the mortality-salience group) would feel temporarily insecure, and the insecurity would trigger greater estimates (hopes?) of future financial well-being. And that is precisely what happened. Compared to those who wrote the essay about music, those thinking of death estimated that their future worth would be significantly higher and that their spending on leisure activities (e.g., vacations) would be greater. In a second study using a similar procedure with two independent groups, participants in another mortality-salience group showed higher levels of greed than those in the music group. The authors believed their study supported the general idea that concern about our inevitable doom creates an insecurity that leads us to think about things that might make us feel more superficially secure—material goods and their consumption.

This study also illustrates a statistical concept called the *outlier*, a concept you first encountered in Chapter 4. This is a data point that is so deviant from the rest of the data that the researcher believes that it cannot reflect reasonable behavior, and its inclusion will distort the results. Outliers can result from such things as a participant misreading the instructions or the data being recorded incorrectly. Because outliers can seriously alter the results (remember from Chapter 4, extreme scores produce means that mislead about typical performance), they are often excluded from the analysis. In the research report, the fact of excluding them, and the criteria used for doing so, must be reported. It is very important to note that there is a danger here, because one does not want to give even the slightest impression that data points are being tossed simply because they mess up a hoped-for result. So it is important, before the study begins, to have agreed-on and precisely defined criteria for throwing out highly deviant data. One commonly used criterion is to exclude data that deviate from the group mean by four or five standard deviations (Sprinthall, 2000), but definitions vary (Hogan & Evalenko, 2006). Remember from Chapter 4 that two standard deviations on either side of the mean of a normal distribution constitute 95% of the data, so four or five standard deviations are going to be pretty extreme. The Kasser and Sheldon (2000) study excluded three outliers—three participants whose future salary estimates were *fifteen* standard deviations above the mean. They must have been *really* insecure.

Research Example 9—Matched Groups

Old movies sometimes feature attempts to extract information from a hero who has been locked up, perhaps tortured, and deprived of sleep for two or three days. Can sleep deprivation affect the responses to interrogation? That was the empirical question asked by Blagrove (1996) in an interesting study using a matched groups design. More specifically, he wanted to know if sleep-deprived people would be influenced by leading questions. He recruited college students for three separate studies, each involving two groups—in each study, some participants were sleep deprived (experimental group) and others were not (control group). The sleep-deprived students spent their time in the laboratory, kept awake for 21 straight hours in the first two studies and 43 hours in the third. Close monitoring by "20 shifts of research assistants" (p. 50) ensured that the subjects remained awake. Nondeprived subjects were allowed to sleep at home. Remember from Chapter 6 that matching is used to create equivalent groups only when the researcher strongly suspects that some factor will correlate with the dependent variable, and if the matching variable can be measured with some precision. Both conditions were met in the Blagrove study. The matching variable was "self-reported habitual sleep durations" (p. 50). Blagrove wanted to make sure that the normal daily amount of sleep was held constant for the two groups to "control for sleep length related group differences in personality and sleep-stage characteristics" (p. 50). The average self-reported sleep times for the two groups were 8.4 and 8.5 hours for the first study, 8.3 and 8.1 for the second, and 8.4 and 8.1 for the third. So the matching procedure was effective.

All participants in the study were given a standardized suggestibility test in which they listened to a story and then responded to misleading questions about it (i.e., questions that could not be directly or accurately answered from information given in the story). After responding, they were given negative feedback about their responses and then questioned again to see if they changed any answers. In general, they were more influenced by the leading questions and more likely to change their answers after being sleep deprived, especially in the third study, in which the sleep deprivation lasted for 43 hours. And using the matching procedure, to ensure that the groups were similar in their typical sleeping patterns, made it possible to attribute the group differences to sleep deprivation and not to any differences in the typical length of sleep for the participants.

Research Example 10—Nonequivalent Groups

One type of research that calls for a nonequivalent group design is one that examines the effects of brain damage that has resulted from an accident of some sort. For obvious ethical reasons, an independent groups design with human subjects is out of the question (any volunteers for the experimental group, those randomly assigned to the group receiving the brain damage?). Although most research studies comparing those with traumatic brain injuries (TBI) look at cognitive factors (e.g., effects on memory or language), an interesting study by McDonald and Flanagan (2004) investigated the abilities of 34 subjects with TBI to process and understand social exchanges. As with many nonequivalent group studies, the researchers tried to reduce the nonequivalence as much as possible, in this case by selecting control group subjects that were "matched on the basis of age, education, and gender" (p. 574).

In the study, both groups viewed videotaped vignettes from a test called "The Awareness of Social Inference Test" (TASIT). The videos portray people having various kinds of social interactions and displaying different emotions. For instance, one TASIT video includes an exchange in which one person is displaying sarcasm, while another video has one person lying to another. McDonald and Flanagan (2004) were interested in determining if those with TBI would be impaired in their ability to (a) accurately detect the basic emotions being felt by those in the tapes (e.g., the anger of someone who was being sarcastic), (b) distinguish sincere from sarcastic comments, and (c) distinguish "diplomatic" lies (told to avoid hurting someone's feelings) from lies told in a sarcastic fashion. Compared to controls, those with TBI were significantly impaired in their abilities to recognize emotions, and to recognize a lack of sincerity. For example, because they had problems detecting anger, they found it hard to distinguish sarcasm from sincerity.

In studies like this, one methodological concern is external validity (Chapter 5). To what extent did the 34 experimental subjects in the McDonald and Flanagan (2004) study represent a typical TBI patient? The researchers were aware of the issue and took pains to select participants who would, as a group, reflect the usual attributes of TBI patients. For example, they compared the number of days of posttraumatic amnesia (76) for their TBI subjects with the number of amnesia days reported "in a consecutive series of 100 people with TBI who were discharged from a comparable brain-injury unit in an independent study" (p. 573), and found no significant difference. From this and other factors, McDonald and Flanagan concluded that their "group was representative of the severity of injury typically seen in this population" (p. 573).

Within-Subjects, Single-Factor Designs

As you already know, any within-subjects design (a) requires fewer participants, (b) is more sensitive to small differences between means, and (c) typically uses counterbalancing to control for sequence effects. A within-subjects design with a single independent variable and two levels will counterbalance in one of two ways. If subjects participate in each condition just once, complete counterbalancing will be used. Half of the participants will experience condition A and then B, and the rest will get B and then A. If participants are tested more than once per condition, reverse counterbalancing (ABBA) could be used. This route was taken by J. Ridley Stroop in the first two of three studies he reported in 1935. This study is high on anyone's "top 10 classic studies" list. For a close look at it, read Box 7.1 before continuing.

Box 7.1

CLASSIC STUDIES—*Psychology's Most Widely Replicated Finding?*

Reverse counterbalancing was the strategy used in a study first published in 1935 by J. Ridley Stroop. The study is so well known that the phenomenon it first demonstrated is now called the "Stroop effect." In an article accompanying a 1992 reprinting of the original paper, Colin MacLeod called the Stroop effect the "gold standard" of measures of attention, and opened his essay by writing that

> it would be virtually impossible to find anyone in cognitive psychology who does not have at least a passing acquaintance with the Stroop effect. Indeed, this generalization could probably be extended to all those who have taken a standard introductory course, where the Stroop task is an almost inevitable demonstration. (MacLeod, 1992, p. 12)

MacLeod went on to state that the Stroop effect is one of psychology's most widely replicated and most frequently cited findings. What did Stroop do?

The original study summarized three experiments completed by Stroop as his doctoral dissertation. We'll focus on the first two because they each illustrate a within-subjects design with one independent variable, tested at two levels, and using reverse counterbalancing. In the first experiment, 14 males and 56 females performed two tasks. Both involved reading the names of color words. Stroop (1992, p. 16) called one of the conditions RCNb ("**R**eading **C**olor **N**ames printed in **b**lack"). Participants read 100 color names (e.g., GREEN) printed in black ink as quickly and accurately as they could. The second condition Stroop (1992, p. 16) called RCNd ("**R**eading **C**olor **N**ames where the color of the print and the word are **d**ifferent"). In this case, the 100 color names were printed in colored ink, but the colors of the ink did not match the color name (e.g., the word GREEN was printed in red ink). The subjects' task was to read the word (e.g., the correct response is "green").

As a good researcher, Stroop was aware of the problems with sequence effects, so he used reverse counterbalancing (ABBA) to deal with the problem. After subdividing each of the stimulus lists into two sets of 50 items, Stroop gave some participants the sequence RCNb–RCNd–RCNd–RCNb, and an equal number of participants the sequence RCNd–RCNb–RCNb–RCNd. Thus, each subject read a total of 200 color names.

Stroop's experiment 1 found *no difference* in performance between the RCNb and RCNd conditions. The average amount of time to read 100 words of each type was 41.0 seconds and 43.3 seconds, respectively. Reading the color names in the RCNd condition was unaffected by having the words printed in contrasting colors.

It was in experiment 2 that Stroop found the huge difference that eventually made his name so well known. Using the same basic design, this time the response was *naming the colors* rather than reading color names. In one condition, NC ("**N**aming **C**olor test"), participants named the colors of square color patches. In the second and key condition, NCWd ("**N**aming **C**olor of **W**ord test, where the color of the print and the word are **d**ifferent"), participants saw the same material as in the RCNd condition of experiment 1, but this time, instead of reading the color name, they were to name the color in which the word was printed. If the letters of the word GREEN were printed in red ink, the correct response this time would be "red," not "green." Participants in 1935 had the same difficulty experienced by people today. Because reading is such an overlearned and automatic process, it interferes with the color naming, resulting in errors and slower reading times. Stroop found that the average color naming times were 63.3 seconds for condition NC and a whopping 110.3 seconds for the NCWd condition. I've taken the four different outcomes, reported by Stroop in the form of tables, and drawn a bar graph of them in Figure 7.2. As you can see, the Stroop effect is a robust phenomenon.

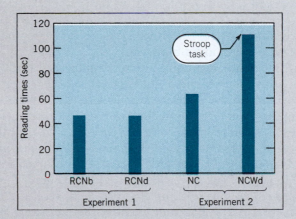

FIGURE 7.2   Combined data from the first two experiments of the original Stroop study (1935).

I mentioned earlier that Stroop actually completed three experiments for his dissertation. The third demonstrated that participants could improve on the NCWd task (the classic Stroop task) if given practice. An unusual aspect of this final study was that in the place of square color patches on the NC test, Stroop, for control purposes, substituted color patches in the shape of swastikas. This "made it possible to print the NC test in shades which more nearly match[ed] those in the NCWd test" (Stroop, 1992, p. 18). The swastika was originally an ancient religious symbol formed by bending the arms of a traditional Greek cross (+). Ironically, Stroop's study was published the same year (1935) that the swastika became officially adopted as the symbol for the National Socialist (or "Nazi" for short) party in Germany.

Another counterbalancing strategy for a study with just two conditions, when each condition is being tested many times, is simply to alternate the conditions (ABAB . . .). Such an approach was taken in the following experiment.

Research Example 11—Repeated Measures

In a study of motion perception and balance, Lee and Aronson (1974) tested some predictions from a theory of perception proposed by James Gibson, mentioned briefly in Chapter 1 as the husband of Eleanor Gibson. In particular, they were interested in how we maintain our balance in a moving environment. Children aged 13 to 16 months were placed in the apparatus pictured in Figure 7.3. When an infant was facing the back wall, the experimenter could move the walls and ceiling either forward or backward, while keeping the floor motionless.

It was hypothesized that moving the room forward (Figure 7.4a) would create an "optic flow pattern" identical to the one produced if the infant's head was moving backward (Figure 7.4b). This, in turn, would trigger a compensating tilt forward by the child. If so, then moving the room forward should cause the infant to lean forward or perhaps fall forward (Figure 7.4c). Just the opposite was predicted when the room was moved backward.

Unlike the situation in a between-subjects study, there is no reason why Lee and Aronson's infants could not experience both experimental conditions: the room moving forward or backward. In fact, there were distinct advantages to having subjects experience both, in order to compare their reactions to each situation. Hence, a within-subjects approach was taken, and the design was a single-factor, repeated-measures design. The single factor, the independent variable, was the direction of the room's movement, either forward or backward, and the infants' body lean or falling was the behavior measured, the dependent variable. Twenty repeated trials were completed per child, with the room's movement alternating from trial to trial. For some children, the alternating sequences began with the room moving forward; for others, the room moved backward on their first trial. Seven participants were tested, ranging in age from 13 to 16 months, but three of them became distressed, and for them the experiment was terminated. The responses of the remaining four participants were recorded by three observers. Some loss of

FIGURE 7.3 The room about to be moved and an infant about to be surprised in Lee and Aronson's (1974) study of perception and balance (courtesy of Dr. David N. Lee, Department of Psychology; University of Edinburgh, Scotland).

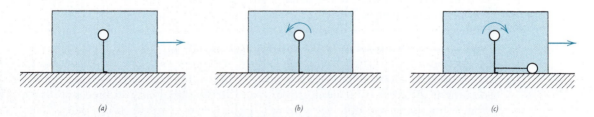

(a)   (b)   (c)

FIGURE 7.4 Predicted effects of moving the room forward in Lee and Aronson's (1974) experiment.

balance in the predicted direction occurred on 82% of the trials. Loss of balance was categorized by the observers as a sway (26% of the trials), a stagger (23%), or a fall (33%). Note the importance of operational definitions here. The researchers needed to be clear about the difference between a "sway" and a "stagger." Even with good definitions, some behaviors might fall into a gray area, and that is why more than one observer was used. Lee and Aronson reported a high degree of consensus among them. You will learn more about this concept of "interobserver reliability" in Chapter 12.

It might have occurred to you that there is a potential problem with a counterbalancing procedure that simply alternates between conditions A and B—participants might easily predict what condition is coming next. However, Lee and Aronson decided that this problem was unlikely to influence their results, given the very young age of their participants. Another reason for their choice of an alternating counterbalancing was practical—with the infants remaining in the moving room throughout the experimental session, once the room had been moved in one direction, the next trial had to be a movement in the opposite direction. To use reverse counterbalancing would have required taking the children out of the room frequently, while the room was being set up in its proper position.

Analyzing Single-Factor, Two-Level Designs

To determine whether the differences found between the two conditions of a single-factor, two-level design are significant or due simply to chance, some form of inferential statistical analysis is required. When interval or ratio scales of measurement are used in the experiment, the most common approach is to use one of two varieties of the *t* test, a procedure mentioned near the end of Chapter 4. Other techniques are required when nominal or ordinal scales of measurement are used or when certain conditions prevent the use of *t* tests. For example, using a *t* test assumes that the data from the two conditions at least approximate a normal distribution. Another assumption is called **homogeneity of variance**, which means that the variability of each of the sets of scores being compared ought to be similar. So, if the standard deviation for one group is significantly larger than the standard deviation for the other group, there is a problem. Tests for homogeneity of variance exist, and if these tests indicate a problem, inferential analyses other than the *t* test can be used. These are called "nonparametric" tests—one common example is the Mann–Whitney *U* test.

There are two varieties of the *t* test for comparing two sets of scores. The first is called a ***t* test for independent samples** (sometimes called a *t* test for independent groups), and, as the name implies, it is used when the two groups of participants are completely independent of each other. This occurs whenever we use random assignment to create equivalent groups, or if the variable being studied is a subject variable involving two different groups (e.g., males vs. females). If the independent variable is a within-subjects factor, or if two separate groups of people are formed in such a way that some relationship exists between them (e.g., participants in group A are matched on intelligence with participants in group B), a ***t* test for related samples** (sometimes called a *t* test for correlated, paired, or dependent samples) is used. For the four single-factor designs just considered, the following *t* tests would be appropriate:

- *t* test for independent samples
  - independent groups design
  - nonequivalent groups design
- *t* test for related samples
  - matched groups design
  - repeated–measures design

In essence, the *t* test examines the difference between the mean scores for the two samples and determines (with some probability) whether this difference is larger than would be expected by chance factors alone. If the difference is indeed sufficiently large, and if potential confounds can be ruled out, then the researcher can conclude with a high probability that the differences between the means reflect some real effect. As you recall from Chapter 4, in addition to determining if the differences are "significant," it is also possible to determine the magnitude of the difference by calculating *effect size*. To learn (or, I hope, review) the exact procedures involved, both in calculating the two forms of *t* test and in determining effect size, consult any introductory statistics text (e.g., Witte & Witte, 2007). You can also work through specific examples of both forms of the *t* test, found in the online "Student Companion Site" (www.wiley.com/college/goodwin). Also at that site, if your school uses SPSS (a common statistical software package), you can use the "SPSS Guide" to learn how to perform both types of *t* tests electronically.

✓ Self Test 7.1

1. There are two different groups in a study, and participants are randomly assigned to one group or the other. What's the design?
2. Ellen signs up for a study in which she completes the Stroop test. Then she is asked to do the task again, but this time the words are turned upside down. What's the design?
3. What is the proper *t* test for a nonequivalent groups design?

Single Factor—More Than Two Levels

When experiments include a single independent variable, using two levels is the exception rather than the rule. Most single-factor studies use three or more levels and, for that reason, they often are called **single-factor multilevel designs**. As was true for two-level designs, these include both between- and within-subjects designs and they include the same four types: independent groups, matched groups, nonequivalent groups, and repeated-measures designs.

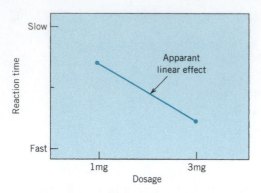

FIGURE 7.5   Hypothetical effects of caffeine on reaction time—two levels.

Between-Subjects, Multilevel Designs

A distinct advantage of multilevel designs is that they enable the researcher to discover **nonlinear effects**. To take a simple between-subjects example, suppose you are interested in the effects of caffeine dosage on reaction time. You set up an experiment that compares two dosage levels (1 mg and 3 mg), get the results in Figure 7.5, and conclude that, as a stimulant, caffeine speeds up reaction time. As the dosage increases, reaction time quickens in a straight-line (i.e., linear) fashion.

Now suppose another researcher does this study but uses a multilevel design that includes four dosages (1 mg, 2 mg, 3 mg, and 4 mg)—an example of *replicating* (1 mg and 3 mg) and *extending* (2 mg and 4 mg) your finding. The study might produce the results in Figure 7.6.

This outcome replicates your results for the 1-mg and 3-mg conditions exactly (dotted line), but the overall pattern for the four conditions calls your conclusion into serious question. Instead of caffeine simply making reaction time faster, the conclusion now would be that (a) adding caffeine quickens reaction time, but only after a level of 2 mg is reached (i.e., no difference between 1 mg and 2 mg), and (b) caffeine quickens reaction time only up to a point; after 3 mg, caffeine begins to slow down reaction time. That is, the outcome is no longer a simple linear result but rather a nonlinear one. In general, the advantage of multilevel designs is that

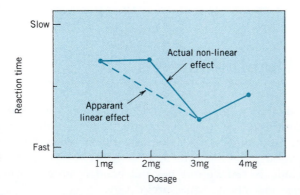

FIGURE 7.6   Hypothetical effects of caffeine on reaction time—four levels.

they are more informative and often provide for more complex and interesting outcomes than two-level designs.

One of psychology's most famous graphs illustrates a nonlinear effect. It shows how the passage of time influences the rate of forgetting, and yields some insight into the common feeling one gets two days after an exam—"I don't remember anything!" The curve comes from the pioneering memory research of Hermann Ebbinghaus, as described briefly in Box 7.2.

Box 7.2

ORIGINS—Nonlinear Results: The Ebbinghaus Forgetting Curve

The nineteenth-century German psychologist Hermann Ebbinghaus (1850–1909) is justifiably famous for his pioneering research on memory and forgetting. At a time when psychology was in its infancy and "how to do psychological research" guides did not exist, Ebbinghaus managed to complete an extended series of studies that set a standard for precision and methodological rigor. His purpose was to examine the formation of associations in the mind, and his first task was to find materials that were devoid of associations. His solution, considered one of the best examples of creativity in scientific psychology, was to string together sequences of consonants, vowels, and consonants. These CVCs are more widely known as nonsense syllables, and Ebbinghaus created about 2,300 of them. For several years, showing either tremendous perseverance or a complete lack of any social life, Ebbinghaus spent hours at a time memorizing and trying to recall various lists of these CVCs. Yes, he was the *only* subject in the research. He systematically varied such factors as the number of syllables per list, the number of study trials per list, and whether the study trials were crammed together or spaced out. He published his result in a small monograph called *Memory: A Contribution to Experimental Psychology* (1885/1964).

In his most famous study, the one resulting in a nonlinear outcome, Ebbinghaus examined the time course of forgetting. His empirical question was this: Once some material has been memorized, how much of that memory persists after varying amounts of time? His procedure was first to commit to memory eight 13-item lists of nonsense syllables, then wait for some period of time, and then attempt to relearn the lists. His time intervals were 20 minutes, 1 hour, 9 hours, 1 day, 2 days, 6 days, and 31 days. Ebbinghaus recorded the total time for both the original learning of the eight lists and the relearning of the lists. Original learning minus relearning yielded a measure of "savings," which was converted to a percentage by dividing by the time of original learning. Thus, if the original learning took 20 minutes and relearning took 5 minutes, 15 minutes or 75% (15/20 × 100) of the original learning time was saved.

His results, which still appear in the memory chapters of most general psychology textbooks, are shown in Figure 7.7. As you can see, recall declined with the passage of time, but the decline was not a steady or linear one. Clearly, it was a nonlinear effect. Forgetting occurred very rapidly at first, but then the rate of forgetting slowed down. Thus, after a mere 20 minutes, only about 60% (58.2, actually) of the original learning had been saved. At the other end of the curve, there wasn't much difference between an interval of a week (25.4% saved) and a month (21.1%).

From the standpoint of methodological control, there are several other interesting things about the Ebbinghaus research. To ensure a constant presentation rate, for example, Ebbinghaus set a metronome to 150 beats per minute and read each CVC exactly on one of the beats. He also tried to study the lists in the same environment and at about the same time of day, and to use no memorization technique except pure repetition. Also, he worked only when sufficiently motivated so that he could "keep the attention concentrated on the tiresome task and its purpose" (Ebbinghaus, 1885/1964, p. 25).

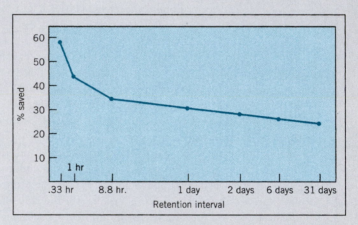

FIGURE 7.7   The Ebbinghaus forgetting curve—a nonlinear outcome.

In addition to identifying nonlinear relationships, single-factor multilevel designs can also test for specific alternative hypotheses and perhaps rule them out. This is a strategy you will recognize from the discussions in Chapters 1 and 3 of the merits of *falsification*. A perfect example is a well-known study by Bransford and Johnson (1972).

Research Example 12—Multilevel Independent Groups

Cognitive psychologists interested in how we comprehend new information have shown that understanding new ideas is easier if they are placed in a meaningful context. For example, understanding a textbook chapter is easier if you have already examined a brief outline of its contents, examined the chapter's objectives, or read the chapter summary before you started to read the chapter itself. The Bransford and Johnson study illustrates these context effects. In their study, participants were asked to comprehend this paragraph. Try it yourself:

> If the balloons popped, the sound wouldn't be able to carry, since everything would be too far away from the correct floor. A closed window would also prevent the sound from carrying, since most buildings tend to be well insulated. Since the whole operation depends on a steady flow of electricity, a break in the middle of the wire would also cause problems. Of course, the fellow could shout, but the human voice is not loud enough to carry that far. An additional problem is that a string could break on the instrument. Then there could be no accompaniment to the message. It is clear that the best situation would involve less distance. Then there would be fewer potential problems. With face to face contact, the least number of things could go wrong. (Bransford & Johnson, 1972, p. 392)

I imagine your reaction to this passage is "Huh?," a response shared by many participants in the original study. However, Bransford and Johnson found that comprehension could be improved by adding some context (meaning). Here's what they did.

They designed a single-factor multilevel independent groups study with five levels of the independent variable. Participants randomly assigned to a control group (no context-1 rep) listened to the paragraph on tape and tried to recall as much as they could of the 14 idea units included in it. They recalled an uninspiring average of 3.6 ideas. A second group (no context-2 reps) heard the story twice to see if recall might improve with simple repetition. It didn't—they recalled just 3.8 ideas. A third group (context before) was first given a 30-second look at the cartoon in Figure 7.8(a). Then they heard and tried to recall the paragraph. They recalled 8.0 ideas out of 14. Clearly, the cartoon gave these participants an overall meaningful context within which to comprehend the sentences of the paragraph. As I am sure you noticed, after looking at the cartoon, the otherwise meaningless collection of sentences in the paragraph now makes sense. But is it necessary to see the cartoon *first*, before reading the passage? Yes. The fourth condition of the study (context after) had subjects listen to the paragraph, *then* see the cartoon, and then recall the paragraph. They recalled 3.6 ideas, just like the first group. Finally, the fifth group was given a partial context. Before listening to the passage, they saw the cartoon in Figure 7.8(b). (partial context). It contains all the elements of Figure 7.8(a), but rearranged in a way that doesn't quite fit with the meaning of the story. Participants in this group recalled an average of 4.0 ideas. In graph form, the results looked like Figure 7.9.

Considering just two groups, "no context-1 rep" and "context before," this study is reasonably interesting, showing a simple improvement in comprehension by adding some context in the form of the cartoon. However, adding the other conditions makes it a *really* interesting study by ruling out (i.e., falsifying) some

FIGURE 7.8 Cartoon providing (a) context and (b) partial context for Bransford and Johnson's (1972) study.

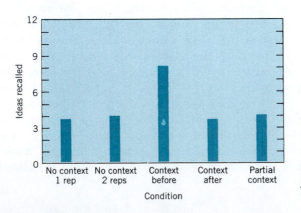

FIGURE 7.9 Data for the five conditions of Bransford and Johnson's study in bar graph form.

alternative factors that might be thought to improve recall in the experiment. Consider these alternatives:

1. It isn't context that matters, it is just practice—give subjects repeated trials and their recall will improve. But simple repetition as an alternative explanation to context can be ruled out by the failure of the "no context-2 reps" condition to produce any increase in recall.

2. It is just showing the cartoon that matters, because the cartoon provides retrieval cues during the memory task that are not present for the one or two repetitions groups. It's not the "context" that matters, simply the presentation of the cartoon image. So it doesn't matter if the cartoon comes before the paragraph or after it. But this explanation can be ruled out by the "context after" condition, which fails to help recall. Because presenting the cartoon after the reading doesn't help, it can be inferred that context improves recall by facilitating the initial processing of the information, not just its subsequent retrieval.

3. The cartoon content just provides additional information that helps subjects, during the test, recall more of the content. But if it is just additional information, then the "partial context" group should also do well. This idea can also be ruled out—recall in the partial context condition is poor. Although this condition contains all of the retrieval cues (images in the cartoon), it lacks a meaningful relationship to the story. Thus, cartoon context improves our understanding of something but *only* if that context is meaningfully related to the paragraph.

The Bransford and Johnson (1972) study, then, is a perfect example of how adding levels of an independent variable can significantly enhance our understanding of some phenomenon, in this case by allowing the researcher to consider and rule out (falsify) explanations that compete with the researcher's preferred explanation. Incidentally, Bransford and Johnson actually reported four experiments in their 1972 paper, the additional studies replicating and extending their finding about the importance of meaningful context with a different set of materials (e.g., a paragraph describing how to do laundry, including sentences like this [p. 722]: "First you arrange things into different groups depending on their makeup") and some other variations in procedure.

Within-Subjects, Multilevel Designs

Whereas a single-factor, repeated-measures design with two levels has limited counterbalancing options, going beyond two levels makes all the counterbalancing options available. If each condition is tested just once per subject, then both full and partial counterbalancing procedures are available. And when each condition is tested several times per subject, both reverse and block randomization procedures can be used. In the following study, each condition was tested just once and a Latin square was used to accomplish counterbalancing.

Research Example 13—Multilevel Repeated Measures

In the Chapter 3 discussion of replication, I briefly mentioned a study by Steele, Bass, and Crook (1999) that failed to replicate a controversial study by Rauscher, Shaw, and Key (1993). The Rauscher study apparently discovered that small but significant improvements in spatial skills could follow from listening to music by Mozart. News of the research reached the popular press, which often distorts accounts of scientific research, and soon stories appeared urging parents to play Mozart to their infants to improve their cognitive abilities. Yet as we saw in Chapter 3, several replication efforts failed. Another study by Ken Steele and his colleagues further questioned the viability of this alleged "Mozart effect."

Steele, Ball, and Runk (1997) included three conditions in their experiment—listening to Mozart for 10 minutes, listening to a recording of soothing environmental sounds (a gentle rainstorm) for 10 minutes, and not listening to anything (sitting quietly for 10 minutes and trying to relax). All 36 participants in the study were tested in each of the three conditions, making this a single-factor, multilevel, repeated-measures design. Although complete counterbalancing would have been easy to implement ($3 \times 2 \times 1$, or six different sequences of conditions, with six participants randomly assigned to each sequence), the authors chose to use a 3×3 Latin square, with twelve participants randomly assigned to each row of the square. To avoid the bias that might result if participants thought they were evaluating the Mozart effect, the participants were "told that the experiment concerned the effect of relaxation on recall" (Steele et al., 1997, p. 1181). Instead of using a spatial skills tasks, Steele et al. used a simple memory task, a reversed digit span procedure—given a stimulus such as "6–8–3–1–7," the correct response would be "7–1–3–8–6." On a given trial, participants would listen to Mozart, listen to gentle rainfall, or sit quietly, and then be given three consecutive digit span tasks. Each digit span included nine numbers, presented in a random order. Thus, a score from 0 to 27 could be earned.

The study did produce some statistically significant findings, but none that would comfort those advocating for the Mozart effect. The average number of digits correctly recalled was virtually identical for all three conditions: 18.53 ($SD = 4.14$) for the Mozart tape, 18.50 ($SD = 6.07$) for the gentle rain tape, and 18.72 ($SD = 5.09$) for the control condition. There was a significant practice effect, however. Regardless of the order in which the conditions were presented, participants improved from the first set of digit span tests to the third set. From the first to the third, the averages were 15.64, 19.14, and 20.97 (SDs of 4.70, 4.87, and 4.29, respectively). So, should parents play Mozart for their children? Sure—it's wonderful music. Will it make them smarter? Apparently not, although it could make them enjoy classical music, an outcome of value by itself.

Presenting the Data

One decision to be made when reporting the results of any research study is how to present the data. There are three choices. First, the numbers can be presented in sentence form, an approach that might be fine for reporting the results of experimental studies with just two or three levels (e.g., the Mozart example), but makes for tedious reading as the amount of data increases. You might have noticed this when reading about the results of the five conditions of the Bransford and Johnson (1972) study. A second approach is to construct a table of results. A table for the Bransford and Johnson study might look like Table 7.2.

TABLE 7.2   *The Bransford and Johnson (1972) Data in Table Format*

Table 1: *Mean Number of Idea Units Recalled as a Function of Different Learning and Recall Contexts*

Condition	Mean Score	Standard Deviation
No context		
1 repetition	3.60	.64
No context		
2 repetitions	3.80	.79
Context		
before	8.00	.65
Context		
after	3.60	.75
Partial		
context	4.00	.60

Note. The maximum score is 14.

A third way to present the data is in the form of a graph, which would portray the Bransford and Johnson study as you've already observed in Figure 7.9. Notice that in an experimental study, a graph always places the dependent variable on the vertical (Y) axis and the independent variable on the horizontal (X) axis. The situation becomes a bit more complicated when more than one independent variable is used, as you will see in the next chapter. Regardless of the number of independent variables, however, the dependent variable *always* goes on the vertical axis.

Deciding between tables and figures is often a matter of the researcher's preference. Graphs can be especially striking if there are large differences to report or (especially) if *interactions* occur (coming in Chapter 8). Tables are often preferred when there are so many data points that a graph would be uninterpretable or when the researcher wishes to inform the reader of the precise values of the means and standard deviations; they have to be guessed at with a graph. One rule you can certainly apply is that you should never present the same data in both table and graph form. In general, you should present data in such a way that the results you have worked so hard to obtain are shown most clearly.

Types of Graphs

Notice that I presented the Bransford and Johnson data in the form of a bar graph (Figure 7.9). Why not present it as a line graph, as in Figure 7.10? Bad idea. The problem concerns the nature of the construct being used as the independent variable and whether its underlying dimension is continuous. A **continuous variable** is one for which a number of intermediate values exist. That is, the variable exists on a continuum. An example might be the dosage level of a drug. In a study

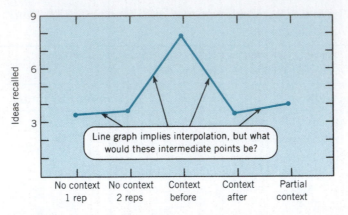

FIGURE 7.10
Bransford and Johnson data inappropriately drawn as a line graph.

comparing 3 mg, 5 mg, and 7 mg of some drug, dosage is a continuous variable. Presumably, we also could use 4-mg or 6-mg dosages if there was a good reason for doing so. For continuous independent variables, it is appropriate to use a line graph to portray the results. That is, because it is reasonable to interpolate between the points of the graph to guess what the effects of intermediate values might be, the line can be used for estimating these in-between effects. Thus, in the drug study, a graph could look like Figure 7.11, and the researcher would be on reasonably solid ground in predicting the effects of intermediate values of the drug, as illustrated by the point marked with an asterisk in Figure 7.12.

Of course, interpolation can be problematic if a study uses two levels of the independent variable, the two levels are far apart, and the relationship is actually nonlinear. Thus, in a drug study comparing 2-mg and 10-mg dosages that produce the solid line in Figure 7.13, interpolating the effects of a 5-mg dosage would produce a large error if the true curve looked like the dotted line. This study would be a good candidate for a single-factor multilevel design.

The situation is different if the independent variable is a **discrete variable**, in which each level represents a distinct category and no intermediate points can occur. In this case no interpolation can be done, and to connect the points with a line is to imply the existence of these intermediate points when in fact they

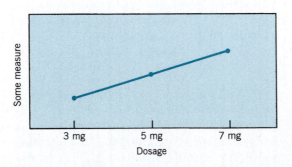

FIGURE 7.11 Appropriate use of a line graph with a continuous variable such as a drug's dosage level.

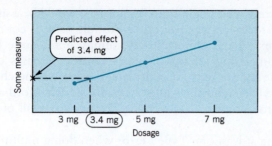

FIGURE 7.12 Interpolating between the points of a line graph.

don't exist. So when using discrete variables, as in the Bransford and Johnson study (Figure 7.9), a bar graph is used. The basic rule is this:

If continuous data: line graph preferred; bar graph acceptable

If discrete data: use a bar graph; a line graph is inappropriate

In general then, bar graphs can be used for both continuous and discrete data, but line graphs should only be used for continuous data. Also, refer back to Box 4.3 for a reminder about the ethics of presenting the data. It is easy to mislead the uninformed consumer of research by doing such things as altering the distances on the *Y*-axis. Your responsibility as a researcher is to present your results honestly and in a way that best illustrate the true outcome of your study.

Analyzing Single-Factor, Multilevel Designs

We have seen that in the case of single-factor, two-level designs with the dependent variable measured on an interval or ratio scale, the null hypothesis can be tested with an inferential statistic called the *t* test. For a multilevel design such as the

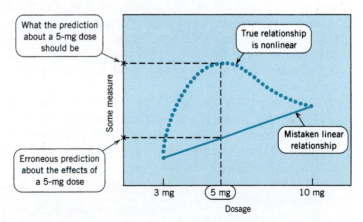

FIGURE 7.13 Problems with interpolation when there is a nonlinear effect and a wide range between levels of the independent variable.

Bransford and Johnson study, you might think the analysis would be a simple matter of completing a series of *t* tests between all of the possible pairs of conditions (e.g., context before vs. context after). Unfortunately, things aren't quite that simple. The difficulty is that completing multiple *t* tests increases the risks of making a Type I error. That is, the more *t* tests you calculate, the greater the chances are of having one accidentally yield significant differences. In the Bransford and Johnson study, you would have to complete 10 different *t* tests to cover all of the pairs of conditions.

The chances of making at least one Type I error when doing multiple *t* tests can be estimated by using this formula:

$$1 - (1 - \text{alpha})^c$$

where c = the number of comparisons being made.

Thus, if all the possible *t* tests are completed in the Bransford and Johnson study, there is a very good chance (4 out of 10) of making at least one Type I error:

$$1 - (1 - .05)^{10} = 1 - (.95)^{10} = 1 - .60 = .40$$

To avoid the problem of multiple *t* tests in single-factor designs, researchers typically use a procedure called a 1-factor (sometimes "1-way") analysis of variance or 1-factor **ANOVA** (**AN**alysis **O**f **VA**riance). The "1-factor" means one independent variable. In essence, a 1-factor ANOVA tests for the presence of some "overall" significance that could exist somewhere among the various levels of the independent variable. Hence, in a study with three levels, the null hypothesis is "level 1 = level 2 = level 3." Rejecting the null hypothesis does not identify exactly which of the " = 's" is really " ≠," however. To determine precisely where the significance lies requires what is called "subsequent testing" or "post hoc (after the fact) analysis." In a study with three levels, subsequent testing would analyze each of the three pairs of comparisons, but only after the overall ANOVA has indicated that some significance exists. A typical procedure is a test called the Tukey's HSD test, with the HSD standing for "honestly significant difference." If the ANOVA does not find any significance, subsequent testing is normally not done, unless some specific predictions about particular pairs of conditions were made ahead of time.

The 1-factor ANOVA yields an "*F* score" or an "*F* ratio." Like the calculated outcome of a *t* test, the *F* ratio examines to what extent the obtained mean differences could be due to chance or are the result of some other factor (presumably the independent variable). Recall from Chapter 4 that an inferential analysis calculates a ratio that looks like this:

$$\text{Inferential statistic} = \frac{\text{Variability between conditions (systematic + error)}}{\text{Variability within each condition(error)}}$$

For a 1-factor ANOVA the inferential statistic is the F ratio. It is typically portrayed in a table called an **ANOVA source table**. Table 7.3 shows you how one of these could be constructed for a 1-factor ANOVA for an independent groups design

TABLE 7.3 *Constructing an ANOVA Source Table for a 1-Factor ANOVA for Independent Groups*

Suppose you are doing an experiment in which three groups of rats are taught to navigate a maze. The independent variable is "delay of reinforcement" and it has three levels. Group 1 rats are given food as soon as they reach the end of the maze, those in Group 2 get food 5 seconds after they reach the end, and those in Group 3 have a 10-second delay in reward. The hypotheses are that (1) learning occurs best for immediate reinforcement and (2) performance suffers in proportion to the increasing delay. The dependent variable is the number of trials taken to learn the maze, with learning operationally defined as two consecutive errorless runs through the maze. Five rats are randomly assigned to each group, making this an independent groups design. The hypothetical results are:

No delay → mean of 13.2 trials (standard deviation of 2.39 trials)

5-sec delay → mean of 20.4 trials (standard deviation of 2.70 trials)

10-sec delay → mean of 21.6 trials (standard deviation of 2.41 trials)

A 1-factor ANOVA is the proper analysis.

Any analysis of variance takes the total amount of variability (variance) in the study and divides it into various "sources." For a 1-factor ANOVA with independent groups, there are two main sources of variance:

1. The variability between groups—between groups 1 and 2, 2 and 3, and 1 and 3. This variance comes from true differences that result from the effects of the independent variable in a well-designed study (and the effects of confounds in poorly-designed studies), as well as some variability due to individual differences among rats in the three groups (which should be minimized or eliminated by a random assignment procedure), and some random factors.

2. The variability within each group. This is the variance that exists among the rats within each group, due to individual differences among them, and some additional random effects. This variability is sometimes called "error variance," although you should not interpret the term "error" to be a mistake of some kind.

An ANOVA source table summarizes the analysis by indicating the sums of squares (*SS*), degrees of freedom (*df*), and mean square (*MS*) for each source of variance, and a final *F* ratio, which determines if differences found among the groups are statistically significant or due to chance. *SS* refers to the sum of squared deviations, a concept introduced in Chapter 4 in Table 4.2, when you learned about standard deviations. Degrees of freedom (*df*) relate to sample size and the number of groups involved in the study. The *df* between groups is equal to the number of groups minus one (in this case $3 - 1 = 2$). The *df* for the error variance is the number of subjects per group minus one, times the number of groups—in this case $[(5 - 1) \times 3] = 12$. (Total degrees of freedom equal the total number of subjects in the study minus one, or $15 - 1 = 14$). *MS* or mean square is another name for variance and in the ANOVA source table, it is found by dividing *SS* by *df* for a particular source (you should check the calculations in the source table). The *F* ratio is found by dividing the variance (*MS*) for the "amount of delay" source of variance by the "error" variance (check this too). Here is the source table for the maze experiment (data from the example used in the online Student Companion Site):

(continued)

TABLE 7.3 *(continued)*

Source of Variance	SS	df	MS	F	p
Reinforcement delay	206.4	2	103.2	16.4	<.01
Error	75.2	12	6.3		
Total	281.6	14			

Recall from Chapter 4 that in any inferential analysis like this one, the researcher hopes for a lot of variability between conditions, and not much variability within each condition. This produces large F ratios, as occurred in this case. Determining whether the F ratio indicates statistical significance involves referring to a Table that you can find in any statistic text (or online—do a Google search for "F distribution table"). In this particular case, the calculated F ratio (16.4) is large enough for the "reject the null hypothesis" decision, with alpha equal to .01. In terms of the language you encountered in Chapter 4, rejecting the null hypothesis at the .01 level means that you believe the probability very low (less than one in a hundred) that the research results are due to chance. With chances this low that the outcome is a random one, it is reasonable to conclude that the effect found in the study is a real one—reinforcement delay hinders maze learning. Please note that when you use a statistical software package such as SPSS, the source table won't just tell you that p is less than .01, it will calculate the exact probability (e.g., $p = .003$) that the results are due to chance.

Remember that after completing a 1-factor ANOVA and finding an overall significant effect, post hoc testing is needed, in order to determine which means are different from the other ones. In this case, a Tukey's HSD test could be done to compare the pairs of means (no delay vs. 5-second delay, no delay vs. 10-second delay, and 5-second delay vs. 10-second delay). These calculations have been completed for you and can be found on the Student Companion Site. The results are that the no delay group learned the maze significantly faster than the other two groups, but that the two delay groups did not differ from each other (makes sense if you look back at the means). In terms of the original hypotheses, the first would be supported by this outcome, but the second would not be supported.

with three levels of the independent variable. The complete calculations for this analysis, as well as a follow-up analysis for effect size, can also be worked through—they are on the Student Companion Site (www.wiley.com/college/goodwin). The site will also show you how to use SPSS to complete a 1-factor ANOVA, as well as a Tukey's HSD test.

Finally, be aware that even though t tests are normally used when the independent variable has just two levels, a 1-factor ANOVA also could be used in that situation. Actually, the t test can be considered a special case of the ANOVA, used when there is a single independent variable with just two levels.

✓ Self Test 7.2

1. There are two main reasons why researchers sometimes use more than two levels of an IV. Which reason is illustrated by the famous Ebbinghaus memory study?
2. Why must a study like the Bransford and Johnson study (effect of context on memory) be portrayed with a bar graph and not a line graph?
3. In the Research Example that examined the so-called Mozart effect, what was the design?

Control Group Designs

I introduced the basic distinction between experimental groups and control groups in Chapter 5. As you recall, although control groups are not always needed, they are especially useful when the research calls for a comparison of some treatment (e.g., a drug effect) with some baseline level of behavior. Experimental groups receive some treatment, while those in the control group do not. In repeated-measures designs, which do not have different groups, a parallel distinction can be made between experimental conditions and control *conditions*, with both conditions experienced by each of the study's participants. Besides the typical control group situation in which a group is left untreated, three other specific types of control groups are worth describing in more detail: placebo controls, waiting list controls, and yoked controls.

Placebo Control Groups

A "placebo" is a substance given to a participant in a form suggesting some specific pharmacological effect when in fact the substance is pharmacologically inactive. Sometimes patients will feel better when given a placebo but told it is drug X, simply because they believe the drug will make them better. In research, members of a **placebo control group** are led to believe they are receiving some treatment when in fact they aren't. You can see why this would be necessary. Suppose you wished to determine if alcohol slows down reaction time. If you used a simple experimental group that was given alcohol and a second group that received nothing to drink, then gave both groups a reaction time test, the reactions indeed might be slower for the first group. Can you conclude that alcohol slows reaction time? No—participants might hold the general belief that alcohol will slow them down, and their reactions might be subtly influenced by that knowledge. To solve the problem, you should include a group given a drink that seems to be alcoholic (and cannot be distinguished in taste from the true alcoholic drink) but is not. This group is the placebo control group. Should you eliminate the straight control group (no drinks at all)? Probably not—these individuals yield a simple baseline measure of reaction time. If you include all three groups and get these average reaction times:

Experimental group:	.32 second
Placebo control:	.22 second
Straight control:	.16 second

you could conclude that what people expect about the effects of alcohol slowed reaction time somewhat (from .16 to .22) but that alcohol by itself also had an effect beyond people's expectations (.22 to .32). By the way, in terms of the various designs introduced earlier in this chapter, this study would be an independent groups, single-factor, multilevel design, assuming subjects would be randomly assigned to groups. If subjects were first matched on some variable (e.g., matched for weight), the study would be a matched groups, single-factor, multilevel design. Can you think why a nonequivalent groups design or a repeated-measures design would be inappropriate here?

Waiting List Control Groups

Waiting list control groups are often used in research designed to assess the effectiveness of some program (Chapter 10) or in studies on the effects of psychotherapy. In this design, the participants in the experimental group are in a program because they are experiencing some type of problem that the program is designed to alleviate; waiting list controls are also experiencing the problem. For instance, a study by Miller and DiPilato (1983) evaluated the effectiveness of two forms of therapy (relaxation and desensitization) to treat clients who suffered from nightmares. They wanted to include a no-treatment control, but to ensure that the clients in all three groups (relaxation, desensitization, control) were generally equivalent to each other, the control group subjects also had to be nightmare sufferers. Having identified a group of nightmare sufferers, they were randomly assigned to the three groups, making this an independent groups, single-factor, multilevel design. For ethical reasons, those assigned to the waiting list were assured that they would be helped, and after the study ended they were given treatment equivalent to that experienced by the experimental groups.

Giving the waiting list participants an opportunity to benefit from some therapy procedure provides an important protection for subject welfare, but it also creates pressures on the researcher to use this control procedure only for therapies or programs of relatively brief duration. In the Miller and DiPilato (1983) study, for example, the subjects in the two experimental groups were in relaxation or desensitization therapy for 15 weeks, and both forms of therapy produced a reduction in nightmares compared to the waiting list control subjects. At the end of 15 weeks, those in the waiting list control group began treatment (randomly assigned to either relaxation or desensitization, because both procedures had worked).

Some might argue that it is unethical to put people into a waiting list control group because they won't receive the program's benefits right away and might be harmed while waiting. This issue can be especially problematic when research evaluates life-influencing programs. Read Box 7.3 for an examination of this issue and a defense of the use of control groups, including waiting lists, in research.

Box 7.3

ETHICS—Who's in the Control Group?

In a study on human memory in which an experimental group gets special instructions to use visual imagery, while a control group is told just to learn the word lists, the question of who is assigned to the control group does not create an ethical dilemma. However, things are not so simple when an experiment is designed to evaluate a program or treatment that, if effective, would clearly benefit people, perhaps even by prolonging their lives. For example, in a well-known study of the effects of personal control on health (Langer & Rodin, 1976), some nursing home residents were given increased control over their daily planning, while control group residents had their daily planning done for them (for the most part) by the nursing staff. On the average, residents in the first group were healthier, mentally and physically, and were more likely to be alive when the authors came back and did an 18-month follow-up study (Rodin & Langer, 1977). If you discovered that one of your relatives had been assigned to the control group, do you think you would be concerned?

In a similar vein, there has been some controversy over the assignment of participants to control groups in studies with cancer patients (Adler, 1992). The research concerned the effects of support groups on the psychological well-being and physical health of women with breast cancer. The findings indicated that women in support groups recovered more quickly and even lived longer than women not placed in these groups (i.e., they are in the control group). Some researchers argued that the results did not reflect the benefits of support groups as much as the harm done to those in the control group who might feel left out or rejected. This could create stress, and it is known that stress can harm the immune system, leading to a host of health-related problems. So is there some truth to Figure 7.14? At the extreme, can being in a control group kill you?

Defenders of the control group approach to evaluating programs make three strong arguments. First, they point out that hindsight is usually perfect. It is easy after the fact to say that "a program as effective as this one ought to be available to everyone." The problem is that *before* the fact it is not so obvious that a program would be effective. The only way to tell is to do the study. Prior to Langer and Rodin's nursing home study, for example, one easily could have predicted that the experimental

FIGURE 7.14   Potential consequences of being assigned to the control group? (© The New Yorker Collection 1993 Donald Reilly from cartoonbank.com. All Rights Reserved.)

group subjects would be unnecessarily stressed by the added responsibility of caring for themselves and drop like flies. Similarly, those defending the cancer studies point out that, when these studies began, few women expressed any preference about their assignment to either an experimental or a control group, and some actually preferred to avoid the support groups (Adler, 1992). Hence, it was not necessarily the case that control group participants will feel left out or overly stressed.

Second, researchers point out that in research evaluating a new treatment or program, the comparison is seldom between the new treatment and no treatment; it is usually between the new treatment and the most favored *current* treatment. So, for control group members, available services are not really being withheld; they are receiving the normal, well-established services. Furthermore, once the study has demonstrated some positive effect of the experimental treatment, members of the control groups are typically given the opportunity to be treated with the new approach.

Third, treatments cost money, and it is certainly worthwhile to spend the bucks on the best treatment. That cannot be determined without well-designed research on program effectiveness, however. In the long run, programs with empirically demonstrated effectiveness serve the general good and may, in many cases, save or prolong lives.

Remember the Chapter 1 discussion of pseudoscience, as illustrated with the case of subliminal self-help CDs? As we saw, there is ample research indicating that any positive effects of these tapes are the result of what people expect to happen. Testing expectancy often involves the use of placebo controls, but consider the following Research Example, which effectively combines both placebos and waiting lists to yield a new interpretation of what these self-help CDs accomplish.

Research Example 14—Using Both Placebo and Waiting List Control Groups

One of the favorite markets for the subliminal self-help business is in the area of weight loss. Americans in particular try to lose weight by attempting an unending variety of techniques, from fad diets to surgery. People are especially willing to try something when minimal effort is involved, and this is a defining feature of the subliminal approach—just pop in a CD and pretty soon your unconscious will be directing your behavior so that weight loss will be inevitable. In a study that creatively combined a placebo control and a waiting list control, Merikle and Skanes (1992) evaluated the effectiveness of self-help weight loss audiotapes. Forty-seven adult females were recruited through newspaper ads and randomly assigned to one of three groups. The experimental group participants ($N = 15$) were given a commercially produced subliminal self-help audiotape that was supposed to help listeners lose weight. Those in the placebo control group ($N = 15$) thought they were getting a subliminal tape designed for weight loss, but in fact they were given one designed to relieve dental anxiety (the researchers had a sense of humor). The two tapes were indistinguishable to ordinary listeners. A third group, the waiting list control ($N = 17$), was told "that the maximum number of subjects was currently participating in the study and that . . . they had to be placed on a waiting list" (p. 774). Those in the experimental and placebo groups were told to listen to their tapes for one to three hours per day and participants in all three groups were weighed weekly for five weeks. The results? As you can see in Figure 7.15, those in the experimental group lost a modest amount of weight (very modest—check out the *Y*-axis), but the *same* amount was also lost by those in the placebo control group. This is the outcome typical with this type of study, indicating that the subliminal tapes have no effect by themselves. The interesting outcome, however, was that the waiting list group also lost weight, about the same amount as the other two groups. This led Merikle and Skanes to conclude that subliminal tapes do not produce their results simply because of a placebo effect. If this had been true, the placebo group participants, believing their mind was being altered, would have lost weight, but the waiting list group folks, not yet in possession of the tapes, would not have lost any weight. Their weight loss led the authors to argue that simply being in an experiment on weight led subjects in all three groups to think about the problem they were experiencing. The subjects in all three groups "may have lost weight simply because participation in the study increased the likelihood that they would attend to and think about weight-related issues during the course of the study" (p. 776). In this study, the waiting list group had the effect of evaluating the strength of the placebo effect and providing an

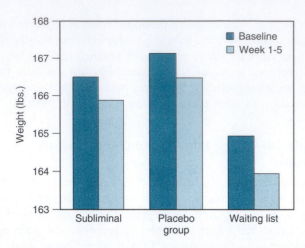

FIGURE 7.15   Results of the Merikle and Skanes (1992) study using placebo and waiting list control groups to evaluate a subliminal self-help program for weight loss.

alternative explanation for the apparent success of subliminal tapes. Also, although the authors didn't mention the term, the study's outcome sounds suspiciously like a Hawthorne effect, which you learned about in Chapter 6. And you might have noticed that the rationale for adding the waiting list control group is another example, like the Bransford and Johnson (1972) memory study described earlier, of adding more than two levels to an independent variable in order to directly test (and potentially rule out) certain hypotheses. The Merikle and Skanes study raises serious questions about the placebo effect hypothesis as an explanation for the effects of subliminal self-help CDs.

One final point worth mentioning about this study is that the second author, Heather Skanes, was the experimenter throughout the study, and the first author, Philip Merikle, arranged the subliminal tape labels. Thus, he was the only one who knew who was getting the weight loss tape (experimental group) and who was getting the dental anxiety tape (placebo group). That is, the authors built a nice double blind control into their study.

Yoked Control Groups

A third type of control group is the **yoked control group**. It is used when each participant in the experimental group, for one reason or another, participates for varying amounts of time or is subjected to different types of events in the study. Each member of the control group is matched or "yoked" to a member of the experimental group so that, for the groups as a whole, the time spent participating or the types of events encountered is kept constant. A specific research example will clarify the concept.

Research Example 15—A Yoked Control Group

A nice example of a yoked control group is a study by Dunn, Schwartz, Hatfield, and Wiegele (1996). The study was designed to evaluate the effectiveness of a psychotherapy technique that was popular (but controversial) in the 1990s. The therapy is called "eye movement desensitization and reprocessing," or EMDR. It is said to be effective as a treatment for anxiety disorders, especially, posttraumatic stress disorder. The essence of the therapy is that the client brings to mind and concentrates on some personal traumatic event. While thinking about this event, the client follows a series of hand movements made by the therapist by moving the eyes rapidly from side to side. During the session, the client continuously rates the level of stress being experienced, and when it reaches a certain low point, the eye movement tracking stops. This might sound a bit fishy to you, as it did to Dunn and his colleagues. They wondered if a placebo effect might be operating—clients think the procedure will work and their expectations and faith in the therapist make them feel better. Most of the support for EMDR has been anecdotal (and you know from Chapter 1 to be skeptical about testimonials), so Dunn decided to use a stronger experimental test.

Dunn et al. (1996) identified 28 college students who had experienced mildly traumatic events (those who they found with more serious trauma were referred to the university counseling center), and after using a matching procedure to create equivalent groups (matching them for age, sex, and the type of traumatic event they reported), randomly assigned them to an experimental and a yoked control group. In the experimental group, participants underwent EMDR. As they thought about their traumatic event and tracked the experimenter's finger with their eyes, they periodically reported their level of stress on a 10-point "SUD" (Subjective Units of Discomfort) scale. Some physiological measures (e.g., pulse) were also recorded. This continued until they reached a SUD level of 0–1 or until 45 minutes had elapsed. Hence, the therapy lasted for varying amounts of time for those in the experimental group, making this study a good candidate for a yoked control group procedure. Participants in the control group were "yoked" in terms of how long the session lasted, so if a subject in the EMDR group took 25 minutes to reach a SUD level of 0–1, a subject in the yoked control group would participate in the control procedures for 25 minutes. The control group did everything the experimental group did (i.e., thought about the trauma, reported SUD), but instead of the eye movements, they focused their visual attention on a nonmoving red dot in the middle of a yellow card. By using the yoked control procedure, Dunn et al. guaranteed that the average amount of time spent in a "session" would be identical for the experimental and control group subjects and that the two groups would do everything the same, except for the eye movements. They also began testing a third yoked group that would only think about the trauma, but not get any form of therapeutic treatment during the session. After just a few subjects were tested, however, this third group was cancelled on ethical grounds—the subjects found the procedure too stressful.

The result was that the EMDR group showed a significant reduction in the SUD score. Unfortunately for advocates of EMDR, the yoked control group also showed a drop, and while the reduction was *slightly* larger for the EMDR group, there were no significant differences between the two groups. These data can be seen in Figure 7.16. The fact that both groups showed essentially the same improvement led Dunn et al. (1996) to conclude that a placebo effect is probably lurking behind any alleged success of EMDR.

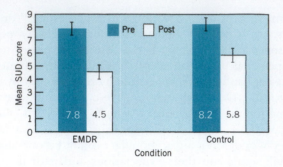

FIGURE 7.16   Results of the Dunn et al. (1996) study evaluating the effectiveness of EMDR therapy.

You will notice that Figure 7.16 also includes vertical lines at the top of each bar. These are called **error bars**, and they indicate the amount of variability that occurred in each condition. In this case, the distance between the top of a bar and the end of the vertical line represents the size of the standard deviation (error bars can sometimes mean other things, such as confidence intervals). Including error bars in graphs enables the researcher to show the reader both central tendency and variability in a graph, and these bars are becoming more common (note that they were not included by the researchers in Figure 7.15, the subliminal self-help study).

One final point about this EMDR study is that it demonstrates that a finding of "no difference" between groups can be important. Recall from Chapter 4 that finding a significant difference when the null hypothesis is indeed false can be "experimenter heaven." Failing to reject a null hypothesis is usually disappointing and can be a difficult finding to interpret, but such an outcome can be useful in a study like the EMDR one. Any time someone advocates a new treatment program of some kind, that person is obligated to show that the program works. This means finding a significant difference between those getting the treatment and those not getting it, and a failure to find such a difference invites skepticism. Recall from Chapter 1 that researchers are skeptical optimists. They are prepared to accept new ideas supported by good research, but very incredulous about claims that are unsupported by empirical evidence.

✓   Self Test 7.3

1.   Look back at the hypothetical reaction time data in the "placebo control groups" section of the chapter. Suppose there was nothing but a placebo effect operating. How would the reaction time numbers change?

2.   In the Research Example evaluating EMDR, why is it that a finding of "no difference" between the experimental and control groups can be a useful outcome?

The designs in this chapter have in common the presence of a single independent variable. In Chapter 8, you will encounter the next logical step—designs with more than one independent variable. These are called "factorial designs."

Chapter Summary

Single Factor—Two Levels

The simplest experimental designs have a single independent variable with two levels of that variable. These designs can include between-subjects variables or within-subjects variables. Between-subjects variables can be directly manipulated or they can be selected as subject factors. If manipulated, participants can be randomly assigned to groups (independent groups design) or matched on some potentially confounding variable, and then randomly assigned (matched groups design). If a subject variable is used, the between-subjects design is called a nonequivalent groups design. Single-factor designs using a within-subjects variable are usually called repeated-measures designs (e.g., the famous Stroop studies). Studies using two levels of the independent variable are normally evaluated statistically with *t* tests (assuming interval or ratio data, normal distributions, and homogeneity of variance).

Single Factor—More Than Two Levels

When only two levels of some experimental variable are compared, the results will always appear to be linear because a graph of the results will have only two points. Some relationships are nonlinear, however (e.g., the Ebbinghaus forgetting curve), and they can be discovered by adding more than two levels to an independent variable. Adding levels can also function as a way to test and perhaps rule out (falsify) alternative explanations of the main result. Like the two-level case, multilevel designs can be either between- or within-subjects designs. Results can be presented visually through the use of bar graphs when the independent variable is a discrete variable or with a line graph if the variable is continuous. Studies using more than two levels of an independent variable are normally evaluated statistically with a 1-factor Analysis of Variance or ANOVA (assuming interval or ratio data, normal distributions, and homogeneity of variance). A significant *F* ratio results in subsequent post hoc testing (e.g., Tukey's HSD test) to identify precisely which means differ from each other.

Control Group Designs

In control group designs, there is at least one condition in which the experimental treatment is absent. Varieties of control groups include placebo controls, often found in drug research; waiting list controls, found in research on the effectiveness of some type of program or therapy; and yoked controls, in which the procedural experiences of the control group participants correspond exactly to those of the treatment group participants.

Chapter Review Questions

1. Consider independent groups designs, matched groups designs, and nonequivalent groups designs. What do they all have in common and how do they differ?

2. In the Research Example that compared sleep-deprived persons with those not so deprived, why was a matched groups design used, instead of an independent groups design, and what was the matching variable?

3. Describe the Stroop effect, the experimental design used by Stroop, and his method for controlling sequence effects.

4. Describe the two varieties of two-sample t tests and, with reference to the four designs in the first part of the chapter (single factor—two levels), explain when each type of test is used.

5. Use the hypothetical caffeine and reaction time study to illustrate how multilevel designs can produce nonlinear effects.

6. Use the Bransford and Johnson experiment on the effects of context on memory to illustrate how a design with more than two levels of an independent variable can test multiple hypotheses and serve the purpose of falsification.

7. Describe when it is best to use a line graph, and when to use a bar graph. Explain why a line graph would be inappropriate in a study comparing the reaction times of males and females.

8. For an independent groups study with one independent variable and three levels, what is the proper inferential statistical analysis, and why is this approach better than doing multiple t tests? How does "post hoc" testing come into play?

9. Use the example of the effects of alcohol on reaction time to explain the usefulness of a placebo control group.

10. Use the subliminal CDs study to illustrate the usefulness of a waiting list control group.

11. Use the study of the effectiveness of EMDR therapy to explain how a yoked control group works.

Applications Exercises

Exercise 7.1   Identifying Variables

As a review, look back at each of the Research Examples in this chapter and identify (a) the independent variable, (b) the levels of the independent variable, and (c) the dependent variable.

1. Research Example 8—Independent Groups
2. Research Example 9—Matched Groups
3. Research Example 10—Nonequivalent Groups
4. Research Example 11—Repeated Measures
5. Research Example 12—Multilevel Independent Groups
6. Research Example 13—Multilevel Repeated Measures
7. Research Example 14—Using Both Placebo and Waiting List Control Groups
8. Research Example 15—A Yoked Control Group

Exercise 7.2   Identifying Designs

For each of the following descriptions of studies, identify the independent and dependent variables involved and the nature of the independent variable (between-subjects or within-subjects; manipulated or subject variable), name the experimental design being used, and identify the measurement scale (nominal, ordinal, interval, or ratio) for the dependent variable(s).

1. In a study of how bulimia affects the perception of body size, a group of bulimic women and a group of same-age nonbulimic women are asked to examine a precisely graded series of 10 drawings of women of different sizes and to indicate which size best matches the way they think they look.

2. College students in a cognitive mapping study are asked to use a direction finder to point accurately to three unseen locations that differ in distance from the laboratory. One is a nearby campus location, one is a nearby city, and the third is a distant city.

3. Three groups of preschoolers (50 per group, assigned randomly) are in a study of task perseverance in which the size of the delay of reward is varied. The children in all three groups are given a difficult puzzle and told to work on it as long as they would like. One group is told that as payment they will be given $5 at the end of the session. The second group will get the $5 after two days from the end of the session, and the third will get the money after four days.

4. To examine whether crowding affects problem-solving performance, participants are placed in either a large or a small room while attempting to solve a set of word puzzles. Before assigning participants to the two conditions, the researcher takes a measure of their verbal intelligence to ensure that the average verbal IQ of the groups is equivalent.

5. In a study of first impressions, students examine three consecutive photos of a young woman whose arms are covered with varying amounts of tattoos. In one photo, the woman has no tattoos; in the second photo she has one tattoo on each arm; in the third photo, she has three tattoos per arm. From a checklist, students indicate which of five different majors the students is likely to be enrolled in and rate the young woman on 10 different 7-point bipolar scales (e.g., one scale has emotionally insecure at one end and emotionally secure at the other end).

6. In an attempt to identify the personality characteristics of cell phone users, three groups of college students are identified—those who do not have a cell phone; those who own a cell phone, but report using less than 2 hours per week; and those who own a cell phone and report using it more than 10 hours per week. They are given a personality test that identifies whether they have an outgoing or a shy personality.

7. A researcher studies a group of 20 men, each with the same type of brain injury. They are divided into two groups in such a way that their ages and educational levels are kept constant. All are given anagram problems to solve; one group is given two minutes to solve each anagram and the second group is given four minutes per anagram.

8. To determine if maze learning is affected by the type of maze used, 20 rats are randomly assigned to learn a standard alley maze (i.e., includes side walls; located on the lab floor); another 20 learn an elevated maze (no side walls; raised above floor level). Learning is assumed to occur when the rats run through the maze without making any wrong turns.

Exercise 7.3   Outcomes

For each of the following studies, decide whether to illustrate the described outcomes with a line graph or a bar graph; then create graphs that accurately portray the outcomes.

1. In a study of the effects of marijuana on immediate memory for a 30-item word list, participants are randomly assigned to an experimental group, a placebo control group, or a straight control group.

   Outcome A. Marijuana impairs recall, while expectations about marijuana have no effect on recall.

   Outcome B. Marijuana impairs recall, but expectations about marijuana also reduce recall performance.

   Outcome C. The apparently adverse affect of marijuana on recall can be attributed entirely to placebo effects.

2. A researcher uses a reliable and valid test to assess the autonomy levels of three groups of first-year female college students after they have been in college for two months. Someone with a high level of autonomy has the ability to function well without help from others, that is, to be independent. Tests scores range from 0–50, with higher scores indicating greater autonomy. One group (R300) is made up of resident students whose homes are 300 miles or more from campus; the second group includes resident students whose homes are less than 100 miles from campus (R100); the third group includes commuter students (C).

   Outcome A. Commuter students are more autonomous than resident students.

   Outcome B. The farther one's home is from the campus, the more autonomous that person is likely to be.

Outcome C. Commuters and R300 students are both very autonomous, while R100 students are not.

3. Animals learn a maze and, in the process of so doing, errors (i.e., wrong turns) are recorded. When they reach the goal box on each trial, they are rewarded with food. For one group of rats, the food is delivered immediately after they reach the goal (0 delay). For a second group, the food appears 5 seconds after they reach the goal (5-second delay).

Outcome A. Reinforcement delay hinders learning.

Outcome B. Reinforcement delay has no effect on learning.

4. Basketball players shoot three sets of 20 foul shots under three different levels of arousal—low, moderate, and high. Under low arousal, every missed free throw means they have to run a lap around the court (i.e., it is a minimal penalty, not likely to cause arousal). Moderate arousal means two laps per miss and high arousal means four laps per miss (i.e., enough of a penalty to create high arousal, perhaps in the form of anxiety). It is a repeated-measures design; assume proper counterbalancing.

Outcome A. There is a linear relationship between arousal and performance; as arousal increases, performance declines.

Outcome B. There is a nonlinear relationship between arousal and performance; performance is good only for moderate arousal.

Answers to Self Tests:

✓ **7.1.**
1. Single-factor, two-level independent groups design.
2. Single-factor, two-level repeated measures design.
3. A *t* test for independent samples.

✓ **7.2.**
1. Find a nonlinear effect.
2. The IV is a discrete variable, with no intermediate points that would allow for extrapolation in a line graph.
3. Single-factor, multilevel repeated-measures design.

✓ **7.3.**
1. Instead of .32 sec, the RT for the experimental group would be .22 sec (same as placebo group).
2. It raises questions about the validity of the new therapy being proposed. Those making claims about therapy are obligated to show that it works (i.e., produces results significantly better than a control group).

CHAPTER 8

Experimental Design II: Factorial Designs

Preview & Chapter Objectives

Chapter 7 introduced you to some basic experimental designs—those involving a single independent variable, with either two or more levels of that variable being compared. The next logical step is to increase the number of independent variables. When a study includes more than a single independent variable, the result is called a factorial design, the focus of this chapter. When you complete this chapter, you should be able to:

- Describe factorial designs using a standardized notation system (2×2, 3×5, etc.).
- Place data accurately into a factorial matrix and calculate row and column means.
- Understand what is meant by a main effect and know how to determine if one exists.

- Understand what is meant by an interaction effect and know how to determine if one exists.
- Know how to interpret interactions and know that the presence of an interaction sometimes lessens or eliminates the relevance of a main effect.
- Identify the varieties of factorials that correspond to the single-factor designs of Chapter 7 (independent groups, matched groups, nonequivalent groups, repeated measures).
- Identify a mixed factorial design and understand why counterbalancing is not always used in such a design.
- Identify a P × E factorial and understand what is meant when such a design produces main effects and interactions.
- Distinguish a mixed P × E factorial from a simple P × E factorial.
- Calculate the number of participants needed to complete each type of factorial design.
- Construct an ANOVA source table for a 2-factor ANOVA for an independent groups design.
- Know how to be an ethically responsible experimenter.

As you have been working your way through this research methods course, you have probably noticed that experimental psychologists sometimes seem to have a language of their own. They talk about operationalizing constructs, rejecting null hypotheses, and eliminating confounds, and when they talk about regression, they are not discussing Freud. You haven't seen anything yet. After mastering this chapter, you will be able to say things like this: "It was a two by three mixed factorial that produced one main effect for the repeated measures variable plus an interaction." Let's start with the basics.

Factorial Essentials

Suppose you are interested in memory and wish to find out if recall can be improved by training people to use visual imagery while memorizing a list of words. You could create a simple two-group experiment in which some people are trained to use visual imagery techniques while memorizing the words ("create a mental image of each word") and some are told to use rote repetition ("just repeat the words over and over to yourself"). Suppose you also wonder about how memory is affected by a word list's presentation rate. Again, you could do a simple two-group study. Some participants see the lists at the rate of 2 seconds per word, others at 4 seconds per word. With a factorial design, *both* of these studies can be done as part of the same experiment.

By definition, a **factorial design** involves any study with more than one independent variable (the terms "independent variable" and "factor" mean the same thing). In principle, factorial designs could involve dozens of independent variables, but in practice these designs usually involve two or three factors, sometimes four.

Identifying Factorial Designs

First, a factorial is described with a numbering system that simultaneously identifies the number of independent variables and the number of levels of each variable. Thus a 2 × 3 (read this as "two by three") factorial design has two independent variables: The first has two levels; the second has three. A 3 × 4 × 5 factorial has three independent variables, with three, four, and five levels, respectively. The hypothetical memory study would be a 2 × 2 design, with two levels of the "type of training" independent variable (imagery and rote repetition) and two levels of the "presentation rate" independent variable (2 and 4 seconds per item).

Second, the total number of conditions to be tested in a factorial study can be identified by looking at all possible combinations of the different levels of each independent variable. In our hypothetical memory study, this produces a display called a **factorial matrix**, which looks like this:

Presentation rate

	2-sec/word	4-sec/word
Imagery		
Rote		

Type of training

Before going on, there's something you should note very carefully. Up to this point in the book, I have been using the concepts "conditions of the experiment" and "levels of the independent variable" as if they meant the same thing. These concepts indeed are interchangeable in single-factor experiments. In factorials, however, this is no longer the case. In all experimental designs, the term "levels" refers to the number of levels of the independent variable. In factorial designs, the term "conditions" equals the number of cells in a matrix like the one you just examined. Hence, the 2 × 2 memory study has *two* independent variables, each with *two* levels. It has *four* different conditions, however, one for each of the four cells. The number of conditions in any factorial design can be determined simply by calculating the product of the numbers in the notation system. Thus, a 3 × 3 design has nine conditions; a 2 × 5 has ten conditions, and a 2 × 2 × 2 has eight conditions. Incidentally, although the use of a factorial matrix is a bit awkward when there are three independent variables, as in the 2 × 2 × 2 just mentioned, a matrix can be drawn. Suppose our memory study added sex as a third factor, in addition to presentation rate and type of training. The factorial matrix could look like this:

	Males		Females	
	2-sec/item	4-sec/item	2-sec/item	4-sec/item
Imagery				
Rote				

Outcomes—Main Effects and Interactions

In factorial studies, two kinds of results occur—main effects and interactions. Main effects refer to the overall influence of the independent variables, and interactions examine whether the variables combine to form a more complex result. Let's look at each in more detail.

Main Effects

In the memory experiment we've been using as a model, the researcher is interested in the effects of two independent variables: type of training and presentation rate. In factorial designs, the term **main effect** is used to describe the overall effect of a single independent variable. So, in a study with two independent variables, such as a 2 × 2 factorial, there can be at most two significant main effects. Determining the main effect of one factor involves combining all of the data for each of the levels of that factor. In the memory study, this can be illustrated as follows. The main effect of type of training is determined by combining the data for those trained to use imagery (for both presentation rates) and comparing it to all of the data for those using rote repetition. Hence, all of the information in the lightly shaded cells (imagery) would be combined and compared with the combined data in the more heavily shaded cells (rote):

		Presentation rate	
		2-sec/word	4-sec/word
Type of training	Imagery		
	Rote		

Similarly, the main effect of presentation rate is determined by combining the data for everyone presented the words at a 2-second rate and comparing that with the data from those presented the words at a 4-second rate. In the following matrix, the effect of presentation rate would be evaluated by comparing all of the information in the lightly shaded cells (2 sec/item) with all of the data in the more heavily shaded cells (4 sec/item):

Presentation rate

	2-sec/word	4-sec/word
Imagery		
Rote		

Type of training

Let's consider some hypothetical data that might be collected in a memory experiment like the example we've been using. Assume there are 25 subjects in each condition (i.e., each cell of the matrix) and their task is to memorize a list of 30 words. The average number of words recalled for each of the four conditions might look like this:

Presentation rate

	2-sec/word	4-sec/word
Imagery	17	23
Rote	12	18

Type of training

Does imagery training produce better recall than rote repetition? That is, is there a main effect of type of training? The way to find out is to compare all of the "imagery" data with all of the "rote" data. Specifically, this involves calculating what are called "row means." The "imagery" row mean is **20** words [(17 + 23)/2 = 40/2 = 20], and the "rote" row mean is **15** words [(12 + 18)/2 = 30/2 = 15]. When asking if there is a main effect of training type, the question is: "Is the difference between the row means of 20 and 15 statistically significant or due to chance?"

In the same fashion, calculating column means allows us to see if there is a main effect of presentation rate. For the 2 sec/item column, the mean is **14.5** words; it is **20.5** words for the 4 sec/item row (you should check this). Putting all of this together yields this outcome:

	Presentation rate		
	2-sec/word	4-sec/word	Row means
Imagery	17	23	**20.0**
Rote	12	18	**15.0**
Column means	**14.5**	**20.5**	

(Type of training labels the rows: Imagery and Rote)

For these data, it appears that imagery improves memory (20 > 15) and that recall is higher if the words are presented at a slower rate (20.5 > 14.5). That is, there seem to be two main effects here (of course, it takes an ANOVA to make a judgment about whether the differences are significant statistically or due to chance). For a real example of a study that produced two main effects, consider this example of the so-called "closing time" effect.

Research Example 16—Main Effects

I don't know how often country music produces empirical questions that intrigue research psychologists, but one example seems to be a song produced by Mickey Gilley in 1975, *The Girls All Get Prettier at Closing Time*, which includes the lyrics: "Ain't it funny, ain't it strange, the way a man's opinion changes, when he starts to face that lonely night." The song suggests that, as the night wears on, men in bars, desperate to find a companion for the night, lower their "attractiveness" threshold—the same woman who only seemed moderately attractive at 10:00 becomes more eye-catching as closing time looms. Yes, pathetic. Nonetheless, several researchers have ventured courageously into bars and clubs on the edges of campuses to test this "closing time" idea, and to determine whether it applies to both men *and* women who are searching for ... whatever. One interesting example is a study by Gladue and Delaney (1990). In addition to resulting in two main effects (sex and time), the study also illustrates several other methodological points.

The Gladue and Delaney (1990) study took place over a 3-month period at a large bar that included a dance floor and had the reputation as being a place where "one had a high probability of meeting someone for subsequent romantic ... activities" (p. 380). The researchers recruited 58 male and 43 female patrons, who made attractiveness ratings of a set of photographs of men and women and also made global ratings of the overall attractiveness of the people who happened to be at the bar—"Overall, how attractive would you rate the men/women in the bar right now" (p. 381). The ratings occurred at 9:00, 10:30, and 12:00 midnight,

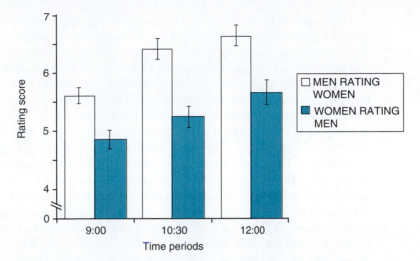

FIGURE 8.1 Main Effects—attractiveness ratings over the course of an evening for males and females rating each other, from the "closing time" study by Gladue and Delaney (1990).

and they were on a 10-point scale, with 10 being the most attractive. For the global ratings, here is the factorial matrix for the results (means estimated from the bar graph in Figure 8.1):

	Time period			
	9:00	10:30	12:00	Row means
Men rating women	5.6	6.4	6.6	**6.2**
Women rating men	4.8	5.2	5.6	**5.2**
Column means	**5.2**	**5.8**	**6.1**	

Both main effects were significant—remember that main effects are determined by examining row and column means. In this case, the average ratings increased for both men *and* women as the night wore on (column means → 5.2 < 5.8 < 6.1). Also, women were generally more discerning—they rated men lower than men rated women during all three time periods combined (row means → 5.2 < 6.2). Figure 8.1 is Gladue and Delaney's (1990) bar graph of the same data—note the use of error bars, as in the EMDR study of Chapter 7 (Research Example 15).

One potential confound in the study was a possible alcohol-use effect. As one drinks more during the course of an evening, others might come to be seen as more attractive. So alcohol consumption could be confounded with the time of the attractiveness rating. Gladue and Delaney (1990) dealt with this by measuring alcohol intake, and eliminated the problem by finding no overall relationship between intake amount and the attractiveness ratings. Another problem was that the global ratings of attractiveness were relatively crude as measures, and open to a number of interpretations. For instance, the actual people in the bar at the three time periods were probably different—people come and go during the evening—so the ratings at the three times might reflect actual attractiveness differences in those at the bar. To account for this problem, Gladue and Delaney also asked their subjects to rate photos of college-age male and female students. The same photos were used for all three time periods. These photos had been pretested for levels of attractiveness, and photos with moderate degrees of attractiveness had been chosen by the researchers. Why moderate? The researchers wished to avoid a problem first mentioned in Chapter 5—*ceiling effects* and *floor effects*. That is, they wanted to use photos for which changes in ratings, either up or down, would be likely to occur during the three time periods. The ratings of these photos produced a more subtle effect than the global ratings. As the time passed, a "closing time" effect occurred for men (confirming Mickey Gilley, I suppose), but it did *not* occur for women; their ratings stayed about the same across all three time periods. This outcome is known as an interaction, our next topic.

✓　Self Test 8.1

1.　A 2 × 3 × 4 factorial has (a) how many IVs, (b) how many levels of each IV, (c) how many total conditions, and (d) how many DVs?
2.　What is the basic definition of a main effect?
3.　A memory study with a 2 (type of instruction) × 2 (presentation rate) factorial, like the example used at the start of the chapter, has these results (DV = words recalled):

　　　Imagery/2 sec rate = 20 words

　　　Imagery/4 sec rate = 20 words

　　　Rote/2 sec rate = 12 words

　　　Rote/4 sec rate = 12 words

　　Are there any apparent main effects here? If so, for which factor? or both? Calculate the row and column means.

Interactions

Main effects are important outcomes in factorial designs, but the distinct advantage of factorials over single-factor designs lies in their potential to show interactive effects. In a factorial design, an **interaction** is said to occur when the effect of one independent variable depends on the level of another independent variable. This is a moderately difficult concept to grasp, but it is of immense importance because interactions often provide the most interesting results in a factorial study. In fact, interactions sometimes render main effects irrelevant. To start, consider a simple example. Suppose I believe that general psychology is best taught as a laboratory self-discovery course rather than as a straight lecture course, but I also wonder if this is generally true or true only for certain kinds of students. Perhaps science majors would especially benefit from the laboratory approach. To test the idea, I need to compare a lab with a lecture version of general psychology, but I also need to compare different types of students, perhaps science majors and humanities majors. This calls for a 2 × 2 design that would look like this:

	Course type	
	Lab emphasis	Lecture emphasis
Science		
Humanities		

Student's major (row label for the two bottom rows)

In a study like this, the dependent variable would be some measure of learning; let's use a score from 1 to 100 on a standardized test of knowledge of general psychology, given during final exam week. Suppose these results occurred:

	Course type	
	Lab emphasis	Lecture emphasis
Science	80	70
Humanities	70	80

Student's major (row label)

Are there any main effects here? No—all of the row and column means are the same: 75. So did anything at all happen in this study? Yes—something clearly happened. Specifically, the science students did better in the lab course, but the humanities students did better in the lecture course. Or to put it in terms of the definition of an interaction, the effect of one variable (course type) depended on the level of the other variable (major). Hence, even if no main effects occur, an interaction can occur and produce an interesting outcome.

This teaching example also highlights the distinct advantage of factorial designs over single-factor designs. Suppose you completed the study as a single-factor, two-level design, comparing lab with lecture versions of general psychology. You would probably use a matched group design, and use student GPA and perhaps major as matching variables. In effect, you might end up with the same people who were in the factorial example. However, by running it as a single-factor design, your results would be:

Lab course: 75   Lecture course: 75

and you might conclude that it doesn't matter whether general psychology includes a lab or not. With the factorial design, however, you know that the lab indeed matters, *but only for certain types of students*. In short, factorial designs can be more informative than single-factor designs. To further illustrate the concept of interactions, in this case one that also failed to find any main effects, consider the outcome of the following study.

Research Example 17—An Interaction with No Main Effects

There has been considerable research indicating that people remember information best if they are in the same general environment or context where they learned the information in the first place. A typical design is a 2 × 2 factorial, with the independent variables being the situation when the material is studied and the situation when the material is recalled. A nice example, and one that has clear relevance for students, is a study conducted by Veronica Dark and a group of her undergraduate students (Grant et al., 1998).

The Grant et al. (1998) study originated from a concern that students often study under conditions that are quite different from the test-taking environment—they often study in noisy environments but take tests in a quiet room. So, in the experiment, participants were asked to study a two-page article on psychoimmunology. Half of the participants studied the article while listening (over headphones) to background noise from a tape made during a busy lunchtime in a cafeteria (no distinct voices, but a "general conversational hum that was intermixed with the sounds produced by movement of chairs and dishes"—p. 619); the remaining participants studied the same article without any background noise (but with the headphones on—can you see why?). After a short break, all of the participants were tested on the material (with short answer and multiple choice questions), also in either a noisy or quiet environment. This 2 × 2 independent groups design yielded the following four conditions:

1. silent study—silent recall
2. noisy study—noisy recall
3. silent study—noisy recall
4. noisy study—silent recall

The results for both the short answer and the multiple choice tests showed the same general pattern; here are the mean scores for the multiple choice results (max score = 16; condition 1, silent study-silent recall, had 9 subjects; the remaining cells had

10 subjects, which is why the row and columns means are a little different from what you would expect if all four cells had an *N* of 10):

	Study condition		
	Silent	Noisy	Row means
Silent during recall	14.3	12.7	**12.8**
Noisy during recall	12.7	14.3	**13.5**
Column means	**12.8**	**13.5**	

This outcome is similar to the pattern found in the hypothetical study about ways of teaching general psychology to science and humanities students. Row and column means were very close (12.8 and 13.5), and they were not significantly different from each other. So, there were no main effects. But examining the four individual cell means shows that an interaction clearly occurred. When the students studied the essay in peace and quiet, they recalled well in the quiet context (14.3) but not so well in the noisy context (12.7); when they studied in noisy conditions, they recalled poorly in a quiet context (12.7) but did well when recalling when it was noisy (14.3). That is, learning was best when the study context matched the recall context. To put it in interaction language, the effect of one factor (where they recalled) depended on the level of the other factor (where they studied). Figure 8.2 presents the data in bar graph form.

This study had some important limitations. First, there were few subjects (total of 39). Second, there were several different experimenters, all undergraduate

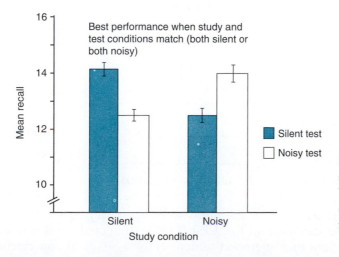

FIGURE 8.2 Bar graph showing an interaction between study and recall conditions (constructed from data in Grant et al., 1998).

students of uncertain training and consistency as experimenters. Nonetheless, the predicted interaction occurred, one that is quite similar to the results of other studies with the same basic design (e.g., Godden & Baddeley, 1975), perhaps an indication of an effect strong enough to overcome some methodological weaknesses.

Can you see the relevance of this for your life as a student? First, unlike much of the research on this context effect, which typically uses lists of words for study, Grant et al. (1998) used study material similar to the kind you would encounter as a student—text information to be comprehended. So the study has a certain amount of *ecological validity* (Chapter 5). Second, although you might conclude from these data that it doesn't matter whether you study in a quiet or noisy environment (just be sure to take the test in the same kind of environment), a fact of academic life is that tests are taken in quiet rooms. Unless you can convince your professors to let you take tests with your iPod going full blast (don't count on it), this study suggests that it is clearly to your advantage to study for exams in a quiet place.

Interactions Sometimes Trump Main Effects

In the opening paragraph describing interactions, you might have noticed a comment about interactions sometimes making main effects irrelevant. This frequently occurs in factorial designs for a specific type of interaction. A good example will make the point. Research Example 7 (Chapter 6) was designed to illustrate the use of a double blind procedure, but it also produced a significant interaction, and two significant but irrelevant main effects. As you recall, the study examined the effect of caffeine on the memory of elderly subjects who were self-described "morning people." When tested in the morning, they did equally well whether taking caffeine in their coffee or having decaf. In the late afternoon, however, they did well with caffeine, but poorly with decaf. Here are the data in factorial matrix form:

	Time of day		
	Morning	Afternoon	Row means
Caffeinated coffee	11.8	11.7	**11.8**
Decaffeinated coffee	11.0	8.9	**10.0**
Column means	**11.4**	**10.3**	

In this experiment, both main effects were statistically significant. Overall, recall was better for caffeine than for decaf (11.8 > 10.0) and recall was also better for morning sessions than afternoon sessions (11.4 > 10.3). If you carefully examine

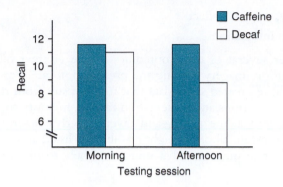

FIGURE 8.3 When an interaction renders main effects meaningless (from Ryan, Hatfield, & Hofstetter, 2002).

the four cell means, however, you can see that performance was about the same for three of the cells, and only declined for the cell with the 8.9 in it—decaf in the afternoon. You can see this effect even more clearly in Figure 8.3—three of the bars are essentially the same height, while the fourth is much lower.

The only really important finding here is that recall declined in the afternoon for seniors drinking decaf—if they drank caffeinated coffee in the afternoon, they did as well as they had in the morning. Thus, you do not really get a true picture of the key result if you report that, overall, caffeine produced better memory than decaf (11.8 > 10.0)—in fact, caffeine's only advantage was in the afternoon; in the morning, whether subjects drank caffeine or decaf did not matter. Similarly, emphasizing the second main effect, that recall was generally better in the morning than in the afternoon (11.4 > 10.3), also gives a false impression of the key result—recall was only better in the morning when decaf was consumed; when caffeine was used, morning or afternoon didn't matter. In short, for this kind of outcome, the interaction is the only important result. The tip-off that you are dealing with the kind of interaction where main effects do not matter is a graph like Figure 8.3, where three of the bars (or points on a line graph) are essentially the same, and a fourth bar (or point) is far removed from the other three.

Combinations of Main Effects and Interactions

The experiment on studying and recalling with or without background noise (Research Example 17) illustrates one type of outcome in a factorial design (an interaction, but no main effects), but there are many patterns of results that could occur. In a simple 2 × 2 design, for instance, there are eight possibilities:

1. a main effect for the first factor only
2. a main effect for the second factor only
3. main effects for both factors; no interaction
4. a main effect for the first factor plus an interaction
5. a main effect for the second factor plus an interaction
6. main effects for both factors plus an interaction

7. an interaction only, no main effects

8. no main effects, no interaction

Let's briefly consider several of these outcomes in the context of the earlier hypothetical experiment on imagery training and presentation rate. For each of the following examples, I have created some data that might result from the study on the effects of imagery instructions and presentation rate on memory for a 30-word list, translated the data into a line graph, and given a verbal description of the results. I haven't tried to create all of the eight possibilities listed above; rather, the following examples illustrate outcomes that might be likely to occur in this type of study.

1. Imagery training improves recall, regardless of presentation rate, which doesn't affect recall. That is, there is a main effect for type of training factor—imagery (22) is better than rote (14). There is no main effect for presentation rate, however—the 2-sec rate (18) equals the 4-sec rate (18).

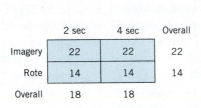

	2 sec	4 sec	Overall
Imagery	22	22	22
Rote	14	14	14
Overall	18	18	

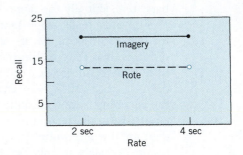

2. Recall is better with slower rates of presentation, but the imagery training was not effective in improving recall. That is, there is a main effect for the presentation rate factor—recall was better at 4-sec/item (22) than at 2-sec/item (14). But there was no main effect for type of training—imagery (18) was the same as rote (18).

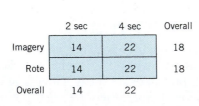

	2 sec	4 sec	Overall
Imagery	14	22	18
Rote	14	22	18
Overall	14	22	

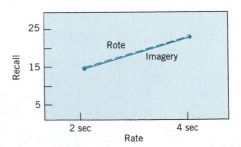

3. Recall is better with slower rates of presentation (20 > 16); in addition, the imagery training was effective in improving recall (20 > 16). In this case, main effects for both factors occur. This is probably the outcome most likely to occur if you actually completed this study.

	2 sec	4 sec	Overall
Imagery	18	22	20
Rote	14	18	16
Overall	16	20	

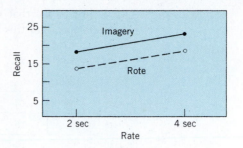

4. At the 2-sec presentation rate, imagery training clearly improves recall (i.e., from 12 to 28); however, at the 4-sec rate, recall is almost perfect (28 = 28), regardless of how subjects are trained. Another way to say this is that when using imagery, presentation rate doesn't matter; but presentation rate does matter when using rote repetition. In short, there is an interaction between type of training and presentation rate. In this case, the interaction may have been influenced by a *ceiling effect*, a result in which the scores for different conditions are all so close to the maximum (30 words in this example) that no difference could occur. Here, the imagery group recalls just about all of the words, regardless of presentation rate. To test for the presence of a ceiling effect, you could replicate the study with 50-item word lists and see if performance improves for the imagery/4-sec group.

	2 sec	4 sec	Overall
Imagery	28	28	28
Rote	12	28	20
Overall	20	28	

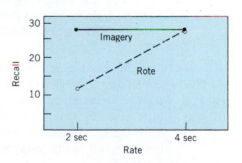

You may be wondering about the obvious main effects that occur in this example. Surely the row (20 and 28) and column (also 20 and 28) means indicate significant overall effects for both factors. Technically, yes, the analysis probably would yield statistically significant main effects in this example, but this is another illustration of the fact that interactions can trump main effects when the results are interpreted—the same point I just made about the caffeine-in-the-afternoon study. For the hypothetical memory study, the main effects are not meaningful; the statement that imagery yields a general improvement in recall is not really accurate. Rather, it only seems to improve recall at the faster presentation rate. Likewise, concluding that 4 seconds per item produces better recall than 2 seconds per item is misleading—it is only true for the rote groups. Hence, the interaction is the key finding here.

5. This is not to say that main effects never matter when an interaction exists, however. Consider this last example:

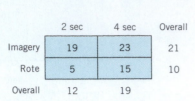

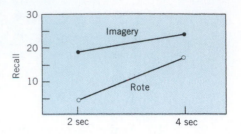

In this case, imagery training generally improves recall (i.e., there's a main effect for type of training: 21 > 10). Also, a slower presentation rate improves recall for both groups (i.e., a main effect for presentation rate also: 19 > 12). Both of these outcomes are worth reporting. Imagery works better than rote at *both* presentation rates (19 > 5 and 23 > 15), and the 4-sec rate works better than the 2-sec rate for *both* types of training (23 > 19 and 15 > 5). What the interaction shows is that slowing the presentation rate improves recall somewhat for the imagery group (23 is a bit better than 19), but slowing the rate improves recall considerably for the control group (15 is a lot better than 5). Another way of describing the interaction is to say that at the fast rate, the imagery training is especially effective (19 is a lot better than 5). At the slower rate, imagery training still yields better recall, but not by as much as the fast rate (23 is somewhat better than 15).

From examining these graphs, you might have noticed a standard feature of interactions. In general, if the lines on the graph are parallel to each other, then no interaction is present. If the lines are nonparallel, however, an interaction probably exists. Of course, this rule about parallel and nonparallel lines is only a general guideline. Whether an interaction exists (in essence, whether the lines are sufficiently nonparallel) is a statistical decision, to be determined by an ANOVA.

Identifying interactions by examining whether lines are parallel or not is easier with line graphs than with bar graphs. Hence, the guideline mentioned in Chapter 7 about line graphs being used only with continuous variables is sometimes ignored by researchers if the key finding is an interaction. For example, a study by Keltner, Ellsworth, and Edwards (1993) showed that when participants were asked to estimate the likelihood of some bad event (e.g., a car accident) occurring, there was an interaction between the emotion they were experiencing during the experiment and whether the hypothetical event was said to be caused by a person or by circumstances. When participants were feeling sad, they believed that events produced by circumstances (e.g., wet roads) were more likely to occur than events produced by individual actions (e.g., poor driving). When participants were angry, however, the opposite happened—they believed that events caused by individuals were more likely. As you can see from Figure 8.4, a line graph was used in the published study even though the *X*-axis uses a discrete variable. Keltner et al. (1993)

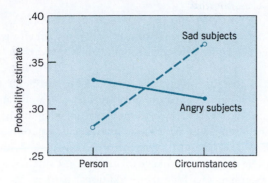

FIGURE 8.4 Using a line graph to highlight an interaction (from Keltner et al., 1993).

probably wanted to show the interaction as clearly as possible, so they ignored the guideline about discrete variables. To repeat a point made earlier, when presenting any data, the overriding concern is to make one's hard-earned results as clear as possible to the reader.

Before we turn to a system for categorizing the different types of factorial designs, you should read Box 8.1. It describes one of psychology's most famous experiments, a classic study supporting the idea that between the time you last study for an exam and the time you take the exam, you should be sleeping. It was completed in the early 1920s, a time when the term "factorial design" had not even been invented, and a time when analysis of variance, the statistical tool most frequently used to analyze factorials, was just starting to be conceptualized. Yet the study illustrates the kind of thinking that leads to factorial studies—the desire to examine more than one independent variable at the same time.

Box 8.1

CLASSIC STUDIES—To Sleep, Perchance to Recall

Although the term "factorial design" and the statistical tools to analyze factorials were not used widely until after World War II, attempts to study more than one variable at a time occurred well before then. A classic example is a study by Jenkins and Dallenbach (1924), which still appears in many general psychology books as the standard example of RI or "retroactive interference"—the tendency for memory to be hindered if other mental activities intervene between the time of study and the time of recall. In essence, the study was a 2 × 4 repeated-measures factorial. The "2" was whether or not activities intervened between learning and a recall test, and the "4" referred to four different retention intervals; recall was tested 1, 2, 4, or 8 hours after initial learning. What made the study interesting (and, eventually, famous) was the factor with two levels. The study's participants spent the time between study and recall either awake and doing normal student behaviors, or asleep in Cornell's psychology lab. The predication, that being asleep would produce less RI, and therefore better recall, was supported.

A close examination of the study illustrates some of the attributes of typical 1920s-era research and also shows that experimenters were just as careful about issues of control then as they are now. First, as you will learn in Chapter 10, research in psychology's early years often featured very few participants. In contrast to what typically happens in memory research today, using many participants and summarizing data statistically, early studies were more likely to include just one, two, or three participants and report extensive data for each—additional participants served the purpose of replication. This happened in the Jenkins and Dallenbach (1924) study; there were just two subjects (referred to as "Observers" or "Os," another typical convention of the time), both seniors at Cornell. When using small numbers of participants, researchers tried to get as much out of them as they could, and the result in this case was what we would call a repeated-measures study today. That is, both students contributed data to all eight cells of the 2 × 4 design, with each student learning and recalling lists eight different times in each of the eight conditions—a total of 64 separate trials. If you are beginning to think that the study was a major undertaking for the two Cornell seniors, you're right. During the study, the two students and Jenkins, who served as experimenter, "lived in the laboratory during the course of the experiments" (p. 606) in a simulated dorm room, and the study lasted from April 14, 1923, to June 7. I'm not sure when Cornell's graduation was that year, but I don't imagine too many seniors today would be willing to give up their last month and a half of college to science!

As good researchers, Jenkins and Dallenbach (1924) were concerned about control, and they used many of the procedures you've been learning about. For instance, they used 10-item lists of nonsense syllables, and the subjects read them aloud during the study trials, until one perfect recitation occurred (i.e., their operational definition of learning). They took measures to ensure a consistent pronunciation of the syllables, and they used counterbalancing to avoid sequence effects in the presentation of the different retention intervals—"[t]he time-intervals between learning and reproduction were varied at haphazard" (p. 607). For the "awake" condition, the students learned their lists between 8 and 10 in the morning, then went about their normal business as students, and then returned to the lab for recall after 1, 2, 4, or 8 hours. For the "asleep" condition, lists were studied between 11:30 at night and 1 in the morning. Students then went to bed, and were awakened for recall by Jenkins 1, 2, 4, or 8 hours later. There was one potential confound in the study—on the awake trials, the students were told when to return to the lab for recall (i.e., they knew the retention interval), but during the asleep trials, students did not know when they would be awakened. Jenkins and Dallenbach were aware of the problem, considered alternatives, but decided their procedure was adequate.

The results? Figure 8.5 reproduces their original graph, showing the data for each student. Each data point is an average of the eight trials for each condition of the study. Several things are clear. First, both students ("H" and "Mc") behaved similarly.

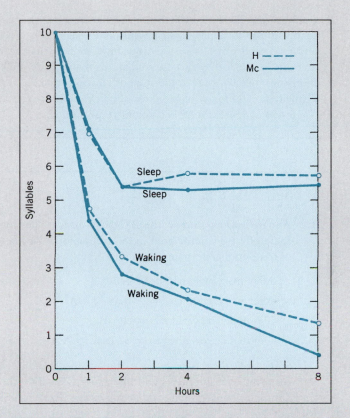

FIGURE 8.5 The Jenkins and Dallenbach study on retroactive interference, showing data for both of the Cornell students who participated, L. R. Hodell (H) and J. S. McGrew (Mc). Keep in mind that the study was completed long before an ethics code would have deleted the participants' names (from Jenkins & Dallenbach, 1924).

Second, and this was the big finding, there was a big advantage for recall after sleeping, compared with recall after being awake. Third, there is the hint of an interaction. As Jenkins and Dallenbach described it: "The curves of the waking experiments take the familiar form: a sharp decline which becomes progressively flatter. The form of the curves of the sleep experiments, however, is very different: after a small initial decline, the curves flatten and a high and constant level is thenceforth maintained" (1924, p. 610).

There was one other intriguing outcome of the study, one never reported in textbook accounts. As the experiment progressed, it became increasingly difficult for Jenkins to wake up the students. It was also hard for Jenkins to "know when they were awake. The Os would leave their beds, go into the next room, give their reproductions, and the next morning say that they remembered nothing of it"

(Jenkins & Dallenbach, 1924, p. 607)! At the time, a semi-asleep state was thought to be similar to hypnosis, so Jenkins and Dallenbach rounded up another student and replicated part of the study, but instead of having the student sleep for varying amounts of time, they had the student learn and recall the lists at different retention intervals while hypnotized (during both learning and recall). They found recall to be virtually perfect for all of the intervals, an early hint at what later came to be called "state-dependent learning" by cognitive psychologists.

✓ Self Test 8.2

1. A maze learning study with a 2 (type of maze—alley maze or elevated maze) × 2 (type of rat—wild or bred in the lab) factorial has these results (DV = number of trials until performance is perfect):

    Alley maze/wild rats = 12 trials

    Alley maze/tame rats = 20 trials

    Elevated maze/wild rats = 20 trials

    Elevated maze/tame rats = 12 trials

    Summarize the results in terms of main effects and interactions.
2. In terms of main effects and interactions, describe the results of the Research Example about studying and taking exams (Research Example 17).

Varieties of Factorial Designs

Like the decision tree in Figure 7.1 for single-factor designs, Figure 8.6 shows you the decisions involved in arriving at one of seven different factorial designs. You'll recognize that four of the designs mirror those in Figure 7.1, but the other designs are unique to factorials. First, while the independent variable must be either a between-subjects or a within-subjects variable in a single-factor design, both types of variables can be present in a factorial design. When this happens, the design is called a **mixed factorial design**. In a mixed design, at least one variable must be tested between subjects, and at least one must be tested within subjects. Second, some between-subjects factorials include both a manipulated independent variable and a subject variable. Because these designs can yield an interaction between the type of person (P) in the study and the environment (E) created in the study, they can be called **P × E factorial designs**, or "Person by Environment designs," with "environment" defined broadly to include any manipulated independent variable. A further distinction can be made within P × E designs, depending on whether the manipulated (environment) variable is a between-subjects or a within-subjects

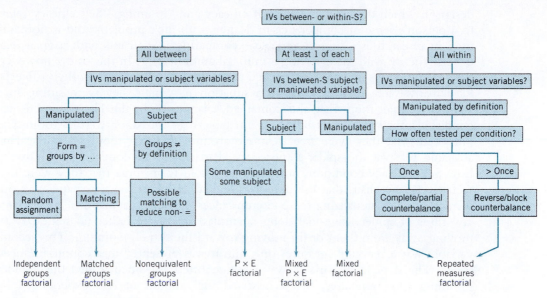

FIGURE 8.6   A decision tree for factorial designs.

factor. If the latter is the case, the P × E design includes both a between–subjects and a within–subjects factor, making the design a **mixed P × E factorial**. Let's examine mixed factorials and P × E factorials in more detail.

Mixed Factorial Designs

In Chapter 6, you learned that when independent variables are between–subjects variables, creating equivalent groups can be a problem, and procedures like random assignment and matching help solve the problem. Similarly, when independent variables are within–subjects variables, a difficulty arises because of potential sequence effects, and counterbalancing is the normal solution. Thus, in a mixed design, the researcher usually gets to deal with both the problems of equivalent groups *and* the problems of sequence effects. Not always, though—there is one variety of mixed design where counterbalancing is not used because sequence effects themselves are the outcome of interest. For example, in learning and memory research, "trials" is a frequently encountered within–subjects independent variable. Counterbalancing makes no sense in this case because one purpose of the study will be to show sequential changes from trial to trial. The following two case studies show mixed designs, one requiring counterbalancing and one in which trials is the repeated measure.

Research Example 18—A Mixed Factorial with Counterbalancing

Riskind and Maddux (1993), perhaps as a consequence of seeing too many bad horror movies involving spiders, were interested in how people manage their emotions in frightening circumstances. They created a 2 × 2 mixed factorial design in which they manipulated self-efficacy and "looming." Self-efficacy refers to a person's sense of competence in dealing with life's problems and is normally used in research as a subject variable—comparing participants with a great deal of self-efficacy with those having a minimal amount of it. In this study, however, the experimenters directly manipulated the feeling of self-efficacy in their subjects. Participants were told to visualize a situation in which they were sitting in a chair in a small room that also contained a tarantula. In the High Self-Efficacy condition, they were instructed to imagine that the door to the room was unlocked, that they were free to move around, and that they had a magazine available to swat the spider if necessary. Participants randomly assigned to the Low Self-Efficacy condition, however, were told to imagine that they were tied securely to the chair, that the door was locked, and that the newspaper was out of reach. While visualizing these circumstances in their imaginations, participants saw films of spiders (five-inch long tarantulas) that were either (a) stationary or moving away from them or (b) moving toward them (i.e., looming). This second variable was a repeated-measures one, and it was presented in a counterbalanced order. The dependent variable was a self-reported assessment called the "Spider Looming Questionnaire," which assessed the amount of fear experienced by subjects.

The outcome, portrayed in Figure 8.7 in both factorial matrix and graph form, is yet another example of how interactions are sometimes more important than main effects. As you can see, differences occurred for both row and column means, and both main effects were statistically significant. More important, however, was the interaction that occurred between the factors. A large amount of fear (4.50, on a 7-point interval scale) occurred when the situation of a bad horror movie was simulated (looming spider plus low self-efficacy), while the film viewers reported only moderate to low amounts of fear in the other three conditions (2.24, 2.64, 2.73). The description of the interaction goes like this: For high self-efficacy participants, fear was fairly low regardless of the relative motion of the spider. On the other hand, for those experiencing low self-efficacy, the amount of fear was clearly affected by whether the spider was looming or not.

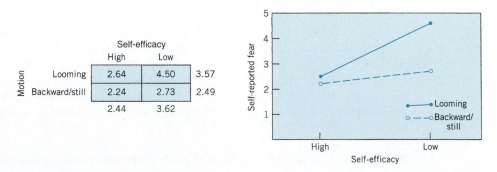

FIGURE 8.7 The interactive effects of looming and self-efficacy on fear (from Riskind & Maddux, 1993).

There is one other methodological point worth mentioning. The questionnaire that subjects filled out also included a *manipulation check*, a concept introduced in Chapter 6. That is, two of the questions (e.g., "I believe I could prevent the spider from harming me if it attacked," Riskind & Maddux, 1993, p. 78) checked to see if the self-efficacy manipulation indeed influenced subjects' temporary feelings of self-efficacy (it did).

Research Example 19—A Mixed Factorial without Counterbalancing

A good example of the situation in which "trials" is the within-subjects factor in a mixed design is a common memory procedure called "release from PI" (Wickens, Born, & Allen, 1963). PI, or proactive interference, is a phenomenon in which the learning and recall of new information is hindered by the prior learning of old information. You might have experienced this if you found it difficult to remember a new phone number because your old one kept coming to mind. The amount of interference is expected to be especially great if the old information is similar to the new information. One way to test the idea that strength of PI is a function of item similarity is to have participants study and recall a sequence of stimulus items that are similar, and then switch to a different type of stimulus item. Presumably, PI should build up from trial to trial for the similar items, and then "release" when the stimulus type changes. Behaviorally, this means that recall accuracy should gradually decrease while PI is accumulating, and then increase again once the release occurs.

Release from PI studies normally use words or nonsense syllables as stimuli, but a clever study by Gunter, Berry, and Clifford (1981) took a different and more applied (and ecologically valid) approach: They used items from television news shows in a series of experiments. We'll consider their experiment 1, which serves as a nice illustration of a mixed factorial design without counterbalancing.

Participants were told they would be seeing clips from a televised news broadcast and would then be tested on the content of the news items. On each trial, they saw a sequence of three stories, then worked on a distractor task (a crossword puzzle) for a minute, and then tried to recall as much as they could about the stories. Each subject experienced four such trials. Half of the subjects were randomly assigned to the release-from-PI condition; they went through three trials in which all the news was from a single general category (e.g., domestic political events) and a fourth ("release") trial with news from a different category (e.g., foreign political events). The remaining subjects were in a control group; all four of their trials were from the same category. Thus, the design was a 2 (release/no release) × 4 (trials) mixed factorial design. Whether or not participants were in the release condition was the between-subjects factor, and trials was the repeated-measures or within-subjects factor.

Figure 8.8 shows the results. That PI was operating is clear from the control group's recall scores; they steadily declined. Release from PI also occurred, as is evident from the recall scores of the experimental group, which declined for trials 1–3, and then shot up on trial 4, the "release" trial.

One of the control features of this study is worth noting. A possible problem was that performance on the release trial might have gone up simply because the foreign news items were easier to recall than the domestic items. To eliminate this

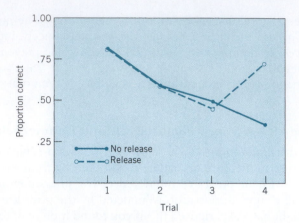

FIGURE 8.8   Release from PI (data from Gunter et al., 1981).

possibility, half of those in the release group saw three domestic trials followed by a foreign trial; the other half saw three foreign trials followed by a domestic trial. Likewise, in the control group, half saw four domestic trials and the remainder saw four foreign trials. The order made no difference to the results.[1]

Factorials with Subject and Manipulated Variables: P × E Designs

Chapter 5 introduced the concept of a subject variable—some already existing attribute of an individual such as age, sex, or some personality characteristic. You also learned to be cautious about drawing conclusions when subject variables are involved. Assuming proper control, causal conclusions can be drawn with manipulated independent variables, but with subject variables such conclusions cannot be drawn. What I am calling P × E designs include both subject (the "P") and manipulated (the "E") variables in the same study. Causal conclusions can be drawn if a significant main effect occurs for the manipulated "Environmental" factor, but they cannot be drawn when a main effect occurs for the subject variable or "Person" factor, and they also cannot be drawn if an interaction occurs. Despite this limitation, designs including both subject and manipulated variables are popular, in part because they combine the two research traditions identified by Woodworth in his famous "Columbia bible" (see the opening paragraphs of Chapter 5). The correlational tradition is associated with the study of individual differences, and the subject variable or "P" factor in the P × E design looks specifically at these differences. A significant main effect for this factor shows that two different *types* of individuals perform differently on whatever behavior is being measured as the dependent variable. The experimental tradition, on the other hand, is concerned with identifying general laws of behavior that apply to some degree to everyone,

---

[1]Calling the design a 2 × 4 emphasizes the two important variables, but technically, this was a 2 × 2 × 4 mixed design, with the second "2" being the between-subjects factor of news category, foreign or domestic. There were no overall differences in recall between foreign or domestic news, so the data for both were combined in Figure 8.8.

regardless of individual differences. Hence, finding a significant main effect for the manipulated or "E" factor in a P × E design indicates that the situational factor is powerful enough to influence the behavior of many different kinds of persons. Consider a hypothetical example that compares introverts and extroverts (the "P" variable) and asks participants to solve problems in either a small, crowded room or a large, uncrowded room (the "E" variable). Suppose you get results like this (DV = number of problems solved):

	E factor		
	Small room	Large room	Row means
Introverts	18	18	**18**
P factor			
Extroverts	12	12	**12**
Column means	**15**	**15**	

In this case, there would be a main effect for personality type, no main effect for environment, and no interaction. Introverts clearly outperformed extroverts (18 > 12), regardless of whether they worked in crowded conditions or not. The researcher would have discovered an important way in which individuals differ, and the differences extend to more than one kind of environment (i.e., both small and large rooms).

A very different conclusion would be drawn from this outcome:

	E factor		
	Small room	Large room	Row means
Introverts	12	18	**15**
P factor			
Extroverts	12	18	**15**
Column means	**12**	**18**	

This yields a main effect for the environmental factor, no main effect for personality type, and no interaction. Here the environment (room size) has produced the powerful effect (18 > 12), and this effect extended beyond just a single type of individual; regardless of personality type, introverted or extroverted, performance deteriorated under crowded conditions. Thus, finding a significant main effect for the "P" factor indicates that powerful personality differences occur, while finding a significant main effect for the "E" factor shows the power of some environmental influence to go beyond just one type of person. Of course, another result could be two main effects, indicating that each factor is important.

The most interesting outcome of a P × E design, however, is an interaction. When this occurs, it shows that for one type of individual, changes in the environment have one kind of effect, while for another type of individual, the same environmental changes have a different effect. Staying with the introvert/extrovert example, suppose this happened:

E factor

	Small room	Large room	Row means
Introverts	18	12	**15**
Extroverts	12	18	**15**
Column means	**15**	**15**	

P factor

In this case, neither main effect would be significant, but an interaction clearly occurred. One thing happened for introverts, and something different occurred for extroverts. Specifically, introverts performed much better in the small than in the large room, while extroverts did much better in the large room than in the small one.

Factorial designs that include both subject variables and manipulated variables are popular in educational research and in research on the effectiveness of psychotherapy (Smith & Sechrest, 1991). In both areas, the importance of finding significant interactions is indicated by the fact that such designs are sometimes called **ATI designs**, or "Aptitude-Treatment Interaction designs." As you might guess, the "aptitude" refers to the nonmanipulated subject (person) variable and the "treatment" refers to the manipulated, environmental variable. An example from psychotherapy research is a study by Abramovitz, Abramovitz, Roback, and Jackson (1974). Their "P" variable was locus of control. Those with an external locus generally believe that external events exert control over their lives, while internals believe that what happens to them is a consequence of their own decisions and actions. In the study, externals did well in therapy that was more directive in providing guidance for them, but they did poorly in nondirective therapy, which places more responsibility for progress on the client. For internals, the opposite was true: They did better in the nondirective therapy and not too well in directive therapy.

ATIs in educational research usually occur when the aptitude or person factor is a learning style variable and the treatment or environmental factor is some aspect of instruction. For example, Figure 8.9 shows the outcome of some educational research reported by Valerie Shute, a leading authority on ATI designs

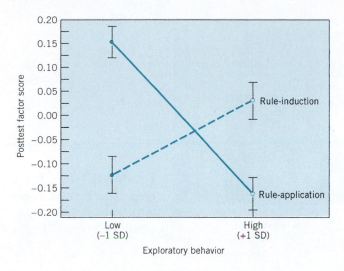

FIGURE 8.9 A P × E interaction between level of exploratory behavior and type of learning environment (from Shute, 1994).

(Shute, 1994). The study compared two educational strategies for teaching basic principles of electricity: rule induction and rule application. Participants were randomly assigned to one strategy or the other. The subject variable was whether learners scored high or low on a measure of "exploratory" behavior. The graph shows that those scoring high on exploratory behavior performed better in a rule induction setting, where they were asked to do more work on their own, whereas those scoring low on exploratory behavior performed better in a rule application environment, where the educational procedures were more structured for them.

P × E factorial designs are also very popular in research in personality psychology, abnormal psychology, developmental psychology, and any research area interested in sex differences. In personality research, the subject variable or P factor will involve comparing personality types; in abnormal psychology, the P factor will be groups of people with different types of mental disorders, and in cross-sectional studies in developmental psychology, the P factor will be age. Sex cuts across all of psychology's subdisciplines. The following experiment uses sex as the subject, or P, factor and illustrates an unfortunate effect of stereotyping.

Research Example 20—A Factorial Design with a P × E Interaction

As parents of a mathematically talented daughter, my wife and I were frustrated on more than one occasion by her experiences in school. For instance, I can recall her being upset at a middle school math teacher who discouraged her from asking questions, and yet seemed to encourage question asking from the boys in the class. Unfortunately, experiences like these do not appear to be rare, and a somewhat distressing study by Inzlicht and Ben-Zeev (2000) shows how stereotypes about young women not being suited for math can affect their actual math performance. Experiment 2 of their study was a 2 × 2 P × E factorial. The first factor, the subject variable, was sex—participants were male and female college students at Brown University. The manipulated or environmental factor was the composition of a

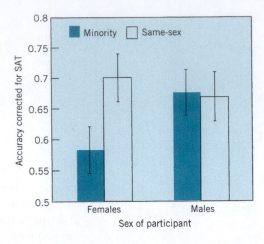

FIGURE 8.10 A P × E interaction: gender and group composition when solving math problems (from Inzlicht and Ben-Zeev, 2002).

three-person group that was given the task of completing a series of math problems. In the "same-sex" condition, all three students taking the test together were either males or females. In the "minority" condition, either males or females would be in the minority; that is, the groups would either include two males and a female or two females and a male. The three-person groups had 20 minutes to solve the math problems and they were informed that, after the session was over, their scores would be made public. Figure 8.10 shows the rather startling interaction.

Notice that, for males, performance was unaffected by who was taking the test with them; they did about the same, regardless of whether they took the test with two other males or with two females. A different story for females, however. They did quite well when they were in a group of other females (slightly better than the males, in fact), but in the situation when a female took the test with two other males, her performance plunged. Keep in mind that the groups didn't even interact; they were just in the same room, taking the test together. Simply being in the room with other males, in the context of a math test, led to a serious drop in performance for women, even women who were highly intelligent (i.e., good enough for admission to a highly selective university). Inzlicht and Ben-Zeev (2000) concluded that the widely held stereotype of men being better at math was evidently sufficient to disrupt the performance of women when they found themselves in the presence of and outnumbered by men. Although they correctly recognized that their study did not directly address the issue of single-sex math classes, Inzlicht and Ben-Zeev argued that "females may in fact benefit from being placed in single-sex math classrooms" (p. 370). On an encouraging note, a more recent study by Johns, Schmader, and Martens (2005) showed that educating females about stereotype threats, or describing the task as "problem solving" rather than a "math test," substantially reduced the problem.

From the standpoint of the concepts you've been learning about in your methods course, there is one other point about the Inzlicht and Ben-Zeev (2000) study worth noting. Remember the concept of falsification (Chapters 1 and 3), the process of ruling out alternative hypotheses? The study I just described was actually experiment 2 of a pair of studies. In experiment 1, Inzlicht and Ben-Zeev (2000) found that the female drop in performance happened when a math test was used, but it did *not* happen with a test of verbal abilities. They contrasted two hypotheses, a "stereotype threat" hypothesis and a "tokenism" hypothesis. The tokenism hypothesis proposes that a person included in a group, but in the minority, perceives herself or himself as a mere token, placed there to give the appearance of inclusiveness. The tokenism hypothesis predicts a decline in female performance *regardless* of the type of test given, and that failed to occur, so Inzlicht and Ben-Zeev argued that the tokenism hypothesis could be ruled out (falsified), in favor of the alternative, which proposed that performance would decline only in a situation that activated a specific stereotype (i.e., the idea that boys are better than girls at math).

In this stereotype threat P × E study, the "E" factor (group composition) was tested as a between subjects factor. If this factor is tested within-subjects, then a P × E design meets the criterion for a mixed design, and can be called a mixed P × E factorial. Such is the case in Research Example 21, which includes a rather disturbing outcome for older drivers.

Research Example 21—A Mixed P × E Factorial with Two Main Effects

Research on the divided attention that results from cell phone use and driving, done by David Strayer and his colleagues (Strayer & Johnston, 2001), was mentioned in Chapter 3 as an example of applied research, contrasted with the basic laboratory research on attention. Another study by this research team (Strayer & Drews, 2004) compared young and old drivers, a subject variable, and also included two types of tasks, driving while using a cell phone, and driving without using one. This second factor was tested within-subjects—both young and old drivers completed both types of tasks. Hence, the design is a mixed P × E factorial—mixed because it includes both within- (cell phone use) and between-subjects (driver age) factors, and P × E because it includes both a manipulated (cell phone use) and a subject (age) variable.

Strayer and Drews (2004) operationally defined their subject variable this way: The 20 younger drivers were those ranging in age from 18 to 25, while the 20 older drivers were between 65 and 74 years old. All the participants were healthy and had normal vision. In a desire to create a procedure with some degree of ecological validity, the researchers used a state of the art driving simulator and a "car-following paradigm" (p. 641), in which drivers followed a pace car, while other cars passed them periodically. Subjects had to maintain proper distance from the pace car, which would hit the brakes frequently (thirty-two times in a ten-minute trial). The dependent variables were driving speed, distance from the pace car, and reaction time (hitting the brakes when the pace car did). There were four ten-minute trials, two with subjects simply driving ("single-task") and two with the subjects driving while carrying on a cell phone conversation (hands-free phone) with an experimenter ("dual-task"). The cell phone conversations were on topics known from a pretesting survey to be of interest to subjects. Because the cell phone factor was a repeated measure, the four trials were counterbalanced "with the constraint that both single- and dual-task conditions were performed in the first half of the experiment and both ... were performed in the last half of the experiment" (p. 642). You might recognize this as a form of block randomization (Chapter 6).

Given the variety of dependent measures, there were several results, but they fell into a general pattern that is best illustrated with the reaction time data. As the factorial matrix here shows, there were main effects for both factors—age and driving condition.

	Driving condition		
	Single-task	Dual-task	Row means
Young drivers	780	912	**846**
Old drivers	912	1086	**999**
Column means	**846**	**999**	

Note: DV = reaction time in ms

Thus, younger drivers (846 ms, or .846 seconds) had quicker reactions overall than older drivers (999 ms), and those driving undistracted in the single-task condition (also 846 ms) were quicker overall than those driving while on the cell phone (also 999 ms). There was no interaction. But a look at the cell means yields another result, one with some interesting implications—the reaction time for older drivers in the single-task condition is identical to the reaction time for younger drivers in the dual-task condition (912 ms). Reaction time for the young people who were using a cell phone was the *same* as for the old folks not using the phone (!). The outcome is sobering for older drivers (who still think they "have it"), while at the same time perhaps of concern to younger drivers. When we discussed this study in class, one of my 20-year-old students asked, "Does this mean that if I talk on my cell while driving, I'll be just like an old person?"

One final point about P × E designs. I created the label not simply because I liked the look of it. Rather, it pays homage to the work of Kurt Lewin (1890–1947), a pioneer in social and child psychology. The central theme guiding Lewin's work was that a full understanding of behavior required studying both the person's individual characteristics and the environment in which the person operated. He expressed this idea in terms of a famous formula, $B = f(P, E)$—Behavior is a joint *f*unction of the *P*erson and the *E*nvironment (Goodwin, 2008). P × E factorial designs, named for Lewin's formula, are perfectly suited for discovering the kinds of interactive relationships that Lewin believed characterized human behavior.[2]

---

[2]One unfortunate implication of Lewin's choice of the label "P" is that a P × E design involves human participants only. Yet it is quite common for such a design to be used with animal subjects (a study in which the subject variable is the species of the primates being tested, for instance).

Recruiting Participants for Factorial Designs

It should be evident from the definitions of the different types of factorial designs that the number of subjects needed to complete a study could vary considerably. If you need 5 participants to fill one of the cells in the 2×2 factorial, for example, the total number of people to be recruited could be 5, 10, or 20. Figure 8.11 shows you why. In Figure 8.11a, both variables are tested between subjects and 5 different participants will be needed per cell, for a total of 20. In Figure 8.11b, both variables are tested within subjects, making the design a repeated-measures factorial. The same 5 individuals will contribute data to each of the four cells. In a mixed design, Figure 8.11c, one of the variables is tested between subjects and the other is tested within subjects. Thus, 5 participants will participate in two cells and 5 will participate in the other two cells, a total of 10.

Knowing how many participants to recruit for an experiment leads naturally to the question of how to treat the people who arrive at your experiment. Box 8.2 provides a hands-on, practical guide to being an ethically competent researcher.

Analyzing Factorial Designs

We have already seen that multilevel, single-factor designs should be analyzed with a 1-factor ANOVA. Similarly, factorial designs using interval or ratio data are analyzed with N-factor ANOVAs, with N referring to the number of independent variables (factors) involved. Hence, a 2×3 factorial would be analyzed by a 2-factor ANOVA and a $2 \times 2 \times 4$ by a 3-factor ANOVA.

When doing a 1-factor ANOVA, just one F ratio is calculated. Then there may be subsequent testing if the F is significant. For a factorial design, however, more than one F ratio will be calculated. Specifically, there will be an F for each possible main effect and for each possible interaction. For example, in the 2×2 design investigating the effects of imagery training and presentation rate on memory, an F ratio will be calculated to examine the possibility of a main effect for type of training, another for the main effect of presentation rate, and a third for the potential interaction between the two. In an $A \times B \times C$ factorial, there will be *seven* F ratios calculated: three for the main effects of A, B, and C; three more for the 2-way interaction effects of $A \times B$, $B \times C$, and $A \times C$; plus one for the 3-way interaction, $A \times B \times C$.

As was the case for 1-factor ANOVAs, subsequent (post hoc) testing may occur with factorial ANOVAs. For example, in a 2×3 ANOVA, a significant F for the factor with three levels would trigger a subsequent analysis (e.g., Tukey's HSD) that compared the overall performance of levels 1 and 2, 1 and 3, and 2 and 3. Following a significant interaction, one common procedure is to complete what is called a **simple effects analysis**. It involves comparing each of the levels of one factor for each level of the other factor. A concrete example will make this clear. Refer back to the point in the chapter where I introduced interactions by discussing a 2×2 factorial with type of course (lab vs. lecture) and type of student (science vs. humanities major) as the factors. As you recall, no main effects occurred

(a) For a 2 × 2 design with 4 different groups and 5 participants per cell—20 subjects needed

S1	S11
S2	S12
S3	S13
S4	S14
S5	S15
S6	S16
S7	S17
S8	S18
S9	S19
S10	S20

(a)

(b) For a 2 × 2 repeated-measures design with 5 participants per cell—5 subjects needed

S1	S1
S2	S2
S3	S3
S4	S4
S5	S5
S1	S1
S2	S2
S3	S3
S4	S4
S5	S5

(b)

(c) For a 2 × 2 mixed design with 5 participants per cell—10 subjects needed

S1	S1
S2	S2
S3	S3
S4	S4
S5	S5
S6	S6
S7	S7
S8	S8
S9	S9
S10	S10

(c)

FIGURE 8.11   Participant requirements in factorial designs.

Box 8.2

ETHICS—On Being a Competent and Ethical Researcher

You learned about the APA code of ethics in Chapter 2, and you have been encountering Ethics boxes in each of the subsequent chapters. Although you should have a pretty good sense of what the ethical requirements of a study are (consent, confidentiality, debriefing, etc.), you might not be quite sure how to put this into actual practice. Hence, this might be a good time to give you a list of practical tips for being an ethically responsible experimenter. Here goes.

- Don't just get to your session on time—be early enough to have all of the materials organized and ready to go when your participants arrive.

- Always treat the people who volunteer for your study with the same courtesy and respect that you would hope to receive if the roles were reversed. Greet them when they show up at the lab and thank them for signing up and coming to the session. They might be a bit apprehensive about what will happen to them in a "psychology" experiment, so your first task is to put them at ease, while at the same time maintaining your professional role as the person in charge of the session. Always remember that they are doing you a favor—the reverse is not true. Smile often.

- Start the session with the informed consent form and don't convey the attitude that this is a time-consuming technicality that has to be completed before the important part starts. Instead, make it clear that you want your participants to have a good idea of what they are about to do. If they don't ask questions while reading the consent form, be sure to ask them if they have any questions when they finish reading. Make sure there are two copies of the signed consent form, one for them to take with them and one for your records.

- Prepare a written "protocol" ahead of time. This is a detailed sequence of steps that you have to complete in order to run the session successfully from start to finish. It helps ensure that each subject has a standardized experience. The protocol usually includes some explicit instructions to be read to the subjects (or it might indicate the point where subjects are given a sheet of paper with written instructions on it).

- Before you test any "real" participants, practice playing the role of experimenter a few times with friends or lab partners. Go through the whole experimental procedure. Think of it as a dress rehearsal and an opportunity to iron out any problems with the procedure.

- Be alert to any signs of distress in your subjects during the session. Depending on the constraints of the procedure, this could mean halting the study and discarding their data, but their welfare is more important than your data. Also, you're not a professional counselor—if they seem disturbed by their participation, gently refer them to your course instructor or the school's counseling center.

- Prepare the debriefing carefully. As a student experimenter, you probably won't be running studies involving elaborate deception or producing high levels of stress, but you will be responsible for making this an educational experience for your participants. Hence, you should work hard on a simplified description of what the study hopes to discover and you should give them the chance to suggest improvements in the procedure or ideas for the next study. So don't rush the debriefing or give a cursory description that gives the impression that you hope they will just leave. And if they seem to want to leave without any debriefing (some will), try not to let them. Debriefing is an important part of your responsibility as a researcher and an educator. (Of course, if they say, "I thought you said we could leave any time," there's not much you can do!)

- Before they go, remind them that the information on the consent form gives them names of people to contact about the study if questions occur to them later. Give them a rough idea of when the study will be completed and when they can expect to hear about the overall results. Also, ask them not to discuss the experiment with others who might be participants. *Leakage* (Chapter 2), a tendency for participants to tell others about the studies they've completed, can be a serious problem, especially at small schools (refer back to Box 6.3 in Chapter 6, for more on the responsibilities of research subjects). If you have been good to them throughout the session, however, that increases the chances of their cooperation in this regard. Also, remember from Chapter 2 that if you have special reasons to be concerned about leakage (e.g., substantial deception in a study), the ethics code allows you to make the debriefing more cursory, as long as you give them the opportunity to receive complete results once the study has been completed.

- As they are leaving, be sure to thank them for their time and effort and be sure you are smiling as they go out the door. Remember that some of the students you test will be undecided about a major and perhaps thinking about psychology. Their participation in your study could enhance their interest.

(row and column means were all 75). A simple effects analysis would make these comparisons:

1. For science majors, compare lab emphasis (mean of 80) with lecture emphasis (70)
2. For humanities majors, compare lab emphasis (70) with lecture emphasis (80)
3. For the lab emphasis, compare science (80) with humanities majors (70)
4. For the lecture emphasis, compare science (70) with humanities majors (80)

For details on how to complete a simple effects analysis, consult any good statistics text (e.g., Witte & Witte, 2007).

In Chapter 7, you learned how to build an ANOVA source table for a 1-factor design for independent groups. Table 8.1 shows you how to create one for a 2 × 2 factorial for independent groups.

TABLE 8.1 *Constructing an ANOVA Source Table for a 2 × 2 Factorial ANOVA for Independent Groups*

Suppose you are doing an experiment on whether violent programs increase aggression in third-grade boys, and you decide to use a 2 × 2 independent groups factorial design. Your first factor (independent variable) is the content of programs that you plan to show the boys—the program includes violence or it doesn't. The second factor is whether or not the boys are made angry during the experiment, right after they see the film. So there are four groups (conditions) → violent content and boys angered; violent content and boys not angered; nonviolent content and boys angered; nonviolent content and boys not angered. After experiencing one of these conditions, each boy is given the opportunity to be aggressive. Let's assume there is a valid measuring tool that yields an aggression score from 0 to 25, with higher numbers showing increased aggression. There are five boys in each group. Here is the factorial matrix and some data:

	Program content		
	Violent	Non-violent	Row means
Made angry	19.6	15.6	**17.6**
Not made angry	17.0	11.4	**14.2**
Column means	**18.3**	**13.5**	

As you recall from Chapter 7, any analysis of variance takes the total amount of variability (variance) in the study and divides it into various "sources." As in the 1-factor example, a 2-factor ANOVA with independent groups includes two main sources of variance:

1. The variability between the different groups.
2. The variability within each group.

For the 2-factor study, however, the between-group variability breaks down further into variance contributed by the first factor (program content), the second factor (anger), and the interaction between the two factors. Each of these three sources of variance will produce its own *F* ratio.

The ANOVA source table for this hypothetical 2 × 2 factorial looks like this. The SS numbers are the result of calculations made on some hypothetical data—these data and all the basic calculations can be found in the online Student Companion Site (www.wiley.com/college/goodwin).

(continued)

TABLE 8.1   *(continued)*

Source of Variance	SS	df	MS	F	p
Program content	110.4	1	110.4	11.2	<.01
Anger	61.2	1	61.2	6.2	<.05
Interaction	4.1	1	4.1	0.4	
Error	159.2	16	9.9		
Total	334.9	19			

An ANOVA source table summarizes the analysis by indicating the sums of squares (*SS*), degrees of freedom (*df*), and mean square (*MS*) for each source of variance, and the final *F* ratios, which determine whether significant main effects and/or an interaction occurred. *SS* again refers to the sum of squared deviations, a concept introduced in Chapter 4 when you learned about standard deviations. Degrees of freedom (*df*) relate to sample size and the number of groups involved in the study. The *df* between groups for each factor is equal to the number of groups per factor minus one (in this case 2−1 = 1 for both factors). The *df* for the interaction is the *df* for the first factor multiplied by the *df* for the second factor. The *df* for the error variance is the number of subjects per group minus one, times the total number of groups—in this case [(5−1) × 4] = 16. (Total degrees of freedom equal the total number of subjects in the study minus one, or 20−1 = 19). As you recall from Chapter 7, *MS* or mean square is another name for variance and in the ANOVA source table, each of the three mean squares is found by dividing *SS* by *df* (you should check the calculations in the source table). Each *F* ratio is found by dividing the variance (*MS*) for each source of between-groups variance by the "error" variance (check this too).

The outcome? Two significant main effects—watching violent programs resulted in more aggression than watching nonviolent programs (18.3 > 13.5), and when the boys were angered, they were more prone to violence than when not made angry (17.6 > 14.2). No interaction occurred.

✓ Self Test 8.3

1. What is the defining feature of a mixed design? In a 3 × 3 mixed design with 20 subjects in the first cell, how many subjects are needed to complete the study?
2. Distinguish a P × E design from an ATI design.
3. If you need a total of 25 participants in a 4 × 4 factorial study, and there are 25 participants in one of the cells, what kind of design is this?

Before closing this chapter, let me make one final point about factorials and the analysis of variance. You've been looking at many factorial matrices in this chapter. They might vaguely remind you of aerial views of farms in Kansas. If so, it's no accident, as you can discover by reading Box 8.3, which tells you a bit about Sir Ronald Fisher, who invented the analysis of variance.

Box 8.3

ORIGINS—Factorials Down on the Farm

Imagine that you're in a small plane flying over Kansas. Looking out the window, you see mile after mile of farms, with their fields laid out in blocks. The pattern might remind you of the factorial matrices that you've just encountered in this chapter. This is because factorial designs and the ANOVA procedures for analyzing them were first developed in the context of agricultural research, devised by Sir Ronald Fisher. The empirical question was, "What are the best possible conditions or combinations of conditions for raising crop X?"

Ronald Aylmer Fisher (1890–1962) was one of Great Britain's best-known statisticians, equal in rank to the great Karl Pearson, who invented the correlation measure we now call "Pearson's r" (next chapter). Fisher created statistical procedures useful in testing predictions about genetics, but he is perhaps best known among research psychologists for creating the Analysis of Variance (ANOVA), which yields the F ratios that allow one to decide about the null hypothesis in experimental research. You can easily guess what the "F" represents.

For about a 15-year period beginning in 1920, Fisher worked at an experimental agricultural station at Rothamsted, England. While there, he was involved in research investigating the effects on crop yield of such variables as fertilizer type, rainfall level, different planting sequences, and different genetic strains of various crops. He published articles with titles like "Studies in Crop Variation. VI. Experiments on the Response of the Potato to Potash and Nitrogen" (Kendall, 1970, p. 447). In the process, he invented ANOVA as a way of analyzing the data. He especially emphasized the importance of using factorial designs, "for with separate [single-factor] experiments we should obtain no light whatever on the possible *interactions* of the different ingredients" (Fisher, 1935/1951, p. 95, italics added). In the real world of agriculture, crop yields resulted from complex combinations of factors, and studying one factor at a time wouldn't allow a thorough evaluation of those interactive effects.

A simple 2 × 2 design for one of Fisher's experiments, with each block representing how a small square of land was treated, might look like Figure 8.12. As with any factorial, this design allows one to evaluate main effects (of fertilizer and type of wheat in this case), as well as the interaction of the two factors. In the example in Figure 8.12, if we assume that the shaded field produces significantly more wheat than the other three (which equal each other), then we would say that an interaction clearly occurred—the fertilizer was effective, but for only one specific strain of wheat.

Fisher first published his work on ANOVA in book form in 1925 (a year after Jenkins and Dallenbach published their classic sleep and memory study), as part of a larger text on statistics (Fisher, 1925). His most famous work on ANOVA, which combined a discussion of statistics and research methodology, appeared 10 years later as *The Design of Experiments* (Fisher, 1935/1951). ANOVA techniques and factorial designs were slow to catch on in the United States, but by the early 1950s, they had become institutionalized as a dominant statistical tool for experimental psychologists (Rucci & Tweney, 1980).

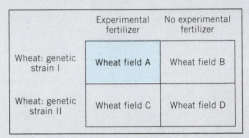

FIGURE 8.12   An agricultural interaction.

This completes our two-chapter sequence about experimental designs. It's a pair of chapters (along with Chapters 5 and 6) sure to require more than one reading and a fair amount of practice with designs before you'll feel confident about your ability to use "experimental psychologist language" fluently and to create a methodologically sound experiment that is a good test of your hypothesis. Next up is a closer look at another research tradition, in which the emphasis is not on examining differences, but in examining degrees of association between measured variables.

Chapter Summary

Factorial Essentials

Factorial designs examine the effects of more than one independent variable. Factorials are identified with a notation system that identifies the number of independent variables, the number of levels of each independent variable, and the total number of conditions in the study. For example, a 2 × 3 ("2 by 3") factorial has two independent variables, the first with two levels and the second with three levels, and six different conditions (2 times 3).

Outcomes — Main Effects and Interactions

The overall influence of an independent variable in a factorial study is called a main effect. There are two possible main effects in a 2 × 3 design, one for the factor with two levels and one for the factor with three levels. The main advantage of a factorial design over studies with a single independent variable is that factorials allow for the possibility of discovering interactions between the factors. In an interaction, the influence of one independent variable differs for the different levels of the other independent variable. The outcomes of factorial studies can include significant main effects, interactions, both, or neither. When a study yields both main effects and interactions, the interactions should be interpreted first, and sometimes an interaction is the important result, while the main effects in the study are irrelevant.

Varieties of Factorial Designs

All of the independent variables in a factorial design can be between-subjects factors or all can be within-subjects factors. Between-subjects factorial designs can include independent groups, matched groups, or nonequivalent groups designs. Within-subjects factorials are also called repeated-measures factorial designs. A mixed factorial design includes at least one factor of each type (between and within). Factorials with at least one subject variable and at least one manipulated variable allow for the discovery of Person × Environment (P × E) interactions. When these interactions occur, they show how stimulus situations affect one type of person one way and a second type of person another way. A main effect for the P factor (i.e., subject variable) indicates important differences between types of individuals that exist in several environments. A main effect for the E factor (i.e., manipulated variable) indicates important environmental influences that exist for several types of persons. In educational research and research on the effectiveness of psychotherapy, these interactions between persons and environments are sometimes called Aptitude-Treatment-Interactions (ATIs). In a mixed P × E design, the E factor is a within-subjects variable.

Chapter Review Questions

1. For a factorial design, distinguish between "levels" and "conditions."

2. What is meant by a main effect? In terms of the contents of a factorial matrix, how does one go about determining if a main effect has occurred?

3. Use the "closing time" study to show that an experiment can result in two important outcomes—two main effects.

4. Use the Grant et al. (1998) experiment (studying in noisy or quiet environments) to illustrate the fact that important results can occur in a study, even if no main effects occur.

5. In a study with both main effects and an interaction, explain why the interaction must be interpreted first, and that the statistically significant main effects might have little meaning for the overall outcome of the study. Use the caffeine study to illustrate.

6. Distinguish between a mixed factorial design and a P × E design. Can a design be both a mixed design and a P × E design? Explain.

7. Use the introvert/extrovert and room size example to show how P × E designs can discover important ways in which (a) individuals differ, and (b) situations can be more powerful than individual differences.

8. Mixed factorial designs may or may not involve counterbalancing. Explain.

9. Describe the basic research design and the general outcome of Jenkins and Dallenbach's famous study on sleep and memory. What was the interaction that might have occurred in their study?

10. What is meant by the concept of leakage and how might it be prevented?

Applications Exercises

Exercise 8.1   Identifying Designs

For each of the following descriptions of studies, identify the independent and dependent variables involved, the levels of the independent variable, and the nature of each independent variable (between-subjects or within-subjects; manipulated or subject variables). Also, describe the number of independent variables and levels of each by using the factorial notation system (e.g., 2 × 3), and use Figure 8.6 to identify the design.

1. On the basis of scores on the Jenkins Activity Survey, three groups of subjects are identified: Type A, Type B, and intermediate. An equal number of subjects in each group is given one of two tasks to perform. One of the tasks is to sit quietly in a small room and estimate, in the absence of a clock, when 2 full minutes have elapsed. The second task is to make the same estimate, except that while in the small room, the subject will be playing a hand-held video game.

2. College students in a cognitive mapping study are asked to use a direction finder to point accurately to three unseen locations that vary in distance from the lab. One is a nearby campus location, one is a nearby city, and the third is a distant city. Half of the participants perform the task in a windowless room with a compass indicating the direction of north. The remaining participants perform the task in the same room without a compass.

3. In a study of touch sensitivity, two–point thresholds are measured on 10 different skin locations for an equal number of blind and sighted adults. Half of the participants perform the task in the morning and half in the evening.

4. Three groups of preschoolers are put into a study of delay of gratification in which the size of the delay is varied. Children in all three groups complete a puzzle task. One group is told that as payment they can have $1 now or $3 tomorrow. The second group chooses between $1 now or $3 two days from now, and the third group chooses between $1 now or $3 three days from now.

For each of the three groups, half of the children solve an easy puzzle and half solve a difficult puzzle. The groups are formed in such a way that the average parents' income is the same for children in each group.

5. In a study of visual illusions and size perception, participants adjust a dial that alters one of two stimuli. The goal is to make the two stimuli appear to be equal in size, and the size of the error in this judgment is measured on each trial. Each participant completes 40 trials. On half of the trials, the pairs of stimuli are in color; on the other half, they are in black and white. For both the colored and the black-and-white stimuli, half are presented at a distance of 10 feet from the participant and half are presented 20 feet away.

6. In a study of reading comprehension, sixth-grade students read a short story about baseball. The students are divided into two groups based on their knowledge of baseball. Within each group, half of the students are high scorers on a test of verbal IQ, while the remaining students are low scorers.

7. In a study on stereotyping, students are asked to read an essay said to be written by either a mental patient or a mental health worker. Half of the subjects given each essay are told that the writer is a male and half are told the writer is a female. Subjects are randomly assigned to the four groups and asked to judge the quality of the essay.

8. In a maze learning study, the performance (number of trials to learn the maze) of wild and lab-reared albino rats is compared. Half of each group of rats is randomly assigned to an alley maze; others learn an elevated maze.

Exercise 8.2 Main Effects and Interactions

For each of the following studies:

a. identify the independent variables, the levels of each, and the dependent variable

b. place the data into the correct cells of a factorial matrix and draw a graph of the results

c. determine if main effects and/or interactions exist and give a verbal description of the study's outcome

For the purposes of the exercise, assume that a difference of **more than 2** between any of the row or column or cell means is a statistically significant difference.

1. A researcher is interested in the effects of ambiguity and number of bystanders on helping behavior. Participants fill out a questionnaire in a room with zero or two other people who appear to be other subjects but aren't. The experimenter distributes the questionnaire and then goes into the room next door. After 5 minutes there is a loud crash, possibly caused by the experimenter falling. For half of the participants, the experimenter unambiguously calls out that he has fallen, is hurt, and needs help. For the remaining participants, the situation is more ambiguous—the experimenter says nothing after the apparent fall.

322

Chapter 8. Experimental Design II: Factorial Designs

The experimenter records how long it takes (in seconds) before a participant offers help. Here are the four conditions and the data:

0 bystanders, ambiguous	24 sec
2 bystanders, ambiguous	38 sec
0 bystanders, unambiguous	14 sec
2 bystanders, unambiguous	14 sec

2. In a maze learning study, a researcher is interested in the effects of reinforcement size and reinforcement delay. Half of the rats in the study are given a 1 cm square block of cheese upon completing the maze; the other half gets a 2 cm square block. Within each reinforcement size group, one-half of the rats are given the cheese on arrival at the goal box and one-half waits for the cheese for 15 seconds after their arrival. Hence, there are four groups and the data (dependent variable was number of errors during ten trials):

small reward, 0 sec delay	17 errors
large reward, 0 sec delay	15 errors
small reward, 15 sec delay	25 errors
large reward, 15 sec delay	23 errors

3. A cognitive psychologist interested in gender and spatial ability decides to examine whether some typical gender differences in a mental rotation task (see Chapter 4 for a reminder of this task) can be influenced by instructions. One set of instructions emphasizes the spatial nature of the task and relates it to working as a carpenter (male-oriented instructions); a second set of instructions emphasizes the problem-solving nature of the task and relates it to working as an interior decorator (female-oriented instructions); the third set of instructions is neutral. An equal number of males and females participate in each instructional condition. Here are the six conditions and the data:

males with male-oriented instructions	26 problems correct
males with female-oriented instructions	23 problems correct
males with normal instructions	26 problems correct
females with male-oriented instructions	18 problems correct
females with female-oriented instructions	24 problems correct
females with normal instructions	18 problems correct

4. A forensic psychologist wishes to determine if prison sentence length can be affected by defendant attractiveness and facial expression. Subjects read a detailed crime description (a felony breaking and entering) and are asked to recommend a sentence for the criminal, who has been arrested and found guilty. A photo of the defendant accompanies the description—half the time the photo is of a woman made up to look attractive and half the time the women is made up to look unattractive. For each type of photo, the woman

is either smiling, scowling, or showing a neutral expression. Here are the conditions and the data:

attractive, smiling	8 years
attractive, scowling	14 years
attractive, neutral	9 years
unattractive, smiling	12 years
unattractive, scowling	18 years
unattractive, neutral	13 years

Exercise 8.3   Estimating Participant Needs

For each of the following, use the available information to determine how many research subjects will be needed to complete the study (*Hint*: One of these is unanswerable without more information):

1. a 3 × 3 mixed factorial; a cell needs 10 participants
2. a 2 × 3 repeated-measures factorial; a cell needs 20 participants
3. a 2 × 4 mixed P × E factorial; a cell needs 8 participants
4. a 2 × 2 × 2 independent groups factorial; a cell needs 5 participants
5. a 2 × 2 matched groups factorial; a cell needs 8 participants
6. a 4 × 4 nonequivalent groups factorial; a cell needs 8 participants

---

Answers to Self Tests:

✓ **8.1.**

1. (a) 3; (b) 2, 3, and 4; (c) 24; (d) no way to know from this information; the factorial notation system only yields information about the IVs.
2. A main effect concerns whether a significant difference exists among the levels of an independent variable.
3. A main effect for the type of instruction factor (row means of 20 for imagery and 12 for rote), but no main effect for presentation rate (both column means are 16).

✓ **8.2.**

1. There are no main effects (row and column means all equal 16), but there is an interaction. Wild rats performed better (fewer trials to learn) in the alley maze, while tame rats performed better in the elevated maze.

2. No overall main effect for whether studying took place in a noisy or a quiet environment; also, no overall main effect for whether recall took place in noisy or quiet environment; there was an interaction—recall was good when study and test conditions matched, and poor when study and test conditions did not match.

✓ 8.3.

1. There is at least one between-subjects factor and at least one within-subjects factor; 60.

2. A P × E design has at least one subject factor (P) and one manipulated (E) factor; an ATI design is a type of P × E design in which the "P" factor refers to some kind of ability or aptitude; these ATI designs are frequently seen in educational research.

3. It must be a repeated-measure factorial design.

CHAPTER 9

Correlational Research

Preview & Chapter Objectives

You have just finished a four-chapter sequence that concentrated on the experimental method in psychology. Four chapters remain, each one dealing with a slightly different research tradition. In this chapter, you will encounter correlational research, an approach that examines relationships between and among variables. You will see that caution is needed to interpret the results of correlational research and that correlational studies can be useful when psychologists try to make predictions about behavior. When you finish this chapter, you should be able to:

- Understand the origins of correlational research in the work of Francis Galton and recognize the significance of Cronbach's "two disciplines" address.

- Distinguish between positive and negative bivariate correlations, create scatterplots to illustrate them, and recognize the factors that can influence the size of correlation coefficients (e.g., range restriction, type of relationship).

- Calculate a coefficient of determination (r^2) and interpret its meaning.
- Understand how a regression analysis accomplishes the goal of prediction.
- Understand how directionality can make it difficult to interpret correlations and how a cross-lagged panel study can help with the directionality problem.
- Understand the third variable problem and how such variables can be evaluated and controlled through a partial correlation procedure.
- Describe the research situations in which correlational procedures are likely to be used.
- Describe the logic of the multivariate procedures of multiple regression and factor analysis, and understand how to interpret the results of these procedures.

Remember Robert Woodworth and the "Columbia bible," his precedent-setting text in experimental psychology (Chapter 5's opening paragraphs)? The book institutionalized the distinction we routinely make today between independent and dependent variables in experimental studies. The second distinction made by Woodworth, between experimental and correlational methods, likewise has had a profound effect on research in psychology. The experimental method manipulates independent variables, according to Woodworth, while the correlational method "[m]easur[es] two or more characteristics of the same individual [and] computes the correlation of these characteristics" (Woodworth, 1938, p. 3). Woodworth took pains to assure the reader that these two research strategies were of equal value. The correlational method was "[t]o be distinguished from the experimental method, [but] standing on a par with it in value, rather than above or below" (Woodworth, 1938, p. 3). After making this assertion, however, Woodworth referred the reader elsewhere for information about correlational research, and devoted the remaining 820 pages of his text to research illustrating the experimental method. The reader could be excused for thinking that correlational research was not quite as important as experimental research.

Psychology's Two Disciplines

The Woodworth text began a process of separation that led eventually to Lee Cronbach's 1957 presidential address to the American Psychological Association, entitled "The Two Disciplines of Scientific Psychology" (Cronbach, 1957). As you can guess, the two disciplines were correlational and experimental psychology. According to Cronbach, correlational psychology is concerned with investigating the relationships between naturally occurring variables and with studying individual differences. The experimental psychologist is not usually interested in individual differences, however, but rather with minimizing or controlling these differences in order to show that some stimulus factor influences every individual's behavior in some predictable way to some measurable degree. The correlationist observes variables and relates them; the experimentalist manipulates variables and observes the outcome. The correlationist looks for ways in which people differ from each other; the experimentalist looks for general laws that apply to everyone.

Cronbach was concerned that correlational psychology held second-class status in scientific psychology, and expressed the belief that it was time for a synthesis to occur, for both approaches to be valued equally by advocates of each, and for research to encompass both strategies. As he put it:

> It is not enough for each discipline to borrow from the other. Correlational psychology studies only variance among organisms; experimental psychology studies only variance among treatments. A united discipline will study both of these, but it will also be concerned with the otherwise neglected *interactions between organismic variables and treatment variables.* (Cronbach, 1957, p. 681, italics added)

As the italicized phrase indicates, Cronbach was calling for an increase in designs like the P × E factorials (P = person or organism; E = environmental treatment) that you learned about in Chapter 8. He was also calling for a renewed appreciation of the correlational method in general, an outcome that has occurred in the last 50 years. Aided by the speed and capacity of modern computers, sophisticated correlational procedures such as multiple regression and factor analysis are in widespread use today. However, many experimental psychology textbooks continue the Woodworth tradition of paying little attention to the correlational method, often devoting just a page or two in a chapter on "nonexperimental" methods. This book is an exception, as you're about to discover. Before diving into a description of the nuts and bolts of correlational research, however, you should read Box 9.1, which describes the origins of the correlational procedure in the attempts by Sir Francis Galton to study the inheritance of genius.

Box 9.1

ORIGINS—Galton's Studies of Genius

When you first encountered him in Chapter 1, Sir Francis Galton (1822–1911) was portrayed as a bit of an eccentric (e.g., trying to measure the usefulness of prayer). However, it would be a mistake to dismiss Galton as a crank. He was a pioneer in the empirical study of intelligence, among the first to make a strong case that genius is inherited and not the result of one's upbringing. Along the way, he invented correlations.

Galton was much impressed by his cousin Charles Darwin's theory of evolution, especially the idea that individual members of a species vary. Individual variations that are useful for survival are then "naturally selected" and passed on to offspring. Galton believed that intelligence was a trait on which people varied, that it was important for survival, and that it seemed to be inherited much like physical characteristics such as eye color and height. He set out to gather evidence for the idea that intelligence was inherited, and produced two books on the subject: *Hereditary Genius* (1869) and *English Men of Science: Their Nature and Nurture* (1874), the latter popularizing the now famous terms "nature" and "nurture." In his books, Galton noted the statistical tendency for "eminence" in specific areas (e.g., science, law) to run in families—eminent lawyers, for example, were more likely to have eminent lawyer sons than would be expected by chance. He discounted the influence of the environment and declared that genius was the result of inheritance.

It wasn't until 1888 that Galton solved the problem of how to express the strength of a tendency for a trait like eminence to run in families; he expressed his ideas in a paper called "Co-relations and Their Measurement" (cited in Fancher, 1990). Using the example of the relationship between parent and child heights, Galton discovered that he could organize his data into a row and column arrangement—see Figure 9.1. The numbers in each cell indicated how many people fell into the categories defined by the row and column headings. Hence, the largest number in those cells indicates that the sample included 14 children who were between 67 and 68 inches tall and whose parents' heights were also between 67 and 68 inches. As you will discover in a few pages, Galton's table is the origin of what are now called "scatterplots" (Figure 9.1 would become a scatterplot if, for the cell with the "14" in it, the cell contained fourteen dots instead).

Second, Galton noticed that while the "co-relations" were imperfect, one regularity occurred quite consistently. Taller-than-average parents had tall children, but they tended to be not quite as tall as Mom and Dad. Shorter-than-average parents

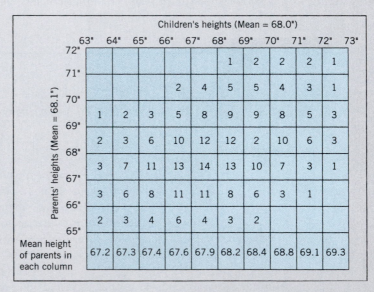

	Children's heights (Mean = 68.0")										
Parents' heights (Mean = 68.1")	63"	64"	65"	66"	67"	68"	69"	70"	71"	72"	73"
72"							1	2	2	2	1
71"					2	4	5	5	4	3	1
70"	1	2	3	5	8	9	9	8	5	3	
69"	2	3	6	10	12	12	2	10	6	3	
68"	3	7	11	13	14	13	10	7	3	1	
67"	3	6	8	11	11	8	6	3	1		
66"	2	3	4	6	4	3	2				
65"											
Mean height of parents in each column	67.2	67.3	67.4	67.6	67.9	68.2	68.4	68.8	69.1	69.3	

FIGURE 9.1 A table used by Galton to correlate the heights of parents and children—an original scatterplot.

had short children, but not quite as short as the parents. That is, the children's heights tended to drift back to, or regress to, the mean for the population. This "regression to the mean" phenomenon, which you already know can threaten a study's internal validity, is one of Galton's more important discoveries.

A third observation made by Galton was that a plot of the average of each column of his scatterplot yielded a more or less straight line. This, in fact, is a type of "regression line," another concept that you'll be encountering shortly. In sum, Galton discovered the main features of a correlational analysis.

Shortly after reading about Galton's work, the young British statistician Karl Pearson continued developing the idea, eventually devising the modern formula for calculating coefficients of correlation. He named it "r" for "regression," in honor of Galton's discovery of the regression to the mean phenomenon. Also following Galton's lead, Pearson believed that correlational analysis supported the idea that many traits were inherited because they ran in families. A feature of correlations that you'll be learning about shortly is that drawing conclusions about causality from them, as both Galton and Pearson did, is a hazardous venture.

Correlation and Regression—The Basics

A correlation exists whenever two variables are associated or related to each other in some fashion. This idea is implied by the term itself: "co" for two and "relation" for, well, relation. In a direct or **positive correlation**, the relationship is such that a high score on one variable is associated with a high score on the second variable; similarly, a low score on one relates to a low score on the other. A **negative correlation**, on the other hand, is an inverse relationship. High scores on one variable are associated with low scores on the second variable, and vice versa. The correlation method was called the Method of Concomitant Variation by John Stuart Mill (refer back to Box 5.1, to review Mill's ideas about the rules of induction). Compared to his Joint Method of Agreement and Difference, which determines the necessary and sufficient conditions for some event to occur, the Method of Concomitant Variation merely states that changes in the value of one variable are accompanied by predictable changes in a second variable.

Positive and Negative Correlations

The relationship between study time and grades is a simple example of a positive correlation. If study time, operationalized as the total number of hours per week spent studying, is one variable and grade point average (GPA) ranging from 0.0 to 4.0 is the second, you can easily see the positive correlation between the two in these hypothetical data from eight students:

	Study hours	GPA
Student 1:	42	3.3
Student 2:	23	2.9
Student 3:	31	3.2
Student 4:	35	3.2
Student 5:	16	1.9
Student 6:	26	2.4
Student 7:	39	3.7
Student 8:	19	2.5

Spending a significant amount of time studying (e.g., 42 hours) is associated with a high GPA (3.3), whereas minimal study time (e.g., 16 hours) is paired with a low GPA (1.9).

An example of negative correlation might be the relationship between goof-off time and GPA. Goof-off time could be operationally defined as the number of hours per week spent in a specific list of activities that might include video game playing, TV watching, and playing golf (of course, these same activities could be called "therapy" time). Here's some hypothetical data for another eight students. This time, examine the inverse relationship between the number of hours per week spent goofing off and GPA:

	Goof-off hours	GPA
Student 1:	42	1.8
Student 2:	23	3.0
Student 3:	31	2.2
Student 4:	35	2.9
Student 5:	16	3.7
Student 6:	26	3.0
Student 7:	39	2.4
Student 8:	19	3.4

Notice that in a negative correlation, the variables go in opposite directions. Large amounts of goof-off time (e.g., 42 hours) accompany a low GPA (1.8); small amounts of goof-off time (e.g., 16 hours) relate to a higher GPA (3.7).

The strength of a correlation is indicated by the size of a statistic called the "coefficient of correlation," which ranges from −1.00 for a perfect negative correlation, through 0.00 for no relationship, to +1.00 for a perfect positive correlation. The most common coefficient is the **Pearson's *r***, mentioned in Box 9.1, and named for Karl Pearson, the British statistician who rivals Sir Ronald Fisher (the ANOVA guy) in stature. Pearson's *r* is calculated for data measured on either an interval or a ratio scale. Other kinds of correlations can be calculated for data measured on other scales. For instance, a correlation coefficient called

Spearman's rho (rhymes with "throw") is calculated for ordinal (i.e., rankings) data. If you look on the Student Companion Site (www.wiley.com/college/goodwin), you will see an example of how to calculate a Pearson's *r* by hand and how to do a correlational analysis with SPSS.

Like means and standard deviations, a coefficient of correlation is a descriptive statistic. The inferential analysis for correlations involves determining if a particular correlation is significantly greater than (or less than) zero. That is, in correlational research, the null hypothesis (H_0) is that the true value of *r* is 0 (i.e., no relationship exists); the alternative hypothesis (H_1) is that $r \neq 0$. Rejecting the null hypothesis means deciding that a significant relationship between two variables exists.

Scatterplots

An indication of the strength of a correlation also can be discerned by examining the modern version of Galton's Figure 9.1, what is now called a **scatterplot** or scattergraph; it provides a visual representation of the relationship shown by a correlation. As shown in the examples in Figure 9.2, perfect positive (9.2a)

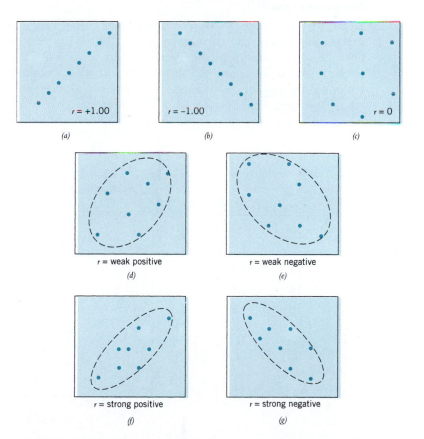

FIGURE 9.2 Varieties of scatterplots.

and perfect negative (9.2b) correlations produce points falling on a straight line, whereas a correlation of zero yields a scatterplot (9.2c) in which the points appear to be randomly distributed on the surface of the graph. Compared to those for relatively weak correlations (9.2d and 9.2e), the points bunch closer together for relatively strong ones (9.2f and 9.2 g). In general, as any correlation weakens, the points on a scatterplot move further away from the diagonal lines that would connect the points in a perfect correlation of +1.00 or −1.00. Note that the dotted line ovals in Figure 9.2 are not a normal feature of scatterplots; I put them there just to show you how the points are more tightly bunched as a correlation strengthens.

Figure 9.3 shows you how a scatterplot is created from a set of data—each point on the scatterplot is an individual subject in the study. Figure 9.4 displays the scatterplots for the hypothetical GPA examples. They indicate a strong positive correlation between study time and GPA and a strong negative one between goof-off time and GPA. The actual correlations are +.88 and −.89, respectively. Your instructor might ask you to verify these Pearson's r's by using the procedures outlined in the Student Companion Site.

Assuming Linearity

So far, the scatterplots we've seen contain points that vary to some degree from the straight line of a perfect correlation of −1.00 or +1.00. Some relationships are not linear, however, and applying Pearson's r to them will fail to identify the nature of the relationship. Figure 9.5 shows a hypothetical example, one of psychology's enduring findings: the relationship between arousal and performance. On tasks that are somewhat difficult, performance is good at moderate levels of arousal but suffers if arousal is very low or very high (e.g., Anderson, 1990). At very low levels of

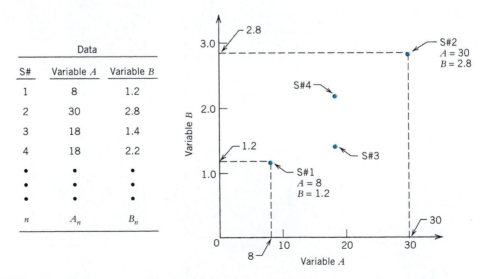

FIGURE 9.3   Creating a scatterplot from a data set.

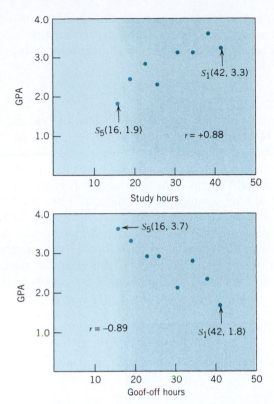

FIGURE 9.4 Scatterplots for some hypothetical GPA data.

arousal the person doesn't have the energy to perform the task, and at very high levels, the intense arousal interferes with the efficient processing of information necessary to complete the task. You can see from the scatterplot that points would fall consistently along this curved line, but trying to apply a linear correlational procedure would yield a Pearson's r of zero or very close to it. You can see how this would happen—the left half of the curve is essentially a strong positive correlation;

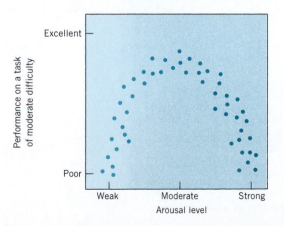

FIGURE 9.5 The curvilinear relationship between arousal level and performance.

the right half is a strong negative correlation, which would cancel out the effect of the left side when calculating a Pearson's *r*. More specialized techniques beyond the scope of this text are needed for analyzing curvilinear relationships like the one in Figure 9.5.

Restricting the Range

When doing a correlational study, it is important to include individuals who provide a wide range of scores. **Restricting the range** of one (or both) of the measured variables weakens the correlation, an effect that you can see in Figure 9.6. Suppose you are investigating the relationship between SAT scores and success in college, the latter measured in terms of GPA at end of the freshman year. Figure 9.6a shows what a scatterplot might look like for a sample of 25 students. The correlation is +.70. Suppose, however, that you decide to study this relationship, but only for students who score 1200 or above on the SAT. Figure 9.6b highlights the points on the scatterplot for such students; these points can form their own scatterplot, as shown in Figure 9.6c. If you now examine 9.6a and 9.6c, it is clear that the correlation is lower for 9.6c. In fact, the correlation for the points in 9.6c drops to +.26.

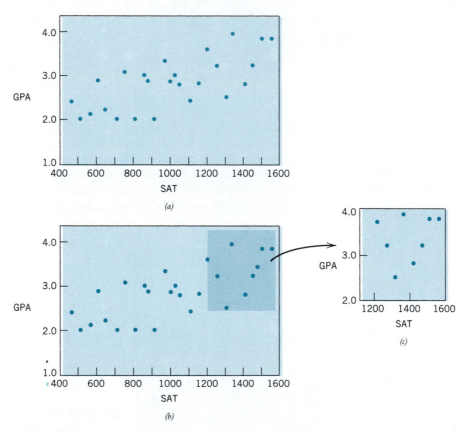

FIGURE 9.6 The effect of a range restriction.

This example has some interesting implications for selective colleges that decide not to consider students whose combined SAT scores fall below 1200. Studies (e.g., Schrader, 1971) have shown the overall correlation between SAT scores and freshman year grades to be somewhere between +.30 and +.40, statistically significant but not huge. That correlation is calculated using students throughout the whole range of SAT scores, however. If the range of SAT scores is restricted to those of 1200 or above, the correlation drops considerably. Procedures exist for "correcting" correlations to account for the restriction problem, but one has to be aware that restricting the range has direct effects on the ability to make predictions. Highly selective schools using an "SAT = 1200" cutoff will certainly be getting a lot of good students, but their ability to predict grades from SAT scores will not be as great as in a school without such a cutoff point. The correlation between SAT and academic success will be higher at the less restrictive school than it will be at the more restrictive school.

Coefficient of Determination—r^2

It is easy to misinterpret the meaning of a particular Pearson's r. If it equals +.70, the relationship is a relatively strong one, but students sometimes look at such a correlation and think that the +.70 somehow relates to 70%, and that the correlation means the relationship is true 70% of the time. This is *not* what a Pearson's r means. A better sense of how to interpret the meaning of a correlation is to use what is called the **coefficient of determination (r^2)**. It is found by squaring the Pearson's r—hence, the coefficient will always be a positive number, regardless of whether the correlation is positive or negative. Technically, r^2 is defined as the portion of variability in one of the variables in the correlation that can be accounted for by variability in the second variable. An example should make this clear.

Suppose you complete a study involving 100 people and you measure an SAT score and a grade point average (GPA) for each person. You correlate the two variables and find a positive correlation. The higher the SAT score, the higher the GPA; conversely, low SAT scores tend to be accompanied by a low GPA. Consider two hypothetical correlations that might result from this study, a perfect +1.00 and +.50. The coefficients of determination will be 1.00 and .25, respectively. To understand what this means, first recognize that the GPAs for the 100 people in the study will probably vary quite a bit, possibly from 0.0 to 4.0. As researchers, we would like to know what produces this variability—why one person gets a 3.8, another a 2.4, and so on. That is, what accounts for individual differences in GPA? There are probably a number of factors in real life that lead to different levels of GPA—study habits, general intelligence, motivation, emotion stability, ability to avoid taking physics courses, and so on. Our hypothetical study has examined one of those factors, a measure of academic ability, as reflected in scores on the SAT. The r^2 provides us with an indication of how much the variability in GPA can be associated with academic ability. In the first outcome, with an r of +1.00 and an r^2 of 1.00, we could conclude that 100% of the variability in GPA can be accounted for with reference to SAT scores. That is, we could say that 100% of the difference between the GPAs of 3.8 and 2.4 (and others) could be attributed to whatever SAT measures. This, of course, would never happen in a real study; human behavior is much too complex. In the second case, with an *r* of +.50 and an r^2 of .25, only a quarter (25%) of the variability in GPA scores can be associated with SAT scores. Presumably, the remaining 75% would be related to other factors, such as the ones listed previously (study habits, etc.). As mentioned earlier, actual research indicates that the correlation between SAT and GPA is in the vicinity of +.30 to +.40. Thus, SAT accounts for about 9% to 16% of the variability in GPA, which might seem rather small to you, and probably accounts for some of the controversy over the value of the SAT.

One final point. Notice, for example, that for a correlation of +.70, the coefficient of determination is .49, while a correlation of +.50 has an r^2 of .25. Although we might be tempted to think that the relationships aren't all that different, that +.70 isn't *that* much bigger than +.50, the reality is that the amount of shared variance is almost twice as much in the first case as in the second. That is, a correlation of +.70 is *much* stronger than a correlation of +.50.

✓ Self Test 9.1

1. Consider the relationship between depression and exercise. Do you think it is a positive or a negative correlation? Explain.
2. Compared to a situation in which both variables involve a wide range of scores, what happens to the correlation when the range of scores is restricted?
3. The hypothetical example involving study time and GPA produced a Pearson's *r* of +.88. What is the coefficient of determination in this case, and what does it mean?

Regression Analysis—Making Predictions

A major feature of correlational research is that predictions about behavior can be made when strong correlations exist. If you know that a statistically significant correlation exists between two variables, then knowing a score on one of the variables enables you to predict a score on the other (if the correlation is not significant, regression analyses should not be done). You can see how this would work with the GPA example. Knowing of the strong relationship between study time and GPA, if I tell you that someone studies 45 hours per week, you could safely predict a relatively high GPA for that student. Similarly, a high GPA allows a prediction about study time. As you'll see later in the chapter, correlational research provides the foundation for using psychological tests to make predictions. Making predictions on the basis of correlational research is referred to as doing a **regression analysis**.

Figure 9.7 reproduces the scatterplots for (a) study time and GPA and (b) goof-off time and GPA, but this time each includes what is called a **regression line**. This line is used for making the predictions and is called a "best-fitting line"; it provides

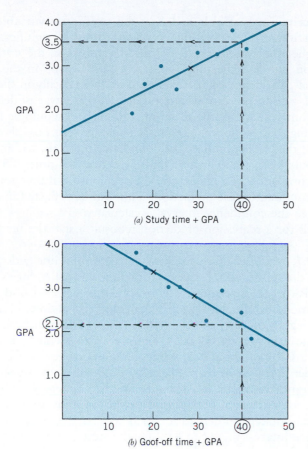

(a) Study time + GPA

(b) Goof-off time + GPA

FIGURE 9.7　Scatterplots with regression lines.

the best possible way of summarizing the points on the scatterplot. More precisely, if you took the absolute values of the shortest distances between each point and the line, those distances would be at a minimum.

The formula for the regression line is essentially the same formula you learned in high school for creating a straight line on a graph with X and Y coordinates:

$$Y = a + bX$$

where a is the place where the line crosses the Y-axis (i.e., the Y-intercept) and b is the slope, the line's relative steepness. X is a known value and Y is the value you are trying to predict. The value of b can be calculated knowing (1) the size of the correlation and (2) the standard deviations for the variables being correlated, and a can be calculated knowing (1) the calculated value of b and (2) the mean scores for the variables being correlated. The Student Companion Site will show you how to do this by hand and with SPSS.

In a regression analysis, the regression equation is used to predict a value for Y (e.g., GPA) based on a given value of X (e.g., study time). Y is sometimes referred to as the **criterion variable** and X as the **predictor variable**. In order to predict with confidence, however, the correlation must be significantly greater than zero. The higher the correlation, the closer the points on the scatterplot will be to the regression line and the more confident you can be in the prediction you make. And that confidence can be expressed mathematically in the form of a confidence interval, a concept I introduced in Chapter 4 as a way of determining a range of scores within which the true mean of a population would be likely to be found. When making a prediction in a regression analysis, it is possible to establish a range of scores for the prediction (i.e., the confidence interval), within which the true prediction would be likely to occur a high percentage of times (95% or 99%). In general, as the correlation gets higher and the relationship is therefore stronger, one can be more confident of the prediction. This will be reflected in a narrower range of scores when the confidence interval is calculated. To see how to calculate confidence intervals for a regression prediction, consult a statistics textbook (e.g., Sprinthall, 2000).

From Figure 9.7, you can also see how a regression line aids in making predictions. Given the relationship between study time and GPA, for example, one could ask what GPA could be expected from someone with 40 study hours. As you can see, the process can be visualized by drawing vertical dotted lines up from the X-axis to the regression line, and then taking a $90°$ left turn until the Y-axis is encountered. The value on the Y-axis is the prediction. Thus, a study time of 40 hours predicts a GPA of about 3.5, while 40 hours of goof-off time predicts a GPA of just under 2.1. The exact predictions, 3.48 and 2.13, respectively, can be calculated by using the regression formula on the Student Companion Site. And because the correlations are both strong (+.88 for study time and −.89 for goof-off time), the confidence intervals for each will have a fairly narrow range. The 95% confidence interval is 2.94 to 4.02 for the study time prediction; hence, we can be 95% confident that the calculated range of GPAs will include the true prediction.

You can be certain that some form of regression analysis has occurred in much of the research you hear about on the news or read about in the popular press—whenever you encounter the terms "risk factor" or "profile" you can be sure that regression analysis has occurred. For instance, a report about "risk factors for heart attacks" will be describing a study in which a significant correlation between, say, smoking and heart disease allows the prediction that heavy smokers will be more likely to develop coronary problems than nonsmokers. That is, smoking predicts heart disease. Another study describing the "profile" of a spouse abuser might include the idea that such behavior is more likely to occur if the abuser is unemployed. Again, this follows from a correlation between unemployment and the tendency to be abusive and allows a prediction, via regression analysis, of the latter from the former.

One final point about a regression analysis is both procedural and ethical. In general, predictions should be made only for people who fall within the range of scores on which the correlation is based. For example, if a regression equation predicting college success is based on a study using middle-class suburban Caucasians whose scores range from 1000 to 1400, then the equation should not be used to predict success for any applicant not within that population.

Interpreting Correlations

With its ability to predict, correlational research gives the researcher a powerful tool. However, great care must be taken in interpreting the results of correlational studies. Specifically, finding a correlation between two variables does not allow the conclusion that one of the variables is causing the other to occur. Unfortunately, a failure to appreciate this fundamental rule makes correlational research the method least understood by the general public. It is not uncommon for news reports to describe correlational research and for the narrative of the report to suggest to the noncritical reader that one variable in the relationship is the cause of the other. The implication of causality occurs many times because the news report will use the term "link," as in, for example, "Researchers have established a link between baldness and heart disease," which turns out to be actual research. In one study, for instance (Lotufo, Chae, Ajani, Hennekens, & Manson, 1999), researchers studying more than 22,000 physicians found that coronary heart disease among these doctors was associated with "vertex" baldness (more so than with frontal baldness or receding hairlines). Most press reports were careful to point out that the link was not a causal one, but the uncritical reader, making more than should be made of the term "link," might be led to conclude that going bald is a direct cause of having a heart attack. I don't know if sales of hair transplants increased after the research was reported, but anyone thinking that eliminating their baldness by investing in transplants would save them from a potential heart attack would be falling prey to the classic misinterpretation of correlational research. If you can see the problem with this line of thinking, then you already have a sense of what is to follow. As you recall from Chapter 1, one of my goals is to help you become a more critical consumer of information. Understanding how to interpret correlational research properly will help you approach that goal because drawing inappropriate conclusions from correlational research occurs quite frequently in popular descriptions of medical and psychological research.

Correlations and Causality

In an experimental study with a manipulated independent variable, we've already seen that cause-and-effect conclusions can be drawn with some degree of confidence. The independent variable of interest is manipulated, and if all else is held constant (i.e., no confounds), the results can be attributed directly to the independent variable. With correlational research, the "all else is held constant" feature is missing, however, and this lack of control makes it impossible to conclude anything about cause and effect from a simple correlation. Let's consider two specific ways in which interpretation problems can occur with correlations. These are referred to as the directionality problem and the third variable problem (Neale & Liebert, 1973).

Directionality

If there is a correlation between two variables, A and B, it is possible that A is causing B to occur (A → B), but it also could be that B is causing A to occur (B → A). That the causal relation could occur in either direction is known as the **directionality problem**. The existence of the correlation *by itself* does not allow one to decide about the direction of causality. For instance, consider a study described recently in the *New York Times*, in which researchers examined the research productivity and beer consumption of ornithologists in the Czech Republic. They found a negative correlation—the more beer consumed by ornithologists, the less productive they were as scientists, a finding not likely to be taken well by those scientists who often claim that their best ideas occur to them in bars or pubs. The *Times* article emphasized the interpretation that probably occurred to you, that spending too much time drinking beer might cause the scientists to have little time left for research. But one researcher, thinking in terms of directionality, suggested that perhaps "those with poor publication records are drowning their sorrows" (For Scientists, 2008). It is also worth noting that the article also illustrated *external validity*, a concept you learned about in Chapter 5. One non-ornithologist critic of the study suggested that perhaps the results were limited to those scientists who studied birds. Another suggested that the results were limited to the Czech Republic, which, the article claimed, had "the highest rate of beer consumption on earth."

Research on the relationship between TV watching and children's aggression typifies the directionality problem. Some of these studies are correlational and take the following general form. Some measure (variable A) of TV watching is made, the number of hours per week perhaps. For the same children, a second measure (variable B) of aggressive behavior is taken. It might be a combined score of teacher ratings of the aggressiveness of those in the study. Suppose this study yields a correlation of +.58, which is found to be significantly greater than zero. What can be concluded?

One possibility, of course, is that watching large amounts of TV inevitably exposes the child to a great deal of violence, and we know that children learn by observation; thus, it would follow that a large dose of TV watching causes children to become aggressive. That is, A $\rightarrow$ B. But could causality be working in the reverse direction? Could it be that children who are already aggressive for some other reason simply like to watch TV more than their nonaggressive peers? Knowing that much of television involves violent programming, perhaps aggressive children choose to watch more of the things that really interest them. In short, perhaps being aggressive causes children to watch more TV. That is, B $\rightarrow$ A.

Solely on the basis of an existing correlation, then, choosing the correct causal direction is not possible. However, there is a way to deal with the directionality problem to some extent. It derives from the criteria for determining causality first described in Chapter 1. As you recall, research psychologists are generally satisfied with attributing causality between A and B when they occur together with some regularity, when A precedes B in time, when A causing B makes sense in relation to some theory, and when other explanations for their co-occurrence can be ruled out.

For the TV and aggressiveness study, all we have is A and B occurring together and the fact that A causing B makes some sense from what is known about observational learning theory. However, using a procedure called a **cross-lagged panel correlation**, it is possible to increase one's confidence about directionality. In essence, this procedure investigates correlations between variables at several points in time. Hence, it is a type of longitudinal design, adding the causal element of A preceding B. The following well-known study illustrates the procedure.

Research Example 22—Correlations and Directionality

Eron, Huesman, Lefkowitz, and Walder (1972) became interested in the same relationship between TV watching and aggression that I've been using as a hypothetical example.[1] In particular, they measured (a) preference for watching violent television programs and (b) peer ratings of aggressiveness. The participants were 875 third graders from a rural area of New York State, first studied in 1960; a modest but significant correlation of +.21 between preference for violent TV and aggressiveness was found. What made the study interesting, however, was that Eron's team returned 10 years later, found 427 of the same students (now arbitrarily labeled "thirteenth graders"), and reassessed the same two variables. By measuring the two variables at two different points in time, six correlations could be calculated. These correlations, as they occurred in the Eron et al. study, are displayed in Figure 9.8.

Of special interest are the diagonal or "cross-lagged" correlations because they measure the relationships between two main variables, but separated in time. If third-grade aggressiveness caused a later preference for watching violent TV (B → A), then we would expect a fair-sized correlation between aggressiveness at

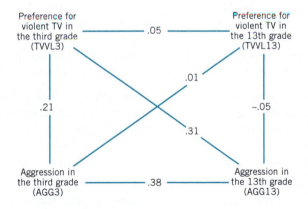

FIGURE 9.8 Results of a cross-lagged panel study of the effects of preference for violent TV programs on later aggression (from Eron et al., 1972).

---

[1] Actually, the study began with another purpose—to see if parental childrearing practices led to aggressiveness in children. But in a questionnaire for parents, Eron included some "filler" questions, items designed to disguise the study's true purpose. One asked parents to list their child's three favorite TV programs. When looking at the data, Eron was surprised to see a relationship emerge—children who preferred violent programs tended to be more aggressive. The entire focus of the study then changed (Huesman & Dubow, 2008). You might recognize this as an example of how *serendipity* (Chapter 3) can determine the direction of research.

time 1 and preference at time 2; in fact, the correlation is virtually zero (+.01). On the other hand, if an early preference for viewing violent TV programs led to a later pattern of aggressiveness (A → B), then the correlation between preference at time 1 and aggressiveness at time 2 should be substantial. As you can see, this correlation is +.31, not large but significant. Based on this finding, as well as on some other indications in their study, Eron and his colleagues concluded that an early preference for watching violent TV is at least partially the cause of later aggressiveness.

Cross-lagged panel correlations must be interpreted cautiously, however (Rogosa, 1980). For one thing, if you examine the overall pattern of correlations in Figure 9.8, you will notice that the correlation of +.31 may be partially accounted for by the correlations of +.21 and +.38. That is, rather than there being a direct path from third-grade preference to thirteenth-grade aggression, perhaps the path is an indirect result of the relationship between preference for violent TV and aggression in the third grade and between the two measures of aggression. A child scoring high on preference for violent TV in the third grade might also be aggressive in the third grade and still be aggressive (or even more so) in the thirteenth grade. Alternatively, it could be that aggressiveness in the third grade produced both (a) a preference for watching violent TV in the third grade and (b) later aggressiveness. Thus, cross-lagged panel correlations help with the directionality dilemma, but problems of interpretation remain. More generally, interpretation difficulties take the form of the third variable problem.

Third Variables

The June 4, 2000, issue of the *New York Times Magazine* contained a playful article entitled "Greens Peace" (Plotz, 2000). In it the author addressed the weighty issue of why some countries seem to be always at war, while others remain relatively peaceful. His answer was golf—countries in which a substantial portion of the population plays golf are less belligerent than countries without golf. As Plotz put it:

> Every peaceful European nation loves golf. But Russia, at war in Chechnya, doesn't hit the links. Non-golf Greece and non-golf Turkey have long warred over non-golf Cyprus. The former Yugoslavia has fragmented into five states. Only peaceful Slovenia swings the sticks. Do India or Pakistan golf? Of course not. Algerians shoot one another; Moroccans next door shoot par. (p. 32)

Although the slogan "make par, not war" (p. 37) has some merit, I think you can see the absurdity of the argument that golf causes peace. And it is only slightly more likely that the reverse is true—that peace causes golf. Rather, if there really is a correlation between peace and golf on a national level, and Plotz doesn't present a Pearson's *r*, of course, its existence is an exaggerated example of what researchers call the **third variable problem**. Because correlational research does not attempt to control extraneous variables directly, these variables might provide the explanation for the correlation found. That is, rather than A causing B or B causing A, some unknown third variable, C, might be causing both A and B to happen. "C" is some uncontrolled third variable (or variables—it is often the case that more than one uncontrolled variable lies behind a correlation). Can you think of some third variables that could produce the alleged golf–peace correlation? Economic prosperity perhaps? Highly prosperous countries might be more likely to be peaceful and also have more time for leisure, including golf.

Other examples of third variables are not quite so absurd as the peace–golf one and can easily mislead someone into making an unwarranted causal connection that could have dramatic effects. In Box 9.1, for example, you learned about Galton's and Pearson's belief that a positive correlation between parents and children on intelligence showed that heredity was the prime cause of differences in level of intellect. Both discounted the effects of the environment (e.g., intelligent parents providing a stimulating environment for their children) as the factor underlying the relationship between parents' and children's abilities. Furthermore, both argued that because inheritance was the cause of intelligence, smart people should be encouraged to have a lot of children. In fact, Galton is the founder of the "eugenics" movement, which advocated, among other things, that Great Britain take steps to improve the overall intelligence of its people through selective breeding. As Galton put it, just as it is possible "to obtain by careful selection a permanent breed of dogs or horses with peculiar powers of running, ... so it would be quite practical to produce a highly-gifted race of men by judicious marriages during several consecutive generations" (Galton, 1869, cited in Fancher, 1990, p. 228). It isn't difficult to imagine the dark side of a eugenics movement, a recommendation that a group deemed "unfit" or "defective" be prevented from reproducing. As you know, such thoughts occurred to leaders in Germany in the 1930s. So it is important to recognize the need for caution when interpreting correlations.

The relationship between watching violent TV programming and children's aggressiveness provides a clear example of the third variable problem. As we've already seen, it is possible that watching TV violence increases aggression (A → B) but that causality in the opposite direction could also occur (B → A). Children who are already aggressive might seek out and watch violent programs. The third possibility is that both A and B result from some third variable, C (C → A and B). For instance, perhaps the parents are violent people. They cause their children to be violent by modeling aggressive behavior, which the children imitate, and they also cause their children to watch a lot of TV. The children might watch TV in order to "lie low" and avoid contact with parents who are always physically punishing them. Another third variable might be a lack of verbal fluency. Perhaps children are aggressive because they don't argue very effectively, and they also watch a lot of TV as a way of avoiding verbal contact with others.

Sometimes, trying to identify third variables is a purely speculative affair. On other occasions, however, one might have reason to suspect that a particular third variable is operating. If so, and if it is possible to measure this third variable, its effects can be evaluated using a procedure called **partial correlation**, which attempts to control for third variables statistically. In effect, it is a post facto (after the fact) attempt to create at least semi-equivalent groups. For example, suppose you know that the correlation between reading speed and reading comprehension is high, +.55 perhaps (example from Sprinthall, 2000). Furthermore, you suspect that a third variable, IQ, might be producing this correlation—high IQ might produce both rapid reading and strong comprehension. To complete a partial correlation, you would correlate (a) IQ and reading speed and (b) IQ and reading comprehension. Let's suppose these correlations turn out to be +.70 and +.72, respectively, high enough for you to suspect that IQ might be an influential third variable. Calculating a partial correlation involves incorporating all three of these correlations (see Sprinthall for the exact procedure). What results is a partial correlation that measures the remaining relationship between reading speed and reading comprehension, with IQ "partialed out" or "controlled." In this case, the partial correlation turns out to be +.10. Thus, when IQ is statistically controlled ("partialed out"), the correlation between speed and comprehension virtually disappears, which means that IQ is indeed an important third variable making a major contribution to the original +.55 correlation between speed and comprehension.

Several partial correlations were calculated in the Eron et al. (1972) study to see if any important third variables might have been responsible for the relatively high correlation (+.31) between third-grade preference for violence and thirteenth-grade aggressiveness. Table 9.1 shows the results for 12 different potential third variables (called "controlled variables" in the table). As you can see, the partial correlations range from +.25 to +.31, indicating that *none* of the 12 factors made a significant contribution to the original correlation of +.31. That is, even taking into account these other factors, the correlation between early preference for violent TV programs and later aggressiveness remained close to +.31. The analysis strengthened their conclusion "that there is a probable causative influence of watching violent television programs in [the] early formative years on later aggression" (Eron et al., 1972, p. 263).

Caution: Correlational Statistics versus Correlational Research

After reading the chapters on experimental design and this one on correlational research, you might be tempted to assume that if you encounter a Pearson's *r* in the description of a study, then the study must be "correlational research." Unfortunately, things are not quite that simple. It is important to make a distinction between the use of correlations as a statistical tool and the use of a correlational design in research. A Pearson's *r* can be calculated whenever you wish to examine the relationship between any two variables. Although this might occur most frequently in a correlational study, it can also occur in an experimental study, in which the researcher calculates a correlation between the independent variable and the dependent variable. Indeed, the determination of *effect size* (Chapter 4) amounts to an estimate of the degree of association between independent and dependent variables.

Just as the presence of a Pearson's *r* in the results doesn't necessarily mean that a correlational research design has been used, the presence of a *t* test or an ANOVA does not necessarily mean that a strictly experimental design has been used. Consider, for example, a study comparing introverts and extroverts on their

TABLE 9.1 *Partial Correlations in Eron, Huesman, Lefkowitz, and Walder's (1972) Study of the Relationship Between a Preference for Watching Violent TV and Aggressive Behavior*

Controlled Variable	Partial Correlation between TVVL3 and AGG13*
None (original correlation)	.31
Third-grade variables	
Peer-rated aggression	.25
Father's occupational status	.31
Child's IQ	.28
Father's aggressiveness	.30
Mother's aggressiveness	.31
Punishment administered	.31
Parents' aspirations for child	.30
Parents' mobility orientation	.31
Hours of television watched	.30
Thirteenth-grade variables	
Father's occupational status	.28
Subject's aspirations	.28
Hours of television watched	.30

*TVVL3 = preference for watching violence on TV in the 3rd grade;
AGG13 = level of aggressiveness in the 13th grade.
Source: Adapted from Eron et al. (1972), Table 4.

level of obedience to authority. One way to perform the study would be to administer a test of introversion and another one of obedience, and then correlate the two. A second approach would be to administer the introversion test, and then select those scoring in the top 25% (i.e., introverted) and bottom 25% (i.e., extroverted) on the test. These subjects could then be placed in an obedience situation and some measure of obedience taken. The obedience scores for the two groups could then be compared with a *t* test or a 1-way ANOVA. Note, however, that these results tell you no more about cause and effect than does the strategy of calculating a Pearson's *r* between the two variables. Thus, the interpretation problems in correlational research exist regardless of how the data are managed in the study.

Finally, you should recognize that the interpretation problems occurring in correlational studies are exactly the same problems that exist in studies described in earlier chapters, in which subject variables were selected as independent variables. The last two chapters described three such designs:

- Single-factor, nonequivalent groups designs (both two-level and multilevel)
- Factorial nonequivalent groups designs
- Factorial P × E designs

✓ Self Test 9.2

1. Suppose the correlation between high school grades and college grades is +.60 (in fact, it is much lower), and you wish to predict academic success in college by looking at high school grades. Which is the criterion variable and which is the predictor variable?

2. Show how the directionality problem makes it difficult to interpret a correlation between depression and a lack of exercise.

3. In the Eron et al. (1972) study on aggression, which techniques were used to address (a) the directionality problem and (b) the third variable problem?

Using Correlations

Considering the pitfalls that exist when trying to interpret correlations, combined with the fact that those envied conclusions about cause and effect can be made only from experiments with manipulated independent variables, why not just do pure experimental studies all the time? That is, why bother with correlational research?

The Need for Correlational Research

The answer has to do with both practical and ethical considerations. On fairly obvious practical grounds, some research is simply not possible as a pure experimental study. As Cronbach put it in his two-disciplines address, the correlational approach "can study what [we have] not learned to control or can never hope to control" (Cronbach, 1957, p. 672). Studying sex differences in behavior, differences between age groups, or differences between personality types are major research areas in which it is not possible to randomly assign. Other correlational studies might involve using data that have been collected for other purposes, again eliminating random assignment. For example, consider an anthropological study that measured handedness by looking at photos of natives from several indigenous cultures using machetes, knifes, and other tools (Faurie & Raymond, 2004). The study found a surprising correlation of +.83 between the percentage of left-handers in a culture and the culture's murder rate. That's right—the more lefties in a culture, the more murders to be found there. Faurie and Raymond interpreted their results in evolutionary terms, arguing that lefties, because they are relatively rare, have distinct advantages in such events as knife fights, because the opponent will find a lefty's motions unusual and hard to predict.

Second, on rather clear ethical grounds, there are some studies that simply cannot be done as experiments with manipulated variables. When the nineteenth-century French physiologist Paul Broca discovered the brain's speech center, later named for him, he did it by noting a relationship between certain types of speech disorders and the extent of brain damage discovered upon a postmortem examination (Goodwin, 2008). *Experimental* evidence that the disorder was caused by the brain damage would require randomly assigning people to a "brain damage" group, which would have portions of their brain pulverized, or to a safer "control" group. Actually, you would also need a third group that could be called a "sham brain damage" group. They would go through most of the same surgical procedures as the brain damage group, except for the actual brain destruction. I think you can appreciate the difficulty of recruiting human volunteers for this experiment. This is one reason why animals are used as subjects in experimental research investigating the relationship between brain and behavior. With humans, the studies are invariably correlational.

Varieties of Correlational Research

Research using correlational procedures can be found in all areas of psychology. Correlations are especially prevalent in (a) research concerning the development of psychological tests, in which reliability and validity are assessed; (b) research in personality and abnormal psychology, two areas that are full of subject variables; and (c) twin studies, research in the Galton tradition that relates to the nature–nurture issue. Let's look at some representative research from each of the three.

Research Example 23—Correlations and Psychological Testing

In Chapter 4 you learned that for a measure to be of value, it must be both reliable and valid. Reliable measures are repeatable and are relatively free from measurement error. A measure is valid if it truly measures the trait in question. A reliable and valid measure of intelligence will yield about the same IQ score on two separate occasions and will be a true measure of intellectual ability and not a measure of something else. Research to establish reliability and validity depends heavily on correlations, as the following series of studies shows.

For measuring IQ scores in children, the big two are the Stanford–Binet IQ Test and the Weschler Intelligence Scale for Children (WISC). In the past few decades, however, a test called the Kaufman Assessment Battery for Children (K·ABC) test has been making inroads (Kaufman & Kaufman, 1983). This test yields a "mental processing" score that is a composite of several subtests for "sequential processing" and "simultaneous processing." These are assumed to be basic mental abilities possessed by the child. In addition, there is a separate "achievement" score to reflect the kind of knowledge derived from school and elsewhere.

The Kaufmans evaluated the reliability of their test in several ways. For example, they used a procedure called **split–half reliability**. This involves taking the items that make up a particular subtest, dividing them in half (e.g., even-numbered vs. odd-numbered items), and correlating the two halves. The correlation should be high if the test is reliable—someone scoring high on one half should score high on the other half as well. A second type of reliability is called **test–retest reliability**, the relationship between two separate administrations of the test. Again, these reliabilities should be high—a reliable test yields consistent results from one testing to another. For the K·ABC, both split-half and test-retest reliabilities were high (correlations in the vicinity of +.90). What about the test's validity?

One indication of a test's validity is its **criterion validity**, the ability of the test to predict some future event. This validity is determined by correlating scores on the test in question (the K·ABC) with scores on some "criterion." The criterion is typically some other test or measurement that is conceptually related to the test in question. For an IQ test, criterion measures are often scores on tests relating to school performance because IQ tests are designed to predict how well someone will perform in school. Scores on a valid test should correlate positively with criterion scores.

Numerous validity studies have been carried out with the K·ABC using a wide range of criterion measures of school achievement (Kaufman & Kaufman, 1983). In general, the results are impressive; for instance, the test is known to be correlated with such criterion measures as the Iowa Tests of Basic Skills and the California Achievement Test, both well established as indicators of school success.

Implied in this K·ABC example is the importance of using good (i.e., reliable and valid) tests. After all, decisions that can affect lives often are made at least in part on the basis of these instruments. Children are placed into gifted programs, managers are promoted, high school students get into good colleges, and psychiatric patients get the correct diagnosis. All of these important decisions are made with the help of psychological tests. Hence, there are ethical issues related to the reliability and validity of these tools. Box 9.2 considers some of them and describes the APA guidelines for the development and use of tests.

Box 9.2

ETHICS—APA Guidelines for Psychological Testing

Section 9 of the 2002 revision of the APA ethics code is called "Assessment." It includes eleven standards that have to do with the development, use, and interpretation of psychological tests. Two standards in particular relate to research issues (American Psychological Association, 2002, pp. 1071–1072):

9.02 Use of Assessments
(a) Psychologists administer, adapt, score, interpret, or use assessment techniques, interviews, tests, or instruments in a manner and for purposes that are appropriate in light of the research on or evidence of the usefulness and proper application of the techniques.
(b) Psychologists use assessment instruments whose validity and reliability have been established for use with members of the population tested. When such validity or reliability has not been established, psychologists describe the strengths and limitations of test results and limitations.

9.05 *Test Construction*

Psychologists who develop tests and other assessment techniques use appropriate psychometric procedures and current scientific or professional knowledge for test design, standardization, validation, reduction or elimination of bias, and recommendations for use.

From these standards, and from the discussion of reliability and validity, it should be clear that there is considerably more to psychological testing than simply making up a questionnaire that seems to make sense and administering it to friends. Yet, that is the typical procedure used when creating most of the pseudoscientific psychological tests found in popular magazines. These tests might appear to be scientific because they include a scoring key (''if you scored between 20 and 25, it means ... ''), but the scales are essentially meaningless because there's never been any attempt to determine their reliability or validity, or to standardize the test so that a specific score you obtain can be compared to norms (i.e., average scores for others like you).

These tests are harmless as long as you understand that they aren't to be taken seriously. Armed with the appropriate skeptical attitude, then, you could explore the following:

- Has stress got you by the neck? (*Self*, April 2000)

- Are you boring? (*Young and Modern*, June/July 1992)

- Test yourself: How angry are you? (*Self*, January 1993)

- What's your secret sexual personality and his? (*Glamour*, June 2000)

To learn how *real* psychological tests are created and validated, take the tests and measurements course that I'm sure your psychology department offers.

Research Example 24—Correlations in Personality and Abnormal Psychology

Besides their use during test development, correlational procedures are important when individual differences in personality traits and differentiating mental disorders are investigated. For example, a study might select a large group of people, give them tests for several different personality traits, and then correlate the scores. From this type of study, one might learn of a positive correlation between introversion and anxiety (introverts tend to be anxious) or of a negative correlation between introversion and sociability (introverts tend to avoid social contact). An example of this correlation strategy is a study by Diener, Wolsic, and Fujita (1995), who wondered about the relationship between physical attractiveness and happiness.

There is a considerable amount of research showing that those who are physically attractive often benefit from their looks. Because of a ''halo'' effect (good qualities assumed to go together), attractive people are often seen as having better social skills, as being more intelligent, and even as being more mentally healthy (Feingold, 1992). And as you recall from the Chapter 6 discussion of types of research requiring a between–subjects design (the "Barbara Helm" study), physical attractiveness might even influence juries. Given all of this, Diener et al. (1995) hypothesized a positive correlation between physical attractiveness (PAtt) and "subjective well-being" (SWB), a term frequently used by researchers as an indicator of "happiness." Diener et al. were careful to point out the directionality problem—if a correlation between PAtt and SWB exists, it could be that attractiveness leads one to be happy, but it could also be that "happy people take better care of their appearance, so they may be more physically attractive" (p. 121). The researchers also pointed out that a third variable, some aspect of personality (e.g., extroversion) could enhance a person's perceived PAtt while also increasing SWB.

There were three different studies completed, but we'll focus on the first one, which examined the correlation between PAtt and SWB (attractiveness and happiness) for a group of 221 college students enrolled in a course on the psychology of happiness. They each filled out three different measures of SWB: a five-item "Satisfaction with Life" survey (sample item: "If I could live my life over, I would change almost nothing."); an overall measure of perceived happiness (scale ranging from "utterly depressed" to "ecstatic, elated, fantastic"; and a measure of "hedonic balance" (measuring frequencies of specific emotions and subtracting the negative ones from the positive ones). Each student also was photographed from the front and in profile, and videotaped while interacting with a stranger. Ten judges then rated each of the 221 student-subjects for physical attractiveness, and the students also rated themselves on how attractive they believed they were.

In a nutshell, the results were that while some of the correlations were statistically significant, all of them were quite low. Here are the basic Pearson's *r* correlations between the various measures of PAtt and SWB (significant correlations with asterisks):

	Satisfaction with Life Scale	**Global Happiness Scale**	**Hedonic Balance Scale**
PAtt judged from frontal view	.17★	.04	.10
PAtt judged from profile view	.24★	.14★	.12
PAtt judged from videotape	.17★	.08	.09
Self-perceived PAtt	.29★	.28★	.30★

As you can see, the correlations between PAtt and SWB were highest when the students were rating themselves for attractiveness; when more objective measures of attractiveness were used, the correlations were decidedly lower. How would you interpret this outcome? Diener et al. (1995) speculated that "happier people tend to perceive themselves as somewhat more attractive than objective ratings might indicate" (p. 122). A little delusion is not always a bad thing.

One of psychology's most famous series of studies is another example of using a correlational strategy to study personality, in this case the personality trait called "achievement motivation." Before reading on, take a look at Box 9.3, which describes a classic study from this tradition, a study suggesting that it might be wise for a culture to ensure that the characters in stories read by children are high achievers.

Box 9.3

CLASSIC STUDIES—*The Achieving Society*

Can you predict the achievement level of an entire society by analyzing the stories told to the children of that society? Yes, according to psychologist David McClelland's classic 1961 book *The Achieving Society*, which documents an extraordinarily ambitious attempt to extend the results of psychological research on achievement into the realm of historical explanation. Along with colleague John Atkinson, McClelland was a pioneer in the study of achievement motivation, the drive to take on challenges and succeed (McClelland, Atkinson, Clark, & Lowell, 1953). Together, they developed ways of measuring the achievement motive, completed countless studies on the correlates of achievement and the environments conducive to developing the need to achieve (*Hint*: Give your children lots of opportunities to be independent), and created a theory of achievement motivation (Atkinson & Feather, 1966). Furthermore, by elaborating on the "interaction between stable motives that characterize the personality and immediate situational influences, the theory of achievement motivation represent[ed] a step toward conceptual integration of 'the two disciplines of scientific psychology'" (Atkinson & Feather, 1966, p. 5) called for by Cronbach (1957) in his famous APA presidential address.

One way of measuring the need for achievement, or "nAch," is to use the Thematic Apperception Test (TAT), in which subjects look at ambiguous pictures and describe what they see in them (Murray, 1943). For instance, a drawing of a young boy staring at a violin might elicit a story about how he is dreaming of being a classical violinist. Someone writing such a story would get a higher score for nAch than someone who wrote a story about the child's planning to take the violin and whack his sister over the head with it. Presumably, the stories people create reflect the underlying motives important to them.

The idea that one could infer motives from stories led McClelland to wonder about the role that children's stories and a culture's myths and fables might play in the developing motives of young people. If these stories are loaded with achievement themes, might not the young children gradually develop the idea that achievement is important? Could it be that the overall level of nAch in a society could be inferred from an interpretation of children's literature, cultural myths, music, and plays? And if children are raised in an environment stressing achievement, might they achieve at a high level as adults?

Such speculation led to McClelland's classic research on achievement in society. He subjected children's literature to the same kind of analysis given TAT stories, and then took various measures of societal economic health and correlated the two. What he found was a positive correlation; as achievement themes increased, actual achievement increased. Of particular interest was the fact that actual achievement lagged behind high levels of achievement in literature by about 50 years—just about the time it would take for children exposed to high-achievement literature to be old enough to have their high levels of nAch affect society.

McClelland's ideas have not gone without criticism. Although his research solves the directionality problem in much the same way that a cross-lagged correlational study does (a 50-year lag), the most obvious problem is the usual one with correlational research—third variables. The relationship between children's literature and later achievement is surely an intriguing one, but historical trends are immensely complicated and susceptible to countless factors. Nonetheless, McClelland's research has become a classic example of trying to extend psychological principles to historical analysis.

Research Example 25—Correlations and Nature-Nurture

As you learned from Box 9.1, Sir Francis Galton was impressed by the tendency for genius to run in families. Studying family resemblance has become a major research strategy that bears on the issue of how heredity and environment interact to produce various traits. The typical procedure is to measure some characteristic for each of many pairs of family members and then to calculate the correlations between them. In twin studies (another method pioneered by Galton), hereditary and environmental factors can be evaluated separately by comparing twins differing in genetic similarity (identical or monozygotic twins vs. fraternal or dizygotic twins) and in the similarity of their home environments (twins reared together in the same home, or those separated and raised in different homes). This research, following Galton's lead, has historically examined the origins of intelligence and found that both genetic and environmental factors influence mental ability (e.g., Bouchard & McGue, 1981). In recent years, however, there have been a number of studies that also demonstrate the heritability of personality traits. One such study is by Tellegen et al. (1988), who found a strong genetic component for basic personality.

Tellegen et al. (1988) compared four different groups—monozygotic twins, some reared together (MZT) and others apart (MZA), and dizygotic twins, also reared either together (DZT) or apart (DZA). All twins took a test called the Multidimensional Personality Questionnaire, which measures eleven different traits and then clusters them into three general personality factors. The first, "positive emotionality," is similar to extraversion—high scorers are outgoing and sociable, and feel confident and self-assured. The second factor is "negative emotionality," associated with alienation, aggression, and a tendency to feel anxious and angry. High scorers on the third factor, "constraint," tend to be conventional, to be unwilling to take risks, and to be generally restrained and cautious. Here are the study's results—correlations among twins in the different categories for each of the three factors.

	MZA	DZA	MZT	DZT
Positive emotionality	.34	−.07	.63	.18
Negative emotionality	.61	.29	.54	.41
Constraint	.57	.04	.58	.25

As you can see, these correlations provide evidence for a genetic component to personality—the correlations for MZ twins are always higher than those for DZ twins. Environment also plays a role, although the comparisons are not as clear—correlations for those raised together are usually, but not in all cases, higher than for those raised apart.

There are two methodological points to note here. First, as you might guess, it is harder to find twins raised apart than those raised together. The sample sizes were:

MZA = 44 pairs   DZA = 27 pairs   MZT = 217 pairs   DZT = 114 pairs

The relatively small number of pairs of twins reared apart (especially DZA) prompted the authors to add a degree of caution to their conclusions. Second, the correlations calculated in the study were not the Pearson's *r*'s that you have been learning about in this chapter. Remember that Pearson's *r* should only be used under certain circumstances (e.g., a linear relationship). One of the other requirements is that the pairs of scores that go into the calculations have to be from the same individual. That is not the case in twin studies, where one score comes from one twin and the second score comes from the other twin. To deal with this problem, a different type of correlation is calculated, and it is called an **intraclass correlation**. There are several varieties of these correlations, and the mathematics need not concern us. In general, they are calculated whenever the pairs of scores are said to be "unordered." Incidentally, intraclass correlations can also be used when calculating interobserver reliability, a concept you will encounter in Chapter 12's description of observational research.

Multivariate Analysis

A **bivariate** approach investigates the relationships between any two variables. A **multivariate** approach, on the other hand, examines the relationships among more than two variables (often many more than two). Up to this point in the chapter, we've been considering the bivariate case, except for the discussion of partial correlation, which evaluates the effects of third variables on the relationship between two other variables. Let me briefly introduce two additional popular multivariate procedures, multiple regression and factor analysis.

Multiple Regression

In the case of simple regression, two variables are involved: the predictor variable and the criterion variable. If SAT scores correlate with freshman year GPA, then the SAT can be used as a predictor of academic success. However, as you know from firsthand experience, phenomena like "success in college" are more complicated than this. SAT scores might predict success, but what about the influence of other factors like "motivation" or "high school grades" or "study time"?

Multiple regression solves the problem of having more than one predictor of some outcome. In a **multiple regression** study, there is one criterion variable and a minimum of two predictor variables. The analysis enables you to determine not just the fact that these two or more variables combine to predict some criterion, but also the relative strengths of the predictors. These strengths are reflected in the multiple regression formula for raw scores, which is an extension of the formula for simple regression:

Simple regression: $Y = a + bX$

Multiple regression: $Y = a + b_1X_1 + b_2X_2 + \cdots + b_nX_n$

where each X is a different predictor score; Y is the criterion, or the score being predicted; and the size of the bs reflect the relative importance of each predictor—they are known as "regression weights" (Licht, 1995). A multiple regression analysis will also yield a multiple correlation coefficient (R) and a multiple coefficient of determination (R^2). R is a correlation between the combined predictors and the criterion, and R^2 provides an index of the amount of variation in the criterion variable than can be accounted for by the combined predictors. Note the use of upper case letters to differentiate the multivariate R and R^2 from the bivariate Pearson's r and r^2. Their interpretations are similar, however. Both R and r tell you about the strength of a correlation, and both R^2 and r^2 tell you about the amount of shared variation.

The advantage of a multiple regression analysis is that when the influences of several predictor variables are combined (especially if the predictors are not highly correlated with each other), prediction improves well beyond the single regression case. For instance, high school grades by themselves predict college success, as do SAT scores. Together, however, they predict better than either one by itself (Sprinthall, 2000). To give you an idea of the types of studies using a multiple regression analysis, consider these two examples:

1. A study predicting the strength of one's belief in materialist values (e.g., placing a high value on the accumulation of wealth) from three variables relating to "food security." Allen and Wilson (1989) found that materialist beliefs could be predicted from (a) childhood experiences in which food was not always plentiful, (b) whether food security was an important current goal for subjects, and (c) a present-day lack of any food insecurity. Having food security as a goal was the strongest predictor. Thus, at least within the confines of this study, the "profile" of someone with strong materialist beliefs was a person who didn't

always get enough food as a child, now gets plenty of food, and spends a fair amount of time thinking about having a sufficient supply of food.

2. A study predicting susceptibility to the common cold from negative life events, perceived stress, and negative affect (Cohen, Tyrell, & Smith, 1993): While you might think that getting a cold is the simple result of standing too close to the person who just sneezed all over your lunch, this study demonstrated that getting colds could be predicted from three variables related to stress. College students exposed to a cold virus were most likely to catch colds if they (a) had recently experienced some stressful event(s), (b) were feeling that current demands on them were overwhelming, and (c) described their general emotional state as negative. Several other personality factors (e.g., extroversion) failed to predict the chances of getting a cold.

Factor Analysis

Another multivariate technique is called **factor analysis**. In this procedure, a large number of variables are measured and correlated with each other. It is then determined whether groups of these variables cluster together to form "factors." A simple example will clarify the idea. Suppose you gave a group of school-age children the following tasks:

- a vocabulary test (VOC)
- a reading comprehension test (COM)
- an analogy test (e.g., doctor is to patient as lawyer is to ???) (ANA)
- a geometry test (GEO)
- a puzzle completion test (PUZ)
- a rotated figures test (ROT)

Pearson's *r*'s could be calculated for all possible pairs of tests, yielding what is called a **correlation matrix**. It might look like this:

	VOC	COM	ANA	GEO	PUZ	ROT
VOC	—	+.76	+.65	−.09	+.02	−.08
COM		—	+.55	+.04	+.01	−.02
ANA			—	−.07	−.08	+.09
GEO				—	+.78	+.49
PUZ					—	+.68
ROT						—

Notice how some of the correlations cluster together (I've circled two clusters). Correlations between vocabulary, reading comprehension, and analogies are all high, as are those between geometry, puzzles, and rotation. Correlations between tests from one cluster and tests from the second cluster are essentially zero. This pattern suggests that the tests are measuring two fundamentally different mental abilities or "factors." We could probably label them "verbal fluency" and "spatial skills."

Factor analysis is a multivariate statistical tool that identifies factors from sets of intercorrelations among variables. It would undoubtedly yield the same two factors we just arrived at by scanning the matrix. The analysis also determines what are called "factor loadings." These, in essence, are correlations between each of the measures and each of the identified factors. In the previous example, the first three measures would be "heavily loaded" on factor 1 (verbal fluency), and the second three would be heavily loaded on factor 2 (spatial skills). Of course, in real research the correlations never cluster together as clearly as in the example I've used, and there is often some debate among researchers about whether the factors identified are truly separate from other factors. Also, there is occasional disagreement over the proper labels for the factors. Factor analysis itself only identifies factors; what they should be called is left to the researcher's judgment.

For the study on genetics and personality, described in Research Example 25, factor analysis was used in the process of creating the personality test that was used (the Multidimensional Personality Questionnaire). Another example of factor analysis is a study by Lawton (1994), who used it in the process of developing a scale to measure two different "wayfinding" strategies. Wayfinding means navigating successfully in the environment—one strategy is to rely heavily on sequences of movements and landmarks (route strategy), while another is to rely more on cardinal directions (N, S, E, W) and the overall geographic orientation (orientation strategy). Factor analysis indicated that the items on the scale developed by Lawton ("Wayfinding Strategy Scale") did indeed fall into two intercorrelated clusters. Here are examples of items indicating each of the two factors:

> Route Strategy Factor: Before starting, I asked for directions telling me how many streets to pass before making each turn.

> Orientation Strategy Factor: I kept track of the direction (north, south, east, west) in which I was going.

Incidentally, Lawton found that females tend to use a Route Strategy, while males tend toward an Orientation Strategy.

✓ Self Test 9.3

1. When assessing split-half reliability, what are the two sets of numbers being correlated?
2. How does multiple regression differ from factor analysis? What do they have in common?

As you can tell from this brief introduction, correlational procedures contribute substantially to modern research in psychology. They are often necessary when experimental procedures cannot possibly be used, and with the development of some highly sophisticated multivariate procedures, questions of cause and effect can be addressed more directly than in the past, when most correlational research was bivariate in nature.

Much correlational research takes place outside the laboratory. In the next chapter, we'll look more closely at applied research by outlining the details of several so-called quasi-experimental designs. We'll also look at program evaluation research as a specific example of applied research that is becoming increasingly important for the social service industry and for education.

Chapter Summary

Psychology's Two Disciplines

Along with experimental research, correlational research has been identified as one of psychology's two traditional approaches to science. Whereas experiments manipulate variables directly and observe the effects, correlational studies observe relationships among naturally occurring variables.

Correlation and Regression—The Basics

Two variables are correlated when a reliable relationship exists between them. The relationship is a direct one in a positive correlation and an inverse one in a negative correlation. The strength of the relationship can be inferred from a scatterplot, from the absolute value of the correlation coefficient (e.g., Pearson's r for interval and ratio data), and from the coefficient of determination, found by squaring the correlation coefficient. Knowing a correlation allows predictions to be made through a process called regression analysis. If there is a significant correlation between two variables, A and B, then knowing the value of A enables the prediction of B with some greater than chance probability.

Interpreting Correlations

A significant correlation between variables A and B does not, by itself, allow us to conclude that A causes B. The directionality problem refers to the fact that causality could be in either of two directions, A causing B or B causing A. The directionality problem can be reduced if there is a time lag between the measurement of A and B, as in a cross-lagged panel correlation. The third variable problem refers to the fact that, for many correlations, the relationship results from one or some combination of uncontrolled variables that naturally covary with the variables being measured. That is, some third variable might cause changes in both variables A and B. The influence of third variables can be evaluated using a partial correlation procedure.

Using Correlations

Correlational studies are often necessary when experiments cannot be carried out for practical or ethical reasons. The method is frequently used in research evaluating psychological tests (i.e., determining reliability and validity), in research concerning individual differences in personality and psychopathology, and in twin studies for studying the relative contributions of heredity and environment to some trait.

Multivariate Analysis

Bivariate correlational analysis studies the relationship between two variables. Multivariate analysis looks at the interrelationships among more than two variables. Multiple regression predicts some outcome (criterion) on the basis of two or more predictor variables. Factor analysis identifies clusters of factors underlying a large number of relationships.

Chapter Review Questions

1. What were the essential points made by Cronbach in his "two disciplines" talk?

2. Describe how the shape of a scatterplot changes when comparing (a) positive and negative correlation, and (b) strong and weak correlations.

3. What is the coefficient of determination and what does it tell you? Use the example of SAT scores and GPA to illustrate.

4. A researcher finds that people with high self-esteem tend to exercise more than people with low self-esteem. Explain the directionality problem and how it could influence the interpretation of this correlation.

5. A researcher finds that children who play lots of video games also tend to be aggressive with their peers at school. Explain the third variable problem and how it could influence the interpretation of this correlation.

6. Use the Eron et al. (1972) study, which found a significant relationship between third-grade TV preferences and thirteenth-grade aggression, to explain the reason why you would use a partial correlation procedure.

7. Define reliability and describe two ways to assess it.

8. Use the research connected with the K·ABC test to illustrate the meaning of criterion validity.

9. In his famous study of achievement motivation through history, David McClelland concluded that societies should encourage independence training in their children, in order to make them high achievers. Describe the method used by McClelland to arrive at this conclusion.

10. Describe how correlational procedures can be used to examine the nature-nurture issue. Why aren't Pearson's *r* correlations calculated in this research?

11. Distinguish between bivariate and multivariate analysis and describe the logic behind the use of a multiple regression procedure.

12. Describe the essential logic of factor analysis.

Applications Exercises

Exercise 9.1   Interpreting Correlations

Each of the following describes the outcome of a hypothetical bivariate correlational study. With both the directionality problem and the third variable problem in mind, describe at least two ways of interpreting each.

1. There is a positive correlation between the level of dominance shown by mothers and the level of shyness shown by children.

2. There is a negative correlation between depression and aerobic fitness level.

3. There is a positive correlation between the number of books found in the home and the college GPAs of the students living in those homes.

4. Happily married couples tend to have more sex (with each other) than unhappy couples.

5. There is a negative correlation between grades and test anxiety.

6. Seating location in class is correlated with grades—the closer to the front, the higher the grade.

Exercise 9.2   Scatterplots, Calculating Pearson's *r*, and Regression

Create a scatterplot for the following data. After guessing what the correlation would be from looking at the plot, use the procedures described in the Student Companion Site (www.wiley.com/college/goodwin) to calculate the actual Pearson's *r*. Then calculate the coefficient of determination, and write a statement that describes the relationship. Finally, formulate the regression equation, and predict the explanatory style of Ed, whose self-esteem is 10, Ted, whose self-esteem is 20, and Fred, whose self-esteem is 30.

1. Variable A = self-esteem: scores range from 0 to 50; higher scores indicate a higher level of self-esteem.

2. Variable B = explanatory style: scores range from 0 to 75; higher scores indicate a negative or pessimistic way of interpreting life's bumps and bruises, and lower scores indicate a positive or optimistic way of interpreting these same outcomes.

Subject No.	Variable A	Variable B
1	42	32
2	22	34
3	16	65
4	4	73
5	46	10
6	32	28
7	40	29
8	12	57
9	28	50
10	8	40
11	20	50
12	36	40

Exercise 9.3   Understanding Scatterplots

Draw scatterplots that would approximately illustrate the following relationships. Write a single statement that summarizes each relationship.

1. A correlation of +.50 between the sequential processing and the simultaneous processing subtests of the K·ABC.

2. A correlation of −.75 between GPA and scores on a test of "soap opera IQ."

3. A correlation of −.02 between intelligence and depression.

4. A correlation of +.90 between tendency to suffer from obsessive-compulsive disorder and love of experimental psychology.

Answers to Self Tests:

✓ 9.1.
   1. Negative; high scores on some measure of depression would be associated with low scores on a measure of exercise, and vice versa.
   2. The size of the correlation will decrease (i.e., move closer to zero).
   3. $r^2 = .77$ means that a little more than three-quarters of the variability in grades (GPA) can be attributed to variation in study time.

✓ **9.2.**

1. Predictor = high school grades; criterion = college grades.
2. Depression could lead to a lack of interest in exercise, but a lack of exercise could also make someone depressed.
3. (a) cross-lagged panel correlation; (b) partial correlation.

✓ **9.3.**

1. The scores from one half of the items (e.g., even numbered items) are correlated with the scores from the remaining items.
2. In multiple regression, two or more variables combine to predict some outcome; in factor analysis, the goal is to identify clusters of variables that correlate highly with each other; both are multivariate techniques, involving the measurement of more than two variables.

CHAPTER 10

Quasi-Experimental Designs and Applied Research

Preview & Chapter Objectives

In this chapter we will consider a type of research design that, like a normal experiment, includes independent and dependent variables, but involves a situation in which research participants cannot be randomly assigned to groups. Because the absence of random assignment means that causal conclusions cannot be made, whereas they can be made with some degree of confidence in a purely experimental study, this design is called quasi-experimental ("almost" experimental). The inability to randomly assign often occurs in applied research that takes place outside of the lab, so one focus of the chapter will be applied research, a strategy you first encountered in Chapter 3, when it was contrasted with basic research.[1]

---

[1]It is important to note that the pairing of quasi-experimental and applied research in this chapter does not mean that quasi-experimental designs are found only in applied research. Such designs might be more likely to be found

You will learn that applied research represents a strong tradition in American experimental psychology and reflects the core American value of pragmatism. Program evaluation is the name given to a form of applied research that uses a variety of strategies to examine the effectiveness of programs designed to help people in various ways. Program evaluation is especially likely to use qualitative analysis. When you finish this chapter, you should be able to:

- Identify the dual functions of applied research.
- Understand why applied psychology has always been an important element in American psychology.
- Identify the design and ethical problems associated with applied research, especially if that research occurs outside of the laboratory.
- Identify the defining feature of a quasi-experimental design, and recognize which designs appearing in earlier chapters were quasi-experimental.
- Describe the features of a nonequivalent control group design and understand why this design is necessarily confounded.
- Understand why matching nonequivalent groups on pretest scores can introduce a regression effect.
- Describe the features of interrupted time series designs and understand how they can be used to evaluate trends.
- Describe several variations on the basic time series design.
- Explain why most archival research is quasi-experimental.
- Describe the advantages and limitations of archival research.
- Describe the strategies that can be used to complete a needs analysis in a program evaluation project.
- Understand the purposes and the procedures involved in the program evaluation procedures of formative evaluation, summative evaluation, and cost-effectiveness evaluation.
- Identify and describe the special ethical problems that often accompany program evaluation research.

As I mentioned at the very beginning of this text, I would like nothing more than to see you emerge from this methods course with a desire to contribute to our knowledge of behavior by becoming a research psychologist. My experience as a teacher in this course tells me that some of you indeed will become involved in research, but that most of you won't. Many of you will become professional psychologists of some kind, however, perhaps working as counselors or personnel specialists or in some other field in which your prime focus will be the delivery of psychological or health-related services (e.g., rehabilitation therapy). As such, you

---

in an applied setting, but they can be found in basic research as well. Furthermore, pairing quasi-experimental and applied does not mean to imply that experimental designs are never used in applied research.

will encounter the worlds of applied research and program evaluation. You may discover you will need to be able to do things like:

- Read, comprehend, and critically evaluate some research literature on the effectiveness of a program that your agency is thinking about implementing.
- Help plan a new program by informing (tactfully) those who are completely ignorant of research design about the adequacy of the evaluation portion of their proposal.
- Participate in an agency self-study in preparation for some type of accreditation process; and possibly, because your agency's director found out that you took this course, design and be in charge of a study to evaluate some agency program.

In other words, this chapter is important whether or not you intend to do research in psychology ever again.

Beyond the Laboratory

You first learned about the distinction between basic and applied research in the opening pages of Chapter 3. To review, the essential goal of basic research in psychology is to increase our core knowledge about human behavior and mental processes. The knowledge might eventually have some application, but that outcome is not the prime motivator—knowledge is valued as an end in itself. On the other hand, applied research is designed primarily for the purpose of increasing our knowledge about a particular real-world problem, with an eye toward directly solving that problem. A second distinction between basic and applied research is that, while basic research usually takes place within the confines of a laboratory, applied research normally occurs outside the lab, in clinics, in social service agencies, in jails, and in business settings. There are exceptions, of course. Some basic research occurs in the field and some applied research takes place in a lab.

To give you a sense of the variety of applied research, consider these article titles from two prominent applied psychology journals: the *Journal of Applied Psychology* and the *Journal of Experimental Psychology: Applied:*

Gender and the Relationship Between Perceived Fairness of Pay or Promotion and Job Satisfaction (Witt & Nye, 1992)

Visual–Spatial Abilities of Pilots (Dror, Kosslyn, & Waag, 1993)

Driven to Distraction: Dual-task Studies of Simulated Driving and Conversing on a Cellular Telephone (Strayer & Johnston, 2001)

Probability and Utility Components of Endangered Species Preservation Programs (DeKay & McClelland, 1996)

These titles illustrate two features of applied research. First, following from our definition, the studies clearly focus on easily recognizable problems ranging from job satisfaction to preserving endangered species. Second, the titles demonstrate that, while the prime goal of applied research is problem solving (e.g., improving driving), these studies also further our knowledge of basic psychological processes (e.g., divided attention). Indeed, there is a close connection between basic and applied research, as illustrated by research designed to evaluate what is called "equity theory" (Adams, 1965). The theory's core premise is that when judging the quality of any interaction with another person, we weigh the relative contribution we make with the relative gain that we receive from the other person. If the costs and benefits are out of whack, we perceive the situation to be inequitable and are motivated to restore the equity balance. For example, in a marriage with both partners working full time, the wife might perceive an inequity if most household chores are her responsibility. She might then initiate various procedures (e.g., negotiation) to restore equity.

Most applied research has the dual function of addressing applied problems directly and providing evidence of basic psychological phenomena that influence theory development. Equity, for example, is frequently studied in applied research settings. The previously mentioned study on gender differences in perceived fairness in pay and promotions deals with an important problem for industry (how to improve job satisfaction), but it also provides some data relevant to broader questions about the adequacy of equity theory. Another illustration of this point comes from the following study, which evaluated a method for improving eyewitness testimony.

Research Example 26—Applied Research

Remember the study in Chapter 8 (Research Example 17) about context–dependent memory, which showed that memory was best if study and recall both occurred under the same conditions (either a noisy or silent environment)? The importance of context for recall, combined with the generally known inaccuracies of eyewitness testimony, led Edward Geiselman and Ronald Fisher to develop a technique called the "cognitive interview." One of its several features is a principle they refer to as "event-interview similarity," in which the interviewer tries to "reinstate in the witness's mind the external (e.g., weather), emotional (e.g., feelings of fear), and cognitive (e.g., relevant thoughts) features that were experienced at the time of the crime" (Fisher, Geiselman, & Amador, 1989, p. 723). In short, the interviewer tries to get the witness to reinstate mentally the *context* of the event witnessed.

Geiselman and his colleagues had previously demonstrated the technique's effectiveness in the controlled laboratory environment, but they were also interested in evaluating it "outside the friendly confines of the laboratory [with] real victims and witnesses of crime" (Fisher et al., 1989, p. 724). With cooperation from the robbery division of the Miami, Florida, police department, they trained seven detectives in the cognitive interview technique. Compared to nine officers in a control group, those given the training elicited more reliable (i.e., corroborated with other information) facts during interviews with eyewitnesses. In Figure 10.1 you can see that both groups performed about the same on a pretest, which

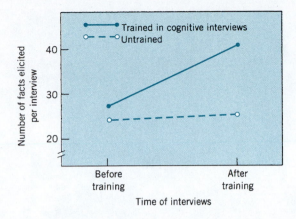

FIGURE 10.1 Effectiveness of the cognitive interview in an applied setting (from Fisher et al., 1989).

summarized a 4-month period during which detectives recorded their interviews with witnesses and separate judges scored the interviews for factual content. After the experimental group completed the training, both groups recorded several additional interviews, which were scored in the same fashion. Clearly, those trained to use the cognitive interview were able to elicit more information from witnesses.

In summary, the Fisher et al. (1989) study is an excellent illustration of how applied research can solve real problems while contributing to our knowledge of some fundamental psychological phenomena. The study shows how a specific interview procedure can improve the efficiency of police work and at the same time provide further evidence for the general importance of context on recall.

Applied Psychology in Historical Context

Because psychology in America developed in an academic setting, you might think that research in psychology traditionally has been biased toward basic research. Not so. From the time psychology emerged as a new discipline in the late nineteenth century, psychologists in the United States have been interested in applied research. For one thing, institutional pressures in the early twentieth century forced psychologists to show how their work could improve society. In order to get a sufficient piece of the academic funding pie at a time when psychology laboratories were brand new entities, psychologists had to show that the ideas deriving from their research could be put to good use.

Psychologists trained as researchers, then, in addition to their prime focus on extending knowledge, often found themselves trying to apply basic research methods to solve problems in areas such as education, mental health, child rearing, and, in the case of Walter Miles, sports. Miles was director of the laboratory at Stanford University in the 1920s. Although devoted to basic research throughout most of his career, he nonetheless found himself on the football team's practice field in 1927, as shown in Figure 10.2 (that's Miles in the suit). Stanford's legendary

Stanford 1927

FIGURE 10.2   Simultaneously testing the reaction times of Stanford football players, circa 1927 (from Archives of the History of American Psychology, University of Akron, Akron, Ohio).

football coach, "Pop" Warner, was known as an innovator, open to anything that might improve his team's performance. Enter Miles, who built what he called a "multiple chronograph" as a way of simultaneously testing the reaction time of seven football players (Miles, 1928). On a signal that dropped seven golf balls onto a cylinder rotating at a constant speed (one ball per player), the players would charge forward, pushing a board that pulled a string that released a second set of golf balls onto the drum. The balls left marks on the cylinder and, knowing the speed of the rotation and the distance between the marks, Miles was able to calculate the players' reaction times. Miles conducted several studies with his multiple chronograph (e.g., Miles, 1931) and demonstrated that it could be a useful tool for identifying the factors that affected a football player's "charging time," but the apparatus never enjoyed widespread use (Baugh & Benjamin, 2006). Nonetheless, it is a good example of an experimental psychologist taking a basic laboratory tool, reaction time in this case, and using it to deal with a concrete problem, how to further advance the efficiency of Stanford's football team.

Walter Miles made just an occasional foray into applied psychology, devoting most of his life to basic experimental research. Other psychologists, however, while trained as experimentalists, turned applied psychology into their primary career. A prime example was Harry Hollingworth, who entered applied psychology simply to make enough money for his talented wife Leta to attend graduate school. The result was a classic study on drug effects, financed by the Coca-Cola Company, whose product had been seized in a raid in Tennessee in 1909, on the grounds that it contained what was considered to be a dangerous drug—caffeine. Box 10.1 elaborates the story and describes an early example of a nicely designed double blind drug effect experiment.

Box 10.1

CLASSIC STUDIES—The Hollingworths, Applied Psychology, and Coca-Cola

In 1911, the Coca-Cola Company was in some danger of having its trademark drink removed from the market or, at the very least, having one of its main ingredients removed from the formula. Under the federal Pure Food and Drug Act, which had been passed five years earlier during a time of progressive reform, Coca-Cola stood accused of adding a dangerous chemical to its drink—caffeine. It was said to be addictive (and they sell it to children!) and its stimulant properties were said to mask the need that we all have for rest when we have become fatigued. In 1909, shipments of Coke syrup were actually seized by federal agents in Tennessee. Two years later, Coca-Cola found itself in court, defending its product. Enter Harry and Leta Hollingworth, and a research story documented by Benjamin, Rogers, and Rosenbaum (1991).

In 1911, Harry Hollingworth was a young professor of psychology at Barnard College in New York City, anticipating a typical academic career of teaching, doing research, and avoiding committee work. His wife Leta also aimed for a professional career as a psychologist. They had married a few years earlier, and the plan was for Leta to teach school in New York while Harry finished graduate studies and began his career. Then Leta would go to graduate school. Unfortunately, Leta soon discovered one of the realities of being a married woman in early twentieth century New York—the city's school board did not allow married women to teach (being married was assumed to be a woman's career). Financial difficulties immediately affected the young couple and, when the Coca-Cola Company offered Harry money for undertaking research of the effects of caffeine, financial necessity prompted him to agree. To his credit, Hollingworth insisted (and Coca-Cola agreed) on being allowed to publish his results, whether or not they were favorable to the company.

Harry and Leta collaborated on the design for the studies they completed, an elaborate series of experiments that lasted for more than a month. With Coca-Cola money, they rented a large apartment in which to conduct the research, with the daily data-collection sessions under Leta's supervision. Five rooms were set up as separate labs, with graduate students serving as experimenters. A variety of mental and physical tests were used, ranging from reaction time to motor coordination. There were sixteen participants used. Methodologically, the Hollingworths put into practice several of the concepts you have been studying in your methods course.

- They used *counterbalancing*. With $N = 16$ and a month's worth of research, you can easily guess that each subject was tested many times. As with any repeated measures design, order effects were controlled through counterbalancing. For example, in one of the studies, participants rotated among five different rooms in the apartment, completing a series of tests in each room. The order in which participants were tested in the rooms was randomized, in essence a partial counterbalancing procedure.

- They used a *placebo* control. Participants were tested after taking pills containing either caffeine or a sugar substance. One set of studies included four groups, a placebo control, and three caffeine groups, each with a different dosage. Hence, the Hollingworths were able to examine not just caffeine effects, but also dosage effects.

- They used a *double blind*. Participants did not know if they were receiving caffeine or a placebo, and the experimenters doing the tests in each room did not know if their subjects had taken caffeine or the placebo (Leta, who was in overall command of the testing, knew).

And the results? Complex, considering the large number of tests used, the various dosages employed, a fair amount of individual variation in performance, and the absence of sophisticated inferential statistical techniques (remember from Box 8.3 that nobody was doing ANOVAs before the mid-1930s). In general, no adverse effects of caffeine were found, except that larger doses, if taken near the end of the day, caused some subjects to have difficulty with sleep. Writing several years later in the textbook *Applied Psychology* (Hollingworth & Poffenberger, 1917), Harry wrote that the "widespread consumption of caffeinic beverages . . . seems to be justified by the results of these experiments" (p. 181). As for the trial, Harry testified on behalf of the company, arguing that there was no scientific basis for banning caffeine in Coca-Cola. The case against Coke was eventually dismissed (on grounds other than caffeine's effects). One final outcome of the study was that it indeed paid for Leta's graduate studies (she eventually became a pioneer in the study and education of gifted children, probably better known than her husband), with enough left over for a European trip.

Psychologists at the beginning of the twenty-first century are as interested in application as were their predecessors at the beginning of the twentieth century. That is, they design and carry out studies to help create solutions to real-world problems while at the same time contributing to the basic core knowledge of psychology. However, applied research projects encounter several difficulties not usually found in the laboratory.

Design Problems in Applied Research

From what you've already learned in Chapters 2, 5, and 6, you should be able to anticipate most of the material in this section. The problems encountered in applied research include:

> ✓ *Ethical dilemmas* (Chapter 2). A study conducted in the field may create problems relating to informed consent and privacy. Also, debriefing may not always be possible. Research done in an industrial or

corporate setting may include an element of perceived coercion if employees believe their job status depends on whether they volunteer to participate in a study (see Box 10.3 for more on ethics and applied research).

✓ *A trade-off between internal and external validity* (Chapter 5). Because research in applied psychology often takes place in the field, the researcher can lose control over the variables operating in the study. Hence, the danger of possible confounding reduces the study's internal validity. On the other hand, external (ecological) validity is often high in applied research because the setting more closely resembles real-life situations, and the problems addressed by applied research are everyday problems.

✓ *Problems unique to between-subjects designs* (Chapter 6). In applied research it is often impossible to use random assignment to form equivalent groups. Therefore the studies often must compare nonequivalent groups. This, of course, introduces the possibility of reducing internal validity by selection problems or interactions between selection and other threats such as maturation or history. When matching is used to achieve a degree of equivalence, regression problems can occur, as will be elaborated in a few pages.

✓ *Problems unique to within-subjects designs* (Chapter 6). It is not always possible to counterbalance properly in applied studies using within-subjects factors. Hence, the studies may have uncontrolled sequence effects. Also, attrition can be a problem for studies that extend over a long period of time.

Before going much farther in this chapter, you should look back at the appropriate sections of Chapters 2, 5, and 6 and review the ideas I've just mentioned. You also might review the section in Chapter 5 about the kinds of conclusions that can be drawn from manipulated variables and subject variables.

✓ Self Test 10.1

1. Applied research is said to have a "dual function." Explain.
2. Use the example of Miles and the Stanford football team to show how basic research and applied research can intersect.
3. How does applied research fare in terms of internal and external validity?

Quasi-Experimental Designs

Strictly speaking, so-called "true" experimental studies include manipulated independent variables and either equivalent groups for between-subjects designs or appropriate counterbalancing for within-subjects designs. Anything less is quasi-experimental ("almost" experimental). In general, a **quasi-experiment** exists whenever causal conclusions cannot be drawn because there is less than complete control over the variables in the study, usually because random assignment is not feasible. Although it might seem that quasi-experiments are therefore lower in status than "true" experiments, it is important to stress that quasi-experiments have great value in applied research. They do allow for a degree of control, they serve when ethical or practical problems make random assignment impossible, and they often produce results that can have clear benefits for people's lives. Thus far we have seen several examples of designs that could be considered quasi-experimental:

- Single-factor nonequivalent groups designs, with two or more levels
- Nonequivalent groups factorial designs
- P × E factorial designs (the P variable, anyway)
- All of the correlational research

In this chapter, we will consider two designs typically found in texts on quasi-experimental designs (e.g., Cook & Campbell, 1979): nonequivalent control group designs and interrupted time series designs. Other quasi-experimental designs exist, but these two are the most frequently encountered. We will also examine a type of research called archival research in this section. Archival research involves answering empirical questions by using information that has already been collected for some other purpose, rather than by collecting new data, and it often includes nonmanipulated independent variables.

Nonequivalent Control Group Designs

In this type of study, the purpose is to evaluate the effectiveness of some treatment program. Those in the program are compared with those in a control group who aren't treated. This design is used when random assignment is not possible, so in addition to the levels of the independent variable, the members of the control group differ in some other way(s) from those in the treatment group. That is, the groups are not equivalent to each other at the outset of the study. You will recognize this as a specific example of the design labeled a "nonequivalent" groups design in Chapters 7 and 8, a type of design comparing nonequal groups, often selected with reference to a subject variable such as age, gender, or some personality characteristic. In the case of a **nonequivalent control group design**, the groups are not equal to each other at the start of the study; *in addition*, they experience different events in the study itself. Hence, there is a built-in confound that can cloud the interpretation of these studies. Nonetheless, these designs can be effective for evaluating treatment programs when random assignment is impossible.

Following the scheme first outlined by Campbell and Stanley (1963), the nonequivalent control group design can be symbolized like this:

Experimental group:	O_1	**T**	O_2
Nonequivalent control group:	O_1		O_2

where O_1 and O_2 refer to pretest and posttest observations or measures, respectively, and T refers to the treatment program that is being evaluated. Because the groups might differ on the pretest, the important comparison between the groups is not simply a test for differences on the posttest, but a comparison of the different amounts of change from pre- to posttest in the two groups. Hence, the statistical comparison is typically between the *change scores* (the difference between O_1 and O_2) for each group. Let's make this a bit more concrete.

Suppose the management of an electric fry pan company wants to institute a new flextime work schedule. Workers will continue to work forty hours per week, but the new schedule allows them to begin and end each day at different times or to put all of their hours into four days if they wish to have a three-day weekend. Management hopes this will increase productivity by improving morale, and designs a quasi-experiment to see if it does. The company owns two plants, one just outside of Pittsburgh and the other near Cleveland. Through a coin toss, the managers decide to make Pittsburgh's plant the experimental group and Cleveland's plant the nonequivalent control group. Thus, the study is quasi-experimental for the obvious reason that workers cannot be randomly assigned to the two plants (imagine the moving costs, legal fees over union grievances, etc.). The independent variable is whether or not flextime is present, and the dependent variable is some measure of productivity. Let's suppose the final design looks like this:

Pittsburgh plant:	pretest:	average productivity for 1 month prior to instituting flextime
	treatment:	flextime instituted for 6 months
	posttest:	average productivity during the sixth full month of flextime
Cleveland plant:	pretest:	average productivity for 1 month prior to instituting flextime in Pittsburgh
	treatment:	none
	posttest:	average productivity during the sixth full month that flextime is in effect in the Pittsburgh plant

Outcomes

Figure 10.3 shows you four different outcomes of this quasi-experiment. All the graphs show positive changes in productivity for the Pittsburgh plant. The question is whether the change was due to program effectiveness or to some other factor(s). Before reading on, try to determine which of the graphs provides the strongest evidence that introducing flextime increased productivity. Also, refer back to the section in Chapter 5 that described "threats to internal validity," and try to identify the threats that make it difficult to interpret the other outcomes.

I don't imagine you found it difficult to conclude that, in Figure 10.3a, something besides the flextime produced the apparent improvement. This graph makes the importance of some type of control group obvious, even if it has to be a nonequivalent control group. Yes, Pittsburgh's productivity increased, but the same thing happened in Cleveland. Therefore, the Pittsburgh increase

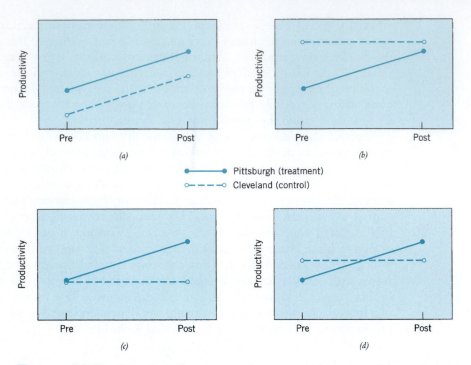

FIGURE 10.3   Hypothetical outcomes of a nonequivalent control group design.

cannot be attributed to the program, but could have been due to several of the threats to internal validity that you've studied. History and maturation are good possibilities. Perhaps a national election intervened between pre- and posttest, and workers everywhere felt more optimistic, leading to increased productivity. Perhaps workers just showed improvement with increased experience on the job.

Figure 10.3b suggests that productivity in Cleveland was high throughout the study but that in Pittsburgh, productivity began at a very low level but improved due to the flextime program. However, there are two dangers here. For one thing, the Cleveland scores might reflect a *ceiling effect* (Chapter 5). That is, their productivity level is so high to begin with that no further improvement could possibly be shown. If an increase could be seen (i.e., if scores on the Y-axis could go higher), you might see two parallel lines, as in Figure 10.3a. The second problem is that because Pittsburgh started so low, the increase there might be a regression effect rather than a true one. Maybe at the start of the study, for some reason, productivity was very low, and then returned to normal.

Figure 10.3c seems at first glance to be the ideal outcome. Both groups start at the same level of productivity, but the group with the program (Pittsburgh) is the only one to improve. This may indeed be the case, and such an outcome generally makes applied researchers happy, but a problem can exist nonetheless. Because of the nonequivalent nature of the two groups, it is conceivable that subject selection could *interact* with some other influence. That is, some factor such as history or maturation could affect one plant but not the other. For example, it's not hard to imagine a selection × history problem here—some historical event affects the Pittsburgh plant but not the Cleveland plant. Perhaps the knowledge that they are participating in a study motivated the Pittsburgh workers (remember Hawthorne?), while Cleveland workers were left in the dark. Perhaps between the pretest and the posttest, the Steelers won yet another Super Bowl, and because workers in Pittsburgh are such avid fans, their general feeling of well-being improved morale and therefore productivity. The Browns, on the other hand, who never win Super Bowls, would be less likely to inspire productivity boosts in the Cleveland plant.

You've probably noted the similarity of Figures 10.3c and Figure 10.1 from the cognitive interview study. Fisher et al. (1989) did not randomly assign detectives to the training and nontraining groups, but they believed the two groups to be roughly equivalent nonetheless, based on a matching procedure using "information gathered in . . . preliminary interviews and the recommendations of the detectives' commanding officer" (Fisher et al., 1989, p. 724). Hence, they believed that the results shown in Figure 10.1 represented a real training effect and that any selection effects, if any, were minimal.

The outcome in Figure 10.3d provides strong support for program effectiveness. Here the treatment group begins below the control group, yet surpasses the controls by the end of the study. Regression can be ruled out as causing the improvement for Pittsburgh, because one would expect regression to raise the scores only to the level of the control group, not beyond it. Of course, selection problems and interactions between selection and other factors are difficult to exclude completely, but this type of crossover effect is considered to be good evidence of program effectiveness (Cook & Campbell, 1979).

Regression and Matching

A special threat to the internal validity of nonequivalent control group designs occurs when there is an attempt to reduce the nonequivalency of nonequivalent groups through a form of a matching procedure. Matching was described in Chapter 6 as an alternative to random assignment under certain circumstances, and it works rather well to create equivalent groups if the independent variable is a manipulated one and participants can be randomly assigned to groups *after* being paired together on some matching variable (see Chapter 6 to review the matching procedure). However, it can be a problem in nonequivalent control group designs when the two groups are sampled from populations that are different from each other on the factor being used as the matching variable. If this occurs, then using a matching procedure can enhance the influence of a **regression effect** and even make it appear that a successful program has failed. Let's look at a hypothetical example.

Suppose you are developing a program to improve the reading skills of disadvantaged youth in a particular city. You advertise for volunteers to participate in an innovative reading program and select those most in need (i.e., those whose scores will be, on average, very low). To create a control group that controls for socioeconomic class, you recruit additional volunteers from similar neighborhoods in other cities. Your main concern is with equating the two groups for initial reading skill, so you decide to match the two groups on this variable. You administer a reading skills pretest to the volunteers in your target neighborhood and to the potential control group participants, and use the results to form two groups that will have the same average score. That is, the matching variable is the reading skills score. Let's say the test has a range from 0 to 100. You decide to select children for the two groups so that the average score is 25 for both groups. The treatment group then gets the program and the control group does not; the design is a typical nonequivalent control group design:

| Experimental group: | pretest | reading program | posttest |
| Control group: | pretest | — | posttest |

Naturally, you're excited about the prospects of this study because you really believe the reading program is unique and will help a lot of children. Hence, you're shocked when these reading scores occur:

| Experimental group: | pre = 25 | reading program | post = 25 |
| Control group: | pre = 25 | — | post = 29 |

Not only did the program not seem to work, but it appears that it even hindered the development of reading skills—the control group apparently improved! What happened?

A strong possibility here is that regression effects resulting from the matching procedure overwhelmed any possible treatment effect. Remember that the experimental group was formed from those with the greatest need for the program because their skills were so weak. If the reading pretest could have been given to all children who fall into this category (i.e., the population called "very weak readers"), the average score might be quite low, let's say 17. When using the matching procedure, however, you were forced to select children who scored much higher than the mean score from this population of "poor readers." Presumably, at least some of the children in this group scored higher than they normally would have on the pretest because no test is perfectly reliable—some degree of measurement error is likely to occur. Therefore, on a posttest, many of these children will score lower (i.e., move back to the mean of 17) simply due to regression to the mean. Let's suppose the program truly was effective and would add an average of 4 points to the reading score. However, if the average regression effect was a loss of 4 points, the effects would cancel each other out, and this would account for the apparent lack of change from pre- to posttest:

$$[25] + [+4] + [-4] = [25]$$

For participants in the control group, just the opposite might have occurred. Suppose their population mean score was higher than 25 (35, perhaps). Maybe they were reasonably poor readers to begin with, but not as bad as the experimental group (i.e., they were from a population called "relatively poor readers"). Selecting participants who scored lower than their population mean, in order to produce pretest scores to match those of the experimental group (i.e., 25), could result in a regression effect producing higher posttest scores. For these children, the posttest

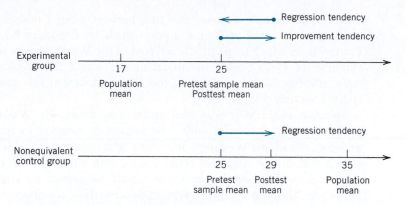

FIGURE 10.4 Hypothetical influences of a regression effect when matching is used with nonequivalent groups, in an attempt to create equivalent groups.

score would result from the same 4-point regression effect used earlier, although this time the regression effect would yield an increase. Thus,

$$[25] + [0] + [+4] = [29]$$

Figure 10.4 shows the problem in visual form. Regression and program improvements cancel each other out in the experimental group, while in the control group, regression is the only factor operating, and it pushes the scores toward the higher end. In sum, the reading program might actually have been a good idea, but the matching procedure caused a regression effect that masked its effectiveness.[2]

This type of regression artifact apparently occurred during the first large-scale attempt to evaluate the effectiveness of Head Start, one of the cornerstone programs of President Lyndon Johnson's "Great Society" initiative in the 1960s (Campbell & Erlebacher, 1970). The program originated in 1965 as an ambitious attempt to give underprivileged preschool children a "head start" on school by teaching them various school-related skills and getting their parents involved in the process. By 1990, about 11 million children had participated, and Head Start is now recognized as perhaps the most successful social program ever run by the federal government (Horn, 1990). Yet in the early 1970s, it was under attack for its "failure" to produce lasting effects, largely on the basis of what has come to be known as the "Westinghouse study" (because the study was funded by a grant to the Westinghouse Learning Corporation and Ohio University), conducted by Victor Cicirelli and his colleagues (1969).

The Westinghouse study documented what it called "fade-out effects"—early gains by children in Head Start programs seemed to fade away by the third grade.

---

[2]Although the practical and ethical realities of applied research in the field might prevent it, a better procedure would be to give a large group of children the reading readiness test, match them on the test, and randomly assign them to a reading program group and a control group.

The implication, of course, was that perhaps federal dollars were being wasted on ineffective social programs, a point made by President Nixon in an address to Congress, in which he explicitly referred to the Westinghouse study. Consequently, funding for Head Start came under attack during the Nixon years. At the same time, the basis for the criticism, the Westinghouse study, was being assaulted by social scientists.

Because Head Start was well under way when the Westinghouse evaluation project began, children couldn't be randomly assigned to treatment and control groups. Instead, the Westinghouse group selected a group of Head Start children and matched them for cognitive achievement with children who hadn't been through the program. However, in order to match the groups on cognitive achievement, Head Start children selected for the study were those scoring well above the mean for their overall group, and control children were those scoring well below the mean for their group. This is precisely the situation just described in the hypothetical case of a program to improve reading skills. Hence, the Head Start group's apparent failure to show improvement in the third grade was at least partially the result of a regression artifact caused by the matching procedure (Campbell & Erlebacher, 1970).

In fairness to the Westinghouse group, it should be pointed out that they would have disagreed vehemently with politicians who wished to cut the program. Cicirelli (1984) insisted that the study "*did not conclude that Head Start was a failure*" (p. 915; italics in the original), that more research was necessary, and that "vigorous and intensive approaches to expanding and enriching the program" (p. 916) be undertaken. Cicirelli (1993) later pointed out that a key recommendation of the Westinghouse study was "not to eliminate Head Start but to try harder to make it work, based on encouraging findings from full-year programs [as opposed to summer-only programs]" (p. 32).

Nonequivalent control group designs do not always produce the type of controversy that engulfed the Westinghouse study. Consider the following two research examples, one an attempt to improve the self-esteem of Little League baseball players through a training program for their coaches, and the second a study of the mental "aftershocks" of an earthquake. The second study shows that nonequivalent control group designs do not always use pretests.

Research Example 27—A Nonequivalent Control Group Design

Coaches can be significant figures in the lives of young children involved in sports. The effects of coaching behavior can be devastating for children whose skills are just developing, if their coach's only goal is to win championships, and anything less than perfect performance produces censure and ridicule. On the other hand, coaches can be marvelous teachers and role models for children in their formative years. Smoll, Smith, Barnett, and Everett (1993) set out to evaluate a training program for coaches aimed at helping them develop the self-esteem of their young athletes. Two weeks before the start of a Little League baseball season, some coaches underwent a program called "Coach Effectiveness Training." The program emphasized several target behaviors that coaches should use—reinforcing effort as well as good performance, providing encouragement and positive instruction after mistakes, and reinforcing team participation and cooperation. The program was evaluated using a nonequivalent control group design. Eight coaches, all from the same league, were in the experimental group. Ten coaches from different leagues were in the control group. Why not make this an experimental design, take a single league, and randomly assign some coaches to each group? Three reasons. First, Smoll's design made it easier to coordinate the training program. Second, it ensured that the average won-lost records of the teams in each group would be 50%. Third, it ensured "that no leakage of information would occur and that guidelines derived from the program would not be communicated to control coaches" (p. 603). Thus, the two groups from the two different leagues were by definition nonequivalent, but the authors also took steps to reduce the nonequivalence as much as possible (while at the same time not doing anything that would introduce a regression artifact), except for the training. The leagues selected "were in similar socioeconomic areas and, according to observations made by the [district] administrator, they included coaches with a similarly wide variety of coaching and leadership styles" (p. 603).

The children being coached by those in the experimental and control groups were evaluated before and after the Little League season. The boys completed a standardized test of self-esteem, and in the posttest they were asked in an interview about their coaches' behaviors. The interviewers were "blind" to (i.e., unaware of) whether the boys were in the experimental or control group (thus, a double blind procedure). Players in the experimental group reported liking their coaches more and liking baseball more. On the measure of self-esteem, there were no overall differences between the two groups of boys, but when Smoll et al. (1993) examined only the boys who scored below the median on the pretest, Figure 10.5 resulted. As you can see, boys with relatively low self-esteem at the start of the season showed a large increase when they were coached by someone from the training program, whereas boys with coaches from the control group kept the same overall level of self-esteem (the apparent decline was not significant). If you consider that low-self-esteem boys might be the most easily discouraged by a bad experience in sport, this is a very encouraging outcome. If coaches do the right things, they can make a big difference in the lives of their young players. Although

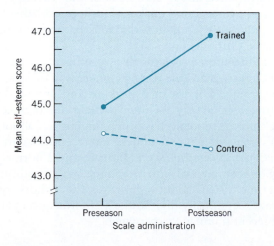

FIGURE 10.5 Changes in self-esteem scores for Little Leaguers before and after the coaches received training about ways to enhance self-esteem (from Smoll et al., 1993).

interpretation problems are inevitable with quasi-experimental designs (e.g., despite the administrator's claim, perhaps the coaches in the experimental group were just better able to relate to their players), this is a really nice study and a good example of the value of applied research.

Research Example 28—A Nonequivalent Control Group Design without Pretests

Nonequivalent control group designs typically include pretests, but that is not always the case. Sometimes these designs occur when an unforeseen opportunity for research makes pretesting impossible. One such event was the 1989 San Francisco earthquake. To James Wood and Richard Bootzin of the University of Arizona, the event suggested an idea for a study about nightmares, a topic already of interest to them (Wood & Bootzin, 1990). Along with some colleagues from Stanford University (located near the quake's epicenter), they quickly designed a study to see if the experience of such a traumatic event would affect dream content in general and nightmares in particular (Wood, Bootzin, Rosenhan, Nolen-Hoeksema, & Jourden, 1992). By necessity, they used a nonequivalent control group design. As is generally the case with this design, the groups were nonequivalent to begin with (students from two different states); in addition, one group had one type of experience (direct exposure to the earthquake), while the second group had a different experience (no direct exposure).

The experimental group consisted of students from Stanford University and San Jose State University who experienced the earthquake. Nonequivalent controls were college students recruited from the University of Arizona. They did not experience the quake, of course, but they were well aware of it through the extensive media accounts. Shortly after the earthquake event (about a week), all participants began keeping a dream log, which was then analyzed for nightmare content and frequency. The results were intriguing. Over the 3 weeks of the study, 40% of San Jose students and 37% of the Stanford students reported having at least one nightmare about an earthquake, while only 5% of the control students at Arizona did. Of the total number of nightmares experienced by the experimental groups, roughly one-fourth were about earthquakes, but virtually none of the control group's nightmares were about quakes. Furthermore, the frequency of nightmares correlated significantly with how anxious participants reported they were during the time of the earthquake.

Well aware of the interpretation problems that accompany quasi-experimental studies, Wood et al. (1992) recognized the dangers inherent in making comparisons between nonequivalent groups. For instance, lacking any pretest ("pre-quake") information about nightmare frequency for their participants, they couldn't "rule out the possibility that California residents have more nightmares about earthquakes than do Arizona residents even when no earthquake has recently occurred" (p. 222). If one lives in California, perhaps earthquake nightmares are a normal occurrence. However, relying partly on their general expertise in the area of nightmare research, and partly on some other survey data about nightmares, the authors argued that the nightmare frequency was exceptionally high in the California group and was likely to be the result of their recent traumatic experience.

Interrupted Time Series Designs

If Wood and his colleagues could have foreseen San Francisco's earthquake, they might have started collecting nightmare data from their participants for several months leading up to the quake and then for several months after the quake. That would have enabled them to determine (a) if the quake truly increased nightmare experiences for the participants in the quake zone, and (b) if the nightmare frequency peaked shortly after the quake and then returned to baseline. Of course, not even talented research psychologists can predict earthquakes, so Wood and his co-workers did the best they could and designed their nonequivalent control group study. If they had been able to take measures for an extended period before and after the event expected to influence behavior, their study would have been called an **interrupted time series design**.

Using the system in Campbell and Stanley (1963) again, the basic time series study can be symbolized like this:

$$O_1 \ O_2 \ O_3 \ O_4 \ O_5 \ \mathbf{T} \ O_6 \ O_7 \ O_8 \ O_9 \ O_{10}$$

where all of the O's represent measures of behavior taken before and after T, which is the point at which some treatment program is introduced or some event (e.g., an earthquake) occurs. T is the "interruption" in the interrupted time series. Of course, the number of measures taken before and after T will vary from study to study and is not limited to a total of five each. It is also not necessary that the number of pre-interruption and post-interruption points be the same number. As a general rule, the more data points, the better, and some experts (e.g., Orwin, 1997) recommend at least *50* pre-interruption data points.

Outcomes

The main advantage of a time series design is that it allows the researcher to evaluate **trends**, predictable patterns of events that occur with the passing of time. For example, suppose you were interested in seeing the effects of a 2-month antismoking campaign on the number of teenage smokers in a community. The program might include some persuasion techniques, peer counseling, showing the teens a smoked-out lung or two, and so on. Assuming that you had a good measure of the smoking behavior, you could take the measure a month before and a month after introducing the program and perhaps get the results in Figure 10.6.

Did the program work? There certainly is a reduction in smoking from pre- to posttest, but it's hard to evaluate it in the absence of a control group (i.e., using a nonequivalent control group design). Yet, even without a control group, it might be possible to see if the campaign worked if not one but several measures were taken both before and after the program was put in place. Consider the possible outcomes in Figure 10.7, which examines the effect of the antismoking campaign by measuring smoking behavior every month for a year before and a year after the program.

Figure 10.7a is a good illustration of how an interrupted time series can identify trends. In this case, the reduction that looked so good in Figure 10.6 is

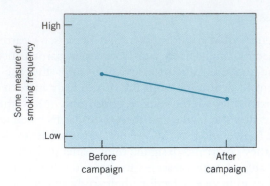

FIGURE 10.6 Incidence of smoking behavior just before and just after a hypothetical antismoking campaign.

shown to be nothing more than part of a general trend toward reduced smoking among adolescents. This demonstrates an important feature of interrupted time series designs—they can serve to rule out (i.e., falsify, remember?) alternative explanations of an apparent change from pre- to posttest.

Two other outcomes that raise questions about the program's effectiveness are seen in Figures 10.7b and 10.7c. In Figure 10.7b, smoking behavior was fairly steady before the campaign and then dropped, but just briefly. In other words, if the antismoking program had any effect at all, it was short-lived. In Figure 10.7c, the decrease after the program was part of another general trend, this time a periodic

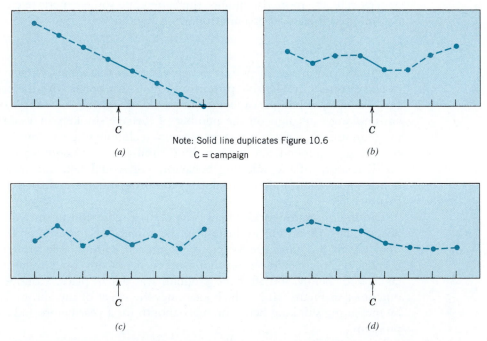

FIGURE 10.7 Hypothetical antismoking campaign evaluated with an interrupted time series design—several possible outcomes.

fluctuation between higher and lower levels of smoking. The ideal outcome is shown in Figure 10.7d. Here the smoking behavior is at a steady and high rate before the program begins, drops after the antismoking program has been put into effect, and remains low for some time afterward. Note also in Figure 10.7d that the relatively steady baseline prior to the campaign enables the researcher to rule out regression effects.

Research Example 29 — An Interrupted Time Series Design

An actual example of an outcome like the one in Figure 10.7d can be found in a study of worker productivity completed at a unionized iron foundry by Wagner, Rubin, and Callahan (1988). They were interested in the effect of instituting an incentive plan in which workers were treated not as individuals but as members of small groups, each responsible for an entire production line. Productivity data were compiled over a period of about 10 years, 4 years prior to introducing the incentive plan and 6 years afterward—there were 114 monthly data points. As you can see from their time series plot in Figure 10.8, productivity was fairly flat and not very impressive prior to the plan but increased steadily after the plan was implemented and stayed high.

This study also illustrates how those conducting interrupted time series designs try to deal with potential threats to internal validity. Figure 10.8 certainly appears to show that the incentive plan worked wonders, but the changes could have been influenced by other factors, including history, instrumentation, and even subject selection. The authors argued that history did not contribute to the change, however, because they carefully examined as many events as they could in the

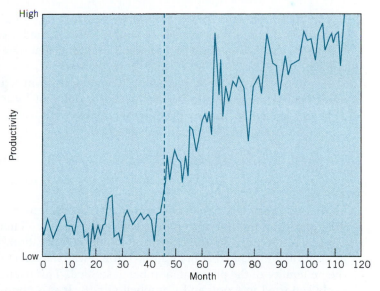

FIGURE 10.8 Interrupted time series design: effect of an incentive plan on worker productivity in an iron foundry (from Wagner et al., 1988).

period before and after the change and could find no reason to suspect that some unusual occurrences led to the jump in productivity. In fact, some events that might be expected to hurt productivity (e.g., a recession in the automobile industry, which affected sales of iron castings) didn't. The researchers also ruled out instrumentation, which could be a problem if the techniques of scoring and recording worker productivity changed over the years. It didn't. Third, although we normally think of subject selection as being a potential confound only in studies with two or more nonequivalent groups, it can occur in a time series study if significant worker turnover occurred during the time of the new plan—the cohort of workers on site prior to the plan could be different in some important way from the group there after the plan went into effect. This didn't happen in Wagner et al.'s study (1988) though. In short, designs like this one, which lack a control group, are susceptible to several threats to internal validity, but these threats often can be ruled out by systematically examining available information, as Wagner and his colleagues did.

Variations on the Basic Time Series Design

Sometimes the conclusions from an interrupted time series design can be strengthened if some type of control comparison can be made. One approach amounts to combining the best features of the nonequivalent control group design (a control group) and the interrupted time series design (long-term trend analysis). The design looks like this:

$$O_1 \ O_2 \ O_3 \ O_4 \ O_5 \ \mathbf{T} \ O_6 \ O_7 \ O_8 \ O_9 \ O_{10}$$
$$O_1 \ O_2 \ O_3 \ O_4 \ O_5 \ \quad \ O_6 \ O_7 \ O_8 \ O_9 \ O_{10}$$

If you will look ahead for a second to Figure 10.11 in Box 10.2, you will see a classic example of this strategy, a study that evaluated a speeding crackdown in Connecticut by comparing fatal accident data from that state with data from similar states.

A second strategy for strengthening conclusions from a time series study can be used when a program is to be introduced in different locations at different times, a design labeled an **interrupted time series with switching replications** by Cook and Campbell (1979), and operating like this:

$$O_1 \ O_2 \ O_3 \ \mathbf{T} \ O_4 \ O_5 \ O_6 \ O_7 \ O_8 \ O_9 \ O_{10}$$
$$O_1 \ O_2 \ O_3 \ O_4 \ O_5 \ O_6 \ O_7 \ \mathbf{T} \ O_8 \ O_9 \ O_{10}$$

With this procedure, the same treatment or program is put into place in two different locations, but at two different points in time. There is no control group, but the design provides the benefit of a built-in replication. If the outcome pattern in location 2 matches that of location 1, the researchers can be more confident about the generality of the phenomenon being studied. This happened in an unpublished study reported in Cook and Campbell (1979). It was completed in the late 1940s and early 1950s, when televisions were just starting to change our lives. A number of Illinois communities were given licenses for new TV stations, but in 1951 there was a freeze on new licenses that wasn't lifted until 1953. That gave researchers an opportunity to study the impact of new televisions on communities at two different times—in the late 1940s, just before the freeze, and right after 1953, with the freeze lifted. Hypothesizing that the new inventions would reduce the amount of reading done, researchers studied library circulation data and found support for their concerns about reading. As TVs began infiltrating communities, library circulation dropped, and the pattern was virtually identical during the two different times examined.

A third elaboration on an interrupted time series design, again in the absence of a control group, is to measure several *dependent* variables, some expected to be influenced by the "interruption," others not expected to change. This was the strategy used in a study by Stolzenberg and D'Alessio (1997). They wished to examine the effect of a California mandatory jail sentencing law, the "three strikes and you're out" policy, on crime rates. The essence of the policy is that jail sentences occur automatically once a person has been convicted of three serious crimes (felonies). Combining data from California's ten largest cities, Stolzenberg and D'Alessio examined two types of crime rates (i.e., two dependent variables). They looked at felonies, supposedly reduced by mandatory sentencing, and relatively minor crimes (misdemeanors). Presumably, these latter crimes would not be affected by the new law. Figure 10.9 shows the results, a good example of the advantages of a time series design. If you look just at the curve for serious crimes right after the law was passed, it actually looks like there is a decline, especially when compared to the flat curve for the nonserious crimes. If you look at the serious crime curve as a whole, however, it is clear that any reduction in serious crime is just part of a trend that had been occurring since around 1992. Overall, the researchers concluded that the "three strikes" law had no measurable effect on crime.

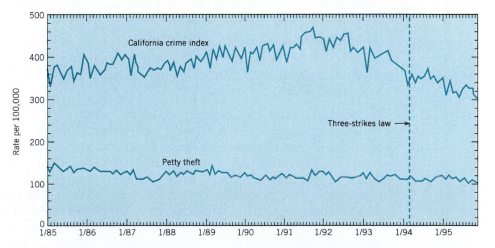

FIGURE 10.9   Interrupted time series using two different dependent measures; the effect of mandatory sentencing on crime rates (from Stolzenberg & D'Alessio, 1997).

> ✓ Self Test 10.2
>
> 1. Why is it said that the nonequivalent control group design has a "built-in confound?"
> 2. If nonequivalent groups are being used and the groups are matched on some pretest score, the results can be distorted by a _____ effect.
> 3. Time series designs sometimes include "switching replications." How does this design differ from the basic interrupted time series design?

Research Using Archival Data

The Stolzenberg and D'Alessio (1997) study demonstrates another feature often seen in quasi-experimental research—the use of **archival data**. Archival data refers to information that has already been gathered for some reason aside from the research project at hand. These data range from public information such as census data, court records (e.g., felonies and misdemeanors), genealogical data, corporate annual reports, and patent office records to more private information such as credit histories, health history data, educational records, personal correspondence, and diaries. The term "archives" refers both to the records themselves and to the places where the records are stored. Archives are located in such places as university libraries, government offices, and computerized databases. Concerning the latter, Table 10.1 lists just a few of the more prominent ones, along with their websites. You can begin to get a sense of the topics that can be studied using archival data from the following titles of research articles:

- Temper and Temperature on the Diamond: The Heat-Aggression Relationship in Major League Baseball (Reifman & Larrick, 1991)
- The Institutionalization of Premarital Cohabitation: Estimates from Marriage License Applications, 1970 and 1980 (Gwaltney-Gibbs, 1986)
- An Archival Study of Eyewitness Memory of the *Titanic*'s Final Plunge (Riniolo, Koledin, Drakulic, & Payne, 2003)

The data extracted from archives sometimes stand on their own, ready for analysis. For example, the archival study on baseball (Reifman & Larrick, 1991) involved examining box scores of major league baseball games over a period of several years. The researchers (a) tabulated where batters were hit by a pitch, and (b) examined weather records to determine the air temperature during games. The idea was to test a notion from the social psychology of aggression, where it has been found that as temperatures increase, people get irritable, and aggressive behavior becomes more likely. Assuming that a hit batsman implies some degree of aggression on the part of the pitcher (arguable), Reifman and Larrick were curious about a correlation between beanballs and heat. They found one—games played in hotter weather produced more hit batters than games in cooler weather.

TABLE 10.1 *Public Databases Available for Online Searches*

Archival research often takes advantage of a number of large-scale online databases. Here are some of them, taken from DeAngelis (2008, pp. 22–23):

- Inter-University Consortium for Political and Social Research (ICPSR)
  - Contains archival data on such topics as substance abuse, criminal justice, and aging
  - www.icpsr.umich.edu
- The DataWeb
  - U. S. Census Bureau data
  - http://Dataferrett.census.gov
- Clinical Trials Network
  - Data from thirteen clinical trials of substance abuse treatments
  - www.nida.nih.gov/ctn
- National Longitudinal Study of Adolescent Health
  - Health and behavior data on 21,000 people first studied in 1994
  - www.cpc.unc.edu/addhealth
- National Institute of Child Health and Human Development study of early child care and development
  - Longitudinal data on more than 1,000 children and families since 1991
  - http://secc.rti.org
- National Institute of Mental Health's human genetics initiative
  - Genetics data on more than 4,000 individuals with specific disorders (e.g., schizophrenia)
  - http://nimhgenetics.org

Sometimes the archival information needs to undergo a **content analysis** before any statistical procedures can be applied. Content analysis can be defined as any systematic examination of qualitative information in terms of predefined categories. For example, in a study looking at how people explain successes and failures in sport, Lau and Russell (1980) content analyzed newspaper quotes from athletes and coaches after wins and losses. Explanations were coded into two general categories, depending on whether some outcome was blamed on internal (our fault) or external (not our fault—lucky breaks, poor officiating, etc.) factors. In general, they found that winners tended to take credit and losers often placed the blame outside themselves. Although content analysis normally occurs with verbal materials, it isn't limited to them. For instance, in a study by Brantjes and Bouma (1991), the drawings of Alzheimer patients were content analyzed and scored in terms of degree of mental deterioration, and then compared to the drawings by those not suffering from the disease.

The most obvious strength of **archival research** is that the amount of information available is virtually unlimited, and the possibilities for archival research are restricted only by the creativity of the investigator. Yet, the fact that archival data already exist also creates problems for researchers. Despite the vast amount of data available, some information vital to a researcher may be missing or the available data may not be representative of some population. In a study that examined the content of advice columns, for example, Schoeneman and Rubanowitz (1985) had to contend with the fact that what eventually is printed in an advice column is just a small proportion of the letters written to advice columnists. Who can say what factors determine the selection of letters for publication?

Another problem with archival research is *experimenter bias* (Chapter 6). In archival research, this bias can take the form of selecting only those records that support one's hypothesis or interpreting the content of records in a way that is biased by one's expectations. The problem can be difficult to avoid completely because the researcher doing archival research is typically faced with much more information than can be used, and the information can often be open to several interpretations. But the problem can also be managed most of the time by using the control procedures described in Chapter 6 (e.g., not disclosing the hypothesis to those responsible for coding or classifying the archival data—in effect, a double blind procedure).

One problem often faced by researchers that does *not* occur with archival research is the problem of participant **reactivity**. For those participating directly in a research study, the knowledge that their behavior is being observed can influence their behavior in ways that yield a distorted result. For instance, if you are a male runner, have you ever noticed that your running form is better and that you run just a little bit faster during that part of the route that takes you by the women's dorm? With archival research, the information for analysis already exists, collected for reasons other than your research project, so reactivity can be ruled out as a factor affecting behavior.

By its nature, archival research does not allow for random assignment in between-subject designs, which makes it quasi-experimental. Like other quasi-experimental research, however, these studies often involve sophisticated attempts to control for potential threats to internal validity. A clever example of this is a study by Ulrich (1984), who demonstrated that recovery from surgery could be influenced by having a room with a view.

Research Example 30—A Quasi-Experimental Design Using Archival Data

One of the more interesting areas of research that has developed in psychology within the past 30 years concerns the relationship between mental and physical well-being. Health psychologists study such problems as the link between stress and illness, the doctor-patient relationship, and, in the case of the Ulrich study, whether such a seemingly minor factor as hospital architecture can affect patient health.

Ulrich examined patient records over a period of about 10 years in a suburban Pennsylvania hospital. He was interested in whether recovery from surgery could be affected by the type of room in which the patient spent postoperative time. In particular, he compared rooms that had windows overlooking a brick wall with rooms having windows that provided a pleasant view of a small group of trees (see

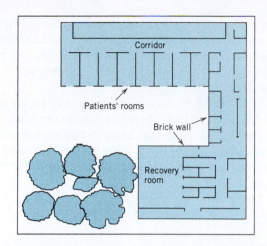

FIGURE 10.10 Floor plan of a hospital used in archival study of recovery from surgery, showing rooms facing either a group of trees or a brick wall (from Ulrich, 1984).

Figure 10.10 for a floor diagram). All of the rooms were the same size, and in each room the beds were arranged so that patients could easily look out of the window.

Because the study was archival, Ulrich could not randomly assign patients to the rooms, so the study was, in effect, a nonequivalent control group design. He did everything possible to make the two groups of patients comparable, though. First, he only used patients recovering from a common type of gallbladder surgery and omitted those under the age of 20 and over 69. Second, he created two similar groups using a variety of matching variables including age, gender, smoking history, and weight. Thus, he examined records for two groups of patients who were generally similar to each other, while still being, by definition, nonequivalent. The independent variable was the type of view they had out of their windows—trees (experimental group) or bricks (control group). And to ensure a similar experience for the experimental group, Ulrich only used records for patients hospitalized between May 1 and October 20 in each of the study's 10 years. Why were those months the only ones selected? Because during the rest of the year, there was no foliage on the trees and the goal was to compare patients who were looking at brick walls with those looking at a fully bloomed and presumably more aesthetically pleasing environment. Ulrich controlled for experimenter bias by having a nurse make the decisions about which records were selected for the study. When making those decisions, she had no way of knowing which room the patients had occupied (another double blind).

From the archival records, Ulrich examined the length of postoperative hospitalization, whether and in what amounts patients requested medication for pain and/or anxiety, the frequency of minor complications such as headache or nausea, and nurses' notes about the patients. What he found was a clear advantage for those recovering in a room with a view. They spent an average of almost one full day less in the hospital after surgery (7.96 vs. 8.70), they requested less pain medication, and when they did request it, they asked for lower doses than patients staring at the bricks. An analysis of nursing records determined that those looking out on the park-like setting were more likely to be perceived as having a positive attitude than the others (but maybe the nurses were affected by the trees too!). The groups did not differ in their requests for antianxiety medication, nor were there differences in minor postoperative complications.

The Ulrich study is one of a growing number that show how physical health can be influenced by any number of nonmedical factors. The study also illustrates how health psychology has become a multidisciplinary field: At the time of the study's publication, Ulrich taught in the Department of *Geography* at the University of Delaware.

In sum, studies employing archival data are an effective way to use information about events that have already occurred and therefore enable the researcher to test hypotheses when variables aren't available for direct experimental manipulation. Considering the vast amount of information out there and its increased availability (e.g., on the Internet), archival research is an approach that promises to become even more visible in the years ahead.

Program Evaluation

Applied research that attempts to assess the effectiveness and value of policies (e.g., California's "three strikes" law) or specially designed programs (e.g., meals on wheels) is sometimes given the name **program evaluation**. This research concept developed in the 1960s in response to the need to evaluate social programs like Head Start, but it is concerned with much more than just answering the question "Did program X work?" More generally, program evaluation includes (a) procedures for determining if a true need exists for a particular program and who would benefit if the program is implemented, (b) assessments of whether a program is being run according to plan and, if not, what changes can be made to facilitate its operation, (c) methods for evaluating program outcomes, and (d) cost analyses to determine if program benefits justify the funds expended. Let's consider each in turn. First, however, you should read Box 10.2, which highlights a paper by Donald Campbell (1969) that is always included at or near the top of the list of the "most important papers about the origins of program evaluation."

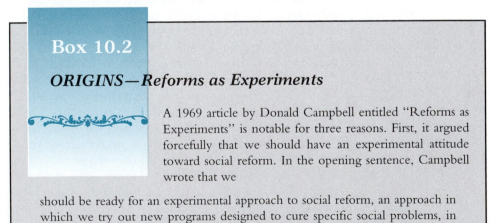

Box 10.2

ORIGINS—Reforms as Experiments

A 1969 article by Donald Campbell entitled "Reforms as Experiments" is notable for three reasons. First, it argued forcefully that we should have an experimental attitude toward social reform. In the opening sentence, Campbell wrote that we

should be ready for an experimental approach to social reform, an approach in which we try out new programs designed to cure specific social problems, in which we learn whether or not these programs are effective, and in which we retain, imitate, modify, or discard them on the basis of apparent effectiveness. (p. 409)

Second, Campbell's article described several studies that have become classics in the field of program evaluation, helped originate and define the field, and provided prototypical examples of designs like the interrupted time series. Perhaps the best-known example is his description of a study to evaluate an effort to reduce speeding in Connecticut (Campbell & Ross, 1968). Following a year (1955) with a record number of traffic fatalities (324), Connecticut Governor Abraham Ribicoff instituted a statewide crackdown on speeding, making the reasonable assumption that speeding and traffic fatalities were related. The following year, the number of deaths fell to 284. This statistic was sufficient for Ribicoff to declare that with "the saving of 40 lives in 1956, a reduction of 12.3% from the 1955 . . . death toll, we can say that the program is definitely worthwhile" (quoted in Campbell, 1969, p. 412). Was it?

I hope you're saying to yourself that other interpretations of the drop are possible. For example, history could be involved; perhaps the weather was better and the roads were drier in 1956. Even more likely is regression—"324" is the perfect example of an extreme score that would normally be followed by regression to the mean. Indeed, Campbell argued that regression contributed to the Connecticut results, pointing out that "[r]egression artifacts are probably the most recurrent form of self-deception in the experimental social reform literature" (p. 414). Such effects frequently occur in these kinds of studies because interventions like a speeding crackdown often begin right after something especially bad has happened. Purely by chance alone, things are not likely to be quite as bad the following year.

Was regression all that was involved here? Probably not. By applying an interrupted time series design with a nonequivalent control (nearby states without a crackdown on speeding), Campbell concluded that the crackdown probably did have some effect, even if it was not as dramatic as was believed by the governor. You can see the results for yourself in Figure 10.11.

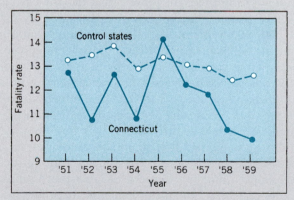

FIGURE 10.11 The Connecticut speeding crackdown, a classic example of an interrupted time series with a nonequivalent control (from Campbell, 1969).

The third reason the Campbell article is so important is that it gave researchers some insight into the political realities of doing research on socially relevant issues. Politicians often propose programs they believe will be effective, and while they might say they're interested in a thorough evaluation, they tend not to be too appreciative of a negative evaluation. After all, by backing the program, they have a stake in its success and its continuance, especially if the program benefits the politician's home state or district. For this reason, politicians and the administrators hired to run programs seldom push for rigorous evaluation and are willing to settle for favorable research outcomes even if they come from flawed designs. For example, Governor Ribicoff was willing to settle for looking at nothing more than traffic fatalities immediately before and right after the crackdown on speeding.

Campbell recommended an attitude change that would shift the emphasis from stressing the importance of a particular program to acknowledging the importance of the problem. This would lead politicians and administrators alike to think of programs as experimental attempts to solve the problem; different programs would be tried until one was found to work. As Campbell put it in the article's conclusion,

> *Trapped administrators* have so committed themselves in advance to the efficacy of the reform that they cannot afford an honest evaluation. . . . *Experimental administrators* have justified the reform on the basis of the importance of the problem, not the certainty of their answer, and are committed to going on to other potential solutions if the first one tried fails. They are therefore not threatened by a hard-headed analysis of the reform. (1969, p. 428; italics in the original)

Planning for Programs—Needs Analysis

An agency begins a program because administrators believe a need exists that would be met by the program. How is that need determined? Clearly, more is required than just an administrative decision that a program seems to make sense. An exercise program in a retirement community sounds quite reasonable, but if none of the residents will participate, much time and money will be wasted. Before any project is planned in any detail, some type of needs assessment must be completed.

Needs analysis is a set of procedures for predicting whether a population of sufficient size exists that would benefit from the proposed program, whether the program could solve a clearly defined problem, and whether members of the population would actually use the program. Several systematic methods exist for estimating need, and it is important to rely on at least some of these techniques because it is easy to overestimate need. One reason for caution follows from the *availability heuristic*, first introduced in Chapter 1's discussion about ways of knowing. Events that grab headlines catch our attention and become more "available" to our memory. Because they come so readily to mind, we tend to overestimate how often they occur. All it takes is one or two highly publicized cases of children being abandoned by vacationing parents for a call to be made for new programs to fix this seemingly widespread problem. Also, a need for some new program can be overestimated by those in a position to benefit (i.e., keep their jobs) from the existence of such a program.

As outlined by Posavac and Carey (2002), there are several ways to identify the potential need for a program. These include:

- *Census data.* If your proposed program is aimed at the elderly, it's fairly obvious that its success will be minimal if there are few seniors living in the community. Census data (www.census.gov) can provide basic demographic information about the number of people fitting into various categories. Furthermore, the information is fine-grained enough for you to determine such things as the number of single mothers under the age of 21, the number of people with various disabilities, or the number of elderly people below the poverty line. In addition to census data, local organizations might have some archival data available. For instance, a corporation thinking of starting a worksite day care center can examine its own files to estimate the number of employees who are working parents of young children. Finally, published research can also provide important information about need. Studies showing long-term decreases in IQ for children raised in impoverished environments provide strong evidence of a need for enrichment programs.

- *Surveys of available resources.* There's no reason to begin a Meals on Wheels program if one already exists in the community and is functioning successfully. Thus, one obvious step in a needs analysis is to create an inventory of existing services. It will include a description of who is providing the services, exactly which services are being provided, and an estimate of how many people are receiving the services. You might discover, for example, that an existing Meals on Wheels program is being run by an agency that is overextended financially and understaffed and, as a result, is meeting no more than 10% of the need. In that case, developing a second program serving different neighborhoods could be worthwhile.

- *Surveys of potential users.* A third needs analysis strategy is to administer a survey within the community, either to a broadly representative sample or to a target group identified by census data. Those participating could be asked whether they believe a particular program is needed. More important, the survey may enable the planner to estimate just how many people would actually use the proposed program.

- *Key informants, focus groups, and community forums.* A **key informant** is someone in the community who has a great deal of experience and specialized knowledge about the problem at hand that is otherwise unavailable to the researcher (Gilchrist & Williams, 1999). Such persons include community activists, clergy, people who serve on several social service agency boards, and so on. Sometimes they might be too close to a problem to judge it realistically, but in general they can be an essential source of information. A **focus group** is a small (7–9 typically) group of individuals who respond to a set of open-ended questions about some topic, such as the need for a particular program (they might also be used to assess a program's progress or its outcome). They are often used as a follow-up to a community survey, but they also can be used as a means to shape the questions that would appear in a survey. Focus group members tend to be similar to each other in age and socioeconomic status, presumably to produce a congenial group that will stay on task. Finally, useful information can sometimes emerge from a **community forum**, an open meeting at which all members of a community affected by some potential program are invited to come and participate. Key informants, focus groups, and forums can all be helpful tools, but the researcher also needs to be careful of weighing too heavily the arguments of an especially articulate (but perhaps nonrepresentative) informant, focus group member, or speaker at a forum.

The past few decades have seen an increased awareness in corporate America that profits are related to worker health. Consequently, companies frequently develop, implement, and evaluate programs for improving the health of their workers. The following study describes a large-scale example, which began with a thorough analysis of need.

Research Example 31 — Assessing Need

A needs analysis project was undertaken by the Du Pont Company prior to starting a program designed to promote healthy behaviors in the workplace (Bertera, 1990). The plan called for implementing a series of changes that would affect over 110,000 employees at 100 worksites. The obvious cost of putting such an ambitious plan into effect made it essential that need be demonstrated clearly.

The Du Pont needs assessment included an analysis of existing data on the frequency of various types of employee illnesses, employee causes of death, and the reasons for employee absence and disability over a 15-year period. One result was that employees making the least amount of money and performing the lowest-ranking jobs were the highest on all major categories of illness. That finding told the evaluators that this particular subgroup of workers needed special attention.

Additional indicators that the health promotion program was needed came from a survey of existing company programs for enhancing health. The survey revealed a wide range of programs run by the medical staffs at the various Du Pont plants, including programs on weight loss, smoking cessation, stress management, and the like. The programs tended to be one-time lectures or films, however, or one-on-one counseling during company physical exams; there was minimal follow-up and no systematic evaluation of effectiveness. Employees were also surveyed to determine their knowledge of health-enhancing behaviors, their intention to change things like their eating habits, their self-assessments of whether their own behaviors were health-enhancing or not, and their preferences for a range of health programs.

On the basis of all of this information, Du Pont developed a comprehensive series of programs aimed at improving the health of its workers. These included training programs that went far beyond one-shot lectures, including creation of local employee Health Promotion Activity Committees, recognition and award programs for reaching certain health goals, and workplace climate changes (e.g., removing cigarette vending machines). Also, all workers completed a Health Risk Survey. The results generated a Health Risk Appraisal, which became part of their personnel files, and included an individualized plan for promoting healthy behaviors. On the basis of their needs assessment the Du Pont Company instituted a company-wide program designed to improve workplace health, specifically targeting "smoking cessation, blood pressure control, and lipid control" (Bertera, 1990, p. 316).

Once the needs analysis is complete and the decision is made to proceed, details of the program can be planned and the program begun. Once the program is under way, the second type of evaluation activity begins.

Monitoring Programs—Formative Evaluation

Programs often extend over a considerable period of time. To wait for a year or so before doing a final evaluation of program effectiveness might be nice and clean from a strictly methodological point of view, but what if it is clear in the first month that problems exist that could be corrected easily? That is, rather than waiting until the program's completion, why not carefully monitor the progress of the program while it is in progress? This monitoring is called **formative evaluation**, and according to one analysis (Sechrest & Figueredo, 1993), it is the most common form of evaluation activity.

A formative evaluation can include several components. For one thing, it determines if the program is being implemented as planned. For example, suppose a local crisis hotline decides to develop a program aimed at the needs of young children who are home alone after school while their parents are working. One important piece of the implementation plan is to make the hotline's phone number available and well known. A formative evaluation would determine whether the planned ads were placed in the newspapers at appropriate times and whether mass mailings of stickers with the hotline's number went out as planned. Also, a sample of residents could be called and asked if they'd heard of the new hotline for kids. There's no point in trying to evaluate the effectiveness of the program if people don't even know about it.

Another general function of the formative evaluation is to provide clear and continuing data on how the program is being used. Borrowing a term from accounting, evaluators sometimes refer to this procedure as a **program audit**. Just as a corporate auditor might look for inconsistencies between the way inventories are supposed to be managed and the way they actually are managed, the program auditor examines whether the program as described in the agency's literature is the same as the program that is actually being implemented.

A final part of a formative evaluation can be a *pilot study* (introduced in Chapter 3). Program implementation and some preliminary outcomes can be assessed on a small scale before extending the program. This happened in the Du Pont study. A pilot program at one of the plants, which showed a significant decline in sick days after implementation of the health promotion program, encouraged program planners and led to an elaboration of the program at other sites (Bertera, 1990). As you can see from Figure 10.12, researchers used a time series design, with data collected over 8 years. (*Note:* By 1982, the results were clear enough that executives began expanding the program to other plants.)

Evaluating Outcomes—Summative Evaluation

Politically, formative evaluations are less threatening than **summative evaluations**, which are overall assessments of program effectiveness. Formative evaluation is aimed at program improvement and is less likely to call into question the very

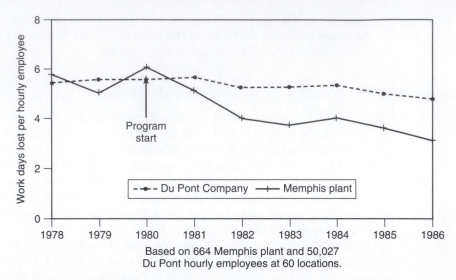

Based on 664 Memphis plant and 50,027
Du Pont hourly employees at 60 locations.

FIGURE 10.12   Effectiveness of a workplace health improvement program,
evaluated via time series (from Bertera, 1990).

existence of a program. Summative evaluation, on the other hand, can do just that.
If the program isn't effective, why keep it, and, by extension, why continue to pay
the program's director and staff (see what I mean about "threatening")? As Sechrest
and Figueredo (1993) stated,

> Summative evaluation and even the rationale for doing it call into question the
> very reasons for existence of the organizations involved. Formative evaluation,
> by contrast, simply responds to the question "How can we be better?" without
> strongly implying the question "How do [we] know [we] are any good at
> all?" (p. 661)

Despite the political difficulty, summative evaluations are the core of the
evaluation process and are an essential feature of any program funded by the federal
government. Any agency wishing to spend tax dollars to develop a program is
obligated to show that those dollars are being used effectively.

The actual process of performing summative evaluations involves applying some
of the techniques you already know about, especially those having to do with
quasi-experimental designs. However, more rigorous experiments with random
assignment are possible sometimes, especially when evaluating a program that has
more people desiring it than space available. In such a case, random assignment
in the form of a lottery (random winners get the program; others wind up in a
waiting list control group) is not only methodologically sound, it is also the only
fair procedure to use.

One problem that sometimes confronts the program evaluator is how to interpret
a failure to find significant differences between experimental and control groups.
That is, the statistical decision is "fail to reject H_0." Such an outcome is difficult
to interpret, as you recall from the discussion in Chapter 4. It could be that there

just isn't any difference, yet there's always the possibility of a Type II error being committed (there really is an effect, but in your study you failed to find it), especially if the measuring tools are not very sensitive or very reliable. The program might indeed have produced some small but important effect, but the analysis failed to discover it.

Although a finding of no difference can be problematic, most researchers believe that such a finding (especially if replicated) contributes important information for decision making, especially in applied research. For instance, someone advocating the continuation of a new program is obligated to show how the program is better than something already in existence. Yet, if differences between this new program and one already well established cannot be shown, then it might be wise to discontinue the new program, especially if it is more expensive than the older one. Indeed, as Yeaton and Sechrest (1986) argue, there may be life-and-death issues involved. They cited a study comparing different treatments for breast cancer that varied in the degree of surgical invasiveness. Survival rates for women undergoing minimally invasive procedures were not significantly different from the rates for women subjected to radical mastectomies. Such an outcome is an example of "failing to reject H_0." Should the results be ignored because no significant differences were found? Of course not. If the same outcome occurs with a less traumatic treatment procedure, why take the more radical step? Of course, the confidence one has in decisions made on the basis of finding no difference is directly related to how often such a finding has been replicated. A recommendation to rely on minimal surgical procedures only follows from repeated failure to find a difference between major and minor procedures.

A "fail to reject H_0" decision also can help evaluate claims made by proponents of some new program. Someone claiming that mandatory jail sentences after a third felony will dramatically reduce serious crime, for instance, is obligated to demonstrate such an effect. The time series study of mandatory sentences previously mentioned (Stolzenberg & D'Alessio, 1997), which found no effect of the "three strikes" program on felony crime rates, is an important finding even though it is a finding of "no effect." If replicated, it would raise serious questions about the value of mandatory sentencing. As another example, recall the study from Chapter 7 (Research Example 15) that examined the effectiveness of EMDR (eye movement desensitization and refocusing) for treating anxiety disorders. A failure to find a difference between those getting the EMDR therapy and a yoked control group raised questions about the value of this supposed revolutionary therapy.

As implied in these "failure to reject H_0" examples, a finding of no difference has important implications for decision making for reasons having to do with cost, and this brings us to the final type of program evaluation activity.

Weighing Costs—Cost-Effectiveness Analysis

Suppose a researcher is interested in the question of worker health and fitness and is comparing two health-enhancement programs. One includes opportunities for exercising on company time, educational seminars on stress management, and a smoking ban. The second plan is a more comprehensive (and more expensive) program of evaluating each worker and developing an individually tailored fitness program, along with financial incentives for things like reducing blood pressure and cholesterol levels. Both programs are implemented on a trial basis in two plants; a third plant is used as a control group. Hence, the design is a nonequivalent control group design with two experimental groups instead of just one. A summative evaluation finds no difference between the two experimental groups in terms of improved worker health, but both show improvements compared to the control group. That is, both health programs work, but the Chevy version works just as well as the Mercedes version. If two programs producing the same outcome differ in cost, why bother with the expensive one?

This corporate fitness example illustrates one type of **cost-effectiveness analysis:** monitoring the actual costs of a program and relating those costs to the effectiveness of the program's outcomes. If two programs with the same goal are equally effective but the first costs half as much as the second, then it is fairly obvious that the first program should be used. A second type of cost analysis takes place during the planning stages for a program. Estimating costs at the outset helps determine whether a program is even feasible and provides a basis for comparison later on between projected costs and actual costs.

Research Example 32—Assessing Costs and Benefits

A study by Erfurt, Foote, and Heirich (1992) provides a good example of a thorough cost-effectiveness analysis. They compared worksite wellness programs that differed in cost at four similar automobile manufacturing plants in Michigan. The program goal was to improve general cardiac fitness. Four different program models were assessed, and they were randomly assigned to the four plants. The four programs were

- Health education (Site A): Designed to increase awareness with periodic health fairs, health education classes for employees, and health-relevant articles in plant newsletters.

- Fitness facility (Site B): Built a physical fitness center with aerobic and strength equipment, staffed with athletic trainers, and available to workers on their own time.

- Health education and follow-up (Site C): Like Site A, but with the addition of wellness counselors who periodically pestered workers about their health-related behaviors and provided counseling about how to make changes in order to reduce health risks.

- Health education, follow-up, and plant organization (Site D): Like Site C, with the addition of creating social support groups (e.g., a buddy system for workers to support each other) and the construction of a one-mile walking path at the plant.

These programs were put into place for 3 years and then assessed for effectiveness and cost. As you might guess, the researchers predicted that health levels (assessed with pre- and posttesting) would be higher at Sites C and D than at A and B, and that health would be better at D than at C. Effectiveness was assessed in terms of changes in such things as blood pressure, smoking rates, and weight. Costs included the salaries for health education staff, the fitness center at Site B and the path at D, and periodic medical screening (e.g., blood pressure).

The results were complex, but there were a number of interesting findings. The key result was that spending lots of money on a fitness center (Site B), which is the typical corporate strategy for improving fitness, was not worth the cost. Comparing Sites B and C, for instance, showed an annual cost per employee of $39.28 at B and $30.96 at C. Yet wellness improved significantly at Site C but not much at B. Wellness was operationally defined by a "risk reduction" factor, a measure of overall reduction in risk of cardiovascular disease. The reduction was 36% at Site B and 48% at C. Risk reduction was also good at Site D (51%), but not especially good at Site A (39%). In short, while health improved at all the plants, the improvement was much greater at Sites C and D, and the costs at C and D were much less than at B (the Site A program was cheapest of all, $17.68, but it was not very effective). The authors concluded that a strategy that emphasized follow-up and social support was both better and more cost-effective than simple education and expensive equipment.

Estimating costs with reference to outcomes can be a complicated process, often requiring the expertise of a specialist in cost accounting. Thus, a detailed discussion of the procedures for relating costs to outcomes is beyond the scope of this chapter, an opinion shared by my wife, who has been a cost accountant and finds my rudimentary knowledge amusing. In addition, it is often difficult if not impossible to put a monetary value on the benefits that might result from the implementation and continuance of some program, especially one involving some aspect of wellness. Some of the basic concepts of a cost analysis can be discovered by reading Chapter 11 of Posavac and Carey's (2002) fine introduction to program evaluation.

A Note on Qualitative Analysis

Chapter 3 first introduced the difference between a quantitative analysis (numbers involved) and a qualitative analysis (numbers not so critical). Although much of the analysis that occurs in program evaluation is quantitative in nature, there is a great deal of qualitative analysis as well, especially in the first three categories of evaluation just described. Thus, during a needs analysis, quantitative data from a community survey and census data can be combined with in-depth interview information from key informants and focus groups. In formative and summative assessments, quantitative data can be supplemented with a qualitative analysis of interviews with agency workers and clients and with direct observations of the program in action. In short, in program evaluation research, it is seldom a question of whether quantitative or qualitative research is better. Rather, although there has been and continues to be some debate about the relative merits of quantitative and qualitative evaluation (e.g., Worthen, 2001), thoughtful program evaluators rely on both. A good example is a study that was designed to evaluate several forms of feedback about energy usage to reduce household energy consumption in the city of Bath in England (Brandon & Lewis, 1999). The most effective condition was one in which residents received immediate feedback via home computers about energy consumption compared to the prior year. The study included both quantitative analysis (changes in energy usage, attitude survey data) and qualitative analysis (content analyses of focus group discussions about energy usage). The authors believed that the focus group results provided the most important outcome—for residents, even those with positive attitudes on environmental issues, the "main issue appeared to be the trade-off between comfort and expenditure with money commonly being identified as the main motivation for conservation among the focus groups" (p. 82).

✓   Self Test 10.3

1.   Archival research does not have to deal with the problem of reactivity. Explain.
2.   What is a formative evaluation and why are these an important component of program evaluation?
3.   How was qualitative analysis used in the study that examined household energy consumption?

As first mentioned in Chapter 5's discussion of external validity, research in psychology is sometimes criticized for avoiding real-world investigations. This chapter on applied research should make it clear that the criticism is without merit. Indeed, concern over application and generalizability of results is not far from the consciousness of all psychologists, even those committed primarily to basic research. It is evident from psychology's history that application is central to American psychology, if for no other reason than the fact that Americans can't help it. Looking for practical applications is as American as apple pie.

The next chapter introduces a slightly different tradition in psychological research—an emphasis on the intensive study of individuals. As you will see, just as the roots of applied research can be found among psychology's pioneers, experiments with small *N* also trace to the beginnings of the discipline. Before moving on to Chapter 11, however, read Box 10.3, which summarizes some of the ethical problems likely to be encountered when doing program evaluation research.

Box 10.3

ETHICS—Evaluation Research and Ethics

Whether evaluating programs that provide services to people, conducting studies in a workplace environment, or evaluating some government service, program evaluation researchers often encounter ethical dilemmas not faced by laboratory psychologists. Some special problems include:

- *Informed consent.* People receiving social services are often powerless. When asked to "volunteer" for a study and sign an informed consent form, they may fear that a failure to "sign up" could mean a loss of services. In situations like this, researchers must take deliberate steps to reassure participants that no coercion will occur. In some cases, witnessed consent verbal rather than written consent might be appropriate.

- *Maintaining confidentiality.* In some research, confidentiality can be maintained by gathering behavioral data from participants but not adding any personal identifiers. In other studies, however, it is necessary for the researcher to know who the participants are. For instance, the researcher might need to recontact participants, especially if the study is a longitudinal one, or a researcher might want to know who replied to a survey so that nonrespondents can be recontacted. In such cases, it is important to develop coding systems to protect the identities of participants. Sometimes, participants in longitudinal studies can use aliases, and survey respondents can send back the anonymous survey and a postcard verifying their participation in separate mailings (Sieber, 1998).

- *Perceived injustice.* As mentioned in Box 7.2, some people might object to being in a control group because they could be missing out on some potentially beneficial treatment. Although most control group members in program evaluation research receive the prevailing treatment, rather than none at all, control group problems can still happen. For example, *leakage* (see Chapter 2 and Box 8.2) can occur if control group members discover important information about the program being offered to someone else. Their resentment of "special treatment" being given to others can seriously affect the outcome. In a study designed to evaluate some worksite changes in a coal mine, for instance, control group miners quickly grew to resent those in the treatment group, whom they felt were getting special attention and did not have to work as hard for the same money (Blumberg & Pringle, 1983). The ill will was even directed at the researchers. Control group workers believed them to be in league with the mine owner in an attempt to break the union. The study as originally designed had to be discontinued.

- *Avoiding conflict with stakeholders.* **Stakeholders** are persons connected with a program in which they have a vested interest, including clients, staff, and program directors. Program evaluators need to be aware of and take steps to avoid potential conflicts with various stakeholders. This means being aware of the needs of stakeholders and explicitly addressing them during the planning stages of the evaluation. For example, program evaluators might build into the initial contract some specific statements about how the results will be reported and what the consequences will be for certain types of outcomes (Posavac & Carey, 2002). A clear understanding ahead of time can help transform "trapped" administrators into "experimental" administrators, to use Campbell's terms.

Chapter Summary

Beyond the Laboratory

The goal of applied research is to shed light on the causes of and solutions to real-world problems. Like basic research, however, the outcomes of applied research also contribute to general theories about behavior (e.g., the cognitive interview study contributes to our basic knowledge about the influence of context on memory). American psychologists always have been interested in applied research, partly because of institutional pressures to show that the "new" psychological science of the late nineteenth century could be put to good use. Applied research can encounter ethical problems (e.g., with informed consent) and problems with internal validity (e.g., nonequivalent groups), but it is often strong in external validity.

Quasi-Experimental Designs

Research in which participants cannot be randomly assigned to conditions is referred to as quasi-experimental research. Nonequivalent control group designs are one example. They typically compare pretest/posttest changes in a group receiving some treatment with pre/post changes in a control group that has been formed without random assignment. Regression effects can make interpretation difficult when nonequivalent groups are forced into a degree of equivalency by matching them on pretest scores. In an interrupted time series design, researchers take several measurements both before and after the introduction of some treatment that is being evaluated. Time series studies enable the researcher to evaluate the effects of trends. Sometimes a nonequivalent control condition, a "switching" replication, or additional dependent measures can be added to the basic time series design. Archival research relies on data (e.g., hospital records) that have been collected for some other purpose, and then reanalyzed for the purpose of answering some empirical question (e.g., can environmental factors affect postoperative recovery?).

Program Evaluation

The field of program evaluation is a branch of applied psychology that provides empirical data about the effectiveness of various human service and government programs. Needs analysis studies determine whether a new program should be developed. Census data, surveys, and other community data can help assess need. Formative evaluations determine whether a program is operating according to plan, and summative evaluations assess program outcomes. Cost analyses help determine whether a program's benefits are worth the funds invested. Program evaluation research typically combines both quantitative and qualitative methods.

Chapter Review Questions

1. Use the study of the cognitive interview as way of (a) distinguishing basic and applied research, and (b) showing that applied research relates to theory development.

2. Describe how Hollingworth was able to use fairly sophisticated methodological controls in his applied study of the effects of caffeine.

3. Describe the essential features of a nonequivalent control group design and explain why Figure 10.3c does not necessarily allow one to conclude that the program was a success.

4. Early program evaluations of Head Start seemed to show that gains made by Head Start children were short-lived; by the third grade, no differences existed between those who had been in the program and those who had not. However, this outcome might have been the result of a regression effect brought about by the matching procedure used to form the groups. Explain.

5. Describe the Research Example that evaluated a "coaches effectiveness training" program and explain why the researchers decided to use a quasi-experimental instead of an experimental design (e.g., using coaches from different leagues).

6. Describe the essential features of an interrupted time series design and three variations on the basic procedure that can strengthen the conclusions drawn from such a design.

7. What are archival data, and why is archival research with independent variables considered to be quasi-experimental?

8. Describe two quantitative and two qualitative procedures that can be used when conducting a needs analysis.

9. Distinguish between formative and summative assessments and explain why agency workers generally prefer the former.

10. A finding of "no difference" sometimes occurs in program evaluation research. Explain why this is not necessarily a bad thing.

11. Briefly describe the attributes of the four main types of program evaluation research.

12. Briefly describe the ethical dilemmas that can face those doing program evaluation research.

Applications Exercises

Exercise 10.1   Identifying Threats to Internal Validity

Threats to internal validity are common in quasi-experimental studies. What follows is a list of some of the threats you've encountered in this chapter and in Chapter 5. For each of the hypothetical experiments that are described, identify which of these threats is most likely to provide a reasonable alternative explanation of the outcome. In some cases, more than one threat could be involved.

Some threats to internal validity	
history	maturation
regression	selection
attrition	selection × history

1. A college dean is upset about the low percentage of freshmen that return to the college as sophomores. Historically, the rate has been around 75%, but in the academic year just begun, only 60% of last year's freshmen return. The dean puts a tutoring program into effect and then claims credit for its effectiveness when the following year's return rate is 65%.

2. Two nearby colleges agree to cooperate in evaluating a new computerized instructional system. College A gets the program and college B doesn't. Midway through the study, college B announces that it has filed for bankruptcy (even though it continues to operate). One year later, computer literacy is higher at college A.

3. Twelve women who volunteer for a home birthing program are compared with a random sample of other pregnant women who undergo normal hospital procedures for childbirth. Women in the first group spend an average of 6 hours in labor, while those in the control group spend an average of 9 hours.

4. A 6-week program in managing test anxiety is developed and given to a sample of first-semester college students. Their anxiety levels are significantly lower at the conclusion of the program than they were at the start.

5. A teacher decides to use an innovative teaching technique in which all students will proceed at their own pace throughout the term. The course will have 10 units, and each student goes to unit N after completing unit $N-1$. Once all 10 units have been completed, the course is over and an A has been earned. Of the initial 30 students enrolled in the class, the final grade distribution looks like this:

    16 earned an A

     2 failed

    12 withdrew from the course during the semester

The instructor considers the new course format an unqualified success.

6. A company decides to introduce a flextime program. It measures productivity for January, runs the program for six months, and then evaluates productivity during the month of June. Productivity increases.

Exercise 10.2 Interpreting Nonequivalent Control Group Studies

A wheel bearing manufacturer owns two plants, both in Illinois. She wishes to see if money for health costs can be reduced if a wellness program is instituted. One plant (E) is selected for a year-long experimental program that includes health screening and individually tailored fitness activities. The second plant (C) is the nonequivalent control group. Absentee-due-to-sickness rates, operationally defined as the number of sick days per year per 100 employees, are measured at the beginning and the end of the experimental year. What follows are four sets of results. Construct a graph for each and decide which (if any) provide evidence of program effectiveness. For those outcomes not supporting the program's effectiveness, provide an alternative explanation for the experimental group's apparent improvement.

Outcome 1 E: pretest = 125 posttest = 100
C: pretest = 125 posttest = 125

Outcome 2 E: pretest = 125 posttest = 100
C: pretest = 100 posttest = 100

Outcome 3 E: pretest = 125 posttest = 100
C: pretest = 130 posttest = 105

Outcome 4 E: pretest = 125 posttest = 100
C: pretest = 110 posttest = 110

Exercise 10.3 Interpreting Time Series Studies

Imagine a time series study evaluating the effects of a helmet law on head injuries among hockey players in amateur city leagues across the nation. Head injuries were significantly lower in the year immediately after the law was passed than in the preceding year. Construct four time series graphs, one for each of the following patterns of results.

1. The helmet law worked.
2. The helmet law seemed to work initially, but its effects were short-lived.
3. The helmet law had no effect; the apparent drop was probably just a regression effect.
4. The helmet law didn't really work; the apparent drop seemed to reflect a general trend toward reduced violence in the sport.

In the section on interrupted time series designs, I described several variations on the basic design. How might each of those be used to strengthen the hockey study?

Exercise 10.4   Planning a Needs Assessment

You are the head of a five-person psychology department at a liberal arts university. One day the dean says to you, "Why don't you develop a master's program in counseling psychology?" The college already has an MBA program and another master's program in physical therapy. Because you've read this chapter, you respond that a thorough needs analysis should be done. The dean tells you to go ahead and even approves a modest budget for the project. Describe the factors that would have to be considered before implementing the new degree and explain the techniques you would use to conduct a needs assessment.

Answers to Self Tests:

✓ **10.1.**

1. The "dual" functions are solving real-world problems, while at the same time contributing to general knowledge about some phenomenon.
2. Miles adapted a basic research methodology, reaction time, to an applied problem, reactions of football linemen.
3. Compared with basic laboratory research, applied research tends to be lower in internal validity and higher in external validity

✓ **10.2.**

1. The groups are nonequivalent; in addition, one group gets one type of treatment, and the other group gets a different treatment (or none at all).
2. Regression
3. In a switching replication, the treatment program is implemented in two different places and at two different times.

✓ **10.3.**

1. The data have already been collected for some other purpose, so subjects could not react in any way to their research participation.
2. Formative evaluation assesses a program that is in progress and allows for program improvements to be implemented before the program has been completed.
3. The researchers used focus groups to assess participants' ideas about energy consumption in the home.

CHAPTER 11

Small *N* Designs

Preview & Chapter Objectives

Up to this point, the research strategies you've encountered typically have tested relatively large groups of participants, specific methodological problems such as creating equivalent groups or avoiding order effects have been dealt with, mean scores have been calculated, inferential analyses like ANOVA have been completed, effect sizes have been calculated, and general conclusions about the effects of independent variables on dependent variables have been drawn. In this chapter, however, you will encounter a very different type of study. These studies closely examine either a single individual or a very small group of individuals. Most of the chapter will concern designs that are often called "single-subject designs" because the behavior of each research subject is considered individually, but they can also be called "small *N* designs" because these studies sometimes use several participants. The data for these subjects *might* be combined statistically, but more often the data for the additional individuals are described individually and used for replication purposes. The chapter will also consider research designs that are called "case studies," in-depth analyses of individuals or events. When you finish this chapter, you should be able to:

- Describe examples of classic studies in psychology's history, all using single individuals or a small number of participants, with the additional subjects used for the purpose of replication (e.g., Dresslar, Thorndike).
- Explain how grouping data from large numbers of participants can yield misleading conclusions about behavior.
- Describe some practical reasons for doing small *N* research.
- Describe B. F. Skinner's basic philosophy about the proper way to conduct research—the experimental analysis of behavior.
- Describe the essential components of any single-subject design.
- Explain the logic of an A–B–A–B withdrawal design.
- Explain the logic of a multiple baseline design and describe three varieties of the multiple baseline procedure.
- Explain the logic of a changing criterion design and relate it to the operant concept of shaping.
- Describe several additional single-subject designs (e.g., alternating treatments design).
- Describe the criticisms that have been directed at small *N* designs in the operant tradition.
- Describe the essential features of case study research and describe the strengths and limitations of this research approach.

The small *N* strategy that will occupy the bulk of this chapter is most frequently associated with the philosophy of science developed by B. F. Skinner, whom you first encountered in Chapter 1. However, it is important to realize that Skinner was not the first to focus on individual research subjects. Rather, small *N* designs have a long history; in fact, the first experimental psychologists used this approach all of the time.

Research in Psychology Began with Small *N*

When psychology emerged as a new science in the second half of the nineteenth century, statistical analysis was also in its infancy. Galton was just beginning to conceptualize correlations, and inferential techniques like ANOVA did not yet exist. Widespread use of large *N* designs and inferential statistics occurred only after Fisher's work on the analysis of variance appeared in the 1930s (see Box 8.3). Before this time, small *N* ruled.

Some of psychology's pioneers used the smallest *N* possible—they studied their own behavior or the behavior of a single individual. You have already learned about two famous examples—Hermann Ebbinghaus's exhaustive study of his own ability to learn and recall lists of nonsense syllables (Box 7.2) and Watson and Rayner's infamous Little Albert experiment (Box 2.1). In Wundt's pioneering laboratory at Leipzig, small *N* designs were also the dominant strategy. Students pursuing the doctorate were assigned specific research topics that typically took a year or so to complete. The studies normally involved a very small number of research participants, with the investigator usually serving as one of the participants. Hence, the separation in role (and status) that exists today between the experimenter giving procedural instructions and a participant following them was not in evidence in those days. In fact, while in the 1890s participants were sometimes called "subjects," they were more likely to be called "observers," because they were typically making observations of their own behavior and mental processes. Whether to use the term subject or observer was an issue as late as 1930 (Danziger, 1985).

Pioneer experimental psychologists sometimes crudely summarized data (e.g., reporting means) from several observers, but more often they reported the data for each person participating. A nice example of this strategy is a study from the laboratory at Clark University completed in the early 1890s. It was an investigation of something called "facial vision," the ability to detect the presence of nearby objects even when they cannot be seen. At one time, blind people were believed to have developed this as a special sense to compensate for their loss of vision. However, Fletcher B. Dressler (1893) was able to show that the skill had more to do with hearing than with vision.

Figure 11.1 is a picture taken in 1892 of the actual experimental setup. As you can see, a blindfolded person (another graduate student, actually) was seated next to a panel made up of four 1-foot squares. From left to right, the squares were either open or filled with (a) wood in a latticed design, (b) wood in a solid panel, or (c) wire screening. The panel hung from the ceiling and could be moved by the experimenter (that's Dressler in the photo) so that each of the squares could be placed next to the blindfolded participant's face. The task was to identify which surface was next to one's face; the participants were Dressler and two other graduate student colleagues.

FIGURE 11.1 Dressler's apparatus for studying facial vision, 1892 (Courtesy Clark University Archives).

TABLE 11.1 *Data from Dressler's Study of Facial Vision*

Subject	Open and Lattice				Lattice and Solid				Solid and Wire			
	R.	W.	R.	W.	R.	W.	R.	W.	R.	W.	R.	W.
J. A. B.	65	15	59	25	58	2	56	0	45	0	46	2
O. C.	72	47	74	46	33	13	28	14	21	4	14	9
F. B. D.	53	24	58	17	69	1	70	4	73	0	77	2

Source: Dressler, 1893, p. 347.

Remarkably, all three students learned to distinguish between pairs of surfaces, as shown in Table 11.1, reproduced from the original article. The data represent the number of right ("R.") or wrong ("W.") responses when making judgments between pairs of surfaces. For example, when comparing the latticed surface with the solid one, F. B. D. (guess who that was) was correct 69 times and wrong just once when the correct answer was "lattice" and was correct 70 out of 74 times when the correct answer was "solid." Similar results occurred for the other two participants.

Notice that while data for all three participants are presented, there are no summary statistics combining the three data sets. This is because the strategy was to show the phenomenon occurring reliably for each participant, not for the average subject. That is, Dressler tested two additional subjects (O. C. and F. B. D.) in order to *replicate* the initial finding (J. A. B.) twice. This replication strategy is a common feature of today's small *N* designs.

Do the results of Dressler's study mean that facial vision as a separate sense truly exists? No. As a good research psychologist, Dressler looked for a more parsimonious explanation and for a way to rule out (falsify) the existence of the special facial sense. He found it by making a small procedural change—he plugged everyone's ears. The result was clear: The "power to distinguish [the panels] was lost entirely" (Dressler, 1893, p. 349). Hence, facial vision turned out to be the ability to detect slight differences in reflected sound waves.[1]

Studies like the one by Dressler, featuring data from one or just a few participants, can be found throughout the early years of experimental psychology, but large *N* studies were not completely absent. For example, some could be found in educational psychology and in child study research (Danziger, 1985). Such studies featured empirical questions such as "What do elementary school children fear?" and they summarized questionnaire results from hundreds of children (e.g., Hall, 1893). These large-scale studies with statistical summaries were not without their critics, however. Leta Hollingworth (1886–1939), an early pioneer in the study of gifted children (refer back to Box 10.1), wrote that "[i]t has become a fashion in educational research to rush forth hastily with a huge load of paper and pencil tests; to spend and hour or two on a hundred children; to rush hastily home to the adding

---

[1]Given this result, what would you as an experimenter do next? For example, what if you varied the distance between the panels and the participant?

machine, there to tabulate the performances of the children, not *one* of which has ever been perceived as an individual child" (quoted in Hollingworth, 1943/1990, pp. 114–115, italics in the original).

One final example of an early small *N* project is worth discussing in some detail. Because the research is an important historical predecessor to B. F. Skinner's work on operant conditioning and foreshadowed the coming of behaviorism when it was completed just over 100 years ago, it can be considered one of the origins of today's small *N* tradition. It also shows that good science can be done with a meager budget (and minimal talent) for apparatus construction. Before continuing, please read Box 11.1.

Box 11.1

ORIGINS—Cats in Puzzle Boxes

Edward L. Thorndike (1874–1959) had a distinguished career as an educational psychologist. He is best remembered among experimental psychologists and historians for his doctoral research, however, in which he studied how cats escape from puzzle boxes (Thorndike, 1898). The research is important for several reasons. It shows how psychology's pioneers relied on the detailed study of individual research participants, it is a good example of how to use parsimonious explanations for behavior, and it is an early example of the kind of research that paved the way for the development of behaviorism, especially the Skinnerian variety.

Studying Individual Cats

To investigate learning in cats, Thorndike built 15 puzzle boxes, each with its own unique escape mechanism. Quite by accident, photos of the actual boxes were discovered in the papers of Robert Yerkes by the historian John Burnham (1972), and two of these photos are reproduced in Figure 11.2. Clearly, Thorndike was not a very talented apparatus builder. In fact, his mechanical aptitude was so minimal that he apparently never learned how to drive a car (Hothersall, 1990). There is an important lesson here, though—consequential research can be done without highly sophisticated equipment. The quality of the idea for the study is more important than the bells and whistles.

Cats were studied individually, and Thorndike described his results cat by cat. The cats learned to escape from the boxes through a process Thorndike (1911/2000) called "trial and error, with accidental success" (p. 150) and according to what he named the "Law of Effect" (p. 244). The cats' actions were initially random and only occasionally, and by accident, successful. Behaviors that worked tended to be repeated ("stamped in" was the phrase Thorndike used), while unsuccessful behaviors were gradually eliminated ("stamped out"). That is, the "effect" of a successful behavior

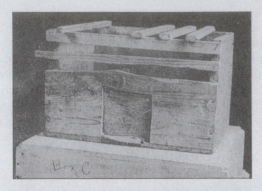

FIGURE 11.2   Two of the puzzle boxes (C and D) built and used by Thorndike in his classic study of cats in puzzle boxes (Courtesy Robert Mearns Yerkes Papers, Manuscripts and Archives, Yale University Library).

was to increase the chances of the behavior occurring on the next trial. The progress of one of Thorndike's cats (no. 10, in Box C) can be seen in Figure 11.3.[2]

Using Parsimonious Explanations

Thorndike's Law of Effect challenged prevailing ideas about the thinking abilities of animals and provided a more parsimonious explanation of problem-solving abilities. He argued that there was no reason to attribute complex thinking processes to animals if their behavior could be explained by a simpler process (i.e., basic trial-and-error learning). Thorndike had little patience with animal researchers who uncritically attributed higher mental processes to animals (e.g., Clever Hans' math skills—Box 3.3), an attitude shaped by Lloyd Morgan, whose famous statement about the need

---

[2]On Thorndike's graphs, the Y-axis was a measure of time to escape (a vertical millimeter in his original graph meant 10 seconds). As for the X-axis, there were no labels, except to note when a significant period of time passed between his consecutive trials. In Figure 11.3 for example, the small unmarked vertical line (just above the "C") meant that a day had elapsed between trials, a "2" was a 2-day gap, "1 h" was an hour, and "78" was 78 hours between consecutive trials (Thorndike, 2000, pp. 38–40).

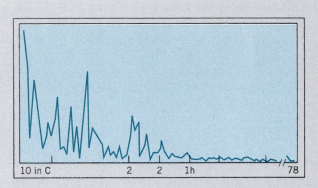

FIGURE 11.3 A record of cat no. 10 learning to escape from Box C (from Thorndike, 1911/2000).

for parsimonious explanations (Chapter 3) appeared about this time. Thorndike was familiar with Morgan's work and might have heard the Englishman give an invited address on animal learning while visiting Harvard in 1896 (Jonçich, 1968).

Anticipating Skinner

The final point worth noting about Thorndike's puzzle box research is that it represented an experimental approach to the study of learning that paved the way for other behavioral researchers. It also provided a model for learning that eventually took the form of B. F. Skinner's experimental analysis of behavior, which you will encounter shortly. Skinner (1953) acknowledged his debt to Thorndike by referring to the latter's work as being among "the first attempts to study the changes brought about by the consequences of behavior" (p. 59).

Reasons for Small *N* Designs

Despite the popularity of large *N* designs in modern psychology, studies using one or just a few individuals continue to make important contributions to our knowledge of behavior. As you will soon discover, these studies cover the entire range from laboratory to field studies and from basic to applied research. There are several reasons why small *N* designs continue to be used.

Misleading Results from Statistical Summaries of Grouped Data

The process of summarizing data from large groups of individuals sometimes yields results that fail to characterize the behavior of the individuals who participated in the study. That is, these outcomes can fail to have what has been called

individual–subject validity (Dermer & Hoch, 1999)—the extent to which a general research result applies to the individual subjects in the study. Although she didn't use this validity term, Hollingworth's concern about large-scale educational psychology studies in psychology's early years was, in essence, a concern about individual-subject validity. And the lack of such validity in large group studies was a central theme in Murray Sidman's *Tactics of Scientific Research* (1960), considered to be the classic text on small N methodology by advocates of the approach. Because group averages can disguise individual differences among the individuals composing those groups, Sidman argued, "[g]roup data may often describe a process, or a functional relation, that has no validity for any individual" (p. 274).

A lack of individual-subject validity can produce erroneous conclusions about behavior. Consider an example from a concept-learning experiment with young children as participants. They are shown a long series of stimulus pairs and have to guess which is correct. If they make the right choice, they are rewarded. The stimuli are in the form of simple geometric objects; Figure 11.4 shows what the stimulus pairs might be for seven of the trials. The plus signs refer to the stimulus in each pair that will be reinforced (with an M&M, perhaps). As you can see, the stimuli vary in shape (triangle or square or circle), color (red or green), and position (left or right). The correct concept in the example is "red"; to accumulate a large pile of M&Ms, the child must learn that shape and position are irrelevant stimulus dimensions. In the language of concept-learning research, color is the "relevant dimension" and red is the "relevant value" on that dimension. The task is considered to be learned when the child reaches some "criterion" score, perhaps 10 consecutive correct choices.

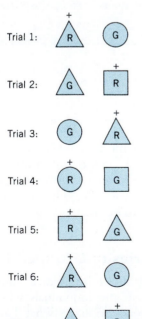

FIGURE 11.4 Typical stimuli used in a discrimination learning study with children.

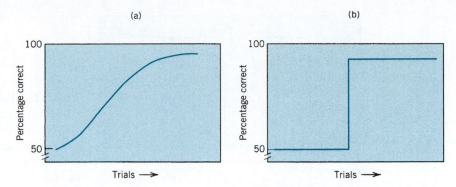

FIGURE 11.5 Concept learning outcomes as predicted by (a) continuity and (b) noncontinuity theory.

An old controversy in the concept-learning literature concerns the manner in which this type of task is learned (Manis, 1971, pp. 64–68). According to "continuity" theory, learning is a gradual process of accumulating "habit strength." Each reinforced trial strengthens the tendency to respond to the relevant dimension and weakens responses to the irrelevant dimensions. A graph of this hypothesized incremental learning process should look something like Figure 11.5a. On the other hand, "noncontinuity" theory holds that the children actively try out different "hypotheses" about the solution during the early trials. While they search for the correct hypothesis, their performance is at chance level (50%), but once they hit on the correct hypothesis, their performance zooms up to 100% accuracy and stays there. Noncontinuity theory predicts that performance should look more like Figure 11.5b.

The history of this issue is long and complicated, and general conclusions are subject to many qualifications, but part of the resolution hinges on how the data are handled. If data from many participants are grouped together and plotted, the result indeed often looks something like Figure 11.5a, and continuity theory is supported. However, a picture more like Figure 11.5b, which supports a noncontinuity theory, emerges when one looks more closely at individual performance, especially on difficult tasks (Osler & Trautman, 1961). Examining performance on trials just before a solution is achieved reveals that accuracy is about 50% (e.g., Trabasso, 1963). After criterion, performance is virtually perfect. That is, participants perform at chance level up to the point when they hit on the correct solution; then their performance improves dramatically. So how does the individual performance illustrated in Figure 11.5b end up as Figure 11.5a when the data are summarized?

The key factor is how long it takes each child to hit on the correct solution; some figure it out quickly, whereas others take longer. This situation is portrayed in Figure 11.6. As you can see, a series of individual curves, when combined, could easily yield the smooth curve of Figure 11.5a. This is a clear instance of how grouped data can create an impression that is not confirmed by examining the behavior of individual participants. When looking at the group curve, one might reasonably conclude that continuity theory works, a conclusion that, in this case,

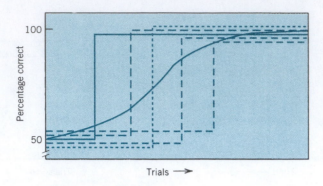

FIGURE 11.6 How grouping data from individual children in a concept-learning experiment can produce a smooth but deceptive learning curve.

would be wrong. As a general rule, any researcher using large *N* designs, especially in research in which learning is involved, should at the very least examine some of the individual data to see if they mirror the grouped data.

Practical Problems with Large *N* Designs

Small *N* designs are sometimes necessary because potential participants are rare or difficult to find. This can happen in clinical psychology, for example, when a researcher wants to study people with a specific psychological disorder, or in cognitive psychology, when individuals might have an unusual type of memory failure as a result of brain damage. A related problem occurs in some animal research, especially if surgery is involved; the surgical environment is expensive, the procedures are time consuming, and ethical considerations exert downward pressure on the size of *N*. The animal colony itself can be difficult to maintain, with costs in these days of animal rights activism including the expense of a security system. In some cases, the species being studied might be hard to obtain, prohibitively expensive, or require long training. For example, the research on teaching sign language to chimpanzees and other apes requires hundreds of hours per animal, and the studies typically extend over many years. In a study teaching sign language to a lowland gorilla (Patterson & Linden, 1981), the ape knew more than 400 different signs at age 10; the study began when the ape was just a year old.

The Experimental Analysis of Behavior

Thus, large *N* designs may occasionally fail to reflect the behaviors of individuals, and they may not be feasible even if they are desired. However, there are also philosophical reasons for preferring small *N* designs. Those reasons were articulated best by the most famous advocate of this approach, B. F. Skinner (1904–1990). As you might recall from Chapter 4, shortly after his death, Skinner was rated the most eminent contemporary psychologist in a survey of historians and heads of psychology departments (Korn, Davis, & Davis, 1991).

Skinner believed passionately that if psychology was to achieve its goals of predicting and controlling behavior, it must study individual organisms intensively and derive general principles only after the exhaustive study of individual cases. That is, psychology should be an inductive science, reasoning from specific cases to general laws of behavior. Indeed, Skinner once said that the investigator should "study one rat for a thousand hours" rather than "a thousand rats for an hour each, or a hundred rats for ten hours each" (Skinner, 1966, p. 21). The goal is to reduce random variability by achieving precise control over the experimental situation affecting the single subject. As Skinner (1956) put it, "I had the clue from Pavlov: control your conditions and you will see order" (p. 223). He called his system the "experimental analysis of behavior," and while you should look elsewhere for a thorough discussion of his ideas (e.g., Skinner, 1953), the essentials are worth mentioning here because they provide the philosophical underpinning for the research designs in applied behavior analysis.

Operant Conditioning

Skinner is best known for his research on **operant conditioning**, a "process in which the frequency of occurrence of a bit of behavior is modified by the consequences of the behavior" (Reynolds, 1968, p. 1). That is, when some behavior occurs in a particular situation, it will be followed by some consequence. If the consequence is positive, the behavior will tend to recur when the individual is in the same situation again. Negative consequences, on the other hand, decrease the future probability of some behavior occurring. If a child's tantrum behavior works (e.g., results in a toy), it will tend to be repeated; if it doesn't, it won't. Note that the definition includes the phrase "frequency of occurrence." Skinner believed that in an experimental analysis of behavior, **rate of response** was the most important dependent variable to measure. If the goals of psychology are to predict and control behavior, and for Skinner those were the only important ones, then the main concern is whether a behavior occurs or doesn't occur and how frequently it occurs per unit of time.

Thus, for the Skinnerian, the behaviors that characterize our lives are controlled by the environment in which we live. To predict and control behavior, according to Skinner, all that is needed is to be able to "specify three things: (1) the occasion upon which a response occurs, (2) the response itself, and (3) the reinforcing consequences. The interrelationships among them are the 'contingencies of reinforcement'" (Skinner, 1969, p. 7).

In the laboratory, operant conditioning is most often studied using an apparatus called an "operant chamber," or "Skinner box." Figure 11.7 shows a typical one designed for rats (Skinner's favorite research subject was the pigeon). The rat is in the process of pressing the lever protruding from the wall. The positive consequence is that a food pellet will be released into the food cup; the rat will then become more likely to press the bar again. A negative consequence could be a brief jolt of electricity across the floor grid, which would reduce the chances of a future bar press.

FIGURE 11.7   An operant chamber with cumulative recorder, as used by rats.

Once bar pressing has been established, it can be brought under the environmental control of stimuli such as the light you can see just above the bar. If food pellets follow bar presses only when the light is on, the animal quickly learns a simple discrimination: Press when the light is on, but don't bother if the light is off. In Skinner's contingencies of reinforcement language, the light being on in the chamber constitutes the "occasion upon which a response occurs," the "response itself" is the bar press, and the food pellet is the "reinforcing consequence."

The rate of bar pressing is recorded and portrayed continuously with an apparatus called a **cumulative recorder**—Figure 11.8a shows one in operation. As the paper is fed out at a constant rate of speed, thereby producing time on the *X*-axis, a pen moves across the paper by a fixed distance every time the animal presses the bar. When a reinforcer follows a response, the pen makes a short vertical marking line. When the pen reaches the top of the paper, it returns immediately to the baseline and starts over. A second pen keeps track of events like the light going on and off. Response rate can be assessed very simply by looking at the slope of the cumulative record. In the cumulative record in Figure 11.8b, the rat is bar pressing very rapidly in the initial portion of the record (perhaps the cue light in the box is on, and it signals that bar pressing produces food) but is hardly pressing at all in the second half (light off, perhaps).

The major publication for basic research in operant conditioning is the *Journal of the Experimental Analysis of Behavior* (*JEAB*), first published in 1958. These recent titles will give you a sense of what you might encounter there:

Contingency tracking during unsignalled delayed reinforcement. (Keely, Feola, & Lattal, 2007)

(a)

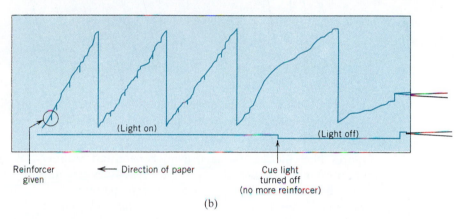

(Light on)   (Light off)

Reinforcer given   ← Direction of paper   Cue light turned off (no more reinforcer)

(b)

FIGURE 11.8   (a) The basic operation of a cumulative recorder (Courtesy Gerbrands Corporation), and (b) a hypothetical cumulative record showing both a high and a low rate of responding.

Resistance to extinction following variable-interval reinforcement: Reinforcer rate and amount (Shull & Grimes, 2006)

Effects of reinforcement history on response rate and response pattern in periodic reinforcement (López & Menez, 2005)

One of the topics you might recall from general psychology concerns so-called "schedules" of reinforcement. A schedule of reinforcement is a rule that determines the relationship between a sequence of behavioral responses and the specific occurrence of a reinforcer. This topic occupied a great deal of Skinner's time in the 1950s, resulting in the massive 739-page *Schedules of Reinforcement*, published in 1957 with a student of Skinner's, Charles Ferster (Ferster & Skinner, 1957). It provides a good illustration of basic research in the experimental analysis of behavior.

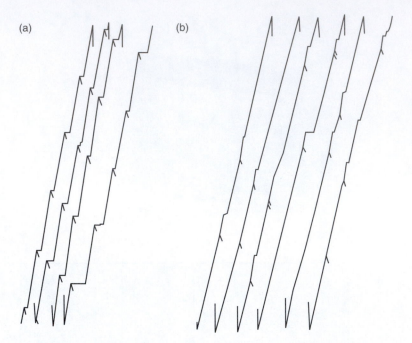

FIGURE 11.9   Cumulative records for (a) FR 200 and (b) VR 360 (from Ferster & Skinner, 1957)

Figures 11.9 and 11.10, taken from Ferster and Skinner (1957), illustrate two common categories of scheduling—ratio schedules and interval schedules. As you can see, different schedules produce different patterns of behavior. Figure 11.9.a shows several cumulative records for a *fixed ratio* schedule, in this case an FR 200. The rule in this case is that a fixed number of responses (in this case, with pigeons as subjects, the response is pecking at a small disk), 200 in this example, must occur before a reinforcer is delivered. Figure 11.9.b shows a *variable ratio* schedule (VR 360). Here the number of responses per reinforcer varies from one reinforcer to the next, with an average number of responses per reinforcer (in this case 360) defining

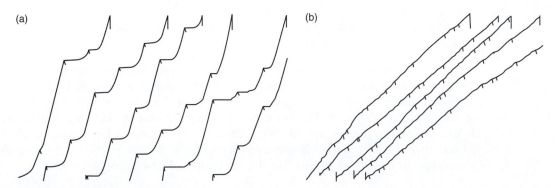

FIGURE 11.10   Cumulative records for (a) FI 4 and (b) VI 2 (from Ferster & Skinner, 1957)

the schedule—yes, pigeons did a lot of key pecking in Skinner's lab, they worked very hard for minimal payoff, and were never able to organize a union. In general, ratio schedules produce high rates of response, especially VR schedules (Skinner pointed out that slot machines are programmed on VR schedules). Figure 11.10 show the records for two versions of interval schedules, fixed and variable. In a *fixed interval* schedule (11.10.a), an FI 4 here, a fixed amount of time must pass (e.g., four minutes), and then the first response after the interval gets rewarded. In a *variable interval* schedule, (11.10.b), that time interval varies, but averages a certain amount of time, a VI 2 here. Interval schedules produce lower response rates than ratio schedules, and the FI schedule produces a telltale scalloping effect, as if the pigeons can keep track of the passage of time, learning that there is no point in key pecking until near the end of the interval.

These are just four examples of dozens of different schedules and schedule combinations studied by Ferster and Skinner (1957). One cannot help but be impressed by the effort here. As Skinner later described it,

> Thousands of hours of data meant thousands of feet of cumulative records. . . .We worked systematically. We would take a protocol and a batch of cumulative records, dictate an account of the experiment, select illustrative records, and cut and nest them in a few figures. In the end, we had more than 1,000 figures, 921 of which went into the book. (Skinner, 1984, p. 109)

Back in Chapter 1, I used Skinner to illustrate how researchers become passionate about their work. The schedules book is a good illustration. The book also exemplifies the small N logic—all of the cumulative records in the book show the behavior of individual pigeons; none show data summary graphs for an "average" pigeon.

Following upon the Ferster and Skinner (1957) book, a fair amount of the subsequent basic research in the experimental analysis of behavior concerned the scheduling of reinforcers. For example, a study by LeFrancois and Metzger (1993) examined how performance on an FI schedule would be affected by different types of prior schedules, for rats bar pressing in a Skinner box. The details need not concern us, but Figure 11.11, portraying the behavior of two different rats in the study, shows that an FI 43s (fixed interval of 43 seconds) can look very different, depending on what preceded it.[3] Skinner often talked about how our current behavior is affected by our "reinforcement history," and this study is a good illustration.

Applied Behavior Analysis

As the historian Laurence Smith (1992) has pointed out, a distinction can be made between two broad categories of scientist. Those representing the "contemplative ideal" focus on trying to understand the basic causes of events in the natural world, while those reflecting the "technological ideal" look for ways to use science to control and change the world. Skinner was firmly in the latter group. Although most of his own research was pure laboratory work, he was always interested in applying the results of an experimental analysis of behavior to real-world problems,

---

[3]The "DRL" in the record stands for **d**ifferential **r**einforcement of **l**ow rates, in this case a rule that a reinforced bar press would occur only if 20 seconds passed without a bar press occurring.

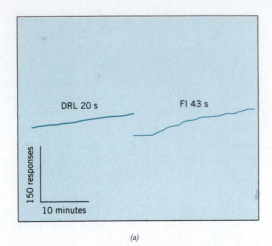
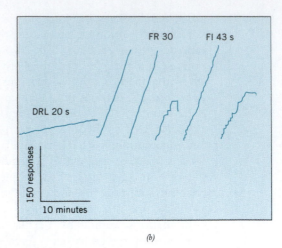

(a)   *(b)*

FIGURE 11.11 Cumulative records from rats experiencing either (a) DRL→FI or (b) DRL→FR→FI (from LeFrancois & Metzger, 1993).

and he made important contributions to education, industry, child rearing, and behavior therapy. His ideas even contributed directly to the NASA space program. On at least two space flights, chimpanzees were given complex operant tasks to learn while being sent into space. One psychologist involved in the space project stated that "[e]very technique, schedule, and programming and recording device we used then and subsequently can be traced to [Skinner] or his students" (Rohles, 1992).

Finally, Skinner was not shy about calling for the redesign of society based on operant conditioning principles, a recommendation that made him a controversial figure. To some, his prescriptions for improving the world seemed ominous, and he was accused of trying to turn everyone into rats or pigeons in Skinner boxes. This issue of control is elaborated in Box 11.2, and you should read it carefully and see if you agree with its conclusion before going on to the descriptions of how conditioning principles can be used to solve a variety of applied behavior problems.

Box 11.2

ETHICS—Controlling Human Behavior

Behaviorists typically describe their goals as the prediction and control of behavior. You might have felt a bit uneasy about "control" because it suggests a deliberate attempt to manipulate behavior, perhaps against a person's will. Because of this implication, behaviorists from Watson to Skinner have been accused of seeking dictatorial control via conditioning. For example, when "Cliff's Notes" summarized Skinner's *Walden Two,* a fictional account of a community established on operant principles, it compared the community to Orwell's nightmare world of *Nineteen Eighty-Four* (Todd & Morris, 1992). The perception of behaviorist as Big Brother overstates the case but is strengthened when one encounters chapters in Skinner's books with headings like "Designing a Culture" (1953) or superficially reads some of Skinner's statements, usually taken out of context.

The notion that one can and perhaps should act to alter behavior follows from the behaviorist's dictum that much of our behavior is conditioned by our learning history. If our experiences will shape behavior *anyway*, why not ensure that productive behaviors are shaped? This attitude is clearly reflected in two famous quotes. They both imply a more extreme environmentalism than their authors really believed, but each shows an almost mischievous willingness to make controversial statements. The first is John Watson's famous claim about child rearing:

> Give me a dozen healthy infants, well-formed and my own specified world to bring them up in and I'll guarantee to take any one at random and train him to become any type of specialist I might select—doctor, lawyer, artist, merchant-chief, and yes, even the beggarman and thief. (1924, p. 82)

The second quote is from Skinner's *Walden Two*. Through the voice of the community's founder and perhaps with Watson's quote in mind, Skinner wrote:

> "What remains to be done?" he said, his eyes flashing. "Well, what do you say to the design of personalities? Would that interest you? The control of temperament? Give me the specifications, and I'll give you the man!" (1948/1976, p. 274)

For Skinner, the controversy over behavior control was a nonissue. It is not a question of deciding whether to control behavior or not, he believed. Behavior *was* controlled by its consequences, period. Given that basic fact, he believed it followed that some effort should be made to create contingencies that would yield productive rather than nonproductive behaviors. Critics remained unconvinced and asked who would be the person deciding which behaviors should be shaped. Skinner believed his critics were missing the point.

One particular manifestation of the controversy over control exists in the clinical environment, where the applied behavior analysis procedures you are about to study have been quite successful in helping people. One especially controversial procedure has been the use of punishment, including electric shock, to alter the behavior of disturbed children. For example, in a study by Kushner (1970), a severely retarded 7-year-old child (mental age of 2) was treated with electric shock for hand biting. The child frequently bled after biting his hand and had suffered serious infections. Attempts to curb the behavior by having him wear boxing gloves or elbow splints failed. The treatment consisted of placing electrodes on the child's thigh and immediately shocking him every time his hand reached his mouth. The result was an almost immediate decline in the behavior that lasted even when the electrodes were removed.

When procedures like this are used in a study evaluating their effectiveness, has the ethical principle of not harming research participants been violated? Defenders of the use of punishment argue that other procedures often don't work with behaviors like self-biting or head banging. As long as appropriate safeguards are in place (e.g., other procedures have been tried unsuccessfully, genuine informed consent from parents or guardians has been obtained), the courts have upheld the use of shock "in extraordinary circumstances such as self-destructive behavior that [is] likely to inflict physical damage" (Kazdin, 1978, p. 352).

Researchers also contend that it is essential to investigate the procedures empirically. With the ultimate goal of finding the best way to help these terribly disturbed children, research evaluating the use of punishment seems to be not only justified but essential.

The applications side of the experimental analysis of behavior is sometimes called **applied behavior analysis**. It includes any procedure that uses behavioral, especially operant, principles to solve real-life problems. To get a sense of the range of environments in which these principles are used, consider the following titles from the *Journal of Applied Behavior Analysis* (or *JABA*), a journal founded in 1968, 10 years after the creation of *JEAB*:

Peer-Mediated Reinforcement Plus Prompting as Treatment for Off-Task Behavior in Children with Attention-Deficit Hyperactivity Disorder (Flood, Wilder, Flood, & Masuda, 2002)

A Single-Subject Approach to Evaluating Vehicle Safety Belt Reminders: Back to Basics (Berry & Geller, 1991)

Behavioral Treatment of Caffeinism: Reducing Excessive Coffee Drinking (Foxx & Rubinoff, 1979)

The designs that we'll be examining in the next section are most frequently applied to clinical settings, but as you can see from this list from *JABA*, the earlier mention of Skinner's applied work, and the designs that follow, operant principles are used in an assortment of circumstances.

✓ Self Test 11.1

1. Explain why the Dressler facial vision study is a good example of falsification thinking.
2. Explain how Thorndike's puzzle box research illustrates a parsimonious conclusion.
3. Those who do research in the experimental analysis of behavior use very small samples and typically don't calculate summary statistics. What strategy do they use instead?

Small *N* Designs in Applied Behavior Analysis

Near the end of their research report on fear conditioning in the Little Albert experiment, Watson and Rayner (1920) described several ways in which the fear might be removed. Although they never tried any of these on Little Albert, the attempt to reduce fear using behavioral methods was made a few years later in a pioneering study by Mary Cover Jones (1924). Taking a 34-month-old boy named Peter who was afraid of rabbits, Jones succeeded in eliminating the fear. Her strategy was to give Peter his favorite food while placing the rabbit at a distance from him and gradually moving the animal closer, a technique similar to modern-day "systematic desensitization" procedures.

Behavioral approaches to therapy did not immediately flourish following Jones's successful treatment of Peter, but they did become popular beginning in the 1950s and especially in the 1960s and 1970s. The impetus was provided by some additional demonstrations of the effectiveness of procedures based on learning principles, along with a developing skepticism of traditional approaches to therapy, especially those relying on Freudian methods (Eysenck, 1952). In the 1960s, several journals featuring behavioral approaches to therapy appeared, including *Behavior Research and Therapy* (1963) and the *Journal of Applied Behavior Analysis* (1968). From that point, research began to appear regularly that included designs attempting to demonstrate that a particular method produced a specific behavioral change in a single subject.

Elements of Single-Subject Designs

The essential logic of single-subject designs is quite simple. Because there are no control groups in these studies, the behavior of a single individual must be shown to change as a result of the treatment being applied and not as a result of some confounding factor. At a very minimum, this requires three elements. First, the target behavior must be operationally defined. It's not sufficient to say simply that an attempt will be made to reduce a child's disruptive classroom behavior. Rather, the behavior must be precisely defined in terms of easily recorded events, such as speaking out in class while someone else is already speaking, leaving one's chair without permission, and so on.

The second feature of any single-subject design is to establish a **baseline** level of responding. This means the behavior in question must be observed for a period of time prior to treatment to determine its typical frequency (i.e., normal rate of response, as Skinnerians would say). It is against this baseline level of responding that the effects of a treatment program can be assessed. The third element is to begin the treatment and continue to monitor the behavior. Congratulations if you've noticed that this sounds just like the logic of the interrupted time series design described in the previous chapter. In both cases, the goal is to be able to evaluate some treatment against an established baseline.

The simplest single-subject design is sometimes referred to as an **A–B design**, with A standing for baseline and B for treatment. The ideal outcome is for the behavior to change when A changes to B. From your knowledge of threats to internal validity, however, I suspect you may be thinking that the A–B design is a weak one. You're right. A change in behavior might be caused by the treatment, but it could also result from a variety of confounding factors, including history, maturation, and even regression. To reduce the viability of alternative explanations such as these, the withdrawal design was developed.

Withdrawal Designs

If a treatment goes into effect and behavior changes, but the change is due perhaps to maturation, then it is unlikely that the behavior will change back to its original form if the treatment is subsequently removed or withdrawn. However, if the treatment is withdrawn and the behavior does return to its baseline level, then it is likely that the behavior is being affected directly by the treatment and not by maturation. This is the logic behind the use of a **withdrawal design** (sometimes referred to as a "reversal" design), the simplest of which is an **A–B–A design**. As you might guess, this design begins just like the A–B design, but after the treatment has been in effect for a while, it is withdrawn (the second A).

If behavior changes correlate precisely with the introduction and removal of treatment, confidence is increased that the treatment is causing the change. That confidence is further strengthened if reintroducing the treatment brings about another change in behavior. For this reason, researchers prefer an **A–B–A–B design** over the A–B–A design. In effect, the treatment program is evaluated twice (replication again). The A–B–A–B design also has the ethical advantage of finishing the experiment with treatment in place. Its ideal outcome, for a behavior that begins with a high rate of occurrence and the goal of treatment is to reduce it (tantrums for example), is shown in Figure 11.12. Note that for the treatment to

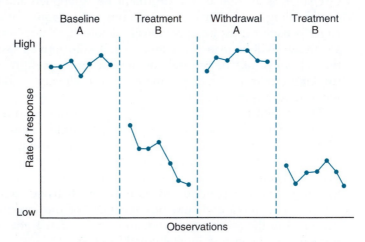

FIGURE 11.12   Ideal outcome of an A–B–A–B withdrawal design

be considered successful, the behavior must return to baseline (or close to it) after the withdrawal, and it must change again when treatment is reinstated. When this result occurs, it is difficult to interpret it in any way other than as the successful application of a treatment program. As an example of how this design is actually used, consider the following study of children with ADHD.

Research Example 33 — An A–B–A–B Design

When you think of attention deficit hyperactivity disorder (ADHD) and how it is treated, I imagine the first thing that comes to mind is medication, a frequent strategy for dealing with this difficult problem. Those in the applied behavior analysis business, however, first think of nonmedical approaches. A case in point is an ambitious attempt by Flood, Wilder, Flood, and Masuda (2002) to train the schoolmates of children with ADHD to help alter off-task behaviors when doing math problems. In keeping with the general small N philosophy, there were only three participants in this study (two boys and a girl), each studied intensively, and each with significant problems staying on task during school. Each was 10 years old, diagnosed with ADHD by their primary physicians, and not taking medication at the time of the study. "Off-task" behavior was operationally defined in the context of doing math problems as "looking away from the assigned task for 3 s[econds] or more (unless participants were counting on their fingers)" (p. 200). Trained observers hidden on the other side of a two-way mirror recorded these behaviors. To be sure that the observers recorded off-task behavior accurately, a second observer was present on 35% of the trials, and when this happened, agreement among observers was about 90%, which is considered good.

The treatment in the Flood et al. (2002) study was to have the each ADHD student paired with a non-ADHD student peer and to have the peer continually reinforce the ADHD student for on-task behavior (e.g., "Wow, we are going fast now," p. 201) and prompt the student when off-task behaviors occurred (e.g., "Let's get moving," p. 201). If the prompting did not get the ADHD subject back on task, the peer confederate "withdrew eye contact and verbal interaction" (p. 201) until the subject returned to the task. As in any A–B–A–B design, baseline was followed by treatment, a withdrawal of the treatment, and then the reintroduction of treatment. As you can see from Figure 11.13, which shows the results for the girl and one of the boys, the off-task behaviors clearly responded to the contingencies — off-task behaviors were quite frequent in the initial baseline, dropped dramatically during treatment, increased again during withdrawal (they labeled it a second "baseline"), and then dropped again during the second treatment period (the outcome for the other boy was essentially the same, but included some slightly different treatment contingencies). Of importance from an educational standpoint, in addition to the change in behavior, the children also solved more math problems during treatment sessions than during baseline sessions. On the other hand, one concern of the researchers was that the study took place in a laboratory environment, rather than a normal school setting, so the extent to which the results might generalize (external validity) to the classroom was not clear.

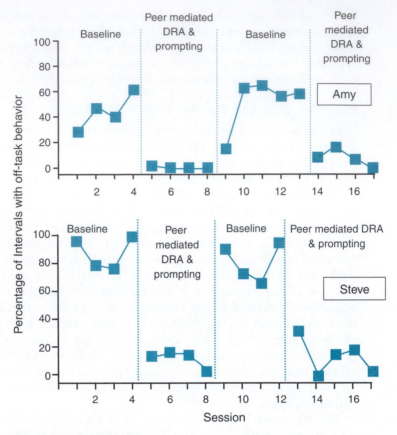

FIGURE 11.13　An A–B–A–B design used by Flood et al. (2002) to increase the on-task behavior of children with ADHD ("Amy" and "Steve")

Multiple Baseline Designs

Sometimes a withdrawal design simply isn't feasible. For example, if the treatment program involves teaching a particular skill, that skill will remain learned even if the program is terminated. That is, when the treatment is withdrawn, as in an A–B–A–B procedure, the behavior will not return to baseline but will remain high. A withdrawal design may also present ethical problems and/or practical ones, especially if the behavior being changed is self-destructive (Barlow, Nock, & Hersen, 2009). If the person being treated is a severely disturbed boy who is systematically banging his head against the wall, and an operant procedure manages to stop the behavior, withdrawing the procedure to see if the head banging resumes is difficult to justify. Also, because this type of research tends to occur in clinical settings, requiring the cooperation of clinical staff, there can be staff resistance to the idea of including the withdrawal of treatment, which might be seen by staff as going backwards ("We just got this behavior stopped and now you want to increase it again?"). Multiple baseline designs solve these types of practical and ethical difficulties.

In a **multiple baseline design**, baseline measures are established and then treatment is introduced *at different times*. There are three varieties. Multiple baselines can be established (a) for the same type of behavior in several individuals, (b) for several behaviors within the same individual, or (c) for the same behavior within the same individual, but in several different settings. There is no hard and fast rule about the number of baselines established per study, but three is considered a minimum (Barlow, Nock, & Hersen, 2009). The logic is the same in all cases. If the behavior is responding to the treatment program that is being examined in the study, then the behavior should change when the program is put into effect, and only then. So, if three different behaviors are being examined, and the treatment program is introduced for each behavior at three different times, then the behaviors should change only after the program is introduced for each, and not before. If all three behaviors change when the program is put into effect for the first behavior, then it is hard to attribute the behavior change to the program—the changes in all three behaviors might be the result of history, maturation, perhaps regression, or some other confound. In general, you can spot a multiple baseline study by looking for several graphs piled on top of each other, with a dotted line moving down from one curve to the next in a stepwise fashion.

The following Research Examples examine each form of the multiple baseline design: changing the same behavior in several individuals, changing several behaviors in the same individual, and changing the same behavior in several different settings. Research Example 35 makes it clear that single-subject research can extend well beyond the clinical environment.

Research Example 34—Multiple Baselines Across Subjects

This study, by Wagaman, Miltenberger, and Arndorfer (1993), illustrates the type of multiple baseline design that is conceptually identical to the strategy used by Dressler (1893) in his facial vision study. That is, this strategy examines the effect of some treatment program on one individual and then replicates it for several others at different times. The behavior in this case was stuttering, and the individuals were eight schoolchildren (six boys, two girls) ranging in age from 6 to 10. The treatment included a simplified form of a procedure called "regulated breathing," in which the children are taught to improve the way they coordinate speaking and breathing. The children were taught at home, and parents were also taught the technique. The program also included elements of social reinforcement (from parents) and awareness training, in which both parents and children were taught to identify every type of speech problem quickly.

This latter feature of the program brings into focus a question that may have occurred to you: How was stuttering defined? Obviously, a program to train full awareness of stuttering must begin with clear operational definitions of the phenomenon. Wagaman, Miltenberger, and Arndorfer (1993) developed specific criteria to identify four categories of stuttering: "(a) word repetitions, (b) part-word repetitions, (c) prolongation of a sound, and (d) blocking or hesitation before the completion of a word" (p. 55). To ensure the reliability of their measures, they tape-recorded all sessions and had multiple raters evaluate the tapes. Agreement among raters was high.

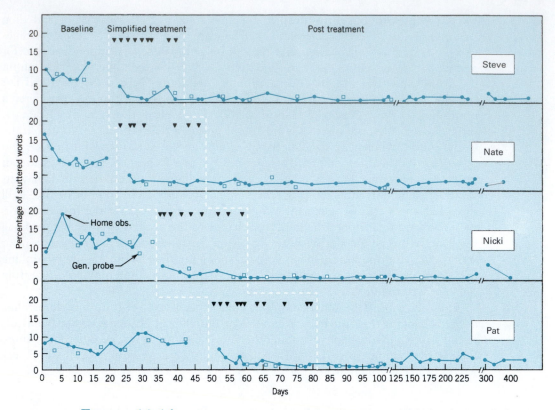

FIGURE 11.14 Decreasing stuttering behaviors in a multiple baseline study by Wagaman, Miltenberger, & Arndorfer (1993).

Figure 11.14 shows what happened for four of the children (curves for the other four were virtually identical). Several points are worth noting. First, as in all single-subject designs, the study began by establishing a baseline, multiple baselines in this case. Second, as is characteristic of multiple baseline studies, the treatment program began at different times. Third, the stuttering behavior for each child clearly responded to treatment, and only after treatment began.

If you count the tiny arrowheads above the treatment portions of the curves, you'll notice that they aren't equal. "Steve," for example, had nine treatment sessions, whereas "Nate" had just seven (the names are fictitious, of course). From what you learned in earlier chapters, you might be wondering if there is a control problem here. Shouldn't the number of training sessions be held constant? Keep in mind, however, that a key element in the philosophy of the small *N* approach is a focus on the individual. Wagaman et al. (1993) were more concerned with ensuring that each child reached a certain level of performance than with keeping the total number of sessions constant. Thus, training for each child continued until each child "consistently achieved the criterion level of stuttering (<3% stuttered words)" (p. 57).

Research in the small *N* tradition is sometimes criticized on the grounds that the results don't generalize beyond the experimental situation and there is a lack of follow-up. The Wagaman et al. (1993) study addressed both problems. First, notice that most of the points in Figure 11.14 are circles, but some are squares; one of them is labeled "gen. probe," for "generalization probe." These squares represent times when the researchers assessed the children's stuttering in the school setting. The circles ("home obs.") refer to sessions in the home. Clearly, even though the training took place at home, the results generalized to the school setting. Second, notice that an extensive follow-up (10 to 13 months) was done for each child, as indicated by the "post treatment" sections of Figure 11.14. Hence, the program not only worked in the short term; its effects lasted.

Research Example 35 — Multiple Baselines Across Behaviors

Ward and Carnes (2002) wished to determine if applied behavior analysis principles could be applied to behavior in a sport environment, in this case to the football field. Several studies had shown that athletic performance can be influenced by publicly posting various measures of behavior (e.g., posting lap times for improving performance of swimmers during team practices), and Ward and Carnes wished to see if the idea could be extended to the performance of linebackers on a football team, especially if performance goals were established by the players themselves. Five linebackers at an NCAA Division II college participated, selected by coaches because they had not performed very well in the prior year and were expected to play a great deal in the coming season that was about to begin. The study took place over that entire season, with measures taken during both practice and games.

Three important defensive behaviors were measured—reads, drops, and tackles, each with a specific operational definition. A "read" meant whether the player "positioned himself to cover a specified area on the field during a pass or . . . run" (Ward & Carnes, 2002, p. 2); a "drop" was whether the player "moved to the correct position described in the play book in response to the positioning of the offense" (p. 2); and a tackle meant stopping the offensive player's forward progress. Both practices and games were videotaped and the behaviors were scored from these tapes by coaches who were not directly involved with the linebackers and who "were not informed of the purpose of the study, the goals the players set, or the sequence of the interventions" (p. 3). That is, a double blind procedure was used. What made the design a multiple baseline is that after baseline measures for reads, drops, and tackles had been established, public posting of players' performance scores during practice occurred in a staggered sequence. That is, as you can see for the case of "John" in Figure 11.15, his performance on reads was the first to be posted publicly (in the locker room); after a period of about two weeks, performance scores for drops was added, and then, after another interval, tackles were added. As you can see, John's performance in all three areas improved right at the point when posting began, and essentially the same result occurred for the other four players. One point to note about the graph is that, while game data were not publicly posted for the players, game performance was plotted on the graph

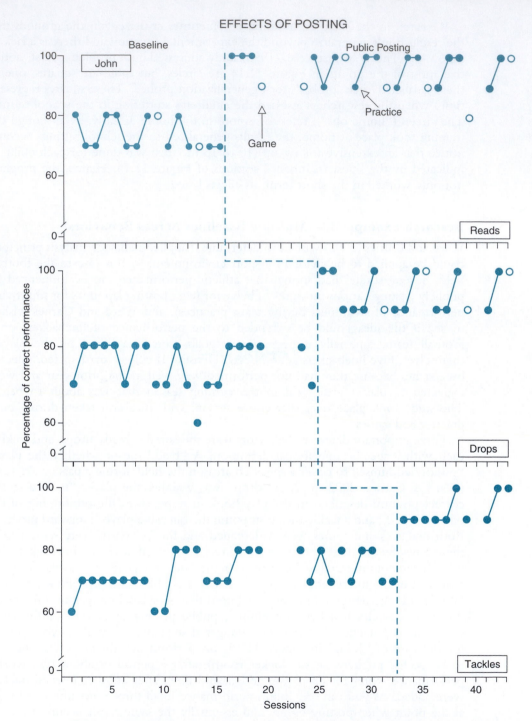

EFFECTS OF POSTING

FIGURE 11.15 A multiple baseline design changing three different linebacker behaviors in the same individual ("John") in a study by Ward and Carnes (2002).

(open circles), and John did quite well, except for one game when reads were a problem. Putting game data on the graph is, in essence, a test of external validity—the extent to which the intervention program (public posting) generalized beyond the practice field. So, linebacker play improved for this team. There was no indication about the effects of the improved linebacker behavior on the team's win–loss record, however.

Research Example 36—Multiple Baselines Across Settings

Kay, Harchik, & Luiselle (2006) used a multiple baseline across settings design to help a 17-year-old male ("George") with autism and mild retardation control a personal hygiene problem—drooling. He seemed unable to control the problem, it was having an adverse effect on his ability to perform in his school environment, and it was causing his peers to avoid him. As with any such research project, the first issue to resolve was exactly how to define the important terms, in this case "drooling." The operational definition chosen was to have an aide count "pools of saliva that were deposited on the surfaces of his immediate work environment" (p. 25). Only those pools that were at least an inch in diameter were counted. As soon as they appeared the aide would wipe them away without comment. As you can see from Figure 11.16, the dependent measure was the average number of pools of saliva per hour.

The treatment program was a combination of training and reinforcement. The training involved teaching George to respond correctly to the prompts "swallow" and "wipe your mouth" (with a tissue). In the intervention phase, the aide checked George every 5 minutes. If his chin was wet, she repeated the training prompts, getting him to swallow and/or wipe his chin. If George's chin was dry, she praised him and gave him a "small edible treat." Although you might think the treat would induce more drooling, it did not—George ate the treat immediately and the procedure actually strengthened his swallowing behavior and reduced drooling.

Baselines were established in three different settings—a classroom, a community vocational site, and a cooking class. Following the typical multiple baseline procedure, the intervention procedure was begun at a different time for each setting. As is clear from Figure 11.16, the intervention was successful, with George's drooling declining steadily after the intervention began in each setting. Furthermore, drooling remained at a low level when the check interval increased from 5 to 15 minutes and when they were eventually discontinued in two of the locations (the researchers maintained the 15 minute checks in the cooking class because of the "particular hygienic concern" [p. 27] there).

Two other methodological points can be made here. First, because some judgment was required about whether a saliva pool was large enough to meet the operational definition, the researchers had a second observer record the pools on 18% of the days of the study. Interobserver agreement (i.e., reliability of the measurement) was excellent, 96%. Second, because an aide was implementing the intervention program, it was important to ensure that the reinforcement contingencies were carried out correctly, thereby maintaining what researchers refer to as "intervention integrity." This was accomplished by the senior author (Kay), who observed the aide on 20% of the days of the study. The aide's accuracy in carrying out the procedures was judged to be virtually perfect, 98%.

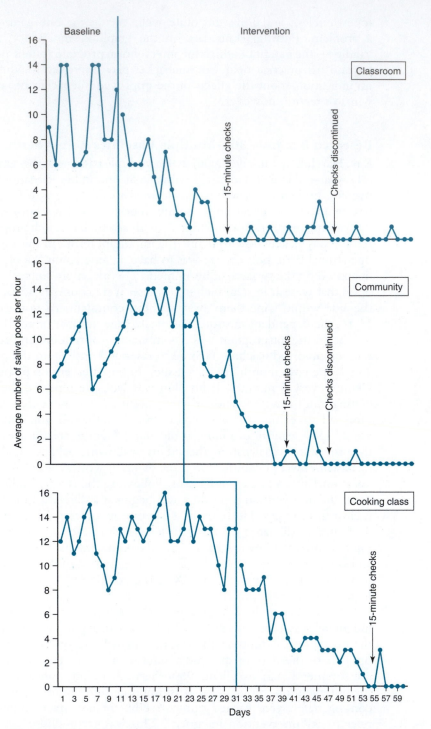

FIGURE 11.16 Data from a multiple baseline across settings study by Kay, Harchik, and Luiselle (2006), designed to eliminate drooling behavior.

Changing Criterion Designs

A third major type of single-subject design, in addition to withdrawal and multiple baseline designs, is called a **changing criterion design** (Hartman & Hall, 1976), a procedure inspired by the operant procedure of **shaping**, in which a behavior is developed by reinforcing gradual approximations to the final, desired behavior. In this design, the target behavior is too difficult for the person to accomplish all at once; it must be shaped in small increments. The procedure begins by establishing the usual baseline; then a treatment is begun and continued until some initial criterion has been reached. Then the criterion is made increasingly stringent until the final target behavior has been achieved. Health-related behaviors, such as developing exercise or diet programs, are perfect candidates for this type of design. For example, a study by Foxx and Rubinoff (1979) tackled the familiar problem of excessive caffeine consumption by introducing a changing criterion approach. For someone who drinks 15–20 cups of coffee a day, changing immediately to 1–2 cups is probably impossible (Are you starting to get a caffeine-withdrawal headache just thinking about it?). Reducing it step by step can be effective, however, especially when there are specific rewards for reaching a series of gradually more demanding criteria. In Research Example 37, the changing criterion approach was applied to another common problem, that of improving the physical conditioning of out-of-shape children.

Research Example 37—A Changing Criterion Design

It's no secret that "the battle of the bulge" is a major obsession for Americans. What is particularly troubling is the number of children with weight problems—by some estimates, as many as one in four children are obese (Gleitman, Fridlund, & Riesberg, 1999)[4] and, for many of them, a lack of exercise contributes significantly to the problem (and the finger exercises of video games don't count). In a nice example of a changing criterion design that also incorporated elements of the withdrawal design, DeLuca and Holborn (1992) set out to see if the exercise behaviors of three obese and three nonobese 11-year-old boys could be shaped. All of the exercise took place on a stationary bicycle, which was specially programmed to ring bells and flash lights to signal moments when reinforcers had been earned. The study began by establishing the usual baseline. For eight consecutive sessions, each boy was simply told to "exercise as long as you like" (p. 672). After an average baseline level of exercise was established, measured in terms of average cycle revolutions per minute, the first criterion was set at 15% above baseline level. Notice that in line with the small N philosophy of focusing on the individual, the first criterion (as well as all subsequent ones) was set not at the same level for all boys, but at a level that was determined with reference to each boy's starting point.

With the establishment of the first criterion, a variable ratio reinforcement schedule began. The boys were again told to exercise as long as they liked, but the bell would ring and the light would go on when they pedaled at a rate that was, on

---

[4]People whose weight is 20% (or more) higher than the average weight for others of their height are said to be obese.

average, 15% higher than their baseline rate. By getting the bell and light to work, they earned points that could accumulate, allowing them to earn valued prizes (e.g., comic books). After another eight sessions, the criterion increased by another 15%, and then increased once more. This was followed by a three-session withdrawal phase, during which the reinforcement contingencies were temporarily suspended. The study then ended with a return to the criterion level in effect just prior to the withdrawal. Figure 11.17 shows the results for four of the boys. Clearly, the level of exercise increased steadily for both the obese and the nonobese boys. Just as clear is the fact that the exercise levels dropped off without the reinforcement contingencies in effect (the withdrawal phase is labeled "BL," for baseline, in the graphs). Note that a possible weakness in the study is the absence of any follow-up data. As you might know from your own experiences with exercise programs, it is notoriously difficult to maintain them for any length of time. It would have been nice to find out if the effects of this operant approach were more lasting than is usually the case.

The DeLuca and Holborn (1992) study illustrates two other points about applied behavior analysis. First, it addresses the question of what constitutes a reinforcer—some boys might be willing to work for comic books, but others might not. To ensure that the boys would be working for outcomes of equal value, DeLuca and Holborn had them complete a "reinforcement survey" at the outset of the study, rating how much they liked certain things on a 10-point scale. Each boy then worked for reinforcers that were highly valued. Second, the researchers directly addressed what applied behavior analysts call **social validity** (Wolf, 1978). This type of validity refers to (a) whether a particular applied behavior analysis program has value for improving society, (b) whether its value is perceived as such by the study's participants, and (c) the extent to which the program is actually used by participants (Geller, 1991). DeLuca and Holborn (1992) assessed social validity by having each boy, his parents, and his homeroom and physical education teachers filled out a "social validation questionnaire" (p. 673), the results of which they described as "uniformly positive." Other indications of program success were anecdotal—all of the boys subsequently participated in track, each of the obese boys convinced his parents to buy him a new bicycle during the program, and all of the boys seemed distressed when the program ended. As previously mentioned, however, the results could have been strengthened with a follow-up 6 months or so later.

Other Designs

The A–B–A–B withdrawal, multiple baseline, and changing criterion designs are not the only ones used in applied behavior analysis. Depending on the problem at hand, many researchers combine elements of the main designs, modify the designs slightly, or create a new design. An example of a modification of the A–B–A–B design is called the **A–B–C–B design**. It is often used in situations in which the treatment program involves the use of contingent reinforcement. That is, during treatment (B), the target behavior is reinforced immediately after it occurs, and reinforcement occurs at no other time. During C, reinforcement is provided, but it is not made contingent on the target behavior. Thus, reinforcement is given

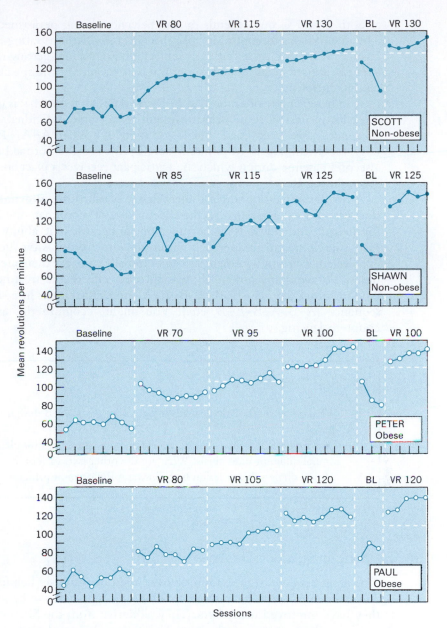

FIGURE 11.17 Data from a changing criterion design to increase the physical conditioning of obese and nonobese 11-year-old boys (from DeLuca & Holborn, 1992).

at both B and C but depends on the behaviors being performed only during B. The design helps to control for placebo effects by demonstrating that the behavior change occurs not just because the subject is pleased about getting reinforcers, happy about being attended to, and so on, but also because of the specific reinforcement contingencies.

Another example of a modified A–B–A–B design is one that is used in evaluating the effectiveness of some drug treatment for a single individual. Several different sequences have been used, but a common one is an **A–A$_1$–B–A$_1$–B design** (e.g., Liberman, Davis, Moon, & Moore 1973). A is the normal baseline, and A$_1$ is a second baseline during which the participant receives a placebo. The real drug is given during B.

A final example of a single-subject design is called the **alternating treatments design**, used when comparing the effectiveness of more than one type of treatment for the same individual. It has become popular because of its ability to evaluate more than a single treatment approach within the same study. After the usual baseline is established, different treatment strategies (usually two) are then alternated numerous times. To avoid any potentially biasing order effects, the treatments are given in random order (e.g., A–B–B–A–B–A–A, etc.) rather than in a simple alternating sequence (A–B–A–B–A–B, etc.). You might recognize this as an example of counterbalancing.

✓ Self Test 11.2

1. What is the methodological advantage of an A–B–A–B design over an A–B–A design?
2. In a multiple baseline design, one variety establishes multiple baselines across several different individuals. What are the other two varieties?
3. Which single subject design best illustrates the operant principle of shaping?

Evaluating Single-Subject Designs

The designs we've been examining have been enormously helpful in assessing the effectiveness of operant and other conditioning approaches to behavior change, and they have improved many lives. They all derive from the Skinner/Pavlov dictum that if conditions are precisely controlled, then orderly and predictable behavior will follow. They have been found to be effective in situations ranging from therapeutic behavior change in individuals to community behavior changes in littering. Small *N* behavioral designs are not without their critics, however.

The most frequent complaint concerns external validity, the extent to which results generalize beyond the specific conditions of the study. If a particular form of behavior therapy is found to be effective for a single individual in a specific situation (e.g., George and his drooling problem), how do we know the therapy is generally effective for other people with the same or a similar problem? Maybe there was something very unusual about the individual who participated in the study. Maybe treatment effects that occur in one setting won't generalize to another.

Advocates reply that generalization is indeed evaluated directly in some studies. The Wagaman et al. (1993) multiple baseline study that helped children overcome stuttering is a good example—the change in stuttering, trained in the home, generalized to the school. And the Ward and Carnes (2002) study examined whether improvement in practice generalized to game performance. Second, although conclusions from single-subject studies are certainly weak if the results aren't replicated, replication and extension are common features of this approach. For instance, the use of "differential attention" to shape behavior (i.e., parents attending to their child's desired behaviors and ignoring undesired behaviors) is now a well-established phenomenon, thanks to dozens of small *N* studies demonstrating its effectiveness for a variety of behaviors. Considering just the population of young children, for example, Barlow, Nock, and Hersen (2009) provided a list of 65 studies on the successful use of differential attention published between 1959 and 1978.

Proponents of single subject designs also point out that external validity is often just as much of a problem for large *N* designs as it is for small *N* designs. For example, a large *N* study on thinking and problem solving using just college students might yield results that would not apply to other, less verbally fluent groups. And as you might recall from Chapter 5's discussion of external validity, some researchers argue that internal validity is always more important than external validity, and small *N* studies tend to be strong in internal validity.

Single-subject designs are also criticized for not using statistical analyses but for relying instead on the mere visual inspection of the data. To some extent, this reflects a philosophical difference between those advocating large and small *N* designs. Defenders of small *N* designs argue that conclusions are drawn only when the effects are large enough to be obvious to anyone. In the multiple baseline study on drooling, for example, all that was reported was the graph (Figure 11.16) and some simple descriptive statistics (percentage of saliva pools during baseline and treatment). In recent years, however, statistical analyses have begun appearing in research reports of single-subject designs. For example, borrowing from program evaluation research, some studies have used time series analyses to separate treatment effects from trend effects (Junginger & Head, 1991). Time series analyses also help with the problem of relatively unstable baselines, which can make a visual inspection of a single-subject graph difficult to interpret. Statistical analyses are now regular features in the *Journal of the Experimental Analysis of Behavior*, traditionally the purest of the pure Skinnerian journals. One operant researcher lamented that in a survey of articles in the 1989 volume of this journal, he found that nearly one-third of the articles used inferential statistics in one form or another and that no more than 10% of the articles included cumulative records (Baron, 1990).

A third criticism of single-subject designs is that they cannot test adequately for interactive effects. As you recall from Chapter 8, one of the attractive features of the factorial design is its ability to identify the interactions between two or more independent variables. Interactive designs for small *N* studies exist, but they are cumbersome. For example, a study by Leitenberg, Agras, Thomson, and Wright (1968) used an A–B–BC–B–A–B–BC–B design to compare two therapy techniques (B and C) and their combination (BC) to help a subject overcome a knife phobia. Notice, however, that technique C never occurred by itself. This required a replication on a second participant, which took the form A–C–BC–C–A–C–BC–C.

One especially important interaction that you learned about in Chapter 8 can result from the P × E design, which includes both a subject (P) and a manipulated (E) variable. One type of P × E interaction occurs when the manipulated factor affects one type of person one way but affects others in a different way. The subject variables in P × E designs are, of course, between-subjects variables, but except for multiple baseline across subjects designs, single-subject designs are within-subjects designs. Thus, P × E interactions analogous to the one just described can be found only in single-subject designs through extensive and complicated replications in which it is found that (a) treatment 1 works well with person type 1 but not with person type 2, and (b) treatment 2 works well with person type 2 but not with person type 1.

A final criticism of small *N* designs in the operant tradition concerns their reliance on rate of response as the dependent variable. This approach seldom includes research using reaction times, whether or not a word is recalled correctly, amount of time spent looking (as in a habituation study), and a number of other dependent variables that shed important light on behavior. Response rate is certainly a crucial variable, but it is difficult to discount the value of the other measures.

Small *N* research is not confined to experimental analysis research and applied behavior analysis. Another small *N* research strategy involves studying individuals in great detail by developing case histories or case studies.

Case Study Designs

During the course of their long and happy (and busy) marriage, Charles and Emma Darwin had ten children. Like many parents, they were especially excited by their firstborn, a boy named William, and Dad began keeping highly detailed notes about his son's progress. He was motivated in part by his life's consuming passion—evolution, in particular the evolution of emotional expression—but he was also a bit like the modern father who winds up with four hundred hours of video on his first child and four hours for his second. Detailed diaries weren't kept for the remaining Darwin children (there were nine others). For William, though, Darwin recorded a wide range of behaviors in detail and eventually published a report called "A biographical sketch of an infant" (Darwin, 1877). He reported, for instance, that young William was able to visually track a candle at nine days and reliably produced what we now call the *rooting reflex*: "surface of warm hand placed to face seemed immediately to give wish of sucking" (quoted in Browne, 1995, p. 425). Darwin's account is a pioneering example of a procedure known as the case study method.

A **case study** in psychology normally refers to a detailed description and analysis of a single individual. The method is occasionally referred to as a "case history" because it involves a close analysis of the history of that person's life or a substantial portion of it. Because the description is typically in narrative form, this method is an example of qualitative research, although it is not uncommon for quantitative data to be included in the write-up. Case studies often include a variety of other methods. For instance, they might involve detailed interviews, both of the person under study and of others who know the person; systematic behavioral observations; psychometric (e.g., IQ test) and physiological (e.g., brain scan) measures; and the incorporation of archival data. In a famous early textbook on personality, Gordon Allport (1937) described a variety of research methods, and then finished with a description of the case study, which he considered the best way to understand the psychology of an individual. In his words,

> This method is logically the last in our series, for it is the most comprehensive of all, and lies closest to the initial starting point of common sense. It provides a framework within which the psychologist can place all his observations gathered by other methods; it is his final affirmation of the individuality and uniqueness of every personality. It is a completely synthetic method, the only one that is spacious enough to embrace all assembled facts. (p. 388)

The case study approach is common in clinical work, in which the case of someone with a particular mental disorder is used to illustrate the factors that lead to and influence the disorder and the methods of treatment for it. The most famous practitioner of this type of case study was Sigmund Freud, who built his personality theory on the basis of detailed case studies of his patients. In more recent years, our understanding of brain function has been enhanced by case studies of those with various types of brain damage, such as those described so eloquently by Oliver Sacks (e.g., *The Man Who Mistook His Wife for a Hat*, 1985).

Although case studies usually involve individuals, the term also applies to an analysis of a specific event that is unique in some way. For example, researchers have done case studies of how nearby residents reacted to a nuclear accident at Three Mile Island in Pennsylvania in 1979 (Aronson, 1999) and whether people retained accurate "flashbulb" memories of where they were and what they were doing when President Kennedy was assassinated in 1963 (Yarmen & Bull, 1978). In addition, case studies often have a broader meaning in disciplines other than psychology. For example, in sociology there are case studies of entire communities. A famous example is a 1949 study of adolescents in a small town in Illinois (Hollingshead, 1949). Case studies have also examined social groups (e.g., fraternities), worker groups (e.g., assembly line workers), and religious groups (e.g., Shakers).

Although case studies in psychology are normally associated with clinical psychology and neuropsychology, experimental psychologists have also completed them, and one of the best-known examples is Alexander Luria's fascinating account of a man who seemed unable to forget anything. This classic study is detailed in Box 11.3, and if you think that having a nearly perfect memory would solve many of your problems as a student, you'll have second thoughts after reading about "S."

Box 11.3

CLASSIC STUDIES — The Mind of a Mnemonist

Case histories often document lives that are classic examples of particular psychological types. In abnormal psychology, for example, the case study approach is often used to understand the dynamics of specific disorders by detailing typical examples of them. Case studies also can be useful in experimental psychology, however, shedding light on basic psychological phenomena. A classic example is the one compiled by Alexander Romanovich Luria (1902–1977), a Russian physiologist/psychologist famous for his studies of Russian soldiers brain-injured during World War II and for his work on the relationship between language and thought (Brennan, 1991).

The case involved one S. V. Sherashevsky, or "S.," as Luria referred to him, whose remarkable memory abilities gave him a career as a stage mnemonist (yes, people actually paid to watch him memorize things) but also caused him considerable distress. The case is summarized in Luria's *The Mind of a Mnemonist* (1968). Luria studied S. for more than 20 years, documenting both the range of S.'s memory and the accompanying problems of his being virtually unable to forget anything. Luria first discovered that there seemed to be no limit on how much information S. could memorize; more astonishing, the information did not seem to decay with the passage of time. He could easily memorize lists of up to 70 numbers and could recall them in either a forward or a reverse order. Also, "he had no difficulty reproducing any lengthy series . . . whatever, even though these had been presented to him a week, a year, or even many years earlier" (Luria, 1968, p. 12).

This is an unbelievable performance, especially considering that most people cannot recall more than seven or eight items on this type of task and that forgetting is the rule rather than the exception. As a student, you might be wondering what the downside to this could possibly be. After all, it would seem to be a wonderful "problem" to have, especially during final exam week.

Unfortunately, S.'s extraordinary memory skills were accompanied by severe deficits in other cognitive areas. For example, he found it almost impossible to read for comprehension. This was because every word evoked strong visual images from his memory and interfered with the overall organization of the idea conveyed by the sentence. Similarly, he was an ineffective problem solver, found it difficult to plan and organize his life, and was unable to think abstractly. The images associated with his remarkable memory interfered with everything else.

Is S. anything more than an idle curiosity, a bizarre once-in-a-lifetime person who doesn't really tell us anything about ourselves? No. He was indeed a very rare person, but the case sheds important light on normal memory. In particular, it provides a glimpse into the functional value of the limited capacity of short-term memory. We sometimes curse our inability to recall something we were thinking about just a few minutes before, but the case of S. shows that forgetting allows us to clear the mind of information that might be useless (e.g., there's no reason to memorize most of the phone numbers we look up) and enables us to concentrate our energy on more sophisticated cognitive tasks such as reading for comprehension. Because S. couldn't avoid remembering everything he encountered, he was unable to function at higher cognitive levels.

One final point. It turns out that S. was not a once-in-a-lifetime case. Another person ("VP") with a similarly remarkable memory was studied by the American psychologists Hunt and Love (1972). Oddly enough, VP grew up in a city in present-day Latvia that was just a short distance from the birthplace of Luria's S.

Evaluating Case Studies

Luria's case study of S. illustrates two strengths of the case study method. First, the method provides a level of detailed analysis not found in other research strategies. Second, although at first glance a case study of such a rare individual might seem to tell us little about ourselves, Luria was able to show that S., in fact, did indicate something important about the value of normal forgetting from short-term memory. Rare cases can shed light on normal behavior, if for no other reason than by contrast. Another strength of the method is that well-chosen cases can provide prototypical descriptions of certain types of individuals. Having a highly detailed "textbook" description of someone suffering from agoraphobia, for instance, gives clinicians a point of comparison for their own clients.

In relation to theory, case studies can provide inductive support for some theory, they can suggest hypotheses for further testing with other methods, and they can serve the purpose of falsification. Concerning the latter, you already know about one famous example, described in Box 3.3. Claims made about the math skills of the horse called Clever Hans were effectively falsified when Pfungst investigated the case.

Case studies also have some important limitations, however. For one thing, their very nature creates problems for experimental control—a case study of one won't have any control groups. Second, conclusions drawn on the basis of a single individual may not generalize; that is, there can be problems with external validity. A third problem is that ample opportunity exists for the theoretical biases of the researcher to color the case description. Is it so surprising to find unending discussions of unresolved Oedipal complexes and various other sexually based problems in case histories written by Freudians?[5] To illustrate, during a session using PsycINFO to find examples for this chapter, I encountered a study called "Ph.D. Envy: A Psychoanalytic Case Study" (Behr, 1992). It described the case

---

[5]Most historians believe that Freud's case histories were written in a way to support his already-existing biases about human nature (Kramer, 2006). That is, having clear in his mind what he thought should be happening with a patient, he looked for and emphasized any supporting evidence (a form of *confirmation bias*).

of a woman with a "profound and debilitating anxiety around not being able to finish her Ph.D. dissertation. . . . [Her] contempt for those without Ph.D.s and the intense envy of those who possessed them led to the psychical equivalence of Ph.D. envy and penis envy" (p. 99). Would her case be described differently by a non-Freudian? Almost certainly.

A fourth limitation of case study methods concerns memory. Participants in case studies of individuals are often required to recall events from the past, and the writers of case histories also have to rely on memories of their encounters with the object of the case. As researchers such as Elizabeth Loftus (1991) have shown repeatedly, memories for the events of our lives are often distorted by circumstances that intervene between the target event and the later recall of it. Take, for example, a New Orleans resident who experienced the devastating Hurricane Katrina in 2005. If asked to describe the experience as part of a case study a year later, some of the information would undoubtedly be accurate. After all, people are not likely to forget water filling the entire first floor of their house. However, during the intervening year, the person has (a) experienced the event; (b) seen endless videos, news stories, TV recreations, and photographs of the event; (c) listened to countless hurricane stories from friends and neighbors; and (d) probably dreamed of the event a few times. As Loftus and her research team have demonstrated (e.g., Loftus & Hoffman, 1989), our subsequent memories are often "constructions" of the event itself and of these later occurrences. That is, we now have a memory that incorporates many elements, only one of which is the event itself. Our memory is by no means a verbatim recording of events.

In sum, case studies are susceptible to biases, they lack control over extraneous variables, and their results may not generalize easily, but they can be useful in generating new research ideas, they can help falsify weak theories, and sometimes they might be the only way to document an extraordinary person or event.

✓ Self Test 11.3

1. Single-subject designs have sometimes been criticized on the grounds of external validity. What does this mean, and how do defenders respond?
2. The case of Clever Hans was described back in Chapter 3, but is used in this chapter to point to a strength of the case study method. Explain.

This chapter has introduced you to a tradition of research in psychology that concentrates on the individual rather than the group. It is an approach ideally suited for some circumstances, such as studying the effects of reinforcement contingencies on behavior and studying individuals in depth. The next chapter completes our analysis of research methods by examining two approaches that are primarily descriptive in nature—observational research and survey research.

Chapter Summary

Research in Psychology Began with Small *N*

Research in psychology's earliest years normally involved a small number of participants, no statistical summaries of data, and, because they had yet to be invented, no inferential statistical analyses. The additional participants served the purpose of replication. Dressler's facial vision study and Thorndike's research on cats escaping from puzzle boxes are good examples.

Reasons for Small *N* Designs

Individual-subject validity is the extent to which a general conclusion drawn from research with large *N* applies to the individual participants in the study. One reason for favoring small *N* designs is that when summarizing data for a large number of individuals, individual-subject validity can be weak. This occurs in some concept learning research, for instance, in which the summarized data imply gradual learning, but an examination of individual behavior implies a more rapid change in performance. Small *N* designs are also favored when studying participants from rare populations or when practical considerations (e.g., expense) make a large *N* design impossible.

The Experimental Analysis of Behavior

The philosophical basis for some small *N* research is the position taken by B. F. Skinner, who argued that if a researcher is able to establish sufficient control over environmental influences, then orderly behavior will occur and can be easily observed (i.e., without statistical analysis). In operant conditioning, behavior is influenced by its consequences and comes under the control of the environment in which it occurs. As a dependent variable, Skinner relied on rate of response. Most of Skinner's work was in basic research (e.g., schedules of reinforcement), but he was a strong advocate for the technological ideal—the practical application of operant principles and techniques to bring about societal change.

Small *N* Designs in Applied Behavior Analysis

Applied behavior analysis is the application of operant principles to improve behavior. Small *N* or single-subject designs are used to evaluate the effectiveness of these applied programs. All single-subject designs carefully define terms, establish baselines, and then apply some intervention technique to be evaluated. Withdrawal designs establish a baseline, apply a treatment, and then withdraw the treatment. If the behavior changes along with the changing conditions, it is assumed that the treatment was effective in altering the behavior. A–B–A–B designs are preferred over A–B–A designs because the study ends with the treatment in effect and the treatment is tested twice. Multiple baseline designs are often used when withdrawal designs are not feasible or ethical. Multiple baselines can be established for several individuals, several behaviors, or several environmental settings. Changing criterion designs are used when the target behavior must be shaped gradually (e.g., weight loss). Small *N* designs have been criticized for being unable to evaluate interactive effects, relying on a single dependent variable, and having limited external validity.

Case Study Designs

Most case studies are detailed analyses of the behavior of single individuals, although some case studies investigate unique events or identifiable groups. They formed the basis for Freud's theories and are often used in a clinical setting to study individuals with various disorders, or the analysis of people with rare attributes (e.g., the memory abilities of S.). They can be useful sources of information and can serve to falsify claims and generate hypotheses for further research, but they are subject to the biases of the investigator, memory failures, and lack of generalizability (external validity).

Chapter Review Questions

1. Describe Dressler's facial vision study and how the results were presented, and explain why he used three participants instead of just one.

2. Explain why Thorndike's research is a good illustration of the principle of parsimony.

3. Explain what is meant by the concept of individual-subject validity.

4. Use the behavior of a rat bar pressing in a Skinner box to illustrate Skinner's claim that behavior can be predicted and controlled if three main factors are known.

5. Skinner's work is said to reflect the "technological ideal." Explain.

6. Describe the three essential elements of every single-subject design.

7. Describe the essential features of a withdrawal design, and distinguish between these designs: A–B–A, A–B–A–B, A–B–C–B.

8. Define a multiple baseline design, explain when it is preferred over a withdrawal design, and describe three varieties.

9. Use the Research Example on exercising for obese and nonobese boys as a way of describing the main features of a changing criterion design. Be sure to work the term "shaping" into your answer.

10. Describe any three ways in which single-subject designs have been criticized. How do advocates for these designs respond?

11. Define the case study method and describe its strengths and limitations.

12. The case study of a very rare individual can also shed light on normal processes. How does the case of "S." illustrate this point?

Applications Exercises

Exercise 11.1   Designing Self-Improvement Programs

Design a changing criterion program for one of the following self-improvement projects. For each project, be sure to define the target behavior(s) operationally, identify what you would use as reinforcement, and indicate what each successive criterion would be.

1. Increase productive study time.
2. Develop an exercise program.
3. Change to healthier eating behaviors.
4. Improve time management.

Exercise 11.2   Hypothetical Outcomes of Applied Behavior Analyses

For each of the following, sketch hypothetical graphs in the single-subject style that illustrate each of the alternative outcomes.

1. A–B–C–B design:

   a. Reinforcement works, but only if it is made contingent on specific behaviors.

   b. Reinforcement works regardless of whether or not it is made contingent on specific behaviors.

2. A–A_1–B–A_1–B design:

   a. The drug worked.

   b. One cannot tell if the drug worked or not; could have been a placebo effect.

3. Multiple baseline across three settings:

   a. The treatment program works.

   b. One cannot discount a history or maturation effect.

4. A–B–A–B design

   a. The treatment program works.

   b. It is hard to tell if the program brought about the change or if some other factor such as maturation was responsible.

Exercise 11.3   Depicting the Results of Applied Behavior Analyses

For each of the following descriptions and data sets, prepare a graph in the single-subject style that would accurately portray the results. Write a brief conclusion.

1. An A–B–A–B design was used to reduce the number of interruptions made in class by a child whose behavior was disrupting his second-grade class. During treatment, the teacher was instructed to ignore the child's interruptions and to pay special attention to the child when he was behaving productively (e.g., doing class work). The number of interruptions per 1-hour recording session were as follows:

    a.   During first A: 12, 12, 7, 6, 6, 9, 8, 10, 9, 11
    b.   During first B: 9, 8, 9, 4, 3, 2, 2, 1, 4, 2
    c.   During second A: 4, 5, 10, 6, 12, 10, 10, 10, 12, 9
    d.   During second B: 9, 9, 2, 1, 1, 1, 0, 3, 4, 1

2. A multiple baseline across persons design was used to improve the foul shooting percentage of three basketball players during practices. A system was used in which successful shots earned points that could later be used to obtain more substantial reinforcers. Each of the following numbers represents the number of foul shots made for each 50 attempted. The numbers that are underlined are baseline data.

    Player 1: <u>32, 29, 38, 31, 33,</u> 44, 36, 37, 44, 41, 40, 38, 45, 42, 40, 44
    Player 2: <u>30, 32, 28, 30, 30, 40, 35, 32, 33,</u> 38, 40, 45, 44, 44, 42, 44
    Player 3: <u>22, 28, 29, 28, 26, 25, 22, 26, 21, 21, 23, 24,</u> 35, 39, 40, 39

Answers to Self Tests:

✓ **11.1.**
1. By plugging their ears, Dresslar and his colleagues were able to rule out the idea that facial vision involved a special sensory process.
2. Thorndike's trial and error explanation for his cats' behavior was more parsimonious than an explanation attributing rational thought to the cats.
3. They portray the data for each participant, with the additional participants serving the purpose of replication.

✓ **11.2.**
1. The treatment program (B) is tried not just once but twice (replication occurs).
2. There can also be multiple baselines for different behaviors and for different environments or settings.
3. Changing criterion design

✓ **11.3.**

1. Some have argued that results from single-subject designs do not generalize beyond the specific situation of the study. Defenders respond that there have been studies that directly test for generalization (e.g., the study on stuttering).

2. A case study can serve the cause of falsification. In the Clever Hans case, the idea that the horse had high-level mathematical skills was falsified.

CHAPTER 12

Observational and Survey Research Methods

Preview & Chapter Objectives

In this final chapter, we will examine two general methods for doing research in psychology that are primarily descriptive in nature—observational research and survey research. Although observations and survey data can be involved in other methods, the major purpose of observational and survey research is to provide accurate descriptions of behavior and mental processes and of the interrelationships among individuals and their environments. They often rely on qualitative analysis of the phenomena being studied, but they can include sophisticated quantitative analysis as well. They can be a rich source of ideas for further research using other methods. When you finish this chapter, you should be able to:

- Distinguish between naturalistic participant and observation methods.

- Articulate the problems that can occur in observational research (control, bias, reactivity, and ethics) and how researchers address those problems.

- Explain why sampling issues are more relevant for survey research than for most other research in psychology.
- Distinguish between probability and nonprobability sampling.
- Describe three varieties of probability sampling and know when each is used.
- Describe four different types of survey research and list the advantages and disadvantages of each.
- Articulate the principles of good survey construction.
- Explain the problems (e.g., social desirability bias, item wording) that can make it difficult to interpret survey data.

As you can tell from the overall structure of this text, center stage has been occupied by the experimental method. It was the direct focus of attention in Chapters 5 through 8, and the earlier chapters, especially the Chapter 3 section on theory, led up to it. As you recall, the starring role for the experiment derives from its potential to yield cause-and-effect conclusions, at least within the constraints of the way in which research psychologists view causality (refer back to Chapter 1). In the last three chapters, you have encountered methods that some might relegate to supporting role status because the conclusions drawn from them can be weaker than those drawn from experiments. However, we've seen that while drawing strong conclusions from correlational, quasi-experimental, and small N studies can be problematic, these methods are essential if we are to understand behavior fully. The same can be said about the two methodological strategies you're about to encounter in this closing chapter. They each have weaknesses, but they are indispensable members of the cast.

Observational Research

As you know from the discussion of psychology's goals in Chapter 1, behavior cannot be predicted, explained, or controlled unless it is first described accurately. The major purpose of observational research is to contribute this descriptive information; these studies provide in-depth accounts of individuals or groups of individuals as they behave naturally in some specific setting.

Varieties of Observational Research

Observational research with the goal of describing behavior can be divided into two broad categories, depending on the degree of experimenter involvement with participants. Sometimes the researcher does not interact in any substantial way with the group being observed, while at other times the researcher is directly involved with the group being studied and might even become a member of it. These types of studies are called "naturalistic observation" and "participant observation," respectively, and I will elaborate on them shortly.

Observational research can also vary in two other ways. First, observational studies vary in terms of the number of different behaviors being observed. Some studies are more global, observing a variety of behaviors, while others focus on some specific behavior. The wide-ranging studies of chimpanzee behavior by Jane Goodall (1990) illustrate the former strategy. An example of the latter strategy is a study by O'Brien, Walley, Anderson-Smith, and Drabman (1982), who observed the specific behavior of "snack selection" by obese and nonobese children at a movie theater. Second, researchers impose varying degrees of structure on the setting being observed. This can range from "zero," when the researcher simply enters some environment and observes behavior without trying to influence it in any way, to "quite a bit," when the researcher creates or identifies a structured setting and observes what occurs in it. The two Research Examples that you will read about in a few minutes illustrate different levels of imposed structure on an observational study. First, let's examine the two main forms of observational study more closely, and examine some of the challenges posed by observational research in general.

Naturalistic Observation

In a **naturalistic observation** study, the goal is to study the behaviors of people or animals as they act in their everyday environments. Settings for naturalistic observation studies range from preschools to malls to the African rain forest, and the individuals observed have included humans of all ages and animals of virtually every species. In some cases, semi-artificial environments are sufficiently "natural" for the research to be considered a naturalistic observation. Studying animal behavior in modern zoos, which often simulate the animals' normal environment to a considerable degree, is an example.

In order for the researcher to feel confident that the behavior being observed is "natural," it is important for the behavior to be unaffected by the experimenter's presence. There are two strategies for accomplishing this. First, in some naturalistic studies the observer is hidden from those being observed. In a study of sharing behavior among preschoolers, for example, observers may be in the next room, viewing the children through a one-way mirror (the observers can see through it; to the child it appears to be a mirror). In a mall, an observer studying the mating rituals of the suburban adolescent could simply sit on a bench in a strategic location and appear to be reading. In other studies, the observer may not be present at all; some naturalistic observation studies use video recorders. The videos are viewed later and scored for the behaviors being investigated.

In some naturalistic observations, especially those involving animals, it can be impossible for the observer to remain hidden—the animals quickly sense the presence of an outsider. Under these circumstances, the observer typically makes no attempt to hide. Rather, it is hoped that after a period of time, the animals will become so habituated to the observer that they will behave normally. With some species, the process can take quite a bit of time. When she first went to study chimpanzees in Tanganyika (now Tanzania), for instance, Jane Goodall (Figure 12.1) had to wait three months before the chimps would let her observe them from a distance of 60 feet (Morell, 1995). After a few more months, they

FIGURE 12.1   Jane Goodall and friend (Kennan Ward/Corbis Images).

became even more accustomed to her. Louis Leakey, her mentor, wrote proudly to a colleague that she "has now had a Chimpanzee family sitting within ten feet of her, behaving in a normal fashion as though she was not there" (quoted in Morell, 1995, p. 249). This habituation strategy is also common to the field of anthropology, in which field workers spend long periods of time living among native members of remote cultures.

Participant Observation

Occasionally, researchers will join a group being observed, or at least make their presence known to the group, thus making the study a **participant observation**. The chief virtue of this strategy is its power to get the investigator as close to the action as possible. Being a participating member of the group can give the researcher firsthand insights that remain hidden to a more remote observer. In some cases, perhaps because a group is closed to outsiders and therefore not available for naturalistic observation (e.g., a college fraternity), participant observation might be the only option. Participant observation is a common technique of qualitative research, because the descriptions often involve a narrative analysis of the group being studied.

One of psychology's classic studies involved participant observation. In it, a small group of social psychologists joined a religious cult in order to examine the kinds of thinking that characterized its members. In particular, they examined this empirical question: If you publicly prophesize the end of the world and the world fails to end, how do you deal with your failed prophecy? The answer was surprising enough to contribute to the development of one of social psychology's best-known theories—the theory of cognitive dissonance that you learned about in Chapter 3.

To learn more about this classic study of what happens when prophecy fails, read Box 12.1.

Box 12.1

CLASSIC STUDIES—When Prophecy Fails

One of social psychology's dominant theories in the 1960s and 1970s was the theory of cognitive dissonance, developed by Leon Festinger. As you recall from the Chapter 3 discussion of theory, this theory proposed that when we experience thoughts that contradict each other, we will be uncomfortable (i.e., we will experience cognitive dissonance) and we will be motivated to reduce the dissonance in some fashion, in order to return to a state of cognitive balance. One prediction derived from the theory is that if we exert a tremendous effort in some way and the outcome is not what we initially expected, we will need to convince ourselves that the effort was worthwhile anyway. Festinger got the chance to test the prediction after encountering a news story with the following headline (Festinger, Riecken, & Schachter, 1956, p. 30):

Prophecy from Planet. Clarion Call to City: Flee That Flood.
It'll Swamp Us on Dec. 21, Outer Space Tells Suburbanite

The story described how a certain Mrs. Keetch had predicted a flood that would destroy most of North America in late December. How did she know? She was in direct contact with aliens from a planet called Clarion who had been visiting Earth in their flying saucers and had seen fault lines that were about to rupture and open the floodgates. Mrs. Keetch gathered a small group of followers, in effect a religious cult, and they became devoted to convincing the world to repent of their sins before it was too late (and time was running out; the story appeared just four months before the predicted catastrophe).

Festinger guessed the flood would not occur, so he became interested in how Mrs. Keetch and the group would react during the aftermath of a failed prophecy. He decided to see firsthand. Over the next several weeks, along with two colleagues and five hired observers, Festinger joined the group as a participant observer. What transpired is described in a delightful book (Festinger et al., 1956) with the same title as this box. There are several points worth noting from a methodological standpoint.

First, recording the data created a number of problems. The observers did not want to reveal their true purpose, so they could hardly take notes during the meetings at Mrs. Keetch's house. Hence, they found it necessary to rely on memory more than they would have liked. The problem was overcome to some degree when they hit on the idea of using the bathroom as a place to write down as much of their narrative data as they could. A second problem was a concern about how the group's behavior might be influenced by their presence. At no point did they believe that the group knew their true purpose, but the researchers were very concerned that their presence strengthened certain of the group's beliefs. Because so many new people seemed to be joining the group over a short period of time, Mrs. Keetch believed (and therefore the group believed) that the mass joining was a "sign from above" that the flood prophecy was correct. Two of the observers were believed by the group to have been "'sent' by the Guardians" (Festinger et al., 1956, p. 242), the residents of Clarion, and one observer was actually believed to be *from* Clarion. Hence, the participant observers probably strengthened the convictions of Mrs. Keetch's small group, the effects of which are difficult to assess. This factor also posed an ethical dilemma. By strengthening the group's convictions, it could be argued that Festinger and his colleagues contributed to their "pathology."

As you know, because you're reading this now, the world didn't end that December 21 in the 1950s. It was not the only failed prophecy. Mrs. Keetch also told the group that the Guardians would send a space ship that would land in her backyard on December 17 to carry them to safety. Of course, the ship didn't arrive and the world didn't end four days later. Did the group become discouraged, give up, call Mrs. Keetch insane, and return to their normal lives? No. In fact, most of them became even *more* vigorous in their proselytizing, at least for a time. Apparently, in order to justify their efforts, they convinced themselves that their work had prevented the catastrophe—the group "spread so much light that God had saved the world from destruction" (p. 169). Hence, rather than quitting after a prophecy fails, one may find that his or her commitment can actually be strengthened. More generally, Festinger concluded that when we expend great effort, dissonance is produced, and we feel internal pressure to convince ourselves that the effort was worthwhile.

YESTERDAY IN THIS SPACE I PREDICTED THAT THE WORLD WOULD COME TO AN END. IT DID NOT, HOWEVER. I REGRET ANY INCONVENIENCE THIS MAY HAVE CAUSED.

©The New Yorker Collection 1995 Mick Stevens from cartoonbank.com. All Rights Reserved.

FIGURE 12.2 Based on Festinger's study, this is an unlikely result of a failed prophecy (© The New Yorker Collection 1995 Mick Stevens from cartoonbank. com. All Rights Reserved).

Challenges Facing Observational Methods

The researcher using observational methods must be prepared to counter several problems, including the absence of control, the possibilities of observer bias and reactivity, and the ethical dilemmas associated with the issues of privacy and consent.

Absence of Control

Some degree of control occurs in observational studies that are structured (see Research Example 39), but in general, the observational researcher must take what circumstances provide. Because of this lack of control, the conclusions from observational studies must be drawn very carefully. If an observer records that child A picks up a toy and shortly thereafter child B picks up a duplicate of the same toy, does it mean that B is imitating A? Perhaps, but other interpretations are possible, the most obvious one being that the toy is simply attractive. When reading accounts of observational research, you won't encounter sentences like "X caused Y to occur."

Despite the lack of control, observational research can be a rich source of ideas for further study and it can sometimes serve the purpose of falsification, an important strategy for theory testing. An observation consistent with theoretical expectations provides useful inductive support, but an observation that contradicts a theory is even more informative. One contradiction won't disprove a theory, as you recall from Chapter 3, but it can call the theory into question. For example, an influential theory of animal aggression in the 1960s (Lorenz, 1966) held that fighting between members of the same species was hardly ever fatal to the combatants, except for humans. For years, those studying aggression argued over the reasons why human aggression seemed to be so different from and so much worse than animal aggression. However, explaining the difference presupposes that the difference truly exists. Goodall's research, however, raised serious questions about the alleged nonfatality of animal aggression. In conflicts over territory among chimpanzees, for example, something analogous to "border wars" occurs (Goodall, 1978). If a lone chimp from one group encounters several chimps from another group, the lone chimp will almost certainly be attacked and is likely to be killed. Such a finding raises serious questions about Lorenz's claim that nonhuman aggression is seldom if ever fatal.

In a more recent example, Boesch–Achermann and Boesch (1993) observed several instances of parent chimpanzees teaching their offspring how to use tools (a hammer/anvil operation) to open several varieties of nuts. This is an important finding that questioned earlier beliefs. As the researchers put it:

> Recent critical reviews of animal learning processes have denied that animals have the ability to imitate, but the teaching instances we observed would have no functional role if the chimpanzees did not have an imitative capacity. Many people still consider pedagogy one of the uniquely human attributes; our observations of chimpanzees indicate otherwise. (p. 20)

Despite control difficulties, observational research can provide important and useful information. It can call some ideas into question, and it can also suggest hypotheses for further study. Hence, the Boesch–Achermann and Boesch study questioned prior claims about the teaching abilities of chimps, but the study could also lead to further research on the teaching capacities of nonhuman primates. For instance, could chimpanzees in captivity that have learned an operant task teach it to their offspring?

Observer Bias

A second problem for those doing observational research comes in the form of experimenter bias. In Chapter 6, you learned that when experimenters expect certain outcomes to occur, they might act in ways that could bring about such a result. In observational research, **observer bias** means having preconceived ideas about what will be observed and having those ideas color one's observations. For example, consider what might happen if someone is studying aggression in preschoolers and believes from the outset that little boys will be more aggressive than little girls. For that observer, the exact same ambiguous behavior could be scored as aggressive if a boy did it but not aggressive if performed by a girl. Similarly, in an animal study, observers with different beliefs about whether animals can be altruistic might interpret certain ambiguous behaviors differently. Biasing can also occur because observational studies can potentially collect huge amounts of information. Deciding what to observe invariably involves reducing this information to a manageable size, and the choices about what to select and what to omit can be affected by preconceived beliefs.

Biasing effects can be reduced by using good operational definitions and by giving observers some training in identifying the precisely defined target behaviors. When actually making the observations, **behavior checklists** are normally used. These are lists of predefined behaviors that observers are trained to spot. Consider, for example, the care taken in a study that observed the behavior of pizza deliverers, whose driving accident rate is three times the national average. Ludwig and Geller (1997) used a checklist "developed over a decade of driver observations and over 2 years of observing pizza deliverers" (p. 254). Part of the list included observations of driver behavior while turning onto a main road from an intersection near the pizza shop. There was a stop sign there, and the behaviors were placed into three categories: a complete stop, a "slow rolling advance," and a "fast rolling advance." Each had its own definition; for instance, the slow rolling advance was defined as when the vehicle moved through the stop sign at "approximately the walking speed of an adult" (p. 255). Observers also recorded oncoming traffic conditions, whether the driver used a directional signal, and whether the driver wore a seat belt.

In addition to defining behaviors with some precision, another way to control for observer bias is to have several observers present and see if their records match. This you might recognize as a form of reliability; in this case it is called **interobserver reliability**, usually measured in terms of the percentage of times that observers agree.[1] Of course, both observers could be biased in exactly the same way, but a combination of checklists, observer training, and agreement among

---

[1] Interobserver reliability is not limited to observational research. As you might recall, you have already encountered the concept several times in this book, in the discussion of using intraclass correlations in Chapter 9's Research Example 24, and in Research Examples 33, 34, and 36 in Chapter 11.

several observers generally controls bias. Bias also can be reduced to the extent that procedures are mechanized. We've already seen that videotaping increases the opportunity for objectivity.

Finally, bias can be reduced by introducing various sampling procedures for systematically selecting a subset of the available information for observation and analysis. For example, a procedure called **time sampling** is sometimes used in observational studies. Rather than trying to maintain a continuous record of everything occurring, behavior is sampled at predefined times and only at those times. These times can be selected according to some rule or they may be randomly selected. Similarly, **event sampling** selects only a specific set of events for observation; others are ignored.

Participant Reactivity

Think about all of the things you do in a typical day. Would you do them all in exactly the same way if you knew you were being observed? Probably not. In all likelihood, you would show **reactivity;** that is, your behavior would be influenced by the knowledge that it was being observed and recorded. Obviously, this problem can occur in observational research and is the reason for the popularity of devices like two-way mirrors. The problem also exists when animals are the subjects of observation and the observers cannot hide. As mentioned earlier, researchers assume that after a period of time the animals will become accustomed to the presence of outsiders, but it is difficult to evaluate the extent to which this occurs. Reactivity can be a special problem for participant observation, in which the observers are involved in the group activities. As you recall from the Festinger prophecy study, the researchers were quite concerned about how their presence might affect the group's behavior.

Reactivity can be reduced by using **unobtrusive measures**. These are any measures taken of behavior, either directly or indirectly, when the subject is unaware of the measurement being made. Direct unobtrusive measures include hidden video or audio recordings or behavior samples collected by hidden observers. Indirect unobtrusive measures record events and outcomes that one assumes have resulted from certain behaviors even though the behaviors themselves have not been observed. Webb, Campbell, Schwartz, Sechrest, and Grove (1981) describe a number of indirect measures, and they can be quite creative. Here's just a sample:

- contents of trash to study eating and drinking habits
- accumulation of dust on library books as an indication of usage
- degree of wear on floor coverings placed in strategic locations to study foot traffic
- analysis of political bumper stickers in an election year

You might also recall from Chapter 10 that one of the strengths of using archival data is that reactivity is avoided.

Ethics

As I am sure you have recognized by now, reducing reactivity raises the ethical problems of invading privacy and lack of informed consent. Wouldn't you be a bit disturbed to discover that researchers were hiding under the bed in your dorm, keeping track of everything you said and did? Believe it or not, that study has already been done, although quite clearly it would not gain IRB approval today. In a 1938 study by Henle and Hubbell, designed to classify conservational speech into "ego-related, social, and object-related" categories (p. 228), the researchers "concealed themselves under beds in students' rooms where tea parties were being held, eavesdropped in dormitory smoking-rooms and dormitory wash-rooms and listened to telephone conversation" (p. 230).

In Box 3.1, I pointed out that some researchers are hesitant to conduct research in the field because of concerns over privacy rights. However, the APA ethics code (see Standard 8.05 in Appendix B) condones the use of naturalistic observation and does not require informed consent or debriefing, provided that certain safeguards are in place. For example, informed consent of participants is not considered essential if behavior is studied in public environments (as opposed to the privacy of one's dorm room), people are not interfered with in any way, and strict confidentiality and anonymity are maintained.

But what about participant observation? You might have been concerned about the lack of consent in Festinger's failed prophecy study (Box 12.1). With good reason, Festinger believed that he and his colleagues would never have been able to join the group if normal consent procedures had been followed, but there is some question about whether an IRB would approve such a study today. Participant observation is a common method among those doing qualitative research, and informed consent of the group being observed from within is now routine and its absence requires a strong justification (Taylor & Bogdan, 1998). Analogous to the habituation rationale for naturalistic observation, it is assumed that even if group members know they are being observed, they will eventually get used to the participant observer and behave naturally. Reality TV shows are based on the same assumption.

To conclude this section on observational research, consider the following two observational studies that illustrate different levels of structure created by the researcher. The first is purely observational, without any direct intervention on the part of the researchers, while the second is highly structured for a specific reason.

Research Example 38—A Naturalistic Observation

School-aged boys generally outperform girls in science, and there is evidence that part of the reason derives from how they are treated by teachers, who seem to expect boys to do better (there are exceptions, of course), and consequently tend to encourage boys in a number of subtle ways (e.g., by responding more completely to science questions from boys). This is disturbing enough, but a study by Crowley, Callahan, Tenenbaum, and Allen (2001) suggests that the differential treatment can begin earlier than the school years and as a part of typical family life. They observed the behavior of parents and their children (both boys and girls) in a science museum and a quick look at Figure 12.3 tells you that big differences occurred. The study also reveals some of the methodological decisions that must be made when doing observational research.

Crowley et al. (2001) set up video cameras and microphones at eighteen different interactive science exhibits in a California science museum. To assure a wide representation of families, they did the study over a 30-month period, included weekdays and weekends, and tested both during the school year and in the summer. Because the museum was a fairly controlled environment, the researchers were able to accomplish one task that is normally not feasible in naturalistic observation—they were able to obtain informed consent. As they entered the museum, families were told that researchers were videotaping activity in the museum (families weren't told that sex differences were being investigated); 90% of families agreed to participate and the children were given a sticker to wear that identified them by age and enabled researchers to identify them easily on the videos. All of the children were younger than 8, and most were under 5.

Crowley et al. (2001) used a form of event sampling. A trial was operationally defined as starting whenever

> the first child from a family—the *target child*—engaged an exhibit and ending when he or she disengaged. The next target child was the first child from a new family who engaged the exhibit after all members of the previous target child's family had disengaged. Thus, each interaction was a unique [event] capturing the complete engagement of a particular child at an exhibit (p. 259, italics in the original).

Trials occurred only if the child engaged the exhibit in the presence of at least one parent. The study included a final total of 351 independent trials.

In addition to defining trials, the researchers also had to develop a scheme to code the verbal interactions. They decided on three categories of parental comment—"explanations," "giving directions," and "talking about evidence" (Crowley et al., 2001, p. 259). For example, a comment that would be coded as an explanation might be something like this: " 'When you turn that fast, it makes more electricity' at an exhibit including a hand-cranked generator" (p. 259). Interobserver reliability was assessed by having more than one rater code the interactions on 20% of the trials; agreement occurred 86% of the time.

As for the results, boys and girls did not differ in terms of how much time they spent at exhibits or in the extent to which they actively engaged the exhibits (e.g., turned the crank at the electricity exhibit). What was very different, however, was the behavior of the parents, both Dads and Moms. Figure 12.3 shows the interactions during which parents gave explanation-type comments. Clearly, boys were much more likely to be given explanations. From the left-hand panel you can see that Dads were slightly worse than Moms, but both favored boys. The right-hand panel shows that the same pattern existed regardless of the age of the child.

As with any good study, Crowley et al. (2001) considered more than one explanation for their results. For example, perhaps the differences resulted from boys just asking more questions of their parents than girls did. Not so. In fact, very few of the explanations from parents were triggered by children's questions and no sex difference occurred in the number of questions asked. In the 60-second intervals prior to any parental explanation, only 15% of boys and 13% of girls asked

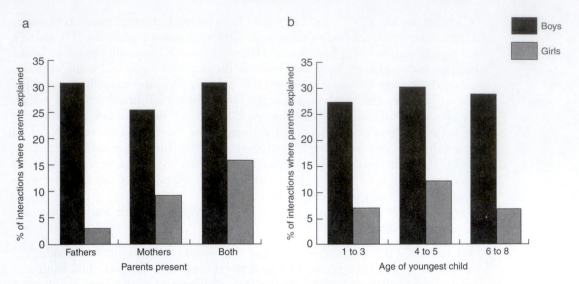

FIGURE 12.3 A substantial difference in how young boys and girls are treated by their parents in science museums, from Crowley et al. (2001).

questions. Hence, although the parents brought both boys and girls to the museum, they treated their children quite differently once there. The fact that differences occurred for children as young as 1–3 years suggests "that parents may be involved in creating gender bias in science learning years before children's first classroom science instruction" (p. 260). You are students now, but you could be parents some day. This study might be worth remembering, especially if you hope to raise a woman scientist.

Research Example 39—A Structured Observational Study

A study by Peterson, Ridley-Johnson, and Carter (1984) is an interesting example of an observational study that adds a structured element to a naturalistic observation. They were interested in helping behavior among school children, a phenomenon that was estimated from prior observations to occur spontaneously no more than once or twice per hour. Because it occurs so infrequently, the researchers decided to create a situation in which helping behavior would be more likely to occur. Thus, one important reason for introducing greater structure into an observational study is to increase the frequency of otherwise rare events.

The structure was created by telling the children they would each have a turn wearing a "supersuit," a "smock of royal blue with a red satin star in the middle of the chest" (Peterson et al., 1984, p. 237). It was fastened with one large button at the back of the neck; pilot testing showed that buttoning it usually required the help of a second person. During free play periods, children took turns wearing the suit, with the order determined by drawing names from a jar. Each child had about 4 minutes to wear the supersuit.

The observations were videotaped, and two observers independently rated the tapes for helping behavior. Interobserver reliability was high: They agreed more than 90% of the time. The coding scheme for defining the behaviors operationally broke them into two general categories: the "donor" behaviors exhibited by potential helpers and the "recipient" behaviors of those wearing the suit. An example of a donor behavior was "*spontaneous helping*—without any direct verbal or physical prompt, the donor offers verbally or physically to fasten the button on the supersuit" (p. 237; italics in the original). An example of a recipient behavior was "*requesting help*—recipient verbally asks for help . . . or approaches the donor, turns so the button at the back is toward the potential donor, and gestures toward it" (p. 238; italics in the original).

The results? Of 56 opportunities for help, spontaneous helping occurred 32 times and prompted helping occurred 13 times. More interesting, however, was the way in which recipients responded to being helped. Surprisingly, Peterson et al. (1984) found that children rarely reinforced others for helping. In fact, "more child recipients actually gave negative consequences (e.g., 'go away' and a shove in response to another child's attempt to help fasten the suit) than positive consequences for helping" (p. 238)! Also, very little reciprocal help (child A helps child B and child B subsequently helps child A) was observed.

The researchers also asked each child to rate the social competence of classmates, and it was determined that most of the helping was done by the most socially competent children. This rating procedure is an example of how an observational study can add elements of other methods. In this case, the added element involved a type of survey, which brings us to that topic.

✓ Self Test 12.1

1. In naturalistic observations of animals, it is usually impossible for observers to be "hidden" from the animals. What is the alternative strategy for reducing reactivity?
2. What is interobserver reliability and what is its purpose?
3. Which ethical problem, typical in observational research, was not a problem in the science museum study?

Survey Research

Survey research is based on the simple idea that if you want to find out what people think about some topic, just ask them. That is, a **survey** is a structured set of questions or statements given to a group of people to measure their attitudes, beliefs, values, or tendencies to act. Over the years, people have responded to surveys assessing everything from political preferences to favorite sexual activities. The method has been around for some time, as you can tell from Box 12.2.

Box 12.2

ORIGINS—Creating the "Questionary"

In his celebrated *Principles of Psychology*, psychology's most famous book, William James (1890/1950) included a chapter on methodology, in which his comments on the original form of survey research were a bit less than complimentary:

> Messrs. Darwin and Galton have set the example of circulars of questions sent out by the hundreds to those supposed able to reply. The custom has spread, and it will be well for us in the next generation if such circulars be not ranked among the common pests of life. (p. 194)

Sir Francis Galton (1822–1911) is normally credited with being the originator of the survey method, although a case can be made that his cousin, Charles Darwin (1809–1882), preceded him. Darwin developed a series of questions on emotional expressions that he distributed to colleagues in different countries (he met many of them during his around-the-world voyage in the 1830s). In what might be the first cross-cultural study, he attempted to determine if facial expressions of emotion were universal, an outcome that would strengthen his belief in the power of evolution. Here are two of the questions he included:

> Is astonishment expressed by the eyes and mouth being opened wide, and by the eyebrows being raised?
> Is contempt expressed by a slight protrusion of the lips and by turning up the nose, and with a slight expiration? (Darwin, 1872, pp. 15–16)

Darwin's correspondents answered yes to these and other questions, perhaps not surprising in light of the way they were worded. You'll soon be reading about "leading" questions. These are both good examples. On the basis of this and other research, Darwin developed an evolutionary theory of facial expressions of emotion. The emotional expression when we feel contempt, for instance, was said to have evolved from the fundamental reaction to bad smells (e.g., turning up the nose).

Galton used the same question-asking strategy and he employed it more often than his cousin. Through survey data, for example, he accumulated information from scientists about the origins of their interests in science, asking them, for instance, "How far do your scientific tastes appear innate?" (quoted from Forrest, 1974, p. 126). Their answers were generally "quite far"—they reported that they seemed to be interested in science for as long as they could recall. Ignoring the possibility that environmental influences (e.g., parental encouragement) could have contributed to their love of science, Galton used the replies to support his strong belief that intellectual ability was primarily innate. He summarized his work in *English Men of Science: Their Nature and Nurture* (Galton, 1874), notable for giving a label (nature-nurture) to an issue that continues to be debated today.

In the United States, the undisputed champion of the survey, which he called a "Questionary," was G. Stanley Hall, who is known in psychology's history as Mr. First (e.g., created the first true experimental lab in America at Johns Hopkins in 1883, began the first psychology journal in the United States in 1887, founded the APA in his study in 1892, and claimed, at least, to have earned the first Ph.D. in psychology in the United States). Hall developed what was called the "child study movement" in the 1880s, an educational effort to study children systematically and find the best ways to educate them. Part of his effort was to develop "questionaries" that were designed to uncover as much as possible about children. These were distributed to teachers, who, in turn, administered them to children. His first study, completed in the early 1880s, was designed to explore "The Contents of Children's Minds" (Hall, 1883/1948). Data were collected from 200 urban (Boston) children just beginning school, and the result was that the children didn't seem to know very much. For instance, 75.5% could not identify what season of the year it was, 87.5% didn't know what an island was, and 90.5% couldn't locate their ribs. Hall also found that children who had been reared in the country, and then moved to Boston, knew more than those reared in the city. This did not surprise Hall, a farm boy himself. Although today we might think that an urban environment would provide a richer variety of experiences and therefore an enhanced knowledge base, few people believed that in the 1880s. Hall was not alone in thinking that urban life stunted intellectual development, and with his characteristic penchant for overstatement, commented that a "few days in the country at this age has raised the level of many a city child's intelligence more than a term or two of school training could do without it" (pp. 261–262).

Survey methodology did not immediately gain respect in psychology. The attitude of William James is pretty clear from this box's opening quote, and his opinion was shared by others. E. B. Titchener, for example, a leading laboratory experimentalist, had this to say about Hall and his methods, in a letter to a colleague of Hall's:

> [Y]ou probably have no idea of the sort of contempt in which Hall's methods and the men trained solely by him are in general held in psychology.... Whenever his questionary papers get reviewed, they get slightingly reviewed. (Titchener, 1906)

Now Titchener tended to be critical of just about everyone, but the attitudes of James and Titchener reflect the fact that survey research only gradually gained acceptance as a legitimate methodological tool.

Unlike most of the methods described in this text, surveying usually requires careful attention to sampling procedures. This point requires some elaboration. For most of the research methods you've read about, the emphasis has been on establishing relationships between and among variables. From some of the research you have read about in this text, for instance, you know that researchers have been interested in such topics as the effects of (a) the movement of a room on children's balance, (b) closing time on perceived attractiveness, (c) coach effectiveness training on children's self-esteem, and (d) looming and self-efficacy on fear of spiders. For studies such as these, researchers naturally hope that the results will generalize beyond the people participating in them, but they assume that if the relationship studied is a powerful one, it will occur for most individuals, regardless of how they are chosen to participate in the study. Of course, whether this assumption turns out to be true depends on the normal processes of replication and extension discussed in several places in this book. So, in a study on the capacity limits of short-term memory in adults, it is not necessary to select a random sample—virtually any group of reasonably fluent adults will do. That is, for most research in psychology, it is sufficient to choose, as participants, what is known as a **convenience sample**. This is a group of individuals who meet the general requirements of the study and are recruited in a variety of ways. Often they are from the "subject pool"—general psychology students being asked to participate in a study or two. You learned about some of the ethical issues related to these pools in Box 5.3. Sometimes a specific type of person is recruited for the study, a convenience strategy that is called "purposive" sampling. For instance, when Stanley Milgram first recruited participants for his obedience studies, he placed ads in the local newspaper asking for volunteers. He deliberately (i.e., purposively) avoided using college students because he was concerned that they might be "too homogeneous a group.... [He] wanted a wide range of individuals drawn from a broad spectrum of class backgrounds" (Milgram, 1974, p. 14).

The Milgram study also illustrates a practical reason for using convenience samples. Recruiting participants for a study can sometimes be time-consuming and frustrating. Milgram could have tried a more sophisticated sampling approach (like the ones you are about to learn), but even if he had, and selected a sample from some larger group, there was no guarantee that the people he selected would be interested in participating in the study. It was simply more efficient to advertise widely and hope to get as many volunteers as possible.

Although convenience samples, combined with the normal processes of replication, are adequate for most research in psychology, they are generally inappropriate for survey research. This is because the goal of most survey research is different—the focus is not on examining relationships among variables; it is on developing an accurate description of the attitudes, beliefs, behavior tendencies, or values of a specifically defined group of people. Good surveys require a form of sampling called probability sampling.

Probability Sampling

This general strategy is used whenever the goal is to learn something specific about an identifiable group of individuals. As a group, those individuals are referred to as a **population**, and any subgroup of them is a **sample**. In **probability sampling**, each member of the population has some definable probability of being selected for the sample. Sometimes it is possible to study all members of a population. For example, if you wanted to learn the attitudes of all of the people in your experimental psychology class about the issue of animal experimentation and did not wish to generalize beyond that class, you could survey everyone in the class.

In this case, the size of the population would be the size of your class. As you might guess, however, the population of interest to a researcher is usually much too large for every member in it to be tested. Hence, a subset of that population, a sample, must be selected.

Even though an entire population is seldom tested in a study, the researcher hopes to draw conclusions about this broader group, not just about the sample. Thus, in survey research, it is important for the sample to reflect the attributes of the target population as a whole. When this happens, the sample is said to be **representative;** if it doesn't happen, the sample is said to be **biased** in some fashion. For instance, if you wanted to investigate student perceptions of college life, it would be a serious mistake to select people from a list that included only those students living in college residence halls. Because off-campus residents and commuter students might have very different attitudes from on-campus residents, the results of your survey would be biased in favor of the latter.

Perhaps the most famous historical example of biased sampling occurred during political polling in the presidential election of 1936. As it had been doing with reasonable success for several previous elections, the magazine *Literary Digest* tried to predict the election outcome by sending out about 10 million simulated ballots to subscribers, to others selected from a sample of phone books from around the country, and to others from motor vehicle registration information (Sprinthall, 2000). Close to 25% (almost 2.5 million) of the ballots were returned to the magazine; of these respondents, 57% preferred the Republican candidate, Alf Landon, and 40% chose the incumbent president, Franklin Roosevelt. In the actual election, Roosevelt won in a landslide with more than 60% of the vote. Can you guess why the sample was biased?

Although the editors of *Literary Digest* were aware that their own subscribers tended to be upper middle class and Republican, they thought they were broadening the sample and making it more representative by adding people chosen from phone books and car registration data. In fact, they were selecting more Republicans. In the midst of the Great Depression, practically the only people who could afford phones and cars were members of the upper middle and upper classes, and these were more likely to be Republicans than Democrats. So, in the survey the magazine actually was asking Republicans how they were going to cast their votes.

You might have noticed another flaw in the *Literary Digest* survey. A large number of ballots was returned, and the magazine was quite confident in its prediction of a Landon victory because the data reflected the views of a substantial number of people—about 2.5 million. Note, however, that not only does the total represent only one-fourth of the ballots originally sent out, but also the returns were from those who *chose* to send them back. So, those responding to the survey tended to be not just Republicans, but Republicans who wished to make their views known (in light of which, the 57% preferring Landon actually looks rather small, don't you think?).

This **self-selection** bias is typical in surveys that appear in popular magazines and in newspapers. A survey will appear, with an appeal to readers to send in a response. Then, a month or so later, the results of those who returned the survey will be reported, usually in a way implying that the results are valid. The person reporting the survey will try to impress you with the total number of returns rather than the representativeness of the sample. An example of this ploy is a well-known report on female sexuality (Hite, 1987). It claimed, among other things, that more than 90% of married women felt emotionally abused in their relationships and a substantial majority reported dissatisfaction in marriage. When criticized because the survey was sent only to a select group of women's organizations and that only 4.5% of 100,000 people returned the survey, the author simply pointed out that 4,500 people were enough for her (just as 2.5 million people were enough for *Literary Digest*). But research that uses appropriate probability sampling techniques generally shows that satisfaction/happiness in marriage is actually quite high. The Hite data were misleading, to say the least.

As a scientific thinker, you should be very skeptical about claims made on the basis of biased samples. The lesson, of course, is that if you want to make an accurate statement about a specific population, you must use a sample that represents that population and you must select the sample directly, not rely simply on who decides to return the survey. If you have no choice but to use data from a self-selected sample, and this happens sometimes, you should at least try to determine if the attributes of the sample (e.g., average age, income) match the attributes of the population you have in mind. Even then you need to be cautious in the conclusions you draw.

Random Sampling

The simplest form of probability sampling is to take a **simple random sample**. In essence, all this means is that each member of the population has an equal chance of being selected as a member of the sample. To select a random sample of 100 students from your school, for instance, you could place all of their names in a large hat and pick out 100. In actual practice, the procedure is a bit more sophisticated than this, however, usually involving software[2] that uses a random number table. To learn the essence of the procedure, work through the example in Table 12.1, which shows you how to use random numbers to select a sample of 5 individuals from a population of 20.

Simple random sampling is often an effective, practical way to create a representative sample. It is sometimes the method of choice for ethical reasons as well. In situations in which only a small group can receive some benefit or must incur some cost, and there is no other reasonable basis for decision-making, random sampling is the fairest method to use. A famous example occurred in 1969 in the midst of the Vietnam War, when a lottery system was established to see who would be drafted in the army. For obvious reasons of fairness, birthdays for each of the 365 days of the year were to have an equal probability of being selected first, second, third, and so on. Unfortunately, the actual procedure had some bias (Kolata, 1986). Capsules, one for every day of the year, were placed in a large drum one month at a time. The January capsules went in first, then the February ones, and so on. The drum was rotated to mix the capsules, but apparently this did not succeed

---

[2]This website allows you to accomplish both to random selection of participants and the random assignment of them to groups: http://www.randomizer.org/

TABLE 12.1 *Selecting a Random Sample Using a Table of Random Numbers*

Task:	Select a random sample of 5 individuals from a population of 20 individuals.
Step 1.	Assign numbers from 01 to 20 to the individuals who make up your population.
Step 2.	Go to a table of random numbers. Here's a portion of one:

```
2  2  1  7  6  8  6  5  8  4  6  8  9  5
1  9  3  6  1  7  5  9  4  6  1  3  7  9
1  6  7  7  2  3  0  2  7  7  0  9  6  1
7  8  0  3  7  6  7  1  6  1  2  0  4  4
0  3  2  8  1  2  2  6  0  8  7  3  3  7
```

Step 3.	Pick a spot to begin searching through the table. This can be anywhere; just be sure that you don't begin any two searches in the same place. Let's suppose you begin with the top number in the third column. It's a 1. You will need to consider pairs of numbers together because the population consists of people numbered 01 through 20. Hence you must use the 1 and the 7 next to it as your starting point.
Step 4.	Your search for a sample of five begins with number 17, which falls within the range of 01 to 20. The first person in your sample, therefore, is person 17.
Step 5.	Continue down the double column until you've found five individuals with numbers between 01 and 20. Here's the table again, with the spacing between columns arranged to make it easier to detect pairs of numbers. The five selected numbers are underlined, the section of the table that needed to be searched is boldfaced, and arrows indicate the direction of search.

```
2  2   1  7   6  8   6  5   8  4   6  8   9  5
1  9   3  6   1  7   5  9   4  6   1  3   7  9
1  6   7  7   2  3   0  2   7  7   0  9   6  1
7  8   0  3   7  6   7  1   6  1   2  0   4  4
0  3   2  8   1  2   2  6   0  8   7  3   3  7
```

Thus the sample consists of population members numbered 17, 3, 12, 2, and 8. Notice that numbers larger than 20 (e.g., 36) are bypassed and if a number repeats itself (17), it is not selected twice.

completely because when the dates were drawn, those capsules entering the drum last tended to be the first to be picked. This was not a good time to have a birthday in December.

There are two problems with simple random sampling. First, there may be some systematic features of the population that you might like to have reflected in your sample. Second, the procedure may be impossible if the population is extremely large. How could you get a list of everyone in the United States in order to select a simple random sample of Americans? The first problem is solved by using stratified sampling, and cluster sampling solves the second difficulty.

Stratified Sampling

Suppose you wanted to measure attitudes about abortion on your campus, and the school's population is 5,000 students, of whom 3,000 are women. You decide to sample 100 students. If you take a simple random sample, there are probably going to be more women than men in your sample, but the proportions in the sample won't match those in the population precisely. Your goal is to make the sample truly representative of the population and, on a question like abortion, there might be important differences of opinion between males and females. Therefore, if your sample happens to be overrepresented with males, it might not truly portray campus attitudes. In a situation like this, it would be a good idea to decide ahead of time that if 60% of the population is female, then exactly 60% of the sample will also be female. That is, just as the population has these two layers (or "strata"), so should the sample.

In a **stratified sample**, then, the *proportions* of important subgroups in the population are represented precisely in the sample. In the previous example, with a goal of a sample of 100, 60 females would be randomly sampled from the list of females, and 40 males would be selected from the list of males. Note that some judgment is required here: The researcher has to decide just how many layers to use. In the case of the abortion survey, males and females were sampled in proportion to their overall numbers. Should each of the four undergraduate classes be proportionately represented also? What about Protestants and Catholics? What about left- and right-handers? Obviously, the researcher has to draw the line somewhere. Some characteristics (religion) may be more critical than others (handedness) in deciding how to stratify the sample. Based on what has occurred in prior research or the goals of the current study, it's up to the researcher to use some good sense.

The intent of a stratified sample, to represent subgroups proportionately, can also be met in a nonprobability convenience sample. When using a subject pool, for instance, if you wished to have 60% females and 40% males in your study, and you hoped to test 100 participants, you could simply sign people up in your study until the 60 females and 40 males had participated. This type of nonprobability sample is called a **quota sample**.

Cluster Sampling

Stratified sampling is an effective procedure, but it still doesn't solve the problem of trying to sample from a huge population, when it is often impossible to acquire a complete list of individuals. **Cluster sampling**, a procedure frequently used by national polling organizations, solves the problem. With this approach, the researcher randomly selects a cluster of people all having some feature in common. A campus survey at a large university might be done this way. If a researcher wanted a cross section of students and stratified sampling was not feasible, an alternative would be to get a list of required "core" classes. Each class would be a cluster and would include students from a variety of majors.

If 40 core classes were being offered, the researcher might randomly select 10 of them and then administer the survey to all students in each of the selected classes.

If the selected clusters are too large, the researcher can sample a smaller cluster within the larger one. Suppose you wanted to find out how students liked living in the high-rise dorms on your campus, which you've defined operationally as any dorm with eight floors or more. Further suppose that fifteen of these buildings exist on your campus, housing a total of 9,000 students. Using cluster sampling, you could first select six of the buildings (each building = a cluster), and then, for each building, randomly select three floors and sample all of the residents (about forty per floor, let's say) of the selected floors in the selected dorms. This would give you an overall sample size of 720 (40 × 3 × 6). Notice that you also could combine some elements of stratified sampling here. If ten of the dorms house women, and men live in the remaining five, you might select your first clusters to reflect these proportions: four female dorms and two male dorms.

Varieties of Survey Methods

Most surveying today occurs in the form of written questionnaires that are sent through the mail or administered in some more direct fashion (e.g., to a class of students). There are other techniques for collecting survey data, however, and each survey type has its strengths and weaknesses. In addition to written questionnaires, survey data are sometimes collected through face-to-face interviews, sometimes through telephone interviews, and more recently, via the Internet. Researchers sometimes combine methods, a "mixed-mode" approach (Dillman, Smyth, & Christian, 2009).

Interviews

You have undoubtedly heard of the Kinsey Report, perhaps the most famous sex survey of all time. Completed in the years just following World War II, it resulted from detailed, face-to-face interviews with thousands of men and women, and it yielded two large books on sexual behavior in America, one for men (Kinsey, Pomeroy, & Martin, 1948) and one for women (Kinsey, Pomeroy, Martin, & Gebhard, 1953). Although you might think that Kinsey's **interview survey** format might have prevented people from describing the intimate details of their sexual attitudes and behaviors, especially considering the historical era in which the studies were done, this apparently did not occur. In fact, conservative postwar America was shocked by the frequency of the reported levels of premarital sex, masturbation, and adultery. The books, although written in dry academic prose and loaded with tables and bar graphs, nonetheless reached best-seller status and made Kinsey a celebrated yet controversial figure. Accused by some of contributing to a moral decline and even of being a Communist, he was regarded by others as a pioneer in the scientific study of an important aspect of human behavior (Christenson, 1971).

The interview format for surveying has the advantages of being comprehensive and yielding highly detailed information. Even though the interviewer typically asks a standard set of questions, the skilled interviewer is able to elicit considerable information through follow-up questions or probes. Having an interviewer present also reduces the problem of unclear questions—the interviewer can clarify on the spot. Sampling is sometimes a problem because, in many cases, sizable segments of the population may not be included if they refuse to be interviewed, cannot be located, or live in an area the interviewer would prefer to avoid. For example, the poor and homeless are usually underrepresented in national surveys using the interview format. Interviews can occur in a group format—the *focus group* procedure described in Chapter 10 is an example.

Besides sampling issues, other major problems with the interview approach are cost, logistics, and interviewer bias. Interviewers need to be hired and trained, travel expenses can be substantial, and interviews might be restricted to a fairly small geographic area because of the logistical problems of sending interviewers long distances. And despite training, there is always the possibility that interviewer bias can affect the responses given in the face-to-face setting. For example, cross-race bias may exist, resulting in systematic differences between interviews with members of one's own race and members of other races.

The careful researcher using interviews will develop a training program to standardize the interview process as much as possible, and sometimes certain types of interviewers may be trained for specific purposes. For example, middle-aged female interviewers may elicit more cooperation in an interview survey of retired women than young male interviewers, who may not get past the door (van Kammen & Stouthamer-Loeber, 1998)

Phone Surveys

A second way to conduct a survey is to pick up the phone and call people. According to Dillman, Smyth, and Christian (2009) **phone surveying** had its peak of popularity in the 1980s—virtually every home had a telephone, households could be selected randomly through a procedure called random-digit-dialing, and people were generally open to being surveyed. And then two things happened that have virtually wiped out the phone surveying business—telemarketing and cell phones. Telemarketing produced a level of annoyance sufficient to lead to the creation of national do-not-call lists, and the marketing strategy also had the effect of creating high levels of suspicion and distrust in the general public, especially when telemarketers begin the call by pretending that they are conducting a survey, when in fact they are selling a product (a ploy known in marketing research as **sugging**—*Selling Under the Guise of a survey*).[3] As for cell phones, they have changed the dynamic of phone surveying. When the only phones in the house were landlines, surveyors would call and the unit of measurement typically would be the "household." With cell phones, however, the unit is the individual, thereby changing the nature of the population. In addition, cell phones are often turned off (except in theaters, restaurants, and classrooms) and it is very easy to screen and delete unwanted calls.

---

[3]Another marketing strategy is called *frugging*—Fund Raising Under the Guise of surveying.

Nonetheless, for what is left of the phone surveying industry, there are some strengths. One obvious advantage over interviews and mailed surveys is cost. The method also combines the efficiency of a mailed survey with the personal contact of an interview. Another clear advantage over the interview is a logistical one; many more participants can be contacted per unit of time. Furthermore, the phone surveyor is not likely to be assaulted, a problem that sometimes occurs when field interviewers venture into high-crime areas. To increase the chances of having people respond to the surveys, one technique used by legitimate surveyors is to precede the call with a brief letter or post card alerting the respondent that a phone call is on the way ("and please cooperate, we could really use your help; and we promise it will be brief"). This is an example of the mixed-mode approach (mixing mail and phone) advocated by Dillman, Smyth, and Christian (2009).

Electronic Surveys

As you recall from the ethics chapter, researchers are increasingly turning to the Internet for data collection. One of the most common forms of Internet data collection involves **electronic surveying** (e-surveying), which is accomplished in one of two ways. First, some e-surveys can be sent via e-mail to a selected sample of individuals. E-mail lists can be purchased or, following the ethically dubious lead of spammers, obtained by using what are called "search spiders" that search the Internet for posted e-mails and accumulate e-mail addresses. A second form of e-survey is one that can be posted on a website, collecting data from those who choose to respond.

The main advantage of e-surveying is that a large amount of data can be collected in a relatively short period of time and for virtually no cost to the researcher. There are costs involved with researcher time and the expense of surveying software, but there are no postage, phone, or interviewer travel costs. It has been estimated that e-survey costs are about one-tenth of the costs of a comparable mailed survey (Anderson & Kanuka, 2003). And with the Internet open 24 hours a day, e-surveying can be completed in less time than other forms of surveys.

Problems exist, however. Although Internet use is widespread, the sample will tend to be biased—responders are unlikely to be representative of all income and education levels, for instance. With e-mail surveys, the researcher runs the risk of having the survey appear to be just another piece of spam or, worse, a potential entry-way for a virus. By one estimate (Anderson & Kanuka, 2003), 85% of e-mail users delete e-mail without reading it, at least some of the time. So, the e-mail survey must have a subject line that will catch the reader's attention. With web-based surveys, the problem (which I suspect you have already recognized) is that the sample is bound to be self-selected, resulting in bias. Furthermore, it could be that there is a teenager out there somewhere with little else to do but respond to your survey several hundred times a day for a week or two. Despite the difficulties, however, e-surveying promises to occupy a large niche in the twenty-first-century survey business. As with phone surveying, savvy researchers can use a mixed mode approach—sending a letter in the mail that appeals to the reader to complete the survey, perhaps including in the letter a website address with a password to enter the survey.

Written Surveys

The traditional survey type is the paper-and-pencil test or **written survey**. Written surveys can be sent through the mail (as you know, because you've probably thrown a few away), they can be administered in a group setting, or they can be put online. Return rate is often a problem. Return rates of 85% or higher are considered excellent (and rare), 70–85% very good, and 60–70% more or less acceptable (Mangione, 1998). Anything below 60% makes researchers nervous about whether the data are representative. Another problem with rate of return occurs when those who return surveys differ in some important way from those who don't return them, a problem called **nonresponse bias** (Rogelberg & Luong, 1998). When this happens, drawing a conclusion about a population is risky at best. The "profile" of the typical nonresponder is an older, unmarried male without a lot of education (Mangione, 1998); nonresponse also occurs when people have some attribute that makes the survey irrelevant for them (e.g., vegetarians surveyed about meat preferences).

The best chance for a decent return rate for a mailed written survey occurs if (a) the survey is brief and easy to fill out; (b) the form starts with relatively interesting questions and leaves the boring items (i.e., demographic information—see below) until the end; (c) before the survey is sent out, participants are notified that a survey is on the way and that their help will be greatly appreciated; (d) nonresponse triggers follow-up reminders, a second mailing of the survey, and perhaps even a phone request to fill out the form; (e) the entire package is highly professional in appearance, with a cover letter signed by a real person instead of a machine; (f) return postage is included; and (g) the recipient has no reason to think the survey is merely step one in a sales pitch (Fowler, 1993; Rogelberg & Luong, 1998). Return rates can also be improved by including a small gift or token amount of money. For example, Dillman, Smyth, and Christian (2009) reported a study that increased response rate from 52% to 64% by adding a token gift of a dollar in the survey mailing. I once filled out a survey about the kinds of features I look for in a social psychology text mainly because it earned me a $5 gift certificate from a chain bookstore.

One important problem that exists with all forms of survey research is a **social desirability bias**. Sometimes people respond to a survey question in a way that reflects not how they truly feel or what they truly believe, but how they think they *should* respond. That is, they attempt to create a positive picture of themselves—one that is socially desirable. For instance, people are likely to distort their voting record, reporting that they vote more often than they actually do (Anderson, Silver, & Abramson, 1988). Another study showed that student-athletes are likely to disguise their levels of anxiety and overstate their degree of self-confidence on surveys (Williams & Krane, 1989). Ensuring participants of complete anonymity can help reduce the bias, but the problem is a persistent one and it is hard to gauge the extent of it. The social psychology literature has a long history of research showing that the attitudes people express on some issue do not always correlate with their behavior. Thus, the results of survey research have to be interpreted with this response bias in mind, and conclusions drawn from surveys can be strengthened to the extent that other research provides converging results.

1. What does it mean to say that a sample is *representative*?
2. What do stratified and quota samples have in common? How do they differ?
3. Compared to written surveys sent through the mail, what is one advantage and one disadvantage of an interview survey?

Creating an Effective Survey

What constitutes a good survey can differ slightly depending on the format (interview, written, etc.). What follows in this section concerns the construction of a written questionnaire survey, but most of the information applies to the other formats as well. When designing a survey, the researcher must create items that effectively answer the empirical question(s) at hand, and must be very careful with the structure and the wording of items.

As with any research in psychology, survey research begins with empirical questions that develop into hypotheses to be tested by collecting data. For example, in a college or university environment, such questions might include focused, single-issue ones:

- Do students feel safe when crossing the campus at night?
- Do students eat balanced, nutritious meals?
- Are faculty more politically liberal than students?

Or they might be more broad-based:

- Are students satisfied with their education at the university?
- Considering college student behavior as a whole, during a typical semester, can it be characterized as health-enhancing or health-inhibiting?

Types of Survey Questions or Statements

Once an empirical question has been framed and its terms defined operationally, the researcher decides on the type of items to use and the wording of those items. Survey items can take a variety of forms. For example, when questions are asked, they can be either open-ended or closed. An **open-ended question** requires a response involving more than just a yes or no answer. Rather, participants must provide narrative information. A **closed question** can be answered with a yes or a no or by choosing a single response from among several alternatives. To illustrate the difference, consider these two ways of asking about school financing:

Open: How do you think we should finance public education?

Closed: Do you think that property taxes should be used to finance public education?

Open-ended questions can be useful for eliciting a wide range of responses, including some not even conceived of by the researchers. They can also increase the respondent's sense of control while filling out the survey. Because they can produce such a wide range of responses, however, open-ended questions are difficult to score and can add considerably to the time required to complete the survey. Hence, they should be used sparingly. One good method is to give respondents an opportunity to elaborate on their responses to closed questions. For example, at the end of a set of closed questions, the survey might provide space for the respondents to comment on their answers to any of the items, especially those for which they gave extreme ratings. Another good use of open-ended questions is in a pilot study as a way of identifying alternatives for a subsequent questionnaire to be composed of closed items. For example, a common open-ended question is sometimes referred to as the "most important problem" item (Schuman & Presser, 1996). An example might be:

> In your judgment, what are the most important problems facing this university today?

This question is likely to elicit a variety of responses in a pilot test, and these responses could become the alternatives in a final item that could ask:

> Which of the following is the most important problem facing this university today? (alternatively, rankings of the items could be requested)
>
> _____ overall quality of teaching
>
> _____ inadequate computer facilities
>
> _____ lack of diversity in the student body
>
> _____ poor quality of dormitory rooms
>
> _____ inadequate career advising

(and so on)

Finally, some survey items can be "partially" open by including a specific checklist, ending it with the category "Other," and allowing respondents to write in their responses.

Written surveys with closed questions often use an interval scale for measuring the responses. As you recall from Chapter 4, with an interval scale there is no true zero point, but the intervals between points on the scale are assumed to be equal. The most common type of interval scale used in surveys is the so-called Likert scale (after the person who invented it, Rensis Likert). A typical Likert scale has anywhere from five to nine distinct points on it (always an odd number—there must be a midpoint that is a "neutral" choice in order for it to be called a Likert scale), with each point reflecting a score on the continuum. For example, on a survey of attitudes toward televised coverage of news, participants might be asked to indicate how much they agree with a series of statements according to a 5-point scale. A sample item might look like this:

> The person anchoring a news show should have at least five years of experience as a professional journalist.

SD   D   U   A   SA

Respondents circle the item on the scale that indicates what they believe. "SD" stands for "strongly disagree," "D" for "disagree," "U" for "undecided," and so on. These points are then typically converted to a 5-point scale (SD = 1, D = 2, etc.). Then, responses from all of the participants could be summarized as a mean and standard deviation. For instance, if the mean score was 4.5, the researcher would conclude that respondents are midway between "agree" and "strongly agree" on this item. Also, scores from several items designed to measure the same issue could be combined into a single mean score.

The above Likert item could be made into a 7-point scale by adding "very strongly agree" and "very strongly disagree." There is no clear advantage to a 5- or a 7- (or more) point scale. A 5-point scale normally provides sufficient discrimination among levels of agreement but might become a de facto 3-point scale in practice, given a tendency for some people to avoid making the choices at each end of the scale. On the other hand, a 7-point scale still yields 5 points if people avoid the extremes, but adding the extra level of discrimination can increase the time it takes to complete the survey. One general rule is to avoid mixing formats. If you decide to use a 5-point Likert scale, use it throughout; don't mix 5- and 7-point scales in the same survey.

One other point about a Likert scale is that when using one, it is normally a good idea to word some of the statements favorably and others unfavorably. In a survey that evaluates teaching, for example, consecutive statements might be phrased like this:

The instructor held my attention during class lectures.

The instructor wrote exams that fairly tested the material covered.

The instructor seemed to be well prepared for class.

The instructor was available for extra help outside of class.

These items are all worded *favorably*, so if a student liked the instructor, that student might race through the survey without reading the items carefully and simply agree with everything. Also, some students might have a response bias called **response acquiescence**—a tendency to agree with statements. To avoid these problems, surveys with Likert scales typically balance favorable and unfavorable statements. This forces respondents to read each item carefully and make item-by-item decisions (Patten, 1998). For example, the above statements could be presented like this, with two items worded favorably and two unfavorably:

The instructor was seldom able to hold my attention during class lectures.

The instructor wrote exams that fairly tested the material covered.

The instructor often appeared to be unprepared for class.

The instructor was available for extra help outside of class.

When items are balanced like this, it is a good idea to emphasize the fact in the instructions.

It is also important to be concerned about the sequencing of the items on your survey. If your research requires that you include questions that some respondents might find sensitive (e.g., frequency of alcohol or drug use, sexual activities), for example, put them near the end of the survey. If you start with them, respondents might stop right away; if they are at the end, respondents have already invested some time and may be more willing to finish the survey. Start the survey with questions that are not especially personal and are both easy to answer and interesting. Also, cluster items on the same general topic in the same place on the survey. For example, if your survey is about satisfaction with college, group the items about courses together, and separate them from items about student activities.

Assessing Memory and Knowledge

In addition to asking about attitudes and opinions, surveys sometimes attempt to assess the respondent's memory or what they know. In this case there are two important guidelines: Don't overburden memory, and use DK ("don't know") alternatives sparingly.

When asking how often respondents have done certain things in their lives, making the interval too long increases the chances of memory errors. For example, on a survey about drinking behavior (assume that the definition of a "drink" has been made clear to the respondent), it is better to ask the person to specify exactly what they have had to drink in the past week than in the past month. Of course, the proper interval will depend on the question being asked. If the activity is a relatively infrequent one (e.g., visiting zoos), a short interval will yield too many scores of zero. One way to aid memory is to provide lists. In a survey about leisure-time activities, for instance, respondents might be asked to examine the past month and indicate how frequently they have rented a movie, gone on a hike, attended the symphony, and so on.

When inquiring about what a person knows, there is always the chance that the honest answer will be "I don't know." Hence, survey items that deal with knowledge often include what is called a **DK alternative** ("don't know"). Some experts discourage the use of DK alternatives because respondents might overuse them, conservatively choosing DK even if they have some knowledge of the issue at hand. Survey results with a lot of DK answers are not very useful. On the other hand, omitting DK as a choice might force respondents to mentally flip a coin on items about which they are truly ignorant (Schuman & Presser, 1996). One way to include DK choices, while at the same time encouraging respondents to avoid overusing them, is to disguise knowledge questions by prefacing them with such statements as "Using your best guess . . . " or "Have you heard or have you read that . . . " (examples from Fink, 1995, p. 76). Also, DK alternatives should be used only when it is reasonable to expect that some respondents will have no idea about what the answer might be (Patten, 1998).

Adding Demographic Information

Demographic information refers to the basic data that serves to identify the survey respondent. These data can include such information as age, sex, socioeconomic status, marital status, and so on. Sometimes the empirical question at hand will determine the type of demographic information needed. In a survey about attitudes toward animal experimentation, for example, it might be useful for the researcher to know whether or not the respondent is a pet owner. Including this demographic information enables the survey researcher to group the results by demographic categories, in this case comparing pet owners and nonowners on attitudes toward animal research.

In general, it is a good idea to put questions about demographic information at the end of a survey. If you start the survey with them, participants might become bored and not attend to the key items as well as they should. Also, you should include only demographic categories that are important for the empirical questions that interest you. The more demographic information you include, the longer the survey and the greater the risk that respondents will tune out. And they might become irritated: Some requests for demographic information (e.g., income) can be perceived as invasions of privacy, even though respondents will have been assured about confidentiality (Patten, 1998). When requesting demographic information, here are some guidelines:

- When asking about age, ask for date of birth.
- When asking for annual income, provide a range to reduce privacy concerns (e.g., $50,000 or less; $50,001–$100,000).
- Don't let the alternatives overlap (e.g., as in the income question just used as an example of providing a range).
- If making comparisons to other surveys, ask for identical demographic information.
- Let the pros do the work—borrow items from the U.S. Census Bureau (www.census.gov); for example, whereas a novice might include "married, single, divorced, and widowed" under marital status, a pro would recognize the ambiguity in "single" and use the census categories—"married, separated, widowed, divorced, never married" (Patten, 1998, p. 27).

A Key Problem: Survey Wording

A major problem in survey construction concerns the wording of the items contained in the survey. Although it is impossible for the survey writer to ensure that all respondents will interpret each question or statement the same way, there are some guidelines that can help in the construction of a good survey. The most important one is to pilot test the instrument on several groups of friends, colleagues, and even some people you don't like. You will be surprised at how often it occurs that you think you have a perfect item and then three friends interpret it three different ways. One tip is to define any terms that you think could be interpreted in different ways.

In addition to pilot testing, there are three specific problems to avoid. These include linguistic ambiguity, asking two questions in one item, and asking leading questions. First, questions can be ambiguous, as when people are asked whether they agree with statements like this:

Visiting relatives can be fun.

What's fun, the relatives who are visiting or the act of visiting the relatives? Second, survey writers sometimes include too much in an item, resulting in an item that actually asks for two responses at once. This is sometimes referred to as a **double-barreled question**. Here's an example:

> It is wrong for female patrons in bars to swear and to buy drinks for men who are unknown to them.

The responder who agrees with the swearing part but disagrees with the drink-buying part would not know how to answer this question. Third, what lawyers refer to as a **leading question** is a question that is structured so that it is likely to produce an answer desired by the asker. Here are two ways of asking about the Clean Air Act that would almost certainly yield different responses:

1. Given the importance to future generations of preserving the environment, do you believe the Clean Air Act should be strengthened, weakened, or left alone?

2. Given the fact that installing scrubbers at utility plants could increase electricity bills by 25%, do you believe the Clean Air Act should be strengthened, weakened, or left alone?

This type of survey bias, the leading question, occurs frequently in the worlds of business or politics, where the intent is to sell a product or a candidate. In politics, for example, it is common for both Republican and Democratic National Committees (RNC and DNC) to send out surveys that include leading questions. For instance, in the 2008 Presidential campaign, Republican candidate John McCain, while trying to make the point that getting out of Iraq would not be easy and that the U.S. might always have some military presence there, made the mistake of mentioning (not "pledging") "100 years" in one of his speeches. In a subsequent survey sent to Democrats by the DNC, this item appeared:

> Do you believe that John McCain's pledge to keep troops in Iraq for another 100 years will be a liability in the General Election?

I never saw the results of this survey, but the outcome for this item would not be hard to guess. Being a Democrat, I wasn't sent the RNC questionnaire, but I am sure it contained items just as biased as this one.

In the world of business, consider this example. In an attempt to outsell McDonald's, Burger King once reported a survey claiming that about 75% of people surveyed preferred their Whoppers to Big Macs. The key question was phrased this way (Kimmel, 2007, p. 208):

> Do you prefer your hamburgers flame-broiled or fried?

Do you see the problem? Burger King's "flame-broiled" method sounds more natural and appetizing than McDonald's "fried" method, so perhaps the outcome was not a surprise. However, another surveyor asked the same question a different way (Kimmel, 2007, p. 208):

> Do you prefer a hamburger that is grilled on a hot stainless steel grill or cooked by passing the raw meat through an open gas flame?

In this case, McDonald's method (the steel grill) was preferred by more than half of the respondents, a figure that rose to 85% when the researcher indicated that after encountering the gas flame, the Burger King burgers were reheated in a microwave oven before being served. The moral of the story: It is probably fair to say that skepticism is the best response when businesses report survey results in their advertising. Unfortunately, this situation lends credence to the widely held belief that surveys can be created and manipulated to produce virtually any outcome.

In addition to these three major problems with wording, here are several other tips about wording (most examples from Fink, 1995):

- Always opt for simplicity over complexity

   Poor: Doctors should be intelligible when explaining a diagnosis to a patient.

   Better: Doctors should use simple and clear language when explaining a diagnosis to a patient.

- Use complete sentences.

   Poor: Place of residence?

   Better: What is the name of the city where you currently live?

- Avoid most abbreviations.

   USC could be University of Southern California, but it could also be the University of South Carolina.

- Avoid slang and colloquial expressions.

   They go out of fashion; by the time you read this, for instance, "information superhighway" will be an overused and outdated expression.

- Avoid jargon.

   As a program evaluator, you might know the difference between "formative" and "summative" evaluations but most survey respondents won't.

- Avoid negatively phrased questions—negative statements are more difficult to process than positive ones.

   Poor: Do you believe that the university should not have the right to search your dorm room?

   Better: Should the university have the right to search your dorm room?

- Use balanced items, not those favoring one position or another.

   Poor: Do you support the use of animals in undergraduate laboratory courses?

   Better: Do you support or oppose the use of animals in undergraduate laboratory courses?

These are just some examples of the issues involved when creating survey items. For more detailed guidance on the construction of reliable and valid survey items, several excellent guides exist (e.g., Converse & Presser, 1986; Fink, 1995; Fowler, 1998; Patten, 1998; Dillman, 2000).

Surveys and Ethics

One point worth noting about survey research is that in some cases, the APA does not require informed consent. In the same standard (8.05) that excuses naturalistic observations from consent, the APA excuses "anonymous questionnaires [assuming that] disclosure of responses would not place participants at risk of criminal or civil liability or damage their financial standing, employability, or reputation, and confidentiality is protected" (APA, 2002, pp.1069–1070). Despite this, it is customary for researchers to include consent language in a cover letter that precedes the survey, or in the opening screens of an online survey.

A final point about survey research and ethics is that decisions affecting people's lives are sometimes made with the help of survey data, and if the surveys are flawed and biased in some way, or poorly constructed, people can be hurt or, at the very least, have their time wasted. Although professional psychologists operating within the APA's ethics code are unlikely to use surveys inappropriately, abuses nonetheless can occur. The problem is recognized by the judicial system, which has established a set of standards for the use of survey data in courts of law (Morgan, 1990). The standards amount to this: If you are going to collect and use survey data, do it as a professional psychologist would. That is, be careful about sampling, survey construction, and data analysis. For an interesting and rather disturbing example of how survey methods can be badly *misused*, read Ethics Box 12.3, which examines the case of a female journalist who was fired from her news anchor job, partly on the basis of a rigged survey.

Box 12.3

ETHICS—*Using and Abusing Surveys*

In early 1981, station KMBC of Kansas City hired Christine Craft, a news journalist from California, to co-anchor its evening news. Less than a year later, she was demoted from that position. The station claimed incompetence, but Ms. Craft sued, arguing that she was hired for her journalistic talent, not her youthful good looks, yet was fired for the latter reason. She won.

On the surface, the station appeared to act prudently, basing its decision not merely on whim but on data collected in a professional phone survey of 400 viewers. However, this case illustrates not the use of survey research, but its misuse. According to Beisecker (1988), the study had several major flaws.

First, although the use of a survey conveys the impression of objectivity, the research was hopelessly biased from the start. One major problem was that the firm doing the research also served as a paid consultant to the station, and those doing the research already knew what decision the station wanted. The resulting bias was reflected in the wording of a phone survey that was used. One purpose of the survey was to compare Ms. Craft with other local news anchors, yet the questions were stacked against her. For example, she did poorly compared to other anchors on a question regarding which news anchor "knows Kansas City best" (p. 23), which is not surprising when one considers that (a) at the time of the survey Ms. Craft had been with the station for all of 6 months and the other anchors had all been at their stations at least a year, and (b) in her early months with KMBC, Ms. Craft had been vigorously promoted as "a fresh new face from California" (p. 23). Also, very few survey items assessed journalistic ability; rather, much of the survey dealt with questions about attractiveness and appearance (e.g., "Her good looks are a big plus for the newscast she's on," p. 23).

In addition to the bias that characterized the project from the start, there were statistical problems serious enough for Beisecker (1988) to conclude that "the research firm did not employ any recognizable statistical tests or principles of statistical inference to justify its generalizations from the sample data" (p. 25). In other words, while the consultant firm reported simple *descriptive* statistics summarizing the survey results, they did not conduct the proper *inferential* statistics that would allow conclusions about the significance of the results. For example, it was reported that among 25- to 34-year-olds in the survey who were asked which channel's news had declined in quality, 30% said KMBC and 16% said a competing channel, KCMO. Much was made of this "2–1 margin," and it was attributed to the allegedly detrimental effects of Ms. Craft's presence. However, the year before (1980), when Ms. Craft was still in California, the *same* question on another survey by the *same* firm yielded 26% for KMBC and 15% for KCMO. An inferential analysis surely would have shown no difference between the numbers for the two years. Not only was the analysis not done, the consultant/researchers conveniently omitted the 1980 data from the 1981 results.

Clearly, survey research can be done well and its results interpreted meaningfully. In the case of Christine Craft, though, the "survey research" basis for her firing had no credibility.

As you recall from Chapter 2, discussions about the use of animals as research subjects often generate more heat than light. One approach to understanding how people feel about the issue is to conduct a good survey. An example of one is in the following study, which closes out our discussion of surveying.

Research Example 40—An Attitude Survey with Cluster Sampling

In 1996, Scott Plous published two different surveys about animal research, one directed at academic psychologists (Plous, 1996a) and a second directed at undergraduate psychology majors (Plous, 1996b). The latter concerns your peer group, so let's consider it in more detail.

First, Plous (1996b) used a sampling procedure that you learned about in this chapter—a "two-stage cluster sampling technique was used to generate a national probability sample" (p. 353). He began by identifying a **sample frame**, which in survey research is defined as the complete list of individuals from whom the sample will be drawn. For Plous, the sample frame was a list of colleges and universities. The initial sample frame included 708 colleges and universities taken from a standard college guide. Excluded from the list were very small schools and schools with a religious affiliation. From the initial list of 708 schools (clusters), 50 were randomly sampled. Psychology department chairs at these schools were contacted, and 42 schools chose to participate. This was a good response rate (87.5%),[4] helped by the fact that Plous had money through a grant to give away a laser printer to one of the departments, as determined by a lottery. Some additional sampling within each department was done. Fifty majors were randomly selected from lists supplied by departments, and the final results were based on the returns of 1,188 undergraduate psychology majors, an overall return rate of 58.75%. This rate was low enough to trigger concerns about representativeness, so Plous examined the sample more closely. For example, government data for 1995 showed that 73.1% of graduating psychology majors were women, and 26.9% were men. This matched Plous's sample almost perfectly—73% female and 27% male. Even without a large return rate, then, the sample looked good.

Students were informed that the survey concerned the use of animals in psychological, not medical, research (while acknowledging some overlap) and animal use in an educational setting. They were then asked a series of closed questions, including the ones in Table 12.2. They were also asked to fill in a table with four columns labeled with different species names (primates, dogs, rats, and pigeons), and three rows labeled in terms of the severity of the experimental procedures used (observation; confinement, but no pain or death; and physical pain and death). For each cell, the students were asked to indicate whether they thought the research would be "usually justified" or "usually unjustified." Because the topic is so controversial, Plous wanted to be sure that the questions would be clear and unbiased. This goal was achieved by doing some pretesting of the items with a separate sample of undergraduate psychology majors.

The results in Table 12.2 show that psychology majors clearly approved the use of animals both for research and teaching purposes. Over 70% either supported or strongly supported animal research (14.3% + 57.4%), about two-thirds believed animal research was necessary for progress to occur in psychology (68.4%), and while most thought that lab work with animals should not be required of psychology majors (54.3%), there was majority support for the use of animals in undergraduate instruction (56.9%). There was concern about pain and suffering, however, with almost unanimous support for protecting the psychological well being of primates (85.1%) and for required assessments of the amount of pain the animals might experience (85.2%). Also, on the 3 × 4 grid, there was little support for procedures involving pain and death; this was true for all four species listed.

And what about the other survey, the one sent to academic psychologists (Plous, 1996a)? Interestingly enough, the results were virtually identical. The only notable difference was for item 1. While 71.7% of psychology majors either strongly supported (14.3%) or supported (57.4%) the use of animals in psychological research, support was even stronger among the psychologists—31.4% strongly supported it and 48.6% supported it (i.e., 80% supporting or strongly supporting).

---

[4]One of the requirements for inclusion was that departments have at least thirty psychology majors. Two of the fifty schools did not meet this criterion and were dropped, so the 87.5% is the result of dividing 42 by 48.

TABLE 12.2 *Attitudes About Animal Research—A Survey of Psychology Majors*

Here is a sample of the items from the survey by Plous (1996a).

In general, do you *support* or *oppose* the use of animals in psychological research?

Strongly support	14.3%
Support	57.4%
Oppose	13.8%
Strongly oppose	4.7%
Not sure	9.8%

Do you believe that the use of animals in psychological research is necessary for progress in psychology, or not?

Yes	68.4%
No	15.7%
Not sure	15.9%

In general, do you *support* or *oppose* the use of animals in undergraduate psychology courses?

Support	56.9%
Oppose	28.4%
Not sure	14.7%

Do you feel that laboratory work with animals should be a required part of the undergraduate psychology major?

Yes	34.1%
No	54.3%
Not sure	11.6%

Federal regulations protect the "psychological well-being" of primates used in research. Do you *support* or *oppose* the idea of protecting the psychological well-being of primates?

Support	85.1%
Oppose	4.0%
Not sure	10.9%

Before being granted approval to run an experiment, investigators in Great Britain, Canada, and the Netherlands are required to assess the degree of pain animals may experience. Would you *support* or *oppose* a similar requirement in the United States?

Support	85.2%
Oppose	7.0%
Not sure	7.8%

Source: Adapted from Plous (1996a), Table 1.

✓ Self Test 12.3

1. On a written survey, what is demographic information and where should it be placed in the survey?
2. Describe an advantage and a disadvantage of including DK alternatives.
3. Plous sent initial requests for cooperation to 708 colleges and universities, excluding very small schools. This list of 708 schools is known as a _____.

With this final chapter on the descriptive methods of observational and survey research, the cast of characters for the production called "research in psychology" is complete. What remains is a brief epilogue that returns to a theme introduced back in Chapter 1, the excitement of doing research in psychology, and includes some ideas about how the methods course might have been good for you.

Chapter Summary

Observational Research

The goal of providing accurate qualitative and quantitative descriptions of behavior can be accomplished by using basic observational methods. In naturalistic observation, the observer is separate from those being observed and the subjects of study are either unaware of the observer's presence or habituated to it. The observer becomes an active member of the group being studied in participant observation studies. Observation studies vary in the amount of structure imposed by the researcher. Lack of control, observer bias, and subject reactivity are three methodological problems that accompany observational research. The researcher also must confront the ethical dilemmas of informed consent and invasion of privacy. Observational research, as well as the other forms of descriptive research described in this chapter, can be used to falsify claims about behavior, and are often a useful source of hypotheses for further investigation.

Survey Research

The primary purpose of survey research is to gather descriptive information about people's self-described attitudes, opinions, feelings, and behaviors. Surveys can be administered in face-to-face interviews, by means of written questionnaires, over the phone, or via the Internet. Unlike most research in psychology, which typically relies on convenience samples, surveys are most effective when administered to a representative sample. Conclusions drawn from survey research can be erroneous if the group sampled does not reflect the population targeted by the survey. Probability sampling is designed to create good samples, and there are three common forms: a simple random sample, a stratified sample, and a cluster sample. In simple random sampling, every member of the population has an equal chance of being selected. Stratified sampling ensures that important subgroups in the population are represented proportionally in the sample. Cluster sampling is used when it is impossible to know all of the members of the population. Quota sampling is a nonprobability sampling technique that has a goal similar to that of stratified sampling (proportionality). Constructing reliable and valid surveys is a major task. Researchers must have clear empirical questions in mind and must exercise great care in the wording and organization of survey items. Survey data can be affected by such respondent biases as social desirability and response acquiescence.

Chapter Review Questions

1. Distinguish between naturalistic and participant observational procedures, in terms of both method and ethics.

2. What is meant by the problem of "reactivity," and how can it be overcome?

3. Give an example to show how observer bias can influence observational research and describe how such bias can be reduced.

4. Describe an example that shows how observational research can serve the purpose of falsification.

5. Distinguish between time and event sampling.

6. Explain why probability sampling is more important for survey research than for other methods.

7. Describe the three forms of probability sampling described in the chapter.

8. Describe the advantages and disadvantages of using face-to-face interviews as a way of doing survey research.

9. Describe two varieties of e-surveys. What are the advantages and disadvantages of e-surveying?

10. If you are conducting a written survey, what can you do to increase the return rate? What is meant by a nonresponse bias?

11. Use the hamburger example to illustrate the dangers of using leading questions in survey research.

12. Use the case of the news journalist Christine Craft to illustrate how survey research can be misused.

13. What is response acquiescence and how can it be avoided?

Applications Exercises

Exercise 12.1   Probability Sampling

1. Use a table of random numbers (you can get one by doing a simple Google search). Use it to select a simple random sample of students from your research methods class. Your instructor will provide a class list and indicate a sample size.

2. Repeat the exercise, but select a stratified sample that reflects the male-female proportions of your methods class.

Exercise 12.2   Improving Poor Survey Items

The following are several examples of items that could be found on surveys. Some are in the form of closed questions, others in the form of agree/disagree statements. For each item, (a) identify what is wrong and (b) rewrite it so as to solve the problem.

1. Have you had an upset stomach lately?
2. Highly prejudiced people are usually hostile and not very smart.
3. In your opinion, how young is the average smoker?
4. Do you agree with most people that violations of seat-belt laws should result in harsh penalties?
5. Most doctors have a superior attitude.
6. People who are overweight lack will power and are usually unhappy.

Exercise 12.3   Defining Behaviors for Observational Research

Imagine that you are in the beginning stages of an observational research study and have to arrive at clear operational definitions for the behaviors you'll be observing. For each of the following hypotheses, operationally define the behaviors to be recorded and describe how you would set up the study (i.e., where you would conduct the study, whether you would create some level of structure, etc.).

1. In the college library, most students spend less than half of their time actually studying.
2. Men interrupt women more than women interrupt men.
3. In a free play situation, older children play cooperatively but younger children engage in parallel play.
4. Teenagers patrolling malls follow clearly defined routes that they repeat at regular intervals.
5. Couples look at each other more when they are dating than when they are married.
6. Dogs are more aggressive within their own territories than outside of them.

Exercise 12.4   Deciding on a Method

For each of the hypotheses listed below, identify the best methodological approach from among the following possibilities. Indicate the reason(s) for your choice. There may be more than one correct answer for some of the items.

naturalistic observation	written survey	interview survey
participant observation	phone survey	e-survey

1. After altering the content of bird feeders, the proportions of two different species of birds at the feeder will change within a few days.

2. When respondents are given the opportunity and encouragement to explain their opinions on controversial issues, their beliefs are usually determined to be based on anecdotal evidence.

3. There is a correlation between personality and online shopping—those who shop online regularly tend to be outgoing, adventurous, and willing to take risks.

4. A national sample (2,000 people) is chosen for a consumer survey on preferred TV shows.

5. College students who major in the physical sciences tend to hold more rigid stereotypes than students who major in the social sciences.

6. When college students enter the cafeteria, males are more likely to be unaccompanied by other students than females; this is especially true for the dinner meal.

7. Members of animal rights groups display a high degree of consistency between their beliefs and their actions.

8. Fraternities and sororities represent well-ordered cultures that reward conformity to unwritten norms for behavior.

Answers to Self Tests:

✓ **12.1.**

1. Researchers stay in the open and assume that, after a period of time, animals will habituate to their presence and act normally.

2. It refers to the extent of agreement among observers about what is being observed; its purpose is to reduce observer bias.

3. Informed consent.

✓ **12.2.**

1. It means that the sample is a good reflection of the wider population; survey results from a representative sample can be generalized to the population.

2. They both represent subgroups proportionately; stratified sampling is probability sampling, whereas quota sampling is nonprobability sampling.

    3. Advantages: follow-up questions, ambiguous questions can be clarified. Disadvantages: cost, logistics, representativeness.

✓ **12.3.**

    1. This is basic information that identifies respondents (e.g., age, gender); it is best to put it at the end of a survey.

    2. Advantage: doesn't force a choice when the respondent truly does not know. Disadvantage: may be chosen too often.

    3. Sample frame.

Epilogue

I sincerely hope that your experience in this research methods course has been a positive and successful one. The course can be difficult, and at times tedious, but I believe it is the most important one in the psychology curriculum, along with your statistics course (the history of psychology course is right up there too). In the letters of recommendation that I write for my students, both for graduate school *and* for jobs, I always look back to how they did in my research methods course, and much of the letter will be framed in terms of the kinds of skills developed in that course. I'd like to close the book by (a) listing those skills, some of which I introduced briefly in Chapter 1, and (b) returning to another theme introduced in Chapter 1, the idea that researchers typically become deeply involved and passionate about their work.

What I Learned in My Research Methods Course

To become a professional psychologist requires an advanced degree, preferably the doctorate, and because graduate study includes a strong dose of research, the undergraduate methods course is an obvious first step toward developing the research skills that will be put to use in graduate school. Yet the majority of undergraduate psychology majors won't go on to earn doctorates in psychology and, as a result, students sometimes question the value of the methods course if their goal is to finish college and get a job. If you're in that category, I'd like to convince you that your chances of getting a decent position and advancing on the job have been improved if you've done well in your methods course. Here's a list of some of the career-enhancing skills you've begun to develop as a result of taking this course. Naturally, if you are heading to graduate school, these skills also apply, and will increase your chances of doing well as you work toward an advanced degree. Here goes:

- Ability to think empirically
    - Framing questions in ways that they can be answered with data
    - Looking for data-based conclusions about behavior
    - Recognizing that conclusions based on data are "working truths," pending further research and replication; it is important to be willing to change your mind about something, if the data warrant a change

- Using logical thinking in the research context, both inductive and deductive varieties
- Ability to examine claims and information about behavior with a critical eye
  - Being skeptical about unsubstantiated, excessive, and/or simplistic claims
  - Looking out for overly strong (i.e., causal) conclusions based only on correlational data
  - Looking carefully at graphs to see that they don't mislead, especially by creating deceptive Y-axes
  - Looking for alternative and more parsimonious explanations for results being used to support some claim
  - Being skeptical about claims based on questionable evidence (e.g., anecdotal data or glowing testimonials, observations affected by bias, results based on an insufficient number of observations)
  - Seeing a red flag whenever claims include the word "prove," as in "listening to Mozart has been *proven* to increase your child's IQ"
- Ability to read difficult material for comprehension
  - Through text reading and especially the reading of original research articles
- Ability to take a vague problem, give it some structure, and work out a systematic plan to solve it
  - Through direct experience in developing, implementing, and completing an empirical research project
  - Through the completion of "what's next?" exercises—designing the next study, based on the results of one just finished
- Ability to search efficiently for important information to help solve problems and organize that information coherently
  - Through experience with PsycINFO and other electronic search tools (finding important information involves more than a Google search)
- Ability to organize, summarize, and interpret data
  - Through lab reports and data summaries for data collection exercises
  - Through the application of descriptive and inferential statistics to evaluate data collected in labs
  - Through the ability to use and correctly interpret SPSS (or other statistics software) procedures
- Improved writing
  - Through learning and using the rules for creating the APA-format lab report, which leads writers to be organized and parsimonious with the language
- Improved communication skills
  - Through experience with oral presentations, posters, lab reports
- Improved computer skills
  - Especially computer statistical packages (e.g., SPSS) and graphing software, but possibly presentation software (e.g., PowerPoint), and possibly through packages or websites that present experiments to be completed by students

This is a rather impressive list, and collectively it could be called "research self-efficacy," but note that I prefaced it by writing that you've *just begun* to develop these skills. To develop them further, as you continue your career as a psychology major with an interest in research, I would suggest the following:

- Seek out opportunities for independent research with your professors. They will be delighted to have you in their labs, and although you might start by doing routine tasks (e.g., data entry), before long you'll be more deeply involved in projects. By the time you graduate, you will probably be a co-author on a conference poster presentation or two, and you might even have completed one or two studies that reflect your own research ideas and for which you are the lead researcher. If you apply to graduate school in psychology, research experience will be high on the list of things that admissions committees hope to see (Landrum & Nelson, 2002).

- Complete an independent research project or a senior thesis, if your school offers them.

- Choose electives likely to have laboratory components. These typically include such courses as Principles of Learning, Cognitive Psychology, Sensation/Perception, and Neuropsychology.

- Go to research conferences and present your research (most likely in poster format). At the very least, you should go to an undergraduate research conference or two. These are small conferences especially designed for undergraduates to present their work. They typically last just a day and feature poster sessions, maybe some oral presentations of research, and an invited address by a prominent researcher. Better yet, submit your work to a regional psychology conference, such as the Southeastern or Midwestern Psychological Association (SEPA, MPA). These are typically three-day conferences that feature talks by prominent psychologists, lots of poster sessions, and opportunities to meet other student researchers. Third, consider going to one of the national conferences of either the American Psychological Association (August every year) or the Association for Psychological Science (June every year). These are larger versions of the regional conferences. Be careful about timing, however. In order to present your research at these regional or national conferences, you will have to submit your work (typically an abstract) sometime in the fall for presentation the following spring or summer. Hence, it's a good idea to be involved in research no later than your junior year.

- Work hard to meet the requirements for Psi Chi, the national honor society in psychology (www.psichi.org). Besides enhancing your resume, membership gives you special opportunities for research. Psi Chi sponsors several research grants and awards, and at all of the regional and national meetings just mentioned, Psi Chi sponsors poster sessions for research by members.

- Submit your work to journals that specialize in undergraduate research. The best known is a journal sponsored by Psi Chi, but others exist. You can find a listing of them, with their website addresses, by looking at Psi Chi's website.

- Find a topic of interest and immerse yourself in it thoroughly. That is, develop a passion for research. This brings us to the book's closing section.

A Passion for Research in Psychology (Part II)

Near the end of his long and productive life, the renowned Russian physiologist Ivan Pavlov was asked by a group of students to write a brief article for their student journal on what it takes to be a great scientist. Pavlov wrote that it took three things. The first was to be systematic in the search for knowledge and the second was to be modest and to recognize one's basic ignorance. The third thing, he wrote, "is *passion*. Remember that science demands [your] whole life. And even if you could have two lives, they would not be sufficient. Science calls for tremendous effort and great passion. Be passionate in your work and in your search for truth" (quoted in Babkin, 1949, p. 110; italics added).

In Chapter 1, you briefly met two famous psychologist/scientists, Eleanor Gibson and B. F. Skinner, and you learned something about the excitement that comes from making important discoveries by doing psychological research. I tried to make the point that perhaps the best reason for doing research in psychology is that it is great fun and can be enormously rewarding, despite the occasional frustrations and setbacks and the guarantee of long hours. That lesson is repeated over and over through the lives of the men and women who are leaders among today's generation of psychological researchers. Two good present-day examples are Elliot Aronson, professor emeritus at the University of California at Santa Cruz, and Elizabeth Loftus of the University of California at Irvine.

Elliot Aronson

Ask psychologists to name the field's most prominent social psychologist, and the name Elliot Aronson (Figure E.1) will be at or near the top of every list. He is known among research psychologists for his long and productive career investigating topics ranging from basic research in prejudice, persuasion, and cognitive dissonance, to applied research in prejudice reduction, condom use, and energy conservation. When the APA named him a recipient of their Award for Distinguished Scientific Contributions, the award citation's final sentence read: "Aronson's vision of social psychology as a rigorous science in the service of humanity stands as a beacon for generations of scientists to come" (Award, 1999, p. 873). He is also recognized by many undergraduates who take the social psychology course, because chances are that he wrote their textbook. Aronson's award-winning (APA's National Media Award in 1973) *Social Animal* (2007) is now in its tenth edition and going strong. You met him earlier in this book (Chapter 3) as the creator of the distinction between experimental and mundane realism and as a key figure in the evolution of cognitive dissonance theory.

Aronson had an enviable list of academic mentors. As an undergraduate at Brandeis University, he wandered into an introductory psychology lecture on prejudice by the famous humanistic psychologist Abraham Maslow. The topic caught the attention of Aronson, who had been on the receiving end of the behavioral products of prejudice while growing up as a Jewish child in the tough working-class town of Revere, Massachusetts. He immediately changed his major

FIGURE E.1 Elliot Aronson. (Courtesy of Public Information Office, University of California, Santa Cruz, photo by Don Harris.)

to psychology and developed a close relationship with Maslow. Later, after earning a Master's degree at Wesleyan College with David McClelland (of achievement motivation fame—see Box 9.3), Aronson went west, arriving at Stanford in the same year that Leon Festinger came there as a new professor. Festinger was just then developing his famous theory of cognitive dissonance, which you read about in Chapter 3 and in the discussion of participant observation in Chapter 12 (Box 12.1). Aronson became Festinger's best-known student, and dissonance theory has remained central to his work ever since. Aronson and his students are responsible for most of the theory's elaboration over the years. A major contribution was Aronson's argument, first articulated in 1960, that cognitive dissonance was strongest and had its most pervasive effects whenever some important aspect of the self-concept was threatened, as when we do something (e.g., cheat on an exam) that is inconsistent with our firmly held beliefs about ourselves (e.g., I am an honest person) (Aronson, 1999).

As you recall from Chapter 3, psychological scientists sometimes develop ideas for research from everyday observations and sometimes as a logical deduction from theory. Aronson does both, often deriving research hypotheses from observations that are then fit into the framework of dissonance theory. When asked about the origins of his ideas for research, Aronson will mention both sources: first, "[j]ust being alive in the world and noticing certain things that pique my curiosity," and second, "from theory or restructuring of theory" (Aronson, personal communication, 2000). For example, for a while, he was stymied by how ineffective it was to use rational arguments as a way of convincing intelligent college students to use condoms in the era of AIDS. Then he hit on an idea that followed from an extension of dissonance theory. Assuming that most people don't like to think of themselves as hypocrites (saying one thing, doing another), Aronson developed a series of studies (e.g., Aronson, Fried, & Stone, 1991) in which college students were induced to give public talks urging condom use and subsequently were confronted with their own failure to use condoms. Feeling hypocritical produced dissonance, which the students reduced by increasing their reported levels of condom use.

Throughout his long career, Aronson's enthusiasm for his science has never wavered. In response to a question about the factors that keep him going as a researcher, he replies simply and elegantly, "Three things: One, I am passionately curious about human social behavior; two, I am excited about trying to find out things that might better the human condition; and finally, doing research is great fun" (Aronson, personal communication, 2000).

Elizabeth Loftus

The work of Elizabeth Loftus (Figure E.2) is a perfect blend of the ideals of basic and applied research, as described in Chapter 3. She has contributed much to our knowledge of the fundamental processes of human memory, while at the same time showing how these principles apply to real-world memory phenomena such as eyewitness memory. Loftus herself identifies this mixture as the most interesting aspect of her work as a research psychologist: "I get to make interesting scientific discoveries and at the same time apply these and other psychological discoveries to the lives of real people" (Loftus, personal communication, 1993).

Loftus is arguably the world's leading expert on the phenomenon of eyewitness memory, part of her broader interest in the factors affecting long-term memory. As a result of her recognized expertise, she has testified in hundreds of court cases in

FIGURE E.2   Elizabeth Loftus. (Courtesy Elizabeth Loftus, University of Washington.)

which eyewitness testimony was a crucial element (Loftus, 1986). As you recall, her research was mentioned briefly in the previous chapter as a caution against relying on the accuracy of case history information when it depends on memory of the distant past. Loftus and her colleagues and research team have completed dozens of studies of the ways in which past memories become distorted by information intervening between the time of the event to be recalled and the time of recall. Most of this research has focused on direct eyewitness recall, but in recent years Loftus has taken on the empirical question of whether memories of childhood sexual abuse can be accurate when remembered many years later. She argues that serious distortions can and do occur.

Loftus's enthusiasm for her research in memory was sparked near the end of her graduate school career at Stanford. Her doctoral dissertation was a basic research project: "An Analysis of the Structural Variables That Determine Problem-Solving Difficulty on a Computer-Based Teletype." If your eyes glaze over as you read the title, Loftus would not be offended. As the project neared its end, she was also "a bit bored with the whole thing" (Loftus & Ketcham, 1991, p. 5). Luckily, she took a social psychology course from Jon Freedman, who sparked her interest in some of the more practical aspects of memory. As Loftus described it:

> In my last six months of graduate school, I spent every free moment in Freedman's lab, setting up the experimental design, running subjects, tabulating the data, and analyzing the results. As the project took shape and [we] realized that we were on to something, that we were actually discovering something new about how the brain works, I began to think of myself as a *research psychologist*. Oh, those were *lovely* words—I could design an experiment, set it up, and follow it through. I felt for the first time that I was a scientist, and I knew with ultimate clarity that it was exactly what I wanted to be doing with my life. (Loftus & Ketcham, 1991, p. 6; first italics in the original; second italics added)

There is a thread that weaves together the work of Gibson and Skinner (as described in Chapter 1) and that of Aronson, Loftus, and other psychological researchers. Pavlov accurately identified this common feature when he exhorted his students to be *passionate* about their work. You can detect this passion if you read carefully the quotes I've chosen, both in Chapter 1 and here. In both the Gibson and Skinner quotes, for example, the concept of beauty appears. For Gibson, the first tentative studies with the visual cliff "worked *beautifully*." When Skinner returned to his jammed pellet dispenser, he found "a *beautiful* curve." Similarly, when Aronson said he is "*passionately* curious" about social behavior, and when Loftus referred to her self-identity as a research psychologist as "*lovely* words," that same intensity of feeling was being expressed.

Furthermore, for psychological scientists, the passionate devotion to their science is connected with a deep-seated conviction that by doing their research, even if it is basic laboratory research with no obvious immediate application, they are contributing to the greater good, that their work will ultimately benefit humanity. This feeling was expressed succinctly in the dedication page of a book written by a former student of Murray Sidman (a pioneer in arguing for small N methods, who was mentioned in Chapter 11). The dedication to her mentor read, "to . . .

Murray Sidman for proving to me that being scientific and data based was the operational definition of caring" (quoted in Sidman, 2007, p. 310).

There are enormous gaps in our knowledge of behavior. Hence, there is ample space available for those with the kind of passion and concern displayed by people like Gibson, Skinner, Aronson, Loftus, and countless other researchers. What could be better than to have a career that is continually exciting and rewarding and helps us to understand the complexities of behavior and mental processes? The invitation is open.

APPENDIX A

Communicating the Results of Research in Psychology

In this appendix, you will learn how to:

- Prepare and write an APA-style laboratory report
- Prepare a professional presentation of your research either as a paper to be read or as a poster to be written and organized

Research Reports, APA Style

You are about to enter the world of the obsessive-compulsive. As you begin to learn about APA-style lab reports, it will seem to you that the list of seemingly arbitrary rules is endless. Take heart. Practically everything you need to know will be found in this appendix. A Google search (just enter "APA style") will also yield a number of guides. For the ultimate source, however, the APA (2001) publishes an encyclopedic *Publication Manual* (*PM*) that can answer any of your format questions. This appendix will teach you the basics and will help you learn how to communicate the results of your research, but at somewhat bloated 439 pages, the *PM* is the ultimate weapon against a botched lab report.

There are two main reasons for the rules that dictate a consistent format for reporting the results of research in psychology. First, research findings accumulate external validity as they are repeated in different labs with different participants and perhaps with slightly varied procedures. In order to replicate a study exactly or make a systematic variation in some procedure, the reader must know precisely what was done in the original study. If the results of a study are written in a known and predictable format, the replication process is made easier. Second, a consistent format makes the review process more efficient and consistent. Thousands of research articles are submitted to dozens of psychological research journals every year. Typically, each article is screened by an editor and then sent to two or three other researchers with expertise in the article's topic. These "peer reviewers" read the article and send the editor a written critique that includes a recommendation about whether the article should be published (most psychology journals reject 70–80% of the articles submitted to them). In the absence of an agreed-on format, the work of the editor and reviewers would be hopelessly complicated. For the purposes of the methods course you are now taking, having a regular format makes it easier for your instructor to grade your lab report fairly.

General Guidelines

One of my beliefs is that the only way to learn how to do research in psychology is to actually do some research. The same principle applies to writing. It is a skill like any other and it improves with practice, assuming that one's efforts are followed by feedback of some kind. Hence, the most basic recommendation I can make is for you to write whenever you can and ask others to read what you've written. When writing a lab report, I would suggest that you find someone who has already completed the research methods course *and* earned a decent grade. As you are writing your report, ask this person to read your work and critique it.

Writing Style

The APA-style laboratory report is not the Great American Novel. Therefore, some literary devices that might enhance a creative writing exercise, such as deliberately creating an ambiguity to hold the reader's attention or omitting details to arouse curiosity, are out of place in scientific writing. Rather, one should always strive for perfect clarity and simplicity of expression. This is easier said than done, of course, but despite the grain of truth in Figure A.1, academic writing is not necessarily stuffy and difficult to follow.

All good writing includes correct grammatical usage. Grammatical errors automatically create ambiguity and awkwardness, so your first step in learning to write

Calvin and Hobbes   by Bill Watterson

FIGURE A.1   Academic writing?

a lab report is to be sure that you know the basic rules of sentence structure. Numerous English usage guides are available, and the *PM* includes a series of guidelines specifically targeted for the kinds of sentences found in scientific writing. One problem that seems especially common in scientific writing, perhaps out of a desire to sound objective, is a tendency to overuse the passive voice. Whenever possible, use the active voice, which generally adds clarity and simplifies sentences. To illustrate,

> Passive: An investigation of sleep deprivation was done by Smith (1992).

> Active: Smith (1992) investigated sleep deprivation.

The *PM*'s guidelines on grammar can be found on pages 40–61.

In addition to grammatical problems, beginning writers of APA lab reports often use some common words inappropriately. For example, although the term "significant" generally means important or meaningful, the writer using the term in this fashion in a lab report might mislead the reader. This is because, in a lab report, "significant" implies "statistically significant," which has a technical definition relating to the rejection of the null hypothesis (refer back to Chapter 4). A reader encountering the word in a lab report might assume that the technical definition is being used even if the writer didn't mean it that way. To eliminate ambiguity, never use this term in the lab report except when it clearly refers to statistical significance.

Two other common problems with word usage concern the confusion between "affect" and "effect" and the use of some plural nouns such as "data." These and related problems are elaborated in Tables A.1 and A.2.

Reducing Bias in Language

For years, linguists and psychologists interested in language use have investigated the connections between language and thinking. Although there is much disagreement over the nature of this relationship, there is a consensus that using language in

TABLE A.1   *Effectively Using the Terms "Affect" and "Effect"*

One of the most common errors found in student lab reports is the failure to distinguish between the different meanings for the words "affect" and "effect."

affect as a noun means an emotional state; thus
- Because of the pressure of a rapid presentation rate, subjects showed increased affect.

affect as a verb means to influence; thus
- Increasing the presentation rate affected recall.

effect as a noun means the result of some event; thus
- The effect of increasing the presentation rate was a decline in recall.

effect as a verb means to bring about or accomplish some result; thus
- We effected a change by increasing the presentation rate.

A common error is to use "effect" as a verb when "affect" should be used; thus

Incorrect:	Changing to a fixed ratio schedule effected the rat's behavior.
Correct:	Changing to a fixed ratio schedule affected the rat's behavior.

A second common error is to use "affect" as a noun when "effect" should be used; thus

Incorrect:	Changing to a fixed ratio schedule had a major affect on the rat's behavior.
Correct:	Changing to a fixed ratio schedule had a major effect on the rat's behavior.

certain ways can reinforce and perpetuate certain concepts, including stereotypes about people. The *PM* makes it clear that "[s]cientific writing should be free of implied or irrelevant evaluation of the group or groups being studied" (2001, p. 63).

A common type of bias in language concerns gender. Language that shows gender bias occurs in two varieties. The first is known as a *problem of designation*. This happens when terms include only masculine terminology but are supposed

TABLE A.2   *Plurals of Words with Latin or Greek Origins*

The plural forms of many words found in scientific writing derive from their origins in Latin and Greek. A failure to recognize the plural form can lead to a grammatical error of disagreement between noun and verb. The most common example is the word *data*, which refers to more than one piece of information and is the plural of *datum*. Although the term "data" is sometimes found in common usage as a singular noun, the *PM* (p. 34) suggests that it be used only in the plural form.

Incorrect: The *data was* subjected to a content analysis.
Correct: The *data were* subjected to a content analysis.

Other examples:

Singular form	Plural form
analys**is**	analys**es**
criteri**on**	criter**ia**
hypothes**is**	hypothes**es**
phenomen**on**	phenomen**a**
stimul**us**	stimul**i**

to refer to both males and females. The most common example is the use of "man" when "person" is intended, as in "Man has long been interested in the causes of mental illness." Some research has shown that even though the intent may be nonsexist when using such language, readers often interpret the language in ways that exclude females. For example, a study by Kidd (1971) found that when people read sentences using "man" or "his" in a supposedly nonsexist fashion, they perceived the sentences as referring to men 86% of the time.

Here are some examples of sentences with problems of designation, along with suggested corrections. As you will see, the problems can be solved fairly easily by rewording, using plurals, or omitting gender designations altogether. The examples are quoted from Table 2.1 of the *PM* (pp. 70–71).

- The client is usually the best judge of the value of his counseling.
  - *Better:* Clients are usually the best judges of the counseling they receive.
- Man's search for knowledge . . .
  - *Better:* The search for knowledge . . .
- Research scientists often neglect their wives and children.
  - *Better:* Research scientists often neglect their spouses and children.

In addition to problems of designation, some sexist language shows *problems of evaluation*. That is, the terms selected for males and females imply judgments of inequality. For example, a writer describing high school athletes may refer to the "men's basketball team" and the "girls' basketball team" (better: "women's basketball team"). Also, using phrases like "typically male" or "typically female" can promote stereotypical thinking, as can using stereotypical descriptors for behaviors that may be identical for males and females (e.g., "ambitious men" but "aggressive women"; "cautious men" but "timid women").

Although the guidelines for gender-neutral language are generally designed to correct problems harmful to women, at least one example addresses an inequality detrimental to men. This occurs when the term "mothering" is used to refer to any behavior involving some kind of supportive interaction between parent and child. Using "mothering" to refer to females and "fathering" to refer to the same behavior in males doesn't work because fathering has a different connotation altogether. The APA recommends that the gender-neutral terms "nurturing" or "parenting" be used here to recognize the fact that males perform these kinds of supportive behaviors also.

Gender bias is not the only form of language bias addressed by the *PM*. The *PM* also urges the writer to be cautious about language bias relating to sexual orientation, racial and ethnic identity, disability, and age. Here are some more examples from Table 2.1 in the *PM*:

- The sample consisted of 200 adolescent homosexuals.
  - *Better:* The sample consisted of 100 gay males and 100 lesbian adolescents.
  - *Note:* more specific, by identifying the numbers of both male and female participants and avoids the use of the term homosexual.
- We studied Eskimos . . .

- *Better:* We studied Inuit from Canada and Aleuts . . .
  - *Note:* more precise, and shows the variety of native tribes from Canada and Alaska.
- . . . disabled person.
  - *Better:* . . . person with a disability.
  - *Note:* emphasis is on the person, rather than the disability.
- . . . depressives.
  - *Better:* . . . people who are depressed.
  - *Note:* emphasis on the person again; the first usage tends to exaggerate the severity of the disorder.

Avoiding Plagiarism

In the section in Chapter 2 on scientific fraud, the discussion centered on data falsification, but plagiarism[1] was also mentioned as a serious problem to be avoided. Standard 8.11 of the 2002 ethics code specifically addresses plagiarism, stating simply that "[p]sychologists do not present portions of another's work or data as their own, even if the other work or data source is cited occasionally" (APA, 2002, p. 1070).

The most obvious form of plagiarism is copying information directly from some source without using quotation marks and then failing to cite the source. The principle is clear: Don't do this under any circumstance, even if the information has been taken from a web page. A second form of plagiarism, sometimes called "accidental plagiarism," is subtler, but no less serious. This occurs when students paraphrase the information from some source, but the sentence structure remains very similar to the original source, and/or concepts they describe in the paraphrase clearly belong to the author of that source. Consider the following example. A student is doing a paper on lying and uses a book called *Telling Lies* by Paul Ekman (1985). The student reads the following passage about a situation in which someone is actually telling the truth but is very nervous and therefore appears to be lying:

> Another equally important source of trouble, leading to disbelieving-the-truth mistakes, is the Othello error. This error occurs when the lie catcher fails to consider that a truthful person who is under stress may appear to be lying . . . Truthful people may be afraid of being disbelieved, and their fear might be confused with the liar's detection apprehension . . .
>
> I have called this error after Othello because the death scene in Shakespeare's play is such an excellent and famous example of it. (Ekman, 1985, pp. 169–170)

---

[1]The term derives from the Latin word *plaga*, meaning a snare or hunting net. The term was eventually applied to the capturing, snaring, or kidnapping of children; thus plagiarism is like "kidnapping" someone's ideas (*Webster's Word Histories*, 1989).

The student decides to paraphrase this information and writes the following in the paper:

> Disbelieving-the-truth mistakes are another kind of problem in the accurate detection of lying. The mistake happens when the person trying to catch someone else lying fails to take into account that a truthful person experiencing stress may seem to be lying. This is known as the Othello error, because of the similarity to the death scene in Shakespeare's famous play. Thus, sometimes you could be telling the truth, yet afraid that nobody will believe you. As a result you would appear to be nervous about being detected.

This paraphrasing is an example of plagiarism on two counts. First, the concept, the "Othello error," has clearly been given that name by Ekman. It is his concept, so his book must be cited. Second, the structure and wording of the paraphrasing is too close to the original in several places. Simply taking an author's words and making a few small changes is not writing—it is plagiarizing. One clear example is when Ekman wrote "This error occurs when the lie catcher fails to consider that a truthful person who is under stress may appear to be lying." The student then wrote, "The mistake happens when the person trying to catch someone else lying fails to take into account that a truthful person experiencing stress may seem to be lying."

Thus, any time you use an idea, term, theory, or research finding that seems to belong to another person, be sure to cite that person's work. To avoid plagiarism, either use direct quotes and clearly attribute the words to the original source or give credit to the creator of an idea, again by the use of a proper citation. When you paraphrase, do not simply replace some of the original author's words with synonyms. Rewrite them in your own words—and still cite the original author, because you will still be using the author's ideas. The writing center at your college or university almost certainly has a set of detailed guidelines for avoiding plagiarism. Go get them. If, by some chance, the center doesn't have a good set of recommendations, there are a number of websites that provide useful information. You can find an excellent one at www.plagiarism.org.

Miscellaneous

Although your instructor may have some specific additions to or deletions from the following checklist, these APA formatting rules are designed to create a document that is physically easy to read.

- Double-space the entire manuscript.
- Make the margins (top, bottom, and sides) one inch throughout the paper.
- Do not change the printing fonts or the font size—stick with one throughout.
  - *PM* recommends that you use either 12 pt. Times Roman or 12 pt. Courier, but I tell my students to use 10 pt. (it might save a page or two).
- Excluding the page header and page number (see below), each page of the manuscript should have no more than 27 lines of text.

- Use a paper clip, not a stapler, to join the pages.
- Be sure to save the file (maybe in two different places) with your manuscript on it.

Main Selections of the Lab Report

The APA-style lab report describing the outcome of an empirical study includes each of the following elements, in this order:

Title page

Abstract

Introduction

Method

Results

Discussion

References

Following the References section, reports include, in this order, separate pages for author notes (these occur in publications, but you probably won't be using them for a class lab report), other footnotes, tables, a list of figures, and the figures themselves. In some cases, an appendix (listing the actual stimulus materials, for instance) might be included. When this happens, the appendix or appendices are placed between the References page(s) and the page with author notes. What follows is a description of how to prepare each main section of the lab report.

Title Page

The title page has a precise format, as you can see from the sample paper at the end of this Appendix. It includes the following elements:

The Manuscript Page Header/Page Number

Found in the upper-right-hand corner, the **manuscript page header** is the first two or three substantive words of the complete title. Five spaces to the right is the number 1, which designates the title page as page 1 of the manuscript. Both the page header and the page number are right-justified (i.e., they are flush with the right-hand margin). Except for pages on which figures (e.g., graphs, diagrams, flow charts) are drawn, *every* page of the manuscript includes the page header and the page number. This helps to identify the manuscript if pages become separated for some reason. Use the Header tool on your word processor to create this.

Running Head

If you examine an article printed in most journals, you will find that, after the first page, the top of every page includes a "header" that is either the author's name (usually even-numbered pages) or a brief version of the full title (usually odd-numbered pages). The latter is called the **running head** because it is found in the header to the published article and runs throughout the article.

To fit into its assigned location, a running head must be brief, yet sufficiently informative to convey the sense of the title. Thus, the running head is not the same thing as the manuscript page header. The only time they are identical is when the first two or three words of the title just happen to provide a good description of the study's content.

The running head is printed at the top of the title page, just below the manuscript page header and page number, and flush with the left-hand margin. It is limited to fifty characters, which include letters, spaces between words, and punctuation marks. For Research Example 12 on context and memory, which had a running head of thirty-one characters, the top of the title page of the submitted manuscript looked like this:

Running head : PREREQUISITES FOR UNDERSTANDING

Title/Author/Affiliation

The title of the article, the name of the person writing the paper (or names, for papers with more than one author), and the college, university, or other professional affiliation of the author(s) go in the middle of the title page, centered between the left and right margins. The first letters of the primary words in the title are capitalized. For a lab report that you do in class, your instructor might want to include the due date here.

Give some thought to the wording of the article's title, which should range from 10 to 12 words (10 for the memory study—"Contextual Prerequisites for Understanding: Some Investigations of Comprehension and Recall"). It should give the reader a clear idea of the article's content and preview the variables being investigated. For example, in an experimental study, a common title format is "The effect of X on Y," which enables the reader to identify the independent (X) and dependent (Y) variables. Thus, a study entitled "The Effects of North Orientation and Target Distance on Pointing Accuracy" tells the reader that participants will be performing some kind of direction-finding task for the dependent measure and that two independent variables will be manipulated, whether or not participants are told the direction of north and the target distance. A second common format is a declarative sentence that summarizes the main result. An example would be Research Example 35, the observational study in the science museum—"Parents Explain More Often to Boys than to Girls During Shared Scientific Thinking." The APA has specific guidelines about authorship when more than one person is involved in a research project (see Standard 8.12 of the APA ethics code in Appendix B). In general, a person should not be an author unless he or she has made a substantial contribution to the work. Being involved in the initial planning and design of the study, collecting some of the data, working on the analysis, and doing some of the writing would constitute a substantial contribution. On the other hand, entering all of the data into a spreadsheet and coordinating the participant pool would not be a contribution sufficient to warrant authorship. On a paper with more than a single author, the first author (i.e., the name listed first on the title page) should be the person who has done the most work. When students work on projects in groups, it is generally a good idea to have one person be the overall leader of the project, carrying responsibilities sufficient to justify first authorship. Author and affiliation information are placed just below the title on the title page. Hence, in the memory and context study, the title, author, and affiliation information probably looked like this on the submitted manuscript.

Contextual Prerequisites for Understanding: Some Investigations of
Comprehension and Recall
John D. Bransford and Marcia K. Johnson
State University of New York, Stony Brook

Abstract

The **abstract** is the first text material to be read in a lab report and the last to be written. It is also the *only* part of the article looked at by many readers, who are forced by the sheer mass of information to read the abstract first in order to determine if the entire article is worth examining in detail. Abstracts are reproduced in PsycINFO.

The abstract contains elements of each of the remaining four major sections, and because it should not exceed 120 words in a single paragraph, it must be very carefully prepared—every word counts. To save space, numbers are never spelled out in the abstract unless they begin sentences, and abbreviations are recommended, if appropriate (e.g., "vs." instead of "versus"). The abstract's opening statement is perhaps the most informative. It always includes a statement of the problem, and it usually informs the reader about the individuals tested and/or the variables under investigation. Here are some samples of the opening sentences of abstracts, taken from three of the research examples used in this text.

- Thirty-four adults with severe traumatic brain injuries (TBI) and 34 matched control participants were asked to interpret videotaped conversational exchanges (McDonald & Flanagan, 2004, p. 572). [Research Example 10]

- Human infants learning to stand use visual proprioceptive information about body sway in order to maintain stable posture (Lee & Aronson, 1974). [Research Example 11]

- Records on recovery after cholecystectomy of patients in a suburban Pennsyl-vania hospital between 1972 and 1981 were examined to determine whether assignment to a room with a window view of a natural setting might have restorative influences (Ulrich, 1984, p. 420). [Research Example 29]

In addition to the meaty opening sentence, an abstract mentions something about the method, briefly summarizes the key results (the second most important sentence), and usually closes with a brief conclusion. The abstract occupies page 2 and only page 2 of the lab report. You should begin a new page when starting the Introduction section.

Introduction

The introduction thoroughly describes the problem being studied and, by reviewing the pertinent research literature, makes it clear what is known and not known about the problem. What is unknown or unclear provides the basis for one or more predictions, and these predictions form the hypotheses for the study. Thus, an introduction includes, normally in this order, a statement of the problem, a review of related research literature, and one or more hypotheses to be tested in the study. In a well-written introduction, the hypotheses are found in or near the final paragraph and flow naturally from the earlier descriptions of the problem and the review of related research. In a poorly written introduction, the hypotheses just seem to pop out at the end of the section and don't seem to have any rational basis. The introduction's literature review only includes studies directly relevant to the study summarized in the lab report.

The introduction begins page 3 of the manuscript and is the only major section of the lab report that is not headed by an identifying label. Rather than being headed with the label "Introduction," the section begins by repeating the article's full title (see sample paper).

APA Citation Format

When reviewing past research related to the problem at hand, you will need to furnish citations for the studies mentioned; the *PM* provides a specific format for this. Sometimes the author's name will be part of the sentence you are writing. If so, the date of publication follows the name and is placed in parentheses. For example:

In a study by Smith (1990), helping behavior declined . . .

If the author's name is not included in the sentence, the name, a comma, and the date are placed in parentheses. For example:

In an earlier study (Smith, 1990), helping behavior declined . . .

If a direct quote is used, the page number is included. For example:

Helping behavior declined when "participants had difficulty determining whether the confederate had fallen onto the live wire" (Smith, 1990, p. 23).

or

In the study by Smith (1990), helping behavior declined when "participants had difficulty determining whether the confederate had fallen onto the live wire" (p. 23).

Every work cited in the introduction (or any other part of the manuscript) must be given a complete listing at the end of the paper. You'll learn how that is accomplished shortly in the description of the "References" section of the report. The *PM* has a thorough guide to citations and can be consulted for virtually any question you may have. Also, you will find the APA's format being used in most of your psychology texts, including this one; hence several models are available to you.

Method

The guiding principle of the method section is that it must be detailed enough for other researchers to read it and be able to replicate the study in their own laboratories. Notice that I've written "other researchers" and not "anyone else." Thus, you can assume that the reader will have some specialized knowledge of methodology. It is enough to say that participants were matched according to variables X, Y, and Z; explaining the matching procedure step by step is not necessary. Similarly, it is enough to describe the type of counterbalancing used (e.g., a 4×4 Latin square) without explaining in great detail why such a control procedure is needed or how the square was constructed.

The method section includes several subsections, which vary depending on the particular study. One subsection always occurs, however, and it is labeled "Participants," or, if animals are being studied, "Subjects." This normally opens the method section and includes a description of those participating in the study. The reader of this subsection should be able to determine the general types of persons who participated in the study, some of their demographic features (average age, for instance), how many there were, and how they were selected. If animals are used, information about the species being studied should be included.

The description of participants is usually followed by a subsection called "Apparatus" if laboratory equipment was used or "Materials" if the experimenter used paper-and-pencil materials such as questionnaires or personality tests. Standard equipment usually can be described with reference to the manufacturer and model number. Apparatus created especially for the study should be described in more detail and perhaps drawn (as in the sample study). Copyrighted surveys or personality questionnaires can simply be listed with the appropriate reference citation.

A third subsection is called "Procedure" or sometimes "Procedure and Experimental Design." It is usually the longest portion of the method section. It describes and operationally defines all of the variables, discusses the design of the study and all of the control features, and reports exactly what happened to the research participants.

Unlike the introduction, the method section does not begin on a new page. It immediately follows the introduction and is labeled with the word "Method," which is centered (refer to the sample paper for the formatting rules for the subsections). This same continuity rule applies to the results and discussion sections.

Results

This section of the report provides a concise yet complete verbal description of the results, along with descriptive and inferential statistics. A typical paragraph in the results section includes a verbal description of some finding, accompanied by the relevant descriptive and inferential statistics supporting the statement. No attempt is made to explain why some prediction succeeded or failed; such interpretation belongs in the discussion section.

A good way to organize the results section is with reference to the sequence of hypotheses in the introduction. For instance, if the introduction ends with three hypotheses, the results section should have a paragraph devoted to each prediction, presented in the same order as in the intro.

Reporting the Data: Statistics

As you recall from Chapter 4, descriptive statistics summarize data, and inferential statistics determine whether it is prudent to reject the null hypothesis(es) or not. The most common descriptive statistics reported are means, standard deviations, and correlation coefficients. Typical inferential statistics include t tests, F ratios from ANOVAs, and chi-square (χ^2) tests. The *PM* (2001, p. 21) also encourages the inclusion of effect size calculations, and it is becoming common to see confidence intervals reported. Procedures for calculating all of these analyses can be found at the Student Companion Site (www.wiley.com/college/goodwin). For now, be aware of two points. First, there are standard abbreviations for statistical terms such as the sample mean (M) and standard deviation (SD). Second, the general rule in reporting statistics is to put the descriptive statistics before the inferential statistics in any given paragraph. A typical results section might have consecutive sentences like this:

> Those given the imagery instructions recalled a mean of 16.52 words ($SD = 2.32$), while those told merely to repeat the words recalled 12.36 words on average ($SD = 3.15$). The difference was significant, $F(1,18) = 12.87$, $p = .018$.

The shorthand method for reporting inferential statistics is basically the same for all types of analysis. The test is identified (e.g., F), the degrees of freedom are listed (1 for the numerator of the F ratio and 18 for the denominator), the calculated value of the test is reported (12.87), and the probability value (e.g., $p = .018$) is indicated. Note that the "F" and "p," as well as the "M" and "SD," as statistical symbols, are italicized. This example illustrates another important point. Whenever means are reported, standard deviations always accompany them.

Portraying the Data: Tables and Figures

Descriptive statistics, especially in factorial designs, are often complicated enough that a paragraph-length description of them can be difficult to follow. To avoid the problem, data are often presented in tables and/or figures. **Tables** are row and column arrangements that typically present means and standard deviations or sets of correlations. **Figures** can be graphs, diagrams, flow charts, sketches of apparatus, or photos. Each has specific formatting rules, some of which can be seen in the sample paper.

It is sometimes difficult to decide whether to use a table or a figure to present the data. In general, a table is preferred if it seems important to report the precise mean scores (on a graph, the exact scores require some guessing) or if there are so many data points that a graph would be hopelessly cluttered. On the other hand, graphs can often illustrate a point dramatically; they are especially useful for showing an interaction effect in a factorial study for example. One certainty is that it is inappropriate to present the same data in two ways—both in a table and as a figure. If a graph is used, it can take several forms; the most common are line graphs and bar graphs. As described and illustrated in Chapter 7, line graphs are normally (but not necessarily) used when the variable on the X-axis is continuous; for discrete variables (e.g., gender), bar graphs should always be used.

When using tables or figures, it is not enough just to present them. In the results section, you must refer the reader to them and point out their important features. Some skill is involved here because you don't want to write a detailed description pointing out every aspect of a table or graph. Thus, in a graph showing a serial position curve in a memory experiment, you might encounter a sentence like this:

> Figure 1 shows that recall was quite high for the first few words of the list, poor for middle words, and almost perfect for the final three words.

As you can tell from the sample paper, tables and figures are not placed in the middle of the text description. Rather, they are placed at the end of the report. Also in the sample paper, notice that the title of the table is included on the same page as the table but the figure titles (called "figure captions") are word processed on a page that is separate from the figures themselves. This is not an arbitrary rule designed to lower your grade and kill trees but follows from the way a manuscript is transformed into a printed journal article. Tables are printed like any other text, as are the figure captions. The figures themselves, however, are submitted as high quality photographs or image files and have to be fitted into their appropriate space (this is why the pages of figures don't include manuscript page headers and page numbers). Hence, the figures and their captions are submitted separately. If you have more than one figure, it is not necessary to create a separate figure caption page for each one; simply list all of the captions on a single page (as in the sample paper).

Discussion

This is the final section of the text material for your lab report and it serves to tie the entire report together. It begins by summarizing the main results with reference to the original hypothesis(es) and then proceeds with its major task—interpretation. This evaluation includes relating the results to any theoretical points raised in the introduction and trying to explain failed predictions. The discussion also addresses the problem of alternative explanations of results. As the author of the article, you will decide on the interpretation that seems most reasonable, but sometimes other alternatives could be conceived. You should mention these alternatives and then explain why you think yours is better.

Finally, the discussion includes an important element of any research program: consideration of the "what's next?" questions you learned about in Chapter 3. That is, writers usually make suggestions about what the next study should be, given the outcome of the one just completed. This, of course, is a natural consequence of the fact that research always answers some questions but raises others. As a student researcher, this part of a journal article is a good place to get ideas for your own research.

References

Unlike the method, results, and discussion sections, the references section starts on a new page and consists of an alphabetized (by author) list of all of the sources cited in the lab report. Each item uses a "hanging indent," which makes it easier to find specific authors when skimming through a reference page. The *PM* includes a complete set of rules for virtually every type of citation; here are examples of the most common ones:

A journal article with one author

Burger, J. M. (2009). Replicating Milgram: Would people still obey today? *American Psychologist, 64,* 1–11.

Note: *American Psychologist* publishes twelve issues per year. A common mistake is to include, along with the volume number (64, in this case), the issue number (1 in this case). It would look like this: 64(1).

However, the only time the issue number is used is when each issue begins with page 1. Almost all journals number their pages consecutively throughout the volume, though (e.g., issue 2 might start with page 154, for example), so adding the issue number adds unnecessary information.

A journal article with more than one author

Hall, J. A., & Veccia, E. M. (1990). More "touching" observations: New insights on men, women, and interpersonal touch. *Journal of Personality and Social Psychology, 59,* 1155–1162.

A magazine

Palmer, J. D. (1982, October). Biorhythm bunkum. *Natural History,* 90–97.

A book that is a first edition

Kimmel, A. J. (1996). *Ethical issues in behavioral research: Basic and applied perspectives*. Malden, MA: Blackwell.

A book that is not a first edition

Kimmel, A. J. (2007). *Ethical issues in behavioral research: Basic and applied perspectives* (2nd ed.). Malden, MA: Blackwell.

A chapter from an edited book

Weiss, J. M. (1977). Psychological and behavioral influences on gastrointestinal lesions in animal models. In J. D. Maser & M. E. P. Seligman (Eds.), *Psychopathology: Experimental models* (pp. 232–269). San Francisco: Freeman.

Electronic sources.

Rules for citing references from websites, electronic databases, e-mail, and so on, have been evolving in recent years and are frequently updated. For the most recent set of guidelines, consult the page on APA's website that is dedicated to this topic: www.apastyle.org/elecref.html.

One final point, and mistakes are often made here, is that before turning in a lab report, you should check the citations in the body of your paper against the list in the References section. Make sure that (a) every source mentioned in the text of your lab report is given a listing in the References section of the paper, and (b) every reference listed in the References section is cited somewhere in the text of your lab report.

Presentations and Posters

If you're lucky, you may find yourself in a position to present the results of some of your research publicly. This can range from a presentation to other psychology students as part of a course requirement to a more formal presentation at a professional conference. For example, as mentioned in the Epilogue, sessions for undergraduate research are scheduled at national meetings of the APA and the Association for Psychological Science (APS) and at regional meetings (e.g., that of the Midwestern Psychological Association, or MPA). Also, a number of colleges and universities host conferences specifically for the purpose of presenting undergraduate research (e.g., my university sponsors a gender conference every year).

Tips for Presenting a Paper

Presentations at professional psychology conferences take one of two forms: papers or, more likely, posters. The paper is the more traditional (but rapidly disappearing) format. In a typical 1-hour session (50 minutes, actually), several researchers (usually four) will each read a paper describing their work. If this happens to you, here are some recommendations:

1. You will be given a time limit—stick to it compulsively. A typical limit is 12 minutes, which allows time for four papers in the session. If you take 20–25 minutes, the person who is scheduled to go last in the session will hate you forever.

2. Prepare a one-page handout that a friend can distribute to the audience just as you are being introduced. The handout should include the title of the paper, your name and affiliation, your hypothesis(es), an abbreviated description of the design, the results, usually as a table or graph, and a concise conclusion. Unfortunately, many in the audience will be thinking about what session they are going to attend in the next hour, planning dinner, or rehearsing their own presentation rather than listening carefully to you, so your handout can be an effective way for them to take useful information away with them.

3. If projection equipment is available, and it usually is, take advantage of it. Learn how to use PowerPoint and deliver your presentation that way.

4. Prepare a normal lab report and then adapt it to the form of a document to be presented orally. This means focusing on the essential points and avoiding picky details. For example, although you should include the model name for

some apparatus in the lab report, the generic name (e.g., "operant chamber") is fine for an oral presentation. The listener should be clear about the purpose of your study, the essential elements of design and control, the results, and what your overall conclusions are. Your presentation should be more conversational than it would be in the more formal lab report.

5. Practice your presentation in front of friends. Ideally, have a video made, learn from it (keep it away from your friends so it doesn't wind up on *YouTube*), and then practice some more. To help with the inevitable anxiety, try to remember that of all the people in the room, you know your project better than anyone.

Tips for Presenting a Poster

Poster sessions have the advantage of allowing the presentation of many more research projects per hour than in a typical paper session and, of course, they eliminate the public-speaking anxiety that accompanies a paper presentation (this could be a disadvantage; learning to speak in public is an important skill). They also increase the chances that you will meet people with research interests similar to yours. At an effective poster session, you will have a half-dozen good conversations, get some ideas for interpreting your results differently perhaps, develop some ideas for "what's next?" questions, and perhaps exchange e-mail addresses.

If you do a poster, you will find yourself in a large room filled with row after row of bulletin boards. On one of these boards, you will arrange a display that enables someone to understand what you have discovered in your research. Some conferences also ask you to prepare copies (usually 50) of a brief version of your paper to be given to those who wish to take one (most of the time, a legal pad for people to write their email addresses on it will do—after you return from the conference, you can send them copies electronically). Here are some tips for presenting a good poster:

1. Layout is critically important. Readers of your poster should be able to figure out the essence of what happened in your study in just a minute or two. If their first response is confusion, they will move on to the next poster. Figure A.2 shows you one possible layout, but the particular conference you're attending might have some specific rules, so pay attention to them. For instance, some smaller conferences publish all of the abstracts in a booklet given to conference attendees. If so, there's no need for you to include an Abstract page in the poster itself. Instead, start with a section called "Introduction" or "Problem Statement."

2. In general, the layout of your poster should be organized and logical. Readers should be able to determine easily the purpose of your study, the method, the results, and your overall conclusions. Be sure the content of the poster flows easily from left to right.

3. It should be possible to read and understand your poster from a distance of 6 feet. Your title should be printed in letters about 2" high and your

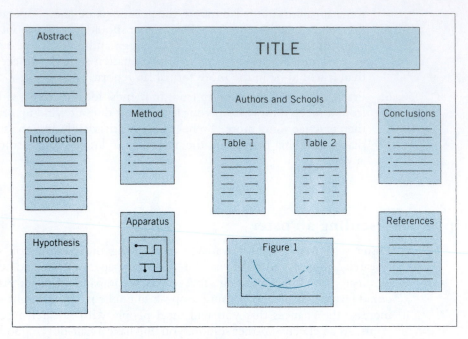

FIGURE A.2   Sample poster layout.

name and university affiliation a bit smaller. The major headings should be set at about 40 pt., things like figure captions at 28 pt., and text no smaller than 24 pt. Use fonts that are easy to read (e.g., Arial, Geneva, Helvetica). Using color conservatively is OK, but don't overuse it to the point of distraction (e.g., don't create a graph with six different colors in it). Mount each page of your poster on backing that is a consistent color. Poster board makes for a good backing, but construction paper will do. If you're lucky, your school will have a print shop that will place your entire poster onto a single sheet of glossy paper. Bring extra pushpins for mounting your poster to the bulletin board; conferences supply pins, but there never seem to be enough.

4. Less is more—edit to the bare bones. Feel free to use bulleted lists instead of long paragraphs, especially for method and results. If readers need more precise detail about some aspect of the study, you'll be there to enlighten them.

5. The poster is essentially a visual form of presentation, so use graphics liberally. In addition to tables and graphs, feel free to include drawings of apparatus, photos of the research environment, diagrams of the research design, and so on. Every graphic should tell an important part of the story of the research, however.

Applications Exercises

Exercise A1.1   True-False

Six of the following ten statements about the APA lab report are true. See if you can identify them.

1. After writing the Abstract, double space and then immediately begin the introduction on the same page.

2. On the title page, the running head will almost always be different from the manuscript page header.

3. In the Results section, if you portray your results with a graph, it is also OK to display them in a table because then the reader gets the exact numbers.

4. An Abstract should be no longer than 120 words.

5. A "what's next" type of paragraph belongs in the Discussion section of the report.

6. Begin each section with a centered label—in the introduction, for example, the word "Introduction" identifies the section.

7. Each item that appears in the Reference section should be found somewhere in the lab report itself.

8. The Method section should contain enough information for replication to be possible.

9. In the Results section, to maintain reader interest, it is important to explain and interpret each result right after you report it.

10. The place to operationally define the independent and dependent variables is the Method section.

Exercise A1.2   Word usage

Each of the following lab report sentences contains an error or, at the very least, wording that could be improved. Fix the sentences.

1. 124 male college students were used in the experiment.

2. The data was then subjected to a 2×3 independent groups ANOVA.

3. The instructions had a strong affect on the participants.

4. The criteria for learning was defined as two consecutive errorless runs through the maze.

5. A study of maze learning was conducted by Tolman.

6. The study tried to get at the essence of man's basic need for achievement.

Exercise A1.3 Referencing—Sharpening your Obsessive-Compulsive Tendencies

Of the following items from a Reference section, one is correct and the remaining seven have exactly one error. Identify the one that is correct and fix the errors.

1. Reynolds, G. S. (1968). *A Primer of Operant Conditioning.* Glenview, IL: Scott, Foresman.

2. Kolata, George B. (1986). What does it mean to be random? *Science, 231,* 1068–1070.

3. Lee, D. N., and Aronson, E. (1974). Visual proprioceptive control of standing in human infants. *Perception and Psychophysics, 15,* 529–532.

4. Miller, A. G. (1972). Role playing: An alternative to deception? *American Psychologist,* 27, 623–636.

5. Geller, D. M. (1982). Alternatives to deception: Why, what, and how? In Sieber, J. E. (Ed.), *The ethics of social research: Surveys and experiments* (pp. 40–55). New York: Springer-Verlag.

6. Bakeman, R., & Brownlee, J. R. (1980). The strategic use of parallel play: A sequential analysis. *Child Development, 51,* 873–878.

7. Brehm, J. (1956). Postdecision changes in the desirability of alternatives. *Journal of Abnormal and Social Psychology, 52(3),* 384–389.

8. Carr, H. A., & Watson, J. B. (1908). Orientation in the white rat. *Journal of Comparative Neurology and Psychology, 18,* pp. 27–44.

Exercise A1.4 Main Sections of the Lab Report

In which section of the lab report (Abstract, Introduction, Method, Results, Discussion) would the following statements most likely be found?

1. We hypothesized that participants given imagery instructions would outperform those given instructions to use rote memorization.

2. There were 3 different groups in the study.

3. A logical next step would be to add another age group to extend the findings to pre-adolescents.

4. Males recalled 45.6 words ($SD = 2.3$), while females recalled 53.5 words ($SD = 1.9$).

5. The experiment was a 2 (sex) × 3 (instructions) mixed factorial.

6. In an earlier study, Smith (1988) found no such effect.

A Sample Lab Report

The following sample lab report is a revised version of a paper that three of my students authored and delivered to an undergraduate research conference. This report is shorter than and not as sophisticated as the articles you'll find in most journals, but it is closer to the kind of lab report that you will be preparing as you begin to learn APA format, so you should find it helpful.

1. The manuscript page header and page number are placed on the same line, separated by 5 spaces, and right-justified. The title page is always page 1.

2. The manuscript page header is the first 2-3 words of the full title.

3. The running head is left-justified and the "h" in "head" is not capitalized.

4. Use all caps for the actual running head, and make the head no more than 50 characters, including spaces. Unlike the page header, the running head should inform the reader about the variables in the study.

5. The title should inform the reader about the variables being investigated in the study. There is no restriction on the length of the title, but the *PM* recommends 10-12 words. This one is 12 words.

6. The title, author(s), and affiliation(s) are centered and located just above the midpoint of the page. Your instructor might ask you to include the date, but for papers submitted to APA journals, the date will be on the cover letter sent by the author to the editor, so the *PM* does not call for a date on the cover page.

①

Effects of North   1

②

③
Running head: ORIENTATION, DISTANCE, AND POINTING ACCURACY

④

⑤

The Effects of a North Orientation and Target Distance on Pointing Accuracy

Aimee Faso, Theresa Yuncke, and Teresa Kottman

Wheeling Jesuit University
⑥

7. Center the label "Abstract." Double space here and throughout the manuscript.

8. There is no paragraph indent at the start of the Abstract.

9. The Abstract should be no longer than 120 words. To save space in the Abstract, print all the actual numbers (3) rather than spelling them out (three), unless a number begins a sentence—then spell it out.

Effects of North   2

Abstract

The ability to point accurately toward fixed geographical targets was examined in a 2 x 2 x 6 factorial design. Seventy-two participants (36 males and 36 females) tried to locate 6 different targets, 3 within walking distance of the laboratory, and 3 that were at least 70 miles from campus. Half the participants were oriented to the compass direction of North; half were not. The North orientation facilitated performance for the 3 distant targets, but did not significantly improve performance for the 3 nearby targets. No gender differences occurred.   ⑨

10. Continue to right justify the page header and page number, but do not right justify the text of the article; just use the normal wrap-around feature of your word processor.

11. Do not include the label "Introduction;" instead, reproduce the title exactly as it is on the title page and center it. Begin a new page for the Introduction.

12. The opening paragraph introduces the topic area of the research and defines some terms (e.g., "cognitive maps").

13. When a reference like this is in parentheses, the ampersand (&) is used; when the reference is in the flow of a sentence, use the word "and."

14. The Introduction describes some prior research but only if it is relevant to your study. Here, the Evans and Pezdek study is described because it introduces the difference between two ways of developing cognitive maps.

15. If the same reference is mentioned more than once in the same paragraph, include the date only for the first mention of the reference.

Effects of North   3   ⑩

⑪

The Effects of a North Orientation and Target Distance on Pointing Accuracy   ⑫

Cognitive maps are mental representations of spatial information

⑬ (Ormrod, Ormrod, Wagner, & McCallin, 1988). They enable us to know

where we are in the geographic environment, and they help us navigate

through the environment in order to move efficiently from point A to point

B. Researchers interested in cognitive mapping have studied such topics

as how the elements of these maps develop (e.g., Cohen, 1985), how

they are structured (e.g., Sholl, 1987), how they are used for navigation

(e.g., Kaplan, 1976), and how accurate we are when using them for

making decisions about where things are located. This last topic was the

focus of the experiment described here.

Evans and Pezdek (1980) demonstrated that people rely on two

methods of developing cognitive maps. First, they use the results of direct

⑭ experience in navigating through the environment. Thus students become

familiar with a campus by moving around in it. They know, for instance,

that to get to the library from the gym, one takes a left at the campus

shop and goes about 200 yards. A second type of cognitive map

knowledge is cartographic: people study maps. Even if we have never

visited Europe, we know that France is just to the south of England and

separated from it by the English Channel. Of course, some cognitive map

knowledge can result both from direct experience and from studying

⑮ maps. Evans and Pezdek asked volunteers to decide as quickly as

possible if sets of three target locations were in the correct spatial

positions with reference to each other. When the locations were states,

subjects used cartographic information when making their decisions.

When the target locations were nearby on-campus locations, however,

they apparently relied on their direct experience.

16. The last portion of the Introduction describes the study's hypotheses and the rationale for the predictions. It isn't enough to write that you expect X to happen; you must make a case for X. This paragraph ends with a specific hypothesis; the sentences leading up to it build the case for that hypothesis.

17. If two or more works are cited within parentheses, separate them with a semicolon and place them in alphabetical order (with reference to the first author's name in a multi-authored article), not chronological order.

18. Do not begin the Method section with a new page. Continue to double space throughout. Center the "Method" label. The goal of a well-written Method section is to make it possible for another researcher to replicate your study, so it is important to be very clear and to be thorough.

19. Subheadings are italicized and left justified.

20. If you begin a sentence with a number, you must spell it out. This sentence cannot begin like this: "72 undergraduates…"

Effects of North   4

(16) Our study had two purposes. First, it was designed to measure how accurately individuals could point toward locations that were either nearby or distant. If distant targets (e.g., cities) are learned and thought of with reference to actual maps, then accuracy in pointing to these targets should be improved if people receive some specific cartographic information such as the direction of "north." If nearby targets are learned by moving through the local environment, however, rather than by using maps, then a north orientation might not be very helpful when pointing to them. On this basis, we hypothesized that when pointing at distant geographic targets, accuracy would be improved by giving subjects a north orientation. When pointing at local targets, however, north orientation was not expected to help.

The second purpose of the study was to explore possible gender differences in using cognitive maps. Some studies (e.g., Kozlowski & Bryant, 1977) have failed to find differences between males and females on a cognitive mapping task, but several (e.g., Herman, Kail, & Siegel, **(17)** 1979; Ward, Newcombe, & Overton, 1986) have found that males use spatial information more efficiently than females. On this basis, we expected that males might point more accurately to geographic targets than females.

Method **(18)**

Participants **(19)**

(20) Seventy-two undergraduate volunteers (36 males and 36 females) from a small private university took part in the study. Experimenters visited freshman- and sophomore-level classes, described the general procedure, and asked for volunteers. No course credit was given. None of the participants were residents of the three distant target cities, but all

21. The rules for reporting numbers are complicated, but in general, actual numbers are used when the number is 10 or greater, and the number is spelled out if it is less than 10. Consult the *PM* (pp. 122-131) for the complete set of rules.

22. Figures are usually graphs, but they can also be other kinds of illustrations, in this case a sketch of the apparatus. The actual figures are placed on separate pages (one figure per page) and placed at the end of the report.

23. Notice that the order in which the variables are described is maintained through the Method and Results sections. Gender is described first, then north orientation, and then target location.

---

were familiar with the cities. Participation required approximately

(21) 10 minutes. The volunteers were tested individually.

Apparatus

Participants pointed toward a series of targets by means of a

(22) goniometer (Figure 1), a device used by physical therapists for measuring angles (e.g., at the elbow). One arm of the goniometer was fixed to a board and the second was free to rotate through 360°. This second arm served as a pointer. The experiment took place in a small classroom that had blackout curtains drawn to prevent subjects from seeing anything outside of the building. Participants stood at a lab table with the goniometer lined up so that its fixed arm was pointing either (a) directly toward north or (b) approximately east/northeast. This latter direction was the result of lining up the goniometer so that the board on which it was fixed was flush with the edge of the lab table.

Procedure

(23) The study used a 2 x 2 x 6 factorial design. The first factor was the subject variable of gender. The second factor was whether or not participants performed the task while knowing the direction of north. The 36 males and 36 females were randomly assigned to the two levels of this north orientation factor, with the restriction that an equal number of males and females be assigned to each group. Thus, 18 males and 18 females were given a north orientation; the remaining 18 males and 18 females were not.

The third factor was the within-subjects variable of target location. Six different targets were used. Three were locations that were either on or within walking distance of the campus: the university's front entrance, a local bar, and a money machine. The remaining locations were distant geographical targets that were at least 70 miles from Wheeling:

24. Something about debriefing might be mentioned, but it is generally not necessary to specify how you conformed to the ethics code; it is assumed that you did. Authors submitting articles to APA journals are required to include a statement in their cover letter confirming that the guidelines were followed faithfully.

25. Do not begin the Results section with a new page. Continue to double space. Center the "Results" label.

26. Report descriptive statistics. In this case, some means are reported in the text, others in Table 1, and still others in graph form (Figure 2). Whenever means are reported, you should also report standard deviations (i.e., the reader should learn about both central tendency and variability).

27. Report inferential statistics, in this case the ANOVA results. Note that the format for reporting an ANOVA includes (a) the name of the test, italicized (F), (b) the degrees of freedom in parentheses (1, 68), (c) the calculated value of F (24.87 in this case) and the probability value, in this case an

estimate ($p < .01$). If the calculated value is less than 1, report it as

shown: $F(1, 68) < 1$. Never place Tables in the body of the

report. As with Figures, place them at the end, prior to the

Figure Captions page.

Effects of North   6

Pittsburgh, Cleveland, and Washington, DC. Target sequence was counterbalanced through the use of a 6 x 6 Latin square. Participants were randomly assigned to a row of the square, with the restriction that equal numbers of males and females were assigned to each row.

The students were told that they would be given a series of locations, some nearby and some far away, and that they were to move the free arm of the goniometer so that it was pointing directly at each location. Those in the north orientation condition were told that the fixed arm of the goniometer was pointed toward north and they could use it as a reference point. Those in the control condition were told nothing about the orientation of the goniometer.

The primary dependent measure was accuracy of pointing. Experimenters determined the correct answers for each location with reference to reliable maps. This made it possible to determine the degree of error for each response. Whether the error was to the "left" or to the "right" of the target was ignored. Hence, the error scores ranged from 0° to 180°. Participants were also asked to describe any strategies they used (24) when performing the task. After completing all six trials and describing any strategies they used, participants were debriefed. Those requesting the final results were sent a brief summary at the conclusion of the study.

Results (25)

The data were analyzed with a 2 (gender) x 2 (orientation) x 6 (target location) analysis of variance, with the level of alpha set at .05. The mean error across all conditions for males was 46.9° ($SD = 16.9$) and for (26) females it was 52.6° ($SD = 15.6$); the difference was not significant, $F(1, 68) < 1$. A main effect for orientation was found, however (27) ($F(1, 68) = 24.87$, $p < .01$). The average error for those given the north

28. Do not begin the Discussion section with a new page and continue to double space. Center the "Discussion" label.

29. When both main effects and interactions occur, it is customary to interpret interactions first. Sometimes the interaction is more important than the main effect (this is one of those times).

30. Results don't always come out as nicely as one hopes. An ambiguous outcome calls for careful interpretation and for further research to determine if the result is reliable.

31. Concentrate on the main finding and try to interpret what it means by relating the result back to the Introduction.

orientation was $33.2°$ (SD = 14.1); it was $66.4°$ (SD = 16.9) for those not told the direction of north. As shown in Table 1, the overall advantage for those given a north orientation occurred both for males and for females.

There was no overall effect for target location, $F(5, 340) < 1$, but there was a significant interaction between north orientation and target location, $F(5, 340) = 7.91$, $p < .01$. A simple effects analysis of the effect of north orientation for each location found that those given the orientation had less error for all three distant locations ($p < .01$). For the closer targets, there were no differences between those given and those not given a north orientation ($p > .05$) for the first two locations, but the north orientation did facilitate performance for the third close location, a money machine just off campus ($p < .05$). These effects can be seen in Figure 2.

Neither the 2-way interaction between gender and location ($F(5, 340) < 1$) nor the 3-way interaction between gender, orientation, and location ($F(5, 340) < 1$) was significant.

Discussion (28)

A significant main effect for north orientation occurred in the study, but (29) the more important result is the interaction between north orientation and location. When pointing to distant targets, participants clearly were aided by being told the direction of north; when the targets were nearby, a north orientation was not as helpful. However, the fact that the north orientation did provide an advantage for one of the three local targets suggests a need for replication before the interaction can be considered a reliable finding. (30)

This outcome is consistent with the research of Evans and Pezdek (1980) in finding that cognitive mapping includes two types of knowledge. (31) One type of spatial knowledge results from the direct experience of moving to and from nearby locations. Such knowledge is perhaps

32. This is a good place to display some "what's next?" thinking.

33. Something should be said about each hypothesis, even when the results are unclear or not significant.

Effects of North   8

organized in terms of local landmarks and direction changes with reference to those landmarks ("take a right at the mailroom"). Hence, pointing accurately to such targets is not as likely to be aided by reference to compass points. Indeed, when explaining their strategies, several participants visualized the trip from the building where they were being tested to the location in question.

The second type of spatial knowledge is more oriented to the compass and results from our experience with maps, which are always oriented to north. When pointing to these locations, we apparently rely on images of the maps we have studied, an idea supported by participants' comments. More than half said that they tried to visualize a map when trying to decide about Pittsburgh, Cleveland, or Washington; none mentioned maps when referring to the nearby locations.

(32) In addition to replicating our results, future research might extend the findings by examining the effects of local landmarks on pointing accurately toward nearby targets. Just as the current study found that cartographic information improved performance for distant targets more than for nearby ones, perhaps the opposite result would occur if participants were given the direction of local landmarks instead of a north orientation. If navigating to nearby targets involves using these landmarks, then pointing accuracy might be improved for them but not for distant targets.

(33) No gender differences were found, perhaps due to the nature of the task. Although several studies have found a slight advantage for males, one other study that failed to find a difference between males and females (Kozlowski & Bryant, 1977) also used a "point to X" procedure.

34. Summarize your conclusions, but try not to be repetitive.

(34)   In summary, our knowledge of geographic locations results from direct experience in traveling to those places and from a more abstract map knowledge. When asked to point to geographic targets, giving people a north orientation enhances their performance when pointing at targets learned with reference to maps; however, a north orientation does not help people point more accurately to nearby targets that are learned by the experience of visiting them.

35. Begin the References section with a new page and continue to double space. Center the "References" label.

36. Note the proper formatting— what is italicized; where the commas and periods are; and what is and is not capitalized.

37. Use a "hanging indent" for each reference.

38. Note that every item in the References section must be mentioned in the lab report somewhere. Likewise, every reference cited in the report must be found in the References section.

   Effects of North   10

References

Cohen, R. (1985). *The development of spatial cognition.* Hillsdale, NJ:

    Erlbaum.

Evans, G. W., & Pezdek, K. (1980). Cognitive mapping: Knowledge of real

 world distance and location information. *Journal of Experimental*

    Psychology: Human Learning and Memory, 6, 13-24.

Herman, J. F., Kail, R. V., & Siegel, A. W. (1979). Cognitive maps of a

    college campus: A new look at freshman orientation. *Bulletin of the*

    Psychonomic Society, 13, 183-186.

Kaplan, R. (1976). Way-finding in the natural environment. In G. T. Moore

    & R. G. Golledge (Eds.), *Environmental knowing* (pp. 46-57).

    Stroudsburg, PA: Dowden, Hutchinson, and Ross.

Kozlowski, L. T., & Bryant, K. J. (1977). Sense of direction, spatial

    orientation, and cognitive maps. *Journal of Experimental Psychology:*

    Human Perception and Performance, 3, 590-598.

Ormrod, J. E., Ormrod, R. K., Wagner, E. D., & McCallin, R. C. (1988).

    Reconceptualizing map learning. *American Journal of Psychology,*

    101, 425-433.

Sholl, J. (1987). Cognitive maps as orienting schemata. *Journal of*

    Experimental Psychology: Learning. Memory. and Cognition, 13, 615-

    628.

Ward, S. L., Newcombe, N., & Overton, W. F. (1986). Turn left at the

    church, or three miles north: A study of direction giving and sex

    differences. *Environment and Behavior, 18,* 192-213.

39. Use a separate page for each Table. Italicize the Table's title.

40. Continue to include the manuscript page header and page number on pages with Tables.

41. Note the horizontal lines used to organize the Table. Never use vertical lines.

42. Organize the Table so that the data that are to be compared (e.g., the means) are grouped together.

43. A note (italicized) operationally defines the dependent variable.

Effects of North   11 ⓐ40

Table 1 ⓐ39

Error Scores as a Function of Gender and North Orientation

ⓐ41

Gender	Mean Error Score		Standard Deviation	
	With North	Without North	With North	Without North
Male	30.7	63.2	10.5	22.9
Female	35.7	69.5	19.1	12.8

ⓐ42

Note. The error score was the difference (in degrees) between the correct

ⓐ43

response and the participant's response.

44. Call this page "Figure Caption" if your report has just a single Figure. Center the "Figure Captions" label.

45. Note the italics. Carry the second line back to the left margin (no hanging indent here). These captions are the descriptions that will appear beneath the Figures when your paper gets published in a journal.

Effects of North   11

Figure Captions

Figure 1. A goniometer. The fixed arm pointed toward north for half of the

participants; the arm free to rotate was used for pointing toward

geographic targets.

Figure 2. Error in pointing to nearby and distant targets for those with or

without a north orientation.

46. Do not include the manuscript page header or the page number on pages with Figures. On the back of this page, write the word "TOP" in pencil to show the orientation of the Figure; also write "Figure 1" and a short article title (or page header) on the back in pencil.

47. If you have more than one Figure, use a separate page for each. All the Figure captions may be placed on a single page, however.

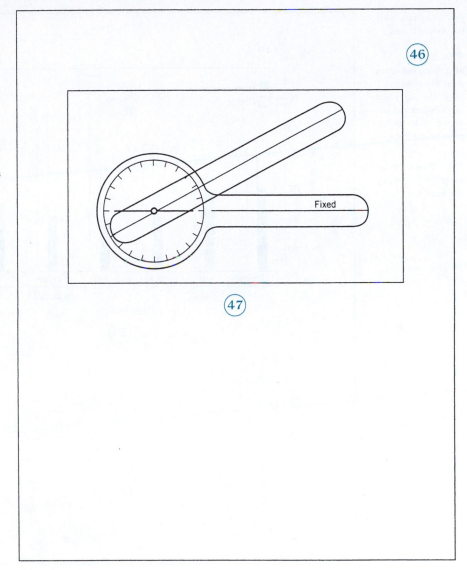

Fixed

48. Carefully label the X- and Y-axes.

49. Place an identifying key so that it fits somewhere below the high point on the Y-axis and to the left of the furthest point on the X-axis.

50. Why is this a bar graph and not a line graph?

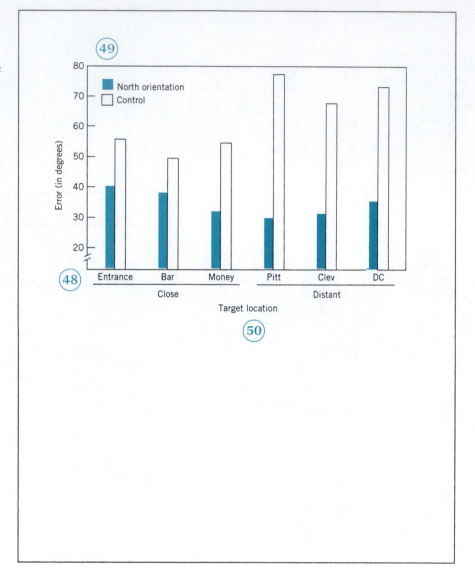

APPENDIX B

The Ethics Code of the American Psychological Association

This appendix contains Category 8 of the APA ethics code for research with human participants, taken from the December, 2002, issue of the *American Psychologist*, APA's main journal.

The APA Ethics Code for Research with Human Participants

Category 8: Research and Publication

8.01 Institutional Approval

When institutional approval is required, psychologists provide accurate information about their research proposals and obtain approval prior to conducting the research. They conduct the research in accordance with the approved research protocol.

8.02 Informed Consent to Research

a. When obtaining informed consent as required in Standard 3.10, Informed Consent, psychologists inform participants about (1) the purpose of the research, expected duration, and procedures; (2) their right to decline to participate and to withdraw from the research once participation has begun; (3) the foreseeable consequences of declining or withdrawing; (4) reasonably foreseeable factors that may be expected to influence their willingness to participate such as potential risks, discomfort, or adverse effects; (5) any prospective research benefits; (6) limits of confidentiality; (7) incentives for participation; and (8) whom to contact for questions about the research and research participants' rights. They provide opportunity for the prospective participants to ask questions and receive answers. (See also Standards 8.03, Informed Consent for Recording Voices and Images in Research; 8.05, Dispensing with Informed Consent for Research, and 8.07, Deception in Research.)

b. Psychologists conducting intervention research involving the use of experimental treatments clarify to participants at the outset of the research (1) the experimental nature of the treatment; (2) the services that will or will not be available to the control group(s) if appropriate; (3) the means by which assignment to treatment and control groups will be made; (4) available treatment alternatives if an individual does not wish to participate in the research or wishes to withdraw once a study has begun; and (5) compensation for or monetary costs of participating including, if appropriate, whether reimbursement from the participant or a third-party payor will be sought. (See also Standard 8.02a, Informed Consent to Research.)

8.03 Informed Consent for Recording Voices and Images in Research

Psychologists obtain informed consent from research participants prior to recording their voices or images for data collection unless (1) the research consists solely of naturalistic observations in public places, and it is not anticipated that the recording will be used in a manner that could cause personal identification or harm or (2) the research design includes deception, and consent for the use of the recording is obtained during debriefing. (See also Standard 8.07, Deception in Research.)

8.04 Client/Patient, Student, and Subordinate Research Participants

a. When psychologists conduct research with clients/patients, students, or subordinates as participants, psychologists take steps to protect the prospective participants from adverse consequences of declining or withdrawing from participation.

b. When research participation is a course requirement or opportunity for extra credit, the prospective participant is given the choice of equitable alternative activities.

8.05 Dispensing with Informed Consent for Research

Psychologists may dispense with informed consent only (1) where research would not reasonably be assumed to create distress or harm and involves (a) the study of normal educational practices, curricula, or classroom management methods conducted in educational settings; (b) only anonymous questionnaires, naturalistic observations, or archival research for which disclosure of responses would not place participants at risk of criminal or civil liability or damage their financial standing, employability, or reputation, and confidentiality is protected; or (c) the study of factors related to job or organization effectiveness conducted in organizational settings for which there is no risk to participants' employability and confidentiality is protected or (2) where otherwise permitted by law or federal or institutional regulations.

8.06 Offering Inducements for Research Participation

a. Psychologists make reasonable efforts to avoid offering excessive or inappropriate financial or other inducements for research participation when such inducements are likely to coerce participation.

b. When offering professional services as an inducement for research participation, psychologists clarify the nature of the services, as well as the risks, obligations, and limitations.

8.07 Deception in Research

a. Psychologists do not conduct a study involving deception unless they have determined that the use of deceptive techniques is justified by the study's significant prospective scientific, educational, or applied value and that effective nondeceptive alternative procedures are not feasible.

b. Psychologists do not deceive prospective participants about research that is reasonably expected to cause physical pain or severe emotional distress.

c. Psychologists explain any deception that is an integral feature of the design and conduct of an experiment to participants as early as is feasible, preferably at the conclusion of their participation, but no later than at the conclusion of the data collection, and permit participants to withdraw their data. (See also Standard 8.08, Debriefing.)

8.08 Debriefing

a. Psychologists provide a prompt opportunity for participants to obtain appropriate information about the nature, results, and conclusions of the research, and they take reasonable steps to correct any misconceptions that participants may have of which the psychologists are aware.

b. If scientific or humane values justify delaying or withholding this information, psychologists take reasonable measures to reduce the risk of harm.

c. When psychologists become aware that research procedures have harmed a participant, they take reasonable steps to minimize the harm.

8.09 Humane Care and Use of Animals in Research

a. Psychologists acquire, care for, use, and dispose of animals in compliance with current federal, state, and local laws and regulations, and with professional standards.

b. Psychologists trained in research methods and experienced in the care of laboratory animals supervise all procedures involving animals and are responsible for ensuring appropriate consideration of their comfort, health, and humane treatment.

c. Psychologists ensure that all individuals under their supervision who are using animals have received instruction in research methods and in the care, maintenance, and handling of the species being used, to the extent appropriate to their role.

d. Psychologists make reasonable efforts to minimize the discomfort, infection, illness, and pain of animal subjects.

e. Psychologists use a procedure subjecting animals to pain, stress, or privation only when an alternative procedure is unavailable and the goal is justified by its prospective scientific, educational, or applied value.

f. Psychologists perform surgical procedures under appropriate anesthesia and follow techniques to avoid infection and minimize pain during and after surgery.

g. When it is appropriate that an animal's life be terminated, psychologists proceed rapidly, with an effort to minimize pain and in accordance with accepted procedures.

8.10 Reporting Research Results

a. Psychologists do not fabricate data.

b. If psychologists discover significant errors in their published data, they take reasonable steps to correct such errors in a correction, retraction, erratum, or other appropriate publication means.

8.11 Plagiarism

Psychologists do not present portions of another's work or data as their own, even if the other work or data source is cited occasionally.

8.12 Publication Credit

a. Psychologists take responsibility and credit, including authorship credit, only for work they have actually performed or to which they have substantially contributed. (See also Standard 8.12b, Publication Credit.)

b. Principal authorship and other publication credits accurately reflect the relative scientific or professional contributions of the individuals involved, regardless of their relative status. Mere possession of an institutional position, such as department chair, does not justify authorship credit. Minor contributions to the research or to the writing for publications are acknowledged appropriately, such as in footnotes or in an introductory statement.

c. Except under exceptional circumstances, a student is listed as principal author on any multiple-authored article that is substantially based on the student's doctoral dissertation. Faculty advisors discuss publication credit with students as early as feasible and throughout the research and publication process as appropriate. (See also Standard 8.12b, Publication Credit.)

8.13 Duplicate Publication of Data

Psychologists do not publish, as original data, data that have been previously published. This does not preclude republishing data when they are accompanied by proper acknowledgment.

8.14 Sharing Research Data for Verification

a.   After research results are published, psychologists do not withhold the data on which their conclusions are based from other competent professionals who seek to verify the substantive claims through reanalysis and who intend to use such data only for that purpose, provided that the confidentiality of the participants can be protected and unless legal rights concerning proprietary data preclude their release. This does not preclude psychologists from requiring that such individuals or groups be responsible for costs associated with the provision of such information.

b.   Psychologists who request data from other psychologists to verify the substantive claims through reanalysis may use shared data only for the declared purpose. Requesting psychologists obtain prior written agreement for all other uses of the data.

8.15 Reviewers

Psychologists who review material submitted for presentation, publication, grant, or research proposal review respect the confidentiality of and the proprietary rights in such information of those who submitted it.

Source: American Psychological Association (2002). Ethical principles of psychologists and code of conduct. *American Psychologist, 57*, 1060–1073.

APPENDIX C

Answers to Selected End-of-Chapter Applications Exercises

Chapter 1. Scientific Thinking in Psychology

1.1 Asking Empirical Questions

1. Is God dead?

Possible empirical questions: To what extent do people of different religious faiths believe in a personal God who is directly involved in their day-to-day lives? For those raised as Christians, did the percentage of them believing in a personal God change over the past 30 years?

3. Are humans naturally good?

Possible empirical questions: Will people be less likely to donate to charity if they believe their donations will be anonymous? How do believers in different religions react to this question and how do nonbelievers react?

5.   What is beauty?

Possible empirical questions: Do 20-year-old men differ from 40-year-old men in terms of how they define beauty in a woman? For men of different cultures, which waist/hip ratio in women is considered most beautiful? Given works of art from three different artistic traditions, how do they vary in terms of "beautiful' ratings?

1.3   Arriving at a Strong Belief

Authority (parents, priests, ministers, or rabbis; perhaps even Charlton Heston on TV as Moses) is an important factor here. In addition, people might have intense emotional experiences (e.g., while looking upon great natural beauty) that they judge to be spiritual in nature. Third, they might use reason to arrive at a belief in God. For instance, they might argue that all events have causes and that ultimately there must be a cause greater than all others (i.e., God).

1.5   Social Cognition and the Psychic Hotline

a.   belief perseverance

After hearing about the "successes" of psychics *repeatedly* on TV infomercials and perhaps from authority figures respected by the individual, a belief might strengthen to the point that it is resistant to evidence.

b.   confirmation bias

The individual ignores evidence questioning the validity of psychic predications and attends only to reports of successful predictions (e.g., those found in supermarket tabloids or reported in great detail by Aunt Edna).

c.   availability heuristic

A favorable initial belief might be formed if there is a high-profile police case in which a psychic has been consulted and appears to have made a dramatic break in the case (of course, the hundreds of failed psychic consultations with police don't make the news).

Chapter 2. Ethics in Psychological Research

2.1   Thinking Scientifically about the Ethics Code

1.   One possible study could examine attitudes toward research and toward psychologists held by students who had been through experiments that either included deception or did not. In addition to the measure of attitudes, students could be asked to rank psychologists, among a number of other professions, on a scale of "trustworthiness."

3.   One possible study could halt the procedure at different points and ask participants to guess the true purpose of the study.

2.2   Recognizing Ethical Problems

1.   This study presents problems relating to consent and privacy violations (unwitting participants could possibly sue for privacy invasions and even bring criminal charges of harassment or criminal trespass—see Box 3.1);

also, not having given consent, there is no possibility to withdraw from the study. To defend the study to an IRB, the researcher would emphasize the importance of understanding how stress affects physiological systems, that the experience was not significantly different from what can happen in any men's room, that proper debriefing would be done, that confidentiality would be maintained (it would not be necessary to know the names of the participants), and that the data would not be used without the person's written permission.

3. This study has serious consent problems and, because participants did not know they were in a research study, they had no knowledge of their right to quit any time. To defend the study to an IRB, the researcher would stress that the study might provide some understanding of a real historical event and yield insight into people's willingness to engage in unlawful activity; this knowledge could eventually be useful to law enforcement. The researcher would also assure the IRB that a thorough debriefing (perhaps with follow-up) would occur, that strict confidentiality would be maintained, and that data would not be used without the person's written permission.

2.4 Decisions about Animal Research

Galvin and Herzog (1992) found that, in general, men were more likely to approve all of the studies than women were. As for the studies themselves, about 80% (combined male and female data, and estimated from a graph) approved both the "rats" and the "bears" studies, about 55% approved the "dogs" study, about 40% approved the "monkeys" study, and about 20% approved the "mice" study.

Chapter 3. Developing Ideas for Research in Psychology

3.1 What's Next?

1. Possible next studies: Compare male and female drivers; vary the age of the drivers; vary the make (and expense) of the car; replicate the study but add a second group in which the driver is said to be listening to a book on tape instead of talking on a cell phone.

3. Possible next studies: Look at sex differences in this spatial ability; vary experience level by comparing freshmen with seniors; compare distant city locations (learned with reference to maps) with campus locations (learned by walking around campus) that are out of sight from the testing point.

3.2 Replicating and Extending Milgram's Obedience Research

1. The roles of teacher and learner could be varied by sex, yielding four different groups: male teacher–male learner; male teacher–female learner; female teacher–female learner; female teacher–male learner (Milgram did not go to this length, but he did vary the sex of the teacher/subject and

found that female teachers delivered about the same level of shocks as the male teachers did).

3. One technique, used by Milgram (1974), would be to give teachers the option of how high to set the shock level; sadists would presumably use high levels. Milgram found that teachers continued to deliver shocks (i.e., continued obeying), but they set very low levels, trying to help the learner as much as possible, apparently. They also tried to press the shock lever as quickly as possible, hoping to deliver minimal pain.

3.3   Creating Operational Definitions

1. *Frustration* could be operationally defined as (a) blood pressure elevated 20% over the baseline level for a person, or (b) amount of time spent pushing against a blockade to keep a child from a desired toy.

3. *Anxiety* could be operationally defined as (a) level of muscle tension in the shoulders, or (b) a person's self-rating of anxiety just before an exam begins, on a scale from 1 to 10.

3.4   Confirmation Bias

See if you can figure out why the correct answer is "E and 7." Hint: These are the only choices allowing for *falsification* of the statement.

Chapter 4. Measurement, Sampling, and Data Analysis

4.1   Scales of Measurement

1. Categories are being used—nominal scale.

3. Rank order is used here—ordinal scale.

5. Nominal scale, assuming the study is set up so that what is measured is whether people help or not (i.e., two categories); could be a ratio scale, though, if the amount of time it takes for someone to help is measured.

7. This is a rank order procedure—ordinal scale.

9. Most psychologists are willing to consider the scales on psychological tests to have equal intervals between choice points—interval scale.

4.2 H_0, H_1, Type I errors, and Type II errors

1. H_0: Male and female participants are equally able to detect deception.

H_1: Females will be better able to detect deception than males, especially when detecting deception in other females (rationale—reading facial expressions of emotion is not a guy thing).

Type I error: Females outperform males, when in fact there are no true differences in the ability to judge deception.

Type II error: No differences are found in the study, but in fact, females are superior to males in judging deception.

3. Depressed and nondepressed patients asked to predict how they will do in negotiating a human maze.

H_0: depressed = nondepressed in their predictions

H_1: predictions of success will be higher for nondepressed than for depressed

Type I: nondepressed predictions significantly better (p < .05), but no true difference exists

Type II: differences in predictions not significant (p > .05), but the nondepressed really do have more confidence in their ability to learn a maze

4.3 Practicing Statistical Analysis

For Psychology majors: mean = 61.8; median = 61.5; mode = 60; range = 25; standard deviation = 8.07; variance = 65.07; 95% CI: 56.03 to 67.57

For Philosophy majors: mean = 53.9; median = 53; mode = 51; range = 24; standard deviation = 8.08; variance = 65.21; 95% CI: 48.12 to 59.68

General conclusion: significantly higher critical thinking scores for Psychology majors, probably because of their research methods course → $t(18) = 2.19$, $p = .04$. And the effect size is large ($d = .98$)

Side-by-Side Stem and Leaf Display

Psychology		Philosophy
9	**4**	3 4 7
5 3	**5**	1 1 5 8
7 5 3 0 0	**6**	1 2 7
4 2	**7**	

Chapter 5. Introduction to Experimental Research

5.1 Identifying Variables

1. There are two independent variables. The first is class; its levels are freshmen and seniors; it is a subject variable. The second is building location; its levels are central and peripheral; it is a manipulated variable. There are also two dependent variables, confidence ratings (interval scale) and pointing accuracy (ratio scale).

3. There are two independent variables. The first, a manipulated variable, is degree of hunger, with two levels operationally defined by the number of hours without food (6 or 12). The second independent variable could be called "tone-food sequencing." Its three levels are (a) tone on and off, then food; (b) tone on, then food; and (c) food, then tone. It is a manipulated variable. There are two dependent variables: how long it takes for saliva to begin, and how much saliva accumulates. Both are ratio.

5. There is one independent variable, which could be called "reinforcement procedure." Its four levels are (a) reinforcement on all 30 trials;

(b) no reinforcement for all 30 trials; (c) no reinforcement for 15 trials followed by reinforcement for 15 trials; and (d) reinforcement for 15 trials followed by no reinforcement for 15 trials. It is a manipulated variable. There are two dependent variables: number of errors and time to completion. Both are ratio.

7. There are two independent variables. The first is the subject variable of sex (two levels—male, female). The second is the type of stimulus materials used; its two levels are stereotypically male and stereotypically female. It is a manipulated variable. The single dependent variable will be an accuracy score (number of correctly identified moved objects) and it is scored on a ratio scale.

5.2 Spot the Confound(s)

1. The independent variable is driver type (four levels, one for each type of driver) and the dependent variable is the distance traveled by a struck golf ball. Confounds are club sequence (the golfers shouldn't all use the clubs in the same order) and golf course hole (some holes might lend themselves to longer distances, if for instance, they are downwind).

Levels of IV	EV1	EV2	DV
Club 1	first to be hit	first hole	distance
Club 2	second to be hit	second hole	distance
Club 3	third to be hit	third hole	distance
Club 4	fourth to be hit	fourth hole	distance

3. The independent variable is memorization strategy (or a similar label), with two levels: imagery and rote repetition. The dependent variable is some measure of recall. Confounds are word type (should all be either concrete or abstract) and presentation mode (should all be either visual or auditory).

Levels of IV	EV1	EV2	DV
imagery	concrete nouns	visual	recall
rote repetition	abstract nouns	auditory	recall

5.3 Operational Definitions (Again)

1. The independent variable is situational ambiguity and, in a helping behavior study, it could be manipulated by staging an emergency (e.g., a person slumped against a wall groaning) and manipulating the level of lighting with perhaps three levels: bright, medium, and dim. These could be operationally defined in terms of some physical measure of brightness. The dependent variable would be helping, and could be operationally defined as occurring whenever a passerby stops and verbally offers aid.

3. One independent variable is the level of bowling skill, and it could be operationalized as a bowler's average score. The second independent variable is whether an audience is present or not, and that could be defined easily enough as a group of people of some fixed number who watch the bowling. The dependent variable would be bowling performance, easily defined as one's total score per game.

5. Two independent variables here—whether or not caffeine is ingested and age—and a single dependent variable that could be operationalized as the number of words recalled after studying a list of 30 words for 2 minutes. Caffeine could be operationally defined by having some subjects drink an 8-ounce cup of caffeinated coffee and others drink an 8-ounce cup of decaffeinated coffee. The drinks could be ingested 20 minutes before doing the memory test, to be sure the caffeine has begun to have an effect. Subjects 20–25 years of age could be compared with those 60–65 years old.

Chapter 6. Control Problems in Experimental Research

6.1 Between-Subject or Within-Subject?

1. The study would need both young and old animals, a between-subjects variable. For each group, some animals would have their visual cortex damaged and others wouldn't, another between-subjects variable.

3. The study would involve comparing the repeated exposure procedure with some other procedure or with the absence of a procedure (control group). In either case, this is a between-subjects situation.

5. This study compares problem solving when done in groups and when done alone. It could be done as a between-subjects variable, but a within-subjects approach would also be fine and might even be preferable, allowing direct comparison within a specific person of whether problem solving works better in a group setting or when one is by oneself.

7. This study compares the degree of suggestibility for two different kinds of clinical patients, and because this is a subject variable, it is a between-subjects variable.

6.2 Constructing a Balanced Latin Square (use the instructions in Table 6.2 to produce these squares)

```
A B D C          A B H C G D F E
B C A D          B C A D H E G F
C D B A          C D B E A F H G
D A C B          D E C F B G A H
                 E F D G C H B A
                 F G E H D A C B
                 G H F A E B D C
                 H A G B F C E D
```

6.3   Random Assignment and Matching
Matching:

Step 1.   Scores on the matching variable—the weights listed in the exercise.

Step 2.   Arrange in ascending order:

> 168, 175, 178, 182, 184, 185, 186, 188, 191, 198, 205,
> 210, 215, 221, 226, 238

Step 3.   Create pairs:

> pair 1: 168 and 175
> pair 2: 178 and 182
> pair 3: 184 and 185
> pair 4: 186 and 188
> pair 5: 191 and 198
> pair 6: 205 and 210
> pair 7: 215 and 221
> pair 8: 226 and 238

From this point answers will vary. For each matched pair, flip a coin to see which of the pair is assigned to the weight loss program and which to the control group. Then calculate a mean weight for each. Follow the procedure in the exercise to accomplish random assignment. Then compare the numbers that result from the two procedures. Chances are the two assigned groups will be closer to each other in average weight when the matching procedure is done.

Chapter 7. Experimental Design I: Single-Factor Designs

7.1   Identifying Variables

1.   Research Example 8—Independent Groups
Independent variable: the essay topic
   levels: thoughts about death
              thoughts about listening to music
Dependent variable: responses to survey on estimates of future well-being (e.g., financial)

3.   Research Example 10—Nonequivalent Groups
Independent variable: traumatic brain injury
   levels: injured
              not injured
Dependent variable: sarcasm detection score

5. Research Example 12—Multilevel Independent Groups
Independent variable: method of study
      levels: with full context (before)
               with full context (after)
               with partial context
               with no context, one repetition
               with no context, two repetitions
Dependent variable: number of idea units recalled

7. Research Example 14—Using Both Placebo and Waiting List Control Groups
Independent variable: type of weight loss tape
      levels: subliminal tape on weight loss
               subliminal tape on dental anxiety (placebo control)
               no tape yet (waiting list control)
Dependent variable: weight loss after five weeks

7.2 Identifying Designs

1. The independent variable is whether or not a person has bulimia; it is a between-subjects variable and a subject variable. The dependent variable is the choice of the body size drawing; assuming equal intervals, it appears to be measured on an interval scale. The design is: single-factor, 2-level, nonequivalent groups.

3. The independent variable is length of the gratification delay; it is a between-subjects manipulated variable. The dependent variable is how long they continue doing the puzzle; it is a ratio scale of measurement. The design is: single-factor, multilevel, independent groups.

5. The independent variable is degree of tattoo coverage; it is a within-subjects manipulated variable. One dependent variable is the judgment about a major; it is measured on a nominal scale (one of five categories). The other dependent variable is the rating scales; depending on the equal interval assumption, this could be either ordinal or interval. The design is: single-factor, multilevel, repeated measures.

7. The independent variable is the length of the time limit for each anagram; it is a between-subjects manipulated variable. The dependent variable is the number of anagrams solved, a ratio measure. The design is: single-factor, 2-level, matched groups.

7.3 Outcomes

1. The independent variable is a discrete variable (type of group in the study), so use a bar graph.

      Outcome A. Marijuana impairs recall, whereas subject expectations about marijuana have no effect on recall.

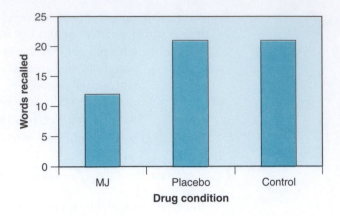

Outcome B. Marijuana impairs recall, but subject expectations about marijuana also reduce recall performance.

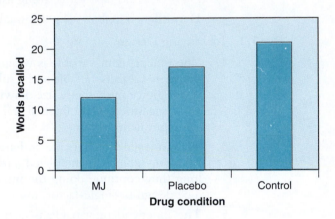

Outcome C. The apparently adverse effect of marijuana on recall can be attributed entirely to placebo effects.

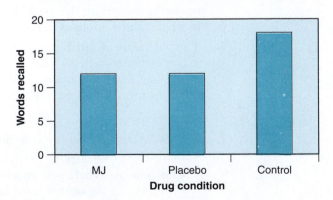

3. The independent variable is a continuous variable (time delay of reinforcement), so a line graph is preferred (a bar graph could be used, however).

Outcome A. Reinforcement delay hinders learning.

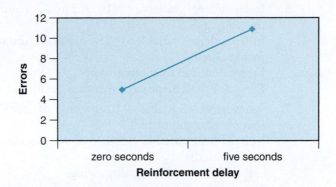

Outcome B. Reinforcement delay has no effect on learning.

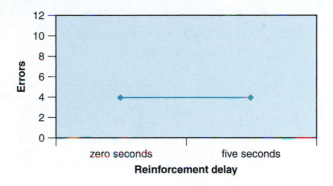

Chapter 8. Experimental Design II: Factorial Designs

8.1 Identifying Designs

1. Independent variable #1: personality type (A, B, intermediate) (between; subject)
   Independent variable #2: cognitive task (video game, no video game) (between; manipulated)
   Dependent variable: accuracy in estimating the passage of 2 minutes
   Design: 2×3 P $\times$ E Factorial

3. Independent variable #1: skin location (10 locations) (within; manipulated)
   Independent variable #2: visual capacity (blind; sighted) (between; subject)

Independent variable #3: time of testing (morning; evening) (between; manipulated)
Dependent variable: threshold judgments
Design: 2 × 2 × 10 Mixed P × E Factorial

5. Independent variable #1: stimulus color (color; b/w) (within; manipulated)
Independent variable #2: stimulus distance (10'; 20') (within; manipulated)
Dependent variable: error score
Design: 2 × 2 Repeated Measures Factorial

7. Independent variable #1: labeling of essay author (patient; worker) (between; manipulated)
Independent variable #2: sex of essay author (male; female) (between; manipulated)
Dependent variable: quality ratings
Design: 2 × 2 Independent Groups Factorial

8.2 Main Effects and Interactions

1. **a.**   IV#1: situational ambiguity (ambiguous, not ambiguous)
IV#2: number of bystanders (0, 2)
DV: time to respond

b.

	0 bystanders	2 bystanders	Row means
Ambiguous	24	38	31
Not ambiguous	14	14	14
Column means	19	26	

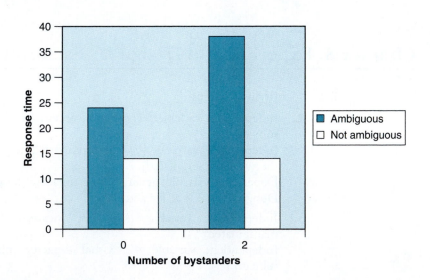

c. There are two main effects and an interaction, but one of the main effects is not relevant. Helping behavior takes longer to occur if the situation is ambiguous, and this is true whether there are 0 (24 > 14) or 2 (38 > 14) bystanders. So the main effect for ambiguity is relevant. There is also a main effect for number of bystanders, but while the number of bystanders affects helping in the ambiguous situation (38 > 24), it is not relevant in the unambiguous situation (14 = 14). So the main effect for number of bystanders is not relevant. The interaction is the key finding and is the reason why the second main effect is not relevant—if the situation is unambiguous, the number of bystanders does not affect helping (14 = 14), but if the situation is ambiguous, helping is slowed by the number of bystanders present (38 > 24).

3. a. IV#1: sex (male, female)

IV#2: instructions (male-oriented, female-oriented, neutral)

DV: problems correct

b.

	Male-oriented	Female-oriented	Neutral	Row means
Males	26	23	26	25
Females	18	24	18	20
Column means	22	23.5	22	

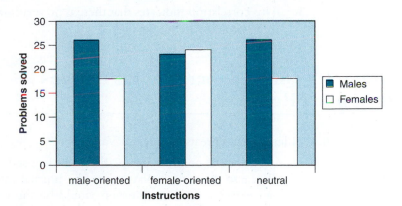

c. There is no main effect for instructions (22 = 23.5 = 22), but there is a main effect for sex (25 > 20) and there is an interaction, which is the key finding. Males outperform females in the neutral condition and when male-oriented instructions are given. With female-oriented instructions, however, no sex difference occurs.

8.3 Estimating Participant Needs

1. 30

3. Cannot be answered without knowing which factor is tested between and which within.

5. 32

Chapter 9. Correlational Research

9.1   Interpreting Correlations

1.   It could be that dominant mothers never allow their children to develop independence, and they become shy as a result (A→B). However, it could also be that naturally shy children cause their mothers to take more control of the relationship (B→A).

3.   It could be that all of the books in the home were read by the children, making them smarter and therefore better students (A→B). It could be that the third variable of parental attitudes toward learning led to (a) lots of books in the home, and (b) reinforcement for their children being good students (C→A&B).

5.   It could be that getting poor grades increases student anxiety (A→B), but it could also be true that anxious students don't prepare well and don't take tests well (B→A).

9.3   Understanding Scatterplots

1.   Use the sample scatterplots found in Figure 9.2 to draw the estimated scatterplot. The Pearson's r of +.50 is relatively strong, indicating some similarity in cognitive function between sequential and simultaneous processing.

3.   This correlation indicates that there is no relationship at all between being intelligent and being depressed.

Chapter 10. Quasi-Experimental Designs and Applied Research

10.1   Identifying Threats to Internal Validity

1.   Without a control group, there are several alternative explanations. Because the 60% is way below the normal retention rate of 75% (i.e., an extreme score), regression would be the most likely threat (65% is heading back in the direction of 75%). History and selection are two other possibilities, but maturation is less likely because two different groups of students would be involved in the study.

3.   This is most likely a selection problem. The women who volunteer are possibly different in some significant way (e.g., more willing to try new things) from the women selected randomly.

5.   Thirty students started the course but only 18 finished it. The problem is attrition, resulting in a group at the end of the course that is systematically different (e.g., more persevering) from those who started the course. This course format might not be effective for the student who needs more direct guidance.

10.2   Interpreting Nonequivalent Control Group Studies

1. It is likely that the program worked—absenteeism drops in the experimental plants, but not in the control plant. It is unlikely but possible, however, that a selection *x* history confound is operating, in which some event affected absenteeism in one plant but not the other.

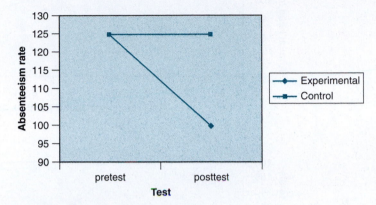

3. There is no evidence that the program worked—absenteeism drops in the experimental plants, but it drops by the same amount in the control plant. The decline could be due to any number of confounds, but also might be part of a general downward trend that could be revealed in a follow-up study by a time series analysis.

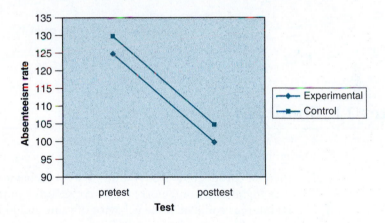

10.3 Interpreting Time Series Studies

1. The law worked (next page; first graph).

3. Probably a regression effect (next page; second graph).

To improve the basic interrupted time series designs, the researchers could (a) use a control group, a league in another city without a helmet law; (b) use a switching replication, comparing with another league that introduced a helmet law at a different time; or (c) add some additional dependent variables that would not be expected to be affected by a helmet law, such as leg injuries.

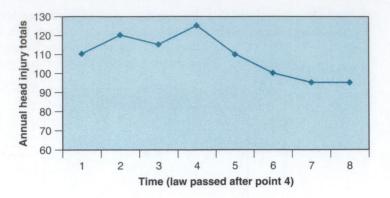

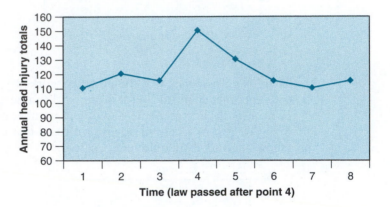

Chapter 11. Small *N* Designs

11.1   Designing Self-Improvement Programs

1.   Increase productive study time: Target behavior could be studying (reading, doing homework) for 30 consecutive minutes without a break. Reinforcer could be some behavior of value and interest (e.g., a period of time reading a mystery novel). Successive criteria could be in 10-minute intervals, with an interval added each week.

3.   Change to healthier eating behaviors: Target behavior could be reducing intake of such junk foods as potato chips and corn chips. Reinforcer could be allowing oneself an extra trip to the driving range. Successive criteria could be defined in terms of a reduction in the number of ounces of chips consumed per week.

11.2   Hypothetical Outcomes of Applied Behavior Analyses

1.   A–B–C–B design

a. Reinforcement works, but only if it is made contingent on specific behaviors.

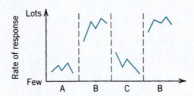

b. Reinforcement works regardless of whether it is made contingent on specific behaviors.

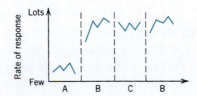

3. Multiple baseline across three settings

a. The treatment program works.

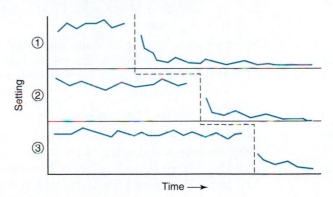

b. One cannot discount a history or maturation effect.

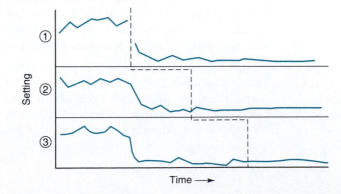

Chapter 12. Observational and Survey Research Methods

12.2   Improving Poor Survey Items

1.   Have you had an upset stomach lately?

a.   "Upset stomach" could be described more precisely, but the major problem is the lack of precision in the "lately"; does it mean within the past week? Month?

b.   After telling the test taker to define an upset stomach as "nauseous to the point where you think you might vomit but you don't," the item could read:

Have you had an upset stomach in the last week? If so, how often?

3.   In your opinion, how young is the average cigarette smoker?

a.   The "how young" could bias the person toward giving a younger age, and some people might even misinterpret the question as a question about when people first start smoking.

b.   *Better:* In your opinion, what is the average age of a typical cigarette smoker?

5.   Most doctors have a superior attitude.

a.   To distinguish M.D.s from Ph.D.s, it might be better to refer to them as "medical doctors."

b.   "Superior attitude" is quite vague and ought to be replaced, perhaps with a description of a specific behavior. The item could read: "Medical doctors are often unwilling to explain their recommendations to patients."

12.3   Defining Behaviors for Observational Research

1.   Studying in the library: probably need to limit the study to students not using computers and using tables where observation is easy. Studying could be defined as reading any printed material and/or writing notes. In a given 15-minute period, the observers could record total time on task (i.e., studying).

3.   Children playing: ages would need to be defined, as well as cooperative play (children playing next to each other and interacting with each other) and parallel play (children playing next to each other but not interacting); study could be done in a preschool with observational two-way mirrors, or a video made for later analysis.

5.   Couples gazing: there would be some structure to this study, perhaps bringing couples (dating couples and married couples) into the lab and asking them to talk to each other about some defined topic for a fixed period of time. Their conversations would be taped and later subjected to analysis (i.e., during the interval, the proportion of time spent in mutual gazing).

12.4   Deciding on a Method

1. This calls for naturalistic observation of the feeding behavior.

3. An e-survey that included a personality assessment, as well as items about shopping, would be the way to go here.

5. The easiest method here would be a written survey about stereotyping administered to classes in the two types of science.

7. This study would require close observation over an extended period of time; participant observation would probably be best.

Appendix A. Communicating the Results of Research in Psychology

Exercise A1.1   True-False

1. After writing the Abstract, double space and then immediately begin the introduction on the same page.

   • False—The intro begins on a new page.

2. On the title page, the running head will almost always be different from the manuscript page header.

   • True—The running head should convey the sense of the title, whereas the manuscript page header is just the first two or three meaningful words of the title.

3. In the Results section, if you portray your results with a graph, it is also OK to display them in a Table because then the reader gets the exact numbers.

   • False—Use either a graph or a table, not both.

4. An Abstract should be no longer than 120 words.

   • True—and never use more than one paragraph.

5. A "what's next" type of paragraph belongs in the Discussion section of the report.

   • True—This is the place for a discussion of potential future research.

6. Begin each section with a centered label—in the introduction, for example, the word "Introduction" identifies the section.

   • False—The intro leads with a centered copy of the article's title.

7. Each item that appears in the Reference section should be found somewhere in the lab report itself.

   • True—Always double-check this.

8. The Method section should contain enough information for replication to be possible.

- True—This is the essential concept to keep in mind as you write a Method section.

9. In the Results section, to maintain reader interest, it is important to explain and interpret each result right after you report it.

   - False—Explanation and interpretation belong in the Discussion section.

10. The place to operationally define the independent and dependent variables is the Method section.

    - True—Part of the process of making it possible to replicate.

Exercise A1.3   Referencing—Sharpening Your Obsessive-Compulsive Tendencies

Of the following items from a Reference section, one is correct and the remaining seven have exactly one error. Identify the one that is correct and fix the errors.

1. Reynolds, G. S. (1968). *A Primer of Operant Conditioning*. Glenview, IL: Scott, Foresman.

   - Reynolds, G. S. (1968). *A primer of operant conditioning*. Glenview, IL: Scott, Foresman.

2. Kolata, George B. (1986). What does it mean to be random? *Science, 231,* 1068–1070.

   - Kolata, G. B. (1986). What does it mean to be random? *Science, 231,* 1068–1070.

3. Lee, D. N., and Aronson, E. (1974). Visual proprioceptive control of standing in human infants. *Perception and Psychophysics, 15,* 529–532.

   - Lee, D. N., & Aronson, E. (1974). Visual proprioceptive control of standing in human infants. *Perception and Psychophysics, 15,* 529–532.

4. Miller, A. G. (1972). Role playing: An alternative to deception? *American Psychologist,* 27, 623–636.

   - Miller, A. G. (1972). Role playing: An alternative to deception? *American Psychologist, 27,* 623–636.

5. Geller, D. M. (1982). Alternatives to deception: Why, what, and how? In Sieber, J. E. (Ed.), *The ethics of social research: Surveys and experiments* (pp. 40–55). New York: Springer-Verlag.

   - Geller, D. M. (1982). Alternatives to deception: Why, what, and how? In J. E. Sieber (Ed.), *The ethics of social research: Surveys and experiments* (pp. 40–55). New York: Springer-Verlag.

Glossary

A priori method A way of knowing, proposed by Charles Peirce, in which a person develops a belief by reasoning and reaching agreement with others who are convinced of the merits of the reasoned argument.

A–A$_1$–B–A$_1$–B A small N design for evaluating placebo effects; A$_1$ is a condition in the sequence in which a placebo treatment is given.

A–B design A small N design in which a baseline period (A) is followed by a treatment period (B).

A–B–A design A small N design in which a baseline period (A) is followed by a treatment period (B) followed by a period in which the treatment is reversed or withdrawn (second A).

A–B–A–B design Like an A–B–A design except that a second treatment period is established (second B).

A–B–C–B design A small N design that compares contingent reinforcement (B) with noncontingent reinforcement (C); allows the researcher to separate the effects of reinforcers and contingency.

Abstract In a lab report, a brief (about 120 words or less) summary of the research being reported.

Alpha level The probability of making a Type I error; the significance level.

Alternating treatments design A small N design that compares, in the same study and for the same participant(s), two or more separate forms of treatment for changing some behavior.

Alternative hypothesis The researcher's hypothesis about the outcome of a study (H$_1$).

Anecdotal evidence Evidence from a single case that illustrates a phenomenon; when relied on exclusively, as in pseudoscience, faulty conclusions can easily be drawn.

ANOVA Short for **AN**alysis **O**f **VA**riance, the most common inferential statistical tool for analyzing the results of experiments when dependent variables are measured on interval or ratio scales.

ANOVA source table A standardized method for displaying the results of an analysis of variance; includes sources of variance, sums of squares, degrees of freedom, mean squares (variance), F ratios, and probability values.

Application A goal of science in which basic principles discovered through scientific methods are applied in order to solve problems.

Applied behavior analysis Research using various methods to evaluate the effectiveness of conditioning procedures in bringing about changes in the rate of response of some behavior.

Applied research Research with the goal of trying to solve some immediate real-life problem.

Archival data Data initially collected for some purpose not related to a current research study, and then used later for a specific purpose in that current research

Archival research A research method in which already existing records are examined to test some hypothesis.

Assent To give assent is to say "yes;" in the SRCD code of ethics for research with children, refers to the willingness on the part of the child to participate in the study.

ATI design Aptitude by treatment interaction design; form of P × E factorial design found in educational research, the goal of which is to examine possible interactions between an aptitude variable (person factor) and a treatment variable (environmental factor).

Attrition A threat to the internal validity of a study; occurs when participants fail to complete a study, usually but not necessarily in longitudinal studies; those finishing the study may not be equivalent to those who started it.

Authority A way of knowing, proposed by Charles Peirce, in which a person develops a belief by agreeing with someone perceived to be an expert.

Availability heuristic   Social cognition bias in which vivid or memorable events lead people to overestimate the frequency of occurrence of these events.

Baseline   The initial stage of a small N design, in which the behavior to be changed is monitored to determine its normal rate of response.

Basic research   Research with the goal of describing, predicting, and explaining fundamental principles of behavior.

Behavior checklists   Lists of behaviors with predefined operational definitions that researchers are trained to use in an observational study.

Belief perseverance   Unwillingness to consider any evidence that contradicts a strongly held view; similar to Peirce's principle of tenacity.

Between-subjects design   Any experimental design in which different groups of participants serve in the different conditions of the study.

Biased sample   A sample that is not representative of the population.

Bivariate analysis   Any statistical analysis investigating the relationship between two variables.

Block randomization   A procedure used to accomplish random assignment and ensure an equal number of participants in each condition; ensures that each condition of the study has a subject randomly assigned to it before any condition has a subject assigned to it again; also used in within-subjects design as a counterbalancing procedure to ensure that when participants are tested in each condition more than once, they experience each condition once before experiencing any condition again.

Carryover effect   Form of sequence effect in which systematic changes in performance occur as a result of completing one sequence of conditions rather than a different sequence.

Case study   A descriptive method in which an in-depth analysis is made of a single individual, a single rare event, or an event that clearly exemplifies some phenomenon.

Ceiling effect   Occurs when scores on two or more conditions are at or near the maximum possible for the scale being used, giving the impression that no differences exist between the conditions.

Changing criterion design   A small N design in which the criterion for receiving reinforcement begins at a modest level and becomes more stringent as the study progresses; used to shape behavior.

Closed question   A type of question found on surveys that can be answered with a "yes" or a "no" or by marking a point on some scale.

Cluster sample   A probability sample that randomly selects clusters of people having some feature in common (e.g., students taking history courses) and tests all people within the selected cluster (e.g., all students in three of the nine history courses available).

Coefficient of correlation   See Pearson's r.

Coefficient of determination   For two correlated factors, the proportion of variance in one factor that can be attributed to the second factor; found by squaring Pearson's r.

Cohort effect   A cohort is a group of people born at about the same time; cohort effects can reduce the internal validity of cross-sectional studies because differences between groups could result from the effects of growing up in different historical eras.

Cohort sequential design   In developmental psychology research, a design that combines cross-sectional and longitudinal designs; a new cohort is added to a study every few years, and then studied periodically throughout the time course of the study.

Community forum   In program evaluation research, a meeting open to community members to discuss the need for, or the operation of, some program.

Complete counterbalancing   Occurs when all possible orders of conditions are used in a within-subjects design.

Confederate   See Experimental confederate.

Confidence interval   An inferential statistic in which a range of scores is calculated; with some degree of confidence (e.g., 95%), it is assumed that population values lie within the interval.

Confidentiality   In research ethics, an agreement on the part of the researcher not to divulge the identity of those participating in a research study.

Confirmation bias   Social cognition bias in which events that confirm a strongly held belief are more readily perceived and remembered; disconfirming events are ignored or forgotten.

Confound   Any extraneous variable that covaries with the independent variable and could provide an alternative explanation of the results.

Construct   A hypothetical factor (e.g., hunger) that cannot be observed directly but is inferred from certain behaviors (e.g., eating) and assumed to follow from certain circumstances (e.g., 24 hours without food).

Construct validity   In measurement, it occurs when the measure being used accurately assesses some hypothetical construct; also refers to whether the construct itself is valid; in research, refers to whether the operational definitions used for independent and dependent variables are valid.

Content analysis A procedure used to systematically categorize the content of the behavior (often verbal behavior) being recorded.

Content validity Occurs when a measure appears to be a reasonable or logical measure of some trait (e.g., as a measure of intelligence, problem solving has more content validity than hat size).

Continuous variable Variable for which an infinite number of values potentially exists (e.g., a drug's dosage level).

Control group A group not given a treatment that is being evaluated in a study; provides a means of comparison.

Convenience sample A non-probability sample in which the researcher requests volunteers from a group of people who meet the general requirements of the study (e.g., teenagers); used in most psychological research, except when specific estimates of population values need to be made.

Convergent validity Occurs when scores on a test designed to measure some construct (e.g., self-esteem) are correlated with scores on other tests that are theoretically related to the construct.

Converging operations Occurs when the results of several studies, each defining its terms with slightly different operational definitions, nonetheless converge on the same general conclusion.

Correlation See positive correlation and negative correlation.

Correlation matrix A table that summarizes a series of correlations among several variables.

Cost-effectiveness analysis Form of program evaluation that assesses outcomes in terms of the costs involved in developing, running, and completing the program.

Counterbalancing For a within-subjects variable, any procedure designed to control for sequence effects.

Creative thinking A process of making an innovative connection between seemingly unrelated ideas or events.

Criterion validity Form of validity in which a psychological measure is able to predict some future behavior or is meaningfully related to some other measure.

Criterion variable In a regression analysis, this is the variable that is being predicted from the predictor variable (e.g., college grades are predicted from SAT scores).

Critical incidents Method, used by ethics committees, that surveys psychologists and asks for examples of unethical behavior by psychologists.

Cross-lagged panel correlation Refers to a type of correlational research designed to deal with the directionality problem; if variables X and Y are measured at two different times and if X precedes Y, then X might cause Y but Y cannot cause X.

Cross-sectional study In developmental psychology, a design in which age is the independent variable and different groups of people are tested; each group is of a different age.

Cumulative recorder Apparatus for recording the subject's cumulative rate of response in operant conditioning studies.

Data-driven Belief of research psychologists that conclusions about behavior should be supported by data collected scientifically.

Debriefing A postexperimental session in which the experimenter explains the study's purpose, reduces any discomfort felt by participants, and answers any questions posed by participants.

Deception A research strategy in which participants are not told of all the details of an experiment at its outset; used for the purpose of avoiding demand characteristics.

Deduction Reasoning from the general to the specific; in science, used when deriving research hypotheses from theories.

Dehoaxing That portion of debriefing in which the true purpose of the study is explained to participants.

Demand characteristic Any feature of the experimental design or procedure that increases the chances that participants will detect the true purpose of the study.

Demographic information Any data that can serve to classify or identify individuals (e.g., gender, age, income).

Dependent variable Behavior measured as the outcome of an experiment.

Description A goal of psychological science in which behaviors are accurately classified or sequences of environmental stimuli and behavioral events are accurately listed.

Descriptive statistics Provide a summary of the main features of a set of data collected from a sample of participants.

Desensitizing That portion of debriefing in which the experimenter tries to reduce any distress felt by participants as a result of their research experience.

Determinism An assumption made by scientists that all events have causes.

Directionality problem In correlational research, this refers to the fact that for a correlation between variables X and Y, it is possible that X is causing Y, but it is also possible that Y is causing X; the correlation alone provides no basis for deciding between the two alternatives.

Discoverability An assumption made by scientists that the causes of events can be discovered by applying scientific methods.

Discrete variable Variable in which each level represents a distinct category that is qualitatively different from another category (e.g., males and females).

Discriminant validity Occurs when scores on a test designed to measure some construct (e.g., self-esteem) are uncorrelated with scores on other tests that should be theoretically unrelated to the construct.

DK alternative In survey research, when assessing levels of participant knowledge, this is an alternative that means "don't know."

Double-barreled question In a survey, a question or statement that asks or states two different things in a single item.

Double blind A control procedure designed to reduce bias; neither the participant nor the person conducting the experimental session knows which condition of the study is being tested; often used in studies evaluating drug effects.

Ecological validity Said to exist when research studies psychological phenomena in everyday situations (e.g., memory for where we put our keys).

Effect size Amount of influence that one variable has on another; the amount of variance in the dependent variable that can be attributed to the independent variable.

Effort justification After expending a large amount of time or effort to obtain some goal, people giving the effort feel pressured to convince themselves that the effort was worthwhile, even if the resulting outcome is less positive than originally thought.

Electronic survey Any survey research that is conducted over the Internet; can be a survey sent via e-mail or a survey posted on a website.

Empirical question A question that can be answered by making objective observations.

Empiricism A way of knowing that relies on direct observation or experience.

Equivalent groups Groups of participants in a between-subjects design that are essentially equal to each other in all ways except for the different levels of the independent variable.

Error bars On bar or line graphs, they indicate the amount of variability around a mean; often reflect standard deviations or confidence intervals.

Error variance Nonsystematic variability in a set of scores due to random factors or individual differences.

E-survey See Electronic survey.

Ethics A set of principles prescribing behaviors that are morally correct.

Evaluation apprehension A form of anxiety experienced by participants that leads them to behave so as to be evaluated positively by the experimenter.

Event sampling A procedure in observational research in which only certain types of behaviors occurring under precisely defined conditions are sampled.

Experiment A research procedure in which some factor is varied, all else is held constant, and some result is measured.

Experimental confederate An individual who appears to be either another subject in an experiment, but is in fact a part of the experiment and in the employ of the experimenter.

Experimental group In a study with an identified control group, the experimental group is given the treatment being tested.

Experimental realism Refers to how deeply involved the participants become in the experiment; considered to be more important than mundane realism.

Experimenter bias Occurs when an experimenter's expectations about a study affect its outcome.

Explanation A goal of science in which the causes of events are sought.

Extension Replicating part of a prior study, but adding some additional features (e.g., additional levels of the independent variable).

External validity The extent to which the findings of a study generalize to other populations, other settings, and other times.

Extraneous variable Any uncontrolled factor that is not of interest to the researcher but could affect the results.

Face validity Occurs when a measure appears, to those taking a test, to be a reasonable measure of some trait; not considered by researchers to be an important indicator of validity.

Factor analysis A multivariate analysis in which a large number of variables are intercorrelated; variables that correlate highly with each other form "factors."

Factorial design Any experimental design with more than one independent variable.

Factorial matrix A row and column arrangement that characterizes a factorial design and shows the independent variables, the levels of each independent variable, and the total number of conditions (cells) in the study.

Falsification Research strategy advocated by Popper that emphasizes putting theories to the test by trying to disprove or falsify them.

Falsifying data   Manufacturing or altering data to bring about a desired result.

Field experiment   An experiment that is conducted outside the laboratory; a narrower term than field research.

Field research   Research that occurs in any location other than a scientific laboratory.

Figures   In a lab report or description of research, these are graphs, diagrams, flow charts, sketches of apparatus, or photos.

File drawer effect   A situation in which findings of no difference fail to be published (the studies are placed in one's files); if there are a large number of such findings, the few studies that do find a difference and get published produce a distorted impression of actual differences.

Floor effect   Occurs when scores on two or more conditions are at or near the minimum possible for the scale being used, giving the impression that no differences exist between the conditions.

Focus group   A small and relatively homogeneous group brought together for the purpose of participating in a group interview on some topic or, in program evaluation research, to discuss the need for or the operation of a program.

Formative evaluation   Form of program evaluation that monitors the functioning of a program while it is operating to determine if it is functioning as planned.

Frequency distribution   A table that records the number of times that each score in a set of scores occurs.

Good subject role   A form of participant bias in which participants try to guess the experimenter's hypothesis and then behave in such a way as to confirm it.

Hawthorne effect   Name often given to a form of participant bias in which behavior is influenced by the mere knowledge that the participant is in an experiment and is therefore of some importance to the experimenter.

Histogram   Graph of a frequency distribution in bar form.

History   A threat to the internal validity of a study; occurs when some historical event that could affect participants happens between the beginning of a study and its end.

Homogeneity of variance   One of the conditions that should be in effect in order to perform parametric inferential tests such as a *t* test or ANOVA; refers to the fact that variability among all the conditions of a study ought to be similar.

Hypothesis   An educated guess about a relationship between variables that is then tested empirically.

Independent groups design   A between-subjects design that uses a manipulated independent variable and has at least two groups of participants; subjects are randomly assigned to the groups.

Independent variable   The factor of interest to the researcher; it can be directly manipulated by the experimenter (e.g., creating different levels of anxiety in subjects), or participants can be selected by virtue of their possessing certain attributes (e.g., selecting two groups who differ in the normal levels of anxiousness).

Individual–subject validity   The extent to which the general outcome of a research study characterizes the behavior of the individual participants in the study.

Induction   Reasoning from the specific to the general; in science, used when the results of specific research studies are used to support or refute a theory.

Inferential statistics   Used to draw conclusions about the broader population on the basis of a study using just a sample of that population.

Informed consent   The idea that persons should be given sufficient information about a study to make their decision to participate as a research subject an informed and voluntary one.

Institutional Review Board (IRB)   University committee responsible for evaluating whether research proposals provide adequate protection of the rights of participants; must exist for any college or university receiving federal funds for research.

Instructional variable   Type of independent variable in which participants are given different sets of instructions about how to perform (e.g., given a list of stimuli, various groups might be told to process them in different ways).

Instrumentation   A threat to the internal validity of a study; occurs when the measuring instrument changes from pretest to posttest (e.g., because of their experience with the instrument, experimenters might use it differently from pretest to posttest).

Interaction   In a factorial design, occurs when the effect of one independent variable depends on the level of another independent variable.

Internal validity   The extent to which a study is free from methodological flaws, especially confounding factors.

Interobserver reliability   The degree of agreement between two or more observers of the same event.

Interquartile range   The range of scores lying between the bottom 25% of a set of scores (25th percentile) and the top 25% of scores (75th percentile); yields a measure a variability unaffected by outliers.

Interrupted time series design Quasi-experimental design in which a program or treatment is evaluated by measuring performance several times prior to the institution of the program and several times after the program has been put into effect.

Interrupted time series with switching replications A time series design in which the program is replicated at a different location and at a different time.

Interval scale Measurement scale in which numbers refer to quantities, and intervals are assumed to be of equal size; a score of zero is just one of many points on the scale and does not denote the absence of the phenomenon being measured.

Interview survey A survey method in which the researcher interviews the participant face to face; allows for more in-depth surveying (e.g., follow-up questions and clarifications).

Intraclass correlation A form of correlation used when pairs of scores do not come from the same individual, as when correlations are calculated for pairs of twins.

Introspection Method used in the early years of psychological science in which an individual would complete some task and then describe the events occurring in consciousness while performing the task.

IRB See Institutional Review Board.

Key informant In program evaluation research, a community member with special knowledge about the needs of a community.

Laboratory research Research that occurs within the controlled confines of the scientific laboratory.

Latin square Form of partial counterbalancing in which each condition of the study occurs equally often in each sequential position and each condition precedes and follows each other condition exactly one time.

Laws Regular, predictable relationships between events.

Leading question In a survey, a question that is asked in such a way that the answer desired by the questioner is clear.

Leakage A tendency for people who have participated in a research study to inform future participants about the true purpose of the study.

Longitudinal study In developmental psychology, a design in which age is the independent variable and the same group of people are tested repeatedly at different ages.

Main effect Refers to whether or not statistically significant differences exist between the levels of an independent variable in a factorial design.

Manipulation check In debriefing, a procedure to determine if subjects were aware of a deception experiment's true purpose; also refers to any procedure that determines if systematic manipulations have the intended effect on participants.

Manuscript page header Found in the upper right-hand corner of a lab report, this is the first two or three words of the complete title; five spaces to the right of the header is the page number, right-justified.

Matched groups design A between-subjects design that uses a manipulated independent variable and has at least two groups of participants; subjects are matched on some variable assumed to affect the outcome before being randomly assigned to the groups.

Matching A procedure for creating equivalent groups in which participants are measured on some factor (a "matching variable") expected to correlate with the dependent variable; groups are then formed by taking participants who score at the same level on the matching variable and randomly assigning them to groups.

Matching variable Any variable selected for matching participants in a matched groups study.

Maturation A threat to the internal validity of a study; occurs when participants change from the beginning to the end of the study simply as a result of maturational changes within them and not as a result of some independent variable.

Mean The arithmetic average of a data set, found by adding the scores and dividing by the total number of scores in the set.

Measurement error Produced by any factor that introduces inaccuracies into the measurement of some variable.

Measurement scales Ways of assigning numbers to events; see nominal, ordinal, interval, and ratio scales.

Median The middle score of a data set; an equal number of scores are both above and below the median.

Median location The place in the sequence of scores where the median lies.

Meta-analysis A statistical tool for combining the effect size of a number of studies to determine if general patterns occur in the data.

Mixed factorial design A factorial design with at least one between-subjects factor and one within-subjects factor.

Mixed P × E factorial design A mixed design with at least one subject factor and one manipulated factor.

Mode The most frequently appearing score in a data set.

Multiple baseline design A small *N* design in which treatment is introduced at staggered intervals when trying to alter (a) the behavior of more than one individual, (b) more than one behavior in the same individual, or (c) the behavior of an individual in more than one setting.

Multiple regression A multivariate analysis that includes a criterion variable and two or more predictor variables; the predictors will have different weights.

Multivariate analysis Any statistical analysis investigating the relationships among more than two variables.

Mundane realism Refers to how closely the experiment mirrors real-life experiences; considered to be less important than experimental realism.

Naturalistic observation Descriptive research method in which the behavior of people or animals is studied as it occurs in its everyday natural environment.

Needs analysis Form of program evaluation that occurs before a program begins and determines whether the program is needed.

Negative correlation A relationship between variables *X* and *Y* such that a high score for *X* is associated with a low score for *Y* and a low score for *X* is associated with a high score for *Y*.

Nominal scale Measurement scale in which the numbers have no quantitative value, but rather serve to identify categories into which events can be placed.

Nonequivalent control group design Quasi-experimental design in which participants cannot be randomly assigned to the experimental and control groups.

Nonequivalent groups design A between-subjects design with at least two groups of participants that uses a subject variable or that creates groups that are nonequivalent.

Nonlinear effect Any outcome that does not form a straight line when graphed; can occur only when the independent variable has more than two levels.

Nonresponse bias Occurs in survey research when those who return surveys differ in some systematic fashion (e.g., political attitudes) from those who don't respond.

Normal curve A theoretical frequency distribution for a population; a bell-shaped curve.

Null hypothesis The assumption that no real difference exists between treatment conditions in an experiment or that no significant relationship exists in a correlational study (H_0).

Objectivity Said to exist when observations can be verified by more than one observer.

Observer bias Can occur when preconceived ideas held by the researcher affect the nature of the observations made.

Open-ended question A type of question found on surveys that requires a narrative response, rather than a "yes" or "no" answer.

Operant conditioning Form of learning in which behavior is modified by its consequences; a positive consequence strengthens the behavior immediately preceding it, and a negative consequence weakens the behavior immediately preceding it.

Operational definitions A definition of a concept or variable in terms of precisely described operations, measures, or procedures.

Operationism Philosophy of science approach, proposed by Bridgman, that held that all scientific concepts should be defined in terms of a set of operations to be performed.

Order effect See sequence effect.

Ordinal scale Measurement scale in which assigned numbers stand for relative standing or ranking.

Outlier In a data set, a data point that is so deviant from the remaining points that the researcher believes that it cannot reflect reasonable behavior and its inclusion will distort the results; often considered to be a score more than three standard deviations from the mean.

P × E factorial design A factorial design with at least one subject factor (P = person variable) and one manipulated factor (E = environmental variable).

Parsimonious Describing theory that includes the minimum number of constructs and assumptions in order to explain and predict some phenomenon adequately.

Partial correlation A multivariate statistical procedure for evaluating the effects of third variables; if the correlation between *X* and *Y* remains high, even after some third factor *Z* has been "partialed out," then *Z* can be eliminated as a third variable.

Partial counterbalancing Occurs when a subset of all possible orders of conditions is used in a within-subjects design (e.g., a random sample of the population of all possible orders could be selected).

Partial replication Repeats a portion of some prior research; usually completed as part of a study that extends the results of the initial research.

Participant See Research participant.

Participant bias Can occur when the behavior of participants is influenced by their beliefs about how they are supposed to behave in a study.

Participant observation Descriptive research method in which the behavior of people is studied as it occurs in its everyday natural environment and the researcher becomes a part of the group being observed.

Participant pool   See Subject pool.

Pearson's *r*   Measure of the size of a correlation between two variables; ranges from a perfect positive correlation of +1.00 to a perfect negative correlation of −1.00; if $r = 0$, then no relationship exists between the variables.

Phone survey   A survey method in which the researcher asks questions over the phone.

Pilot study   During the initial stages of research it is common for some data to be collected; problems spotted in this trial stage enable the researcher to refine the procedures and prevent the full-scale study from being flawed methodologically.

Placebo control group   Control group in which some participants believe they are receiving the experimental treatment, but they are not.

Plagiarism   Deliberately taking the ideas of someone and claiming them as one's own.

Population   All of the members of an identifiable group.

Positive correlation   A relationship between variables X and Y such that a high score for X is associated with a high score for Y and a low score for X is associated with a low score for Y.

Posttest   A measurement given to participants at the conclusion of a study after they have experienced a treatment or been in a control group; comparisons are made with pretest scores to determine if change occurred.

Power   The chances of finding a significant difference when the null hypothesis is false; depends on alpha, effects size, and sample size

Predictions   A goal of psychological science in which statements about the future occurrence of some behavioral event are made, usually with some probability.

Predictor variable   In a regression analysis, the variable used to predict the criterion variable (e.g., SAT scores are used to predict college grades).

Pretest   A measurement given to participants at the outset of a study, prior to their being given a treatment (or not treated, when participants are in a control group).

Probability sampling   Method of selecting research participants according to some systematic sampling procedure; see also Simple random sample, Stratified sample, Cluster sample.

Productivity   With reference to theory, this refers to the amount of research that is generated to test a theory; theories that lead to a great deal of research are considered productive.

Program audit   An examination of whether a program is being implemented as planned; a type of formative evaluation.

Program evaluation   A form of applied research that includes a number of research activities designed to evaluate programs from planning to completion.

Programs of research   Series of interrelated studies in which the outcome of one study leads naturally to another.

Progressive effect   In a within-subjects design, any sequence effect in which the accumulated effects are assumed to be the same from trial to trial (e.g., fatigue).

Protocol   A detailed description of the sequence of events in a research session; used by an experimenter to ensure uniformity of treatment of research participants.

Pseudoscience   A field of inquiry that attempts to associate with true science, relies exclusively on selective anecdotal evidence, and is deliberately too vague to be adequately tested.

Psychophysics   One of experimental psychology's original areas of research; investigates the relationship between physical stimuli and the perception of those stimuli; studies thresholds.

Qualitative research   A category of research activity characterized by a narrative analysis of information collected in the study; can include case studies, observational research, interview research.

Quantitative research   A category of research in which results are presented as numbers, typically in the form of descriptive and inferential statistics.

Quasi-experiment   Occurs whenever causal conclusions about the effect of an independent variable cannot be drawn because there is incomplete control over the variables in the study; random assignment not possible in these studies

Quota sample   A non-probability sample in which the proportions of some subgroups in the sample are the same as those subgroup proportions in the population.

Random assignment   The most common procedure for creating equivalent groups in a between-subjects design; each individual volunteering for the study has an equal probability of being assigned to any one of the groups in the study.

Range   In a set of scores, the difference between the score with the largest value and the one with the smallest value.

Rate of response   The favored dependent variable of researchers working in the Skinnerian tradition; refers to how frequently a behavior occurs per unit of time.

Ratio scale   Measurement scale in which numbers refers to quantities and intervals are assumed to be of equal size; a score of zero denotes the absence of the phenomenon being measured.

Reactivity Occurs when participants' behavior is influenced by the knowledge that they are being observed and their behavior is being recorded in some fashion.

Regression analysis In correlational research, knowing the size of a correlation and a value for variable X, it is possible to predict a value for variable Y; this process occurs through a regression analysis.

Regression effect The tendency for regression to the mean to occur.

Regression line Summarizes the points of a scatterplot and provides the means for making predictions.

Regression to the mean If a score on a test is extremely high or low, a second score taken will be closer to the mean score; can be a threat to the internal validity of a study if a pretest score is extreme and the posttest score changes in the direction of the mean.

Reliability The extent to which measures of the same phenomenon are consistent and repeatable; measures high in reliability will contain a minimum of measurement error.

Repeated-measures design Another name for a within-subjects design; participants are tested in each of the experiment's conditions.

Replication The repetition of an experiment; exact replications are rare, occurring primarily when the results of some prior study are suspected to be erroneous.

Representative sample A sample with characteristics that match those same attributes as they exist in the population.

Research participant Any person who takes part in and contributes data to a research study in psychology.

Research team A group of researchers (professors and students) working together on the same research problem.

Response acquiescence A response set in which a participant has a tendency to respond positively to survey questions, all else being equal.

Restricting the range Occurs in a correlational study when only a limited range of scores for one or both of the variables is used; range restrictions tend to lower correlations.

Reverse counterbalancing Occurs in a within-subjects design when participants are tested more than once per condition; subjects experience one sequence, and then a second with the order reversed from the first (e.g., A–B–C–C–B–A).

Risk In the ethical decision making that goes into the planning of a study, refers to the chance that participating in research would have greater costs than benefits to the participant.

Running head Found on the title page of a lab report and at the top of odd-numbered pages of a printed research article; provides a brief (no more than 50 characters, including spaces and punctuation) summary of the title of the article.

Sample Some portion or subset of a population.

Sample frame List of individuals from whom the sample will be drawn; with cluster sampling, a list of groups from which a sample of groups will be selected.

Scatterplot A graph depicting the relationship shown by a correlation.

Science A way of knowing characterized by the attempt to apply objective, empirical methods when searching for the causes of natural events.

Self-selection problem In surveys, when the sample is composed of only those who voluntarily choose to respond, the result can be a biased sample.

Sequence effect Can occur in a within-subjects design when the experience of participating in one of the conditions of the study influences performance in subsequent conditions (see Progressive effect and Carryover effect).

Serendipity The process of making an accidental discovery; finding X when searching for Y.

Shaping Operant procedure for developing a new behavior that underlies the changing criterion design; behaviors are reinforced as they become progressively close to a final desired behavior.

Simple effects analysis Following an ANOVA, a follow-up test to a significant interaction, comparing individual cells.

Simple random sample A probability sample in which each member of the population has an equal chance of being selected as a member of the sample.

Single-factor design Any experimental design with a single independent variable.

Single-factor multilevel designs Any design with a single independent variable and more than two levels of the independent variable.

Situational variable Type of independent variable in which subjects encounter different environmental circumstances (e.g., large vs. small rooms in a crowding study).

Social desirability bias A type of response bias in survey research; occurs when people respond to a question by trying to put themselves in a favorable light.

Social validity   The extent to which an applied behavior analysis program has the potential to improve society, whether its value is perceived by the study's participants, and whether participants actually use the program.

Split-half reliability   A form of reliability in which one-half of the items (e.g., the even-numbered items) on a test are correlated with the remaining items.

Stakeholders   In program evaluation research, persons connected with a program who have a vested interest in it; includes clients, staff, and program directors.

Standard deviation   A measure of the amount of deviation of a set of scores from the mean score; the square root of the variance.

Statistical conclusion validity   Said to exist when the researcher uses statistical analysis properly and draws the appropriate conclusions from the analysis.

Statistical determinism   An assumption made by research psychologists that behavioral events can be predicted with a probability greater than chance.

Stem and leaf display   A method of displaying a data set that combines the features of a frequency distribution table and a histogram into one display.

Stratified sample   A probability sample that is random, with the restriction that important subgroups are proportionately represented in the sample.

Subject   Name traditionally used to refer to a human or animal research participant; humans volunteering for research are now referred to either as subjects or as research participants, while nonhuman animals are typically referred to as subjects.

Subject pool   Group of students asked to participate in research, typically as part of an introductory psychology course requirement; sometimes called a "participant pool."

Subject selection effect   A threat to the internal validity of a study; occurs when those participating in a study cannot be assigned randomly to groups; hence the groups are nonequivalent.

Subject variable   A type of independent variable that is selected rather than manipulated by the experimenter; refers to an already existing attribute of the individuals chosen for the study (e.g., gender).

Sugging   A marketing strategy in which an attempt to sell a product is made by disguising the sales pitch with what appears to be a legitimate survey; the term is short for **S**elling **U**nder the **G**uise of a survey.

Summative evaluation   Form of program evaluation completed at the close of a program that attempts to determine its effectiveness in solving the problem for which it was planned.

Survey   A descriptive method in which participants are asked a series of questions or respond to a series of statements about some topic.

Systematic variance   Variability that can be attributed to some identifiable source, either the systematic variation of the independent variable or the uncontrolled variation of a confound.

***t* test for independent samples**   An inferential statistical analysis used when comparing two samples of data in either an independent groups design or a nonequivalent groups design.

***t* test for related samples**   An inferential statistical analysis used when comparing two samples of data in either a matched groups design or a repeated-measures design.

Tables   In a research report, these are summaries of data or descriptions of research design that are laid out in a row and column arrangement.

Task variable   Type of independent variable in which participants are given different types of tasks to perform (e.g., mazes that differ in level of difficulty).

Testing   A threat to the internal validity of a study; occurs when the fact of taking a pretest influences posttest scores, perhaps by sensitizing participants to the purpose of a study.

Test–retest reliability   A form of reliability in which a test is administered on two separate occasions and the correlation between them is calculated.

Theory   A set of statements that summarizes and organizes existing information about some phenomenon, provides an explanation for the phenomenon, and serves as a basis for making predictions to be tested empirically.

Third variable problem   Refers to the problem of drawing causal conclusions in correlational research; third variables are any uncontrolled factors that could underline a correlation between variables X and Y.

Time sampling   A procedure in observational research in which behavior is sampled only during predefined times (e.g., every 10 minutes).

Time series design   See Interrupted times series design.

Trends   Predictable patterns of events that occur over a period of time; evaluated in time series studies.

Type I error   Rejecting the null hypothesis when it is true; finding a statistically significant effect when no true effect exists.

Type II error Failing to reject the null hypothesis when it is false; failing to find a statistically significant effect when the effect truly exists.

Unobtrusive measures Any measure of behavior that can be recorded without participants knowing that their behavior has been observed.

Validity In general, the extent to which a measure of X truly measures X and not Y (e.g., a valid measure of intelligence measures intelligence and not something else).

Variance A measure of the average squared deviation of a set of scores from the mean score; the standard deviation squared.

Waiting list control group Control group in which participants aren't yet receiving treatment but will, eventually; used to ensure that those in the experimental and control groups are similar (e.g., all seeking treatment for the same problem).

Withdrawal design Any small N design in which a treatment is in place for a time and is then removed to determine if the rate of behavior returns to baseline.

Within-subjects design Any experimental design in which the same participants serve in each of the different conditions of the study; also called a "repeated-measures design."

Written survey A survey method in which the researcher creates a written questionnaire that is filled out by participants.

Yoked control group Control group in which the treatment given a member of the control group is matched exactly with the treatment given a member of the experimental group.

References

ABRAMOVITZ, C. V., ABRAMOVITZ, S. I., ROBACK, H. B., & JACKSON, M. C. (1974). Differential effectiveness of directive and nondirective group therapies as a function of client internal-external control. *Journal of Consulting and Clinical Psychology, 14,* 849–853.

ADAIR, J. G. (1973). *The human subject: The social psychology of the psychological experiment.* Boston: Little, Brown.

ADAMS, J. S. (1965). Inequity in social exchange. In L. BERKOWITZ (Ed.), *Advances in experimental social psychology* (pp. 267–299). New York: Academic Press.

ADLER, T. (1992, September). Debate: Control groups—bad for cancer patients? *APA Monitor, 23,* 34.

ADLER, T. (1992, November). Trashing a laboratory is now a federal offense. *APA Monitor, 23,* 14.

ALLEN, M. W., & WILSON, M. (2005). Materialism and food security. *Appetite, 45,* 314–323.

ALLPORT, G. W. (1937). *Personality: A psychological interpretation.* New York: Henry Holt.

American Heritage dictionary of the English language (3rd ed.) (1992). Boston: Houghton-Mifflin.

American Psychological Association (1953). *Ethical standards of psychologists.* Washington, DC: Author.

American Psychological Association (1973). *Ethical principles in the conduct of research with human participants.* Washington, DC: Author.

American Psychological Association (1982). *Ethical principles in the conduct of research with human participants.* Washington, DC: Author.

American Psychological Association (1985). *Guidelines for ethical conduct in the care and use of animals.* Washington, DC: Author.

American Psychological Association (2001). *Publication manual of the American Psychological Association* (5th ed.). Washington, DC: Author.

American Psychological Association (2002). *Ethical principles of psychologists and code of conduct. American Psychologist, 57,* 1060–1073.

ANASTASI, A., & URBINA, S. (1997) *Psychological testing* (7th ed.). Englewood Cliffs, NJ: Prentice Hall.

ANDERSON, B., SILVER, B., & ABRAMSON, P. (1988). The effects of race of the interviewer on measures of electoral participation by blacks. *Public Opinion Quarterly, 52,* 53–83.

ANDERSON, C. A., & BUSHMAN, B. J. (2001). Effects of violent video games on aggressive behavior, aggressive cognition, aggressive affect, physiological arousal, and prosocial behavior: A meta-analytic review of the scientific literature. *Psychological Science, 12,* 353–359.

ANDERSON, C. A., LINDSAY, J. J., & BUSHMAN, B. J. (1999). Research in the psychological laboratory: Truth or triviality? *Current Directions in Psychological Science, 8,* 3–9.

ANDERSON, J. E. (1926). Proceedings of the thirty-fourth annual meeting of the American Psychological Association. *Psychological Bulletin, 23,* 113–174.

ANDERSON, K. J. (1990). Arousal and the inverted-U hypothesis: A critique of Neiss's "reconceptualizing arousal." *Psychological Bulletin, 107,* 96–100.

ANDERSON, T., & KANUKA, H. (2003). *E-research: Methods, strategies, and issues.* Boston: Houghton Mifflin.

Anonymous advertisement (1881, October). *Phrenological Journal, 73,* old series, 3–4.

ARONSON, E. (2007). *The social animal* (10th ed.). New York: Worth.

ARONSON, E. (1999). Dissonance, hypocrisy, and the self-concept. In E. HARMON-JONES & J. MILLS (Eds.), *Cognitive dissonance: Progress on a pivotal theory in social psychology* (pp. 103–126). Washington, DC: American Psychological Association.

ARONSON, E., & MILLS, J. (1959). The effects of severity of initiation on liking for a group. *Journal of Abnormal and Social Psychology, 59,* 177–181.

ARONSON, E., FRIED, C., & STONE, J. (1991). Overcoming denial and increasing the intention to use condoms through the induction of hypocrisy. *American Journal of Public Health, 81,* 1636–1638.

ARONSON, E., & METTEE, D. (1968). Dishonest behavior as a function of different levels of self-esteem. *Journal of Personality and Social Psychology, 9,* 121–127.

Asch, S. (1956). Studies of independence and conformity: A minority of one against a unanimous majority. *Psychological Monographs, 70* (Whole No. 416).

Atkinson, J. W., & Feather, N. T. (1966). *A theory of achievement motivation.* New York: Wiley.

Award for distinguished scientific contributions: Eliot Aronson (1999). *American Psychologist, 54*, 873–884.

Azar, B. (2002, February). Ethics at the cost of research? *Monitor on Psychology, 33*(2), 38–40.

Babkin, B. P. (1949). *Pavlov: A biography.* Chicago: University of Chicago Press.

Bahrick, H. P. (1984). Semantic memory content in permastore: Fifty years of memory for Spanish learned in school. *Journal of Experimental Psychology: General, 113*, 1–29.

Bakan, D. (1966). The influence of phrenology on American psychology. *Journal of the History of the Behavioral Sciences, 2*, 200–220.

Bandura, A. (1986). *Social foundations of thought and action: A social cognitive theory.* Englewood Cliffs, NJ: Prentice Hall.

Bandura, A., Ross, D., & Ross, S. A. (1963). Imitation of film-mediated aggressive models. *Journal of Abnormal and Social Psychology, 66*, 3–11.

Barber, T. X. (1976). *Pitfalls in human research.* New York: Pergamon Press.

Barlow, D. H., Nock, M. K., & Hersen, M. (2009). *Single case experimental designs: Strategies for studying behavior change.* Boston: Allyn & Bacon.

Baron, A. (1990). Experimental designs. *The Behavior Analyst, 13*, 167–171.

Baugh, F. G., & Benjamin, L. T., Jr. (2006). Walter Miles, Pop Warner, B. C. Graves, and the psychology of football. *Journal of the History of the Behavioral Sciences, 42*, 3–18.

Baumeister, R. F. (2008). Free will in scientific psychology. *Perspectives on Psychological Science, 3*, 14–19.

Baumrind, D. (1964). Some thoughts on ethics of research: After reading Milgram's "Behavioral study of obedience." *American Psychologist, 19*, 421–423.

Baumrind, D. (1985). Research using intentional deception: Ethical issues revisited. *American Psychologist, 40*, 165–174.

Beauchamp, T. L., & Childress, J. F. (1979). *Principles of biomedical ethics.* New York: Oxford University Press.

Behr, W. A. (1992). Ph.D. envy: A psychoanalytic case study. *Clinical Social Work Journal, 20*, 99–113.

Beisecker, T. (1988). Misusing survey research data: How not to justify demoting Christine Craft. *Forensic Reports, 1*, 15–33.

Benedict, J., & Stoloff, M. (1991). Animal laboratory facilities at "America's Best" undergraduate colleges. *American Psychologist, 46*, 535–536.

Benjamin, L. T. Jr., Cavell, T. A., & Shallenberger, W. R. (1984). Staying with initial answers on objective tests: Is it a myth? *Teaching of Psychology, 11*, 133–141.

Benjamin, L. T., Jr., Rogers, A. M., & Rosenbaum, A. (1991). Coco-Cola, caffeine, and mental deficiency: Harry Hollingworth and the Chattanooga trial of 1911. *Journal of the History of the Behavioral Sciences, 27*, 42–55.

Berry, T. D., & Geller, E. S. (1991). A single-subject approach to evaluating vehicle safely belt reminders: Back to basics. *Journal of Applied Behavior Analysis, 24*, 13–22.

Bertera, R. L. (1990). Planning and implementing health promotion in the workplace: A case study of the Du Pont Company experience. *Health Education Quarterly, 17*, 307–327.

Blagrove, M. (1996). Effects of length of sleep deprivation on interrogative suggestibility. *Journal of Experimental Psychology: Applied, 2*, 48–59.

Blumberg, M., & Pringle, C. D. (1983). How control groups can cause loss of control in action research: The case of Rushton coal mine. *Journal of Applied Behavioral Science, 19*, 409–425.

Boesch-Achermann, H., & Boesch, C. (1993). Tool use in wild chimpanzees: New light from dark forests. *Current Directions in Psychological Science, 2*, 18–21.

Boorstin, D. J. (1985). *The discoverers.* New York: Vintage Books.

Boring, E. G. (1950). *A history of experimental psychology* (2nd ed.). Englewood Cliffs, NJ: Prentice Hall.

Bouchard, T. J., & McGue, M. (1981). Familial studies of intelligence: A review. *Science, 212*, 1055–1059.

Brady, J. V. (1958, April). Ulcers in "executive" monkeys. *Scientific American, 199*, 95–100.

Brady, J. V., Porter, R. W., Conrad, D. G., & Mason, J. W. (1958). Avoidance behavior and the development of gastroduodenal ulcers. *Journal of the Experimental Analysis of Behavior, 1*, 69–72.

Bramel, D., & Friend, R. (1981). Hawthorne, the myth of the docile worker, and class bias in psychology. *American Psychologist, 36*, 867–878.

Brandon, G. & Lewis, A. (1999). Reducing household energy consumption: A qualitative and quantitative field study. *Journal of Environmental Psychology, 19*, 75–85.

Bransford, J. D., & Johnson, M. K. (1972). Contextual prerequisites for understanding: Some investigations of comprehension and recall. *Journal of Verbal Learning and Verbal Behavior, 11*, 717–726.

BRANTJES, M., & BOUMA, A. (1991). Qualitative analysis of the drawings of Alzheimer's patients. *The Clinical Neuropsychologist, 5*, 41–52.

BREHM, J. W. (1956). Postdecision changes in the desirability of alternatives. *Journal of Abnormal and Social Psychology, 52*, 384–389.

BRENNAN, J. F. (1991). *History and systems of psychology.* Englewood Cliffs, NJ: Prentice Hall.

BRIDGMAN, P. W. (1927). *The logic of modern physics.* New York: Macmillan.

BROADBENT, D. E. (1958). *Perception and communication.* New York: Pergamon Press.

BROWN, M. F. (1992). Does a cognitive map guide choices in the radial-arm maze? *Journal of Experimental Psychology: Animal Behavior Processes, 18*, 56–66.

BROWNE, J. (1995). *Charles Darwin: Voyaging.* Princeton, NJ: Princeton University Press.

BRYAN, J. H., & TEST, M. A. (1967). Models and helping: Naturalistic studies in aiding behavior. *Journal of Personality and Social Psychology, 6*, 400–407.

BURGER, J. (2009). Replicating Milgram: Would people still obey today? *American Psychologist, 64*, 1–11.

BURKS, B. S., JENSEN, D. W., & TERMAN, L. (1930). *Genetic studies of genius, Vol. 3. The promise of youth: Follow-up studies of a thousand gifted children.* Stanford, CA: Stanford University Press.

BURNHAM, J. C. (1972). Thorndike's puzzle boxes. *Journal of the History of the Behavioral Sciences, 8*, 159–167.

BURTON, A. M., WILSON, S., COWAN, M., & BRUCE, V. (1999). Face recognition in poor-quality video: Evidence from security surveillance. *Psychological Science, 10*, 243–248.

BYRNE, G. (1988, October 7). Breuning pleads guilty. *Science, 242*, 27–28.

CAMPBELL, D. T. (1969). Reforms as experiments. *American Psychologist, 24*, 409–429.

CAMPBELL, D. T., & ERLEBACHER, A. (1970). How regression artifacts in quasi-experimental evaluations can mistakenly make compensatory education look harmful. In J. HELLMUTH (Ed.), *Compensatory education: A national debate* (pp. 185–210). New York: Brunner-Mazel.

CAMPBELL, D. T., & ROSS, H. L. (1968). The Connecticut crackdown on speeding: Time series data in quasi-experimental analysis. *Law and Society Review, 3*, 33–53.

CAMPBELL, D. T., & STANLEY, J. C. (1963). *Experimental and quasi-experimental designs for research.* Chicago: Rand-McNally.

CARELLO, C., ANDERSON, K. L., & KUNKLER-PECK, A. J. (1998). Perception of object length by sound. *Psychological Science, 9*, 211–214.

CARNAP, R. (1966). *An introduction to the philosophy of science.* New York: Basic Books.

CARR, H. A., & WATSON, J. B. (1908). Orientation in the white rat. *Journal of Comparative Neurology and Psychology, 18*, 27–44.

CATTELL, J. M. (1895). Proceedings of the third annual meeting of the American Psychological Association. *Psychological Review, 2*, 149–172.

CECI, S. J., & BRUCK, M. (2009). Do IRBs pass the minimal harm test? *Perspectives on Psychological Science, 4*, 28–29.

CHERRY, E. C. (1953). Some experiments on the recognition of speech, with one and with two ears. *Journal of the Acoustic Society of America, 25*, 975–979.

CHRISTENSEN, L. (1988). Deception in psychological research: When is its use justified? *Personality and Social Psychology Bulletin, 14*, 664–675.

CHRISTENSON, C. V. (1971). *Kinsey: A biography.* Bloomington: Indiana University Press.

CICIRELLI, V. G. (1984). The misinterpretation of the Westinghouse study: A reply to Zigler and Berman. *American Psychologist, 39*, 915–916.

CICIRELLI, V. G. (1993). Head Start evaluation. *APS Observer, 6*(1), 32.

CICIRELLI, V. G., COOPER, W. H., & GRANGER, R. L. (1969). The impact of Head Start: An evaluation of the effects of Head Start on children's cognitive and affective development. *Westinghouse Learning Corporation,* OEO Contract B89-4536.

COHEN, J. (1988). *Statistical power analysis for the behavioral sciences* (2nd ed.). Hillsdale, NJ: Lawrence Erlbaum Associates.

COHEN, J. (1994). The earth is round ($p < .05$). *American Psychologist, 49*, 997–1003.

COHEN, S., TYRELL, D. A., & SMITH, A. P. (1993). Negative life events, perceived stress, negative affect, and susceptibility to the common cold. *Journal of Personality and Social Psychology, 64*, 131–140.

COILE, D. C., & MILLER, N. E. (1984). How radical animal activists try to mislead humane people. *American Psychologist, 39*, 700–701.

CONVERSE, J. M., & PRESSER, S. (1986). *Survey questions: Hand crafting the standardized questionnaire.* Newbury Park, CA: Sage.

COOK, T. D., & CAMPBELL, D. T. (1979). *Quasi-experimental design and analysis issues for field settings.* Chicago: Rand-McNally.

CORNELL, E. H., HETH, C. D., KNEUBUHLER, Y., & SEH-GAL, S. (1996). Serial position effects in children's route reversal errors: Implications for police search operations. *Applied Cognitive Psychology, 10*, 301–326.

COULTER, X. (1986). Academic value of research participation by undergraduates. *American Psychologist, 41*, 317.

CRONBACH, L. J. (1957). The two disciplines of scientific psychology. *American Psychologist, 12*, 671–684.

CRONBACH, L. J., HASTORF, A. H., HILGARD, E. R., & MACCOBY, E. E. (1990). Robert R. Sears (1908–1989). *American Psychologist, 45*, 663–664.

CROWLEY, K., CALLAHAN, M. A., TENENBAUM, H. R., & ALLEN, E. (2001). Parents explain more often to boys than to girls during shared scientific thinking. *Psychological Science, 12*, 258–261.

DALLENBACH, K. M. (1913). The measurement of attention. *American Journal of Psychology, 24*, 465–507.

DAMASIO, A. R. (1994). *Descartes' error: Emotion, reason, and the human brain.* New York: Avon Books.

DANZIGER, K. (1985). The origins of the psychological experiment as a social institution. *American Psychologist, 40*, 133–140.

DARLEY, J. M., & LATANÉ, B. (1968). Bystander intervention in emergencies: Diffusion of responsibility. *Journal of Personality and Social Psychology, 8*, 377–383.

DARWIN, C. (1872). *The expression of the emotions in man and animals.* London: Murray.

DARWIN, C. (1877). A biographical sketch of an infant. *Mind, 2*, 285–294.

DEANGELIS, T. (2008, September). Information gold mines. *GradPSYCH, 6*(3), 20–23.

DEKAY, M. L., & MCCLELLAND, G. H. (1996). Probability and utility components of endangered species preservation programs. *Journal of Experimental Psychology: Applied, 2*, 60–83.

DELUCA, R. V., & HOLBORN, S. W. (1992). Effects of a variable-ratio schedule with changing criteria on exercise in obese and nonobese boys. *Journal of Applied Behavior Analysis, 25*, 671–679.

DENNIS, W. (1941). Infant development under conditions of restricted practice and of minimum social stimulation. *Genetic Psychology Monographs, 23*, 143–189.

Department of Health and Human Services (1983). Federal regulations for the protection of human research subjects. In L. A. PEPLAU, D. O. SEARS, S. E. TAYLOR, & J. L. FREEDMAN (Eds.), *Readings in social psychology* (2nd ed.). Englewood Cliffs, NJ: Prentice Hall.

DERMER, M. L., & HOCH, T. A. (1999). Improving descriptions of single-subject experiments in research

texts written for undergraduates. *Psychological Record, 49*, 49–66.

DEWSBURY, D. A. (1990). Early interactions between animal psychologists and animal activists and the founding of the APA committee on precautions in animal experimentation. *American Psychologist, 45*, 315–327.

DIENER, E., & CRANDALL, R. (1978). *Ethics in social and behavioral research.* Chicago: The University of Chicago Press.

DIENER, E., FRASER, S. C., BEAMAN, A. L., & KELEM, R. T. (1976). Effects of deindividuation variables on stealing among Halloween trick-or-treaters. *Journal of Personality and Social Psychology, 33*, 178–183.

DIENER, E., MATTHEWS, R., & SMITH, R. (1972). Leakage of experimental information to potential future subjects by debriefing subjects. *Journal of Experimental Research in Personality, 6*, 264–267.

DIENER, E., WOLSIC, B., & FUJITA, F. (1995). Physical attractiveness and subjective well-being. *Journal of Personality and Social Psychology, 69*, 120–129.

DILLMAN, D. A., SMYTH, J. D., & CHRISTIAN, L. M. (2009). *Internet, mail and mixed-mode surveys: The tailored design method* (3rd ed.). New York: Wiley.

DOMJAN, M., & PURDY, J. E. (1995). Animal research in psychology: More than meets the eye of the general psychology student. *American Psychologist, 50*, 496–503.

DONNERSTEIN, E. (1980). Aggressive erotica and violence against women. *Journal of Personality and Social Psychology, 39*, 269–277.

DRESSLER, F. B. (1893). On the pressure sense of the drum of the ear and "facial-vision." *American Journal of Psychology, 5*, 344–350.

DROR, I. E., KOSSLYN, S. M., & WAAG, W. L. (1993). Visual-spatial abilities of pilots. *Journal of Applied Psychology, 78*, 763–773.

DUNLAP, R. E., VAN LIERE, K. D., MERTIG, A. G., & JONES, R. E. (2000). Measuring endorsement of the New Ecological Paradigm: A revised NEP scale. *Journal of Social Issues, 56*, 425–442.

DUNN, T. M., SCHWARTZ, M., HATFIELD, R. W., & WIEGELE, M. (1996). Measuring effectiveness of Eye Movement Desensitization and Reprocessing (EMDR) in non-clinical anxiety: A multi-subject, yoked control design. *Journal of Behavior Therapy and Experimental Psychiatry, 27*, 231–239.

DUTTON, D. G., & ARON, A. P. (1974). Some evidence for heightened sexual attraction under conditions of high anxiety. *Journal of Personality and Social Psychology, 30*, 510–517.

EBBINGHAUS, H. (1964). *Memory: A contribution to experimental psychology* (H. A. RUGER & C. A. BUSSENIUS,

Trans.). New York: Dover. (Original work published 1885)

EKMAN, P. (1985). *Telling lies: Clues to deceit in the marketplace, politics, and marriage*. New York: W.W. Norton.

ELKINS, I. J., CROMWELL, R. L., & ASARNOW, R. F. (1992). Span of apprehension in schizophrenic patients as a function of distractor masking and laterality. *Journal of Abnormal Psychology, 101*, 53–60.

ELMES, D. G., KANTOWITZ, B. H., & ROEDIGER, H. L., III. (2006). *Research methods in psychology* (8th ed.). Belmont, CA: Wadsworth.

ERFURT, J. C., FOOTE, A., & HEIRICH, M. A. (1992). The cost-effectiveness of worksite wellness programs for hypertension control, weight loss, smoking cessation, and exercise. *Personnel Psychology, 45*, 5–27.

ERON, L. D., HUESMAN, L. R., LEFKOWITZ, M. M., & WALDER, L. O. (1972). Does television violence cause aggression? *American Psychologist, 27*, 253–263.

EYSENCK, H. J. (1952). The effects of psychotherapy: An evaluation. *Journal of Consulting Psychology, 16*, 319–324.

FADEN, R. R., & BEAUCHAMP, T. L. (1986). *A history and theory of informed consent*. New York: Oxford University Press.

FANCHER, R. E. (1990). *Pioneers of psychology* (2nd ed.). New York: W.W. Norton.

FAURIE, C., & RAYMOND, M. (2004). Handedness, homicide and negative frequency–dependent selection. *Proceedings of the Royal Society*. Retrieved 03/22/06 from www.isem.univ-montp2.fr/GE/Adaptation/Bibliographie/fauriePRSLB2004.pdf

FEINBERG, J. (1974). The rights of animals and unborn generations. In W. T. BLACKSTONE (Ed.), *Philosophy and environmental crisis* (pp. 43–68). Athens: University of Georgia Press.

FEINGOLD, A. (1992). Good-looking people are not what we think. *Psychological Bulletin, 111*, 304–341.

FERNALD, D. (1984). *The Hans legacy*. Hillsdale, NJ: Erlbaum.

FERSTER, C., B., & SKINNER, B. F. (1957). *Schedules of reinforcement*. New York: Appleton-Century-Crofts.

FESTINGER, L. (1957). *The theory of cognitive dissonance*. Stanford, CA: Stanford University Press.

FESTINGER, L. (1999). Reflections on cognitive dissonance: Thirty years later. In E. HARMON-JONES & J. MILLS (Eds.), *Cognitive dissonance: Progress on a pivotal theory in social psychology* (pp. 381–385). Washington, DC: American Psychological Association.

FESTINGER, L., RIECKEN, H. W., & SCHACHTER, S. (1956). *When prophecy fails*. Minneapolis: University of Minnesota Press.

FINK, A. (1995). *How to ask survey questions*. Thousand Oaks, CA: Sage.

FISCHMAN, M. W. (2000). Informed consent. In B. D. SALES & S. FOLKMAN (Eds.), *Ethics in research with human participants* (pp. 35–48). Washington, DC: American Psychological Association.

FISHER, C. B., & FYRBERG, D. (1994). Participant partners: College students weigh the costs and benefits of deceptive research. *American Psychologist, 49*, 417–427.

FISHER, R. A. (1925). *Statistical methods for research workers*. London: Oliver & Boyd.

FISHER, R. A. (1951). *The design of experiments* (6th ed.). New York: Hafner. (Original work published 1935)

FISHER, R. P., GEISELMAN, R. E., & AMADOR, M. (1989). Field test of the cognitive interview: Enhancing the recollection of actual victims and witnesses of crime. *Journal of Applied Psychology, 74*, 722–727.

FLOOD, W. A., WILDER, D. A., FLOOD, A. L., & MASUDA, A. (2002). Peer-mediated reinforcement plus prompting as treatment for off-task behavior in children with attention-deficit hyperactivity disorder. *Journal of Applied Behavior Analysis, 35*, 199–204.

FLOURENS, P. (1978). Phrenology examined (C. D. Meigs, Trans.). In D. N. ROBINSON (Ed.), *Significant contributions to the history of psychology. Series E. Volume II.* Washington, DC: University Publications of America. (Original work published 1846)

FOLKMAN, S. (2000). Privacy and confidentiality. In B. D. SALES & S. FOLKMAN (Eds.), *Ethics in research with human participants* (pp. 49–57). Washington, DC: American Psychological Association.

FORREST, D. W. (1974). *Francis Galton: The life and work of a Victorian genius*. New York: Taplinger.

For scientists, a beer test shows results as a litmus test (2008). www.nytimes.com/2008/03/18/science

FOWLER, F. J., Jr. (1993). *Survey research methods* (2nd ed.). Newbury Park, CA: Sage.

FOWLER, F. J., Jr. (1998). Design and evaluation of survey questions. In L. BICKMAN & D. J. ROG (Eds.), *Handbook of applied social research methods* (pp. 343–374). Thousand Oaks, CA: Sage.

FOXX, R. M., & RUBINOFF, A. (1979). Behavioral treatment of caffeinism: Reducing excessive coffee drinking. *Journal of Applied Behavior Analysis, 12*, 335–344.

FRAYSSE, J. C., & DESPRELS-FRAYSEE, A. (1990). The influence of experimenter attitude on the performance of children of different cognitive ability levels. *Journal of Genetic Psychology, 151*, 169–179.

FRIEDMAN, H, S., TUCKER, J. S., SCHWARTZ, J. E., TOMLINSON-KEASEY, C., MARTIN, L. R., WINGARD, D. L., & CRIQUI, M. H. (1995). Psychological and behavioral predictors of longevity: The aging and death of the "Termites." *American Psychologist, 50,* 69–78.

FULERO, S. M., & KIRKLAND, J. (1992, August). *A survey of student opinions on animal research.* Poster presented at the annual meeting of the American Psychological Association, Washington, DC.

GALLUP, G. G., & BECKSTEAD, J. W. (1988). Attitudes toward animal research. *American Psychologist, 43,* 74–76.

GALLUP, G. G., & EDDY, T. J. (1990). Animal facilities survey. *American Psychologist, 45,* 400–401.

GALLUP, G. G., & SUAREZ, S. D. (1985a). Alternatives to the use of animals in psychological research. *American Psychologist, 40,* 1104–1111.

GALLUP, G. G., & SUAREZ, S. D. (1985b). Animal research versus the care and maintenance of pets: The names have been changed but the results remain the same. *American Psychologist, 40,* 968.

GALTON, F. (1869). *Hereditary genius.* London: Macmillan.

GALTON, F. (1872). Statistical inquiries into the efficacy of prayer. *Fortnightly Review, 12,* 125–135.

GALTON, F. (1874). *English men of science: Their nature and nurture.* London: Macmillan.

GALTON, F. (1948). An inquiry into human faculty and its development. In W. DENNIS (Ed.), *Readings in the history of psychology* (pp. 277–289). New York: Appleton-Century-Crofts. (Original work published 1883)

GALVIN, S. L., & HERZOG, H. A. (1992). The ethical judgment of animal research. *Ethics & Behavior, 2,* 263–286.

GARDNER, G. T. (1978). Effects of federal human subjects regulations on data obtained in environmental stressor research. *Journal of Personality and Social Psychology, 36,* 628–634.

GELLER, D. M. (1982). Alternatives to deception: Why, what, and how? In J. E. SIEBER (Ed.), *The ethics of social research: Surveys and experiments* (pp. 40–55). New York: Springer-Verlag.

GELLER, E. S. (1991). Editor's introduction: Where's the validity in social validity? *Journal of Applied Behavior Analysis,* Monograph *#5,* 1–6.

GERAERTS, E., BERNSTEIN, D. M., MERCKELBACH, H., LINDERS, C., RAYMAEKERS, L., & LOFTUS, E. F. (2008). Lasting false beliefs and their behavioral consequences. *Psychological Science, 19,* 749–753.

GIBSON, E. J. (1980). Eleanor J. Gibson. In G. LINDSEY (Ed.), *A history of psychology in autobiography. Volume 7* (pp. 239–271). San Francisco: W. H. Freeman.

GIBSON, E. J., & WALK, R. D. (1960). The "visual cliff." *Scientific American, 202,* 64–71.

GILCHRIST, V. J., & WILLIAMS, R. L. (1999). Key informant interviews. In B. F. CRABTREE & W. L. MILLER (Eds.), *Doing qualitative research* (2nd ed.) (pp. 71–88). Thousand Oaks, CA: Sage Publications.

GILLESPIE, R. (1988). The Hawthorne experiments and the politics of experimentation. In J. G. MORAWSKI (Ed.), *The rise of experimentation in American psychology* (pp. 114–137). New Haven, CT: Yale University Press.

GILLIGAN, C. (1982). *In a different voice: Psychological theory and women's development.* Cambridge, MA: Harvard University Press.

GLADUE, B. A., & DELANEY, H. J. (1990). Gender differences in perception of attractiveness of men and women in bars. *Personality and Social Psychology Bulletin, 16,* 378–391.

GLEITMAN, H., FRIDLUND, A. J., & RIESBERG, D. (1999). *Psychology* (5th ed.). New York: W.W. Norton.

GODDEN, D. R., & BADDELEY, A. D. (1975). Context-dependent memory in two natural environments: On land and under water. *British Journal of Psychology, 66,* 325–331.

GOODALL, J. (1978). Chimp killings: Is it the man in them? *Science News, 113,* 276.

GOODALL, J. (1990). *Through a window: My thirty years with the chimpanzees of Gombe.* Boston: Houghton Mifflin.

GOODWIN, C. J. (2008). *A history of modern psychology* (3rd ed.). New York: Wiley.

GOODWIN, K. A., MEISSNER, C. A., & ERICSSON, A. (2001). Toward a model of false recall: Experimental manipulation of encoding context and the collection of verbal reports. *Memory & Cognition, 29,* 806–819.

GRANT, H. M., BREDAHL, L. C., CLAY, J., FERRIE, J., GROVES, J. E., McDORMAN, T. A., & DARK, V. J. (1998). Context-dependent memory for meaningful material: Information for students. *Applied Cognitive Psychology, 12,* 617–623.

GREEN, B. F. (1992). Exposé or smear? The Burt affair. *Psychological Science, 3,* 328–331.

GREENBERG, M. S. (1967). Role playing: An alternative to deception. *Journal of Personality and Social Psychology, 7,* 152–157.

GREENWALD, A. G., SPANGENBERG, E. R., PRATKANIS, A. R., & ESKENAZI, J. (1991). Double-blind tests of subliminal self-help audiotapes. *Psychological Science, 2,* 119–122.

GROSE, P. (1994). *Gentleman spy: The life of Allen Dulles.* Boston: Houghton-Mifflin.

GUNTER, B., BERRY, C., & CLIFFORD, B. R. (1981). Proactive interference effects with television news items:

Further evidence. *Journal of Experimental Psychology: Human Learning and Memory, 7,* 480–487.

Gwaltney-Gibbs, P. A. (1986). The institutionalization of premarital cohabitation: Estimates from marriage license applications, 1970 and 1980. *Journal of Marriage and the Family, 48,* 423–434.

Hall, G. S. (1893). *The contents of children's minds on entering school.* New York: Kellogg.

Harmon-Jones, E., & Mills, J. (Eds.). (1999). *Cognitive dissonance: Progress on a pivotal theory in social psychology.* Washington, DC: American Psychological Association.

Harris, B. (1979). Whatever happened to Little Albert? *American Psychologist, 34,* 151–160.

Hartman, D. P., & Hall, R. V. (1976). The changing criterion design. *Journal of Applied Behavior Analysis, 9,* 527–532.

Henle, M., & Hubbell, M. B. (1938). "Egocentricity" in adult conversation. *Journal of Social Psychology, 9,* 227–234.

Herzog, H. (1993). Human morality and animal research. *The American Scholar, 62,* 337–349.

Hilgard, E. R. (Ed.) (1978). *American psychology in historical perspective.* Washington, DC: American Psychological Association.

Hilgard, E. R. (1987). *Psychology in America: A historical survey.* San Diego, CA: Harcourt Brace Jovanovich.

Hilgartner, S. (1990). Research fraud, misconduct, and the IRB. *IRB: A Review of Human Subjects Research, 12,* 1–4.

Hite, S. (1987). *Women and love.* New York: Knopf.

Hobbs, N. (1948). The development of a code of ethics for psychology. *American Psychologist, 3,* 80–84.

Hogan, T. P., & Evalenko, K. (2006). The elusive definition of outliers in introductory statistics textbooks for behavioral sciences. *Teaching of Psychology, 33,* 252–256.

Holahan, C. K., Sears, R. R., & Cronbach, L. J. (1995). *The gifted group in later maturity.* Palo Alto, CA: Stanford University Press.

Holden, C. (1987, March 27). NIMH finds a case of "serious misconduct." *Science, 235,* 1566–1577.

Hollingshead, A. B. (1949). *Elmstown's youth.* New York: Wiley.

Hollingworth, H. L. (1990). *Leta Stetter Hollingworth: A biography.* Bolton: Anker Publishing Co. (Original work published 1943)

Hollingworth, H. L., & Poffenberger, A. T. (1917). *Applied psychology.* New York: D. Appleton.

Holmes, D. S. (1976a). Debriefing after psychological experiments. I. Effectiveness of postdeception dehoaxing. *American Psychologist, 31,* 858–867.

Holmes, D. S. (1976b). Debriefing after psychological experiments. II. Effectiveness of postexperimental desensitizing. *American Psychologist, 31,* 868–875.

Holmes, D. S., McGilley, B. M., & Houston, B. K. (1984). Task-related arousal of Type A and Type B persons: Level of challenge and response specificity. *Journal of Personality and Social Psychology, 46,* 1322–1327.

Horn, J. L. (1990, October). Psychology can help kids get a Head Start. *APA Monitor, 22,* 3.

Hothersall, D. (1990). *History of psychology* (2nd ed.). New York: McGraw-Hill.

Hubel, D. H. (1988). *Eye, brain, and vision.* New York: Scientific American Library.

Hubel, D. H., & Wiesel, T. N. (1959). Receptive fields of single neurons in the cat's striate cortex. *Journal of Physiology, 148,* 574–591.

Huesmann, R., & Dubow, E. (2008). Leonard D. Eron (1920–2007). *American Psychologist, 63,* 131–132.

Huff, D. (1954). *How to lie with statistics.* New York: W.W. Norton.

Hull, D. B. (1996). Animal use in undergraduate psychology programs. *Teaching of Psychology, 23,* 171–174.

Hunt, E., & Love, T. (1972). How good can memory be? In A. W. Melton & E. Martin (Eds.), *Coding processes in human memory* (pp. 237–260). Washington, DC: V. H. Winston.

Hunt, R. R., & Ellis, H. C. (2004). *Fundamentals of cognitive psychology* (4th ed.). New York: McGraw-Hill.

Inzlicht, M., & Ben-Zeev, T. (2000). A threatening intellectual environment: Why females are susceptible to experiencing problem-solving deficits in the presence of males. *Psychological Science, 11,* 365–371.

Jaffe, E. (2005). How random is that? *APS Observer, 18*(9), 20–30.

James, W. (1950). *Principles of psychology.* Vol. *1.* New York: Dover. (Original work published 1890)

Jenkins, J. G., & Dallenbach, K. M. (1924). Minor studies from the psychological laboratory of Cornell University: Oblivescence during sleep and waking. *American Journal of Psychology, 35,* 605–612.

Ji, L., Peng, K., & Nisbett, R. E. (2000). Culture, control, and perception of relationships in the environment. *Journal of Personality and Social Psychology, 78,* 943–955.

Johns, M., Schmader, T., & Martens, A. (2005). Knowing is half the battle: Teaching stereotype threat as a means of improving women's math performance. *Psychological Science, 16,* 175–178.

Jonçich, G. (1968). *The sane positivist: A biography of Edward L. Thorndike.* Middletown, CT: Wesleyan University Press.

JONES, J. H. (1981). *Bad blood: The Tuskegee syphilis experiment*. New York: Free Press.

JONES, M. C. (1924). A laboratory study of fear: The case of Peter. *Pedagogical Seminary, 31*, 308–315.

JOYNSON, R. B. (1989). *The Burt affair*. London: Routledge.

JUNGINGER, J., & HEAD, S. (1991). Time series analyses of obsessional behavior and mood during self-imposed delay and responsive prevention. *Behavior Research and Therapy, 29*, 521–530.

KASSER, T., & SHELDON, K. M. (2000). Of wealth and death: Materialism, mortality salience, and consumptive behavior. *Psychological Science, 11*, 348–351.

KAUFMAN, A. S., & KAUFMAN, N. L. (1983). *KABC: Kaufman Assessment Battery for Children. Interpretive Manual.* Circle Pines, MN: American Guidance Service.

KAY, S., HARCHIK, A. E., & LUISELLI, J. K. (2006). Elimination of drooling by an adolescent student with autism attending public high school. *Journal of Positive Behavior Interventions, 8*, 24–28.

KAZDIN, A. E. (1978). *History of behavior modification: Experimental foundations of contemporary research*. Baltimore: University Park Press.

KEELY, J., FEOLA, T., & LATTAL, K. A. (2007). Contingency tracking during unsignalled delayed reinforcement. *JEAB, 88*, 229–247.

KEITH-SPIEGEL, P., & KOOCHER, G. P. (2005). The IRB paradox: Could the protectors also encourage deceit? *Ethics and Behavior, 15*, 339–349.

KELTNER, D., ELLSWORTH, P. C., & EDWARDS, K. (1993). Beyond simple pessimism: Effects of sadness and anger on social perception. *Journal of Personality and Social Psychology, 64*, 740–752.

KENDALL, M. G. (1970). Ronald Aylmer Fisher, 1890–1962. In E. S. PEARSON & M. G. KENDALL (Eds.), *Studies in the history of statistics and probability* (pp. 439–447). London: Charles Griffin.

KENT, D. (1994). Interview with APS president-elect Richard F. Thompson. *APS Observer, 7*, 4, 10.

KERSTING, K. (2005, April). "Trust your first instincts": Fallacious folklore? *Monitor on Psychology, 36*(4), 24.

KIDD, V. (1971). A study of the images produced through the use of the male pronoun as the generic. *Moments in Contemporary Rhetoric and Communication, 1*, 25–30.

KIM, K., & SPELKE, E. S. (1992). Infants' sensitivity to effects of gravity on visible object motion. *Journal of Experimental Psychology: Human Perception and Performance, 18*, 385–393.

KIMMEL, A. J. (2007). *Ethical issues in behavioral research: A survey*. Malden, MA: Blackwell.

KINSEY, A. C., POMEROY, W. B., & MARTIN, C. E. (1948). *Sexual behavior in the human male*. Philadelphia: W. B. Saunders.

KINSEY, A. C., POMEROY, W. B., MARTIN, C. E., & GEBHARD, P. H. (1953). *Sexual behavior in the human female*. Philadelphia: W. B. Saunders.

KIRK, R. E. (1968). *Experimental design: Procedures for the behavioral sciences*. Belmont, CA: Brooks/Cole.

KITAYAMA, S., MARKUS, H. R., MATSUMOTO, H., & NORASAKKUNKIT, V. (1997). Individual and collective processes in the construction of the self: Self-enhancement in the United States and self-criticism in Japan. *Journal of Personality and Social Psychology, 72*, 1245–1267.

KLINE, R. B. (2004). *Beyond significance testing: Reforming data analysis methods in behavioral research*. Washington, DC: American Psychological Association.

KOHLBERG, L. (1964). Development of moral character and moral behavior. In L. W. HOFFMAN & M. L. HOFFMAN (Eds.), *Review of child development research* (Vol. 1). New York: Sage.

KOLATA, G. B. (1986). What does it mean to be random? *Science, 231*, 1068–1070.

KOOCHER, G. P., & KEITH-SPIEGEL, P. (1998). *Ethics in psychology: Professional standards and cases* (2nd ed.). New York: Oxford University Press.

KORN, J. H. (1988). Students' roles, rights, and responsibilities as research participants. *Teaching of Psychology, 15*, 74–78.

KORN, J. H. (1997). *Illusions of reality: A history of deception in social psychology*. Albany: SUNY Press.

KORN, J. H., DAVIS, R., & DAVIS, S. F. (1991). Historians' and chairpersons' judgments of eminence among psychologists. *American Psychologist, 46*, 789–792.

KRAMER, P. D. (2006). *Freud: Inventor of the modern mind*. New York: Harper Collins.

KRAUT, R., OLSON, J., BANAJI, M., BRUCKMAN, A., COHEN, J., & COUPER, M. (2004). Psychological research online. *American Psychologist, 59*, 105–117.

KRUGER, J., WIRTZ, D., & MILLER, D. T. (2005). Counterfactual thinking and the first instinct fallacy. *Journal of Personality and Social Psychology, 88*, 725–735.

KRUPAT, E. (1975). Conversation with John Darley. In E. KRUPAT (Ed.), *Psychology is social: Readings and conversations in social psychology*. Glenview, IL: Scott, Foresman.

KRUTA, V. (1972). Marie-Jean-Pierre Flourens. In C. C. GILLESPIE (Ed), *Dictionary of scientific biography (Vol. V)*. New York: Scribner's.

KUHN, T. S. (1970). The function of dogma in scientific research. In B. A. BRODY (Ed.), *Readings in the philosophy of science* (pp. 356–373). Englewood Cliffs, NJ: Prentice Hall.

KUSHNER, M. (1970). Faradic aversive controls in clinical practice. In C. NEURINGER & J. L. MICHAEL (Eds.), *Behavior modification in clinical practice.* New York: Appleton-Century-Crofts.

LANDRUM, R. E., & CHASTAIN, G. (1999). Subject pool policies in undergraduate-only departments: Results from a nationwide survey. In G. CHASTAIN & E. R. LANDRUM (Eds.), *Protecting human subjects: Department subject pools and Institutional Review Boards* (pp. 25–42). Washington, DC: American Psychological Association.

LANDRUM, R. E., & NELSON, L. R. (2002). The undergraduate research assistantship: An analysis of the benefits. *Teaching of Psychology, 29,* 15–19.

LANGER, E. J., & RODIN, J. (1976). The effects of choice and enhanced personal responsibility for the aged: A field experiment in an institutional setting. *Journal of Personality and Social Psychology, 34,* 191–198.

LAU, R. R., & RUSSELL, D. (1980). Attributions in the sports pages. *Journal of Personality and Social Psychology, 39,* 29–38.

LAVRAKAS, P. J. (1998). Methods for sampling and interviewing in telephone surveys. In L. BICKMAN & D. J. ROG (Eds.), *Handbook of applied social research methods* (pp. 429–472). Thousand Oaks, CA: Sage.

LAWTON, C. A. (1994). Gender differences in wayfinding strategies: Relationship to spatial ability and spatial anxiety. *Sex Roles, 30,* 765–779.

LEAK, G. K. (1981). Student perception of coercion and value from participation in psychological research. *Teaching of Psychology, 8,* 147–149.

LEE, D. N., & ARONSON, E. (1974). Visual proprioceptive control of standing in human infants. *Perception and Psychophysics, 15,* 529–532.

LeFRANCOIS, J. R., & METZGER, B. (1993). Low-response-rate conditioning history and fixed-interval responding in rats. *Journal of the Experimental Analysis of Behavior, 59,* 543–549.

LEITENBERG, H., AGRAS, W. S., THOMSON, L. E., & WRIGHT, D. E. (1968). Feedback in behavior modification: An experimental analysis. *JABA, 1,* 131–137.

LEPPER, M. R., ROSS, L., & LAU, R. R. (1986). Persistence of inaccurate beliefs about the self: Perseverence effects in the classroom. *Journal of Personality and Social Psychology, 50,* 482–491.

LIBERMAN, R. P., DAVIS, J., MOON, W., & MOORE, J. (1973). Research design for analyzing drug–environment–behavior interactions. *Journal of Nervous and Mental Disease, 156,* 432–439.

LICHT, M. M. (1995). Multiple regression and correlation. In L. G. GRIMM & P. R. YARNOLD (Eds.), *Reading and understanding multivariate statistics* (pp. 19–64). Washington, DC: American Psychological Association.

LOFTUS, E. F. (1979). *Eyewitness testimony.* Cambridge, MA: Harvard University Press.

LOFTUS, E. F. (1986). Ten years in the life of an expert witness. *Law and Human Behavior, 10,* 241–263.

LOFTUS, E. F., & HOFFMAN, H. G. (1989). Misinformation and memory: The creation of new memories. *Journal of Experimental Psychology: General, 118,* 100–104.

LOFTUS, E. F., & KETCHAM, K. (1991). *Witness for the defense: The accused, the eyewitness, and the expert who puts memory on trial.* New York: St. Martin's Press.

LÓPEZ, F., & MENEZ, M. (2005). Effects of reinforcement history on response rate and response pattern in periodic reinforcement. *JEAB, 83,* 221–241.

LORENZ, K. (1966). *On aggression.* New York: Harcourt Brace Jovanovich.

LOTUFO, P. A., CHAE, C. U., AJANI, U. A., HENNEKENS, C. H., & MANSON, J. E. (1999). Male pattern baldness and coronary heart disease: The physician's health study. *Archives of Internal Medicine, 160,* 165–171.

LUDWIG, T. D., & GELLER, E. S. (1997). Assigned versus participative goal setting and response generalization: Managing injury control among professional pizza deliverers. *Journal of Applied Psychology, 82,* 253–261.

LURIA, A. R. (1968). *The mind of a mnemonist.* New York: Basic Books.

MacLEOD, C. M. (1992). The Stroop task: The "gold standard" of attentional measures. *Journal of Experimental Psychology: General, 121,* 12–14.

MANGIONE, T. W. (1998). Mail surveys. In L. BICKMAN & D. J. ROG (Eds.), *Handbook of applied social research methods* (pp. 399–427). Thousand Oaks, CA: Sage.

MANIS, M. (1971). *An introduction to cognitive psychology.* Belmont, CA: Brooks/Cole.

MARCEL, A. J. (1983). Conscious and unconscious perception: Experiments on visual masking and word recognition. *Cognitive Psychology, 15,* 197–237.

MAREAN, G. C., WERNER, L. A., & KUHL, P. K. (1992). Vowel categorization by very young infants. *Developmental Psychology, 28,* 396–405.

MAYER, F. S., & FRANTZ, C. M. (2004). The connectedness to nature scale: A measure of individuals' feeling in community with nature. *Journal of Environmental Psychology, 24,* 503–515.

McCLELLAND, D. C. (1961). *The achieving society.* Princeton, NJ: Van Nostrand.

McClelland, D. C., Atkinson, J. W., Clarke, R. A., & Lowell, E. L. (1953). *The achievement motive*. New York: Appleton-Century-Crofts.

McCord, D. M. (1991). Ethics-sensitive management of the university human subject pool. *American Psychologist, 46*, 151.

McDonald, S., & Flanagan, S. (2004). Social perception deficits after traumatic brain injury: Interaction between emotion recognition, mentalizing ability, and social communication. *Neuropsychology, 18*, 572–579.

McGraw, K. O., Tew, M. D., & Williams, J. E. (2000). The integrity of Web-based experiments: Can you trust the data? *Psychological Science, 11*, 502–506.

McGraw, M. (1941). Neural maturation as exemplified in the changing reactions of the infant to pin prick. *Child Development, 12*, 31–42.

Merikle, P. M., & Skanes, H. E. (1992). Subliminal self-help audiotapes: A search for placebo effects. *Journal of Applied Psychology, 77*, 772–776.

Middlemist, R. D., Knowles, E. W., & Matter, C. F. (1976). Personal space invasions in the lavatory: Suggestive evidence for arousal. *Journal of Personality and Social Psychology, 33*, 541–546.

Miles, W. R. (1928). Studies in physical exertion I: A multiple chronograph for measuring groups of men. *American Physical Education Review, 33*, 379–387.

Miles, W. R. (1930). On the history of research with rats and mazes: A collection of notes. *Journal of General Psychology, 3*, 324–337.

Miles, W. R. (1931). Studies in physical exertion II: Individual and group reaction time in football charging. *Research Quarterly, 2*(3), 5–13.

Miles, W. R. (1933). Age and human ability. *Psychological Review, 40*, 99–123.

Milgram, S. (1963). Behavioral study of obedience. *Journal of Abnormal and Social Psychology, 67*, 371–378.

Milgram, S. (1974). *Obedience to authority: An experimental view*. New York: Harper & Row.

Mill, J. S. (1843). *A system of logic, ratiocinative and inductive, being a connected view of the principles of evidence, and the methods of scientific investigation*. London: Longmans, Green.

Mill, J. S. (1869). *The subjection of women*. London: Longmans, Green, Reader, Dyer.

Miller, A. G. (1972). Role playing: An alternative to deception? *American Psychologist, 27*, 623–636.

Miller, N. (1985). The value of behavioral research on animals. *American Psychologist, 40*, 423–440.

Miller, W. R., & DiPilato, M. (1983). Treatment of nightmares via relaxation and desensitization: A controlled evaluation. *Journal of Consulting and Clinical Psychology, 51*, 870–877.

Minton, H. L. (1987). *Lewis M. Terman and mental testing: In search of the democratic ideal*. In M. M. Sokal (Ed.), *Psychological testing and American society, 1890–1930* (pp. 95–112). New Brunswick, NJ: Rutgers University Press.

Minton, H. L. (1988). Charting life history: Lewis M. Terman's study of the gifted. In J. G. Morawski (Ed.), *The rise of experimentation in American psychology* (pp. 138–162). New Haven, CT: Yale University Press.

Mook, D. G. (1983). In defense of external invalidity. *American Psychologist, 38*, 379–387.

Morell, V. (1995). *Ancestral passions: The Leakey family and the quest for humankind's beginnings*. New York: Simon & Schuster.

Morgan, C. L. (1903). *Introduction to comparative psychology*. London: Walter Scott.

Morgan, F. W. (1990). Judicial standards for survey research: An update and guidelines. *Journal of Marketing, 54*, 59–70.

Moses, S. (1991, July). Animal research issues affect students. *APA Monitor, 22*, 47–48.

Mowrer, O. H., & Mowrer, W. M. (1938). Enuresis—a method for its study and treatment. *American Journal of Orthopsychiatry, 8*, 436–459.

Murphy, G. L. (1999). A case study of a departmental subject pool and review board. In G. Chastain & R. E. Landrum (Eds.), *Protecting human subjects: Departmental subject pools and institutional review boards* (pp. 131–156). Washington, DC: American Psychological Association.

Murray, B. (2002, February). Research fraud needn't happen at all. *Monitor on Psychology, 33*(2). Retrieved August 7, 2008 from http://apa.org/monitor/feb02/fraud.html

Murray, H. A. (1943). *Thematic apperception test*. Cambridge, MA: Harvard University Press.

Myers, D. G. (1990). *Social psychology* (3rd ed). New York: McGraw-Hill.

Myers, D. G. (1992). *Psychology* (3rd ed.). New York: Worth.

Neale, J. M., & Liebert, R. M. (1973). *Science and behavior: An introduction to methods of research*. Englewood Cliffs, NJ: Prentice Hall.

Neisser, U. (1976). *Cognition and reality*. San Francisco: W. H. Freeman.

Neisser, U. (1981). John Dean's memory: A case study. *Cognition, 9*, 1–22.

NORCROSS, J. C., HANYCH, J. M., & TERRANOVA, R. D. (1996). Graduate study in psychology: 1992–1993. *American Psychologist, 51,* 631–643.

O'BRIEN, T. P., WALLEY, P. B., ANDERSON-SMITH, S., & DRABMAN, R. S. (1982). Naturalistic observation of the snack-eating behavior of obese and nonobese children. *Addictive Behaviors, 7,* 75–77.

ORNE, M. T. (1962). On the social psychology of the psychology experiment: With particular reference to demand characteristics and their implications. *American Psychologist, 17,* 776–783.

ORNE, M. T., & SCHEIBE, K. E. (1964). The contribution of nondeprivation factors in the production of sensory deprivation effects. *Journal of Abnormal and Social Psychology, 68,* 3–12.

ORWIN, R. G. (1997). Twenty-one years old and counting: The interrupted time series comes of age. In E. CHELIMSKY & W. R. SHADISH (Eds.), *Evaluation for the 21st century* (pp. 443–465). Thousand Oaks, CA: Sage Publications.

OSLER, S. F., & TRAUTMAN, G. E. (1961). Concept attainment II: Effect of stimulus complexity upon concept attainment at two levels of intelligence. *Journal of Experimental Psychology, 62,* 9–13.

PARSONS, H. M. (1974). What happened at Hawthorne? *Science, 183,* 922–932.

PATTEN, M. L. (1998). *Questionnaire research: A practical guide.* Los Angeles: Pryczak.

PATTERSON, F. G., & LINDEN, E. (1981). *The education of Koko.* New York: Holt, Rinehart, & Winston.

PECK, F. S. (1978). *The road less traveled.* New York: Simon & Schuster.

PETERSON, L., RIDLEY-JOHNSON, R., & CARTER, C. (1984). The supersuit: An example of structured naturalistic observation of children's altruism. *Journal of General Psychology, 110,* 235–241.

PLOTZ, D. (2000, June 4). Greens peace. *New York Times Magazine, 32,* 37.

PLOUS, S. (1996a). Attitudes toward the use of animals in psychological research and education: Results from a national survey of psychologists. *American Psychologist, 51,* 1167–1180.

PLOUS, S. (1996b). Attitudes toward the use of animals in psychological research and education: Results from a national survey of psychology majors. *Psychological Science, 7,* 352–358.

PLOUS, S., & HERZOG, H. (2001). Reliability of protocol reviews for animal research. *Science, 293,* 608–609.

POLLICK, A. (2007). IRBs: Navigating the maze. *APS Observer, 20*(10), 16–21.

POPPER, K. R. (1959). *The logic of scientific discovery.* New York: Basic Books.

POSAVAC, E. J., & CAREY, R. G. (2002). *Program evaluation: Methods and case studies* (6th ed.). Englewood Cliffs, NJ: Prentice Hall.

PRATKANIS, A. R., ESKENAZI, J., & GREENWALD, A. G. (1994). What you expect is what you believe (but not necessarily what you get): A test of the effectiveness of subliminal self-help audiotapes. *Basic and Applied Social Psychology, 15,* 251–276.

RAUSCHER, F. W., SHAW, G. L., & KEY, K. N. (1993). Music and spatial task performance. *Nature, 365,* 611.

REDELMEIER, D. A., & TIBSHIRANI, R. J. (1997). Association between cellular-phone calls and motor vehicle collisions. *The New England Journal of Medicine, 336,* 453–458.

REIFMAN, A. S., & LARRICK, R. R. (1991). Temper and temperature on the diamond: The heat–aggression relationship in major league baseball. *Personality and Social Psychology Bulletin, 17*(5), 580–585.

RESNICK, J. H., & SCHWARTZ, T. (1973). Ethical standards as an independent variable in psychological research. *American Psychologist, 28,* 134–139.

REYNOLDS, G. S. (1968). *A primer of operant conditioning.* Glenview, IL: Scott, Foresman.

REYNOLDS, R. I. (1992). Recognition of expertise in chess players. *American Journal of Psychology, 105,* 409–415.

RINIOLO, T. C., KOLEDIN, M., DRAKULIC, G. M., & PAYNE, R. A. (2003). An archival study of eyewitness memory of the *Titanic's* final plunge. *The Journal of General Psychology, 130,* 89–95.

RISKIND, J. H., & MADDUX, J. E. (1993). Loomingness, helplessness, and fearfulness: An integration of harm-looming and self-efficacy models of fear. *Journal of Social and Clinical Psychology, 12,* 73–89.

ROCKEFELLER, J. D. IV. (1994). Is military research hazardous to veterans' health? Lessons spanning half a century: A report examining biological experimentation on U.S. military [online]. www.trufax.org/trans/roc00.html

RODIN, J., & LANGER, E. J. (1977). Long-term effects of a control-relevant intervention with the institutionalized aged. *Journal of Personality and Social Psychology, 35,* 897–902.

ROEDIGER, R. (2004). What should they be called? *APS Observer, 17*(4), 5, 46–48.

ROEDIGER, H. L., & MCDERMOTT, K. B. (1995). Creating false memories: Remembering words not presented in lists. *Journal of Experimental Psychology: Learning, Memory, and Cognition, 21,* 803–814.

ROGELBERG, S. G., & LUONG, A. (1998). Nonresponse to mailed surveys: A review and guide. *Current Directions in Psychological Science, 7,* 60–65.

ROGOSA, D. (1980). A critique of cross-lagged correlation. *Psychological Bulletin, 88,* 245–258.

ROHLES, F. H., Jr. (1992). Orbital bar pressing: A historical note on Skinner and the chimpanzees in space. *American Psychologist, 47,* 1531–1533.

ROMANES, G. J. (1886). *Animal intelligence.* New York: D. Appleton.

ROSENBERG, M. J. (1969). The conditions and consequences of evaluation apprehension. In R. ROSENTHAL & R. L. ROSNOW (Eds.), *Artifact in behavioral research* (pp. 280–349). New York: Academic Press.

ROSENTHAL, R. (1966). *Experimenter effects in behavioral research.* New York: Appleton-Century-Crofts.

ROSENTHAL, R. (1979). The file drawer problem and tolerance for null results. *Psychological Bulletin, 86,* 638–641.

ROSENTHAL, R. (1994). Science and ethics in conducting, analyzing, and reporting psychological research. *Psychological Science, 5,* 127–133.

ROSENTHAL, R., & FODE, K. L. (1963a). Three experiments in experimenter bias. *Psychological Reports, 12,* 491–511.

ROSENTHAL, R., & FODE, K. L. (1963b). The effect of experimenter bias on the performance of the albino rat. *Behavioral Science, 8,* 183–189.

ROSNOW, R. L., GOODSTADT, B. E., SULS, J. M., & GITTER, A. G. (1973). More on the social psychology of the experiment: When compliance turns to self-defense. *Journal of Personality and Social Psychology, 27,* 337–343.

RUCCI, A. J., & TWENEY, R. D. (1980). Analysis of variance and the "second discipline" of scientific psychology: A historical account. *Psychological Bulletin, 87,* 166–184.

RYAN, L., HATFIELD, C., & HOFSTETTER, M. (2002). Caffeine reduces time-of-day effects on memory performance in older adults. *Psychological Science, 13,* 68–71.

SACKS, O. (1985). *The man who mistook his wife for a hat: And other clinical tales.* New York: Touchstone.

SAMELSON, F. (1992). Rescuing the reputation of Sir Cyril [Burt]. *Journal of the History of the Behavioral Sciences, 28,* 221–233.

SANFORD, E. C. (1914). Psychic research in the animal field: Der Kluge Hans and the Elberfeld horses. *American Journal of Psychology, 25,* 3–31.

SCHAIE, K. W. (2005). *Developmental influences on adult intelligence: The Seattle Longitudinal Study.* New York: Oxford University Press.

SCHAIE, K. W. (1988). Ageism in psychological research. *American Psychologist, 43,* 179–183.

SCHLAGMAN, S., SCHULZ, J., & KVAVILASHVILI, L. (2006). A content analysis of involuntary autobiographical memories: Examining the positivity effect of old age. *Memory, 14,* 161–175.

SCHNEIRLA, T. C. (1929). Learning and orientation in ants. *Comparative Psychology Monographs, 6* (No. 4).

SCHOENEMAN, T. J., & RUBANOWITZ, D. E. (1985). Attributions in the advice columns: Actors and observers, causes and reasons. *Personality and Social Psychology Bulletin, 11,* 315–325.

SCHRADER, W. B. (1971). *The predictive validity of the College Board Admissions tests.* In W. H. ANGOFF (Ed.), *The College Board Admission Testing Program.* New York: College Entrance Examination Board.

SCHUMAN, H., & PRESSER, S. (1996). *Questions and answers in attitude surveys: Experiments on question form, wording, and content.* Thousand Oaks, CA: Sage.

SCOTT-JONES, D. (2000). Recruitment of research participants. In B. D. SALES & S. FOLKMAN (Eds.), *Ethics in research with human participants* (pp. 27–34). Washington, DC: American Psychological Association.

SEARS, D. O. (1986). College sophomores in the laboratory: Influences of a narrow data base on psychology's view of human nature. *Journal of Personality and Social Psychology, 51,* 515–530.

SECHREST, L., & FIGUEREDO, A. J. (1993). Program evaluation. In L. W. PORTER & M. R. ROSENZWEIG (Eds.), *Annual Review of Psychology. Volume 44* (pp. 645–674). Palo Alto, CA: Annual Reviews.

SHELDON, W. H. (1940). *The varieties of human physique: An introduction to constitutional psychology.* New York: Harper & Row.

SHELDON, W. H. (1942). *The varieties of temperament: A psychology of constitutional differences.* New York: Harper & Row.

SHEPARD, R. N., & METZLER, J. (1971). Mental rotation of three-dimensional objects. *Science, 171,* 701–703.

SHERROD, D. R., HAGE, J. N., HALPERN, P. L., & MOORE, B. S. (1977). Effects of personal causation and perceived control on responses to an environment: The more control, the better. *Journal of Personality and Social Psychology, 13,* 14.

SHOOK, N. J., & FAZIO, R. H. (2008). Interracial roommate relationships: An experimental test of the contact hypothesis. *Psychological Science, 19,* 717–723.

SHULL, R. L., & GRIMES, J. A. (2006). Resistance to extinction following variable-interval reinforcement: Reinforcer rate and amount. *JEAB, 85,* 23–29.

SHUTE, V. J. (1994). Learners and instruction: What's good for the goose may not be good for the gander. *Psychological Science Agenda*, 7(3), 8–9, 16.

SIDMAN, M. (1960). *Tactics of scientific research*. New York: Basic Books.

SIDMAN, M. (2007). The analysis of behavior: What's in it for us? *Journal of the Experimental Analysis of Behavior*, 87, 309–316.

SIEBER, J. E. (1998). Planning ethically responsible research. In L. BICKMAN & D. J. ROG (Eds.), *Handbook of applied social research methods* (pp. 127–156). Thousand Oaks, CA: Sage.

SIEBER, J. E., & SAKS, M. J. (1989). A census of subject pool characteristics. *American Psychologist*, 44, 1053–1061.

SIGALL, H., & OSTROVE, N. (1975). Beautiful but dangerous: Effects of offender attractiveness and nature of the crime on juridic judgment. *Journal of Personality and Social Psychology*, 31, 410–414.

SILVERMAN, I. (1975). Nonreactive methods and the law. *American Psychologist*, 30, 764–769.

SINGER, P. (1975). *Animal liberation*. New York: Avon.

SKINNER, B. F. (1953). *Science and human behavior*. New York: Free Press.

SKINNER, B. F. (1956). A case history in scientific method. *American Psychologist*, 12, 221–233.

SKINNER, B. F. (1966). Operant behavior. In W. K. HONIG (Ed.), *Operant behavior: Areas of research and application* (pp. 12–32). New York: Appleton-Century-Crofts.

SKINNER, B. F. (1969). *Contingencies of reinforcement*. Englewood Cliffs, NJ: Prentice Hall.

SKINNER, B. F. (1976). *Walden Two*. New York: Macmillan. (Original work published 1948)

SKINNER, B. F. (1979). *The shaping of a behaviorist*. New York: New York University Press.

SKINNER, B. F. (1984). *A matter of consequences*. New York: New York University Press.

SMALL, W. S. (1900). An experimental study of the mental processes of the rat. *American Journal of Psychology*, 11, 80–100.

SMITH, D. (2003). What you need to know about the new code. *Monitor on Psychology*, 34(1), 62–65.

SMITH, L. D. (1992). On prediction and control: B. F. Skinner and the technological ideal of science. *American Psychologist*, 47, 216–223.

SMITH, S., & SECHREST, L. (1991). Treatment of aptitude × treatment interactions. *Journal of Consulting and Clinical Psychology*, 59, 233–244.

SMITH, S. S., & RICHARDSON, D. (1983). Amelioration of deception and harm in psychological research: The important role of debriefing. *Journal of Personality and Social Psychology*, 44, 1075–1082.

SMOLL, F. L., SMITH, R. E., BARNETT, N. P., & EVERETT, J. J. (1993). Enhancement of children's self-esteem through social support training for youth sport coaches. *Journal of Applied Psychology*, 78, 602–610.

Society for Research in Child Development. (1996). Ethical standards for research with children. *SRCD directory of members*, 337–339.

SOKAL, M. M. (Ed.) (1981). *An education in psychology: James McKeen Cattell's journal and letters from Germany and England, 1880–1888*. Cambridge, MA: MIT Press.

SOKAL, M. M. (1992). Origins and early years of the American Psychological Association, 1890–1906. *American Psychologist*, 47, 111–122.

SPATZ, C. (1997). *Basic statistics: Tales of distributions* (6th ed.). Pacific Grove, CA: Brooks/Cole.

SPELKE, E. S. (1985). Preferential looking methods as tools for the study of cognition in infancy. In G. GOTTLIEB & N. KRASNEGOR (Eds.), *Measurement of audition and vision in the first year of postnatal life* (pp. 323–363). Norwood, NJ: Ablex.

SPELT, D. (1948). The conditioning of the human fetus in utero. *Journal of Experimental Psychology*, 38, 338–346.

SPRINTHALL, R. C. (2000). *Basic statistical analysis* (6th edition). Boston: Allyn and Bacon.

SPURZHEIM, J. G. (1978). Outlines of phrenology. In D. N. ROBINSON (Ed.), *Significant contributions to the history of psychology. Series E. Volume II*. Washington, DC: University Publications of America. (Original work published 1832)

STEELE, K. M., BALL, T. N., & RUNK, R. (1997). Listening to Mozart does not enhance backwards digit span performance. *Perceptual and Motor Skills*, 84, 1179–1184.

STEELE, K. M., BASS, K. E., & CROOK, M. D. (1999). The mystery of the Mozart effect: Failure to replicate. *Psychological Science*, 10, 366–369.

STERNBERG, R. J., GRIGORENKO, E. L. (1999). A smelly 113° in the shade (Or, why we do field research). *APS Observer*, 12(8), 10–11, 20–21.

STOLZENBERG, L., & D'ALESSIO, S. J. (1997). "Three strikes and you're out": The impact of California's new mandatory sentencing law on serious crime rates. *Crime and Delinquency*, 43, 457–470.

STRAYER, D. L., & DREWS, F. A. (2004). Profiles in driver distraction: Effects of cell phone conversations on younger and older drivers. *Human Factors*, 46, 640–649.

STRAYER, D. L., & JOHNSTON, W. A. (2001). Driven to distraction: Dual-task studies of simulated driving and conversing on a cellular telephone. *Psychological Science*, 12, 462–466.

STROOP, J. R. (1992). Studies of interference in serial verbal reactions. *Journal of Experimental Psychology: General, 121,* 15–23. (Original work published 1935)

SULLIVAN, D. S., & DEIKER, T. E. (1973). Subject-experimenter perceptions of ethical issues in human research. *American Psychologist, 28,* 587–591.

TAYLOR, D. W., GARNER, W. R., & HUNT, H. F. (1959). Education for research in psychology. *American Psychologist, 14,* 167–179.

TAYLOR, S. J., & BOGDAN, R. (1998). *Introduction to qualitative research methods: A guidebook and resource* (3rd ed.). New York: Wiley.

TELLEGEN, A., LYKKEN, D. T., BOUCHARD, T. J., WILCOX, K. J., SEGAL, N. L., & RICH, S. (1988). Personality similarity in twins reared apart and together. *Journal of Personality and Social Psychology, 54,* 1031–1039.

TERMAN, L. M. (1925). *Genetic studies of genius, Vol. 1. Mental and physical traits of a thousand gifted children.* Stanford, CA: Stanford University Press.

TERMAN, L. M., & ODEN, M. H. (1947). *Genetic studies of genius, Vol. 4. The gifted child grows up: Twenty-five years' follow-up of a superior group.* Stanford, CA: Stanford University Press.

TERMAN, L. M., & ODEN, M. H. (1959). *Genetic studies of genius, Vol. 5. The gifted group at mid-life: Thirty-five years' follow-up of the superior child.* Stanford, CA: Stanford University Press.

THOMAS, E. (1995). *The very best men.* New York: Simon & Schuster.

THORNDIKE, E. L. (1898). Animal intelligence: An experimental study of the associative processes in animals. *Psychological Review Monographs, 2* (No. 8).

THORNDIKE, E. L. (2000). *Animal intelligence: Experimental studies.* New Brunswick, NJ: Transaction Publishers. (Original work published 1911)

TITCHENER, E. B. (1906, June 6). *Letter to L. N. Wilson.* Wilson Papers, Clark University, Worcester, MA.

TODD, J. T., & MORRIS, E. K. (1992). Case histories in the great power of steady misrepresentation. *American Psychologist, 47,* 1441–1453.

TOLMAN, E. C. (1959). Principles of purposive behavior. In S. KOCH (Ed.), *Psychology: A study of a science. Volume 2: General systematic formulations, learning, and special processes* (pp. 92–157). New York: McGraw-Hill.

TOLMAN, E. C., TRYON, R. C., & JEFFRIES, L. A. (1929). A self-recording maze with an automatic delivery table. *University of California Publications in Psychology, 4,* 99–112.

TOMAS, V. (Ed.). (1957). *Charles S. Peirce: Essays in the philosophy of science.* New York: Liberal Arts Press.

TOMLINSON-KEASEY, C. (1990). The working lives of Terman's gifted women. In H. Y. GROSSMAN & N. L. CHESTER, (Eds.), *The experience and meaning of work in women's lives* (pp. 213–239). Hillsdale, NJ: Lawrence Erlbaum.

TRABASSO, T. (1963). Stimulus emphasis and all-or-none learning in concept identification. *Journal of Experimental Psychology, 65,* 398–406.

TRAFIMOW, D., MADSON, L., & GWIZDOWSKI, I. (2006). Introductory psychology students' perceptions of alternatives to research participation. *Teaching of Psychology, 33,* 247–249.

TRIANDIS, H. C. (1995). *Individualism and collectivism.* Boulder, CO: Westview Press.

TRYON, R. C. (1929). The genetics of learning ability in rats: Preliminary report. *University of California Publications in Psychology, 4,* 71–89.

TUCKER, W. H. (1997). Re-reconsidering Burt: Beyond a reasonable doubt. *Journal of the History of the Behavioral Sciences, 33,* 145–162.

TUKEY, J. W. (1977). *Exploratory data analysis.* Reading, MA: Addison-Wesley.

TVERSKY, A., & KAHNEMAN, D. (1973). Availability: A heuristic for judging frequency and probability. *Cognitive Psychology, 5,* 207–232.

TWENEY, R. D. (1987). Programmatic research in experimental psychology: E. B. Titchener's laboratory investigations, 1891–1927. In M. G. ASCH & W. R. WOODWARD (Eds.), *Psychology in twentieth-century thought and society* (pp. 34–57). New York: Cambridge University Press.

ULRICH, R. E. (1991). Animal rights, animal wrongs and the question of balance. *Psychological Science, 2,* 197–201.

ULRICH, R. S. (1984). View through a window may influence recovery from surgery. *Science, 224,* 420–421.

VAN KAMMEN, W. B., & STOUTHAMER-LOEBER, M. (1998). Practice aspects of interview data collection and data management. In L. BICKMAN & D. J. ROG (Eds.), *Handbook of applied social research methods* (pp. 375–397). Thousand Oaks: CA: Sage.

VANDEHEY, M. A., MARSH, C. M., & DIEKHOFF, G. M. (2005). Providing students with instructors' notes: Problems with reading, studying, and attendance. *Teaching of Psychology, 32*, 49–52.

WAGAMAN, J. R., MILTENBERGER, R. G., & ARNDORFER, R. E. (1993). Analysis of a simplified treatment for stuttering in children. *Journal of Applied Behavior Analysis, 26*, 53–61.

WAGNER, J. A., III, RUBIN, P. A., & CALLAHAN, T. J. (1988). Incentive payment and nonmanagerial productivity: An interrupted time series analysis of magnitude and trend. *Organizational Behavior and Human Decision Processes, 42*, 47–74.

WALKER, A. J. (1996). Couples watching television: Gender, power, and the remote control. *Journal of Marriage and the Family, 58*, 813–823.

WARD, P., & CARNES, M. (2002). Effects of posting self-set goals on collegiate football players' skill execution during practice and games. *Journal of Applied Behavior Analysis, 35*, 1–12.

WASON, P. C., & JOHNSON-LAIRD, P. N. (1972). *Psychology of reasoning: Structure and content*. Cambridge, MA: Harvard University Press.

WATSON, J. B. (1907). Kinesthetic and organic sensations: Their role in the reactions of the white rat to the maze. *Psychological Review Monograph Supplements, 8* (No. 33).

WATSON, J. B. (1924). *Behaviorism*. New York: W.W. Norton.

WATSON, J. B. (1928). *Psychological care of infant and child*. New York: W.W. Norton.

WATSON, J. B., & RAYNER, R. (1920). Conditioned emotional reactions. *Journal of Experimental Psychology, 3*, 1–14.

WEBB, E. J., CAMPBELL, D. T., SCHWARTZ, R. D., SECHREST, L., & GROVE, J. B. (1981). *Nonreactive measures in the social sciences* (2nd ed.). Boston: Houghton Mifflin.

Webster's word histories. (1989). Springfield, MA: Merriam-Webster.

WEISS, J. M. (1968). Effects of coping response on stress. *Journal of Comparative and Physiological Psychology, 65*, 251–260.

WEST, S. G., GUNN, S. P., & CHERNICKY, P. (1975). Ubiquitous Watergate: An attributional analysis. *Journal of Personality and Social Psychology, 32*, 55–65.

WESTMAN, M., & EDEN, D. (1997). Effects of respite from work on burnout: Vacation relief and fade-out. *Journal of Applied Psychology, 82*, 516–527.

WICKENS, D. D., BORN, D. G., & ALLEN, C. K. (1963). Proactive inhibition and item similarity in short-term memory. *Journal of Verbal Learning and Verbal Behavior, 2*, 440–445.

WILKINSON, L., & APA Task Force on Statistical Inference. (1999). Statistical methods in psychology journals: Guidelines and explanations. *American Psychologist, 54*, 594–604.

WILLIAMS, J. M., & KRANE, V. (1989). Self-report distortion on self-report questionnaires with female collegiate golfers. *The Sport Psychologist, 3*, 212–218.

WINER, B. J., BROWN, D. R., & MICHAELS, K. M. (1994). *Statistical principles in experimental design* (3rd ed.). New York: McGraw-Hill.

WINSTON, A. S. (1990). Robert Sessions Woodworth and the "Columbia Bible": How the psychological experiment was redefined. *American Journal of Psychology, 103*, 391–401.

WITKIN, H. A., & GOODENOUGH, D. R. (1977). Field dependence and interpersonal behavior. *Psychological Bulletin, 84*, 661–689.

WITMER, L. (1893, July 14). *Letter to Hugo Münsterberg*. Münsterberg Papers, Boston Public Library, Boston, MA.

WITT, L. A., & NYE, L. G. (1992). Gender and the relationship between perceived fairness of pay or promotion and job satisfaction. *Journal of Applied Psychology, 77*, 910–917.

WITTE, R. S., & WITTE, J. S. (2007). *Statistics* (8th ed.). New York: Wiley.

WOLF, M. M. (1978). Social validity: The case for subjective measurement, or how behavior analysis is finding its heart. *Journal of Applied Behavior Analysis, 11*, 203–214.

WOOD, J. M., & BOOTZIN, R. R. (1990). The prevalence of nightmares and their independence from anxiety. *Journal of Abnormal Psychology, 99*, 64–68.

WOOD, J. M., BOOTZIN, R. R., ROSENHAN, D., NOLEN-HOEKSEMA, S., & JOURDEN, F. (1992). Effects of the 1989 San Francisco earthquake and content of nightmares. *Journal of Abnormal Psychology, 101*, 219–224.

WOODWORTH, R. S. (1938). *Experimental psychology*. New York: Henry Holt.

WORD, C. O., ZANNA, M. P., & COOPER, J. (1974). The nonverbal mediation of self-fulfilling prophecies in interracial interaction. *Journal of Experimental Social Psychology, 10,* 109–120.

WORTHEN, B. R. (2001). Whither evaluation? That all depends. *American Journal of Evaluation, 22,* 409–418.

WUNDT, W. (1904). *Principles of physiological psychology* (5th ed.) (E. B. TITCHENER, Trans.). New York: MacMillan. (Original work published 1874)

YARMEN, A. D., & BULL, M. P. (1978). Where were you when President Kennedy was assassinated? *Bulletin of the Psychonomic Society, 11,* 133–135.

YEATON, W. H., & SECHREST, L. (1986). Use and misuse of no-difference findings in eliminating threats to validity. *Evaluation Review, 10,* 836–852.

ZAJONC, R. B. (1990). Leon Festinger (1919–1989). *American Psychologist, 45,* 661–662.

ZEIGARNIK, B. (1967). *On finished and unfinished tasks.* In W. D. ELLIS (Ed.), *A source book of Gestalt psychology* (pp. 300–314). London: Routledge and Kegan Paul. (Original work published 1927)

Name Index

Subject Index